Oxford Revision Guides

AS & A Level

PSYCHOLOGY

Through Diagrams

Grahame Hill

OXFORD
UNIVERSITY PRESS

OXFORD
UNIVERSITY PRESS

Great Clarendon Street, Oxford OX2 6DP

Oxford University Press is a department of the University of Oxford.
It furthers the University's objective of excellence in research, scholarship,
and education by publishing worldwide in

Oxford New York

Auckland Bangkok Buenos Aires Cape Town Chennai
Dar es Salaam Delhi Hong Kong Istanbul Karachi Kolkata
Kuala Lumpur Madrid Melbourne Mexico City Mumbai Nairobi
São Paulo Shanghai Taipei Tokyo Toronto

Oxford is a registered trade mark of Oxford University Press
in the UK and in certain other countries

© Grahame Hill 2009

British Library Cataloguing in Publication Data

Data available

ISBN- 978-0-19-918094-3

10

Typeseting, artwork and design by Steve Evans Design and Illustration

Printed in Great Britain by Bell and Bain Ltd, Glasgow

Contents

Contents (cont.)

Contents (cont.)

Contents by specification

Content by specification (cont.)

OCR SPECIFICATION - AS LEVEL EXAMINATION		
Unit Reference	**Topic**	**See book pages**
Unit 1 - G541 Psychological Investigations	• **Techniques for Collecting/Analysing Data** ➤ Self-report; Experiments; Observation; Correlation	31-34
	• **Outline of an existing piece of research** ➤ Strengths/weaknesses of methods, improvements, etc.	26-27, 31-40
	• **Data produced by a piece of research** ➤ Descriptive statistics, tables, graphs, conclusions, etc.	41-42
	• **Outline of a proposed piece of research** ➤ Hypotheses, variables, sampling, procedures, etc.	29-40
Unit 2 - G542 Core Studies	• **15 Core Studies:** ➤ Cognitive psychology - Loftus and Palmer (1974), Baron-Cohen et al. (1997), Savage-Rumbaugh (1986) ➤ Developmental psychology - Samuel & Bryant (1984), Bandura, Ross & Ross (1961), Freud (1909) ➤ Physiological psychology - Maguire et al. (2000), Dement and Kleitman (1957), Sperry (1968) ➤ Social psychology - Milgram (1963), Reicher and Haslam (2006), Piliavin, Rodin & Piliavin (1969) ➤ Individual differences - Rosenhan (1973), Thigpen and Cleckley (1954), Griffiths (1994)	*14, 99, 220,* 221, 178-180, 181, 135, 136 *113-117,* 118, *72, 251,* 73, *141-142, 175,* 176 16, *79,* 80, *89,* 90, *81-83,* 84, 85 *17, 45,* 50, *51-52, 48-49,* 47, *60-61,* 62 *161-166,* 167, *168,* 169, *199, 202,* 200
	• **Issues, debates, perspectives, methods of studies.**	12-17, 26, 31-34, 38-40

OCR SPECIFICATION - A2 LEVEL EXAMINATION		
Unit Reference	**Topic**	**See book pages**
Unit 3 - G543 Options in Applied Psychology	• **Forensic Psychology** ➤ Turning to crime ➤ Making a case ➤ Reaching a verdict ➤ After a guilty verdict	*76,* 214, 215-219 220-226 *48-49,* 53, 227-230 *46-47,* 231-233
	• **Health and Clinical Psychology** ➤ Healthy living ➤ Stress ➤ Dysfunctional behaviour ➤ Disorders	203-207 192-197 161-167, 182-185, 189 170-175, 177, 182-185, 189
	• **Psychology of Sport and Exercise** ➤ Sport and the individual ➤ Sport performance ➤ Social psychology of sport ➤ Exercise psychology	234, *235-236,* 237-238 239, 243 241-242 --------
	• **Psychology of Education** ➤ Teaching and learning ➤ Student participation ➤ The social world of reaching and learning ➤ Enabling learning: dealing with diversity	114-120, 129, 130-132, 244-248 -------- 123-124, 145, 249 ---------
Unit 4 - G544 Approaches and Research Methods in Psychology	• **Research Methodology and Project Design**	29-44
	• **Synoptic questions on:** ➤ Approaches and perspectives ➤ Methods ➤ Issues and debates	11-16 31-38 18-28, 38-39

Content by specification (cont.)

EDEXCEL SPECIFICATION - AS LEVEL EXAMINATION		
Unit Reference	**Topic**	**See book pages**
Unit 1 Social and Cognitive Psychology	• **Social Psychology - obedience & prejudice** ➢ Definition / Terminology / Content of the approach ➢ Studies in detail / Key issue ➢ Methodology / How Science Works / Practical	17, 50-52, 59 *51*, 77 26, 33, 35, 38, 40
	• **Cognitive Psychology - memory & forgetting** ➢ Definition / Terminology / Content of the approach ➢ Studies in detail / Key issue ➢ Methodology / How Science Works / Practical	14, 97-102 *97-98, 102*, 103, 220, 224 29-31, 36-38, 41-42, 263
Unit 2 Understanding the Individual	• **Psychodynamic approach: Freud** ➢ Definition / Terminology / Content of the approach ➢ Studies in detail / Key issue ➢ Methodology / How Science Works / Practical	12, 141-142, 144, 157-158 103, 176, 187-188, *222* 26, 33-35, 39-40, 42-44
	• **Biological approach** ➢ Definition / Terminology / Content of the approach ➢ Studies in detail / Key issue ➢ Methodology / How Science Works / Practical	16, 22, 78, 83, 86, 157-158 219 26, 29-31, 36-37, 41-44, 79, *86*
	• **Learning approach** ➢ Definition / Terminology / Content of the approach ➢ Studies in detail / Key issue ➢ Methodology / How Science Works / Practical	13, 72, 130-132, 146, 157-158, 184-185 73, 177, 213 26, 31-32, 38, 40-44

EDEXCEL SPECIFICATION - A2 LEVEL EXAMINATION		
Unit Reference	**Topic**	**See book pages**
Unit 3 Applications of Psychology	• **Criminological Psychology** ➢ Definition / Terminology / Content of the application ➢ Studies in detail / Key issue ➢ Methodology / How Science Works / Practical	72, 214, 220-221, 233, 251 215, 217-218, 220-221, 226 26-27, 31, 38, 40
	• **Child Psychology** ➢ Definition / Terminology / Content of the application ➢ Studies in detail / Key issue ➢ Methodology / How Science Works / Practical	147-153, 178, 180 152-153, 180 32, 38-40
	• **Health Psychology: substance misuse** ➢ Definition / Terminology / Content of the application ➢ Studies in detail / Key issue ➢ Methodology / How Science Works / Practical	184, 198-199, 201-204 203-204 26, 40
	• **Sport Psychology** ➢ Definition / Terminology / Content of the application ➢ Studies in detail / Key issue ➢ Methodology / How Science Works / Practical	234-236, 238-240, 243 ---------- 33, 40
Unit 4 How Psychology Works	• **Clinical Psychology** ➢ Definition / Terminology / Content of the application ➢ Studies in detail / Key issue ➢ Methodology / How Science Works / Practical	161, 164-167, 169-177, 182-185, 187–191 167 34, 38, 86
	• **Issues and Debates** ➢ Contributions to society ➢ Ethical issues / Research methods ➢ Key issues / Debates / Application of knowledge	12-17, *182-189, 199, 215-218* 26-27, 29-44 12-19, 21-28

Content by specification (cont.)

AQA SPECIFICATION B - AS LEVEL EXAMINATION		
Unit Reference	**Topic**	**See book pages**
Unit 1 - PYSB1 Introducing Psychology	• **Approaches** ➢ Key approaches to psychology ➢ Biopsychology • **Gender Development** ➢ Gender development • **Research Methods** ➢ Methods of research ➢ Representing data, descriptive statistics ➢ Ethics	 12-16, *86, 130-131*, 141-142, *146* 78-79, *80*, 81-83, *84*, 86 156-158 29-40 41-42 26-27
Unit 2 - PSYB2 Social Psychology, Cognitive Psychology and Individual differences	• **Social Psychology** ➢ Social influence ➢ Social cognition • **Cognitive Psychology** ➢ Remembering and forgetting ➢ Perceptual processes • **Individual Differences** ➢ Anxiety disorders ➢ Autism	 45, 48-53, 241, 243 55-59 95-103 105-107, *110-111* 174-177, 182-190 178-181, *184-185*, 186

AQA SPECIFICATION B - A2 LEVEL EXAMINATION		
Unit Reference	**Topic**	**See book pages**
Unit 3 - PSYB3 Child development and Applied Options	• **Child Development** ➢ Social development ➢ Cognitive development ➢ Moral development • **Applied Psychology** ➢ Cognition and law ➢ Schizophrenia and mood disorders ➢ Stress and stress management ➢ Substance abuse ➢ Forensic psychology	 147-151, 154-155 *113*, 114-122 123-125 103, 112, 220-224 170-173, 182-185, 189-191 192-194, 196-197 198-199, 201-206 214-215, 217-218, 231-233
Unit 4 - PSYB4 Approaches, Debates and Methods in psychology	• **Approaches in Psychology** ➢ Biological, Behaviourist, Social Learning, Cognitive, Psychodynamic and Humanist approaches ➢ Comparison of approaches • **Debates in Psychology** ➢ Debates in psychology • **Methods in Psychology** ➢ Inferential statistics ➢ Issues in research	 12-16, *24, 72, 78, 86, 130-132,* *141-146, 165-166* 12-16, *170-177* 18-25 43-44 31-40, 26-28

N.B.

Page numbers in normal text indicate directly relevant subject matter while page numbers in italics indicate useful background reading and links.

This revision guide provides less coverage of the Edexcel specification and the 'Psychology of Sport and Exercise' and 'Psychology of Education' options in Unit 3 of the OCR specification. It is imperative to obtain a detailed copy of the specification you are studying to ensure adequate knowledge of all examination material and requirements.

How the specifications are assessed

Specifications in outline (as at June 2008)

		AQA a www.aqa.org.uk/	Edexcel www.edexcel.org.uk/	AQA b www.aqa.org.uk/	OCR www.ocr.org.uk
AS	**Unit 1** Title	Cognitive, Developmental, Research methods	Social and Cognitive Psychology	Introducing Psychology	Psychological Investigation
	Unit 1 Exam	50% of AS (25% of A Level) 1½ hours *Compulsory structured questions*	40% of AS (20% of A Level) 1 hour 20 mins *Compulsory structured questions*	50% of AS (25% of A Level) 1½ hours *Compulsory structured questions*	30% of AS (15% of A Level) 1 hour *Compulsory structured questions*
	Unit 2 Title	Biological, Social, Individual differences	Understanding the Individual	Individual differences, Social Psychology and Cognitive Psychology	Core Studies
	Unit 2 Exam	50% of AS (25% of A Level) 1½ hours *Compulsory structured questions*	60% of AS (30% of A Level) 1 hour 40 mins *Compulsory structured questions*	50% of AS (25% of A Level) 1½ hours *Candidates answer 3 questions*	70% of AS (35% of A Level) 2 hours *Compulsory questions + limited choice*
A2	**Unit 3** Title	Topics in Psychology	Applications of Psychology	Child Development & Applied Options	Options in Applied Psychology
	Unit 3 Exam	50% of A2 (25% of A-Level) 1½ hours 3 essay questions from 8 topics: *Biological rhythms; Perception; Relationships; Aggression; Eating behaviour; Gender; IQ & learning; Cognition & development.*	40% of A2 (20% of A-Level) 1½ hours Questions to be answered on 2 of 4 applications: *Criminological psychology; Child psychology; Health psychology - substance misuse; Sport psychology*	50% of A2 (25% of A-Level) 2 hours *Candidates answer 3 questions*	50% of A2 (25% of A-Level) 1½ hours Questions to be answered on 2 of 4 applications: *Forensic psychology; Health & clinical psychology; Psychology of sport and exercise; Psychology of education.*
	Unit 4 Title	Psychopathology, Psychology in Action and Research Methods	How Psychology Works	Approaches, Debates & Methods	Approaches and Research Methods
	Unit 4 Exam	50% of A2 (25% of A-Level) 2 hours a) *Psychopathology - 1 essay from 3* b) *Psychology in action - 1 question from 3* c) *Research methods - 1 compulsory structured question*	60% of A2 (30% of A-Level) 2 hours a) *Clinical psychology - compulsory questions* b) *Issues & debates - compulsory questions then 1 essay from two options*	50% of A2 (25% of A-Level) 2 hours *Candidates answer 3 questions*	50% of A2 (25% of A-Level) 1½ hours a) *Research methods - compulsory questions* b) *Approaches, debates etc. - 1 from 2 questions*
	NB:	Optional choices in Unit 3 and Unit 4 a & b	Exam questions may be asked on practical work conducted while studying the units	Questions may be asked on practical work conducted while studying the units	Optional choices in Unit 3

Assessment Objectives and AS/GCE weightings (%)

	Descriptor	AQA a		Edexcel		AQA b		OCR	
		AS	GCE	AS	GCE	AS	GCE	AS	GCE
AO1	For example, demonstrate knowledge and understanding of relevant psychological concepts, theories, findings and debates.	37.5	34	35-40	30-35	37	32	35	30
AO2	For example, analyse, evaluate, apply and draw connections between different areas of scientific knowledge in psychology.	37.5	39	30-35	36.5-41.5	35	41	33	41.5
AO3	For example, describe, use, communicate, analyse, interpret, explain and evaluate the ethics of research techniques and data in psychology.	25	27	30-35	27-32	28	27	32	28.5

Stretch and challenge

Psychology examinations aim to stretch and challenge candidates with:

1. **extended** written responses
2. **command words** e.g. assess, evaluate, discuss etc.
3. **application** of knowledge to new situations
4. **synoptic** assessment of links between specification areas

In order to secure higher level marks candidates must address the **precise** demands of the questions posed.

Units covered in this Oxford Revision Guide

The **AS** and **A2** specifications of all 4 main UK examination boards are covered. However, the Edexcel specification and OCR unit 3 sport and education options have more limited coverage than other areas.

Candidates must be able to expand upon the summaries in this guide and practise applying their knowledge to the exam questions of their specification.

1.1 Introduction – what is psychology?

DEFINITIONS

The word 'Psychology' is derived from two Greek roots: 'Psyche', meaning 'mind' or 'soul' and 'Logos', meaning 'study of'. Psychology, therefore, literally means 'study of the mind'. However, a more recent definition by Atkinson *et al.* (1991) suggests that psychology is:

'The scientific study of behaviour and mental processes'

Just giving this simple definition, however, is a bit misleading, since psychologists now and throughout their history have not only disagreed about the definition of psychology, but have also strongly disagreed about *what* should be studied in the subject and *how* it should be studied.

THE HISTORY OF PSYCHOLOGY

WHERE DID PSYCHOLOGY COME FROM?
Psychology developed from three main areas of study:

PHILOSOPHY
- Many of the problems which psychology has investigated were first most clearly outlined by Greek philosophers such as Socrates, Plato, and Aristotle in the 5th century BC. Two more recent philosophical influences on the development of psychology as a science were:
1 **Empiricism** – which argued that humans should only measure data that is *objectively observable,* such as behaviour.
2 **Positivism** — which argued that the *methods* and principles of *science* should be applied to human behaviour.

BIOLOGY
Biology has had two important influences:
1 Evolution – Darwin's suggestion that humans have *evolved* from other animals. The discoveries in *genetics* that followed from his evolutionary theory have had many important implications for the study and understanding of behaviour.
2 Physiology – the discoveries, mostly by the medical profession, of the structure and function of the brain, nervous, and endocrine systems have significantly contributed to the understanding of behaviour.

PHYSICS
- A subject that because of its great success has been adopted as the ideal model by scientists in psychology, who have borrowed its *scientific methods* and *principles.*
- Physicists, such as Fechner, started applying their subject to human behaviour and experience (psychophysics) in the nineteenth century, with some success.

WHEN DID PSYCHOLOGY START?
The date **1879** is usually said to be the start of psychology as a **separate scientific discipline,** since it was when Wilhelm Wundt created the first psychology laboratory in Leipzig. Wundt is, therefore, regarded as the 'founding father' of psychology, although Americans tend to suggest that William James should have this honour since his 1890 book (which took 12 years to write) entitled *Principles of Psychology* was a major landmark in psychology's literature and he began teaching a course on the relationship between physiology and psychology at Harvard University in 1875.

HOW DID PSYCHOLOGY DEVELOP?
- **Structuralism** – was the first approach to investigating psychology, pioneered by Wundt himself, who thought that the object of psychological investigation should be the *conscious mind,* and that it should be studied by *introspection* (looking inwards at one's own mental experience) in order to *break it down* into its component parts (such as images, sensations and feelings) like the science of chemistry had done with chemicals. One structuralist, Titchener, claimed there were a total of 46,708 basic sensations that combined to form the structure of the human mind, but the approach was very limited in its ability to explain and was replaced by functionalism.
- **Functionalism** – the approach William James advocated. James was influenced by Darwin's views and argued that the workings of the mind are functional, to survive and adapt, so we should investigate *what behaviour and thoughts are for.* Many of James's insights remain valid today, but functionalism was superseded by the next two very powerful approaches that both started around the turn of the century.
- **Psychoanalysis** – was in fact a method of *therapy* developed by Sigmund Freud in Austria, but in many major books, such as *The interpretation of dreams* (1900), Freud began describing in detail an underlying theory of the human mind and behaviour that has had an enormous (and controversial) impact on psychology. Freud argued that the proper object of psychological investigation should be the *unconscious mind,* and that our behaviour is determined by processes of which we are not aware.
- **Behaviourism** – Behaviourists, such as John Watson, were extremely critical of all the approaches that concerned themselves with 'minds', and proposed that psychology should only investigate *observable behaviour* if it wanted to be an objective science. This approach dominated experimental psychology until the 1950s, when a strong resurgence of interest in the 'mind' developed in the form of the cognitive and the humanistic approaches, which suggested that behaviourism ignored all the most important and interesting things that go on in our heads.
- **Cognitive psychology** – aims to investigate the mind by using *computer information processing* ideas to arrive at testable *models* of how the brain works, and then applying *scientific methods* to confirm these models. The cognitive approach has enjoyed much success and is a very dominant one in psychology today.
- The **Humanistic approach**, however, has had less of an impact on psychology, since it has deliberately adopted a *less scientific* view of the human mind by arguing that psychology should focus on each *individual's conscious experience* and *aims* in life.
- The **Biological approach** has advanced *evolutionary, physiological,* and *genetic* explanations for human behaviour throughout the history of psychology.

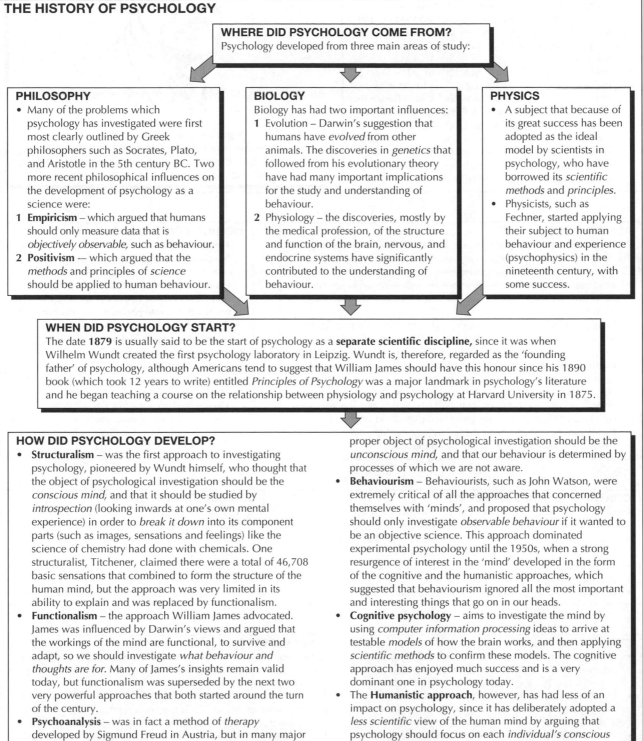

1.2 The psychodynamic approach

ORIGINS AND HISTORY

- The psychodynamic approach was mainly initiated by *Sigmund Freud*, a Viennese doctor who specialised in neurology. Freud became interested in hysteria – the manifestation of physical symptoms without physical causes – and became convinced that **unconscious mental causes** were responsible not just for this disorder but for many disorders and even 'normal' personality. Freud developed psychoanalysis – a set of techniques for **treating** the unconscious causes of mental disorders and built up an underlying explanatory **psychoanalytic theory** of how human personality and abnormality develop from childhood.
- Freud's theory and approach were influenced by the ideas and society of his time, particularly by his early work with Charcot, the Parisian hypnotist, and Breuer the pioneer of the cathartic method. Freud's psychoanalytic approach had a great impact on psychology and psychiatry, and was developed in different ways by other **psychodynamic** theorists (those influenced by psychoanalytic assumptions) such as Jung, Adler, Klein, Anna Freud (his daughter) and Erikson.

Sigmund Freud (1856 - 1939)

'…I set myself the task of bringing to light what human beings keep hidden within them… the task of making conscious the most hidden recesses of the mind is one which it is quite possible to accomplish'.

ASSUMPTIONS

Psychoanalysis, as developed by Freud, had a very fixed set of assumptions that later psychodynamic theorists agreed with to differing extents. The most common shared assumptions of the approach are:

- *Unconscious processes* – many important influences on behaviour come from a part of the mind we have no direct awareness of, the unconscious.
- *Psychodynamic conflict* – different parts of the mind are in constant dynamic struggle with each other (often unconsciously) and the consequences of this struggle are important in understanding behaviour.
- *Emotional drives* – Freud believed behaviour is motivated by sexual and aggressive drives. The drives create psychic energy that will build up (like steam in a steam engine) and create tension and anxiety if it cannot be released in some form. While not all psychodynamic theorists agree with Freud's view, they do see emotional motivation as important.
- *Development* – personality is shaped by relationships, experience and conflict over time, particularly during childhood.

METHODS OF INVESTIGATION

- Freud used the **case study** method when treating his clients (seeing them individually and investigating them in detail), often using the clinical interview method to probe their past and question their behaviour. He **deeply** analysed and **interpreted** the **symbolism** of all they said and did. These methods remain the norm for most psychodynamic theorists.
- Two particular techniques Freud used were:
  Free association – the uninhibited expression of thought associations, no matter how bizarre or embarrassing, from the client to the analyst.
  Dream analysis – the 'royal road' to the unconscious, the analyst attempts to decode the symbols and unravel the hidden meaning of a dream from the dreamer's report.

CONTRIBUTION TO PSYCHOLOGY

Freud used his theory to explain a vast number of topics, such as:

- *Personality development* – due to fixation / defence mechanisms.
- *Moral / gender development* – the result of the Oedipus complex.
- *Aggression* – caused by hydraulic drives and displacement.
- *Abnormality* – the consequence of early trauma and repression.
- *Memory* – Forgetting caused by repression.

+ Slips of the tongue, the shaping of civilisation and customs, etc.

CONTRIBUTION TO SOCIETY

- The purpose of psychoanalysis was as a therapy to treat mental disorder. Once the unconscious cause of disorder was identified through dream interpretation, etc., then a cure could be effected by getting it 'out in the open' to be discussed, resolved and controlled.
- Psychoanalysis can be applied to art and literature.

STRENGTHS

- Freud's ideas made a large impact on psychology and psychiatry and are still discussed and used today, around a 100 years after he started developing them.
- Freud thought case studies like 'Little Hans' and 'Anna O', his belief in determinism and his detailed collection of data provided scientific support for his theory.
- Psychodynamic therapies drew attention to the psychological causes of mental disorder.
- Psychoanalysis has enormous explanatory power and has something to say on a huge variety of important topics.
- Later psychodynamic theory tried to deal with the weaknesses of psychoanalysis and develop the strengths.

WEAKNESSES

Psychodynamic psychology has been accused of:

- Having vague concepts that can be used to explain anything but which can predict very little.
- Having concepts that are difficult to test and verify scientifically. Experimental research that has been conducted often fails to support psychodynamic ideas, and that which does seem to support them can often be attributed to alternative causes.
- Using unrepresentative samples and techniques that were not fully objective and therefore open to bias.
- Being linked with unsuccessful psychodynamic therapies.
- Having many concepts that can be explained by more scientific approaches such as cognitive psychology.

1.3 The learning theory approach

ORIGINS AND HISTORY

- The learning theory approach in psychology was initiated mainly by the behaviourists, who were influenced by the philosophy of **empiricism** (which argues that knowledge comes from the environment via the senses, since humans are like a 'tabula rasa', or blank slate, at birth) and the physical sciences (which emphasise scientific and objective methods of investigation).
- **Watson** started the behaviourist movement in 1913 when he wrote an article entitled 'Psychology as the behaviourist views it', which set out its main principles and assumptions. Drawing on earlier work by Pavlov, behaviourists such as Watson, Thorndike and Skinner proceeded to develop theories of **learning** (such as classical and operant conditioning) that they attempted to use to explain virtually **all** behaviour.
- The behaviourist approach dominated experimental psychology until the late 1950s, when its assumptions and methods became increasingly criticised by ethologists and cognitive psychologists. The behaviourist theories have been modified to provide more realistic explanations of how learning can occur, for example by psychologists such as Bandura with his social learning theory.
- Social Learning Theory argues that important cognitive processes occur between stimulus and response.

John Watson
'Give me a dozen healthy infants ... and my own specified world to bring them up in and I'll guarantee to take any one at random and train him to become any type of specialist I might select – doctor, lawyer ... and yes, even beggarman and thief.'

ASSUMPTIONS
The behaviourists believed:
1. the majority of all behaviour is **learned** from the **environment** after birth (behaviourism takes the nurture side of the nature-nurture debate), and so
   a psychology should investigate the **laws** and **products** of learning
   b behaviour is **determined** by the environment, since we are merely the total of all our past learning experiences, freewill is an illusion.
2. only **observable** behaviour not minds should be studied if psychology is to be an objective science, since we cannot see into other people's minds, and if we ask them about their thoughts they may lie, not know, or just be mistaken. Most learning theorists still adopt this scientific approach.

METHODS OF INVESTIGATION
The behaviourists adopted a very scientific approach, using strict laboratory experimentation, usually conducted on animals such as rats or pigeons. Animals were tested because the behaviourists believed:
- the laws of learning were universal
- there was only a quantitative difference between animals and humans
- animals are practically and ethically more convenient to test

CONTRIBUTION TO PSYCHOLOGY
The behaviourists' discoveries concerning the laws of learning were vigorously applied to explain many aspects of behaviour, such as:
- **Language acquisition,** e.g. Skinner's theory.
- **Moral development,** e.g. conditioned emotional responses of guilt and conscience.
- **Attraction,** e.g. Byrne & Clore's reinforcement affect model.
- **Abnormality,** e.g. the classical conditioning of phobias and their treatment.
+ aggression, prejudice, gender role identity, etc.

CONTRIBUTION TO SOCIETY
- The behaviourist learning theory approach has produced many practical applications for education (such as programmed learning) and the treatment of those suffering behavioural disturbances (such as systematic desensitisation for phobias, behaviour shaping for autism, and token economies for institutionalised patients).
- Operant conditioning principles have been used in training animals to perform tasks, from circus animals to guide dogs.
- Watson applied behaviourist theory to both child rearing and advertising, while Skinner offered many suggestions regarding the large scale manipulation of behaviour in society in his books such as *Beyond Freedom and Dignity* and *Walden Two*.

STRENGTHS
Behaviourism contributed to psychology in many ways:
- Behaviourism was very scientific and its experimental methodology left a lasting impression on the subject.
- It provided strong counter-arguments to the nature side of the nature-nurture debate.
- The approach is very parsimonious, explaining a great variety of phenomena using only a few simple (classical and operant) principles.
- Behaviourism has produced many practical applications, some of which have been very effective.
- Social learning theory has overcome some of the weaknesses of the behaviourists' theories.

WEAKNESSES
Behaviourist views have been criticised by other approaches for a number of reasons.
- Ethologists argued that the behaviourists ignored innate, built-in biases in learning due to evolution, but also disagreed with the behaviourists' use of animals and laboratory experimentation, saying that there is a biologically qualitative difference between humans and other animals and that experiments only demonstrate artificial, not natural learning.
- Cognitive psychologists think that behaviourism ignores important mental processes involved in learning; while the humanistic approach disliked their rejection of conscious mental experience.

1.4 The cognitive approach

ORIGINS AND HISTORY

- The cognitive approach began to revolutionise psychology in the late 1950s and early 1960s, to become the dominant paradigm in the subject by the 1970s. Interest in mental processes had been gradually resurrected through the work of people like Tolman and Piaget, but it was the arrival of the **computer** that gave cognitive psychology the terminology and metaphor it needed to investigate human minds.
- Cognitive psychology compares the human mind to a computer, suggesting that we too are **information processors** and that it is possible and desirable to study the **internal mental processes** that lie between the stimuli we receive and the responses we make. Cognition means 'knowing' and cognitive processes refer to the ways in which knowledge is gained, used and retained. Therefore, cognitive psychologists have studied perception, attention, memory, thinking, language, and problem solving.
- Cognitive psychologists believe these internal mental processes (our programming) can be investigated scientifically by proposing models of psychological functions and then conducting research to see, when people are given an input of information, whether their output of behaviour/verbal report matches what the models would predict.

E. Loftus

'... cognition refers to all those processes by which sensory input is transformed, reduced, elaborated, stored, recovered and used... cognition is involved in everything a human being might possibly do.'
Neisser (1966)

ASSUMPTIONS

Cognitive psychologists assume that:

1 The study of **internal mental processes is important in understanding behaviour** – cognitive processes **actively** organise and manipulate the information we receive – humans do not just passively respond to their environment.

2 Humans, like computers, are **information processors** – regardless of our hardware (brains or circuits) both receive, interpret and respond to information – and these processes can be modelled and tested **scientifically**.

METHODS OF INVESTIGATION

Cognitive psychologists mostly use:

- **Experimentation** – usually conducted in the laboratory, e.g. memory experiments conducted under strictly controlled conditions, where independent variables such as the time delay before recall are manipulated to find the effect on the amount of information retained.
- **Case studies** – for example the study of brain damaged patients such as those with anterograde amnesia in memory research.

CONTRIBUTION TO PSYCHOLOGY

Cognitive psychologists have sought to explain:

- **Memory,** e.g. Atkinson and Shiffrin's multi-store model of the input, storage and loss of information, etc.
- **Perception,** e.g. Gregory's theory on the role of mental processes in influencing/organising visual stimuli
- **Attention,** e.g. Broadbent's filter model
- **Artificial intelligence,** e.g. Rumelhart and McClelland's parallel distributed network models
- **Social cognition,** e.g. the effects of stereotypes on interpersonal perception
- **Abnormality,** e.g. Beck's ideas on the errors of logic and negative thinking of depressed patients.

CONTRIBUTION TO SOCIETY

Cognitive psychology has had a broad range of applications, for example to:

- **Memory** – to help improve memory through mnemonic devices or to aid the police in eyewitness testimony
- **Education** – Information processing theory has been applied to improve educational techniques
- **Therapy** – such as the use of Ellis's rational emotive therapy to restructure faulty thinking and perceptions in depression, for example. When combined to form cognitive-behavioural techniques, effectiveness is improved
- **Health promotion** – e.g. the health belief model and the following (or not) of health advice.

STRENGTHS

Cognitive psychology is probably the most dominant approach today:

- It investigates many areas of interest in psychology that had been neglected by behaviourism; yet, unlike psychoanalysis and humanism, it investigates them using more rigorous scientific methods.
- In contrast to the biological approach, it bases its explanations firmly at a functional, psychological level, rather than resorting to reductionism to explain human behaviour.
- The approach has provided explanations of many aspects of human behaviour and has had useful practical applications.
- Cognitive psychology has influenced and integrated with many other approaches and areas of study to produce, for example, social learning theory, cognitive neuropsychology, social cognition, and artificial intelligence.

WEAKNESSES

Cognitive models have been accused of being:

- over simplistic – ignoring the huge complexity of human functioning compared to computer functioning
- unrealistic and over hypothetical – ignoring the biological influences and grounding of mental processes
- Too cold – ignoring the emotional life of humans, their conscious experience and possible use of freewill.

1.5 The humanistic approach

ORIGINS AND HISTORY

- The humanistic movement developed in America in the early 1960s, and was termed the third force in psychology since it aimed to replace the two main approaches in the subject at that time, behaviourism and psychoanalysis. Influenced by gestalt psychology's idea of studying **whole units,** and existential philosophy with its belief in **conscious free will,** humanists argued that behaviourism's artificial and dehumanising approach and psychoanalysis's gloomy determinism were insufficient to provide a complete psychology.
- The humanistic approach aimed to investigate all the uniquely **human** aspects of **experience** such as love, hope, creativity, etc. and emphasised the importance of the individual's interaction with the environment. Humanists, such as **Maslow,** believed that every individual has the need to **self-actualise** or reach their potential, and **Rogers** developed client-centred therapy to help individuals in this process of self-actualisation.
- In line with its person-centred, idiographic, holistic approach and belief in freewill, humanistic psychology rejects the traditional scientific and experimental approach to Psychology.

Carl Rogers
'Humanistic psychology has as its ultimate goal the preparation of a complete description of what it means to be alive as a human being.' Bugental (1967)

ASSUMPTIONS

Bugental (1967), the first president of the American Association for Humanistic Psychology, described some of its fundamental assumptions:

- A proper understanding of human nature can only be gained from **studying humans,** not other animals.
- Psychology should research areas that are **meaningful** and important to human existence, not neglect them because they are too difficult. Psychology should be **applied** to enrich human life.
- Psychology should study **internal experience** as well as external behaviour and consider that individuals can show some degree of **free will.**
- Psychology should study the **individual** case (an idiographic method) rather than the average performance of groups (a nomothetic approach).
- In general, humanistic psychologists assume that the **whole person** should be studied in their environmental **context.**

METHODS OF INVESTIGATION

Humanists take a phenomenological approach, investigating the individual's conscious experience of the world. For this reason they employ the idiographic case study method, and use a variety of individualistic techniques such as:

- flexible open ended interviews
- the Q-sort technique, where the participant is given one hundred different statements on cards, such as 'I don't trust my emotions' or 'I have an attractive personality' which they have to sort into piles for personal relevance.

CONTRIBUTION TO PSYCHOLOGY

The humanistic approach has been applied to relatively few areas of psychology compared to other approaches. The main areas of explanation have been in:

- **Personality/self identity,** e.g. Rogers's self theory
- **Motivation,** e.g. Maslow's hierarchy of needs and self-actualisation
- **Abnormality,** e.g. due to imposed conditions of worth by others or the inability to accept the true self. Humanists are against the nomothetic classification of abnormality

CONTRIBUTION TO SOCIETY

The humanistic approach's primary application has been to therapeutic treatment for anybody suffering 'problems with living'. Some humanistic therapies include:

- client-centred therapy – whereby the client is encouraged to develop positive self-regard and overcome mismatch between their perceived self, true self, and ideal self
- gestalt therapy – developed by Fritz Perls, the aim is to help the client become a 'whole' (gestalt) person by getting them to accept every aspect of themselves.

STRENGTHS

The humanistic approach has contributed to psychology by:

- re-emphasising the need to study consciousness and human experience for a complete study of the subject
- serving as a valuable agent of criticism against the extremes of the earlier major approaches
- highlighting the value of more individualistic and idiographic methods of study, particularly in the areas of personality and abnormality
- emphasising the importance of self-actualisation, responsibility, freedom of choice, and social context in therapy.

WEAKNESSES

Humanistic psychology has not, however, had the significant impact on mainstream academic psychology that the other approaches have. This is probably because humanists deliberately take a less scientific approach to studying humans since:

- their belief in free will is in opposition to the deterministic laws of science
- they adopt a more idiographic approach, seeking the more unique aspects of individuals, rather than producing generalised laws of behaviour that apply to everyone
- the issues they investigate, such as consciousness and emotion, are amongst the most difficult to objectively study.

1.6 The biological approach

ORIGINS AND HISTORY

- Sometimes known as the physiological, biopsychological, neurophysiological, nativist (considering nature rather than nurture) or innate approach.
- The biological approach to psychological matters has integrated with and run parallel to the rest of psychological thought since early Greek times – the Greek physician Galen suggested that personality and temperament may be linked to the levels of body fluids such as blood and bile in the body.
- As knowledge of human anatomy, physiology, biochemistry, and medicine developed, important insights for human behaviour and experience were gained. Penfield, for example, mapped the role of various areas of the cerebral cortex through microelectrode stimulation with conscious patients. Sperry investigated the effects of splitting the cerebral hemispheres on consciousness and psychological function.
- The field will progress still further as the technology to isolate the effects of genes and scan the living brain develops.

Roger Sperry
'All that is psychological is first physiological' Anon.

ASSUMPTIONS
Biologically orientated psychologists assume that:
- all that is psychological is first physiological – that is since the mind appears to reside in the brain, all thoughts, feelings and behaviours ultimately have a physical/biological cause
- human genes have evolved over millions of years to adapt physiology and behaviour to the environment. Therefore, much behaviour will have a genetic basis
- psychology should, therefore, investigate the brain, nervous system, endocrine system, neurochemistry, and genes
- it is also useful to study why human behaviour has evolved in the way it has, the subject of evolutionary/sociobiological theory.

METHODS OF INVESTIGATION
Common techniques include:
- laboratory experimentation – e.g. stimulating, giving drugs to, or removing parts of the brain to see what effect it has on behaviour
- laboratory observations – controlled observations of physical processes, e.g. sleep or the scanning of the structure and activity of the brain
- correlations – e.g. between twins and adopted family members to discover the genetic influence on intelligence or mental disorders.

CONTRIBUTION TO PSYCHOLOGY
Physiological researchers have contributed to an understanding of:
- **Gender development** – e.g. the influence of genetic and hormonal predispositions on gender behaviour and identity
- **Aggression** – e.g. investigating the role of the limbic system
- **Abnormality** – e.g. the dopamine hypothesis and enlarged ventricle theory of schizophrenia
- **Memory** – e.g. brain scans of areas involved during memory tests or the effect of brain damage on memory
- **Motivation** – e.g. the role of the hypothalamus in homeostasis
- **Awareness** – e.g. biological theories of sleep, dreams and body rhythms
- **Localisation of function** – e.g. the effect on behaviour of brain damage to certain areas.

CONTRIBUTION TO SOCIETY
Physiology's main applications have been to:
- **Therapy** – e.g. drug treatment, psychosurgery, or electroconvulsive therapy for mental disorders such as schizophrenia or depression
- **Health** – e.g. research on the causes, effects and management of stress
- **Industry** – e.g. research on jet lag and shift work
- **Sport** – e.g. the effect of arousal on performance
- **Education** – e.g. the genetic basis of ability.

STRENGTHS
Physiology has contributed to psychology in many ways:
- The approach is very scientific, grounded in the hard science of biology with its objective, materialistic subject matter and experimental methodology.
- It provides strong counter-arguments to the nurture side of the nature-nurture debate.
- Physiology's practical applications are usually extremely effective, e.g. the treatment of mental disorder.
- The physiological approach has contributed to psychologists' understanding of a very wide range of phenomena.

WEAKNESSES
- Reductionism – the biopsychological approach explains thoughts and behaviour in terms of the action of neurones or biochemicals. This may ignore other more suitable levels of explanation and the interaction of causal factors.
- The approach has not adequately explained how mind and body interact – consciousness and emotion are difficult to study objectively.
- Over simplistic – biopsychological theories often over-simplify the huge complexity of physical systems and their interaction with environmental factors.

1.7 The social psychological approach

ORIGINS AND HISTORY
- Researchers can be said to adopt a social psychological approach when they focus their research on *social behaviour* (between individuals or groups) and tend to regard *other people* and *social contexts* as just as, if not more, important as influences upon people as their dispositions and personality characteristics.
- Social behaviours include those most important to us such as attraction, helping, prejudice and aggression, while the influences studied include those of individuals (e.g. leadership and obedience), groups (e.g. conformity and crowding), societies (e.g. social norms and expectations) and culture (e.g. history, politics and language).
- Social psychology has a long history within scientific psychology, e.g. Triplett's (1898) social facilitation experiment. Like most psychological research, social psychologists began by investigating social processes and influence as they applied to the *individual*. Most of this research came from America and dominated social psychology, but a more sociological and European approach was gradually incorporated to take more account of social, historical and political contexts and collective/shared representations and identities.
- Social constructionism has taken the social approach one step further by suggesting our society, culture and language affect the very way we define psychological concepts and the process of scientific investigation itself – making unbiased study difficult if not impossible.

Stanley Milgram
Social psychology can be defined as 'the scientific investigation of how the thoughts, feelings and behaviours of individuals are influenced by the actual, imagined or implied presence of others', G. Allport (1935).

ASSUMPTIONS
Social psychologists assume that, for anyone who has been raised in a society:
1 All behaviour occurs in a social context, even when nobody else is physically present.
2 A major influence on people's behaviour, thought processes and emotions are other people and the society they have created.

METHODS OF INVESTIGATION
Social psychologists have used a very wide range of methods, e.g.
- Field experiments – e.g. Piliavin and others changed the type of victim requiring help in the everyday environment of a subway.
- Laboratory experiments – e.g. Milgram changed various social variables to affect obedience under controlled conditions.
- Surveys – e.g. questionnaires have been used on many people to measure the frequency and reasons for prejudiced attitudes.
- Observation / content analysis – e.g. to record discrimination.

CONTRIBUTION TO PSYCHOLOGY
Social psychologists have sought to explain:
- *Social influence* e.g. conformity, obedience, leadership, social facilitation and crowd behaviour.
- *Social cognition* e.g. social identity / categorisation, attitudes, attribution, stereotyping and emotion.
- *Social behaviour* e.g. inter-personal and inter-group aggression, discrimination, attraction and helping.
- *Social development* e.g. gender, self, attachment and intellectual development over time as a result of changing roles, social expectations, social circumstances and cultural influences.

CONTRIBUTION TO SOCIETY
Social psychology has had a broad range of applications, for example to:
- *Criminology* – e.g. attribution theory and jury decision-making.
- *Education* – e.g. the labelling and stereotyping of students' educational performance.
- *Industry* – e.g. in leadership/management selection and group productivity.
- *Sport* – e.g. team and audience effects on performance.
- *The environment* – e.g. the effects of architecture and crowding on behaviour or attitude change towards the environment.
- *Health* – e.g. social factors affecting the exposure and reaction to stress.

STRENGTHS
Social psychology is still an important approach today.
- Social influences have been shown to be involved in, and have a strong effect upon, people's behaviour, thinking and emotions – often stronger than dispositional influences.
- The approach has provided explanations for a great many phenomena.
- The approach has had many useful practical applications in a wide range of areas.
- The approach has provided evidence for its concepts and theories using a wide range of methods, often conducted in a scientifically objective manner.

WEAKNESSES
At times the social psychological approach has:
- Underestimated what people bring with them into social situations – individual differences (whether inherited or learnt) do affect the results of social psychological studies but are sometimes explored less.
- Provided only 'superficial snapshots of social processes' (Hayes, 1995), ignoring their development over time and the broader social, political, historical and cultural context that the research takes place in. For example American researchers measuring what their students find attractive in a photograph of a face in laboratory conditions at a particular time in history.

2.1 Psychology and science 1

To fully investigate whether psychology, despite its problems, is justified in calling itself a science, we must first outline what a science consists of, and then see how well psychology matches these criteria.

A science consists of various components:
- A **subject matter**
- Good **theories** and **hypotheses**
- Scientific **methodology**

THE SCIENTIFIC METHOD

Within a paradigm

hypotheses are derived

from theories

to be tested in scientific ways

against the world/reality

to support or refute those theories

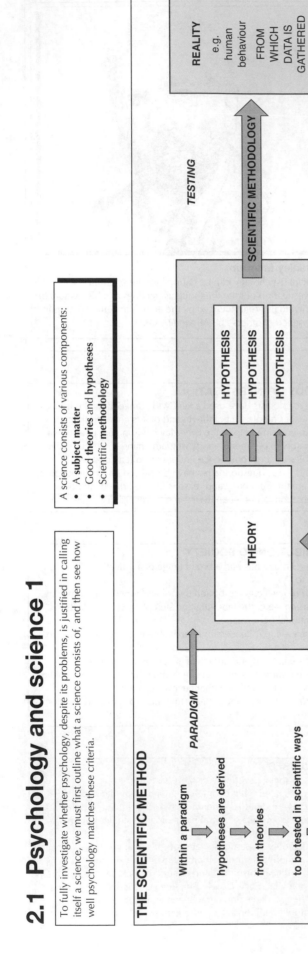

PARADIGM

THEORY

HYPOTHESIS
HYPOTHESIS
HYPOTHESIS

TESTING

SCIENTIFIC METHODOLOGY

FEEDBACK SUPPORT/REFUTE

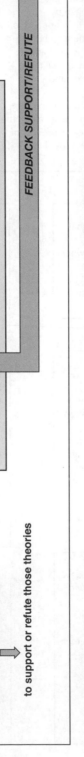

REALITY

e.g. human behaviour

FROM WHICH DATA IS GATHERED

A SUBJECT MATTER

- The subject matter of a science is what the science is about. There should be agreement amongst researchers about *what* should be studied and *how*. **Kuhn** (1962) used the term 'paradigm' to describe this **shared set of assumptions, methods and terminology**.
- According to Kuhn's theory of the progression of science, paradigms go through changes over time, through three historical stages:

  a **Pre-science**, where there is no universally accepted paradigm.
  b **Normal science**, where researchers work sharing the same paradigm.
  c **Revolution**, where conflicting evidence becomes so overwhelming that a *paradigm-shift* occurs to a new perspective.

- Thus, the majority view at one time was that the Earth was flat and was the centre of the Universe, but this view became more and more criticised until it was superseded. Similarly, the Newtonian paradigm of physics was replaced by Einstein's which better fitted the facts of, for example, planetary motion.

PSYCHOLOGY'S SUBJECT MATTER

Does psychology have a unified subject matter and paradigm?
Kuhn argues that psychology is in a state of **pre-science**, because there are so many conflicting approaches to the subject that there is **no overall paradigm**. However, it could be argued that psychology has already gone through **several paradigm shifts**, from structuralism, to behaviourism, to cognitive psychology. Perhaps psychology is in the process of selecting the best set of approaches to form an integrated paradigm. Certainly most psychologists accept the definition of Psychology as the study of *mind* **and** behaviour.
Valentine (1982) proposes that **behaviourism** is the closest psychology has come to having a unified **paradigm**, since it had a clear subject matter (observable behaviour), assumptions (environmental determinism, learning, etc.), methods (strict laboratory experimentation), and terminology (conditioning, reinforcement, etc.). This paradigm dominated psychology for many years.
Other philosophers of science, such as **Feyerabend** (1975), argue that **science** does **not** progress in an **orderly** way through paradigms, but does and should progress **anarchistically** – as each researcher sticks tenaciously to their own theories, often in the face of opposition from others. Feyerabend argues that conforming to paradigms may limit creativity and progress, 'The only principle that does not inhibit progress is anything goes'. This view seems much more realistic of how psychology has developed, with many psychologists working as individuals or in small teams to defend their own particular area of research in the subject.

2.2 Psychology and science 2

THEORIES AND HYPOTHESES

A science should involve theories which should provide hypotheses to be tested in order to support or refute the theories. The theories themselves should provide general laws or principles to fulfil the aims of science – **understanding, prediction,** and **control.**

1 Understanding – Theories should provide understanding by being
- **orderly** (theories should organise facts and find regularities and patterns to generate laws).
- **internally consistent** (different parts of the theory should not contradict each other).
- **parsimonious** (provide the greatest possible explanation in the most economic way).
- **true!** (theories should correctly explain reality).

2 Prediction – A good theory should generate lots of **bold, precise hypotheses** to stimulate research to support or refute the theory.
- According to **Karl Popper** (1959) scientific theories should be **refutable** (able to be shown wrong) and research should aim to falsify rather than support theories – since it is all too easy to find support to fit your theory, especially if you expect to find it. **Falsification** is best achieved by advancing bold and precise hypotheses, and if a theory is falsified then it should be rejected. Thus Popper is suggesting that science advances through refutation rather than support. This is why we ensure we include a null hypothesis.
- Another philosopher of science, **Imre Lakatos,** suggests that theories should be given a chance to prove themselves first, so they can develop. Lakatos proposes that theories or paradigms should have a **hard core** of crucial assumptions and a **protective belt** of auxiliary hypotheses – this belt can support being falsified to a certain extent (perhaps the first experiments made type 2 errors) but the hard core should remain unfalsified for the theory to remain credible. Good theories, he added, should also provide a **positive heuristic** – a future research program to generate new hypotheses and to produce unexpected findings.
- Theories provide laws and principles to predict the future, but this can only occur if
  - **a** a **deterministic/**nomothetic view is taken, rather than a freewill or idiographic approach.
  - **b induction** is accepted, i.e. that we can generalise from a limited number of observations to general laws. Induction can **never prove** anything 100%, however, because it is impossible to observe all possible data at any one time and we can never prove that our next observation will not refute our law. Induction is the basis for inferential statistics which talk about the **probability** of chance factors causing the results.

3 Control – Theories should be **useful** and have **practical implications,** such as solving problems and improving the human condition. However, complete control may be impossible in practice, due to the complexity of situations and the probabilistic nature of scientific laws. Knowing the high probability that something will occur 99/100 will not guarantee that it will occur on a certain occasion. Ethical issues are also raised concerning control – who should have it and whose purposes should it serve?

SCIENTIFIC METHODOLOGY

- A science should test its hypotheses in fair and objective ways, meaning its terms should be operationalised and its methods should be standardised, controlled and replicable.

PSYCHOLOGICAL THEORIES AND HYPOTHESES

The different approaches to psychology fulfil these principles to varying degrees:

1 Psychoanalysis has **great explanatory power** and understanding of behaviour, but has been accused of only explaining behaviour after the event, **not predicting** what will happen in advance and of being **unfalsifiable/**unrefutable. Some have argued that psychoanalysis has approached the status more of a religion than a science, but it is not alone in being accused of being unfalsifiable (evolutionary theory has too – why is anything the way it is? Because it has evolved that way!) and like all theories that are difficult to refute – the possibility exists that it is actually right. Kline (1984) argues that psychoanalytic theory **can** be broken down into testable hypotheses and tested scientifically. For example, Scodel (1957) postulated that orally dependent men would prefer larger breasts (a positive correlation), but in fact found significantly the opposite (a negative correlation). Although Freudian theory could also be used to explain this finding (through reaction formation – the subjects were showing exactly the opposite of their unconscious impulses!), Kline has nevertheless pointed out that theory would have been refuted by *no significant correlation.*

2 The **humanistic approach** in psychology deliberately steps away from a scientific viewpoint, **rejecting determinism** in favour of freewill, aiming to study the **individual** to arrive at a unique and in depth understanding. The humanistic approach does not have an orderly set of theories (although it does have some core assumptions) and is not interested in prediction and controlling people's behaviour – the individuals themselves are the only ones who can and should do that. **Miller** (1969) in 'Psychology as a Means of Promoting Human Welfare' criticises the controlling view of psychology, suggesting that understanding should be the main goal of the subject as a science, since he asks who will do the controlling and whose interests will be served by it?

3 Behaviourism had **parsimonious** theories of learning, using a few simple principles (reinforcement, behaviour shaping, generalisation, etc.) to explain a vast variety of behaviour from language acquisition to moral development. It advanced **bold, precise and refutable hypotheses** (such as Hull's drive theory equations) and possessed a **hard core of central assumptions,** such as determination from the environment (it was only when this assumption faced overwhelming criticism by the cognitive and ethological theorists that the behaviourist paradigm was overthrown). Behaviourists firmly believed in the scientific principles of **determinism** and orderliness, and thus came up with fairly consistent **predictions** about when an animal was likely to respond (although they admitted that perfect prediction for any individual was impossible). The behaviourists used their predictions to **control** the behaviour of both animals (pigeons trained to detect life jackets) and humans (behavioural therapies) and indeed Skinner, in his book *Walden Two* (1948), described a whole society controlled according to behaviourist principles.

4 Cognitive Psychology – adopts a scientific approach to unobservable mental processes by advancing precise models and conducting experiments upon behaviour to confirm or refute them.

- Full understanding, prediction and control in psychology is probably unobtainable due to the huge complexity of environmental, mental and biological influences upon even the simplest behaviour.

PSYCHOLOGICAL METHODS

- Behaviourist, cognitive and biopsychological approaches have used the most objective method, the laboratory experiment. Humanists point out many problems of using this method for human study.

2.3 Peer review and validating research

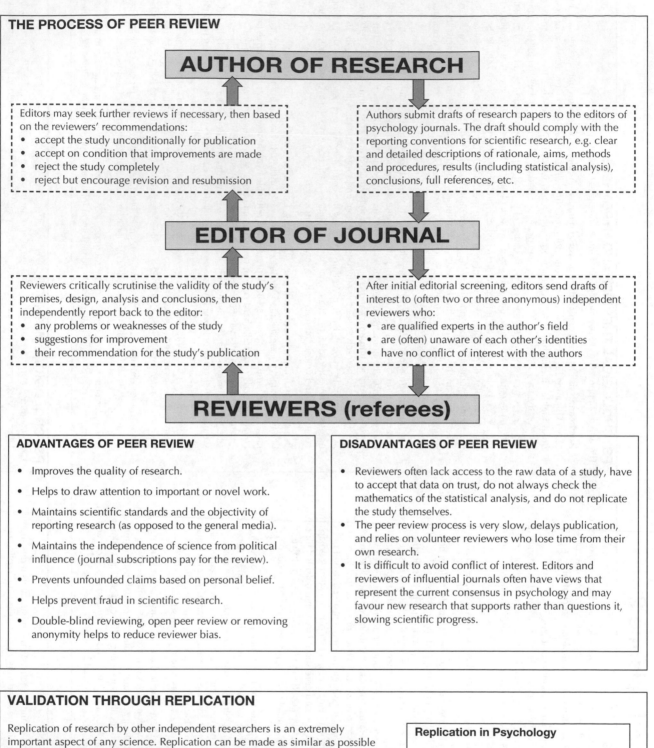

THE PROCESS OF PEER REVIEW

AUTHOR OF RESEARCH

Editors may seek further reviews if necessary, then based on the reviewers' recommendations:
- accept the study unconditionally for publication
- accept on condition that improvements are made
- reject the study completely
- reject but encourage revision and resubmission

Authors submit drafts of research papers to the editors of psychology journals. The draft should comply with the reporting conventions for scientific research, e.g. clear and detailed descriptions of rationale, aims, methods and procedures, results (including statistical analysis), conclusions, full references, etc.

EDITOR OF JOURNAL

Reviewers critically scrutinise the validity of the study's premises, design, analysis and conclusions, then independently report back to the editor:
- any problems or weaknesses of the study
- suggestions for improvement
- their recommendation for the study's publication

After initial editorial screening, editors send drafts of interest to (often two or three anonymous) independent reviewers who:
- are qualified experts in the author's field
- are (often) unaware of each other's identities
- have no conflict of interest with the authors

REVIEWERS (referees)

ADVANTAGES OF PEER REVIEW

- Improves the quality of research.
- Helps to draw attention to important or novel work.
- Maintains scientific standards and the objectivity of reporting research (as opposed to the general media).
- Maintains the independence of science from political influence (journal subscriptions pay for the review).
- Prevents unfounded claims based on personal belief.
- Helps prevent fraud in scientific research.
- Double-blind reviewing, open peer review or removing anonymity helps to reduce reviewer bias.

DISADVANTAGES OF PEER REVIEW

- Reviewers often lack access to the raw data of a study, have to accept that data on trust, do not always check the mathematics of the statistical analysis, and do not replicate the study themselves.
- The peer review process is very slow, delays publication, and relies on volunteer reviewers who lose time from their own research.
- It is difficult to avoid conflict of interest. Editors and reviewers of influential journals often have views that represent the current consensus in psychology and may favour new research that supports rather than questions it, slowing scientific progress.

VALIDATION THROUGH REPLICATION

Replication of research by other independent researchers is an extremely important aspect of any science. Replication can be made as similar as possible to the original study or can be modified to test the effect of changing certain variables and procedures. It serves to test:
- The reliability of the methods and procedures used in the original study – are they clear, precise, objective and standardised enough to allow proper replication.
- The validity of the operationalisation of variables in the study – does a different way of testing the key variables on the same population give the same result?
- The generalisability of the findings – can the same results and conclusions of the study be found in other samples and populations (how much of a general law do the findings of the study represent?).

Unfortunately, if a study's results are not exactly replicated by other researchers, it is sometimes difficult to identify whether procedural variables, participant variables or researcher effects are responsible.

Replication in Psychology

➤ Milgram's (1963) study of obedience has been replicated with many different variations.

➤ Haney, Banks and Zimbardo (1973) was partially replicated by Reicher and Haslam (2006).

➤ Asch's (1951, 1952, 1956) studies of conformity have not always been replicated with the same results by studies conducted in later decades or on different populations.

2.4 Ethnocentrism and cultural bias

EXAMPLES OF CULTURAL BIAS IN PSYCHOLOGY

Social influence – Cross-cultural replications of obedience and conformity studies have revealed wide differences in resistance to influence.
Interpersonal relationships – Cultural bias in Western research on this topic, is revealed by its focus on:
- brief, new acquaintances, rather than long term, kin relationships.
- the idea that marriage on the basis of romantic love is more desirable than on the basis of companionate love.

Helping behaviour – Western economic theories on the costs and rewards of helping behaviour may not be suitable for other cultures.
Abnormality – The increased diagnosis of mental disorder in immigrants may reflect prejudice or misunderstanding by a native diagnoser.
Psychometric testing – IQ and personality tests have been culturally biased in terms of content, phrasing, application, and assessment.

THEORETICAL BIAS

Cultures differ in many important ways from each other, for example in terms of their values, norms of behaviour and social structure – such as whether they emphasise individualism or collectivism, masculine or feminine values, etc. (Triandis, 1990).

Since cultural values strongly shape the construction of theories, a major problem is **ethnocentrism**, which involves:
- inappropriately generalising the values and research findings of one culture to another without bothering to test other cultures. This limits the validity of theories and neglects important cross-cultural differences.
- imposing those values upon other cultures when conducting cross-cultural research. This distorts the validity of research, over-emphasises differences and can lead to unfavourable comparisons being made.

Nobles (1976) points out that the 'Eurocentric' approach (based on concepts such as 'survival of the fittest', 'competition' and 'independence') to the study of African people (who believe in 'the survival of the tribe', 'co-operation' and 'interdependence') amounts to an act of scientific colonialism.

REPORTING BIAS

- **Interpretation of results**
  Results that show cultural differences may be reported in a way that make non-American/European cultures appear deviant from the 'norm' or inferior.
- **Selection of material to be published**
  The predominantly white establishment in American and European psychology has filtered out research on black psychology, leading to the need to publish journals and books specifically for black psychology. Around two thirds of psychology in the world is North American.
- **Use of results**
  Results may be interpreted to fit political ideology and thus 'scientifically sanction' racist policies such as the eugenics driven policy of restricting immigration into the USA during the 1920s and 1930s based on the results of (biased) IQ tests.

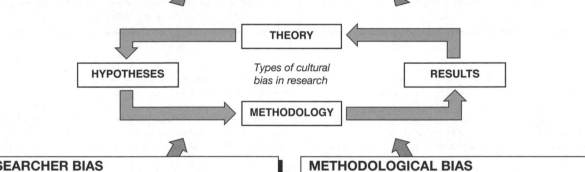

Types of cultural bias in research

THEORY — HYPOTHESES — METHODOLOGY — RESULTS

RESEARCHER BIAS

Cultural bias in research is likely to be caused by:
- **Lack of researchers**
  Researcher bias may occur because researchers from other cultures are not appointed to, or promoted in, academic positions in universities. 'Token' black psychologists in a predominantly white department, for example, may find themselves marginalised into areas outside mainstream psychology.
- **Nature of researchers**
  Culturally biased or racist researchers are likely to propose hypotheses that:
  - a investigate stereotypical differences between 'races' (arbitrary and over-simplified categories based on skin colour) which may ignore cultural influences and perpetuate the stereotypes.
  - b do not investigate important cross-cultural differences or similarities.

METHODOLOGICAL BIAS

Cultural bias in the methodology of studies is found in:
- The biased sampling of subjects – the vast majority of the most famous studies in American and European psychology only used white subjects. Reviews of research in these countries frequently reveal less than 5% of subjects tested are not white.
- The use of Eurocentric scientific methods (based on 'control over nature', objective 'separateness' from the subject, and the investigation of individual 'differences' and 'uniqueness'), such as the laboratory experiment, is alien to the African concepts of 'oneness with nature', 'groupness' and 'similarity' (Nobles, 1976). These methods represent an imposed 'etic' (the study of a culture from the outside) when ecologically valid data can only be gained from an 'emic' study (from within the culture). Imposed 'etics' can lead to very culturally biased tests such as those on IQ described by Gould (1982).

CONSEQUENCES OF CULTURAL BIAS

Nobles (1976) argues that Western psychology has been a tool of oppression and dominance. Cultural bias has also made it difficult for psychologists to separate the behaviour they have observed from the context in which they observed it.

VALIDITY OF CULTURAL BIAS

Culturally biased views have been exposed as false in many areas of psychology.

REDUCING CULTURAL BIAS

Equal opportunity legislation aims to rid psychology of cultural bias and racism, but we must be aware of merely swapping old, overt racism for new, more subtle forms of racism (Howitt and Owusu-Bempah, 1994).

2.5 The nature-nurture debate

NATURE → NURTURE

APPROACH

Roots of the approach – nativist philosophy, biology (physiology and genetics), evolutionary theory.
Causes of behaviour – genetic determinism, inherited influence, maturational blueprint, neurochemical and hormonal influences, brain activity.
Methods employed – gene/chromosome mapping, twin and adoption studies, brain scanning, brain stimulation or damage studies, drug testing.
Implications – due to biological determinism, behaviour can only be changed through physical means, such as selective breeding (eugenics), gene therapy, brain surgery, or drugs.
Criticisms – reductionist, may neglect environmental influences.

Roots of the approach – empiricism philosophy, behaviourism, social psychology.
Causes of behaviour – the mind is regarded as a 'tabula rasa' (blank slate) at birth; therefore, knowledge and behaviour are the result of experience and learning from the environment.
Methods employed – use of classical and operant conditioning techniques to affect behaviour, manipulation of social environment to change behaviour.
Implications – due to environmental determinism, behaviour can be easily changed through manipulating reinforcement and environmental conditions. Anybody could be trained to do anything.
Criticisms – reductionist, may neglect innate influences.

AREAS OF EXPLANATION

Perception – Research conducted by Fantz, Bower, and Gibson and Walk on new-born babies indicated pattern detection, size constancy and depth perception are innate abilities.
Aggression – The ethologist Lorenz and psychoanalyst Freud believed aggression is an innate drive. Bio-psychologists have examined the role of hormones and brain areas in aggression.
Sex-role behaviour – Bio-psychologists propose gender identity is a direct result of genetic and hormonal influences.
Abnormality – The biomedical approach has isolated genetic and neurochemical causes of mental disorders.
Language acquisition – Chomsky proposed language is gained through the use of an innate language acquisition device.

Perception – Research into perception by Hebb on cataract removal and Turnbull on cross-cultural differences indicated that perceptual identification is a learnt ability.
Aggression – Social learning theory argues that aggression is learnt from the environment through observation and imitation. Social psychologists study conformity to aggressive norms.
Sex-role behaviour – Cultural relativism and learning theory argue that gender is socially constructed and reinforced.
Abnormality – The environment plays a role in the development of phobias, post-traumatic stress disorder, and anorexia.
Language acquisition – Skinner argued that language is learnt from other people via natural behaviour shaping techniques.

While some researchers have aimed to investigate the relative contributions of innate and environmental factors in psychology, it is now accepted that the two influences form a **continuum** and interact so thoroughly with each other that they are virtually inseparable. Even seemingly direct genetic influences, such as those on the physical development of the brain, are affected by environmental factors, from the inside of the womb to the pollution of the atmosphere. Many genes could impose a **susceptibility** to develop in certain ways or provide a 'norm of reaction' – a genetic potential that may or may not be realised by environmental circumstances. In a similar way, environmental experiences are **mediated** by not only innate abilities but even by the physical structure of the body, e.g. what gender or skin colour it has.

EXAMPLES OF NATURE–NURTURE INTERACTION IN PSYCHOLOGY

Perception – Blakemore and Cooper showed restricted environmental experience could physically affect the visual cortex of the brain.
Cognitive development – Piaget suggested that innate schemata develop and expand through interaction with the environment to adapt the child to its surroundings, although development was always limited by biological maturation.

Abnormality – Many mental disorders, such as schizophrenia, may have a genetic predisposition – those with an inherited susceptibility may be more likely to develop the disorder if they experience certain stressful environmental conditions. Animal studies have looked at the effect of aversive environmental stimuli upon the brain's neurotransmitters to explain depression.

Sex-role behaviour – The Biosocial approach proposes that factors such as the physical sex and innate temperament of a new born baby elicits sex typing behaviour from the people around it, leading to a self-fulfilling prophecy in terms of its gender identity.

THE STANDING OF THE DIFFERENT APPROACHES IN PSYCHOLOGY

NATURE ←——————————————————→ NURTURE

BIOPSYCHOLOGY
Focuses on genetic, physiological, hormonal and neurochemical explanations of behaviour.

PSYCHOANALYSIS
Focuses on instinctual drives of sex and aggression, expressed within the restrictions imposed by society via the ego and superego.

COGNITIVE PSYCHOLOGY
Focuses on innate information processing abilities or schemata that are constantly refined by experience.

HUMANISM
While accepting basic physiological needs, the focus is upon the person's experience of their social and physical environment.

BEHAVIOURISM
Focuses on the acquisition of virtually all behaviour from the environment via conditioning.

2.6 The reductionism vs. holism debate

REDUCTIONISM

HOLISM AND INTERACTIONISM

ASSUMPTIONS

Reductionism involves explaining a phenomenon by **breaking** it **down** into its **constituent parts – analysing it.** Reductionism works on the scientific assumption of **parsimony** – that complex phenomena should be explained by the **simplest underlying principles** possible.

Holism looks at same/higher level explanations. Interactionism shows how **many aspects** of a phenomenon or **levels** of explanation can **interact together** to provide a **complete** picture. Both approaches involve taking a gestalt approach, assuming that **'the whole is greater than the sum of its parts'**.

EXAMPLES IN PSYCHOLOGY

There have been many reductionist attempts to explain behaviour in psychology, for example:
- Structuralism – one of the first approaches to psychology pioneered by Wundt and Titchener involved trying to break conscious experience down into its constituent images, sensations, and feelings.
- Behaviourism – assumed that complex behaviour was the sum of all past stimulus-response learning units.
- Biopsychology – aims to explain all at the psychological or mental level in terms of that at the physiological, neurochemical or genetic level. Ultimately, psychology would be replaced by biology and the other natural sciences lower down on the reductionist ladder.

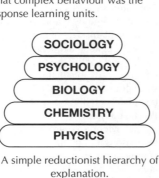

A simple reductionist hierarchy of explanation.

Other approaches have proposed higher level holistic and/or interactionist explanations of human behaviour, for example:
- **Humanistic psychology** – investigates all aspects of the individual as well as the effect of interactions between people. Gestalt therapy developed by Fritz Perls aims to enable people to accept and cope with all aspects of their life and personality.
- **Social psychology** – looks at the behaviour of individuals in a social context. Group behaviour may show characteristics that are greater than the sum of the individuals which comprise it (or *less* in the case of social loafing!).
- **Psychoanalysis** – Freud adopted an interactionist approach, in that he considered that behaviour was the result of dynamic interaction between id, ego, and superego.
- **Abnormal psychology** – mental disorders are often explained by an interaction of biological, psychological, and environmental factors. Schizophrenia may be due to a genetic predisposition triggered by environmental stress. An eclectic approach to therapy is often taken using drugs and psychotherapy.
- **Perception** – illusions show that humans perceive more than the sum of the sensations of the retina.

FOR

- Reductionist explanations in psychology adopt a very **scientific** and **analytical** approach, which has worked very well with the natural sciences.
- By breaking phenomena down into smaller simple components (as behaviourism did with stimulus-response units) these constituent parts are often more **easily tested.**
- By explaining behavioural phenomena in terms of their underlying physical basis, psychology gains the scientific **support** and **credibility** of these well established and robust sciences, and **unifies** with them to provide a **consistent** picture of the universe.

- The interactionist approach can **integrate** many **different levels** of explanation to provide a more **complete** and **realistic** understanding of behaviour.
- Holism does **not ignore** the **complexity** and the **'emergent properties'** of higher level phenomenon. For example, there may be aspects of crowd behaviour that could not be explained in terms of the individuals in that crowd.
- **Functional** explanations are only possible at higher levels – examining the social reasons **why** we show a certain aggressive behaviour is often more useful than providing a detailed neuronal, hormonal and physiological explanation of the act.

AGAINST

- **Oversimplification** – reductionist explanations often ignore many important interactions and the emergent properties of phenomena at higher levels. The whole may be greater than the sum of its parts.
- **Value of explanation** – higher level explanations may be less detailed and more useful than lower level ones. The **meaning** of an action, such as a hand wave, is only gained from its situation (e.g. greeting or drowning) not its underlying physiological description.
- **Validity of reductionism** – Rose (1976) argues that different levels of discourse cannot be substituted for each other. This raises the problem of the relationship between the **mind** and the **brain** – is a feeling of pain the same as the activation of nerve cells in a particular part of your brain? A neurologist may follow the 'neuronal path' of a pin prick up the arm and into a reception area of the brain, but the neurologist would have to rely on your conscious (psychological level) verbal report to know whether you *felt* pain or not.

- There is a great **practical difficulty** in investigating the integration of explanations from different levels. Research into mental disorders is beginning to understand the interaction of environmental, psychological, and biological explanations of disorders like depression.
- Holistic explanations of psychological phenomena that assume the mind is not the same as the body, tend to **ignore** the huge **influence** of biology on behaviour.
- Holistic explanations tend to get more **hypothetical** and divorced from physical reality the higher they go up the reductionist ladder. Higher level theories appear to **lack** the **predictive** power of the physical sciences (although there is a corresponding increase in the complexity of the systems investigated).

2.7 The freewill vs. determinism debate

 FREEWILL

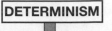 DETERMINISM

ASSUMPTIONS

The freewill approach assumes that humans **are free to choose their behaviour,** that they are essentially **self-determining.** Freewill does not mean that behaviour is uncaused in the sense of being completely random, but assumes that influences (biological or environmental) can be rejected at will.
Soft determinism (William James, 1890) suggests that freewill is not freedom from causation, but freedom from coercion and constraint – if our actions are voluntary and in line with our conscious desired goals then they are free.

The determinism approach assumes that **every physical event is caused,** and, since human behaviour is a physical event, it follows that it too is caused by preceding factors.
If all events are caused and perfect knowledge is gained of the current state of the universe, it follows that future events are entirely **predictable.**
Determinism, with its emphasis on **causal laws** is, therefore, the basis of science, which aims to reveal those laws to provide prediction and **control** of the future.

EXAMPLES IN PSYCHOLOGY

Humanistic psychology, proposed by the likes of Rogers and Maslow, is the strongest advocate of human freewill, arguing that we are able to direct our lives towards self-chosen goals. The emphasis on freewill is most apparent in humanistic based therapies, where the terms client and facilitator are used to indicate the voluntary nature of the situation, and the idea that the individual has the power to solve their own problems through insight. Humanistic therapies are usually non directive.
Cognitive psychology appears to adopt a soft determinism view considering problem solving and attentional mechanisms as the 'choosers' of thought and behaviour. While it seems that we select what we pay attention to, these mechanisms operate with the parameters of their innate capabilities and our past experience (just as a computer cannot choose to do something it was not built or programmed for) e.g. 'perceptual set' suggests that we are not free to choose what we see. However, language and metacognitive abilities may allow humans to choose from among many possible influences (Johnson-Laird,1988).

The majority of approaches in psychology adopt a fairly strict deterministic view of human behaviour.
Behaviourism took an extreme environmental determinism approach, arguing that learning from the environment 'writes upon the blank slate of our mind at birth' to cause behaviour. Watson's belief that the deterministic laws of learning could predict and control the future were reflected in his claim that he could take any infant at random and turn them into any type of specialist he might select. Skinner argued that freewill is completely an illusion created by our complexity of learning.
Psychoanalysis took the view of unconscious determinism - that our behaviour is controlled by forces of which we are unaware - the reasons for our actions are merely rationalised by our conscious minds. Later psychoanalysts, such as Erikson, looked at more conscious ego processes than Freud, however.
Biological approaches to psychology look at the deterministic influence of genetics, brain structure and biochemistry. Sociobiologists investigate evolutionary determinism.

FOR

- **Introspection** upon our decisions when many possible and equally desirable options are available often seems to indicate free choice. Subjective impressions should be considered.
- Even if humans do not have freewill, the fact that **they think they do** has many implications for behaviour. Rotter (1966), for example, has proposed that individuals with an external locus of control who feel that outside factors (e.g. chance) control their life, suffer more from the effects of stress than those who feel they can influence situations (an internal locus of control). Brehm (1966) argued people react if their freedom is threatened.

- The illusion of freewill is shattered very easily by **mental disorders** (obsessive compulsives lose control of their thoughts and actions, depressives their emotions) and psychoactive drugs (which can produce involuntary hallucinations and behaviour).
- Determinism is one of the key assumptions of **science** – whose cause and effect laws have explained, predicted and controlled behaviour (in some areas) above the levels achieved by unaided commonsense.
- The **majority** of all psychologists, even those sympathetic to the idea of freewill, accept determinism to some degree.

AGAINST

- It is **difficult to define** what freewill is and what the 'self' that 'does the choosing' consists of. Philosophers such as Descartes regarded it as the non-physical soul or spirit, while the existentialist philosopher Sartre preferred to think that freewill was a product of consciousness.
- The **evidence** for the existence of freewill is mostly **subjective** – where 'objective' studies have been conducted the results are a little disturbing – Libet (1985a) claims that the brain processes that initiate the movement of a hand occur almost half a second *before* the moment a subject reports choosing to move it!
- A pure freewill approach is **incompatible** with the deterministic assumptions of **science.**

- Determinism is **inconsistent** with society's ideas of self-control and responsibility that underlie all our moral and legal assumptions. Only extreme examples of determinism are taken into account (e.g. insanity).
- Determinism can never lead to complete prediction, due to
  a The vast complexity of influences upon any behaviour
  b The nature of induction – never being able to prove 100%
  c The notions of unpredictability (e.g. Heisenberg's 'uncertainty principle') and non-causality that physics has produced
- Determinism is **unfalsifiable since** it always assumes a cause exists, even if one has not been found yet.

2.8 The idiographic vs. nomothetic debate

NOMOTHETIC APPROACH	IDIOGRAPHIC APPROACH

DEFINITIONS

The approach of investigating **groups** of people to try to find **general laws** of behaviour that apply to everyone.

The approach of investigating **individuals** in personal, in-depth, detail to achieve a **unique understanding** of them.

ASSUMPTIONS AND METHODS

The nomothetic approach (from the Greek word `nomos` meaning `law`) assumes that since individuals are merely complex combinations of many universal laws, people are best studied by **large scale**, preferably experimental, methods to identify those laws.

Differences between people are only **quantitative** so an individual will be **compared to others**, classified with others, measured as a score upon a dimension, or be a **statistic** supporting a general principle.

The idiographic approach (from the Greek 'idios' meaning `private or personal`) assumes that since each human is unique, they are best investigated by the **case study method** to provide a detailed understanding of the individual.

Differences between people are **qualitative** so study should focus on the unique aspects of, and variability within, a person's thinking and behaviour. By studying these **personal variables**, norms or trends, predictions can be made – but only for that particular individual.

EXAMPLES FROM PSYCHOLOGY

Nomothetic research is the main approach taken in scientifically-orientated psychology:
The **behaviourist** experiments on learning were conducted on many subjects (mostly rats and pigeons), replicated until the general principles of learning were well established, then even generalised as **universal laws** of nature to humans.
The social psychology **experiments** of Asch and Milgram used the nomothetic approach, aiming to reach conclusions about people in general by comparing groups of participants.
All psychological theories that propose generalised principles of behaviour have nomothetic assumptions – Eysenck's personality theory places individuals along a universal **dimension** of extroversion, intelligence tests measure people along a **scale** of IQ scores, and **classification manuals** for mental disorder, e.g. the DSMIV, classify people as suffering from particular **types** of disorder.

The idiographic approach is taken, in its pure form, more rarely in psychology than the nomothetic approach:
Humanistic psychologists focus on the unique characteristics and life experiences of individuals. Some, such as Szasz (1972), have rejected the grouping of individuals into general diagnostic categories like 'schizophrenia', preferring to focus on their unique 'problems with living'.
In personality research Allport (1961) made the distinction between common and **individual traits**, while Kelly (1955) tried to identify the way individuals perceive the world in terms of **personal constructs**.
Freud (1909) used the clinical case study method and aimed to identify the unique life experiences in a patient's history that led to their psychological problems. Nevertheless, he did argue that there were similar processes and mental structures present in everyone that created certain types of problem.

EVALUATION

The nomothetic approach is in tune with the deterministic, law-abiding nature of science, and has been applied very successfully in other **sciences** as well as psychology.
The ability to generalise laws and compare groups of people is very useful in **predicting** and **controlling** behaviour in general. For example, personality questionnaires and mental disorder classification manuals have been used in the selection of personnel and the diagnosis and treatment of disorders.
The drawback, however, is that this approach leaves us with a more **superficial understanding of any one person** – you and I may have the same IQ, but I may have answered different questions to you. Also a piece of nomothetic research may tell me I have a 1% chance of becoming schizophrenic, but it will not tell me if I am in that 1%.

The idiographic approach provides a more complete and global **understanding** of the **individual**. In some counselling and psychotherapy the goal is **greater self-understanding**. Nomothetic generalisations may be too vague or inaccurate for the individual.
An idiographic approach may help to balance the neglect of uniqueness in Psychology – a science dominated by experiments that actively try to control and eliminate individual differences (subject variables).
Replication and prediction for an individual is possible in an idiographic approach, but we **cannot legitimately generalise** (apply) findings to other people, which limits its usefulness and application in psychology.
The idea that people are so unique they cannot be compared in any way seems contradicted by psychological research.

COMPROMISE

Clearly both approaches seem necessary for a complete study of Psychology – if the aims of science are to *describe, understand, predict* and *control*, then idiographic methods may be more suitable for the first two aims and nomothetic methods for the latter two.
As Kluckholm and Murray (1953) comment, every person is in some respects 1) like no other person, 2) like some other people, and 3) like all other people. If there were no common points between individuals then nobody would be able to understand each other!
In the case of abnormality, nomothetic classification allows research to be carried out on groups of people suffering similar symptoms in the hope that a similar cause and cure can be identified, while an idiographic approach may be useful to deal with the particular and perhaps unique set of problems encountered by each patient.

2.9 Ethical guidelines for conducting research

ETHICAL GUIDELINES FOR THE USE OF ANIMALS IN RESEARCH

The Experimental Psychology Society (1986) has issued guidelines to control animal experimentation based on the legislation of the 'Animals (Scientific Procedures) Act' (1986). In general all researchers should:

1 Avoid or minimise stress and suffering for all living animals.
2 Always consider the possibility of other options to animal research.
3 Be as economical as possible in the numbers of animals tested.

However, before any animal is tested a Home Office Licence to conduct animal research has to be acquired. The Home Office provides legislation for and monitors:

- **The conditions under which animals are kept** – cage sizes, food, lighting, temperature, care routine, etc. all have to be suitable for the species and its habits.
- **The researchers conducting the research** – all involved have to demonstrate they have the necessary skills and experience to work with the particular species they wish to study in order to acquire their personal licences.
- **The research projects allowed** – applications must be submitted outlining the project's aims and possible benefits as well as the procedures involved (including the number of animals and the degree of distress they might experience). Projects are only approved if the three requirements above are met and the levels of distress caused to the animals are justified by the benefits of the research. The conditions of the licence have to be strictly adhered to regarding the numbers, species and procedures (e.g. limits on the maximum level of electric shock) allowed. Research on endangered species is prohibited unless the research has direct benefits for the species itself, e.g. conservation.

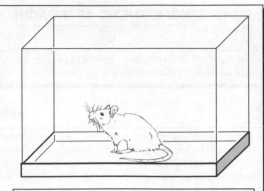

Bateson (1986) has specified some of the factors involved in deciding on the viability of animal research. Often the decision will involve a trade off between
a. The certainty of benefit from the research.
b. The quality of the research.
c. The amount of suffering involved for the animals.
Home Office licences are most likely to be awarded if factors 'a' and 'b' are high, and factor 'c' is low.

ETHICAL ISSUES IN HUMAN RESEARCH

The aim of Psychology is to provide us with a greater understanding of ourselves and, if required, to enable us to use that understanding to predict and control our behaviour for **human betterment**. To achieve this understanding psychologists often have no other choice but to investigate human subjects for valid results to be obtained. Humans, however, not only experience physical **pain** and **anxiety** but can also be affected mentally – in terms of **embarrassment** or **loss of self-esteem** for example. Humans also have **rights** of **protection** and **privacy** above the levels granted to other animals, and so this leads us to ethical dilemmas:

- How far should psychologists be allowed to go in pursuing their knowledge?
- Should humankind aim to improve itself by allowing people to be dehumanised in the process?
- Do the **ends** of psychological research **justify** the **means**?
- Can we ever know whether a piece of research will justify abusing the rights of individuals before we conduct it?

The existence of ethical constraints is clearly a serious but necessary limitation on the advancement of Psychology as a science and the major professional psychological bodies of many countries have published ethical guidelines for conducting research. In Britain, the British Psychological Society (1993) has published the "***Ethical Principles for Conducting Research with Human Participants***", which guides psychologists to consider the implications of their research (e.g. by asking members of the target population if they would take offence to the research) and deals with a number of methodological ethical issues such as:

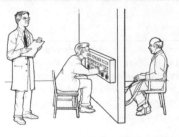

CONSENT – Researchers are obliged, whenever possible, to obtain the participants' **informed** consent – *all* aspects of the research that might affect their willingness to give consent should be revealed. Consent is especially an issue when testing involves children or those unable to give it themselves, e.g. people with serious brain damage. Authority or payment must not be used to pressure participants into consent.

DECEPTION – The BPS Ethical Principles (1993) states that "Participants should never be deliberately misled without extremely strong scientific or medical justification. Even then there should be strict controls and the disinterested approval of independent advisors". Many psychology studies would not achieve valid results due to demand characteristics if deception was not employed, and so a cost-benefit analysis of the gains vs. the discomfort of the participant must be considered.

DEBRIEFING – Involves clarifying the participants' understanding of the research afterwards and discussing or rectifying any consequences of the study to ensure that they leave the study in as similar a state as possible to when they entered it. This is especially important if deception has been employed and the procedures could cause long term upset.

WITHDRAWAL FROM THE INVESTIGATION – Any participant in a psychological study should be informed of their right to withdraw from testing whenever they wish.

CONFIDENTIALITY – Under the Data Protection Act (1984) participants and the data they provide should be kept anonymous unless they have given their full consent to make their data public. If participants are dissatisfied after debriefing they can demand their data is destroyed.

PROTECTION OF PARTICIPANTS – Participants should leave psychological studies in roughly the same condition in which they arrived, without suffering physical or psychological harm. The risk of harm should not be greater than that found in everyday life.

OBSERVATIONAL RESEARCH – Hidden observational studies produce the most ecologically valid data but inevitably raise the ethical issue of invasion of privacy.

2.10 Ethical issues and human psychological research

CONSENT

Milgram (1963) – The subjects in Milgram's study had volunteered to participate in a study of learning, not obedience. Having not been told of the researcher's objectives, they did not give their informed consent.

Bystander intervention studies – Such as those conducted by Darley and Batson (the 'Good Samaritan' study) or Piliavin (subway studies) where subjects were not asked for their consent at all. However, one could argue that people see the plight of others every day without consent.

Zimbardo et al. (1973) – The subjects in the prison simulation experiment signed a formal 'informed consent' statement specifying there would be a loss of some civil rights, invasion of privacy and harassment.

DECEPTION

Milgram (1963) – The subjects were led to believe they were giving real electric shocks to another in an experiment on learning rather than obedience. Orne and Holland (1968) suggested that the subjects were involved in a 'pact of ignorance' with the experimenter – they did not really believe they were harming anyone.

Rosenhan (1973) – In the study 'On being sane in insane places' eight 'normal' people gained admission to psychiatric hospitals merely by pretending to hear voices and faking their name and occupation. One might argue that this case of deception was one that the victims were able to avoid.

Drug testing – Often involves the use of placebo control groups. Patients may be given either the real drug or pills that have no effect, but are not told which they have been given. Perhaps a necessary case of deception but what about the patients' rights to receive the best care?

Craik and Tulving (1975) – Tested Levels of Processing ideas by using incidental learning – subjects were not told they would be tested on their memory. A minor case of deception.

CONFIDENTIALITY

Confidentiality is of particular importance in case studies, especially involving data gained as part of a client–patient relationship. There are many examples in psychology of pseudonyms used to maintain anonymity, e.g. Genie, H.M., Anna O, etc.

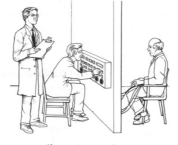

Milgram's experiment

OBSERVATIONAL RESEARCH

Hidden observational studies produce the most ecologically valid data but inevitably raise the ethical issue of privacy. The importance of this issue will be greater in certain areas of psychology (e.g. intimate behaviour in interpersonal relationships) than others (e.g. crowd behaviour).

WITHDRAWAL

Milgram (1963) – The study abused the right of subjects to withdraw from a psychology study – those wishing to leave were told 'you have no other choice, you *must* go on'. However, subjects had the right to leave and they were not physically restrained.

Zimbardo et al (1973) – Stopped their prison simulation study after just six days instead of the two weeks it was meant to run because of extreme reactions shown by the participants.

DEBRIEFING

Milgram (1963) – All subjects were fully debriefed and reassured after the experiment. They were shown that the learner was unharmed and had not received any shocks.

PROTECTION OF PARTICIPANTS

Milgram (1963) – Baumrind (1964) criticised Milgram's study as being unethical because it caused distress and anguish to the subjects. One had a seizure and all subjects could have suffered psychological damage. Milgram himself commented that 'In a large number of cases the degree of tension reached extremes that are rarely seen in sociopsychological laboratory studies'.
However, the results obtained were completely unexpected (Milgram asked for estimates beforehand), and although the subjects appeared uncomfortable with their obedience, Milgram concluded that 'momentary excitement is not the same as harm'. Milgram argued that it was the shocking nature of his findings that provoked a moral outrage.
A follow-up opinion survey conducted a year later found that 84% were 'glad to have been in the experiment', 15% were neutral, and only 1.3% were 'sorry or very sorry to have been in the experiment'. Around 80% of the respondents said there should be more experiments like Milgram's conducted, and around 75% said they had learnt something of personal value from their experience. The subjects were examined one year after the experiment by a psychiatrist who found no signs of harm.

Zimbardo et al. (1973) – Zimbardo's prison simulation procedures were more stressful than the volunteer students playing the prisoner role expected. A surprise city police arrest and processing was followed by brutal treatment from the students playing the role of the guards, which caused psychological stress in the form of crying, rage and depression, and even the development of a psychosomatic rash.

Watson and Rayner (1920) – Conditioned a phobia of rats into an emotionally stable 11-month-old infant, 'Little Albert', by repeatedly startling the child with a loud noise every time a white rat was presented. The fear response generalised to other objects including rabbits, fur coats and even facial hair (including that on a Santa Claus mask!) but was never removed from the subject.

Bandura et al. (1961) – Showed how aggression could be learnt in children through observational learning in their Bobo Doll experiment. However, is it right to produce aggression in children experimentally, even if they may acquire it from their own environment anyway?

2.11 The ethics of socially sensitive research

Many of the studies conducted and topics researched in psychology have wider implications for those who are investigated and society as a whole. The ethics of socially sensitive research involves the psychologist being aware of:
- The implications of investigating certain controversial topics.
- The possible uses to which their research findings will be put.
- The amount of influence the psychologist has on public policy.
- The basis or validity of their research findings in controversial areas.
- The availability, understanding and interpretation of the data they provide.

Deciding what to research

Even the very act of phrasing hypotheses – deciding who and what is to be investigated – has ethical implications.

- Investigating potentially socially sensitive areas, such as race and its effects on IQ or the genetic basis of homosexuality, may serve to legitimise or perpetuate socially constructed differences and prejudices. Alternatively, one might argue that the only way to dispel such prejudices or tackle genuine difference is to investigate them objectively and scientifically to reach the truth. Avoiding controversial topics just because they are controversial (and may involve stress to the researchers) could be regarded as an avoidance of social responsibility.
- Whether objectivity in the phrasing and investigation of research hypotheses is possible is debatable. As the humanist psychologist Rogers (1956), in his debate with the behaviourist Skinner, commented 'In any scientific endeavour – whether "pure" or "applied" science – there is a prior subjective choice of the purpose or value which that scientific work is perceived as serving'.
- We must remember that what is investigated, even in seemingly pure academic research, is subject to social values. Much psychology, especially in the USA, has been (and still is) funded by the military and large businesses, for example Zimbardo's research into the psychological effects of imprisonment was funded by the US navy.

The use of knowledge

Psychologists should consider how their findings will be used and who will be affected by them.

- Knowledge is rarely neutral in practice, it can be used to improve the human condition or worsen it. The application of psychological knowledge to warfare is a good example. Watson (1978) has commented 'Psychology can be a worrying science in the hands of the military' – research on deindividuation and attitude change can be used to train soldiers to kill or brainwash prisoners of war, yet psychological research on intergroup conflict and post-traumatic stress disorder can also help prevent war or treat the victims of it.
- Even the same research findings, such as those on the operant conditioning of animals, can be applied to train animals to help the disabled, e.g. guide-dogs, or to deliver explosive weapons, e.g. 'Project Pigeon' (Skinner, 1960).

The influence of the psychologist in society

The impact of socially sensitive research depends upon the influence the psychologists have in a society. Segall (1976) in 'Human Behaviour and Public Policy' identifies three main ways in which psychologists could affect political and social policies, by acting as:

- expert witnesses, e.g. giving evidence in court cases. The problem with this role for psychologists is that they lose control of their knowledge – policy makers can use or reject psychological expertise and knowledge at will. On the plus side, opposing psychological views can be presented for judgement, reducing the possibility of biased views influencing outcomes, e.g. alternative views on the value of testimony retrieved under hypnosis.

- Policy evaluators, e.g. helping research the impact of proposed political and social measures, such as new laws. Psychological research on the harmful effects of American school segregation for blacks and whites was influential in causing desegregation laws. The problems of this role for psychologists are that it is dependent upon the quality of research and prevailing social conditions of the time.
- Social-psychological engineers – to devise ways of ensuring desirable behaviour. Skinner (1971) advocated this view for psychologists in his book *Beyond Freedom and Dignity*. The problems with this role for psychologists are those of behavioural control in general (Who decides what behaviour is desirable? Who controls the controllers? etc.) and the possible unreliability of psychological research.

It follows that the potentially harmful effects of socially sensitive research become magnified with the power of psychologists in society.

The basis of psychological knowledge

With socially sensitive research, the psychologist must be particularly careful to avoid bias and error, and thus must make clear their **theoretical background**, the **limitations of their research** and the **generalisability of their findings.** Howitt (1991) argues that, since it is impossible to be objective and value free, psychologists should always be cautious when applying their findings. There are many examples of biased or faulty psychological research influencing social views and policies.

- Bowlby's (1951) maternal deprivation research drew attention to the adverse effects of early disrupted child-care but wrongly added support to the social view that it was the role of the woman to care for children.
- Gould (1981) in 'The Mismeasure of Man' describes how biased IQ tests carried out by Yerkes on immigrants to the USA led to eugenicists limiting immigration from Europe for people wanting to escape Nazi persecution.
- Cyril Burt's questionable view that 80% of IQ was genetically determined, influenced ideas on selective education at age 11.
- Gerard (1983) argued that the Social Science Statement supporting the 1954 Brown vs. Board of Education U.S. Supreme Court Decision which led to school desegregation was based on 'well meaning rhetoric rather than solid research'.

Although the premature application of psychology to political issues diminishes public confidence in the social sciences, all knowledge is relative to the time and decisions have to be made on currently available knowledge.

The availabilty of research

In the case of socially sensitive research, psychologists have a responsibility to clarify the communication of findings to the media, public and policy makers to minimise any distortion or abuse of findings (they may only want to hear findings that confirm their own prejudices or policies). Miller (1969) argues that psychological knowledge should be freely given away to the public to prevent its exploitation.

3.1 Variables

WHAT DO PSYCHOLOGISTS INVESTIGATE?

VARIABLES

A variable is any object, quality or event that changes or varies in some way. Examples include: aggression, intelligence, time, height, amount of alcohol, driving ability, attraction.

OPERATIONALISATION

Many of the variables that psychologists are interested in are **abstract concepts,** such as aggression or intelligence. Operationalisation refers to the process of making variables physically measurable or testable. This is done in psychology by recording some aspect of **observable behaviour** that is assumed to be indicative of the variable under consideration. For example:
Aggression – a psychologist may record the number of punches thrown.
Intelligence – a psychologist may record the number of puzzles solved in an hour, or calculate the score on an IQ test.

Reification (regarding hypothetical variables like intelligence as having a real physical existence) is a danger, however.

INVESTIGATING VARIABLES

OBSERVATIONS, CASE STUDIES, SURVEYS, ETC.

In these methods variables are precisely measured in varying amounts of detail.

CORRELATIONS

Variables are measured and compared to see how they co-vary with each other (what relationship they have together).

EXPERIMENTS

One variable (the **independent variable**) is **altered** to see what **effect** it has on another variable (the **dependent variable**).
The independent variable is the variable that is manipulated in two or more conditions to see what effect it has on the dependent variable.
The dependent variable is the main measured outcome of the experiment, hopefully due to the manipulation of the independent variable.
For example, the independent variable (IV) of alcohol could be manipulated to see what effect it had on the dependent variable (DV) of driving ability by testing in two conditions, one with no alcohol and the other with four pints of lager.
However, many **extraneous variables** (other variables that could potentially influence the dependent variable apart from the independent variable), could spoil the experiment and so **controls** are employed to prevent extraneous variables from becoming confounding variables (those that actually affect the dependent variable strongly enough to distort the effect of the independent variable). Extraneous variables can be either **random** (unsystematic variables that can affect the dependent variable but should not affect one condition more than another) or **constant** (those that have a systematic effect on one condition more than another). While random errors will reduce the accuracy of the results, only constant errors usually truly confound the experimental results.

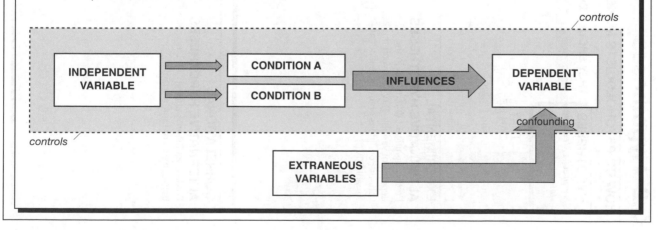

3.2 Hypotheses

HOW DO PSYCHOLOGISTS MAKE THEIR PREDICTIONS?

HYPOTHESES are *precise, testable statements*

THEY SHOULD BE

THEY CAN BE

BOLD
2-tailed (non-directional) hypotheses simply predict an effect, such as a difference or correlation.

1-tailed (directional) hypotheses predict a particular direction in the effect, e.g. that one condition will do better than another, or that a positive correlation will occur.

PRECISE
Precise hypotheses should contain fully **operationalised variables** and the words **'statistically significant'** if inferential statistics are to be conducted on the results.

REFUTABLE
To be scientific every hypothesis should be capable of being **shown to be wrong**. For this reason a **null hypothesis** is proposed that states that there will be **no significant effect** (either difference or correlation). Sometimes, however, it is the null hypothesis which researchers wish to study.

EXPERIMENTAL ALTERNATIVE HYPOTHESES
Predict significant differences in the dependent variable [DV] between the various conditions of the independent variable [IV].

BOLD

2 - tailed
There will be a significant **difference in** [the DV] **between** [condition A of the IV] **and** [condition B of the IV].

1 - tailed
There will be a significant **increase in** [the DV] **in** [condition A of the IV] **compared to** [condition B of the IV].
or
There will be a significant **decrease in** [the DV] **in** [condition A of the IV] **compared to** [condition B of the IV].

PRECISE

2 - tailed example
There will be a **statistically significant** difference in **I.Q. scores** between **male subjects** and **female subjects**.

1 - tailed examples
There will be a **statistically significant** increase in **I.Q. scores** in **male subjects** compared to **female subjects**.
or
There will be a **statistically significant** decrease in **I.Q. scores** in **male subjects** compared to **female subjects**.

REFUTABLE

2 - tailed example
There will be **no** statistically significant difference in I.Q. scores between male subjects and female subjects.

1 - tailed examples
There will be **no** statistically significant increase in I.Q. scores in male subjects compared to female subjects.
or
There will be **no** statistically significant increase in I.Q. scores in female subjects compared to male subjects.

CORRELATIONAL ALTERNATIVE HYPOTHESES
Predict significant patterns of relationship between two or more variables.

BOLD

2 - tailed
There will be a significant **correlation between** [variable 1] and [variable 2].

1 - tailed
There will be a significant **positive correlation between** [variable 1] and [variable 2].
or
There will be a significant **negative correlation between** [variable 1] and [variable 2].

PRECISE

2 - tailed example
There will be a **statistically significant** correlation between **hours of psychology revision conducted** and **A level grade gained in psychology**.

1 - tailed example
There will be a **statistically significant** positive correlation between **hours of psychology revision conducted** and **A level grade gained in psychology**.

REFUTABLE

2 - tailed example
There will be **no** statistically significant correlation between hours of psychology revision conducted and A level grade gained in psychology.

1 - tailed example
There will be **no** statistically significant positive correlation between hours of psychology revision conducted and A level grade gained in psychology.

3.3 Experimental methods

HOW DO PSYCHOLOGISTS INVESTIGATE THEIR HYPOTHESES?

EXPERIMENTS

An experiment involves the **manipulation of the independent variable** to see what effect it has on the dependent variable, while attempting to **control** the influence of all other **extraneous variables**.

	LABORATORY	FIELD	NATURAL/QUASI
TYPES	The researcher **deliberately manipulates** the independent variable while maintaining **strict control** over extraneous variables through standardised procedures in a controlled environment.	The researcher **deliberately manipulates** the independent variable, but does so in the subject's own **natural environment.**	The independent variable is **changed by natural occurrence**; the researcher just records the effect on the dependent variable. Quasi experiments are any where control is lacking over the IV.
EXAMPLES	**BANDURA ET AL. (1961)** Bandura manipulated the independent variable of 'exposure to aggression' to see what effect it had on the dependent variable of 'imitation of aggression in children' under controlled laboratory conditions by randomly allocating children to either a condition where they saw: • an adult being violent towards a Bobo Doll, or • an adult showing no violence. The number of aggressive acts shown by each child was later also measured in the laboratory.	**FESHBACH AND SINGER (1971)** Feshbach and Singer manipulated the independent variable of 'exposure to aggression' to see what effect it had on the dependent variable of 'imitation of aggression in children' by showing boys in a residential school either: • aggressive television or • non-aggressive television. This field study was conducted over 6 weeks, during which the boys' aggression was rated.	**JOY ET AL. (1977)** Joy et al. investigated the independent variable of 'exposure to aggression' to see what effect it had on the dependent variable of 'imitation of aggression in children' by measuring levels of aggression in children of a small Canadian town: • before television was introduced to the town, and • after television was introduced to the town.
STRENGTHS	The most scientific method because the: • manipulation of the independent variable indicates **cause and effect.** • laboratory **increases control** and accurate measurement of variables thus more **objectivity.** • laboratory standardisation means greater ability to replicate (repeat again) the study.	• Has **greater ecological validity** than laboratory experiments, since behaviour occurs in its own natural environment. • **Less bias** from sampling (subjects do not have to be brought into the laboratory) and demand characteristics (if subjects are unaware of being tested).	• Has **great ecological validity**, since a 'natural' change (not induced directly by the experimenter) occurs in a natural environment. • **Very little bias** from sampling or demand characteristics (if subjects are unaware of being observed by experimenters).
WEAKNESSES	• **Total control** over all variables is **not possible.** • **Artificial** laboratory conditions may produce unnatural behaviour that **lacks ecological validity** (results do not generalise to real life). • Results more likely to be **biased** by sampling, demand characteristics, experimenter expectancy. • May raise ethical problems of deception, etc.	• **More bias** likely from extraneous variables, due to **greater difficulty of controlling** all aspects of experiment outside the laboratory. • More **difficult to replicate** exactly. • More **difficult to record data** accurately. • **Ethical problems** of consent, deception, invasion of privacy, etc.	• **Hard to infer cause and effect** due to **little control** over extraneous variables and no direct manipulation of the independent variable. • **Virtually impossible to replicate** exactly. • Bias if subjects are aware of being studied. • **Ethical problems** of consent, deception, invasion of privacy, etc.

3.4 Non-experimental methods 1. Observation

HOW DO PSYCHOLOGISTS INVESTIGATE THEIR HYPOTHESES?

OBSERVATIONS

Observations involve the precise measurement of naturally occurring behaviour in an objective way.

Observers may be disclosed so subjects know they are being studied, or undisclosed (hidden/covert).

	NATURALISTIC	CONTROLLED	PARTICIPANT
TYPES	Naturalistic observations involve the recording of spontaneously occurring behaviour in the subject's own natural environment.	Controlled observation involves the recording of spontaneously occurring behaviour, but under conditions contrived by the researcher (e.g. in the laboratory).	Participant observations involve the researcher becoming involved in the everyday life of the subjects, either with or without their knowledge.
EXAMPLES	• Fagot's (1973) naturalistic observation of parent-child interaction in gender socialisation in the home. • Sylva et al.'s (1980) naturalistic observation of types of play in children's playgroups. • Ethological observations of animal behaviour in the animal's natural habitat.	• Sleep studies – laboratory equipment is needed to record eye movements and changes in brain activity as subjects naturally fall to sleep. • Parent-child interaction – observed through one way mirrors. • Human sexual response, e.g. Masters and Johnson's work.	• Rosenhan (1973) used eight 'normal' undisclosed participant observers to gain admittance to psychiatric hospitals through faking symptoms and then record their experiences of being a psychiatric inpatient. • Whyte's (1955) participant observation of Italian gang behaviour in the USA.
STRENGTHS	• **High ecological validity** (realism) of observed behaviour if observer is hidden. • Can be used to **generate ideas** for or **validate findings** from experimental studies. • Sometimes the only ethical or practical method.	• **More control** over environment which leads to **more accurate** observations. • Greater control leads to **easier replication.** • Usually avoids ethical problems of consent, unless research purpose and observer are hidden.	• Very **high ecological validity** if participant observer undisclosed, less if disclosed depending upon level of integration with subjects. • Extremely **detailed** and **in depth knowledge** available, not gained from any other method.
WEAKNESSES	• **Cannot legitimately infer cause and effect** relationships between variables that are only observed but not manipulated. • **Lack of control** over conditions makes **replication more difficult.** • **Ethical problems** of invasion of privacy.	• **Participant reactivity** may distort the data if subject is aware of being observed, e.g. abnormal sleep patterns in unnatural laboratory conditions. • **Lower ecological validity** than naturalistic observations, can cause demand characteristics. • Cause and effect can not be inferred.	• **Difficult to record data promptly** and **objectively,** and impossible to **replicate** exactly. • Observer's behaviour may **influence subjects.** • **Ethical problems** of deception with undisclosed participant observations. • Cause and effect cannot be inferred.

3.5 Non-experimental methods 2. Questioning

HOW DO PSYCHOLOGISTS INVESTIGATE THEIR HYPOTHESES?

QUESTIONING PEOPLE

There are many techniques for gathering **self report** data, which can be employed in varying detail - from the superficial survey of many people to the in-depth assessment of individuals.

Techniques	Examples	Strengths	Weaknesses
INTERVIEWS All interviews involve direct verbal questioning of the subject by the researcher, but differ in how structured the questions are:		Generally, interviews generate a large amount of detailed data, especially about internal mental states/beliefs.	Generally interviews rely on self report data which may be untrue. Cause and effect cannot be inferred.
• **Structured interviews** – contain fixed predetermined questions and ways of replying (e.g. yes/no) known as 'closed' questions or 'fixed response' questions	Usually used in large scale interview-based surveys, e.g. market research, for nomothetic, quantitative data.	Easy to quantify and analyse. Reliable, replicable and generalisable.	Less validity – distorts/ignores data due to restricted answers or insensitivity.
• **Semi-structured interviews** – contain guidelines for questions to be asked, but phrasing and timing are left up to the interviewer and answers may be open-ended.	Schedule for affective disorders and schizophrenia – a diagnostic interview. Most employment interviews.	Fairly flexible and sensitive. Fairly reliable and easy to analyse.	Flexibility of phrasing and timing could lead to lower reliability. Open-ended answers are more tricky to analyse.
• **Clinical interview** – semi-structured guidelines but further questioning to elaborate upon answers. 'Open' questions provide more qualitative data.	Piaget's interviewing of his children. Freud's interviewing of his patients.	Very flexible, sensitive and valid. Fairly reliable and easy to analyse.	Flexibility leads to more difficulty in replication and bias from interviewer.
• **Unstructured interview** – may contain a topic area for discussion but no fixed questions or ways of answering. Interviewer helps and clarifies interview.	Often used in humanistic based therapy interviews for freely-expressed, idiographic, qualitative data.	Highly detailed and valid data. Extremely flexible, natural and un-constrained.	Very unstandardised, therefore, not very replicable, reliable or generalisable. Difficult to quantify and analyse.
QUESTIONNAIRES Questionnaires are written methods of gaining data from subjects that do not necessarily require the presence of a researcher. They include:		Generally questionnaires collect large amounts of standardised data relatively quickly and conveniently.	Generally questionnaires lack flexibility, are based on self report data and are biased by motivation levels.
• **Opinion surveys**, e.g. attitude scales and opinion polls. Questions can be closed or open-ended and should be precise, understandable and easy to answer.	Likert attitude scales – a five-point rating scale, from 'strongly disagree' to 'strongly agree' via 'neutral'.	Highly replicable and easy to score (unless open-ended answers).	Biased by socially desirable answers, acquiescence (agreeing with items) and response set (replying in the same way).
• **Psychological tests**, e.g. personality and I.Q. tests. Items need to be standardised for a population and tested to show reliability, validity and discriminatory power.	Eysenck's personality inventory (to measure extroversion for example) or Bem's sex role inventory (to assess gender role identity).	Highly replicable and standardised between individuals. Easy to score.	Difficult to construct highly reliable and valid tests.

3.6 Non-experimental methods 3. Case study and correlation

HOW DO PSYCHOLOGISTS INVESTIGATE THEIR HYPOTHESES?

TECHNIQUES AND EXAMPLES

CASE STUDY
An idiographic method involving the **in-depth** and **detailed** study of an **individual** or particular group. The case study method is often applied to unusual or valuable examples of behaviour which may provide important insights into psychological function or refutation of psychological theory. Examples of case studies include: Freud's studies of his patients and Piaget's studies of his children.

CORRELATIONS
A method of data analysis which measures the relationship between two or more variables to see if a trend or systematic pattern exists between them. Inferential statistics can be used to arrive at a correlation coefficient which indicates the strength and type of correlation, ranging from:

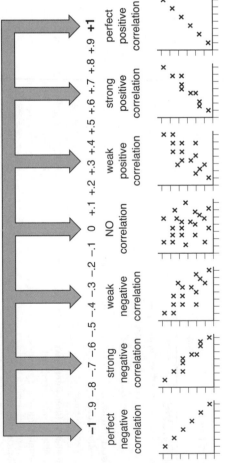

−1 −.9 −.8 −.7 −.6 −.5 −.4 −.3 −.2 −.1 0 +.1 +.2 +.3 +.4 +.5 +.6 +.7 +.8 +.9 **+1**

perfect negative correlation — strong negative correlation — weak negative correlation — NO correlation — weak positive correlation — strong positive correlation — perfect positive correlation

- A **positive** correlation occurs when one variable **increases** as another variable **increases.**
- A **negative** correlation occurs when one variable **increases** as another variable **decreases.**

STRENGTHS

Highly detailed and in depth data is provided which superficial methods might miss or ignore.

High ecological validity of data obtained.

Often the only method suitable for studying some forms of behaviour, e.g. investigating the acquisition of human language in primates.

Often the only method possible due to rarity of behaviour, e.g. natural cases of human environmental deprivation, such as the case of Genie.

Precise information on the degree of relationship between variables is available in the form of the correlation coefficient. It can readily quantify observational data.

No manipulation of behaviour is required.

Strong significant correlations can suggest ideas for experimental studies to determine cause and effect relationships.

WEAKNESSES

No cause and effect can legitimately be inferred.

Lack of generalisability to the population due to single cases being too small and unrepresentative a sample.

Low reliability due to:
- many case studies involving recall of past events, which may be open to memory distortion
- subject reactivity
- lack of observer objectivity.

Difficult or impossible to replicate.

Time consuming and expensive.

No cause and effect can be inferred, e.g. one variable cannot be said to cause an increase or decrease in the other variable – their association could be explained by a third variable.

Correlations should be plotted out on scattergrams to properly illustrate the relationship between variables – a zero correlation coefficient may not form a random pattern.

For example, this pattern would not yield a significant correlational result.

3.7 Sampling

HOW DO PSYCHOLOGISTS SELECT THEIR SUBJECTS?

SAMPLING

- Sampling is the process of selecting subjects to study from the **target population** (a specified section of humankind).
- Since the results of the study on the sample will be generalised back to the target population (through inference), samples should be as **representative** (typical) of the target population as possible.
- Samples should be of a sufficient size (e.g. 30) to represent the variety of individuals in a target population, but not so large as to make the study uneconomical in terms of time and resources.

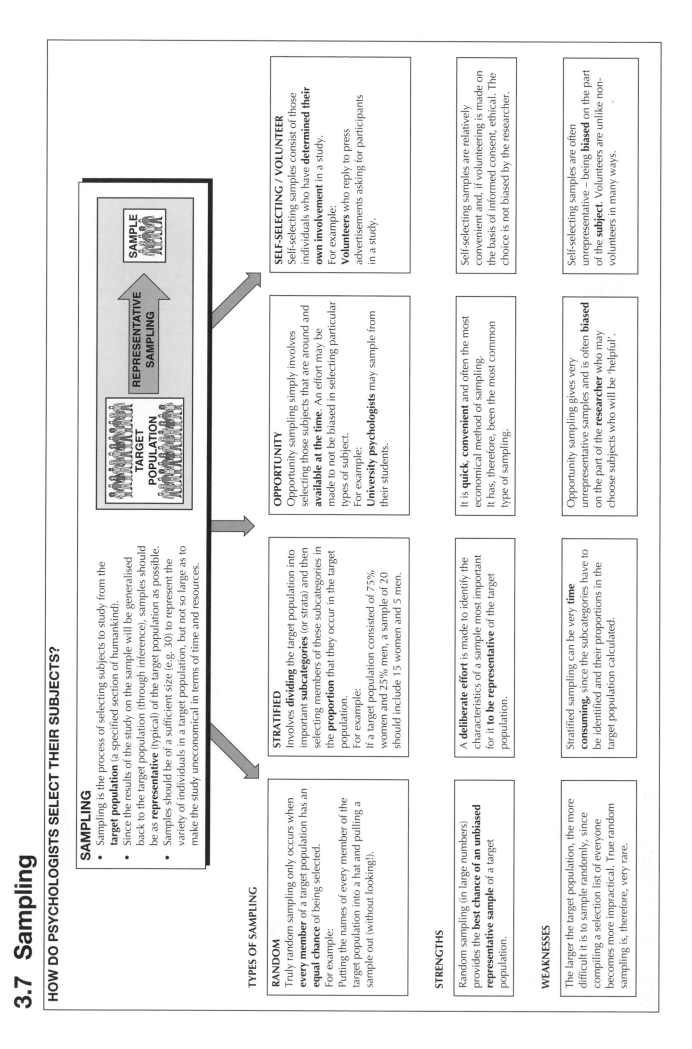

TYPES OF SAMPLING

RANDOM
Truly random sampling only occurs when **every member** of a target population has an **equal chance** of being selected.
For example:
Putting the names of every member of the target population into a hat and pulling a sample out (without looking!).

STRATIFIED
Involves **dividing** the target population into important **subcategories** (or strata) and then selecting members of these subcategories in the **proportion** that they occur in the target population.
For example:
If a target population consisted of 75% women and 25% men, a sample of 20 should include 15 women and 5 men.

OPPORTUNITY
Opportunity sampling simply involves selecting those subjects that are around and **available at the time**. An effort may be made to not be biased in selecting particular types of subject.
For example:
University psychologists may sample from their students.

SELF-SELECTING / VOLUNTEER
Self-selecting samples consist of those individuals who have **determined their own involvement** in a study.
For example:
Volunteers who reply to press advertisements asking for participants in a study.

STRENGTHS

Random sampling (in large numbers) provides the **best chance of an unbiased representative sample** of a target population.

A **deliberate effort** is made to identify the characteristics of a sample most important for it **to be representative** of the target population.

It is **quick, convenient** and often the most economical method of sampling. It has, therefore, been the most common type of sampling.

Self-selecting samples are relatively convenient and, if volunteering is made on the basis of informed consent, ethical. The choice is not biased by the researcher.

WEAKNESSES

The larger the target population, the more difficult it is to sample randomly, since compiling a selection list of everyone becomes more impractical. True random sampling is, therefore, very rare.

Stratified sampling can be very **time consuming,** since the subcategories have to be identified and their proportions in the target population calculated.

Opportunity sampling gives very unrepresentative samples and is often **biased** on the part of the **researcher** who may choose subjects who will be 'helpful'.

Self-selecting samples are often unrepresentative – being **biased** on the part of the **subject**. Volunteers are unlike non-volunteers in many ways.

3.8 Experimental design

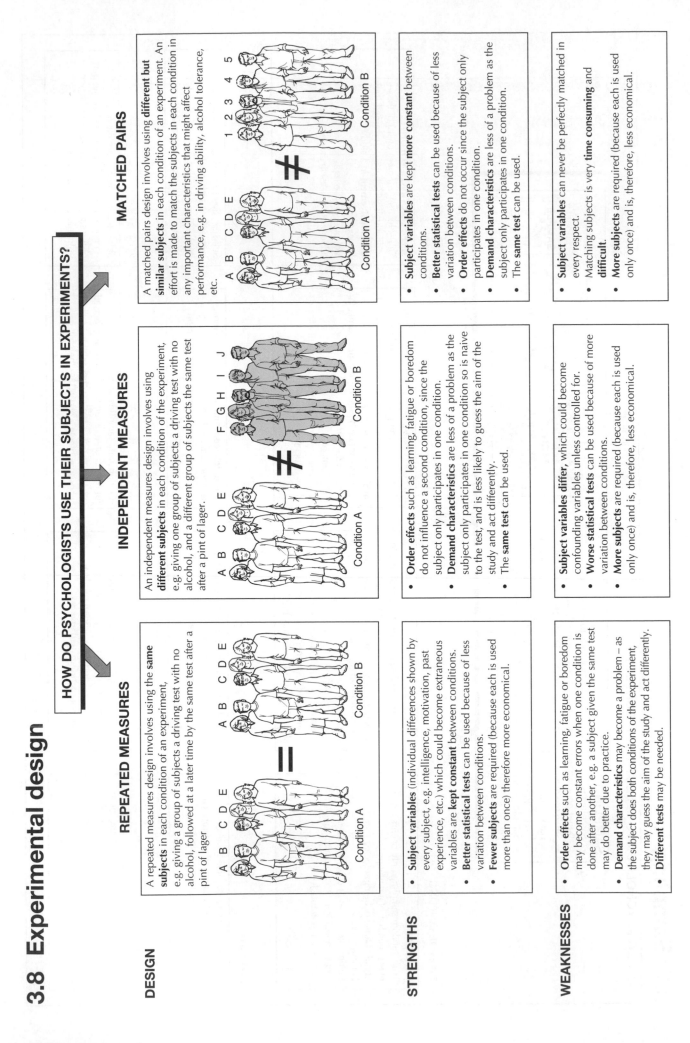

REPEATED MEASURES

DESIGN

A repeated measures design involves using the **same subjects** in each condition of an experiment, e.g. giving a group of subjects a driving test with no alcohol, followed at a later time by the same test after a pint of lager

Condition A   Condition B

STRENGTHS

- **Subject variables** (individual differences shown by every subject, e.g. intelligence, motivation, past experience, etc.) which could become extraneous variables are **kept constant** between conditions.
- **Better statistical tests** can be used because of less variation between conditions.
- **Fewer subjects** are required (because each is used more than once) therefore more economical.

WEAKNESSES

- **Order effects** such as learning, fatigue or boredom may become constant errors when one condition is done after another, e.g. a subject given the same test may do better due to practice.
- **Demand characteristics** may become a problem – as the subject does both conditions of the experiment, they may guess the aim of the study and act differently.
- **Different tests** may be needed.

INDEPENDENT MEASURES

An independent measures design involves using **different subjects** in each condition of the experiment, e.g. giving one group of subjects a driving test with no alcohol, and a different group of subjects the same test after a pint of lager.

Condition A   Condition B

- **Order effects** such as learning, fatigue or boredom do not influence a second condition, since the subject only participates in one condition.
- **Demand characteristics** are less of a problem as the subject only participates in one condition so is naive to the test, and is less likely to guess the aim of the study and act differently.
- The **same test** can be used.

- **Subject variables differ**, which could become confounding variables unless controlled for.
- **Worse statistical tests** can be used because of more variation between conditions.
- **More subjects** are required (because each is used only once) and is, therefore, less economical.

MATCHED PAIRS

A matched pairs design involves using **different but similar subjects** in each condition of an experiment. An effort is made to match the subjects in each condition in any important characteristics that might affect performance, e.g. in driving ability, alcohol tolerance, etc.

Condition A   Condition B

- **Subject variables** are kept **more constant** between conditions.
- **Better statistical tests** can be used because of less variation between conditions.
- **Order effects** do not occur since the subject only participates in one condition.
- **Demand characteristics** are less of a problem as the subject only participates in one condition.
- The **same test** can be used.

- **Subject variables** can never be perfectly matched in every respect.
- Matching subjects is very **time consuming** and **difficult**.
- **More subjects** are required (because each is used only once) and is, therefore, less economical.

3.9 Controlling extraneous variables and bias

HOW DO PSYCHOLOGISTS CONTROL EXTRANEOUS VARIABLES AND BIAS IN THEIR STUDIES?

TYPE OF PROBLEM	PROBLEM	METHOD OF CONTROL
SUBJECTS	**INDIVIDUAL DIFFERENCES** Subject variables can become a problem especially in an independent measures design, creating random or even constant confounding effects.	**Sample large** and **randomly** to gain a representative sample. Use a repeated measures or matched pairs design. **Allocate** subjects **randomly** to each condition of an independent measures experiment to balance out subject variables.
METHOD	**ARTIFICIALITY** Laboratory environments and operationalised variables may lack ecological validity.	Use a **non**-laboratory environment instead, e.g. field study. Broaden or increase the number of definitions for the operationalised variable.
DESIGN	**ORDER EFFECTS** Where learning, boredom or fatigue can influence the second condition of an experiment using a repeated measures design.	Use independent measures design instead. Delay or change the second test. **Counterbalance** the conditions, by getting half the subjects to perform condition A before condition B, and the other half to perform condition B before condition A, thereby balancing the order effects equally between conditions.
	DEMAND CHARACTERISTICS Working out the aim of the study and behaving differently (e.g. trying to please the researcher or spoil the study).	Use independent measures design to stop exposure to both conditions of the experiment, therefore reducing chances of guessing the aim of the study. Use **deception** to hide research aim. However, there are ethical problems with this. Use **single blind method** – the subject does not know which condition of the experiment they are in, e.g. whether they have been given placebo or real pills.
	EXPERIMENTER EXPECTANCY Where the expectations of the researcher influence the results either by consciously or unconsciously revealing the desired outcome or through unconscious procedural or recording bias. Also known as **investigator effects** (a more general term that can be used for non-experimental research as well).	Use **double blind method** – neither the subject nor the researcher carrying out the procedure and recording the results knows the hypothesis or which condition the subjects are in. Use **inter-observer reliability** measures to overcome biased observation. An observer with no vested interest in the result, simultaneously, but separately, rates the same piece of behaviour with the researcher. When results are compared, a high positive correlation should be expected.
PROCEDURE	**DISTRACTION AND CONFUSION** Both sources of extraneous variables which could confound studies unless controlled for.	Standardised instructions should be given in a clear and simple form and the subject should be asked if they have questions, so each participant receives equal information. Standardised procedures should be employed so each subject is tested under equal conditions with no distractions.

3.10 Reliability and validity of studies

HOW DO PSYCHOLOGISTS TEST THE QUALITY OF STUDIES?

RELIABILITY
The reliability of a method of measurement (whether it be an experimental test, questionnaire or observational procedure) refers to how **consistently** it measures.

INTERNAL RELIABILITY
Internal reliability refers to **how consistently a method measures within itself**. If methods of measurement were not **standardised** they would give distorted final scores.
For example, internal reliability would be lacking if
- a ruler consisted of variable centimetres,
- an I.Q. test was made up of half ridiculously easy questions and half ridiculously difficult questions (virtually everyone would score half marks and be equally intelligent!) or
- different observers using the same observational definitions simultaneously scored the same individual differently.

Internal reliability could be checked for test items by the **split half method** – correlating the results of half the items with the other half (e.g. the odd numbers with the even numbers of the test) and gaining a high positive correlation coefficient.

EXTERNAL RELIABILITY
External reliability refers to **how consistently a method measures over time when repeated**. Methods of measurement should give similar scores when repeated on the same people under similar conditions.
For example external reliability would be lacking if
- a ruler measured an unchanging object different lengths each time it was used,
- an I.Q. test scored the same person a genius one day but just average a week later.

External reliability could be checked for test items by the **test-, re-test method** – correlating the results of the test conducted on one occasion with the results of the test conducted on a later occasion (with the same subjects) and gaining a high positive correlation coefficient.

VALIDITY
The validity of a method of measurement (whether it be an experimental test, questionnaire or observational procedure) refers to whether it **measures what it is supposed to measure** – how realistically or truly variables have been operationalised.

INTERNAL VALIDITY – refers to whether a study's results were really due to the variables the researchers suggest were tested by their methodology (and not confounding ones).

EXTERNAL VALIDITY – refers to whether the results can be generalised if conducted in different environments or using different participants.

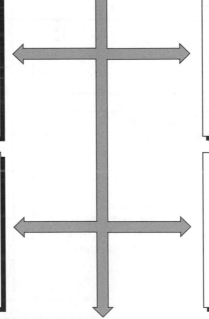

FACE/CONTENT VALIDITY
Face or content validity involves **examining** the content of the test to see if it **looks** like it measures what it is supposed to measure.
For example, examining the test items of an intelligence test to see if they seem to measure general intelligence, not just general knowledge or linguistic comprehension.

CONCURRENT VALIDITY
Concurrent validity involves **comparing** a **new** method or test **with** an already well **established** one that claims to measure the same variable(s). A high positive correlation should be gained between the results of the two tests.
For example, correlating the results from the same people tested by a new intelligence test and an older established one.

CONSTRUCT VALIDITY
Construct validity refers to whether the test or method can be used to **support** the **underlying theoretical constructs** concerning the variable that it is supposed to be measuring.
For example, if theory suggests the offspring of two highly intelligent parents raised in a stimulating environment should be intelligent, an I.Q. test should confirm this.

PREDICTIVE VALIDITY
Predictive validity refers to whether the test will **predict future performance** indicated by its results.
For example, high scorers on an I.Q. test at a young age should be predicted to later perform better in studies or jobs requiring intelligence.

ECOLOGICAL VALIDITY
Ecological validity refers to whether a test or method measures behaviour that is representative of naturally occurring behaviour. Too specifically operationalised tests or those conducted under contrived conditions may not reflect spontaneously occurring, natural behaviour. For example, do the items on an intelligence test represent all the types of behaviour we would describe as intelligent in everyday life?
However, since there is difficulty in saying what conditions are 'natural' or 'normal' (laboratories are human social situations too, while some field studies may be conducted under very unusual circumstances) ecological validity is perhaps best measured by the extent to which research findings can be generalised to other research settings.

3.11 Timing and location of investigations

WHEN SHOULD PSYCHOLOGISTS INVESTIGATE?

CROSS-SECTIONAL STUDIES
In cross-sectional studies subjects of **different** ages are investigated **at one particular point in time**. It is a form of independent measures design.

LONGITUDINAL STUDIES
In longitudinal studies the **same** subjects are investigated **over a long period of time**. It is a form of repeated measures design.

WHERE SHOULD PSYCHOLOGISTS INVESTIGATE?

CROSS-CULTURAL STUDIES
In cross-cultural studies subjects from **different cultures** are given the same test and their results are compared.

EXAMPLES

ASCH (1951)
Asch's findings on conformity were not replicated by some later researchers, indicating that his findings may have been influenced by factors present in his society *at that particular time*.

Kohlberg (1981) compared the moral development of three groups of boys aged 10, 13 and 16.

KOHLBERG (1971)
Kohlberg conducted a twenty year longitudinal study of moral reasoning.

Developmental psychologists concentrate on how abilities and behaviour may vary over time, from infancy to adulthood, and so may find that studying the same subjects over a long period of time is the most accurate way of discovering the principles and processes of development.

MEAD (1935)
Mead studied three different tribes in New Guinea and compared their gender role behaviours.

Cross-cultural studies have investigated whether variation occurs in different countries in conformity, obedience, intelligence, perception and attachment – to name just a few examples in psychology.

STRENGTHS

- Immediate results can be gained, therefore, they are convenient.
- Cheaper and less time consuming than longitudinal studies.
- Less likelihood of losing subjects between conditions.

- Less bias from subject variables.
- In some areas of psychology, such as mental illness, a longitudinal study may be the only way of determining how a disorder progresses.

- Combats an ethnocentric culturally biased view of human psychology.
- Widens the generalisability of results.
- Provides data on cultural differences or similarities which may increase understanding of psychological development.

WEAKNESSES

- Cross-sectional studies may be overly influenced by the social environment of the time, and therefore need to be regularly replicated.
- All disadvantages of independent measures design, e.g. subject confounding variables, greater number of subjects needed, etc.
- Cohort effect may bias data.

- Time consuming, expensive and high likelihood of losing subjects between conditions.
- Extremely difficult or impossible to replicate exactly.
- Longitudinal studies can be carried out retrospectively by examining the history of subjects, but this has many disadvantages, such as memory distortion and lack of objectivity.

- More time consuming, difficult (due to language barriers, etc.) and expensive.
- Open to ethnocentric misinterpretation when researchers from one culture investigate another culture.
- Subject reactivity may increase with a cross-cultural observer, producing untypical behaviour.

3.12 Data recording techniques

TECHNIQUES	ADVANTAGES	DISADVANTAGES
BEHAVIOUR SAMPLING METHODS		
• **Event sampling.** Key behavioural events are recorded every time they occur.	Limits the behaviours observed, thus reducing the chance that the behaviour of interest will be missed.	It is difficult to observe all incidents of key behaviour over large areas. Other important behaviour may be ignored.
• **Time sampling.** Behaviour is observed for discrete periods of time.	Reduces the amount of time spent in observation and thus may increase accuracy.	Behaviour may be missed if random time samples are not taken across the day.
• **Point sampling.** The behaviour of just one individual in a group at a time is recorded.	Increases the accuracy of observation and number of behaviours that can be recorded.	May miss behaviour in others that is important for an understanding of the individual.
DATA RECORDING TECHNIQUES		
• **Frequency grids.** Nominal data is scored as a tally chart for a variety of behaviours.	Quick and easy to use and can record a larger number of behaviours at a time.	Nominal data provides little information, e.g. it cannot say how long or intensely a behaviour was shown.
• **Rating scales.** Scores ordinal level data for a behaviour, indicating the degree to which it is shown.	Provides more information on the behaviour.	Rating using opinion rather than fixed scales, such as timing, introduces subjectivity.
• **Timing behaviour.**	High accuracy of data.	Loss of descriptive detail of behaviour.
DATA RECORDING EQUIPMENT		
• **Hand-written** notes or coding systems.	Less intimidating than more mechanical methods of recording.	Data may be missed or subjectively recorded.
• **Audio-tape** recording.	Accurately records all spoken data for later leisurely and accurate analysis.	Omits important gestures and non-verbal communication accompanying speech.
• **Video.**	Accurately records all data in view for later analysis – increases objectivity.	May produce participant reactivity and unnatural behaviour due to intimidation.
• **One way mirrors** in laboratories.	Reduces participant reactivity.	Unethical if subjects are not informed.
CONTENT ANALYSIS A **quantitative** method for analysing the **communication** of people and organisations, e.g. in their conversations, or media records. The researcher first decides what media they are going to sample and then devises the **coding units** they are interested in measuring, e.g. the frequency of, or amount of time and space devoted to, certain words or themes.	Content analysis is a useful tool for gathering data on a variety of topics, from rhetorical devices used in political speeches to the stereotyping or aggressive content of books and films. It can be used to assess what is omitted from speech, not just what is included. The data gained is usually of high ecological validity. Multiple coders can improve inter-rater reliability.	It is sometimes difficult to arrive at objectively operationalised coding units and the technique can be time consuming. Content analysis can be used to examine the function that a person's or organisation's communication serves, e.g. justifying or criticising, but the analyst's interpretations are also open to interpretation!
QUALITATIVE DATA ANALYSIS The analysis of qualitative data in its own right, without reducing it to quantitative numbers, can be very useful. Qualitative data can be gained from a variety of methods, such as observations, interviews, case studies and even experiments – descriptions of how subjects behaved and what they said is presented as **transcripts**, **quotes** and **commentary** on important themes.	Qualitative data is useful to describe information lost in the quantified and narrowed analysis of figures. Interviews with subjects after experiments can often reveal the causes of their behaviour and provide ideas for future research. However, qualitative analysis can be a useful research tool in its own right – arriving at an in-depth analysis and discussion of the meaning of behaviour, not just its frequency.	Qualitative analysis is often attacked for its lack of objectivity. However, • techniques exist to check its reliability and validity, e.g. triangulation (using more than one method of investigation) and repetition of the research cycle (to check previous data). • subjective opinion and participant consultation is regarded as a strength by many researchers, e.g. feminists.

3.13 Numerical descriptive statistics

HOW DO PSYCHOLOGISTS SUMMARIZE THEIR DATA NUMERICALLY?

LEVELS OF DATA

NOMINAL
Nominal data is a simple **frequency headcount** (the number of times something occurred) found in **discrete categories** (something can only belong to one category).

For example, the number of people who helped or did not help in an emergency.

Nominal data is the simplest data.

ORDINAL
Ordinal data is measurements that can be put in an **order**, **rank** or **position**.

For example, scores on unstandardised psychological scales (such as attractiveness out of 10) or who came 1st, 2nd, 3rd, etc. in a race.

The **intervals** between each rank, however, are **unknown,** i.e. how far ahead 1st was from 2nd.

INTERVAL AND RATIO
Both are measurements on a **scale**, the **intervals** of which are **known and equal**. **Ratio** data has a **true zero** point, whereas **interval** data can go into **negative** values.

For example, **temperature** for interval data (degrees centigrade can be minus) **length** or **time** for ratio data (no seconds is no time at all).

The most **precise** types of data.

MEASURES OF CENTRAL TENDENCY

MODE
The value or event that occurs the most frequently.
The most suitable measure of central tendency for nominal data.
Not influenced by extreme scores; useful to show most popular value.
Crude measure of central tendency; not useful if many equal modes.

MEDIAN
The middle value when all scores are placed in rank order.
The most suitable measure of central tendency for ordinal data.
Not distorted by extreme freak values, e.g. 2, 3, 3, 4, 4, 4, 4, 4, 5, 5, 6, 42.
However, it can be distorted by small samples and is less sensitive.

MEAN
The average value of all scores.
The most suitable measure of central tendency for interval or ratio data.
The most sensitive measure of central tendency for all data.
However, can be distorted by extreme freak values.

MEASURES OF DISPERSION

	ADVANTAGE	DISADVANTAGE
RANGE the difference between the smallest and largest value, plus 1. For example, 3, 4, 7, 7, 8, 9, 12, 4, 17, 17, 18 **(18 – 3) +1 = Range of 16**	• Quick and easy to calculate.	• Distorted by extreme 'freak' values, an extra value of 43 would give a range of 41.

SEMI-INTERQUARTILE RANGE
When data is put in order, find the first quartile (Q1) and third quartile (Q3) of the sample, subtract the Q1 value from the Q3 value and divide the result by two.
For example,
3, 4, 7, 7 8, 9, 12, 14, 17, 17, 18
    ↑   ↑   ↑
    Q1 Q2   Q3
    7   17
17 – 7 = 10 10 ÷ 2 = **Semi-interquartile range of 5**
	• Less distorted by any extreme 'freak' values.	• Ignores extreme values.

STANDARD DEVIATION
The average amount all scores deviate from the mean. The difference (deviation) between each score and the mean of those scores is calculated and then squared (to remove minus values). These squared deviations are then added up and their mean calculated to give a value known as the variance. The square root of the variance gives the standard deviation of the scores.
 	
score mean   d   d
                        squared
6 – 10 = –4   16
8 – 10 = –2   4
10 – 10 =   0   0
12 – 10 = +2   4
14 – 10 = +4   16
                         40
mean of 40 = 8 = variance
square root of variance
= standard deviation = 2.8
	• The most sensitive measure of dispersion, using all the data available.
	• Can be used to relate the sample to the population's parameters.
		• A little more time consuming to calculate but no important disadvantages.

3.14 Graphical descriptive statistics

HOW DO PSYCHOLOGISTS SUMMARIZE THEIR DATA PICTORIALLY?

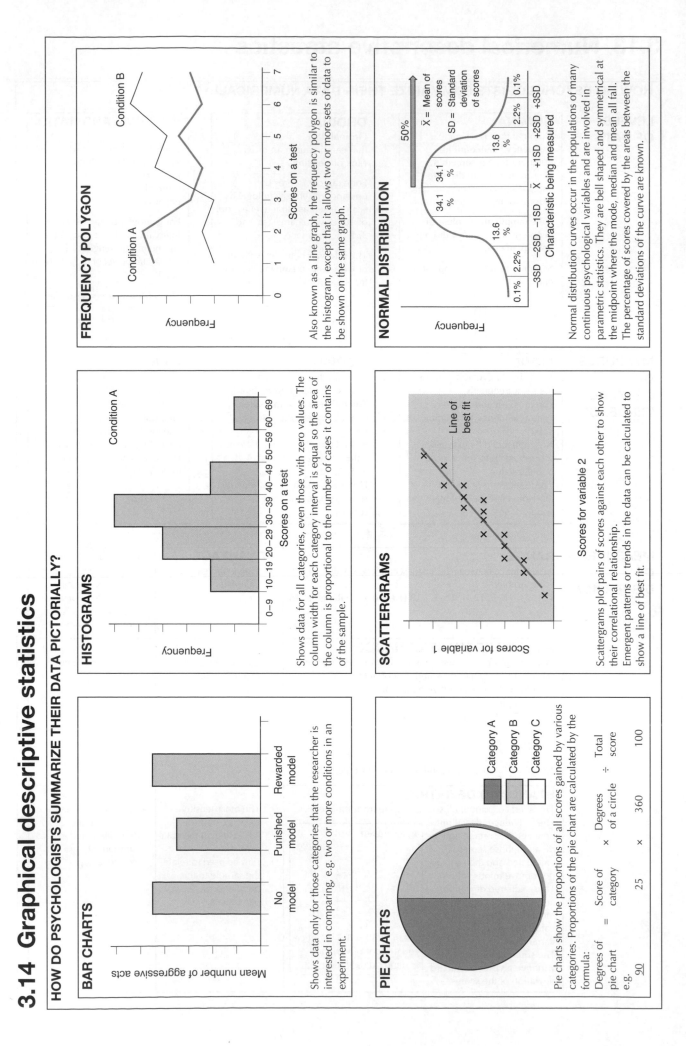

BAR CHARTS

Mean number of aggressive acts

No model | Punished model | Rewarded model

Shows data only for those categories that the researcher is interested in comparing, e.g. two or more conditions in an experiment.

HISTOGRAMS

Condition A

Frequency

0–9 10–19 20–29 30–39 40–49 50–59 60–69

Scores on a test

Shows data for all categories, even those with zero values. The column width for each category interval is equal so the area of the column is proportional to the number of cases it contains of the sample.

FREQUENCY POLYGON

Condition A Condition B

Frequency

0 1 2 3 4 5 6 7

Scores on a test

Also known as a line graph, the frequency polygon is similar to the histogram, except that it allows two or more sets of data to be shown on the same graph.

PIE CHARTS

Category A
Category B
Category C

Pie charts show the proportions of all scores gained by various categories. Proportions of the pie chart are calculated by the formula:

Degrees of pie chart = Score of category × Degrees of a circle ÷ Total score

e.g.

90 = 25 × 360 ÷ 100

SCATTERGRAMS

Scores for variable 1

Line of best fit

Scores for variable 2

Scattergrams plot pairs of scores against each other to show their correlational relationship.
Emergent patterns or trends in the data can be calculated to show a line of best fit.

NORMAL DISTRIBUTION

Frequency

50%

X̄ = Mean of scores
SD = Standard deviation of scores

0.1% 2.2% 13.6% 34.1% 34.1% 13.6% 2.2% 0.1%

−3SD −2SD −1SD X̄ +1SD +2SD +3SD

Characteristic being measured

Normal distribution curves occur in the populations of many continuous psychological variables and are involved in parametric statistics. They are bell shaped and symmetrical at the midpoint where the mode, median and mean all fall. The percentage of scores covered by the areas between the standard deviations of the curve are known.

3.15 Inferential statistics

HOW DO PSYCHOLOGISTS KNOW HOW SIGNIFICANT THEIR RESULTS ARE?

WHAT IS MEANT BY SIGNIFICANCE?

DEFINITION: A significant result is one where there is a **low probability that chance factors** were responsible for any observed difference, correlation or association in the variables tested.

FOR EXAMPLE

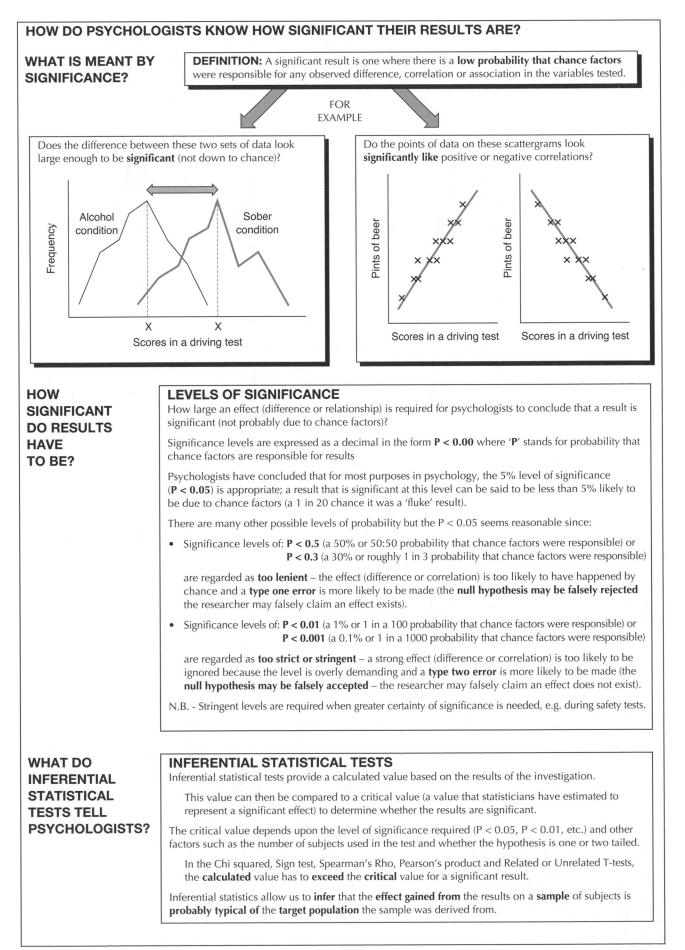

Does the difference between these two sets of data look large enough to be **significant** (not down to chance)?

Frequency

Alcohol condition

Sober condition

X   X

Scores in a driving test

Do the points of data on these scattergrams look **significantly like** positive or negative correlations?

Pints of beer

Pints of beer

Scores in a driving test

Scores in a driving test

HOW SIGNIFICANT DO RESULTS HAVE TO BE?

LEVELS OF SIGNIFICANCE

How large an effect (difference or relationship) is required for psychologists to conclude that a result is significant (not probably due to chance factors)?

Significance levels are expressed as a decimal in the form **P < 0.00** where 'P' stands for probability that chance factors are responsible for results

Psychologists have concluded that for most purposes in psychology, the 5% level of significance (**P < 0.05**) is appropriate; a result that is significant at this level can be said to be less than 5% likely to be due to chance factors (a 1 in 20 chance it was a 'fluke' result).

There are many other possible levels of probability but the P < 0.05 seems reasonable since:

- Significance levels of: **P < 0.5** (a 50% or 50:50 probability that chance factors were responsible) or **P < 0.3** (a 30% or roughly 1 in 3 probability that chance factors were responsible)

  are regarded as **too lenient** – the effect (difference or correlation) is too likely to have happened by chance and a **type one error** is more likely to be made (the **null hypothesis may be falsely rejected** the researcher may falsely claim an effect exists).

- Significance levels of: **P < 0.01** (a 1% or 1 in a 100 probability that chance factors were responsible) or **P < 0.001** (a 0.1% or 1 in a 1000 probability that chance factors were responsible)

  are regarded as **too strict or stringent** – a strong effect (difference or correlation) is too likely to be ignored because the level is overly demanding and a **type two error** is more likely to be made (the **null hypothesis may be falsely accepted** – the researcher may falsely claim an effect does not exist).

N.B. - Stringent levels are required when greater certainty of significance is needed, e.g. during safety tests.

WHAT DO INFERENTIAL STATISTICAL TESTS TELL PSYCHOLOGISTS?

INFERENTIAL STATISTICAL TESTS

Inferential statistical tests provide a calculated value based on the results of the investigation.

This value can then be compared to a critical value (a value that statisticians have estimated to represent a significant effect) to determine whether the results are significant.

The critical value depends upon the level of significance required (P < 0.05, P < 0.01, etc.) and other factors such as the number of subjects used in the test and whether the hypothesis is one or two tailed.

In the Chi squared, Sign test, Spearman's Rho, Pearson's product and Related or Unrelated T-tests, the **calculated** value has to **exceed** the **critical** value for a significant result.

Inferential statistics allow us to **infer** that the **effect gained from** the results on a **sample** of subjects is **probably typical of** the **target population** the sample was derived from.

3.16 Choosing inferential statistical tests

HOW DO PSYCHOLOGISTS CHOOSE AN APPROPRIATE STATISTICAL TEST?

1 TEST OF DIFFERENCE OR RELATIONSHIP REQUIRED?
2 WHAT EXPERIMENTAL DESIGN HAS BEEN USED?
3 WHAT LEVEL OF DATA IS BEING USED?
4 ARE ALL THREE PARAMETRIC CONDITIONS MET?
   a Interval or ratio data
   b Both sets of data normally
      distributed or from normally
      distributed populations
   c Both sets of data have
      similar variance.

PARAMETRIC TESTS
The most powerful and sensitive tests.

TESTS OF RELATIONSHIP

ASSOCIATION
OR
CORRELATION

TESTS OF DIFFERENCE

	INDEPENDENT MEASURES DESIGN	REPEATED MEASURES OR MATCHED PAIRS DESIGN	ASSOCIATION / CORRELATION
NOMINAL DATA	CHI SQUARED TEST	SIGN TEST	CHI SQUARED TEST
ORDINAL DATA	MANN WHITNEY U TEST*	WILCOXON SIGNED RANKS TESTS*	SPEARMAN'S RHO CORRELATION
INTERVAL OR RATIO DATA	UNRELATED T-TEST	RELATED T-TEST	PEARSON'S PRODUCT MOMENT CORRELATION COEFFICIENT

1 2 3 4

* NB The two ordinal level tests of difference are the only ones where the calculated value of the test has to be LESS THAN the critical value.

4.1 Social power

DEFINITION
Social power refers to the influence a person has to change another's thoughts, feelings, or behaviour. There are many sources of power, many ways in which it can work and many effects it can have on those who have it and those who yield to it.

NORMS OF POWER
Power relations are embedded in the hierarchical nature of society. Zimbardo *et al.*'s (1973) prison simulation experiment showed how the role of prison guard and the power that went with it could be readily assumed by subjects selected on the basis of their normality. Clearly, the norms of guard power (operating from coercive and legitimate power bases) can be readily understood (although exaggerated by media portrayal) and conformed to by anyone.

THE IMPACT OF POWER
According to **social impact theory** (Latane, 1981), the strength of influence felt by a target is determined by three factors:
- The **strength** (or importance) of the influencer,
- The **number** of influencers,
- The **immediacy** (or closeness) of the influencer/s.

Increases in each of the above factors will cause the power of influence to increase, while decreases in these factors (or an increase in the target's strength or number) will have the opposite effect. For example, you are more likely to be influenced by several very important people standing in front of you, than by one unimportant person talking over the telephone.

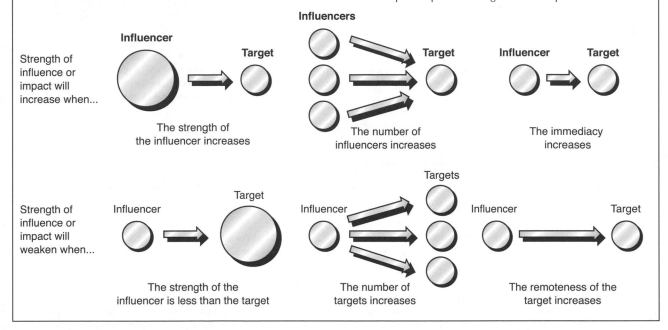

Strength of influence or impact will increase when...

Influencer → **Target**
The strength of the influencer increases

Influencers → **Target**
The number of influencers increases

Influencer → **Target**
The immediacy increases

Strength of influence or impact will weaken when...

Influencer → **Target**
The strength of the influencer is less than the target

Influencer → **Targets**
The number of targets increases

Influencer → **Target**
The remoteness of the target increases

TYPES OF POWER
Raven and others have identified six different (although they can operate simultaneously) sources or *bases of power*.

1 Reward power
This influence is based on the ability to provide what others **want** or to remove what they do not want. Many people possess this source of power (e.g. parents, employers, friends), but note that they offer many different types of reward (e.g. love, money, approval). This power only works as long as the rewards can be given by the influencer and are wanted by the receiver.

2 Coercive power
This involves the ability to **punish**, by inflicting some form of negative stimulus (e.g. disapproval, ridicule, pain) or by removing pleasant stimuli (e.g. affection, wages). This power base requires constant supervision, since it produces negative feelings and attitudes in its victims who only tend to comply behaviourally to demands rather than really accepting them.

3 Referent power
This is the influence a person has because they are **respected** or admired. The target wishes to identify with (be like) the influencer and is more likely to follow their wishes. Role models and idols have this power, but only maintain it as long as they are liked or respected.

4 Legitimate power
This is where the target accepts the **norms** (probably internalised) that the influencer should have (has the right to) influence over them. The legitimacy of the power obviously depends on the situation – we accept that a referee can tell us what to do in a football match, but not outside of that situation.

5 Expert power
The power an influencer has because the target believes they possess **superior knowledge** in a desired area. We are thus at the mercy of our doctor's advice in matters of health, and at the mercy of garage mechanics when our cars need servicing.

6 Informational power
One person or a group of people, expert or otherwise, can have power if they provide socially accepted **information**. This ties in with the social reality hypothesis and Festinger's social comparison theory (we look to others to know how to react in certain situations).

4.2 'A study of prisoners and guards in a simulated prison' Haney, Banks, and Zimbardo (1973)

AIM
To demonstrate the situational rather than the dispositional causes of negative behaviour and thought patterns found in prison settings by conducting a prison simulation with 'normal' subjects playing the roles of guard and prisoner.

METHOD
Subjects: 22 male subjects selected (through personality assessment) from an initial pool of 75 volunteers based on their stability, maturity and lack of involvement in anti-social behaviour. They were mostly Caucasian, middle class, college students, who were strangers to each other and were randomly allocated to either prisoner or guard roles. Prisoners signed a consent document which specified that some of their human rights would be suspended and all subjects were to receive $15 a day for up to 2 weeks.

Apparatus: Prison – a basement corridor in Stanford University Psychology department converted into a set of 2 x 3 metre prison cells with a solitary confinement room (a tiny unlit closet), a 'yard' room and an observation screen (through which covert video and audiotape data recording could take place).
Uniforms – to facilitate role identification, guards were given khaki shirts and trousers, batons and reflecting sunglasses. Prisoners wore loose fitting smocks with identification numbers,

no underwear, a lock and chain around one ankle, and a nylon stocking cap to cover their hair.

Procedure: The procedure, as with the apparatus, was designed to establish 'functional equivalents' for the experience of prison life.
- Prisoners were arrested by real police outside their houses by surprise, taken to a real police station for finger-printing and processing, and were then driven blindfolded to the mock prison (where they were stripped naked, 'deloused', and dressed in prisoner's uniform). Prisoners remained in the 'prison' 24 hours a day and followed a schedule of work assignments, rest periods, and meal/toilet visits.
- Guards worked only 8 hour shifts, and were given no specific instructions apart from to 'maintain a reasonable degree of order within the prison necessary for its effective functioning' and a prohibition against the use of physical violence.

RESULTS
The effects of imprisonment were assessed by video and audio tape observation of behaviour and dialogue, self-report questionnaires, and interviews. The experiment had to be terminated after 6 days, instead of the intended 14, because of the pathological (abnormal) reactions shown by both prisoners and guards.

- **Effects on prisoners** – subjects showed what was termed the 'Pathological Prisoner Syndrome' – disbelief was followed by rebellion which, after failure, was followed by a range of negative emotions and behaviours. All showed passivity (some becoming excessively obedient) and dependence (initiating very little activity without instruction). Half the prisoners showed signs of depression, crying, fits of rage, and acute anxiety, and had to be released early. All but two of those who remained said they would forfeit the money if they could be released early.

The experimenters proposed that these reactions were caused by a loss of personal identity, emasculation, dependency, and learned helplessness brought about by the arbitrary and unpredictable control, and the norms and structures of the prison system.

- **Effects on guards** – subjects showed what was termed the 'Pathology of Power' – huge enjoyment of the power at their disposal (some worked extra time for no pay, and were disappointed when the study was over) led to the guards abusing it and dehumanising the prisoners. All prisoners' rights were redefined as privileges (going to the toilet, eating, and wearing eye-glasses became rewards), and punishment with little or no justification was applied with verbal insults. Although not all guards initiated aggressive action, none contradicted its use in others.
The experimenters proposed that these reactions were caused by a sense of empowerment legitimised by the role of 'guard' in the prison system.

EVALUATION
Methodological: Lack of ecological validity – A role play simulation lacks 'mundane realism' and may produce artificial results. The experimenters admit factors, such as the lack of physical violence and minimum duration of the sentence, limit the generalisability of the simulation, but point out that most of the functional equivalents of the prison system were implemented and that most of the subjects' excessive reactions went beyond the demands of the role play (prisoners called each other by their ID numbers in private, and guards showed aggression even when they thought they were not being observed).

Data analysis – Was mostly qualitative rather than quantitative.

Ethical problems – 1 The study was ethically approved beforehand – perhaps the dramatic and disturbing results cause the ethical objections, but these came from the subjects not the experimenters.

2 The subjects had signed an informed consent document, but were unaware that they would be arrested in public and of exactly how realistic their imprisonment would be.

3 The experiment was terminated early and debriefing and assessment of the subjects took place weeks, months and years afterwards.

Theoretical: The research provides support for social psychological explanations of behaviour, has wide ranging implications for the usefulness and ethics of existing penal systems, and has been used to facilitate our understanding of the psychological effects of imprisonment.

Links: Social influence – particularly power, leadership, obedience (see Milgram) and conformity.

4.3 Rethinking the psychology of tyranny: The BBC prison study Reicher and Haslam (2006)

BACKGROUND

This study investigates the social psychology of tyranny ('an unequal social system involving the arbitrary and oppressive use of power by one group or its agents over another') – 'how we come to condone the tyranny of others or else act tyrannically ourselves.' The researchers wished to partially replicate Haney, Banks and Zimbardo's (1973) influential but ethically debatable Stanford Prison Experiment (SPE), and to question the traditional social psychological analysis of its results – namely that automatic deindividuation and conformity to social roles tends to lead groups to extreme antisocial behaviour.

Reicher and Haslam suggest a Social Identity approach may provide a better explanation of the SPE and tyranny. This approach argues that people do not automatically act in terms of group membership or social roles, but only do so if 'they internalise such membership as part of their self-concept'. The Social Identity approach proposes that people positively valued due to their group membership (e.g. dominant groups) are likely to identify with, and act in terms of, the group. However, for people negatively valued because of their group membership (e.g. subordinate groups) collective action depends upon:

- The permeability of category boundaries – when these are seen as permeable people think they can advance to a more desirable group and so act individually, but when perceived as impermeable people think they cannot change so are more likely to identify with their present group.
- The *security* of intergroup relations – when group differences are seen as illegitimate and unstable, people are more aware of cognitive alternatives to the status quo, see the possibility of change and may challenge inequality.

AIMS

In general, the authors aimed to:

i provide detailed data on the developing interactions between two groups of unequal power and privilege

ii develop practical and ethical procedures for conducting important large-scale studies in social psychological research

iii analyse the conditions under which people will:
- define themselves in terms of, and act on, group identities.
- accept or challenge group inequalities

In particular, the following predictions were based on the Social Identity approach:

1 Dominant group members (the guards) will identify with their group from the start and impose their power.
2 Subordinate group members will only identify and challenge inequality if relations are seen as impermeable and insecure.

METHOD

Design
Experimental case study

Independent variables (4):
Independent measures design:
1 Amount of power (guard vs. prisoner).
Repeated measures design:
2 Group permeability (before vs. after being told it was no longer possible for prisoners to become guards on day three).
3 Legitimacy (before vs. after being told there were in fact no psychological differences between prisoners and guards to justify their allocation to different groups) – this variable was not tested.
4 Cognitive alternatives (before vs. after the introduction of a new prisoner who was an experienced trade union official on day five).

Dependent variables recorded:
1 Social variables: social identification, awareness of cognitive alternatives, right-wing authoritarianism
2 Organisational variables: compliance with rules
3 Clinical variables: self-efficacy, depression
Quantitative measurement via daily psychometric tests and qualitative behaviour analysis of audio and video recordings.

Participants
15 men, randomly divided into two groups of five guards and 10 prisoners (after being matched for racism, authoritarianism and social dominance), selected as being pro-social and well-adjusted (by psychometric testing, independent clinical assessment and character references), of a variety of ages and backgrounds, from 332 applicants recruited from national press advertisements.

Procedure
Participants spent 8 days under constant video surveillance in a purpose-built, controlled institutional environment resembling a prison that aimed to create 'inequalities between groups that were real to the participants.'

Prisoners had their heads shaved and had basic uniforms (t-shirts with a 3-digit number, loose trousers, sandals), and basic food and living conditions in lockable 3-person cells.

Guards had better uniforms, food and accommodation, plus control over keys and resources to use as rewards or punishments. They were shown the prison timetable/chores and had complete freedom in how they implemented their responsibility for the smooth running of the prison (with the exception of physical violence).

RESULTS

- Guards did not internalise their role nor develop and act in terms of a group identity (perhaps due to negative views of the role).
- Prisoners acted in their own individual interests to be promoted to the guard group until group impermeability was introduced on day three, after which a group identity formed and prisoners rebelled causing the collapse of the prison system by day six.
- After the collapse, a self-governing commune was created, but a lack of group identity led some participants to favour a more tyrannical new system and authoritarianism scores increased.

DISCUSSION

- Research on significant social psychology issues can be ethical. Independent clinical psychologists and an ethics committee able to change or terminate the study were present throughout.
- A Social Identity approach was mostly supported. People did not automatically conform to group roles nor act tyrannically in groups, indeed groups helped resist tyranny. Failing, powerless groups, however, can lead to tyranny.

4.4 Studies of conformity

CONFORMITY DEFINITIONS AND TYPES

Definition: 'Yielding to group pressure' Crutchfield (1962). According to Aronson (1976) the pressure can be real (involving the physical presence of others) or imagined (involving the pressure of social norms/expectations). Kelman (1958) suggests that the yielding can take the form of

- compliance – A change in behaviour without a change in opinion (just going along with the group),
- internalisation – A change in both behaviour and opinion (the group's and your own opinions coincide), or
- identification – The individual changes their behaviour and opinions to identify with the influencing group.

CONFORMITY STUDIES

Jenness (1932)

Asked subjects to estimate the number of beans in a bottle, first individually and then as a group. When asked individually again, the subjects showed a shift towards the group's estimate rather than their own. This was rather a simple experiment, however.

Sherif (1935)

Asked subjects to estimate how far a spot of light in a completely dark room moved. Sherif kept the point of light stable, but due to the autokinetic effect illusion (caused by small eye movements) each individual reported fairly consistent estimates that often differed from other subjects.

However, when subjects were put in groups, their estimates converged towards a central mean, despite not being told to arrive at a group estimate and despite denying that they had been influenced by the others in post experimental interviews.

Asch (1951, 1952, 1956)

Asch wanted to test conformity under non ambiguous conditions and, therefore, devised a very simple perceptual task of matching the length of a line to one of three other comparison lines. The task was so easy that control subjects made almost no errors. In the experimental condition only one real (naive) subject was tested at a time, but was surrounded by seven confederates of the experimenter, who were also supposed to be subjects but had been told beforehand to all give the same wrong estimate on 12 out of the 18 trials. The only real subject was second to last to give their estimate, and was, therefore, faced with either giving their own opinion or conforming to the group opinion on the critical trials.

The average rate of conformity was 32%. 74% conformed at least once and 26% never conformed. Asch conducted variations to identify factors influencing conformity, such as:

- increasing the group size – Asch found little increase above 3 or 4, although other studies have found that larger groups will increase conformity but at a decreasing rate.
- providing support for the subject – when Asch provided an ally that agreed with the naive subject's estimates, conformity dropped to 5.5%. It seems that the unanimity of the group is important. If the ally changed to the group's estimates, then the naive subject would often follow suit.
- increasing the difficulty of the task – when the comparison lines were made closer in length, the rate of conformity increased.
- when the naive subject could write down their response, conformity dropped.

Even subjects that did not conform, felt strong social pressure to do so. One was heard to exclaim 'I always disagree – darn it!', and on being debriefed, commented 'I do not deny that at times I had the feeling "to heck with it, I'll go along with the rest"'.

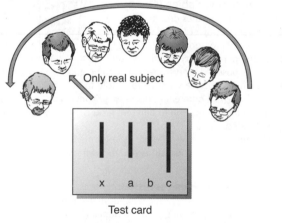

Direction that answers were given in

Only real subject

x a b c

Test card

Crutchfield (1954)

Crutchfield tested for conformity without physical presence by placing subjects in individual cubicles with electronic display boards which supposedly let each subject know what the others had answered. In fact, he allowed each subject to believe they were the last to answer and presented them with uniformly wrong group answers on half the tasks.

With this more efficient and standardised procedure Crutchfield tested over 600 subjects using a variety of stimuli such as Asch's line comparison tests, obviously incorrect factual statements, and personal opinions. He found 30% conformity in Asch's line test, 46% conformity to the suggestion that a picture of a star had a larger surface area than a circle (when it was a third smaller), and 37% agreement to the statement 'I doubt that I would make a good leader' (which none agreed to when asked on their own).

Criticisms of conformity studies

- Artificiality – the above studies used well controlled and standardised procedures but mostly reflect conformity under laboratory conditions, with meaningless stimuli.
- The high conformity found may only reflect the norms prevalent in the USA in the 1950s. Replications have found widely varying rates of conformity in more recent times and when the studies have been conducted cross culturally.
- Ethics – subjects were deceived.

4.5 Theories of conformity

CRUTCHFIELD'S CONFORMING PERSONALITY THEORY (1955)

After Crutchfield had tested his subjects for conformity, he also gave them a number of personality and I.Q. type tests, and found, for example, that those subjects who conformed the most typically

- were less intellectually competent – perhaps they were more open to the expert power of others
- had less ego strength – perhaps making them less confident in their own opinion
- had less leadership ability – perhaps making them less able to assert their own opinion
- were more narrow minded / authoritarian – perhaps inclining them to stick to the majority answer

However, if conforming personalities exist, then they should conform in a variety of situations, but McGuire (1968a) has found inconsistency of conformity across different situations.

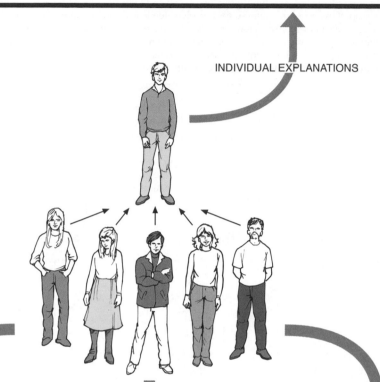

INDIVIDUAL EXPLANATIONS

SOCIAL THEORIES OF CONFORMITY

INFORMATIONAL SOCIAL INFLUENCE

Deutsch and Gerard (1955) have suggested that one motive for conformity is based on the **need** that everyone has **for certainty**.

When individuals are placed in ambiguous/**uncertain conditions**, they are more likely to refer to others to know how to react (Festinger called this **social comparison**).

Under these conditions, other people possess informational or **expert power** and individuals may show **internalisation** conformity – both their behaviour and opinions coincide with the group's.

Informational influence explains the conformity found in Sherif's study and much of the conformity in Asch's tasks – especially when the difficulty of the task was increased. A few of Asch's subjects seemingly experienced perceptual distortion, but the majority believed that the group's judgement was superior.

NORMATIVE SOCIAL INFLUENCE

Deutsch and Gerard (1955) have proposed that another motive for conformity is based upon the **need** for **social acceptance** and **approval**.

When individuals are put into a potentially **embarrassing situation**, such as disagreeing with the majority, they are faced with a **conflict** between their own and others' opinions.

Under these conditions other people have **reward** or **coercive power** which may lead individuals into **compliance** – publicly agreeing with the group, but privately maintaining their own opinions.

Normative influence explains some of Asch's conformity results, especially in the private answer variation. Some of his subjects reported private disagreement with the group's answers, commenting 'If I'd been the first I probably would have responded differently'.

REFERENT SOCIAL INFLUENCE

Turner (1991) suggests that people have a tendency to categorise themselves as members of different groups (Social Identity Theory) and argues that we are most likely to conform to the norms of those groups that we feel we are members of.

This occurs because people expect to agree with the members of such groups, but do not necessarily expect their views to coincide with those of other groups and are therefore less likely to conform to out-group than in-group pressure.

Under these conditions, members of the in-group possess **informational**, and perhaps also **reward** and **referent power**, which may lead the individual to **identification** conformity – their behaviour and beliefs coinciding with the group's, while they feel they are members of that group.

4.6 Milgram's (1963) study of obedience

AIM
To investigate how far people will go in obeying an authority figure.

PROCEDURE
Subjects were led to believe that the experiment was investigating the effects of punishment on learning. The subjects were tested one at a time and were always given the role of teacher (through a fixed lottery). The subject saw his apparent co-subject (in reality an actor) strapped into a chair with electrodes attached to him, since he was to be the 'learner'. The subject ('teacher') was told the shocks would cause no permanent tissue damage and was given a trial shock of 45 volts.

The subject then started the experiment in the shock generator room next door by testing the learner over an intercom, and was told by the experimenter (the authority figure) to administer increasing levels of electric shock for each wrong answer (which the actor gave often). In the basic set-up of the experiment the subject received feedback reactions from the learner he was 'electrocuting' only by a thump on the wall at 300 volts followed by no further reply. The experiment finished when either the subject refused to continue (disobeyed the experimenter's request), or had reached the maximum shock on the scale (450 volts). The subject was then fully debriefed as to the real nature of the experiment, re-introduced to the learner in a friendly way and reassured that no damage had been done since the learner had not really received any shocks at all!

Subjects
They were 40 males between the ages of 20 and 50 from a range of occupations and were drawn from the New Haven area. They were obtained by newspaper ad's for participation in a study of learning at Yale University and were paid $4.50 just for turning up.

The learner
An actor was required to play the role of the learner – an Irish-American, 47-year-old accountant who appeared mild-mannered and likeable.

Apparatus
Two rooms in the Yale Interaction Laboratory were used – one for the learner containing an 'electric chair' and an answering device, the other for the teacher and experimenter with an electric shock generator. The generator did not actually give shocks to the learner, and was used to measure the dependent variable of obedience. It was a convincing machine with a row of 30 switches ranging from 15 to 450 volts in increments of 15 volts, and was marked with descriptive terms of the shock effects – ranging from 'slight shock' through to 'Danger: severe shock' and 'XXX'.

The experimenter
He was 31 years old, dressed in a grey laboratory coat, and appeared somewhat stern and impassive through the experiment. If at any point the subject showed reluctance to administer the shock, he would command them to continue with standardised prompts ranging from "please continue" to "You have no other choice, you *must* go on".

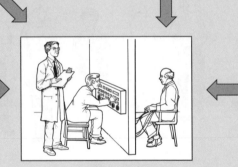

RESULTS
Levels of obedience expected
Psychology students and professional colleagues were asked what percentage of subjects would administer the highest degree of shock (450 volts) – the answers ranged from 1 to 3, with a mean of 1.2.

Levels of obedience obtained
65% of subjects continued to the maximum shock level of 450 volts. No subject stopped before 300 volts.

Subjects' realisation of shock effects
In the post-experimental interview the subjects were asked "How painful to the learner were the last few shocks that you administered to him?". The mean response was 13.42 out of 14 – 'extremely painful' on the scale.

Behavioural reactions to the study
"In a large number of cases the degree of tension reached extremes that are rarely seen in sociopsychological laboratory studies. Subjects were observed to sweat, tremble, stutter, bite their lips, groan and dig their fingers into their flesh. These were characteristic rather than exceptional responses to the experiment... One sign of tension was the regular occurrence of nervous laughing fits... Full-blown, uncontrollable seizures were observed for 3 subjects. On one occasion we observed a fit so violently convulsive that it was necessary to call a halt to the experiment. In the post experimental interviews subjects took pains to point out that they were not sadistic types, and that the laughter did not mean they enjoyed shocking the victim". Milgram (1963).

EVALUATION OF METHODOLOGY
Experimental validity
The procedure was well standardised and obedience was accurately operationalised as the amount of voltage given. Orne and Holland (1968) however, have argued that the subjects did not really think that the learner would come to harm. They suggested that the subjects were involved in a *'pact of ignorance'* with the experimenter and obeyed in much the same way as a member of a magician's audience will comply and put their head under a guillotine which has just split a cabbage head in two! The genuine distress of the subjects, their ratings of the shock pain and their comments during debriefing count against this criticism, as does the study by Sheridan and King (1972).

Ecological validity
Some psychologists have suggested that the experiment is an artificial test of obedience and therefore **lacks 'mundane realism'** or ecological validity. Milgram argues that while there are important differences between experimental and real life obedience, there is a fundamental similarity in the psychological processes at work – especially the process of agency.

The subjects were also American, male and volunteers – an unrepresentative sample that may have already been more obedient and helpful, but later studies have found similarly high rates of obedience using other samples and more everyday tasks and contexts (see replications and field studies of obedience). The methodology also caused numerous ethical problems (see ethics and obedience studies).

4.7 Studies of obedience

MILGRAM'S VARIATIONS ON THE BASIC STUDY

Milgram decided to conduct many **variations** of the study to determine the key factors that were responsible for the obedience (overall 636 subjects were tested during the 18 different variation studies). In the basic set-up of the experiment the subject received feedback reactions from the learner he was 'electrocuting' only by a thump on the wall at 300 volts followed by no further reply, but in a later condition vocal feedback was given (this was standardised by the use of a tape recording).

The table below shows some of the different variables that were carefully manipulated to see the effect on obedience (measured by the percentage that gave the maximum 450 volt shock).

Vocal feedback condition	
At **75 volts**	moans / groans.
At **150 volts**	requests to be excused from the experiment.
At **195 volts**	yelled "Let me out! My heart's bothering me."
At **285 volts**	agonised scream
At **300 volt**	kicked the wall and begged to be released.
At **315 volts**	no further responses.

65%	Remote – victim condition.	The victim in a separate room and no feedback until a bang on the wall at 300 volts. No subject stopped before 300 volts.
62.5%	Vocal – feedback condition.	With the verbal protestations, screams, wall pounding and ominous silence after 300 volts. Only a few stopped before 300 volts.
92.5%	Two teacher condition.	The subject was paired with another teacher (a confederate) who actually delivered the shocks while the subject only read out the words.
47.5%	Shift of setting condition.	The experiment was moved to a set of run down offices rather than the impressive Yale University.
40%	Proximity condition.	Learner moved into the same room so the teacher could see his agonised reactions.
30%	Touch proximity condition.	The teacher had to force the learner's hand down onto a shock plate when he refused to participate after 150 volts.
20%	Absent experimenter condition.	The experimenter has to leave and give instructions over the telephone. Many subjects cheated and missed out shocks or gave less voltage than ordered to.
10%	Social support condition.	Two other subjects (confederates) were also teachers but soon refused to obey. Most subjects stopped very soon after the others.

REPLICATIONS OF MILGRAM'S STUDY

Varying the subjects   **Gender** – women were found to show similar levels of obedience by Milgram, but other studies have found both lower levels (when asked to electrocute another woman) and higher levels (when asked to electrocute a puppy).
Nationality – cross-cultural studies have found varying obedience levels – higher in Holland, Austria and Germany, but lower in Britain and Australia. The different procedures used in these studies make proper comparison difficult.

Varying the victim   **Gender** – a female victim has occasionally reduced obedience
Species – Sheridan and King (1972) found 75% obedience when real electric shocks were used on puppies.

Varying the setting   See field experiments…

Field experiments on obedience

High levels of obedience have been shown many times under real life conditions.

Hofling _et al._ (1966) investigated obedience in American hospitals. They found that 95.5% (21 out of 22) of the nurses tested obeyed an unknown doctor's telephone instructions to administer twice the maximum allowed dose of a drug (in fact a harmless placebo) that was clearly labelled with warnings against such an action and that was not on the ward stock list for the day. This was in contrast to 21 out of 22 nurses who replied that they would not have obeyed the doctor and broken the hospital regulations for medication when asked how they would have reacted in the same situation.

This study was conducted under slightly unusual conditions however (although in a natural environment it still lacked ecological validity), and the results have not been replicated when the procedure was changed to make it more realistic, i.e. a drug known to the nurses, and with others around to consult.

Bickman (1974) investigated obedience on the streets of New York. He revealed that when an experimenter was dressed in a guard's uniform and told passers-by to pick up paper bags or give a coin to a stranger there was 80% obedience, compared to 40% when the experimenter was dressed more 'normally'. A milkman's uniform, however, did not have the same effect as the guard's on obedience.

Meeus and Raaijmakers (1986) investigated obedience in a business setting in Holland. They had an experimenter ask subjects to act as interviewers, supposedly in order to test the effects of stress on job applicants by delivering 15 increasingly distressing and insulting remarks to applicants (in fact confederates) at a time of high unemployment. 91.5% of their subjects obeyed the experimenter and made all 15 remarks despite the psychological distress shown by the applicants.

4.8 Explanations of obedience

EXPLANATIONS OF OBEDIENCE STUDIES

SOCIAL POWER EXPLANATIONS

THE IMPACT OF POWER – *Social impact theory* (Latane and Wolf) explains factors that affected obedience in Milgram's studies

1 The impact of the **experimenter's power on the subject** – The experimenter was close (immediacy of influence was high) and important (strength of influence was high) to the subject. When the experimenter gave instructions over the telephone obedience decreased (as immediacy decreased). When there were a number of (confederate) teachers who disobeyed in the social support condition, the subjects' obedience decreased as the experimenter's power and authority was spread amongst many teachers, having less impact on each one (diffusion of impact).

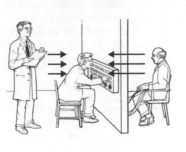

2 The impact of the **learner's distress on the subject** – The subject was not in close proximity to the learner (low immediacy of influence). When the consequences of the shocks were made more immediate (when the learner was brought into the same room) the impact of the learner's distress increased and obedience decreased. When there were two teachers, and the naive subject only had to read out the questions, he felt even less individually responsible for his actions (diffusion of impact) and obedience increased.

TYPES OF POWER USED
- The location of respectable Yale university added **legitimate power** to the situation (obedience decreased when the location changed).
- The experimenter represented scientific authority and possessed expert and legitimate power (obedience decreased when he was absent), especially with his grey laboratory coat which represents the power that uniform has in our society – see studies by Haney, Banks and Zimbardo (1973) and Bickman (1974).

MILGRAM'S AGENCY THEORY
- Milgram (1974) suggests that when faced with commands from legitimate authority figures we lose our sense of responsibility for our own actions and become the agents of others' wishes (the state of agency). Thus the high levels of obedience found in Milgram's studies resulted from the experimenter as the authority figure **taking responsibility** for the consequences of the obedience.
- According to Milgram (1974) agency involves a **cognitive shift in viewpoint** that results in people switching from their normal **autonomous state** (where they feel in control of, and responsible for, their actions) to the **agentic state** (where they regard themselves as "the instrument for carrying out another person's wishes").
- The purpose of the agentic state is to allow human hierarchical social systems to function properly – if people did not automatically yield to those of higher status then society would be disorganised and unable to achieve its collective goals efficiently (or at all) and disobedient, lower ranking individuals would constantly risk punishment from those above them in the hierarchy.
- Milgram proposed the agentic state was a product of evolution and pointed out that we grow up in a society where we constantly submit to those in authority from the moment we are born, e.g. to parents, teachers and employers.
- The agentic state can account for the horrific acts committed in the name of obedience – for example soldiers who have committed atrocities arguing they were only following orders and were not responsible for their actions.

AUTHORITARIAN PERSONALITY THEORY

What is it?	How does it affect obedience?	Evaluation
Adorno *et al.* (1950) suggest people with authoritarian personalities are: • preoccupied with power, • submissive to authority figures, • hostile and contemptuous towards people of lower status, • inflexible in beliefs and values, • rigid, rule-following in thinking, • prone to categorise people into 'us' and 'them' groups, often due to harsh and disciplinarian parental upbringing which produces unconscious feelings of hostility that may be displaced onto safer targets. Adorno *et al.* measured these traits with personality questionnaires like the F - Scale (Fascist tendencies).	The theory predicts people with authoritarian personalities are more likely to obey authority figures and support harsher measures. This may be because: • They are more vulnerable to the legitimate power of authority figures. • They feel hostile or contemptuous towards the lower status of the victim of obedience. • They feel less able to resist following rules/instructions. • They identify less with the victim than the authority figure.	• Studies have found an association between authoritarianism and obedience, willingness to accept tyranny and support of harsher sentencing as jury members. • It is uncertain how much behaviour is determined by personality traits as opposed to external social influences in different obedience situations. • Much of the theory was based on debatable Freudian concepts. • F-Scales were scored so agreement to all statements, such as 'Obedience and respect for authority are the most important virtues a child can learn', meant authoritarianism, but scores could have been due to response set.

4.9 Independent behaviour

TYPES OF RESISTANCE

Independent behaviour – involves the true rejection of social influence to behave in accord with one's own internal attitudes, regardless of whether they coincide with the influencer's.

Anti-conformity – involves resisting social influence by deliberately opposing the majority and refusing to behave like them. This behaviour is still affected by society, however.

EXAMPLES OF RESISTING INFLUENCE IN PSYCHOLOGY

Independence in conformity studies

- Asch's (1951) conformity experiment showed high rates of resistance (average non-conformity on the critical trials was 68%, 26% did not conform at all, and all 50 were resistant at least once in the original test). In post-experimental interviews with the independent subjects, he found some resisted based on confidence of opinion (see locus of control), others were withdrawn and acted on the basis of being an individual (see reactance below) and the rest were filled with tension and doubt but felt it necessary to deal adequately with the task (perhaps conforming to the role of 'conscientious participant').
- Crutchfield (1954) found non-conformity ranging from 54% to 70%, depending on the type of task used to test conformity.

Independence in obedience studies

- Milgram's (1963) experiment found low levels of disobedience (only 35% refused to give the maximum shock).
- Hofling *et al.* (1966) found less than 5% disobedience to authority in a hospital setting.

EXPLANATIONS OF INDEPENDENT BEHAVIOUR

Situational influence

SOCIAL IMPACT THEORY

This theory suggests independence only occurs when social conditions allow it to be expressed – ***reductions in the impact of others' power*** relative to the individual's desire to express their independence are *necessary*.

Evaluation

- Reducing the importance/strength of the influencer – when Milgram's obedience experiment was moved to a location with less legitimate and expert power, disobedience increased from 35% to 52.5%.
- Reducing the immediacy of the influencer – when Milgram's authority figure gave instructions by telephone, disobedience increased from 35% to 80%.

SOCIAL SUPPORT

Social Impact theory also suggests that diffusion of impact over many targets reduces the effect of social influence on each individual, but social support also

- breaks the consensus of the majority.
- introduces the possibility of, and support structure for, dissent. A norm for resistance and the opportunity of minority influence is created.

Evaluation

Resistance is significantly increased by social support:

- Just one ally in Asch's study increased non-conformity from an average of 68% to 95%.
- Two other 'teachers' (actors) disobeying in Milgram's study increased the real subjects' disobedience to 90%.
- Gamson *et al.* (1982) found 97% of groups showed dissent and 50% completely rebelled to unfair requests from authority figures – probably because the groups provided a greater opportunity for dissent to be expressed and discussed, and social support to justify and implement rebellion.

However, it is difficult to know if resistance in groups is just *conformity* to others rebelling or true independence.

Individual differences

LOCUS OF CONTROL (LOC)

Rotter (1954, 1966) proposed that people with an:

- ***internal*** locus of control believe their ***own personality*** and behaviour determine the outcomes of events
- ***external*** locus of control believe the results of their actions are more affected by ***chance or other people***.

It has been suggested that those with a ***high internal*** LOC (as measured, for example, by Rotter's I-E Scale) may be ***more independent***, perhaps because they:

- rely less on external explanations and have more self-confidence (to resist informational social influence)
- feel more responsible for the outcomes of their actions (so reducing agentic shift in obedience situations)

Evaluation

Odell (1959) was the first to find a correlation ($r = .33$, $P<0.05$) between internal LOC and independence of judgement, while Ritchie and Phares (1969) found people with an internal LOC were not just resistant to changing ideas (i.e. stubborn!), but were less likely to change opinions as a result of high status influence than those with an external LOC (Lefcourt, 1982). Crutchfield found non-conformers had higher self-confidence than conformers.

PSYCHOLOGICAL REACTANCE

Brehm (1966) argued people have a psychological need for individual freedom and that perceived constraints on independence activate a physiological arousal state of reactance which leads to resistance to assert their freedom.

Evaluation

Reactance may just reflect American cultural values of freedom and individualism. The society that one is raised in can affect the level of independence. Berry (1966, 1967) discovered that people living in an individualistic hunting society where self-reliance is highly valued, showed more independent behaviour than members of a collectivistic agricultural society who were more dependent upon co-operation, agreement and conformity.

4.10 Social influence research and social change

SOCIAL CHANGE

Social change can refer to:

1 **The ability of individuals or social groups to change their identity, power and status within a society** – in this case the research of the *Social Identity approach* can be used to explain how and why social change occurs and how power imbalance and tyranny can be overcome.

2 **The large-scale changing of general social norms and views** – since conformity and obedience to majority social norms acts to prevent social change in society, social influence research into *minority influence* can help explain how social change occurs.

THE SOCIAL IDENTITY APPROACH

The Social Identity approach (Tajfel, 1978, Turner 1985) suggests that people allocate themselves to groups and gain their identities and self-esteem from those groups. For people who are negatively valued because of their current group membership (e.g. subordinate groups), social change depends upon the permeability of social group boundaries:

- When group boundaries are perceived as *permeable*, people think they can advance to desirable groups so *act individually* to *change group*, e.g. by changing aspects of appearance or behaviour to become accepted.
- When group boundaries are perceived as *impermeable*, people think they cannot change so are more likely to *identify with their present group*. Social change will then depend on *collective action* by the group to improve their identity, status and power, e.g. challenging inequalities or redefining their own group identity. Collective action against dominant groups depends upon the *security of intergroup relations* – when people see group differences as illegitimate and unstable, and are more aware of cognitive alternatives to the status quo, they see the possibility of change and may challenge inequality.

Evaluation

- The 'Black is Beautiful' campaign showed redefining collective action.
- The Reicher and Haslam (2006) BBC Prison Study of tyranny supports the Social Identity approach to social change.

MINORITY INFLUENCE

At times minority groups may not only resist, but actually influence majority groups in society to cause social change. Throughout history minorities (often defined in terms of political power rather than just number) such as scientific, religious, women's and black rights groups have changed the majority viewpoint (Kuhn called this a 'paradigm shift'). In fact, without minorities to introduce change and innovation, conformity to the majority status quo would stagnate progress in society.

HOW DO MINORITIES CAUSE CHANGE?

Dual Process theory – Moscovici (1980) argued that since minorities do not have the informational and normative influence of the majority (in fact they are often ridiculed by them), they must exert their influence through their *behavioural style* – how they express their views.

Consistency of viewpoint over time and between members of the minority group is the most important aspect of this style since this not only draws attention to the minority view and gives the impression of certainty and coherence, but also causes doubt about majority norms.

Other important features of behavioural style are *investment* (the minority has made sacrifices for the view), *autonomy* (the view is made on principle without ulterior motives) and *flexibility* (the consistent viewpoint must not be seen as too rigid and dogmatic). This behavioural style means minorities and majorities exert influence through 2 different processes (thus *dual* process theory):

- Majorities influence minorities quickly through compliance (the minority changes public behaviour but not private opinions)
- Minorities influence majorities more slowly through conversion (the majority gradually change their private opinions before their public behaviour), which can cause majority internalisation (both public and private acceptance of the minority view).

Moscovici argues that conversion occurs because minority views encourage cognitive conflict and therefore greater processing in the long term which may restructure the majority group's attitudes.

Evaluation – alternative theories of changing social views

- Social Identity Theory suggests opinion change is more likely if in-group rather than out-group members express minority views.
- Social Impact Theory suggests minority views have increasing impact when high profile (greater immediacy) and advanced by many people (increasing number of influencers) of higher status (increasing strength of influence).

EVIDENCE FOR MINORITY INFLUENCE

Moscovici *et al.* (1969) tested subjects in groups of 6 on their ability to judge the colour of 36 blue slides of varying brightness. Unknown to the rest of the subjects, 2 in each group were confederates who acted as a minority group. They found that when the minority:

- *consistently* judged the slides to be green rather than blue, the majority followed them on 8.42% of trials.
- *inconsistently* judged the slides to be green rather than blue (on 2 in every 3 trials), the majority followed them on only 1.25% of trials.

Furthermore, in later individual tests the subjects exposed to the minority were more likely (than control groups with no minority) to report ambiguous green/blue slides as green, *especially* if they had previously resisted the minority view, indicating a longer-term influence.

Nemeth *et al.* (1974) replicated Moscovici *et al.*'s study but had their 2 confederates:

- Randomly say green on half the trials and green/blue on the other half. This caused no minority influence because of the inconsistency.
- Consistently say green or green/blue depending on the brightness of the slides. This consistency led to 21% minority influence.
- Say green on every trial. This consistency caused no minority influence, perhaps because it was seen as being rigid and unrealistic.

Maass and Clark (1983) found publicly expressed views on gay rights followed the majority but privately expressed views shifted towards the minority viewpoint, indicating minorities cause a change in private opinions/attitudes *before* a change in public behaviour.

5.1 Theories of attribution

WHAT IS ATTRIBUTION?

Social psychologists who have investigated social cognition (how we understand and think about people and social situations) have pointed out that people do not just passively observe their own and others' actions, but try to work out or explain what caused them. Attribution refers to the process of deciding what caused behaviour – whether:

1   the person performing the actions was responsible (an **internal / dispositional attribution** where the cause seems due to some aspect of the individual, i.e. their personality, ability, mood, etc.) or
2   the social situation and circumstances they were experiencing were responsible (an **external / situational attribution** where the cause seems due to some external influence, i.e. environmental factors, other people, chance, etc.).

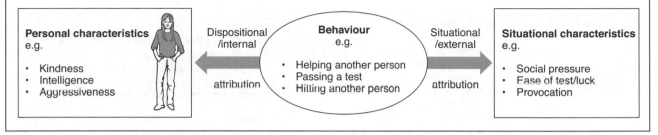

Personal characteristics e.g.

- Kindness
- Intelligence
- Aggressiveness

Dispositional /internal attribution

Behaviour e.g.

- Helping another person
- Passing a test
- Hitting another person

Situational /external attribution

Situational characteristics e.g.

- Social pressure
- Ease of test/luck
- Provocation

THEORIES OF HOW ATTRIBUTIONS ARE MADE

CORRESPONDENT INFERENCE THEORY
Jones and Davis (1965), Jones and McGillis (1976)

Correspondent inference theory **explains dispositional attributions** by suggesting that people attempt to find a *match* (correspondence) *between* the *behaviour* they observe and *underlying stable qualities in the person* that produced it. Internal, dispositional inferences are made in two main stages:

1   **Attributing intention** – did the person/actor deliberately mean to perform the behaviour or was it an accident? This is decided by whether the actor:
   - *knew the effects* their actions would have
   - *had the ability* to perform those actions.
2   **Attributing disposition** – this is achieved by assessing, for example, the:
   - *non-common effects* of the behaviour – actions that have non-common (unusual) effects are seen as more likely to reflect individual dispositions than behaviour that produces common effects.
   - *social desirability* of the behaviour – the more socially *undesirable* a behaviour is perceived as being, the more likely it is to be attributed to dispositional causes.

Evaluation
- Jones, Davis and Gergen (1961) found participants rated taped applicants' statements for the job of an astronaut or submariner more dispositionally (greater correspondent inference) when they were inconsistent with expectations (i.e. claiming they were 'inner-directed' when required to relate well to others in the enclosed confines of a submarine).
- Jones and Harris (1967) found more dispositional inferences were made in the USA for students who freely chose to deliver unpopular speeches (e.g. supporting Fidel Castro).
- Correspondent inference theory emphasised the idea that attribution may be *biased* towards dispositional causes (due to factors like hedonic relevance). This was supported by later research on attributional bias.
- The theory focuses on the *social comparison* of the individual's behaviour with that of others, looking for *unexpected* variations. It ignores, however, comparison with the individual's own *past behaviour* and the fact that behaviour that *fulfils expectations* or stereotypes is also useful in the attribution of causes. *Unintentional* behaviour is important for dispositional attribution too, e.g. clumsy actions.

KELLEY'S CO-VARIATION MODEL
Kelley (1967, 1972)

The co-variation model explains how **dispositional** or **situational attributions** are made of *people we know*, based upon our past knowledge of their behaviour and that of others. Attributions are made based on how the following sources of information co-vary with each other:

1   **Consensus** – concerns variation across people and refers to the extent to which *other people* behave in the same way to the same stimuli as the known person.
2   **Consistency** – concerns variation across time and refers to the extent to which the known person has behaved in the same way to the same stimuli on *past occasions*.
3   **Distinctiveness** – concerns variation across stimuli and refers to the extent to which the known person behaves in the same way to *different* (but perhaps similar) *stimuli*.

	Type of attribution		
	Dispositional	**Situational**	
Consensus	*LOW*	*HIGH*	*LOW*
Consistency	*HIGH*	*HIGH*	*LOW*
Distinctiveness	*LOW*	*HIGH*	*HIGH*

Evaluation
- McArthur (1972) gave participants descriptions like 'John laughed at the comedian' with different combinations of consensus, consistency and distinctiveness information, and found they generally attributed as the model predicted (apart from a tendency to prefer dispositional attributions and use less consensus information).
- Alloy and Tabachnik (1984) concluded that people find working out the co-variations difficult. Given that humans are usually cognitive misers (preferring to use the least mental effort possible), researchers like Hilton and Slugoski (1986) with their Abnormal Conditions Focus Model suggest mental 'shortcuts' are taken – only certain types of information are preferred for certain attributions (e.g. using just low consensus for internal attributions).
- People may often lack knowledge about others' behaviour and thus consensus, consistency and distinctiveness information. Under these conditions Kelley (1972) suggests we use causal schemata such as multiple sufficient causes, discounting and augmentation principles.

5.2 Bias in attribution

WHAT IS ATTRIBUTION BIAS?
Social psychologists have found that attributional decisions about one's own and others' behaviour are not always made in a logical and objective manner (as some 'normative' theories of attribution suggest) but may become distorted or biased since:

1 People are 'cognitive misers' – we do not wish to spend more mental effort than necessary and so may not examine all the attributional evidence available or may simply take mental short cuts to reach quick conclusions.
2 The information available may be insufficient or be received in ways that highlight some aspects more than others, e.g. due to viewpoint, salience or importance.
3 The information may be used in ways that maximise its use to us, e.g. for predicting future behaviour or maintaining our self-esteem.

FUNDAMENTAL ATTRIBUTION ERROR
What is it?
The fundamental attribution error (Ross, 1977) is the general *tendency* people have *to make internal, dispositional attributions* for *others' behaviour* rather than external, situational ones, when there may be equally convincing evidence for both types of cause. The fundamental attribution error (FAE) tendency to attribute dispositionally and hold the person and their characteristics responsible for behaviour increases with the *seriousness of the consequences* of the behaviour and its *personal (hedonic) relevance* to us.

Why does it occur?
Focus of attention – observers are more likely to notice the actor and their behaviour than the situation and more diffuse circumstances influencing behaviour.
Predictability of behaviour – attributions to personal, stable characteristics rather than changeable situational ones fulfil the observer's need to be able to predict and control the world.
Linguistic ease – the English language makes it easier to describe actors and their actions in the same way (e.g. we talk of 'aggressive' behaviour resulting from an 'aggressive' *person* rather than *situation*), thus facilitating the attributional link between them (Nisbett and Ross, 1980).

Evaluation
- Ross *et al.* (1977) randomly assigned college students to be either 'questioners' (to invent and ask challenging questions based on their own expertise) or 'answerers' in a quiz. They found that the 'questioners' were rated as having better general knowledge ability (despite not actually answering any questions themselves!) than the 'answerers', by both the 'answerers' and observers of the quiz (but not themselves). This dispositional attribution ignored the 'questioners' situation of being able to create the questions and supports the FAE since later tests given by the researchers found no difference in general knowledge between the 'questioners' and 'answerers'.
- The FAE explains attributions in other studies, e.g. the tendency of observers of the Milgram experiment to attribute the potentially serious consequences of the participants' obedience to personal characteristics rather than social pressure (Bierbrauer, 1979).
- However, the FAE may not be as fundamental a tendency as first thought, Miller (1984) found cross-cultural variations in attributional tendencies with Indian-Hindus tending to prefer situational attributions to a greater degree than Americans.
- The FAE ignores attributions made by the actor about their own behaviour.

ACTOR-OBSERVER EFFECT
The actor-observer effect (Jones and Nisbett, 1972) refers to the tendency of people to attribute internal / dispositional causes when observing others' behaviour (as in the fundamental attribution error), but *attribute external / situational causes to their own behaviour* (when they are the actors).

Why does it occur?
Focus of attention – observers are more likely to notice the actor and their behaviour, while actors look out at, and therefore focus more on, factors in the environment.
Access to information – actors have more knowledge of intention and past behaviour (consistency information) than observers who therefore rely more on the FAE.

Evaluation
- Nisbett et al (1973) found that male college students were more likely to *attribute* their *own choice* of girlfriend and major study subject *to external factors* (e.g. she is a relaxing person, chemistry is a high paying field), but their *best friend's choices* to *dispositional factors* (e.g. needing someone to relax with, wanting to make a lot of money).
- Storms (1973) got actors to make more dispositional attributions by showing them videotapes of their behaviour, thus refocusing their attention as observers on to themselves.
- The actor–observer effect tends to focus on cognitive rather than motivational factors and so does not take into account whether the behaviour to be attributed was successful or not.

SELF-SERVING BIAS
The self-serving bias effect (Miller and Ross, 1975) refers to the tendency of *actors* to *attribute successful behaviour to dispositional causes*, but *unsuccessful behaviour to situational ones*, thus qualifying the actor–observer effect. The self-serving bias can lead to self-handicapping behaviour.

Why does it occur?
Motivational factors – Miller (1978) suggested that attribution is used to maintain self-esteem and for impression management of esteem in the eyes of others. Dispositional attributions of successful behaviour provide self-enhancement, situational attributions of unsuccessful behaviour provide self-protection.
Cognitive factors – since people usually expect to succeed based on their own abilities, unexpected/unintended failure is perceived as due to external factors.

Evaluation
- Kingdon (1967) interviewed successful and unsuccessful politicians and found that they tended to attribute their successes to dispositional factors, e.g. hard work and their reputation, and their defeats to external factors, e.g. national trends and lack of campaign money.
- Johnson et al (1964) found that students asked to teach other pupils attributed responsibility for increased performance to their teaching, but decreased performance to the student. However, this effect has not always been found with experienced teachers (e.g. Ross et al, 1974).
- Cross-cultural differences have been found, with more self-effacing and modest participants from China and Japan showing less self-serving bias than American participants.

5.3 Factors affecting impression formation

CENTRAL TRAITS

Asch (1946) proposed the idea of central traits – personality characteristics that have a greater impact on the formation of impressions about other people because they correlate highly with certain other traits and so allow more inferences to be drawn about a person than *peripheral* traits.

Asch found subjects given the adjective '***warm***' in the middle of a list of adjectives about a hypothetical person rated that person as ***more generous, wise, happy and good-natured*** than a control group without the word 'warm'. Substituting the word 'cold' for 'warm' caused significantly less favourable ratings than the control group, whereas substitution with the words 'polite' or 'blunt' caused fewer differences from the control. Thus 'warm' and 'cold' are central traits, but 'polite' and 'blunt' are peripheral traits.

Response trait	Control	Polite	Blunt	Warm	Cold
'Generous' rating	55%	56%	8%	91%	8%

Evaluation
- Kelley (1950) supported Asch's results with a replication of greater ecological validity using students' ratings of a lecturer introduced as either 'warm' or 'cold'.
- The impact of central traits can depend on the context.
- Asch explained central traits using Gestalt psychology; others favour implicit personality theory explanations.

PRIMACY AND RECENCY EFFECTS

Asch (1946) also investigated the primacy effect on impression formation, proposing that information presented first has a greater impact (first impressions are important).

Asch gave one group of subjects a list of adjectives about a hypothetical person that started with positive traits and ended with more negative ones, then gave a second group the same list in the reverse order. Those given the desirable traits first rated the person favourably on other adjectives, whereas the opposite was true if negative traits were first.

Response trait	Positive traits first	Negative traits first
'Generous' rating	90%	10%

Luchins (1957) supported the primacy effect with a more ecologically valid experiment that changed the presentation order of descriptions of introvert or extrovert behaviour, but also found that a recency effect (***information presented last has a stronger influence*** on impression formation) could occur after a longer time delay before judgement or with people we already know well rather than strangers.

Evaluation
- It is unclear whether the primacy effect is due to the later traits being reinterpreted, rejected or less attended to.
- The effects are important for witness ordering in trials.

CENTRAL TRAITS
PRIMACY/RECENCY

SOCIAL SCHEMAS
STEREOTYPING

1. She must also be generous, wise, happy and good-natured.
2. She must also be ungenerous, unwise, unhappy and bad-natured.
3. She is going to be helpful.
4. She made a mistake because she is less intelligent, like all blond women.
5. She must be a nice person, I think I will like her.
6. I do not think I will like her.

1. She is 'intelligent, skilful, industrious, *warm*, determined, practical, cautious.'
2. 'intelligent, skilful, industrious, *cold*, determined, practical, cautious'
3. She is *working* as a *volunteer* today.
4. She is a *blond woman*.
5. '*intelligent, industrious*, impulsive, critical, stubborn, envious'
6. She is '*envious, stubborn*, critical, impulsive, industrious, intelligent'.

SOCIAL SCHEMAS

A social schema is an ***internal cognitive representation*** of an external social object or situation acquired from experience. The schema contains an interrelated set of concepts, beliefs, attitudes and expectations about these social objects or situations that help us to:
- Understand and deal with the external social world quickly and with limited information.
- Fill in missing information and make assumptions based on our schema's previous knowledge.

Each person has many social schemas (or schemata) relating to specific people, social roles, social situations (in which case they are termed 'scripts') and social groups (in which case they are also called 'stereotypes').

The schema is activated by a cue (e.g. the sight of a friend, a conversation about a traffic warden or entering a restaurant) and our thoughts, feelings and behaviour are automatically directed and ***influenced*** by ***past expectations*** and attitudes.

Evaluation
- Schema assumptions can be wrong, adversely affect interactions or cause mistakes (e.g. assuming your friend wants to go out drinking again, feeling hostile before any interaction occurs, or waiting to be served at a buffet).

STEREOTYPING

A stereotype is a ***cognitive representation of a social group*** that helps simplify the social world and allow assumptions to be made about a person based on limited information (an observable cue, such as gender, skin colour or accent). However, unlike more specific and accurate schemas created from direct personal experiences, stereotypes are:
- often acquired more indirectly from other people and social norms so represent less verified shared beliefs.
- too ***over-generalised*** in content to represent the variability of individual members accurately.
- likely to ***exaggerate*** the perceived ***similarities*** within groups as well as the ***differences*** between groups.
- prone to ***confirmatory bias*** (leading people to selectively attend to information that confirms the stereotype).

Evaluation
- Impression formation stereotype distortion appears in many areas, e.g. job selection, jury decision-making.
- Stereotype bias applies more to private, first impressions, e.g. Kruglanski and Freund (1990) found negative ratings of a dissertation were more influenced by the ethnic group of the writer when the evaluators were under time pressure and thought they would not be judged.

5.4 Attitudes

THE STRUCTURE OF ATTITUDES

The three-component model suggests it is useful to distinguish between cognitive, affective and behavioural aspects of attitudes.

COGNITIVE COMPONENT

The cognitive component of an attitude refers to the emotionally neutral **beliefs and knowledge** a person has about something or someone (e.g. their thoughts about objects or people). Cognitive beliefs:
- are acquired from personal experience and social norms.
- can be represented as schemas or stereotypes.

AFFECTIVE COMPONENT

The affective component of an attitude refers to the **values and feelings** a person has about something or someone (e.g. how much they like or hate the object of the attitude). Emotional evaluations are acquired from more personal:
- positive or negative experiences with the attitude object.
- inner needs and desires, e.g. for resources or status.

BEHAVIOURAL COMPONENT

The behavioural or 'conative' part of an attitude refers to the **physical actions** a person performs relating to the object of the attitude (what, if anything, people actually do about their thoughts and feelings).

Evaluation of the three-component model
- Stereotypes are important in explaining prejudiced attitudes. However, on their own they do not explain the strong affect (like or hate) felt towards others.
- Critics (e.g. Petty and Cacioppo, 1981) of the three-component model of attitudes say the affective aspect is the only one of importance.
- Factors like frustration, competition and the need for positive self-esteem are needed to explain the affective, emotional feelings of prejudice.
- Critics of the three-component model argue that the cognitive and affective components do not always predict behaviour, making the concept of attitudes worthless. For example, LaPiere (1934) found prejudiced attitudes towards Chinese people were not well associated with actual discrimination.
- However, attitude predictive power is improved by:
  1 increasing the precision of correspondence between attitudes measured and behaviour predicted, e.g. Davidson and Jaccard's (1979) correlation study of oral contraceptive attitudes and actual use.
  2 providing more detailed models of the relationship between thoughts, feelings and behaviour, e.g. Ajzen's (1988) Theory of Planned Behaviour with its notion of 'perceived behavioural control'.

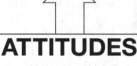

ATTITUDES

- Definition – 'a learned predisposition to respond in a consistently favourable or unfavourable manner with respect to a given object' (Newcomb, 1950 – quoted in Pennington, 1986)
- Importance – attitudes are central to social psychology and an understanding of topics like prejudice and persuasion.

THE FUNCTIONS OF ATTITUDES

THE ADAPTIVE FUNCTION

Attitudes serve to adapt their owners to the physical and social world and allow people to achieve their goals by directing people:
- away from undesirable behaviour / situations to avoid dissatisfaction.
- towards desirable behaviour / situations to increase satisfaction.
- towards people who share similar attitudes to gain social acceptance and group unity (to achieve group goals).

Evaluation
Cognitive consistency and similarity of attitudes are important in social interactions to be accepted by others (Heider's Balance Theory, 1958).

KNOWLEDGE FUNCTION

Attitudes impose structure and meaning on the physical and social world and store key information on how to deal with it. This allows:
- More simplified and rapid access to personal knowledge when decision making is required.
- Greater predictability when interacting with the physical or social environment, reducing the anxiety of uncertainty.

Evaluation
Festinger (1957) found cognitive dissonance/anxiety occurs when a person's attitudes are in conflict (and thus cannot properly fulfil their knowledge function).

EGO-EXPRESSIVE FUNCTION

Attitudes allow us to clarify and express our identity (in terms of our beliefs, values and feelings) to ourselves and other people. This:
- contributes to the development of our personal self-concept and identity.
- enables people to identify and join others with similar attitudes to acquire group-level identities.

Evaluation
However, it has been suggested that attitudes about the self are perhaps more important for the function of ego **defence**, e.g. using positive self attitudes to protect our self-image.

5.5 Theories of prejudice

STEREOTYPING
- As Pennington (1986) notes, stereotyping involves
  a **categorising** people into groups based on visible **cues**, such as gender, nationality, race, religion, bodily appearance, etc.
  b assuming **all** members of a group share the **same characteristics**.
  c **assigning individuals to these groups** and presuming they possess the same characteristics based on little information other than their possession of the noticeable trait or cue.
- While stereotyping is an **in-built cognitive process**, it is important to realise that the **cues** seen as important to categorise (e.g. gender, skin colour, religion, etc.) and the **content** of the stereotype itself (e.g. personality traits) are not fixed, but historically determined and **changeable** over time.
- Stereotypes serve to **exaggerate** the **similarities within groups** ('those people are all the same') and exaggerate the **differences between groups** ('they are not like us').
- Stereotyping, therefore, literally involves **pre-judging** an individual, and, although it serves the important **functions** of categorising and generalising knowledge, it can lead to **unrealistic perceptions**, and **inter-group hostility**.

Evidence
- Karlins *et al.* (1969) showed how the content of stereotypes concerning 'Americans' and 'Jews' changed over a 40 year period – the former seeming to become more 'materialistic' and the latter appearing to be less 'mercenary', for example.
- Many studies have shown how stereotyping can lead to prejudice, e.g. Buckhout (1974) and Duncan (1976).

Evaluation
- McCauley & Stitt (1978) propose that stereotypes are now best regarded as **probabilistic beliefs**. People are asked to estimate what percentage of a group would possess certain characteristics, and this is compared to the estimate for people in general, to arrive at a diagnostic ratio.
- Although the contents of stereotypes are usually derogatory, and stereotyping accounts for the **thinking** in prejudice, it does **not** explain the **strong negative emotions** nor all the discriminatory **behaviour** shown in society.

INTERGROUP CONFLICT THEORY
- According to Sherif, the prejudice in society is caused by:
  a The existence of groups
  b **Competition** between those groups
- Conflict exists between groups because each group will struggle to obtain limited resources. Sherif argued that competition will always provoke prejudice, and conducted a field study to investigate this idea.

Evidence
- Sherif *et al.* (1961) conducted a field study in Robbers' Cave State Park in America. Two groups of 11 boys were created and a tournament was set up between them that was sufficient to produce fighting and name calling.
- The basis of many wars has been resource competition.

Evaluation
- Tyerman and Spencer's (1983) study on groups of boy scouts showed that competition is not always sufficient to cause conflict and discrimination.
- Sherif's study was ethically dubious given that its goal was to deliberately create prejudice and fighting over penknives was involved.

THE PROCESS OF STEREOTYPING

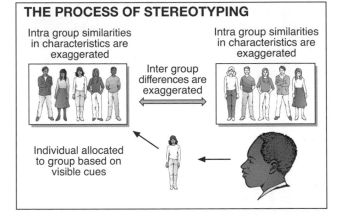

Intra group similarities in characteristics are exaggerated

Intra group similarities in characteristics are exaggerated

Inter group differences are exaggerated

Individual allocated to group based on visible cues

MINIMAL GROUP THEORY
- Minimal group theory suggests that merely dividing people into groups is sufficient to cause prejudice to occur between them. Tajfel and Turner (1979) explain this phenomena in terms of their social identity theory (SIT), which proposes that
  a people allocate themselves to groups and gain their identity from those groups
  b people need to feel good about themselves and, therefore, seek positive self-esteem
  c people will want to feel they are in the best group and will, therefore, act to make it so, even if that means putting other groups down

Evidence
- Tajfel *et al.* (1971) conducted a study on Bristol schoolboys, who they assigned to meaningless groups, in some cases completely randomly by the toss of a coin. Tajfel found that the individual members would not only allocate more points to their own group members but would often maximise the difference between the groups – even if it meant their own group receiving fewer points overall.

Evaluation
- Tajfel's results have received cross-cultural confirmation, but his experiments have been accused of artificiality and demand characteristics. The study may only reflect the norms of competition found in many societies – co-operative societies may not show the minimal group effect (Wetherall, 1982).

AUTHORITARIAN PERSONALITY
Adorno *et al.* (1950) found authoritarian personalities are:
- hostile and contemptuous towards people of lower status
- inflexible and conventional in beliefs and values
- rule-following in thinking, and intolerant of ambiguity
- prone to categorise people into 'us' and 'them' groups.

This can lead to greater prejudice / discrimination as they *displace* their hostility onto minority groups and *project* their own negative traits onto others (Freudian concepts).
They may also see their own group/values as superior to other groups and rely more on stereotyping and stereotypes.

Evidence
- The association between authoritarianism and prejudice has been supported both cross-culturally (e.g. in the USA and India) and with different targets (e.g. the mentally ill, and AIDS victims).

Evaluation
- Personality theories of prejudice cannot account on their own for very sudden increases in prejudice at certain times in history, in certain places, against certain targets.
- Pettigrew (1958) found prejudice of white against black South Africans was not due to levels of authoritarianism.

5.6 Factors affecting the decision to help

INFORMATION PROCESSING OF EMERGENCIES

Latane and Darley (1970) proposed an information processing explanation of helping behaviour that identifies several stages involved in the decision making process of whether to help another.

Is the situation needing help **NOTICED?**
— NO → **HELP NOT GIVEN**

↓ YES

Is the situation **DEFINED** as an emergency?
— NO →

↓ YES

Does the potential helper **TAKE RESPONSIBILITY?**
— NO →

↓ YES

Does the potential helper decide **HOW** to help?
— NO →

↓ YES

Does the potential helper **ACT** upon the chosen way to help?
— **NO**

YES → **HELP GIVEN**

NATURE OF BYSTANDER

Personal factors affecting the decision to help include
- the past reinforcement history of the individual for helping behaviour plus internalised norms
- the level of moral development reached
- the personality of the individual (those who are emotionally empathetic may help more)
- similarity to the victim (the greater the similarity, the greater the help given)
- the individual's relationship to the victim (greater helping if genetically related or friend)
- the mood of the bystander (good moods lead to more help)

COSTS AND REWARDS OF HELPING

Exchange theory – Proposes that the decision to help is made on rational grounds, by calculating the profits of intervening. If the costs of helping (e.g. loss of time, money, health) outweigh the rewards (e.g. praise) then help is unlikely. Experiments support this theory, but it may be over-rationalistic, ignoring the emotions aroused by the distress of victims.

		Costs of helping victim	
		LOW	HIGH
Costs of not helping victim	HIGH	Direct help	Indirect or no help
	LOW	Help depends on norms	No help

Arousal: cost-reward model – Piliavin et al. (1981) suggested different kinds of helping situation may cause different motives for helping: 'one kind is triggered by quick, non-rational emotional arousal in response to emergencies, the other kind is influenced more by the potential helper's analysis of the costs and benefits of helping'

THE COSTS OF HELPING IN DIFFERENT SITUATIONS

THE COST OF TIME

Darley and Batson's (1973) 'Good Samaritan' study operationalised the cost of time for subjects by telling them that they were either on time, behind schedule or ahead of schedule to deliver a talk in the next building on the 'Good Samaritan'. Of those who had plenty of time to reach the building 63% helped a man in the corridor on the way who was slumped in a doorway, compared to 45% of those who were on schedule and 10% who thought they were late.

THE COST OF HELPING DIFFERENT VICTIMS

Piliavin et al. tested helping behaviour for different victims by having confederates collapse in subway trains under different conditions. When the confederate
- had a walking cane, help occurred quickly and frequently
- had a bottle and smelt of alcohol, help occurred slowly and less frequently
- had (fake) blood dribbling from their mouth, help occurred frequently but indirectly

The costs of helping and not helping were different in each condition.

5.7 The situational determinants of helping behaviour

THE REACTIONS OF OTHERS

Pluralistic ignorance – if several people are present and nobody shows signs of concern or action, then the situation may be socially defined as 'in need of no action'. This is a form of informational social influence, bystanders look to each other to know how to react.

Latane and Rodin (1969)

Subjects sitting in a waiting room went to help a female experimenter (they had heard her fall over next door) more often and more quickly when alone than when in the company of a confederate of the experimenter who did nothing.

Latane and Darley (1968)

Subjects completing a questionnaire in a waiting room that began to fill with smoke were more likely to report the smoke when alone than when in a group of three (despite being unable to see clearly after 6 minutes!).

Aaarrhh!!!!

THE NUMBER OF BYSTANDERS

Social impact theory (Latane, 1981) suggests that a diffusion of responsibility occurs when many witnesses are present – the impact of a victim's plight is felt less strongly for each subject and so more witnesses can actually mean less helping.

Darley and Latane (1968)

Individual subjects, who were meant to be discussing social problems with other participants in separate cubicles over an intercom system (to prevent embarrassment), heard one of the group (in fact a tape recording of a confederate – there were no other real participants) explain that he was prone to have seizures when under stress – and later proceeded to have one!
The experimenters measured the percentage who helped within 4 minutes.

When the subject thought there were:

a   2 in the group, 85% intervened.
b   3 in the group, 62% intervened.
c   5 other subjects, 31% intervened.

...er-if could-er
-er somebody er
-er-give me a
little-help...

THE NORMS OF SOCIETY

Different social norms or expectations to help in certain situations may influence helping behaviour. Most societies conform to norms of reciprocity (help is given to those who are likely to return the favour); social responsibility (helping dependent others, e.g. beggars); and neighbourliness (helping those who live locally). However, norm theory does not predict which norms will be conformed to when there is a conflict between them, e.g. helping a beggar who is dependent but not likely to reciprocate the favour.

ENVIRONMENTAL LOCATION

Help is less likely to be given in built up urban areas than more rural areas, perhaps because of stimulus overload (Milgram, 1970), greater risks due to crime levels or the more impersonal environment of largely populated areas.

AMBIGUITY

Help is more likely to be given in clear-cut and emergency situations.

THE PROXIMITY OF BYSTANDERS

Social impact theory (Latane, 1981) suggests that as the remoteness between the bystander and victim increases (the greater the distance between them), the less directly responsible the bystander will feel. Someone requesting donations in front of you is more likely to be helped than someone asking by telephone.

Piliavin et al.'s (1969) subway studies revealed that help was offered just as frequently on crowded subways as uncrowded ones, suggesting that it is more difficult to refuse help in an immediate, face-to-face, non-remote situation, such as the enclosed space of a subway.

5.8 'Good Samaritanism: an underground phenomenon?' Piliavin, Rodin, and Piliavin (1969)

BACKGROUND
Social psychologists were prompted into investigating helping behaviour by the case of Kitty Genovese (a woman stabbed to death over a period of 30 minutes in front of 38 unresponsive witnesses). Most studies were conducted under strict laboratory conditions, using non-visual emergency situations. The main theories of helping behaviour involved diffusion of responsibility and the economic analysis of costs and rewards for helping.

AIM
To investigate, under real life conditions, the effect on the speed and frequency of helping, and the race of the helper, of
- the type of victim (drunk or ill)
- the race of the victim (black or white)
- the presence of helping models (present or absent)
- the size of the witnessing group

METHOD
Design
Field experiment

Independent variables (4):
- Type of victim (drunk or ill)
- Race of victim (black or white)
- Presence of helping models (present or absent)
- Size of the witnessing group

Dependent variables recorded:
- Frequency of help
- Speed of help
- Race of helper
- Sex of helper
- Movement out of area
- Verbal comments

Subjects
New York subway travellers between 11am and 3 pm, approximately 45% black, 55% white, mean of 8.5 bystanders in critical area, opportunity sample.

Situation
Non stop 7.5 minute journey in subway carriage

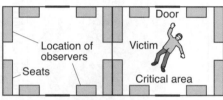

Procedure
4 teams of 4 researchers
- 2 female who recorded reactions
- 2 male, one acting victim, one model

Victims – 3 white, 1 black, all aged between 26–35, dressed and acted identically. Instructed to collapse after 70 seconds and remain on floor until helped.
Model instructed to help 70 seconds after collapse until end if no other help.

103 trials conducted in total, of which: 38 involved drunk victim (smelt of alcohol and carried a bottle in paper bag). 65 involved sober victim carrying a cane.

RESULTS	DISCUSSION OF RESULTS
1 Frequency of help was impressive – overall 93% helped spontaneously (before the model), 60% of which involved more than one helper. Help was so spontaneous that the model's effect could not be properly studied.	Unlike earlier studies of helping behaviour, bystanders were continuously and visually presented with the emergency situation, making it difficult to ignore.
2 No diffusion of responsibility was found with group size.	Immediate situations decrease diffusion of impact.
3 A victim who appeared ill was more likely to receive help than one who appeared drunk. There was 100% help for the cane victim (of which 63 out of 65 trials involved spontaneous help) but 81% help for the drunk victim (of which 19 out of 38 trials involved spontaneous help). Help was also offered more quickly for the cane victim (a median of 5 seconds compared to 109 second delay with the drunk victim).	The Arousal: Cost-Reward Model proposes that the decision to help depends upon the costs and rewards of helping versus not helping. Therefore, less help for drunk victim since costs of helping are high (perhaps dangerous), costs of not helping are low (no blame), and rewards are low (probably less gratitude).
4 There was a tendency for same race helping to be more frequent, especially in the drunk condition.	Less costs of helping same race in terms of public censure, more witness arousal empathy with victim.
5 Men were significantly more likely to help the victim than women.	Less cost for men in terms of ability to physically help.
6 The longer the emergency continued without help being given: a The less impact the model had on the other bystanders. b The more likely bystanders were to leave the area. c The more likely it was that observers would discuss their behaviour.	Arousal: Cost-Reward Model argues that bystander arousal produced by the plight of others can be reduced by leaving the area or rationalising the decision not to help (e.g. by regarding the victim as undeserving) if help is not given.

STRENGTHS OF STUDY
- High ecological validity – study took place under naturally occurring conditions.
- Highly standardised procedure
- Yielded a lot of detailed data.
- Proposed a theoretical explanation to account for levels of helping in all conditions of the experiment.

WEAKNESSES OF STUDY
- Methodological weaknesses – conditions are under less strict control in field experiments than laboratory experiments. Insufficient trials conducted in some conditions of the experiment to yield reliable data, e.g. there were fewer drunk victims, only 8 black cane carriers.
- Ethical weaknesses – deception, lack of consent, no debriefing, and the production of anxiety and/or inconvenience for the bystanders are all ethically problematic.

6.1 Factors influencing the formation of attraction

SITUATIONAL FACTORS

PROXIMITY

This factor refers to the physical or functional distance between individuals, what Kerckoff (1974) called our 'field of availables', and suggests that the smaller the distance separating individuals, the greater the chance of attraction taking place. This factor is necessary for other influences, for example

- those who live near us are more likely to share our beliefs, social class, education, etc. (see similarity)
- we have to be close to somebody in order to reward them (see learning theory)
- proximity allows increased exposure, which leads to familiarity (see familiarity)

Evidence

Festinger et al. (1950) studied student friendship patterns in university campus housing and found that the students were most friendly with those living next door, less friendly with those living two doors away and least friendly with those living at the end of the corridor. Segal (1974) studied police cadets who were assigned to their rooms and classroom seats alphabetically, and found that they were more likely to rate someone as a friend who was close in the alphabet to them. Newcomb (1961) conducted a two year study of liking patterns in rented accommodation. The best predictor of liking in the second year was familiarity.

Evaluation

Proximity provides the minimum conditions necessary for attraction to start and maintain itself, but note that too close a proximity can invade our personal space and make us feel uncomfortable until our relationship has developed – the better we know someone the closer we allow them!

EXPOSURE AND FAMILIARITY

Zajonc investigated the 'mere exposure effect', which suggests that, all other things being equal, people prefer stimuli that they have seen more often. Close proximity clearly increases the chance of repeated exposure, which may lead to familiarity and a sense of trust.

Evidence

Zajonc et al. (1971) asked subjects to evaluate photos of strangers and found that those strangers who appeared more often than others were rated more positively. This effect has also been found for repeated exposure of music, paintings, and political candidates. Segal (1974) studied student friendship patterns in university campus housing and found that the students were most friendly with those living next door, less friendly with those living two doors away and least friendly with those living at the end of the corridor. Bossard (1931) found that couples in Chicago who lived within one block of each other were more likely to get married than those who lived two blocks apart, whereas Clarke (1952) found that more than 50% of people marrying in Colombus Ohio lived within walking distance of each other.

Evaluation

Repeated exposure may give a greater chance that negative characteristics will be found in other people or that boredom or stimulus satiation may occur, in which case the proverb 'familiarity breeds contempt' may be supported. Most research however has supported the link between familiarity and attraction.

PERSONAL FACTORS

PHYSICAL ATTRACTIVENESS

A strong research finding is that people are not only drawn towards those who are physically attractive, but see these people as psychologically attractive as well – having a whole host of other positive traits (such as popularity, warmth, generosity, etc.).

Evidence

Dion (1972) using photographs of 7-year-old children found that attractive children were less likely to be thought of as anti-social than unattractive children.

Walster et al. (1966), using the 'computer dance' procedure, found the most important factor in determining whether a woman would be asked for a second date was her physical attractiveness, regardless of the man's.

Evaluation

Physical attractiveness is not absolute or objective ('beauty is in the eye of the beholder'), and can be influenced by a number of characteristics, such as

- culture – Garfield (1982) found that different cultures have different conceptions of beauty, and even in the same culture norms of attractiveness will vary
- gender – in 'western cultures' men seem to be more attracted by physical beauty, whereas women's preferences are not predominantly physical – Sigall and Landy (1973) found that the physical attractiveness of the male's partner increased his status in the eyes of other males, whereas the reverse was not true for women
- context – the perception of a person's beauty can change with circumstances – those who disagree with us may lose their physical appeal. Efran (1974) found good looking criminals received more lenient sentences unless their looks were involved in the crime.

SIMILARITY

Although, ideally, we would want the most attractive person possible, in reality we tend to be attracted by similarity – not just of looks, but also of beliefs, attitudes and values ('birds of a feather flock together'). Rubin (1973) suggested similarity is rewarding because we are more likely to agree with similar people, which leads to more joint activities and confidence in ourselves and our opinions, and facilitates communication.

Evidence

Griffit and Veitch (1974) studied 13 males who spent 10 days in a nuclear fall-out shelter, and concluded that those who were the most similar liked each other the best by the end.

Cann et al. (1995) found attraction was greater towards a stranger who had similar attitudes. However, agreement that the same joke was funny had the strongest effect on attraction.

Evaluation

Winch (1955) has argued that in some cases complementarity is more important than similarity in determining the formation of attraction (i.e. 'opposites attract'). Snyder and Fromkin (1980) suggest that we dislike people who are too like us, as we like to see ourselves as unique. Rosenbaum (1986) proposed that although similar attitudes do not have much effect on liking, we are repulsed by dissimilar attitudes. This idea is not well supported.

RECIPROCAL LIKING

A more subtle form of similarity is that we like people who like us. Aronson proposed the reward-cost principle, which states that we will be attracted to those who like us and consistently make positive comments about us, as opposed to those who do not (presumably because it increases our self esteem).

Aronson and Linder's (1965) 'gain-loss' theory is somewhat less obvious – we like people more who start off by disliking us and then change their mind, than we do those who liked us all along, and the same theory applies for those who start by liking us and then change to dislike.

Evidence

Aronson and Linder (1965) found experimental support for the 'gain-loss' theory by letting subjects overhear (a confederate's) opinions of them. When the confederate started off by stating negative things about the subject and then switched to positive things, the subject rated the confederate more positively.

Evaluation

In general our liking depends upon how much we respect the opinions and motivations of the people who praise us. If the praise is seen as false flattery, then dislike occurs.

6.2 Theories of relationships

ECONOMIC THEORIES

- Researchers such as Homans and Blau explain relationships in terms of economic transactions – an assessment of the costs and rewards involved in interacting with others.
- **Exchange theory** – suggests that the attraction of others depends upon the profit they provide for us – the rewards of interacting with them (e.g. stimulation, money, love) minus the costs (e.g. effort, time, money) – relative to the profits of other relationships.
- **Equity theory** – proposes that participants in a relationship seek a fair (equitable) return of rewards in proportion to their initial investment in their relationship (the rewards that they bring to it).

Relationship formation and maintenance

- Exchange and equity theories predict that relationships will be maintained when
  a both partners are satisfied with their 'comparison levels' of rewards (the agreed ratio of costs and rewards) in their current relationship (Thibaut & Kelley, 1959)
  b the comparison level for alternative relationships is low
  c the costs of leaving the relationship are high
  d partners are similar in their ability to reward each other

Relationship breakdown

The theories predict relationship breakdown when
  a one or both partners are dissatisfied with their comparison levels of rewards
  b the comparison level for alternative relationships is high (there are better relationships elsewhere)
  c the costs of leaving the relationship are low (one or both partners are able to leave the relationship with little loss)
  d partners are not similar in the ability to reward each other

Evaluation of theories

- It is difficult to quantify all psychological costs and rewards in a relationship to test the theories.
- However, just using the variable of physical attraction, Murstein (1972) found couples in intimate relationships were more likely to be equally attractive.
- The theory is rather 'mercenary', not dealing with emotions which can over-ride the calculation of profit in relationships.
- The theory is derived from the values of capitalistic societies.
- The theory may not apply to certain relationships, e.g. family.

LEARNING THEORY

- Byrne and Clore (1970) use the learning theory principles of classical and operant conditioning to explain attraction in terms of
  a a conditioned emotional responses
  b the consequences of interpersonal behaviour
- The reinforcement an individual provides depends upon what basic human needs they can satisfy for the other person, such as the need for resources (e.g. food), love, sex, etc.

Relationship formation and maintenance

- Learning theory predicts relationships will be maintained if
  a partners are associated (by classical conditioning) with pleasant stimuli and life experiences such as successful careers or happy domestic environments
  b partners positively reinforce each other with pleasant stimuli such as interaction, sex, presents, etc.

Relationship breakdown

- Learning theory predicts relationship breakdown when
  a partners are associated with unpleasant life experiences, such as unemployment, poverty, etc. (classical conditioning)
  b partners do not reinforce each other with pleasant stimuli (boredom) or inflict more negative than positive stimuli on each other (operant conditioning)

Evaluation of theory

- The theory links well with the economic theory notions of cost and rewards.
- Veitch & Griffith (1976) found the attraction shown towards a stranger depended upon whether he was associated with good or bad news.
- Some relationships exist despite very few rewards and the giving, not just receiving, of reinforcement (due to the norm of reciprocity) is regarded as important.

COGNITIVE THEORY

- Heider (1958) proposed balance theory, which argues that people strive for 'cognitive consistency' in their liking and disliking of others, and are motivated to achieve balanced relationships.

Relationship formation and maintenance

- A cognitive triad is a pattern of relationships involving three people. The triad will be balanced, and consistent relationships maintained, if the multiplication of the signs leads to a '+'.

A balanced triad where relationships are consistent.

– = negative feeling
+ = positive feeling

Ex-boyfriend
Boyfriend + Girlfriend

Relationship breakdown

- Unbalanced liking patterns are due to inconsistent attitudes in relationships and produce unpleasant 'cognitive dissonance' that people are motivated to reduce by changing their attitudes.

An unbalanced triad where the relationships are causing cognitive dissonance

Ex-boyfriend
Boyfriend + Girlfriend

Evaluation of theory

- Aronson & Cope (1968) found subjects liked a professor more when he showed hostility towards a graduate who had previously upset the subject.
- The theory realises that relationships are influenced by more than two people.
- The triad models only involve three people and ignore the strength of liking.

EVOLUTIONARY THEORIES

- Sociobiological theorists, such as Dawkins (1989), aim to account for attraction and relationships by looking at the evolutionary survival functions of it.

Relationship formation and maintenance

- Friendship and affiliation has probably evolved due to the advantages of increased protection and hunting efficiency that groups provide.
- Male–female bonds may have evolved to help care for helpless human infants. As the brain and head size of babies increased, they had to be born at earlier and less developed stages. The extra care required would involve both parents and attachment bonds that kept them together would be selected by evolution because of the increased survival rate of their offspring.

Relationship breakdown

- Unfaithfulness may be genetically advantageous for both sexes:
  a **The male** optimal method of passing on genes is to mate with many females, since they cannot guarantee the offspring are their own and produce many gametes.
  b **Females** produce and invest in a limited number of eggs, and so mating with a male of better genetic quality without discovery, will make their offspring fitter as well as receiving care from the current partner.
- Pair bonding in humans may only have evolved to last long enough to provide care for helpless human infants.

Evaluation of theories

- The theories propose that there are conflicting evolutionary tendencies to bond yet cheat, which perhaps explains the difficulty of maintaining intimate relationships.
- These ideas have ethical implications – what is natural is not necessarily moral.

6.3 The breakdown of attraction

In addition to providing theories that explain the breakdown of relationships, social psychologists have identified the important factors and processes that are involved.

FACTORS LEADING TO BREAKDOWN OF RELATIONSHIPS

ENVIRONMENTAL FACTORS

PHYSICAL ENVIRONMENT
- **Distance** – Relationships involving a lack of proximity are difficult to maintain due to the lack of reinforcement, ability to share activities and intimacy, plus the inevitable extra costs involved (links with learning and exchange theories).
- **Hardship** – Lack of resources may cause frustration and aggression which may be directed at the partner (links with frustration-aggression theory). Negative emotions produced by hardship may become associated with the partner (by classical conditioning).

SOCIAL ENVIRONMENT
- **'Field of availables'** – The greater the number and quality of alternative partners in a social environment, the greater the comparison level for alternatives (this links with exchange theory).
- **Family and friends** – Competition for intimacy and attention or dissimilarity of attitudes and beliefs between one partner and the friends and/or family of the other partner (this links with cognitive balance theory) can cause problems.

INTER-PERSONAL FACTORS

BOREDOM
- **Lack of stimulation** – Unhappiness due to lack of stimulation and reinforcement (this links with learning theory) can lead to break-up in itself or by facilitating unfaithfulness by increasing the appeal of alternative relationships (this links with exchange theory).
- **Reduction in stimulation** – Sex is one of the most powerful reinforcers, but its frequency rapidly declines during the first four years of a relationship (Udry, 1980). However, 41% of married couples still have sex twice a week compared to 23% of single people.

CONFLICT
Only 1.2% of married couples report never having disagreements (McGonagle et al, 1992). Important factors in conflict are:
- **Rule-breaking** – Argyle and Henderson (1984) found the breaking of implicit rules of trust and intimacy were major factors in relationship break-down.
- **Compromise difficulties** – the discovery of differences over time reduces similarity, and the time-commitment of relationships reduces an individual's ability to achieve goals and indulge hobbies.
- **Conflict maintenance** – The tendency to respond in equally negative and destructive ways perpetuates conflict.

INDIVIDUAL FACTORS

BACKGROUND
According to Duck (1988) relationships are more likely to breakdown between individuals who:
- **Differ in demographic background** – perhaps due to dissimilarity of cultural attitudes and expectations.
- **Marry very early** – either in their relationship (due to lack of time for compatibility assessment) or in terms of age (due to lack of coping skills).
- **Have experienced a lack of relationship commitment** – either in their family or personal life.
- **Come from lower socio-economic or education levels.**

SOCIAL SKILLS
Baron & Byrne (1997) suggest lack of social skills can influence breakdown:
- **Coping strategies** – couples who differ in the way they cope with stress are less satisfied with their relationship (Ptacek & Dodge, 1995).
- **Conflict avoidance** – more men than women believe that avoiding conflict is a legitimate way of dealing with it. This can lead to a perpetuation of conflict and a lack of resolution.
- **Emotional expressiveness** – those unable to express emotions are less happy in relationships (King, 1993).

PROCESSES INVOLVING THE BREAKDOWN OF RELATIONSHIPS

DUCK'S STAGES IN PERSONAL RELATIONSHIP BREAKDOWN

INTRA-PSYCHIC PHASE
personal assessment of costs and rewards

DYADIC PHASE
confrontation and negotiation with partner

SOCIAL PHASE
involvement and use of social network

GRAVE DRESSING PHASE
retrospective analysis and public distribution of break-up story

CONFLICT
Rusbult and Zembrodt (1983) categorised four methods of dealing with relationship dissatisfaction.

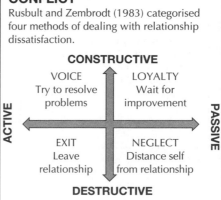

CONSTRUCTIVE

VOICE
Try to resolve problems

LOYALTY
Wait for improvement

ACTIVE — PASSIVE

EXIT
Leave relationship

NEGLECT
Distance self from relationship

DESTRUCTIVE

6.4 Evolutionary explanations of animal behaviour

THE THEORY OF EVOLUTION

Charles Darwin's claim that humans evolved from other animals provided the starting point for comparative psychology. The basic principles of evolutionary theory are

- **genetic mutation and phenotype variation** – during reproduction, genetic mutation and chromosome variation occurs, which affects the physiology and behaviour of the offspring
- **adaptation** – some genetic mutation and chromosome variation results in changes of physiology and behaviour that allows an organism to adapt itself better to its particular environment (ecological niche)
- **selective pressure** – those aspects of the environment that favour certain characteristics of animal physiology and behaviour over others
- **natural selection** – individuals with adaptive physiology and behaviour will be more likely to survive in their environment and compete successfully with other members of their species who do not have the same advantage
- **fitness** – increased survival chances and competitiveness means an increased likelihood of producing more offspring, who will also possess the favourable genetic mutations (survival of the fittest)
- **evolution** – species develop from other species, genetically and physically, over very long periods of time (though not necessarily in a smoothly continuous way). A species exists when the genetic variation of a group becomes different enough from the species it evolved from to prevent reproduction occurring with it

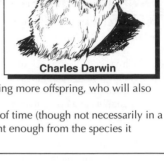
Charles Darwin

SOCIOBIOLOGY

- Sociobiology is the theoretical system applied to social ethology, and, unlike previous approaches, examines the evolution of social behaviour in terms of the survival consequences it has for the genes each animal possesses. Genes are regarded as the fundamental unit of evolution, their 'purpose' is merely to replicate copies of themselves. Behaviour evolves not for the good of the species or even the individual, but for the good of the genes. According to Dawkins (1976) all animals are merely 'survival machines' to carry our 'selfish genes' and the more adaptive their physiology and behaviour, the greater their fitness (ability to produce offspring that will themselves pass on copies of their genes).
- By focusing on genes, the idea of inclusive fitness and the social co-evolution of evolutionary stable strategies between and within species, sociobiologists such as Wilson, Hamilton, Trivers, and Dawkins have been able to explain many aspects of human and non-human social behaviour (including altruism, a topic that presented many problems to previous explanatory theories).
- Sociobiology has extended its theoretical basis to incorporate the idea of cultural evolution and the interaction it might have with genetic evolution. Here the concept of the 'meme' has been proposed – an **idea** or concept that forms the basic **unit** of cultural evolution, which replicates itself from one **mind** to another and is subject to the same evolutionary pressures and laws as genes.
- Sociobiological theory has proposed some powerful arguments for the origin of animal and human behaviour, but has been criticised theoretically and ethically, so its ideas should be applied with caution.

E.O. Wilson

EVALUATION OF EVOLUTIONARY EXPLANATIONS

Advantages

- The study of evolutionary processes places behaviour in an important environmental and historical **context**.
- Evolutionary findings tend to counterbalance the nurture approach – showing how learning can be subject to genetically evolved biases.
- Evolutionary theory is supported by comparative research of behavioural similarities between species and analysis of the function of behaviour in its environmental setting. Studies of mutation rates in DNA also support evolution's assumptions.

Disadvantages

- It is wrong to assume that behaviour must always have evolved for a particular purpose, it may be just a by-product or left-over of evolution. To give a famous dinosaur example – Tyrannosaurus Rex arms did not evolve to be so small for a reason, they were left over from evolutionary ancestors that walked on all fours.
- It is wrong to assume adaptation is an optimal solution – evolutionary adaptation always builds on past adaptation, which may not be an ideal base.
- 'Armchair adaptionism' (Lea, 1984) – it is easy to think up theoretical speculations or stories to explain evolutionary function, rather than rely on empirical research. Evolutionary theory may produce contradictory theories for the same behaviour.
- Evolutionary theory is reductionist and may be seen as overly deterministic. Other levels of explanation are necessary, e.g. social/psychological.
- Evolutionary explanations of behaviour tend to underestimate or ignore the learning capabilities which influence behaviour and that may even over-ride the influence of genetic evolution on behaviour.
- Evolutionary explanations may overexaggerate similarities between species and show anthropomorphism – a tendency to project human traits on to animals, e.g. saying a cat that is rubbing itself against your legs (probably to mark its territory) 'loves' you.
- Sociobiological ideas may be misunderstood or misapplied, e.g. to justify eugenic or capitalist politics (the latter may even have influenced sociobiological theory).

6.5 Sexual selection and human reproductive behaviour 1

What is sexual selection?

EVOLUTION
Occurs due to **variations** in characteristics between individuals being **inherited** due to those features being better **adapted** (allowing survival and reproduction) to **selective pressures**. These selective pressures come from two sources.

NATURAL SELECTION
Refers to selective pressures on individuals' characteristics from the physical environment, e.g. climate, predators, food scarcity, etc. Characteristics will therefore evolve that increase the ability to survive and thus have the **opportunity** to reproduce.

SEXUAL SELECTION
Refers to selective pressures on individuals' characteristics from the social environment, e.g.:
- **intersexual** competition (the **mate choice** and preference of the opposite sex)
- **intrasexual** competition (the **mate competition** between members of the same sex)

Characteristics will therefore evolve that increase the **access** to reproduction.

Why does sexual selection occur?
Sexual selection occurs as a result of the different levels of parental investment between males and females, as well as between different individual men or women, that encourages them to choose and compete over members of the opposite sex who appear to invest the most in reproduction and parenting. Overall, in humans, it is the female who biologically invests more than the male.

THE EVOLUTION OF SEX DIFFERENCES IN PARENTAL INVESTMENT
Why do human females invest more than males?
- Anisogamy – females invest in producing relatively few, large, long lasting and energy rich gametes (ovum), while men produce many, short lived and rapidly renewable gametes (sperm).
- Gestation and lactation – females provide more resources by developing the zygote internally for nine months (gestation) and producing milk for offspring nutrition (lactation).
- Parental certainty – because of anisogamy and internal conception, the female always knows the offspring are hers, whereas the male does not necessarily have this guarantee.
- Commitment to resources – because of the previous factors and the helpless nature of human infants, females are likely to continue caring for offspring after birth to ensure their survival and avoid wasting an already significant investment of time and effort.

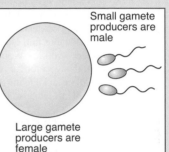

Small gamete producers are male

Large gamete producers are female

Abandon care of offspring to mate more often

Care for fewer offspring to help them survive

Male investment after conception is more uncertain due to lack of paternal guarantee (caring for the offspring of other males will increase their reproductive success at the expense of one's own) and the ease of desertion to mate again (due to their lack of initial investment and the fact that females are left 'holding the baby'). Further male investment depends upon:
- The number and availability of other females – a low female-to-male ratio, a high degree of competition from other males (mate competition), and a low appeal of the male to other females (mate choice) will all increase the likelihood of investing in offspring care rather than attempting to mate again.
- The likelihood of infant survival – increased male care may occur when harsh climate, many predators or lack of food and other social support means helpless human infants are less likely to survive with only the mother's care.

What are the effects of sexual selection on human reproductive behaviour?

SEXUAL SELECTION AND HUMAN MATING STRATEGIES/SYSTEMS
The sex differences in parental investment have implications for male and female mate choice and competition in terms of the **number** and **duration** of sexual relationships that they should prefer. The optimal evolutionary strategies are for females to prefer quality and commitment, but males to prefer quantity, quality and exclusive access without commitment. In practice environmental conditions and mate competition will combine with mate choice preferences to produce different types of mating strategies or systems.

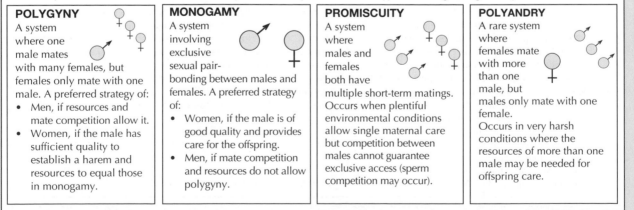

POLYGYNY
A system where one male mates with many females, but females only mate with one male. A preferred strategy of:
- Men, if resources and mate competition allow it.
- Women, if the male has sufficient quality to establish a harem and resources to equal those in monogamy.

MONOGAMY
A system involving exclusive sexual pair-bonding between males and females. A preferred strategy of:
- Women, if the male is of good quality and provides care for the offspring.
- Men, if mate competition and resources do not allow polygyny.

PROMISCUITY
A system where males and females both have multiple short-term matings. Occurs when plentiful environmental conditions allow single maternal care but competition between males cannot guarantee exclusive access (sperm competition may occur).

POLYANDRY
A rare system where females mate with more than one male, but males only mate with one female. Occurs in very harsh conditions where the resources of more than one male may be needed for offspring care.

6.6 Sexual selection and human reproductive behaviour 2

SEXUAL SELECTION AND HUMAN MATE CHOICE, PREFERENCES AND BEHAVIOUR

The sex differences in parental investment also have implications for male and female mate choice and competition in terms of the **type of sexual partner** that they should prefer and the **kinds of reproductive behaviour** they should show. Inter-sexual competition (mate choice) and intra-sexual competition (mate competition) will have a number of effects on males and females:

FOR MALES

Males invest less biologically than females but will invest time and effort competing with males for access to females and seeking for resources.

If environmental conditions are favourable, the male optimal evolutionary strategy is to prefer quantity, quality and exclusive access with minimal commitment of resources to each partner, so as to father as many offspring as possible.

Preferred features in females

The features males have evolved to find attractive in females are those concerning signs of the following qualities:

- The ability to conceive, birth and raise children – signs of fertility are those associated with youth and reproductive physique. Men thus find women more attractive if they:
  Look younger – younger women are more likely to conceive and have a longer reproductive life ahead of them. Childlike facial features, such as big eyes, small noses and full lips will also be preferred as signs of 'beauty'.
  Possess an 'hour-glass' figure – wide hips may indicate ability to deliver children, a narrow waist indicates a lack of pregnancy. Larger breasts and buttocks also indicate nutritional health (suitable fat deposits) and the ability to nurture, and will therefore be found attractive.
- Physical/genetic health – physical signs of these that will be found attractive include clear skin, glossy hair, high energy levels and symmetrical facial and bodily features (indicating genetic and nutritional health).
- Chastity and sexual faithfulness – these are harder to assess after loss of virginity but will increase paternity likelihood.

Reproductive behaviour

Because of initial parental investment and mate preferences, males are likely to have evolved to:

- Be less choosy, which may lead to greater infidelity with females of variable quality.
- Be more attracted/aroused by physical characteristics.
- Exaggerate their resources and fake commitment.
- Be more jealous and disturbed by sexual infidelity in their female partners (since it reduces paternal certainty).
- Approve of marriage contracts to encourage sexual exclusivity with females.

FOR FEMALES

Females invest more biologically than males, only require one male to fertilise them, and cannot afford to waste their greater investment.

The optimal evolutionary strategy for females is therefore to prefer males with signs of quality, resources and commitment, so as to ensure as many of their own offspring survive as possible with this extra, and in some cases vital, investment.

Preferred features in males

The features females have evolved to find attractive in males are those concerning signs of the following qualities:

- The ability to provide resources – signs of this are the possession of resources or traits that help compete for them. Females therefore find males more attractive if they:
  Have status and dominance – usually shown by older males since they may have had more time to acquire resources and prove they are capable of competing successfully for them.
  Possess promising qualities – such as drive, ambition, intelligence, skill and/or strength to gain resources in the future. Such qualities will be also seem desirable because they may be inherited by the mother's sons (thus increasing the chance of grandchildren).
- Physical/genetic health – physical signs of these that will be found attractive include size, musculature, clear skin, glossy hair, high energy levels and symmetrical facial and bodily features (indicating genetic and nutritional health).
- Commitment of resources – through pre-mating signs of kindness, generosity and resource sharing.

Reproductive behaviour

Because of initial parental investment and mate preferences, females are likely to have evolved to:

- Be choosier, which may lead to infidelity occurring only with males of higher quality.
- Be more attracted/aroused by psychological characteristics.
- Emphasise or exaggerate their physical attributes.
- Be more jealous and disturbed by emotional infidelity in their male partners (since it indicates risk of abandonment and thus loss of resources).
- Approve of marriage contracts to encourage commitment of resources from males.

EVIDENCE AND EVALUATION

- A comparison of male-female body size differences and male testicle size between humans and species of primate indicates that humans seem biologically best adapted to polygyny in the form of serial monogamous relationships.
- Buss's (1989) questionnaire survey of over 10,000 people from 37 cultures found high levels of cross-cultural agreement (ranging from 92 to 100%) for the evolutionary predictions that women value earning potential in their partners more than men, while men value physical attributes and younger partners more than women. Questionnaires and physiological measures have also found that men are more distressed than women at the thought of sexual infidelity in their partners.
- The content analysis of Lonely Hearts personal advertisements in the USA, Britain, Holland and India has consistently revealed that men tend to seek attractiveness and offer resources, while women tend to offer attractiveness and seek resources as evolutionary theory predicts (Dunbar, 1995).
- Singh (1993) found men rating body shapes preferred a low waist-to-hip ratio of 0.7, regardless of exact body weight.
- Averaged composite faces of men and women containing more symmetry have been rated as more attractive than less symmetrical faces, while women with symmetrical breasts have been found to be more fertile and men with symmetrical bodies have greater mating success.
- However, in many studies the effects of socially created norms have not been completely excluded as explanations.

6.7 Parent – offspring conflict

Evolutionary explanations of parent-offspring conflict

Trivers (1974) pointed out that according to the *Sociobiological theory* of the 'selfish gene', although parents and offspring are obviously genetically related, they only possess 50% of their genes in common and so some degree of conflict of interests will occur between them. Parents will want to invest in the survival of *many* offspring, both present and future, whereas each offspring is primarily interested in its *own* survival. Parent-offspring conflict can take different forms.

FEEDING AND WEANING CONFLICT

Feeding conflict occurs between parents and their offspring throughout the duration of parental care, while weaning conflict only occurs towards the end of parental care. According to evolutionary theory:

- *Parents* want to invest in all offspring (present and future) so, to reserve care resources of time and energy for future offspring, they will only give each current offspring the minimum care necessary for its survival. Once this is done, it is in the parents' interest to stop caring (wean the infant) and start producing new young. There will therefore be a time when offspring are demanding more care than the parents are willing to provide – the weaning conflict.
- *Offspring*, however, are expected to demand more investment than the minimum to receive the extra, although diminishing, benefits of parental care until: 1) they are large enough to better feed themselves rather than rely on the parent to do so; 2) they need to become independent to raise their own offspring; 3) their selfishness leads to a greater genetic cost in lost siblings (who also share copies of their genes). Offspring are thus often adapted to demand more food than the parent is willing to give them and evolve ways to manipulate their parents to gain extra attention.

Evaluation

- Exaggerated gaping and begging signals are shown by chicks in a nest. Herring gulls deliberately crouch in their nest to hide their size to obtain extra parental care.
- Hinde (1977) found weaning occurs in Rhesus monkeys at around 15 weeks when the parent actively encourages infant independence.
- Nash (1978) observed that older female baboons were more likely to show longer parental care than younger female baboons that had greater chances to reproduce again.
- Human babies and infants show loud crying behaviour to gain parental attention and resources.

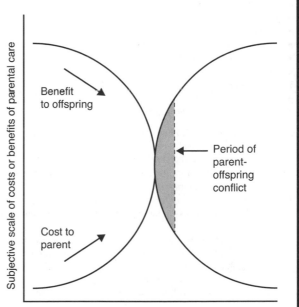

Parent – offspring conflict adapted from Trivers (1974)

- Human cultural norms affect the physical weaning of infants from their mother's milk as well as the age and extent of offspring independence from parental investment, e.g. Erikson's concept of the 'adolescent moratorium' (socially-authorised delay in becoming an adult) found in Western cultures.

SELECTIVE PARENTAL INVESTMENT

Although parents gain *evolutionary fitness* by caring for all their children, under certain conditions (especially lack of environmental resources) preferential *favouritism* is shown. For example:

- *Offspring with no genetic relationship* to a new parent joining the family unit may receive less favour.
- *Older offspring* may be favoured in harsh conditions because they have already survived the dangers of infancy, e.g. predation or disease.
- *Weaker or deformed offspring* may receive less favour because of lower fitness (ability to reproduce and pass on genes).

These factors can result in:

- Parental neglect, mistreatment or even infanticide.
- Sibling competition (for greater parental attention and resources). Whether the siblings in a species fight for favouritism, dominance or to kill each other depends on the degree of offspring competition at any one time and whether the fitness gained from the extra care outweighs the genetic loss of the sibling.

Evaluation

- In some species 'if food supplies take a turn for the worse, parents may stop feeding the weakest of a litter, eat it, or feed it to its siblings' (Polis, 1981 quoted in Lea, 1984).
- Infanticide is a fairly common occurrence in species such as lions and langur monkeys where adult males gaining control of a harem of females kill the offspring of previous males.
- Human children are cross-culturally at higher risk of neglect, abuse, beating, and infanticide 1) by stepfathers (Daly and Wilson, 1985), 2) by their own parents in times of famine, 3) in poor families (Sedlak, 1991), and 4) if they have physical deformities or serious psychological disorders (Miller, 2000).
- In societies limited to one child or where male offspring are favoured, infanticide/abortion of daughters is much higher.
- Spotted hyena pups (born at the same time) bite each other, wounding or killing their siblings so they cannot go outside to be fed by the mother when she returns from hunting.
- Human and chimpanzee children (born sequentially) often act in a babyish way after a younger sibling is born (Trivers, 1985) to compete for parental attention.
- Evolutionary effects on human parental investment are complicated by human learning abilities and cultural norms.

6.8 The influence of childhood/adolescent experience on adult relationships

ATTACHMENTS IN INFANCY

Bowlby suggested from his work on infant attachment that a child's first relationship creates a 'working model' that could influence later relationships with other people. Other researchers have agreed, proposing that infant attachments can even influence intimate adult relationships, for example Shaver *et al.* (1988) point out the similarities between the two as:

- Intense orientation towards a specific other
- Proximity seeking
- Distress on separation/grief at loss
- Extensive eye-contact
- Provision of care-giving

To which Stern (1993) adds:
- Kissing and caressing
- Intimate speech patterns and 'baby talk'

Hazan and Shaver (1987) have shown that adult romantic relationships seem to follow the *three major patterns* of mother-infant attachment type revealed by Ainsworth *et al.*'s (1971) Strange Situation scenario, even in terms of their *proportions* in the general population, namely:

1 Securely attached adult lovers (56%) find relationships rewarding and are less anxious about their partner abandoning them.
2 Anxious/Ambivalent adults (19%) experience uncertainty, fear abandonment and can put too much pressure on their partners.
3 Avoidant adults (25%) dislike getting too close to others and are reluctant to commit themselves to an intimate relationship.

Horowitz *et al.* (1993) elaborated on this idea, suggesting adults form positive or negative models of themselves and their partners, which result in secure, preoccupied, fearful or dismissive attitudes to the relationship.

Evaluation

Durkin (1995) makes the following points:
- Feeney *et al.* (1993) found:
  1 secure adults reported more loving and satisfying relationships.
  2 anxious/ambivalent adults had more, though shorter, intimate relationships.
  3 avoidant adults reported fewer and less intense love relationships, but more positive attitudes towards casual, uncommitted sex.
- Many other factors influence the formation of adult relationships, e.g. exchange theory, and relationship satisfaction also depends on aspects of the partner's character.
- The use of questionnaires to assess adult attachment type can result in demand characteristics and over-generalisation about the similarity of different relationships.
- The participant's memory of distant early relationships may not be accurate.

PSYCHODYNAMIC DEVELOPMENT

- Freud argued that:
  1) interactions with our parents and gratification of the libido during the **psychosexual** stages of development,
  2) the outcomes of the Oedipus Complex, and
  3) our ability to direct our libido towards objects external to the family during the genital stage, all play a role in later sociability, sexual preferences, and the ability to develop intimate adult relationships.
- Erikson's **psychosocial** theory of development suggested that the outcomes of psychosocial conflicts in childhood (e.g. trust vs. mistrust, ages 0 to 1) and adolescence (e.g. identity vs. role confusion, ages 12 to 18), can affect the formation of adult relationships, for example by causing a fear that intimacy/commitment will cause a loss of individual identity.
- Later psychodynamic approaches have focused more on the 'internal working models of relationships' and related **unconscious emotions** created from early parent-infant interactions that can show '**transference**' onto later adult relationships (Lemma-Wright, 1995). This can cause adults to end up in relationships affected by those they had with their parents as infants.

Evaluation

- Research supporting psychodynamic theories on how early experience affects adult relationships comes more from therapy sessions than scientific experimentation.
- The internal models and emphasis on early care-giver attachment of later psychodynamic theories brings them closer to other lines of research in this area.

SOCIAL LEARNING

- Social learning theory would suggest that children automatically acquire their *expectations* and *behaviour* relating to adult relationships from the **observational learning of adult models**, which may lead to later imitation.
- Models of adult relationships can be found in a culture's media and society, but perhaps more obviously and importantly in the child's own home. Parental models of gender role and relationship behaviour, as well as the perceived warmth/quality of interactions can influence the later adult behaviour of both young children and adolescents.

Evaluation

- As Shaffer (1996) notes, studies of the effects of divorce show that:
  1 Girls from divorced families are more likely to show a persistent lack of self-confidence in their relationships with men (Hetherington *et al.*, 1989).
  2 Adolescents from divorced families are more likely to fear their own marriages will be unhappy (Franklin *et al.*, 1990).
  3 Adults whose parents divorced are more likely than those from intact families to have an unhappy marriage and divorce themselves (Amato and Keith, 1991).
- Conformity to cultural and peer norms of behaviour can override the effects of parental modelling, for example in the case of certain second-generation immigrant children living in western cultures who later reject arranged marriages and their parents' cultural norms of relationships.
- Rather than early observational learning and later imitation of adult relationship behaviour, divorce could have other more direct effects on children that can influence later relationships.

6.9 Cultural differences in relationships

WHY STUDY CROSS-CULTURAL DIFFERENCES IN RELATIONSHIPS?
Moghaddam *et al.* (1993) point out many differences between Western and non-Western cultures that can profoundly affect the nature of relationships. Hui and Triandis's (1986) 'individualistic' and 'collectivistic' dichotomy, as well as Hsu's (1983) distinction between 'continuous' and 'discontinuous' societies, illustrate some of these differences and their effects.

WESTERN CULTURES
Western cultures tend to be more:

Individualistic – emphasising the individual, their goals, rights, attitudes and needs. As a consequence there is:
- A focus on first acquaintances, close friendships and intimate partnerships between *two individuals*.
- A strong social norm of *monogamous* relationships and marriages (reflected in the society's laws).
- An emphasis on *voluntary choice* in relationships due to:
  a The Western lifestyle of high mobility and easy long-distance communication, giving *greater availability* of relationships.
  b The notion of *romantic love* – that choosing a perfect match whom you love deeply is necessary to fulfil one's own needs.
- A tendency for relationship interactions to be more governed by individual, economic-based resource allocation and voluntary reciprocity (the returning of favours based on individual responsibility).

Discontinous – youth and progress are emphasised and change is regarded as both important and inevitable. Consequently:
- There may be an increase in the preference for temporary relationships and increased rates of divorce.
- Rules in relationships may be less important, since if they are broken the relationships can be left and others found.

NON-WESTERN CULTURES
Non-Western cultures tend to be more:

Collectivistic – emphasising the group, its decisions, attitudes, needs and one's duties towards it. As a consequence there is:
- More emphasis on *long-term kinship* and *social group relationships*, often involving more than two people.
- A higher frequency of *polygamous* relationships and marriages (reflected in the society's laws).
- A lack of *voluntary choice* in relationships due to:
  a More stationary lifestyles, with less long-distance communication, leading to *less availability*.
  b Obligations to *family and social norms*. *Marriage* is supposed to take into account the wishes of others and is frequently *arranged*.
- A tendency for relationship interactions to be more governed by group need or equality-based resource sharing and obligatory reciprocity (the returning of favours as an important social responsibility).

Continuous – showing a concern for heritage, customs, tradition and respect for the wishes of one's elders. Consequently:
- Change is viewed with suspicion, perhaps leading to greater stability in relationships.
- Rules in relationships are strictly and formally adhered to because of the need to maintain long-term, stable relationships.

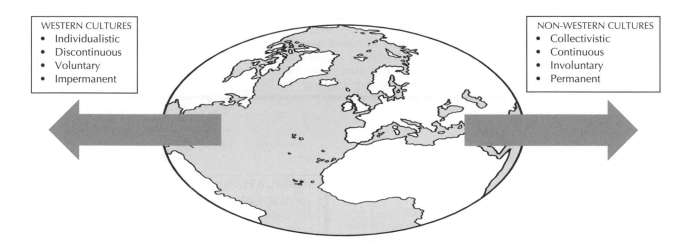

WESTERN CULTURES
- Individualistic
- Discontinuous
- Voluntary
- Impermanent

NON-WESTERN CULTURES
- Collectivistic
- Continuous
- Involuntary
- Permanent

Evaluation
- The research on Western relationships has seriously restricted implications for non-Western societies and has neglected certain kinds of relationship in its own society, e.g. the more collectivisitic relationships of rural communities and relationships with family members. However, due to the greater worldwide media control of Western nations, their cultural values are increasingly affecting non-Western values.
- There is a Western (ethnocentric) tendency to assume that Western relationships are superior due to ideological dogma. However, cross-cultural study of relationships points out reasons for their frequent failure in Western societies – the individualistic values of independence, satisfaction of personal needs and personal control inherently conflict with the intimacy, sharing and compromise demanded by relationships, making them more difficult to maintain. In collectivistic societies the norms of dependency, sharing and lack of personal control aid the maintenance of relationships. Gupta and Singh (1982), for example, found that newly-weds in India who married out of love reported more intense feelings of love than those from arranged marriages. However, this pattern had reversed after five years and became more exaggerated after ten years.
- Studies have revealed similarities across cultures, however, for example in terms of feelings of sexual jealousy (although it may be triggered and expressed in different ways) and the notion of romantic love (although it may vary in commonness).

7.1 Social learning theory and aggression

SUPPORTING EVIDENCE

Bandura *et al.* (1963) allowed one group of children to watch an adult model perform certain aggressive acts with an inflatable 'Bobo doll' which were unlikely to occur normally, such as throwing the doll up in the air, hitting it with a hammer and punching it while saying things like 'pow' and 'boom'. When these children were left in a playroom with the inflatable doll, they frequently imitated the same acts of aggression, compared to a control group who had not seen the model and showed none of the behaviours.

Bandura (1965) used a similar experimental set-up, but showed different consequences for the model's aggression to three groups of children. One group saw the model's aggression being rewarded, one group saw the model being punished for the aggression, and another group saw no specific consequences.

When allowed to enter the playroom, the children who had seen the model punished showed less imitative aggression than the other two groups. However, if all the children were offered rewards for doing what the model had done, all groups showed high levels of imitation. The children in the model punished group had clearly learnt the aggression by observation, but had not shown their potential to imitate it because they expected negative consequences.

SOCIAL LEARNING THEORY AND AGGRESSION

Social learning theory was developed mainly by Bandura and Walters, and suggests that much behaviour, including aggression, is **learnt** from the environment (rather than being instinctual) through reinforcement and the process of **modelling**. Modelling involves learning through the **observation** of other people (models), which may lead to **imitation** if the behaviour to be imitated **leads to desirable consequences**.

Bandura distinguished between the learning of behaviour and the performance of it. Behaviour may be learnt from models through observation, but the likelihood of it being imitated depends on the perceived consequences of the model's actions – if a child sees a model's behaviour being rewarded, this acts as vicarious (indirect) reinforcement for the child who will proceed to imitate it. If the child sees others punished for their actions then, although the behaviour is learnt, it is less likely to be imitated. The social learning theory can easily be applied to explain the learning and performance of aggressive behaviour. Models can be parents, peers or media characters (thus this theory has implications for the portrayal of behaviour like violence on television).

EVALUATION
Methodological
Bandura's social learning theory laboratory experiments have been accused of being overly **artificial** (hitting a Bobo doll is not the same as inflicting aggression on a real person) and of inducing **demand characteristics** (the children may have believed that they were meant to behave aggressively).
However, other experimental studies have demonstrated that children are more likely to hurt other children after viewing violent behaviour (Liebert and Baron, 1972).

Theoretical
The theory neglects the role of innate factors in behaviour like aggression. However, social learning theory does provide a more credible explanation of the transmission of behaviour like violence than the traditional behaviourist view of learning, and has investigated the types of models and behaviours that are most likely to be imitated. Social learning theory provides a more complete approach to explaining learning and has attempted to integrate cognitive and even psychoanalytic concepts with traditional behaviourist learning theory.

IMPLICATIONS FOR REDUCING/CONTROLLING AGGRESSION

The implication of social learning theory is that if aggressive behaviour is not observed or reinforced in a society, then it will not naturally occur.

However many examples of aggression already frequently occur in the great majority of societies, and so the theory would be more realistically applied to reducing aggression.

This could be achieved by ensuring that aggression is not reinforced, or that negative consequences are seen to follow it. The direct punishment of aggression raises problems though, since it may itself be perceived as an aggressive act that is socially approved of – indeed research consistently demonstrates that 'aggression breeds aggression'. Munroe and Munroe (1975) found cross-culturally that childhood aggression is highest in societies whose families highly punish their children for showing aggression.

Social learning theory would suggest that media violence should be dramatically reduced.

7.2 'Transmission of aggression through imitation of aggressive models' Bandura, Ross, and Ross (1961)

AIM
To demonstrate that learning can occur through mere observation of a model and that imitation can occur in the absence of that model. More specifically:
- Children shown aggressive models will show significantly more imitative aggressive behaviour than those shown non-aggressive or no models.
- Children shown non-aggressive, subdued models will show significantly less aggressive behaviour than those shown aggressive or no models.
- Boys should show significantly more imitative aggression than girls, especially with the male rather than female aggressive model.

METHOD
Subjects: 72 children, 36 boys and 36 girls, aged 37–69 months (with a mean age of 52 months) were used.

Design: Laboratory experiment, in which the independent variable (type of model) was manipulated in three conditions:
- Aggressive model shown
- Non-aggressive model shown
- Control condition, no model shown

The dependent variable was the amount of imitative behaviour and aggression shown by the children.

A matched pairs design was used with 24 children (12 boys and 12 girls) assigned to each condition, with an effort made to match subjects according to pre-existing levels of aggression. In addition to the above manipulations, in the experimental conditions:
- Half the subjects observed a same sex model.
- The other half observed opposite sex models.

Procedure: In the experimental conditions children were individually shown into a room containing toys and played with some potato prints and pictures in a corner for 10 minutes while either:
- The non-aggressive adult model (either male or female) played in a quiet and subdued manner for 10 minutes, or
- The aggressive model distinctively aggressed against a 5 foot inflated Bobo doll by **a** sitting on it and repeatedly punching it on the nose, **b** striking it on the head with a mallet, and **c** throwing it up in the air and kicking it around the room. The aggressive model also uttered verbally aggressive statements such as 'sock him in the nose', 'throw him in the air' and 'pow', as well as two non-aggressive statements – 'he keeps coming back for more' and 'he sure is a tough fella'.

All children (including the control group) were then individually taken to a different experimental location and subjected to mild aggression arousal by being stopped from playing with some very attractive toys. This arousal took place in order to give all groups an equal chance of showing aggression and also to allow the group shown the non-aggressive model to demonstrate an inhibition of aggressive behaviour.

All children were then shown into another room which contained both aggressive toys (e.g. a 3 foot high Bobo doll, a mallet, dartguns, and a tether ball) and non-aggressive toys (e.g. a tea set, dolls, and colouring paper), and were observed through a one-way mirror for 20 minutes.

Observers recorded (with inter-scorer reliabilities of .90 correlation coefficient) behaviour in the following categories:

- **Imitation behaviour of aggressive model**:
  a physical aggression, e.g. sitting on the doll and repeatedly punching it on the nose.
  b Verbal aggression, e.g. 'sock him' or 'pow'.
  c Non-aggressive speech, e.g. 'he sure is a tough fella'.
- **Partial imitation behaviour of aggressive model**, e.g. mallet aggression against other objects or sitting on the Bobo doll without punching it.
- **Non-imitative physical and verbal aggression**, e.g. just punching the Bobo doll, physical aggression with other objects and verbal non-imitative remarks 'shoot the Bobo' or 'horses fighting, biting'.
- **Non-aggressive behaviour**, e.g. non aggressive play or sitting quietly.

RESULTS
1. Children in the aggressive model condition showed significantly more imitation of the model's physical and verbal aggression and non-aggressive verbal responses than children who saw the non-aggressive model or no model at all in the control condition.
2. Children in the aggressive model condition usually showed more partial imitation and non-imitative physical and verbal aggression than those who saw the non-aggressive model or no model at all, but not always to a significant degree.
3. Children in the non-aggressive model condition showed very little aggression, although not always significantly less than the no model group.
4. Children who saw the same sex model were only likely to imitate the behaviour significantly more in some of the categories. For example, boys would imitate male models significantly more than girls for physical and verbal imitative aggression, non-imitative aggression and gun play; girls would imitate female models more than boys for verbal imitative aggression and non-imitative aggression only, but not significantly.

EVALUATION
Methodological:

Procedure –	Not completely standardised presentation of model's behaviour (later experiments used videotape presentation)
Artificiality –	Bizarre acts of aggression were shown and imitated against a Bobo doll, not a real person.
Ethical problems –	Aggression was induced in, and taught to, children. Exposure to an adult stranger's aggression may have been frightening for the children.

Theoretical: The research provides reasonable support for the social learning theory idea that behaviour can be acquired through observation rather than direct personal experience, and that reinforcement is not required for learning to occur. This study has important implications for the effects of media violence on children.

Links: Social learning theory, aggression, socialisation, gender differences.

7.3 Social psychological theories of (institutional) aggression

DEINDIVIDUATION THEORY

Deindividuation occurs when a person is no longer identified as an individual. It can occur:

- When surrounded by large numbers of other people.
- When clothing makes individual identification difficult or impossible, i.e. when in uniform or disguise.

Deindividuation of the:

- aggressor can lead to a loss of inhibitions and an abdication of personal responsibility, making aggression more permissible or easily expressed.
- victim of aggression can lead to dehumanisation and a disregard of the individuality/rights of victims (by the aggressor), and feelings of loss of identity (in the victim).

Zimbardo (1970) found twice the level of electric shock was given to a victim by hooded subjects than those wearing normal clothes and name tags.

Application to institutional aggression

- In prisons, deindividuation as a result of guard and prisoner uniforms plus large numbers can lead to:
  1 the abuse of prisoners by guards (e.g. the Abu Ghraib prisoners in Iraq had bags placed over their heads and were dehumanised and mistreated by certain US military police).
  2 the abuse of prisoners by other prisoners.
  3 prisoner feelings of powerlessness (e.g. the Stanford Prison Simulation) and depression (e.g. prison suicide).
- In the army, uniforms reduce personal identity and responsibility for socially-permitted aggression.

Evaluation

- Some psychologists would argue that deindividuation is really only a social factor that facilitates the expression of aggression rather than being a fundamental cause of it.

FRUSTRATION-AGGRESSION THEORY

In proposing their Frustration-Aggression theory, Dollard *et al.* (1939) suggested that, '... aggression is always a consequence of frustration and, contrariwise ... the existence of frustration always leads to some form of aggression.'
According to the Frustration-Aggression theory, aggression is an **innate drive response** to frustrating *external* **stimuli** from the environment.

- The frustrating stimuli can be any **social** conditions that thwart our satisfaction, e.g. bad housing, unemployment.
- The aggressive response can take many forms, such as overt aggressive behaviour against the cause of frustration, or indirect release through **displacement** of aggression onto scapegoats, or even aggressive fantasy.

Barker *et al.* (1941) found children frustrated by being kept waiting a long time before they could play with toys were more aggressive and destructive (throwing and stamping on the toys) than a second non-frustrated control group.
Hovland and Sears (1940) found a significant correlation between economic frustration (measured in terms of the price of cotton) and displaced aggression on scapegoats (measured in terms of the number of lynchings of black people) in the southern states of America between 1882 and 1930.

Application to institutional aggression

- Prisons are a source of many sources of environmental frustration, e.g. overcrowding, limited resources, lack of freedom, guard control, etc.
- Aggression that cannot be directed at the source of frustration, e.g. the guards, may be displaced onto lower-status scapegoats, e.g. other new or 'weak' prisoners.
- McCain *et al.* (1980) found that more crowded prisons experienced higher amounts of aggressive and disruptive behaviour.

Evaluation

- Aggression is not always caused by frustration – there are many other theories that can explain the occurrence of aggression without frustration, e.g. imitation according to social learning theory or conformity to aggressive norms.
- Frustration does not always lead to aggression – frustration can lead to a range of responses, for example despair or depression (Seligman). Berkowitz (1968) suggested that frustration causes anger or a 'readiness' to aggress, but argues that aggression will only result if there are aggressive cues or provocative stimuli in the environment.

SOCIAL NORM CONFORMITY THEORY

Research indicates that aggression can be produced and shaped through conformity to norms of aggression in society.

- Different groups in society may produce different norms of aggression, both in terms of when aggression should be expressed and how it should be expressed.
- Cross-cultural differences in aggression can be explained by the different expected norms of each culture.

Marsh (1978) studied the norms of aggression involved in football hooliganism – violence was expected by the group in order to save face, but once a rival fan had been kicked to the floor and been made to bleed, the combat was finished – anyone going excessively further than that was described as a 'nutter', a clear deviant from the group norm.
Anderson (1994) has discovered similar norms governing predominantly teenage violence in inner cities of the USA, which revolve around the expectations of receiving 'respect'.

Application to institutional aggression

- Haney, Banks and Zimbardo's (1973) Stanford prison simulation found that participants selected for their normal personalities readily understood and conformed to the norms of power associated with the role of being a guard, resulting in the guards abusing their power and treating the prisoners aggressively (although physical violence was prohibited).
- In prison institutions and those of the armed forces, social pressure to conform to norms of aggression is even more powerful.

Evaluation

Reicher and Haslam (2006) found in their own prison simulation that participants asked to be guards were reluctant to conform to and identify with the role, perhaps reflecting the negative social attitudes towards the norms associated with it.

7.4 The role of neural, hormonal, and genetic factors in aggression

NEURAL FACTORS AND AGGRESSION

Brain structures
Neurophysiologists have identified many structures in the brain that seem to play different roles in the expression and type of aggressive behaviour shown, e.g.:

- The **hypothalamus** – electrical stimulation and ablation studies in animals have shown the hypothalamus to be important for the expression of anger and aggression. In cats, threat attack or 'sham rage' (aggressive posturing and hissing) has been produced by stimulation of the medial hypothalamus, while predatory aggression (actual attack behaviour, often silent) was triggered by stimulation of the lateral hypothalamus (Flynn, 1967).
- The **amygdala** – and limbic system structures of the temporal lobe play an important role in the expression of many emotions. Psychosurgery to destroy the amygdala has decreased aggressive behaviour in humans. Charles Whitman, a man who shot 38 people, was later found to have had a temporal lobe tumour.
- The **frontal lobes** of the cortex – appear to have a role in the inhibition, control and direction of aggressive behaviour in line with environmental situations. Brower and Price's (2001) research review concluded that certain injuries to the frontal lobe can be associated with increased aggressive dyscontrol (impulsive rather than premeditated aggression) in humans.

Neurotransmitters
Lack of the neurotransmitter **serotonin** has been associated with increased aggression in animal studies, perhaps due to a reduction of its inhibiting effect, e.g. drugs that block the action of serotonin increase aggression in rats.

Evaluation
- Isolating precise areas responsible for aggression is to oversimplify the massive interconnectedness of the brain. Delgado (1967) stimulated the aggression centres of monkeys by remote control and found that their aggression was not indiscriminate but directed according to their position on the dominance hierarchy – showing the influence of the reasoning parts of the brain.
- Cases of brain damage may be too rare to account for the widespread occurrence of aggression, although frontal lobe dysfunction may be more common than we think.
- There are ethical and practical difficulties investigating human brains, and there are problems generalising research on animals to humans (e.g. underestimating the influence of human learning and social/cultural norms).

HORMONAL FACTORS AND AGGRESSION

Some suggest that **testosterone** causes human aggression since physical violence is cross-culturally most common among those who would be expected to have the highest levels of the hormone, i.e. young adult males. Olweus (1985, cited in Durkin 1995) proposed that testosterone could stimulate/irritate young males, making them more susceptible to impulsive and aggressive responses.

- Studies that have injected testosterone into young male animals or castrated them have found corresponding increases or decreases in aggressive behaviour, but injecting testosterone into humans does not have the same effect. Castration of violent sexual offenders, however, can (but not always) produce decreases in aggression, although we cannot guarantee lower testosterone is the key cause.
- Studies of criminals with a history of violence have shown them to have higher levels of testosterone compared with non-violent criminals, and hormonal changes in women before menstruation can produce aggressive behaviour (Floody, 1983), although this finding is not universal.
- Archer's (2005, cited in Pakes and Winstone, 2007) research review has concluded that testosterone levels have a low but positive correlation with levels of aggression in humans, but a higher one with measures of dominance.

Evaluation
- Correlation is *not causation* – testosterone might be a cause or effect of aggression, or both may be affected by a *third* factor, e.g. social dominance.
- Testosterone levels can rise *after* aggressive or dominant acts.
- Dominant but non-aggressive criminals also have higher levels of testosterone.
- Susman *et al.* (1987, cited in Durkin) found an association between hormone levels and aggressiveness in boys, but not girls who showed the *same* levels of aggression.
- Hormones may influence aggressive responses but ignore social contexts and learning, e.g. the reinforcement consequences for those responses.

GENETIC FACTORS AND AGGRESSION

Some researchers have argued that aggression could have a genetic basis. As Kornadt (2002) reports, findings are mixed but indicate some genetic influence:

- **Selective breeding** studies for aggressiveness in animals has supported a genetic basis – strains of aggressive and non-aggressive animals have been produced, despite cross-fostering, e.g. raising aggressive strains with non-aggressive animal parents (Lagerspetz and Lagerspetz, 1971).
- The Danish Twin Study of 7000 **twins** revealed a concordance rate for aggressiveness of 35% for monozygotic (identical) twins, but only 13% for dizygotic twins (Christiansen, 1974).
- Rushton *et al.* (1986) measured aggressiveness using questionnaires on 573 adult twins (both male and female, average age 30) and found correlation coefficients of $r = 0.40$ for monozygotic twins and $r = 0.04$ for dizygotic twins, indicating a heritability estimate of 72% for aggressiveness.

Evaluation
- Twin studies still indicate an important influence of environmental factors in the development of aggression.
- Twin studies do not reveal how genes affect aggression. Case studies may shed more light on this, e.g. Brunner *et al.*'s (1993) study of a Dutch family where impulsive aggressive tendencies were inherited by the males only.
- The use of self-report questionnaires rather than objective measures of aggression may limit the validity of Rushton *et al.*'s study.

7.5 Evolutionary explanations of human aggression

EVOLUTIONARY THEORY OF AGGRESSION

Evolutionary psychologists consider the evolutionary **adaptive function** of aggression, suggesting aggressive behaviour evolved due to **natural or sexual selection** to allow animals to **defend** themselves and to **compete** for food and mates. Ardrey suggests animals have a **'territorial imperative'** – the desire to obtain and defend territory to secure access to food and mates. The concept of 'aggression' is therefore primarily applied to intra-species rather than inter-species (e.g. predation) situations.

Although aggression is a highly adaptive behaviour, it is also an extremely risky behaviour to indulge in since it is returned by other organisms and may result in death before genes have been passed on. For this reason animals, including humans, should only show aggression in certain contexts to achieve specific survival goals.

Buss and Shackelford (1997) propose an evolutionary psychological account of human aggression, arguing that aggressive behaviour has evolved to solve seven adaptive problems of social living:

1 **Co-opting the resources of others** – aggression to gain territory/resources, e.g. children bullying others for money or toys, adult mugging and warfare.

2 **Defending against attack** – aggression to prevent the loss of resources and status necessary for reproductive fitness, e.g. fighting 'to stick up for yourself'.

3 **Inflicting costs on same-sex rivals** – aggression to aid intra-sexual (between members of the same sex) competition for mates and resources, e.g. men fighting over women.

4 **Negotiating status and power hierarchies** – aggression to gain prestige and dominance among same-sex members, e.g. gang violence 'to prove oneself'/ boxing, and to aid sexual selection by opposite-sex members, e.g. women attracted by dominant, powerful men.

5 **Deterring rivals from future aggression** – aggression to maintain dominance and fear in others (see status above), e.g. making threatening gestures, reinforcing aggressive reputations, maintaining an aggressive appearance (gang tattoos, war paint, scars, etc.).

6 **Deterring mates from sexual infidelity** – aggression against opposite-sex members to maintain the fidelity of desired long-term mates and ensure paternity, e.g. wife-battering (see infidelity and jealousy below).

7 **Reducing resources expended on genetically unrelated children** – aggression against non-related offspring to keep resources for the propagation of one's own genes, e.g. child abuse and infanticide by step-parents.

INFIDELITY AND JEALOUSY

A good example of the power of evolutionary explanations to account for specific types of aggression is in the context of infidelity and sexual jealousy. Due to **male-female differences** in **parental investment, parental certainty, optimal mating strategy**, and **sexual selection**, evolutionary theory predicts:

- Human **males** have a greater survival need to **compete** with **other males** for access to choosy females. Lower status men or those less able to attract a mate are especially willing to take greater risks by using aggression or face genetic extinction.
- Human **females** can always guarantee offspring are their own and **compete** with **other women** more for the quality rather than the availability of men, so women should take fewer risks with physical violence and choose more indirect forms of aggression.
- Human **males** cannot risk wasting investment on offspring that are not their own, so should show **more jealous violent aggression relating to female fidelity** – both **towards male competitors** and their own **long-term female mates** if infidelity is suspected or the female partner wishes to leave for another man (especially if she is young and reproductively valuable).

Buss and Shackelford (1997) provide the following examples of research evidence that confirm these evolutionary predictions:

INTRA-SEXUAL JEALOUSY AGGRESSION

Male-male aggression
- Cross-culturally, human violent aggression and homicide is far more common in males, against other males (Daly and Wilson, 1988).
- Homicide is more common in poor and unmarried men than richer, married ones (Wilson and Daly, 1985).
- Sexual jealousy produces more male-male homicides than female-female.

Female-female aggression
- Female aggression is more verbal against other women to maintain status and reduce the attractiveness of competitors, especially by using verbal criticism of the physical unattractiveness of other females and their promiscuity (for men looking for *long-term* mates with sexual fidelity) to lower their appeal in the eyes of men (Buss and Dedden, 1990).

INTER-SEXUAL JEALOUSY AGGRESSION

- Most male non-sexual aggression against women involves girlfriends and spouses due to sexual jealousy.
- In a study of 36 Baltimore spousal homicides, 25 were attributed to jealousy, and the wives were the victims in 24 of these cases (Guttmacher, 1955).
- In a study of battered women, 57 out of 60 attributed the violence to their husband's extreme jealousy and possessiveness (Hilberman and Munson, 1978).
- Young wives/girlfriends are more likely to be killed than older ones (Daly and Wilson, 1988).
- In 100 cases of spousal violence, the husbands' frustration over their inability to control their wives and accusations of infidelity were the most reported causal factors (Whitehurst, 1971).
- Verbal aggression and non-lethal physical violence against mates is often similar in men and women, but spousal homicide by women is less frequent and often due to defense against a jealous abusive husband (Daly and Wilson, 1988).

7.6 Explanations of group display

WHAT IS GROUP DISPLAY?

- Group display is the **spontaneous manifestation of collective group behaviour** – how individuals in a group or crowd act in a **uniform** (or similar), **coordinated** but unplanned way.
- Psychologists have long been interested in group display to understand and predict the behaviour of violent crowds, e.g. lynching mobs, but group display has also been studied in more contemporary and (often) less violent contexts, e.g. crowds at sporting events. A number of theories relevant to explaining group display have been proposed.

ETHOLOGICAL THEORY

Lorenz argued that some species have **evolved** threat **rituals** (stereotyped displays) and aggressive collective behaviour to defend and compete for territories and resources against other groups. Rituals serve to settle potentially aggressive disputes before resorting to damaging violence. Lorenz argued that humans have also evolved aggressive group action (warfare), territoriality and collective threat displays, e.g. grimacing, aggressive posturing and shouting.

Evaluation
- Generalising from other animals ignores human learning.

COLLECTIVE UNCONSCIOUS THEORY

Le Bon's (1895) book 'The Crowd' argued that individuals in a crowd lose their conscious individual personalities to the primitive, animalistic, spirit of the crowd. Individuals undergo a radical transformation once in the grip of the 'law of mental unity of crowds', descending 'several rungs in the ladder of civilisation', possessing 'a sort of collective mind' and showing impulsive, irritable, highly suggestible and overly emotional behaviour and an incapacity to reason. The theory suggests group display occurs through:
- **Contagion** (crowd behaviour spreads amongst its members like an involuntary disease)
- **Suggestibility** (crowd member or leader suggestions are accepted uncritically due to loss of conscious personality)
- **Anonymity** (due to sheer numbers the individual feels a sense of invincible power and lack of responsibility).

The crowd has the following effect upon its members:
- **Homogeneity of personality** – all members behave in the same way (group display).
- **Intellectual retardation** – crowds are intellectually inferior to the individuals who compose it, showing rapid shifts of attention and uncritical acceptance of ideas.
- **Violent action and exaggerated emotionalism** – with a loss of constraints, savage and destructive behaviour is shown. Crowd members become excited and impulsive.

Evaluation
- Le Bon does not distinguish between types of crowds – they are often peaceful and together for enjoyment and celebration, e.g. at concerts, football matches, parties, etc.
- Crowd behaviour is not always wild and unruly and does not necessarily involve a loss of individual identity.

SOCIAL IDENTITY THEORY

Reicher (1982a) argues that rather than losing their identity (see collective unconscious theory) or automatically conforming to group norms, individuals in a crowd act in a rule-governed and coherent manner, but only in line with the values, norms and **goals** of **groups** they **identify** with.

Evaluation
- Reicher used social identity theory and the St Paul's riot in Bristol to show how crowd behaviour was not wild or irrational, but defined and directed by the group identity assumed by the individuals. Violence was spontaneous and uniform (group display), e.g. collective brick throwing, but governed and limited by the aims of being a member of the St Paul's community (crowd aggression was directed at the police only and restricted to the St Paul's area). Rather than mindless mob violence, the crowd directed traffic flow through the area and families shopped during the riot. Behaviour not in line with the crowds' identity was frowned upon and discouraged, e.g. when riot stones hit targets other than the police.

EMERGENT NORM THEORY

Turner and Killian (1972) explain behavioural contagion in crowds by proposing that collective crowd action is **triggered off by the first people to show a clear pattern of behaviour.** Their actions define the **norm** of behaviour (the appropriate thing to do) as **social comparison theory** and **informational social influence** suggest that people in a crowd are uncertain how to react and look to others for information. Thus if the emergent norm becomes 'applaud the performance', 'Mexican wave', 'lynch the criminal' or 'burn the witch' then crowd members follow the established pattern.

Evaluation
- Reicher (1982) disagrees with the idea that norms are only established by a small number of initial actors because this ignores pre-existing, whole-group identities.

SOCIAL NORM CONFORMITY THEORY

Marsh (1978) found that regularly occurring crowds develop implicit **roles** and **norms** that guide and regulate behaviour. Individuals conform to socially expected group displays, mainly for reasons of **normative social influence**.

Evaluation
- Marsh's study of football crowds on the terraces found evidence for conformity to norms. He even distinguished different groups among supporters (e.g. 'novices', 'rowdies' and 'nutters') each with their own rules and norms of behaviour. Group displays of violence were not wild and undirected, but tended to have constraints and be more verbal and ritualised than physically damaging.

8.1 The nervous and endocrine systems

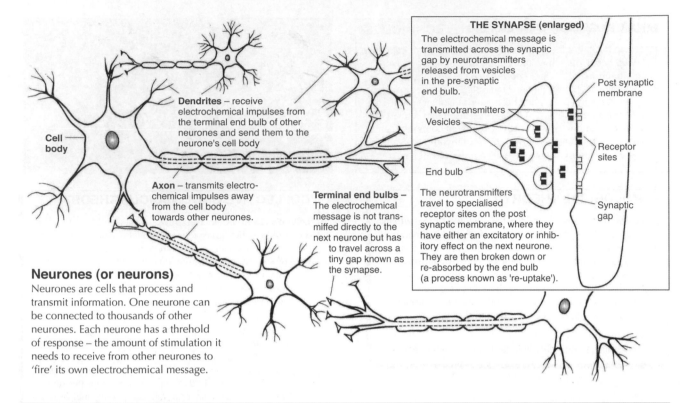

Dendrites – receive electrochemical impulses from the terminal end bulb of other neurones and send them to the neurone's cell body

Cell body

Axon – transmits electrochemical impulses away from the cell body towards other neurones.

Terminal end bulbs – The electrochemical message is not transmitted directly to the next neurone but has to travel across a tiny gap known as the synapse.

THE SYNAPSE (enlarged)
The electrochemical message is transmitted across the synaptic gap by neurotransmitters released from vesicles in the pre-synaptic end bulb.

Neurotransmitters

Vesicles

End bulb

Post synaptic membrane

Receptor sites

Synaptic gap

The neurotransmitters travel to specialised receptor sites on the post synaptic membrane, where they have either an excitatory or inhibitory effect on the next neurone. They are then broken down or re-absorbed by the end bulb (a process known as 're-uptake').

Neurones (or neurons)
Neurones are cells that process and transmit information. One neurone can be connected to thousands of other neurones. Each neurone has a threhold of response – the amount of stimulation it needs to receive from other neurones to 'fire' its own electrochemical message.

THE NERVOUS SYSTEM
The nervous system is made up of 10-12 billion neurones of 3 main types:
- **Sensory neurones**, which respond to external stimuli such as touch and light.
- **Motor neurones**, which carry messages to muscles, organs or glands.
- **Association neurones** (by far the most common type), which transmit and integrate information between other neurones.

The nervous system includes:
- The **central nervous system** (CNS) which consists of the brain and spinal cord.
- The **peripheral nervous system** (PNS) which consists of 43 pairs of peripheral nerves whose function is to link the senses to the CNS and the CNS to the muscles and organs. The PNS functions through two main systems:
  1. The **somatic nervous system** – this allows communication and voluntary interaction with the outside world via the sensory and motor neurones.
  2. The **autonomic nervous system** – this connects the CNS to internal glands, organs and involuntary muscles in order to regulate internal processes without conscious control. It has two branches that interact to govern many aspects of behaviour, e.g. homeostasis:
     a. The sympathetic branch – prepares the body for action by increasing heartbeat, breathing, blood sugar levels, and adrenaline release.
     b. The parasympathetic branch – acts to conserve and restore body energy when relaxed.

THE ENDOCRINE SYSTEM
The endocrine glands secrete hormones into the blood stream to affect behaviour.
There are many endocrine glands throughout the body which are regulated by the pituitary gland (sometimes referred to as the 'master gland'), which is itself controlled by the hypothalamus of the brain.

Pituitary gland – secretes many hormones from its anterior and posterior sections, e.g. for growth, maternal care, etc.

Pineal gland – secretes melatonin involved in regulating body rhythms.

Thyroid gland – secretes thyroxin, which affects body metabolism.

Pancreas – secretes insulin and glucagon to control blood sugar levels.

Adrenal glands – secrete corticosteroids involved in muscle development and epinephrine/norepinephrine involved in activating the sympathetic nervous system.

Gonads – secrete androgens involved in masculine characteristics (and possibly behaviour) and oestrogen and progesterone which regulate the female menstrual cycle.

8.2 Methods of investigating brain function – measurement

MEASURING/OBSERVATIONAL TECHNIQUES

DIRECT RECORDING OF NEURONAL ACTIVITY

Microelectrodes are inserted into single neuronal cells and record their electrochemical activity, e.g.

Hubel and Wiesel measured the activity of single neuronal cells in the visual cortex of monkeys. By keeping the head still, various visual stimuli could be presented to different areas of the retina to discover both the area the cell represented and the stimuli it most responded to.

EVALUATION
Advantages
- Extremely precise – a very accurate way of studying the living function of neurones.

Disadvantages
- Very time-consuming – thousands of neurones occupy even a tiny area of brain.
- Too focused – it neglects the interactions between nerve cells that are responsible for brain functions.
- Invasive method – it, thus, has ethical problems, especially if applied to humans.

EXTERNAL RECORDING OF BRAIN ACTIVITY

Aims to detect brain activity from measurements made at the surface of the skull, e.g.
- electroencephalograms (EEG) – electrodes are attached to areas of the scalp, and the electrical activity of the brain beneath that they detect is amplified to reveal the frequency of the 'brain wave'. The frequency is the number of oscillations the wave makes in a second and ranges from 1–3 hertz (delta waves) to 13 hertz or over (beta waves).
- evoked potentials – record the change in the electrical activity of an area of brain when an environmental stimuli is presented or a psychological task is undertaken.

Electrooculargrams (EOG) measure electrical activity of eye movements, whereas Electromyograms (EMG) record activity from muscles to measure tension or relaxation.

EVALUATION
Advantages
- Non-invasive techniques – no alteration or intervention makes these methods of measuring brain activity more natural and ecologically valid.
- Practically useful – these methods can distinguish between levels of sleep and different types of subject, e.g. brain damaged, epileptic, those with Alzheimer's disease, etc.

Disadvantages
- Crude measure – the activity of millions of neurones is measured and averaged. EEGs indicate the activity level but not the precise function of the neurones involved.

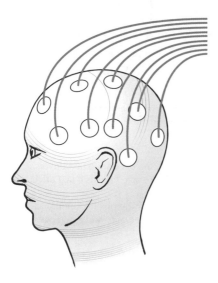

SCANNING TECHNIQUES
1 **STILL PICTURES** – detailed three dimensional or cross-sectional images of the brain can be gained by the following non-invasive techniques:
   a **Computerised Axial Tomography** (CAT scan) – is produced by X-ray rotation.
   b **Magnetic Resonance Imaging** (MRI scan) – where magnetic fields are rotated around the head to produce an extremely detailed picture.

2 **DYNAMIC PICTURES** – moving coloured images of brain activity levels in different parts of the brain over time can be gained by techniques such as:
   a **Positron Emission Tomography** (PET scan) – which detects the metabolism level of injected substances (e.g. glucose) made mildly radioactive to show which parts of the brain are most active (using up energy) over a period of minutes.
   b **Functional Magnetic Resonance Imaging** (F-MRI scan) – shows metabolic activity second by second without injected tracers.
   c **Magnetoencephalography** (MEG scan) – detects actual nerve cell firing over thousandths of a second.

EVALUATION
Advantages
- Detailed knowledge – scans can gain information about the brain structure and function of conscious patients, some while they are performing psychological tasks.

Disadvantages
- Scanning techniques – are expensive and scans can be difficult to interpret and are sensitive to disruption, e.g. by small movements.

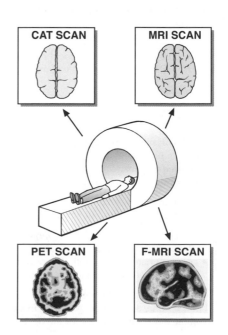

8.3 Navigation related structural change in the hippocampi of London taxi drivers. Maguire *et al.* (2000)

INTRODUCTION

The hippocampus is a structure found inside each hemisphere of the brain that is thought to play a role in spatial memory and navigation. Maguire *et al.* report that previous research has found:

- Certain birds and small mammals that show behaviour requiring navigation and spatial memory (e.g. food storage) have increased hippocampal volumes relative to their brain and body size, and can even show a greater increase in volume during seasons that demand more spatial ability.
- Differences in the structure of the healthy human brain exist between different groups of subjects, e.g. males and females, or musicians and non-musicians.

However, there are still questions surrounding:

- The precise role of the hippocampus in humans.
- Whether human hippocampi can undergo structural changes with extensive experience of spatial/navigational behaviour.
- Whether differences in human brain structure are predetermined (e.g. by the genes) or the result of 'plastic'/morphological/structural change caused by environmental stimulation.

London taxi drivers are ideally suited for a study of the effects of spatial navigation experience on the human hippocampus since they have to acquire extensive spatial/navigational information ('The Knowledge') on the city of London to pass their licensing test and carry out their job.

AIMS

In general, the authors aimed to investigate:

1 navigational experience and the role played by the hippocampus in humans
2 whether the healthy human brain can undergo 'plastic' (structural) changes in response to extensive navigational experience.

In particular, based on past research, they expected taxi drivers to show significant (p<0.05) structural differences in their hippocampi compared to non-taxi drivers.

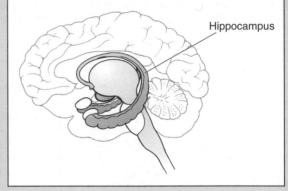

Hippocampus

METHOD

Design
Natural experiment
Independent measures design/matched pairs

Independent variable:
Amount of navigational experience tested in two conditions:

- Licensed London taxi drivers with a minimum of 18 months job experience (in addition to an average of about two years acquiring 'The Knowledge')
- Non-taxi drivers (control group).

Dependent variable:
Volume of the hippocampi, including their anterior, body and posterior sections.

N.B. A **correlation** was also conducted on the taxi drivers between the amount of time spent as a taxi driver (training + job) and their hippocampal volume.

Participants
Taxi drivers – 16 healthy, right-handed, male, London taxi drivers. Average age 44 (range 32 to 62 years), average time as a taxi driver 14.3 years (range 1.5 to 42 years).
Controls – (50 for the VBM template, 16 for the pixel counting) matched for health, handedness, sex, average age, and age range.

Procedure
Structural MRI (magnetic resonance imaging) scans of taxi drivers and non-taxi drivers were analysed by:
VBM (voxel-based morphometry) – an automatic procedure that 'normalised' the scans to a template (to eliminate overall size of brain as a variable) and compared the taxi drivers' brains with a control group of 50 non-taxi drivers to see if any differences in structure were to be found anywhere in the brain.
Pixel counting – an experienced observer (blinded to the subjects' identities and the VBM results) compared the volume of anterior, body and posterior cross-sections of the taxi drivers' hippocampi with those of a precisely matched control group.

RESULTS

VBM analysis – despite *no significant differences elsewhere* in the brain between the two groups, *taxi drivers* had significantly *increased* grey matter volume in the right and left *posterior hippocampus* compared to controls.

Pixel counting – despite no significant difference in the overall volume of the hippocampi between the two groups:

- taxi drivers had a significantly *larger* volume in the *posterior hippocampi* compared to controls.
- controls had a significantly *larger* volume in the *anterior hippocampi* compared to taxi drivers.

Correlations – a significant *positive* correlation was found between *time* as a taxi driver and *right posterior hippocampal volume* (but a *negative* one for the right *anterior* section).

DISCUSSION

Taken together, the experiment and correlation indicate:

- Human spatial representations and navigational experience are stored in the posterior hippocampus.
- The structural rearrangement of the hippocampi in taxi drivers reflects, rather than causes (as a pre-existing, predisposition), the amount of navigational ability.
- The healthy human brain can change in structure in response to environmental stimulation. This has implications for rehabilitation after brain damage, although this study only applies to the hippocampus.
- The methods of measurement were objective and well-controlled (by computer or blind assessment).
- The study does not show *how* the brain changes occur.

8.4 Methods of investigating brain function – alteration

ALTERATION/EXPERIMENTAL TECHNIQUES

ACCIDENTAL DAMAGE
Researchers use these natural experiments to compare the alteration in psychological functioning with the location of damage (by scan, surgery or autopsy). Damage may be caused by
- **strokes/tumours** – e.g. blood clot damage has revealed much about the location of motor, sensory, and linguistic functioning in the brain.
- **head trauma** – e.g. a railroad construction accident blew a 3 foot long metal rod through Phineas Gage's left frontal lobe in 1848, changing his personality to make him impulsive and irritable.
- **virus** – e.g. the virus herpes simplex damaged the temporal lobe and hippocampus of Clive Wearing causing anterograde amnesia.

EVALUATION
Advantages
- The altering damage occurs 'naturally' so there are less ethical problems compared to other methods.

Disadvantages
- Lack of precision – the exact extent of damage is not controllable and may be difficult to assess.
- Comparison problems – comparison of the functioning in the individual before and after the damage is less objective, since it is often based on retrospective accounts of previous behaviour and abilities.
- Confounding variables – other non-physical effects of the damage may be responsible for behavioural differences. Social reactions to Phineas Gage's physical deformity may have affected his personality.

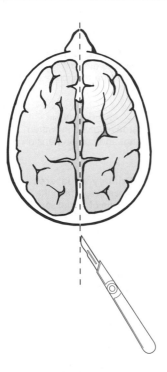

DELIBERATE DAMAGE
ABLATION/LESION STUDIES – aim to investigate function by removing areas of the brain or destroying links between areas. Some of the psychological functions investigated have included
- **Motivation** – ablation studies on the hypothalamus of rats have caused disrupted eating behaviour.
- **Aggression** – removing the amygdala of some animals has reduced their aggression.
- **Memory** – Lashley removed large portions of rat brains to find the location of memory.
- **Consciousness** – Sperry cut the corpus callosum of epileptic patients, producing a 'split mind'.
- **Psychopathology** – prefrontal lobotomy was performed on mental inmates to control behaviour.

EXPERIMENTAL EXPOSURE EFFECTS – aim to influence brain physiology by using environmental distortion or deprivation. Common examples are found in perceptual studies, e.g. Blakemore and Cooper's study of the visual cortex of cats exposed to an environment of vertical lines.

EVALUATION
Advantages
- Greater control – greater precision in the location of damage and the ability to compare behaviour before and after alteration leads to higher certainty over the effects of the damage.

Disadvantages
- Ethical problems of intervention – the deliberate change of behaviour is radical and irreversible.
- Non-human findings – may not be legitimately generalised to humans due to qualitative differences.
- Plasticity – the brain is a very flexible system which can compensate for damage. Removing one part of it will only show the performance of the rest of the system, not necessarily the missing part.

STIMULATION OF THE BRAIN
ELECTRICAL STIMULATION – aims to stimulate brain areas with microelectrodes to reveal their function through behavioural change. Examples include
- animal studies – Delgado stimulated areas of the limbic system to provoke aggression in monkeys and inhibit aggression in a charging bull (while standing in front of it!) by remote control.
- human studies – Penfield stimulated areas of the cortex in patients undergoing brain surgery and found locations that would produce body movement (primary motor cortex), body sensations (primary sensory cortex), memories of sound (temporal lobe) and visual sensations (visual cortex).

EVALUATION
Advantages
- Less harmful – the aim is to stimulate the brain rather than damage it (therefore more ethical).
- More valid – stimulation seems a better way of investigating the 'living' function of brain areas.

Disadvantages
- Invasive technique – the techniques still involve surgical operation, which can be risky.
- Interconnectedness – it is not easy to know exactly how far the stimulation has spread to other areas and the behaviour produced may not be natural, indeed it is often more stereotyped.

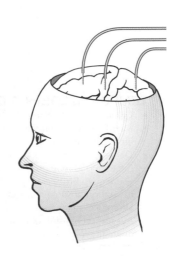

8.5 Localisation of brain function – exterior structure

LEFT SIDE VIEW OF BRAIN

FRONTAL LOBE OF CORTEX
- Involved in planning, initiative, and voluntary motor control. The frontal cortex is a very highly developed area in humans compared to other animals.
- Micro-electrode stimulation of the primary motor cortex produces twitches of movement in body parts.
- Damage causes lack of insight, loss of primitive reflex suppression, behavioural inertia (lack of spontaneity and initiative), and an inability to adjust behaviour to make it appropriate to the situation.

PARIETAL LOBE OF CORTEX
- Involved in sensing and monitoring of body parts.
- Micro-electrode stimulation to the primary sensory cortex produces sensations in various parts of the body.
- Contains many sensory association areas, such as the visual association area necessary for object recognition (damage does not cause blindness but visual agnosia – the inability to recognise the identity of whole objects by sight). Also integrates information from different sensory areas to enable cross-modal matching (e.g, pairing up the sight and sound of an object).

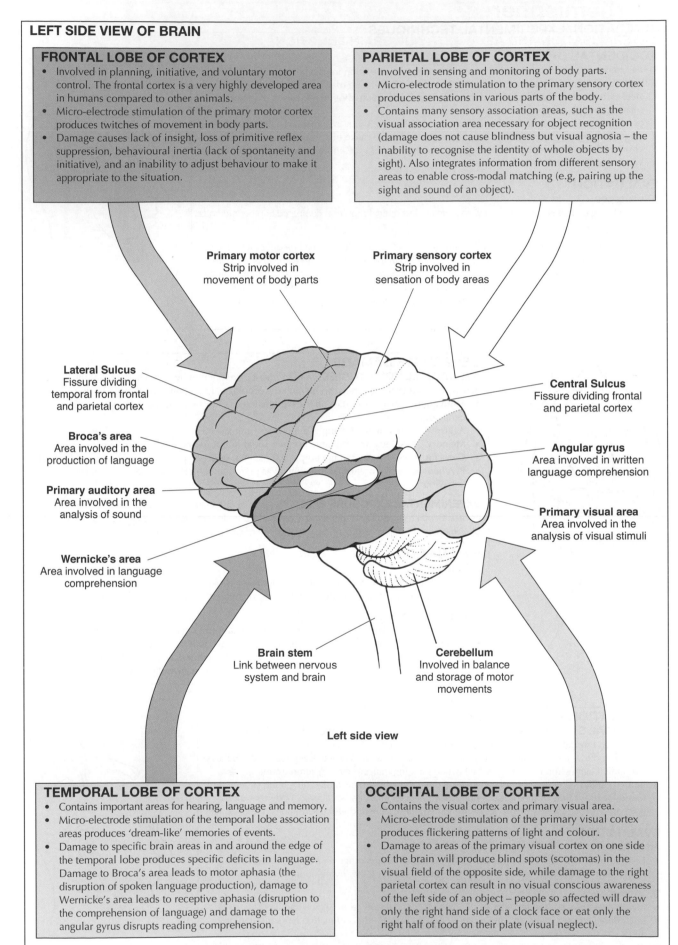

Primary motor cortex
Strip involved in movement of body parts

Primary sensory cortex
Strip involved in sensation of body areas

Lateral Sulcus
Fissure dividing temporal from frontal and parietal cortex

Central Sulcus
Fissure dividing frontal and parietal cortex

Broca's area
Area involved in the production of language

Angular gyrus
Area involved in written language comprehension

Primary auditory area
Area involved in the analysis of sound

Primary visual area
Area involved in the analysis of visual stimuli

Wernicke's area
Area involved in language comprehension

Brain stem
Link between nervous system and brain

Cerebellum
Involved in balance and storage of motor movements

Left side view

TEMPORAL LOBE OF CORTEX
- Contains important areas for hearing, language and memory.
- Micro-electrode stimulation of the temporal lobe association areas produces 'dream-like' memories of events.
- Damage to specific brain areas in and around the edge of the temporal lobe produces specific deficits in language. Damage to Broca's area leads to motor aphasia (the disruption of spoken language production), damage to Wernicke's area leads to receptive aphasia (disruption to the comprehension of language) and damage to the angular gyrus disrupts reading comprehension.

OCCIPITAL LOBE OF CORTEX
- Contains the visual cortex and primary visual area.
- Micro-electrode stimulation of the primary visual cortex produces flickering patterns of light and colour.
- Damage to areas of the primary visual cortex on one side of the brain will produce blind spots (scotomas) in the visual field of the opposite side, while damage to the right parietal cortex can result in no visual conscious awareness of the left side of an object – people so affected will draw only the right hand side of a clock face or eat only the right half of food on their plate (visual neglect).

8.6 Localisation of brain function – the cerebral hemispheres

LATERALISATION AND ASYMMETRY OF BRAIN FUNCTION

Most functions of the brain are contralaterally controlled – the sense information and functions of one side of the body are received and controlled by the hemisphere on the **opposite side of the brain**. Thus, touch, sound, and sight (but not smell) information received from the right side of the body is processed in the left hemisphere, which also controls right hand side body movements. Many functions are, therefore, duplicated in both hemispheres. However, there are some differences (asymmetries) in function between them.

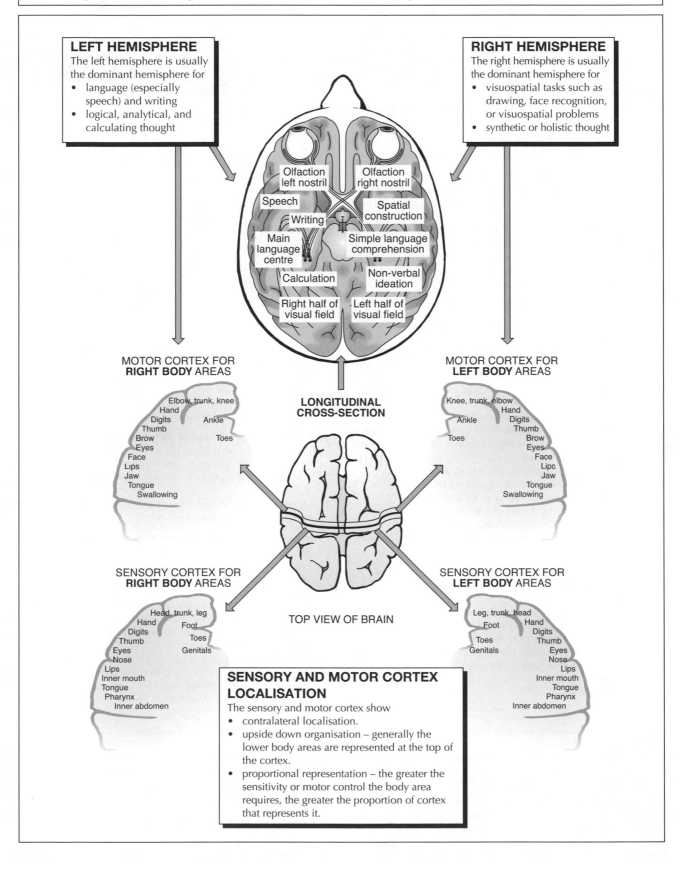

LEFT HEMISPHERE
The left hemisphere is usually the dominant hemisphere for
- language (especially speech) and writing
- logical, analytical, and calculating thought

RIGHT HEMISPHERE
The right hemisphere is usually the dominant hemisphere for
- visuospatial tasks such as drawing, face recognition, or visuospatial problems
- synthetic or holistic thought

Olfaction left nostril
Olfaction right nostril
Speech
Spatial construction
Writing
Main language centre
Simple language comprehension
Calculation
Non-verbal ideation
Right half of visual field
Left half of visual field

LONGITUDINAL CROSS-SECTION

MOTOR CORTEX FOR **RIGHT BODY** AREAS

Elbow, trunk, knee
Hand
Digits
Thumb
Ankle
Brow
Toes
Eyes
Face
Lips
Jaw
Tongue
Swallowing

MOTOR CORTEX FOR **LEFT BODY** AREAS

Knee, trunk, elbow
Hand
Ankle
Digits
Thumb
Toes
Brow
Eyes
Face
Lips
Jaw
Tongue
Swallowing

SENSORY CORTEX FOR **RIGHT BODY** AREAS

Head, trunk, leg
Hand
Foot
Digits
Toes
Thumb
Eyes
Genitals
Nose
Lips
Inner mouth
Tongue
Pharynx
Inner abdomen

TOP VIEW OF BRAIN

SENSORY CORTEX FOR **LEFT BODY** AREAS

Leg, trunk, head
Foot
Hand
Toes
Digits
Genitals
Thumb
Eyes
Nose
Lips
Inner mouth
Tongue
Pharynx
Inner abdomen

SENSORY AND MOTOR CORTEX LOCALISATION
The sensory and motor cortex show
- contralateral localisation.
- upside down organisation – generally the lower body areas are represented at the top of the cortex.
- proportional representation – the greater the sensitivity or motor control the body area requires, the greater the proportion of cortex that represents it.

8.7 'Hemisphere deconnection and unity in conscious awareness' Sperry (1968)

AIM
To present studies investigating the behavioural, neurological and psychological consequences of surgery in which the two cerebral hemispheres are deconnected from each other by severing the corpus callosum. Sperry uses these studies to argue that the 'split brain' shows characteristics during testing that suggest each hemisphere
- has slightly different functions
- possesses an independent stream of conscious awareness and
- has its own set of memories which are inaccessible to the other

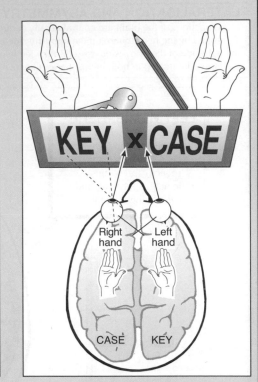

METHOD
Subjects: A handful of patients who underwent hemispheric deconnection to reduce crippling epilepsy.

Design: A natural experiment. Severing the corpus callosum prevents communication between the left and right hemispheres.

Procedure: Since each hemisphere receives information from, and controls the functioning of, the opposite side of the body, the capabilities of each can be tested by
- presenting visual information to either the left or right visual field when the subject is focusing straight ahead. If this is done at fast speeds (about 1 tenth of a second) the eye does not have time to move and re-focus. Thus information presented to the left visual field, will be received by the right hemisphere of the brain
- presenting tactile information to either the left or right hand behind a screen (to remove visual identification). Thus tactile information from objects felt by the right hand will be received by the left hemisphere.

RESULTS
Visual stimuli presented in one visual field at a time
- Objects shown once to a visual field are only recognised if presented again in the same visual field, not the other – implying different visual perception and memory storage for each hemisphere.
- Objects presented in the right visual field, and therefore received in the left hemisphere, can be named verbally and in writing, indicating the presence of speech comprehension and production as well as writing ability.
- Objects presented in the left visual field, and therefore received in the right hemisphere, can <u>not</u> be named verbally or in writing, but can be identified through pointing, indicating that the right hemisphere has language comprehension but not speech or writing.
  These tests imply that the two hemispheres of the brain have different abilities and functions.

Different visual stimuli presented simultaneously to different visual fields
- If different visual stimuli are presented simultaneously to different visual fields, e.g. a dollar sign to the left, a question mark to the right, and the subject is asked to draw with the left hand (out of sight) what was seen, the subject draws the stimuli from the left visual field (the dollar sign). If asked what the *left hand has just drawn*, the subject's verbal, left hemisphere replies with what was seen in the right visual field (the question mark).

- If two related words are simultaneously presented to the different visual fields, e.g. 'key' to the left and 'case' to the right, the left hand will select a key from amongst a variety of objects, whereas the right hand will write what it saw in the right visual field (a case) without being influenced by the meaning of the word in the left visual field.

Tactile stimuli presented to different hands
- If an object has been felt by the left hand only, it can be recognised by the left hand again but cannot be named by the subject or recognised by the right hand from amongst other objects.
  These tests imply that one side of the brain does not know what the other side has seen or felt.

Tests of the non-dominant right hemisphere
- The left hand can pick out semantically similar objects in a search for an object presented to the left visual field but not present in the search array of objects, e.g. a watch will be selected in response to a picture of a wall clock. The left hand can sort objects into meaningful categories.
- The right brain can solve simple arithmetical problems (pointing out the correct answer) and is superior in drawing spatial relationships.
- The right brain appears to experience its own emotional reactions (giggling and blushing in embarrassment at a nude pin-up presented to the left visual field) and can show frustration at the actions of the left hemisphere.

EVALUATION
Methodological: *Validity* – Being a natural experiment there is a lack of control over variables – in particular the subjects' mental abilities may have been atypical before the operation.

Theoretical: There do seem to be functional asymmetries between the hemispheres. However, research has revealed many individual differences – the above findings appear most typical of right-handed men. It should not be forgotten that the left and right hemispheres share many functions and are highly integrated.

Applications: The research has implications for helping patients with brain damage.

Links: Cortical functions, consciousness, psychosurgery.

8.8 Evaluation of neurophysiological findings

THE LIMITATIONS OF NEUROPHYSIOLOGICAL FINDINGS

- Neurophysiology often explains the hardware and function of different parts of the brain but often **ignores** the effect of **environmental experience** upon it. Some studies have looked at this issue, however, such as Blakemore & Cooper's (1970) exposure of animals to environments of vertical lines, and the effect of this on the striate visual cortex.

- Physiological explanations have not dealt with the **'mind body' problem** – they do not say how the physical structure and activity of the brain gives rise to the apparently non-physical conscious sensations and experience of mental life.

- There are many **limitations** of some of the **methods** used to identify brain activity, e.g. electrical stimulation of the brain may have a spreading activation effect to other areas (see methods of investigating brain function).

- The idea that neurophysiological explanations are sufficient to explain psychological functioning is dubious. In the case of visual perception, for example, Marr (1982) pointed out that the **aims** and **cognitive processes** of vision had to be considered rather than just the hardware. Indeed, once the processes by which perception occurs have been identified, the psychologist could change the hardware from the brain to a computer's circuits. There is, however, the possibility that vision could only be achieved by the complex biological hardware of the brain, but on the other hand, this biological complexity may also make a clear and useful explanation of perception impossible if the functions are spread in a parallel way over millions of neurones.

- Focusing just on the physiology of the brain may lead researchers to ignore the important implications that **psychological** research and theory has for the functions of brain areas. Hubel and Wiesel's 'bottom-up' description of feature detection in the cells of the visual cortex only focused on the 'input' from the retina, and thus ignored the 'top-down' influences of past experience and expectation that many psychologists such as Gregory (1970) have long pointed out. Recent investigations of the neural activity of cells that respond to the input of visual stimuli are now stressing the importance of the brain's background state of activity - 'It seems that the output of an individual neurone also depends on what the brain happens to be thinking about at the time' (McCrone, cited from *New Scientist*, December 1997). Maunsell and Treue (1996), for example, found the visual movement detection cells of monkeys would show increased activity to moving dots that they had been trained to pay attention to, compared to dots they could see but were not 'interested' in.

Integration of cortical areas devoted to speaking a written passage

Retinal information sent to the primary visual cortex is analysed to detect the lines and curves of letters in the text. Words are distinguished in the angular gyrus and transformed into a form that can be recognised and interpreted for meaning by Wernicke's area. Once the written passage has been understood and held in memory, Broca's area is involved in the formation of spoken words and the motor cortex initiates the physical production of them.

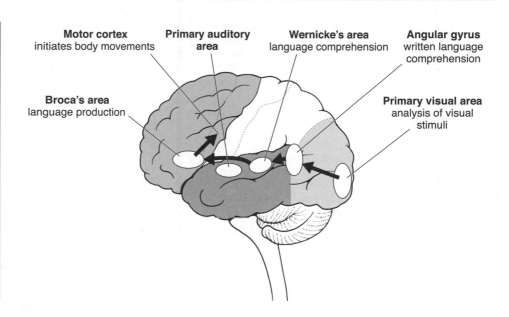

Motor cortex initiates body movements

Primary auditory area

Wernicke's area language comprehension

Angular gyrus written language comprehension

Broca's area language production

Primary visual area analysis of visual stimuli

ARGUMENTS AGAINST LOCALISATION OF FUNCTION

- **Localisation is not always clear cut.** In the case of brain asymmetry, for example, there are many variations in the location of function in the two cerebral hemispheres between male and female subjects and left and right handed subjects. The findings usually reported on the location of cerebral functioning are most representative of right-handed, male subjects.

- **The brain shows 'plasticity'.** According to some researchers, the brain is very flexible and can physically adjust the location of function if brain damage occurs (e.g. the recovery of language in children with left cerebral hemisphere damage), or specialisation to environmental conditions is required (e.g. blind Braille readers show an increase in the sensory cortex surface area devoted to the right forefinger, compared to non-Braille readers and their own left forefingers).

- **The brain is hugely integrated.** There are many different brain areas involved in abilities such as vision (Maunsell and Newsome, 1987, proposed there were at least 19 visual areas in macaque monkeys) and research needs to focus on how these areas **interact** together to produce function. The diagram above shows how just some of the areas involved in language interact in a simple task. Researchers such as Lashley believe in holism – that many functions are distributed across the whole brain. Lashley (1929) destroyed virtually all parts of rat brains in varying amounts to find the location of memory, and concluded that the 'law of mass action' applied memory loss is related to the amount of damage inflicted upon a rat brain, not the location of it. Neuroscientists are currently accepting the view that the brain is a very dynamic system and that activity in one area of the brain is influenced by the background activity of the rest of the brain. We must 'stop thinking of neurones as if they are exchanging messages… most of the 5000 input lines to the average brain cell are actually parts of feedback loops returning via neighbouring neurones, or those higher up the hierarchy. Barely a tenth of the connections come from sense organs or mapping levels lower in the hierarchy. Every neurone is plumbed into a sea of feedback' (McCrone, cited in *New Scientist*, December, 1997).

8.9 The genetic basis of behaviour

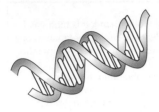
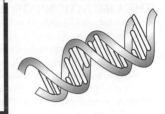

GENETIC INFLUENCES ON BEHAVIOUR

The inherited basis of human behaviour has long interested philosophers, genetic biologists, psychologists, politicians and the general public, and has generated a great deal of debate and controversy. An understanding of the assumptions and methods of the biological approach in this area can help explain the implications of research into the genetic basis of behaviour.

GENETIC RESEARCH ASSUMPTIONS

Genotype and phenotype

- The **genotype** refers to a person's 'genetic blueprint' – the **total pattern of chromosomes** (each containing thousands of genes) inherited from each parent, with the DNA 'instructions for building a new person'.
- The **phenotype** refers to the set of characteristics a person actually develops – **the physical realisation** or embodiment of the genetic instructions based on the environmental resources available.

Behavioural genetics is the attempt to discover the influence of inherited **genetic** factors on individual differences in **behaviour** and **mental abilities** – based on the assumption that genetic factors must influence such characteristics to some extent, since they are produced by bodies which are constructed from the instructions contained in the DNA.

Family genetic relatedness

During human reproduction, a fertilised egg (zygote) receives 23 chromosomes from the mother and 23 from the father. This means the average number of genes shared by two 'blood relatives' can be calculated.

For example, in terms of **average genetic makeup** (genotype), any one individual **shares**:

- 100% with a monozygotic (same egg)/identical twin.
- 50% with a dizygotic (different egg)/fraternal twin.
- 50% with a parent, brother or sister.
- 25% with a related uncle, aunt, niece or nephew.

Evaluation

Researchers have differed in their assumptions over exactly how strong genetic influences are, creating an over-simplified division of nature vs. nurture. Gene–environment interaction is actually highly complicated, since research shows that:

- A variety of environmental factors, from womb and food nutrition to pollution and social stimulation, influence phenotype development from a genotype.
- Environmental factors can even affect the genotype itself – switching genes on or off.
- A single human characteristic can be influenced by many genes (pleiotropy), not all of which may be present or expressed in a particular person.
- Some genes, e.g. those involved in Huntingdon's disease, have more direct and inevitable effects than others, e.g. those involved in Alzheimer's disease.

GENETIC RESEARCH METHODS

Family/Twin resemblance correlations

These measure the degree of similarity (concordance) of characteristics between genetically related (e.g. parent/offspring, sibling/sibling, etc.) and unrelated individuals on the assumption that the closer the genetic relationship, the greater the similarity of traits. Comparing the concordance rates of monozygotic and dizygotic twins is particularly valuable since twins are born at the same time to similar environments, but each type differs in the proportion of genes shared.

Evaluation

With these studies it is difficult to discover the relative effects of genetic and environmental influences – the closer the genetic relatedness people have, the more likely they are to share similar family environments (especially for identical twins who are treated more alike than non-identical, e.g. brother and sister, twins).

Adoption studies

Adoption studies help control for the similar environments related individuals are more likely to share, especially if correlations are made between monozygotic twins raised in different families.

Evaluation

Since adoption studies are natural experiments, they can never completely control environmental effects, e.g. separated twins may be placed in similar adoptive families and still shared womb environment.

Selective breeding studies

Animals with similar characteristics are mated to see if their offspring are more likely to show the trait when raised alone or by parents who do not possess it.

Evaluation

Controlled human breeding studies are not ethical.

Molecular genetics

Modern technology allows the extraction of genetic material from individuals with a certain characteristic to see how it differs from that of people without the characteristic. This can reveal the coding of the genes correlated with the characteristics and their location amongst the 46 human chromosomes.

Evaluation

Molecular genetics research has found that individuals can possess the genes associated with a characteristic, without necessarily developing it themselves.

9.1 Body rhythms 1

WHAT ARE BODY RHYTHMS AND WHAT CAUSES THEM?
Body rhythms are biological processes that show cyclical variation over time. Many processes show such cyclical variation in both plants and animals over a variety of time periods, ranging from hours or days to years, and reflect the influence of the Earth's rotation upon its living inhabitants through the physical changes in the environment it produces. Body rhythms seem governed by internal, inbuilt mechanisms (termed 'endogenous pacemakers' or 'body clocks') as well as external environmental stimuli (termed 'zeitgebers' or 'time-givers').

CIRCADIAN RHYTHMS

- Circadian rhythms cycle over 24 hours ('circa' = approximately, 'diem' = day). Humans show physiological changes over a 24 hour cycle in hormone levels, body temperature and heart, respiration and metabolic rate. Of most interest to psychologists however, has been the circadian sleep-waking cycle because of the dramatic changes in behaviour it produces.

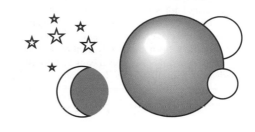

THE SLEEP-WAKING CYCLE

The circadian sleep-waking rhythm determines our alertness and activity levels during the day and night. In humans it is regulated by:

- **The endogenous pacemakers or internal body clock** of the *suprachiasmatic nucleus* (SCN) and the *pineal gland*. The SCN is part of the hypothalamus that regulates sleep-waking patterns by sending messages to the pineal gland to release melatonin – which is thought to stimulate the production of serotonin in the raphe nucleus to initiate sleep. Removal of the SCN in hamsters randomises their sleep–waking patterns. The sleep-waking body clock seems to be the product of evolution and is largely inherited, SCN cells will fire in a rhythmic way even if removed and placed in culture. In humans it seems to naturally run on a slightly longer cycle than a day (around 25 hours) but there seem to be inherited individual differences between people. If the SCN of mutant hamsters which causes different sleep-waking patterns is transplanted into normal hamsters who have had their SCN removed, they adopt the mutant's circadian patterns. The sleep-waking circadian rhythm can be adjusted to a certain degree by zeigebers, but seems mostly regulated by the internal body clock.
- The major **external re-setter (zeitgeber)** of the circadian body clock in humans is light, which is detected at the retina and can influence (via interconnecting nerve fibres) the SCN to synchronise our rhythms to the 24 hour cycle of the day. This has been demonstrated by studies that have removed the zeitgeber of light such as *Siffre's cave study*. However, while the cycle/rhythm can slowly adjust to new starting points (as happens when zetigebers change due to human activities such as shift work or travel over time zones) and can be resisted with a struggle (e.g. in sleep deprivation studies) the basic pattern or ratio of sleep-waking activity is remarkably consistent due to its biological basis. Similar sleep-waking patterns are found cross-culturally, despite cultural zeitgebers such as siestas and environmental zeitgebers in countries who experience whole summers or winters of lightness and darkness (such as those in the arctic circle). The inflexibility of the rhythm has also been demonstrated under controlled laboratory conditions, where exposure to different ratios of light and dark hours do not affect the sleeping patterns of subjects beyond certain limits.

PSYCHOLOGICAL AND PHYSIOLOGICAL CHANGES OF THE CIRCADIAN RHYTHM

	PSYCHOLOGICAL EXPERIENCE	PHYSIOLOGICAL CORRELATES		
		EEG	EOG	EMG
WAKING STATES (Approx. 16 hours)	**Alertness** – involves open-eyed active consciousness with the full ability to concentrate on a task. **Relaxation** – involves a passive but awake conscious experience although the eyes may be shut.	Beta waves (13 hertz or above) Alpha waves (8 to 12 hertz)	Eye movements reflect task Eye movements reflect cognition	Muscle activity reflects task Muscle activity reflects relaxation
SLEEP STATES (Approx. 8 hours – around 80% NREM 20% REM in adults)	**NON-REM SLEEP** – involves a series of stages. **Stage 1:** Lightest stage of sleep. Easily awakened.	Theta waves (4–7 hertz)	Slow rolling eye movements	Muscles relaxed but active
	Stage 2: Light sleep. Fairly easily awakened. Some responsiveness to external and internal stimuli – name calling produces K-complex activity.	Theta waves sleep spindles, K-complexes	Minimal eye movement	Little muscle movement
	Stage 3: Deep sleep. Difficult to awaken. Very unresponsive to external stimuli.	Delta waves (1–3 Hz) 20-50% of the time	Virtually no eye movement	Virtually no muscle movement
	Stage 4: Very deep sleep. Very difficult to awaken. Very unresponsive to external stimuli.	Delta waves over 50% of the time	Virtually no eye movement	Virtually no muscle movement
	REM SLEEP It is difficult to awaken people from rapid eye-movement (REM) sleep. If woken, individuals report vivid dreaming far more often than if woken from non-REM sleep (Dement and Kleitman, 1957).	High levels of mixed wave brain activity	Eye movement – may reflect dream content	Muscles in a state of virtual paralysis

9.2 Disrupting biological rhythms

WHAT PHYSIOLOGICAL CONCEPTS ARE RELEVANT?

- Physiological research into body rhythms such as the human sleep-waking circadian rhythm has revealed that both inner biological factors (**endogenous pacemakers** or body clocks) and external environmental factors (**zeitgebers**) can influence our pattern of sleeping and waking activity.
- However, research has also shown that the sleep-waking body clock is fairly consistent and slow to adjust, while zeitgebers such as work patterns and travel across time zones can change very quickly. Such a **mismatch between our natural body rhythms and activity patterns** can produce negative effects, which have been investigated by physiologically orientated psychologists.
- The **pattern of adjustment** is also important. Siffre, a French cave explorer, spent 6 months in a cave underground which effectively removed the external zeitgebers of the world above such as light levels and human activity patterns. No time cues were given via his telephone contact with the outside world and artificial lights were switched on when he woke up and off when he fell asleep. Under these conditions his natural body rhythms lengthened to around 25 hours so by the time he left the cave he had experienced fewer 'days' than everyone else. This means that adjustment to new zeitgebers is easier if they involve a **lengthening** of the day, since the **circadian cycle** itself seems to have a natural tendency to lengthen.

SHIFT WORK

Much shift work has involved three 8-hour working periods rotating anti-clockwise, e.g. from night shift to evening shift to day shift (a 'phase advance' rather than 'phase delay' schedule), frequently on a weekly basis or less. Physiological research on body rhythms informs us this can produce long-term disorientation, stress, insomnia, exhaustion and negative effects on reaction speed, co-ordination skill, attention and problem solving, since such work schedules:

1. Create a mismatch or desynchronisation between the body rhythms of arousal and the zeitgebers of activity levels.
2. Do not allow enough adjustment time for body rhythms to catch up with (become 'entrained' by) new activity levels.
3. Delay the catching up (entrainment) of body rhythms by shortening rather than lengthening the day.

This increases the chances of accidents occurring due to human error, even when other factors such as reduced hours of sleep, night-time supervision levels, etc. are taken into account.

Czeisler *et al.* (1982) studied a group of industrial workers who were following such a shift pattern and their suggestion that they moved clockwise in shifts (a phase delay schedule) on a three week rather than one week basis led to better worker health and morale, as well as higher productivity levels.

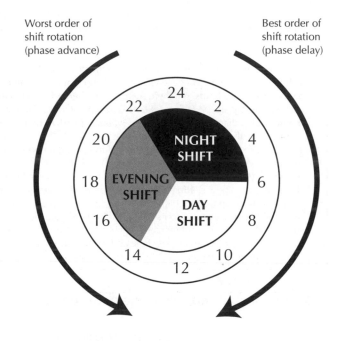

Worst order of shift rotation (phase advance)

Best order of shift rotation (phase delay)

JET LAG

Rapid air travel across time zones can produce jet lag – general disorientation and symptoms similar to those described for shift work, though not always as severe. This also:

1. Results from a mismatch or desynchronisation between the body rhythms of the old time zone, stored in the body clock you take with you, and the zeitgebers of the new time zone, such as human activity levels (e.g. mealtimes) and light levels.
2. Is harder to adjust to if the zeitgebers shorten the day and the circadian cycle – causing a phase advance. This explains why rapid travel from the west to the east across many time zones tends to produce worse jet lag than travelling from east to west (which lengthens the day and causes phase delay).

The influence of zeitgebers and endogenous pacemakers on jet lag are harder to identify since many other variables involved in travelling could cause the symptoms, such as stress, excitement, unfamiliarity and restricted posture.

Slower travel over fewer time zones as well as taking drugs that affect melatonin activity at appropriate times may reduce the severity of jet lag symptoms.

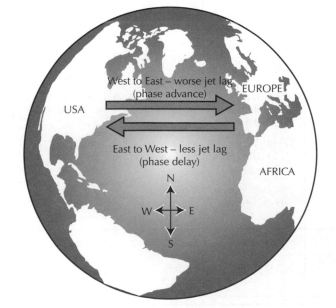

9.3 Body rhythms 2

PSYCHOLOGICAL AND PHYSIOLOGICAL CHANGES

THE ROLE OF ENDOGENOUS PACEMAKERS AND ZEITGEBERS

CIRCANNUAL RHYTHMS
(Rhythms lasting about a year)

- Much behaviour in animals varies over a yearly cycle, such as hibernation, mating and migration.
- Some humans show Seasonal Affective Disorder (SAD) – a strong variation in mood over the year, usually involving depression during the winter months.

- A key external zeitgeber that regulates physiology and behaviour in yearly cycles is light levels. Greater winter darkness stimulates the pineal gland to produce melatonin – a hormone involved in controlling energy levels and mood.
- However, many environmental and psychological factors can lead to winter depression, e.g. the colder weather.

INFRADIAN RHYTHMS
(Rhythms lasting longer than 24 hours)

- The intradian rhythm of menstruation in women occurs over a 28-day cycle and is associated with physiological changes and discomfort relating to the shedding of the lining of the uterus wall and the behavioural changes of pre-menstrual syndrome (PMS).
- The psychological effects that are suggested to occur begin around five days before menstruation in some women and can include mood change, irritability, dizziness and changes in energy levels and eating habits. The severity of the physiological symptoms varies among women and the extent of psychological changes associated with PMS has been the subject of some debate between psychologists.

- The endogenous pacemaker of the pituitary gland and its triggering of hormones such as prostaglandin internally regulate the menstrual cycle. The endogenous regulation of PMS via cycles in the endocrine system is supported by the finding of PMS cross-culturally.
- The menstrual cycle can be quite variable at first and is open to modification by external stimuli – zeitgebers such as light levels (indicating a role for melatonin) and the presence of other women (studies show frequent interaction with particular women can cause synchronisation of menstruation, possibly due to pheromones – released chemically active scents). Since not all women experience it, PMS may result from psychological factors too.

ULTRADIAN RHYTHMS
(Rhythms lasting less than 24 hours)

DIURNAL (day) RHYTHMS
- Individuals seem to vary in their activity levels, some being more alert and receptive to information in the morning, others in the evening.
- Horne and Osterberg (1976) used their 'Morningness-Eveningness' questionnaire to confirm this distinction, although research findings on the effect of time of day upon performance have been mixed.

- Morning types seem to reach their physiological peak (as measured by body temperature, metabolic rate, etc.) earlier than evening types, indicating perhaps a 'phase advance' in their endogenously regulated circadian rhythms (Marks and Folkhard, 1985).
- However, these variations could be the result (rather than the cause) of zeitgebers such as the subject's lifestyle and activity levels during the day.

NOCTURNAL (night) RHYTHMS
- The stages of sleep are cycled through around 5 times per night in the following way:
  Relaxation to first cycle – may involve hypnagogic experiences, e.g. dream images or falling sensations.
  First cycle – Descent to deep stage 4 sleep (which lasts approx. 40 minutes), ends with a short REM period.
  Second cycle – Gradual descent to deep stage 4 sleep (approx. 30 minutes), ends with a short REM period.
  Third cycle – Mostly stage 2 sleep followed by up to 40 minutes of REM sleep.
  Fourth cycle – Around an hour of stage 2 sleep followed by around an hour of REM sleep.
  Fifth cycle – Stage 2 sleep followed by a shorter REM period or waking (possibly with hypnagogic experiences).
- The level of dreaming and alertness is determined by when during the cycles a person is awoken. The deepest NREM sleep usually occurs in the first half of a night, while the most vivid dreaming REM sleep usually occurs in the second half.

- The ultradian rhythm of alternating NREM and REM sleep results from the alternating activity of the endogenous pacemakers of the:
  1. raphe nuclei (which releases inhibiting, NREM sleep-producing serotonin) and
  2. locus coeruleus (which releases activating, REM sleep inducing acetylcholine and noradrenaline).
- Destruction of the locus coeruleus stops REM sleep
- Destruction of the raphe nuclei causes sleeplessness
- Zeitgebers like alcohol can disrupt the cycle.

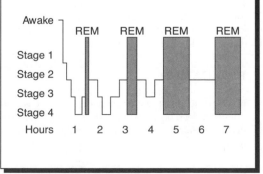

9.4 'The relation of eye movements during sleep to dream activity: an objective method for the study of dreams' Dement and Kleitman (1957)

AIM
Aserinsky and Kleitman found a relationship between rapid eye movement (REM) during sleep and reports of dreaming. Dement and Kleitman aimed to provide a **more detailed** investigation of how objective, physiological aspects of rapid eye movement relate to the subjective, psychological experience of dreaming reported by subjects, by testing whether:

- significantly **more dreaming** occurs **during REM sleep** than non-REM sleep under controlled conditions.
- there is a **significant positive correlation** between the objective length of **time** spent **in REM** and the subjective **duration of dreaming** reported upon waking.
- there is a significant **relationship** between the **pattern of rapid eye movements** observed during sleep and the **content** of the **dream** reported upon waking.

METHOD
Subjects: 7 adult males and 2 adult females – 5 of which were intensively studied, 4 of which were used to confirm results.

Design: Laboratory experimentation and observation.

Procedure: Subjects slept individually in a quiet dark laboratory room after a normal day's activity (except that alcohol and caffeine were avoided during the days before testing). Electrodes were connected near the eyes to register eye movement and on the scalp to measure brain waves during sleep – these were the objective measures of REM sleep. Subjects were awoken at various times during the night (fairly evenly distributed across the average sleeping time of the subjects) by a loud doorbell noise, and immediately reported into a recording device whether they had been dreaming and the content of the dream *before* any contact with the experimenter (to avoid bias). Subjects were never usually told whether their eyes had been moving before being awoken. Dreaming was only counted if a fairly detailed and coherent dream was reported – vague impressions or assertions of dreaming without recall of content were not counted.

STUDY ONE
Subjects were awoken in one of four different ways during either REM or non-REM sleep, and were compared to see if they had been dreaming.
- 2 subjects were awoken randomly
- 1 subject was awoken during 3 REM sleep periods followed by 3 non-REM periods, and so on
- 1 subject was awoken randomly, but was told he would only be awoken during periods of REM sleep
- 1 subject was awoken at the whim of the experimenter

STUDY TWO
Subjects were awoken either 5 or 15 minutes after REM sleep began and were asked to decide whether the duration of their dream was closer to 5 or 15 minutes.
The length of the dream (measured in terms of the number of words in their dream narratives) was also correlated to the duration of REM sleep before awakening.

STUDY THREE
Subjects were awoken as soon as one of four patterns of eye movement had occurred for 1 minute, and were asked exactly what they had just dreamt.
- Mainly vertical eye movements
- Mainly horizontal eye movements
- Both vertical and horizontal eye movements.
- Very little or no eye movement

RESULTS
Generally, REM periods were clearly observed in all subjects and distinguished from non-REM sleep periods. REM sleep periods occurred at regular intervals specific to each subject (although on average occurring every 92 minutes) and tended to last longer later in the night.

STUDY ONE
Regardless of how subjects were awoken, significantly more dreams were reported in REM than non-REM sleep.
When subjects failed to recall dreams from REM sleep, this was usually early in the night.
When subjects recalled dreams from non-REM sleep it was most often within 8 minutes after the end of a REM period.

STUDY TWO
Subjects were significantly correct in matching the duration of their dream to length of time they had shown REM sleep for both the 5-minute periods (45 out of 51 estimates correct) and 15-minute periods (47 out of 60 estimates correct).
All subjects showed a significant positive correlation at the P< 0.05 level or better between the length of their dream narratives and duration of REM sleep before awakening.

STUDY THREE
There was a very strong association between the pattern of REMs and the content of dream reports.
- The 3 vertical REM periods were associated with dreams of looking up and down at cliff faces, ladders, and basketball nets.
- A dream of two people throwing tomatoes at each other occurred in the only mainly horizontal REM period.
- 21 periods of vertical and horizontal REMs were associated with dreams of looking at close objects.
- 10 periods of very little or no REMs were associated with dreams of looking at fixed or distant objects.

EVALUATION

Methodological: Dreams may be recalled easier in REM than non-REM sleep because the latter is a deeper stage of sleep – perhaps dreams occur in deeper sleep, but are more difficult to recall from it.

The study used a limited sample, mostly men, therefore showed a lack of generalisability.

Theoretical: The research provides support for the idea that dreams can be studied in an objective way. This then opens up areas of research for the effect of environmental stimuli on dreaming.

Links: Sleep and dream research. Laboratory studies.

9.5 The nature of sleep

THE NATURE OF SLEEP – WHAT IS IT?

1 Sleep is part of the *circadian sleep-waking body rhythm* – representing the lowest point in measurements of the daily cyclical variation in conscious awareness and physical activity levels.
Evidence – see research on circadian rhythm physiological measures of body temperature, brain wave activity, etc.

2 Sleep consists of *two distinct types* – REM (rapid eye movement) and NREM (non-rapid eye movement) sleep.
Evidence – see research on difference in EEG, EOG and EMG measurements between REM and NREM sleep.

3 Sleep is also an *ultradian rhythm* – showing cyclical variations in the depth of NREM sleep and the occurrence of REM sleep.
Evidence – see research on ultradian rhythm sleep cycles gained from controlled laboratory observations.

4 Sleep is a psychological and possibly biological *need* – sleep deprivation causes an intensified desire to sleep.
Evidence – see research on the negative effects of sleep deprivation in humans and other animals.

5 Sleep is an *active neurological process* – specialised parts of the brain actively initiate sleep.
Evidence – see research on brain areas and sleep, e.g. the role of the:
- Suprachiasmatic nucleus and pineal gland in sleep onset.
- Raphe nuclei and inhibiting serotonin in initiating NREM sleep.
- Reticular activating system in lowered NREM cortical activity.
- Locus coeruleus and acetylcholine in initiating REM sleep.
- Pons in the muscular paralysis of REM sleep.

Thalamus
Pineal gland
Hypothalamus
Supra-chiasmatic nucleus
Optic chiasm
Eyeball
Raphe nucleus
Pons
Locus coeruleus
Medulla
Reticular activating system

LIFESPAN CHANGES IN SLEEP

What changes occur in sleep over the lifespan?

There are changes in the approximate average hours of total sleep per day, time spent in REM, and sleep pattern with age:

Age	Sleep per day	% REM sleep	Sleep pattern
Newborns	16 hours	50%	Fragmented sleep periods over the 24 hours
Four-month infants	14 hours	40%	Sleep fragmented, but shows a strong nocturnal shift
One-year-old infants	13 hours	30%	Nocturnal sleep established, daytime naps
Four-year-old infants	11 hours	20%	Nocturnal sleep, often with a single daytime nap
12 year-old children	10 hours	18.5%	Nocturnal sleep, no daytime naps required
Adolescents	8.5 hours	20%	Delta wave decline starts, increased daytime sleepiness
Young adults	7.75 hours	22%	Adult ultradian pattern well established
Middle-aged adults	7 hours	19%	Stage 4 NREM deep sleep starts to disappear
The elderly	6 hours	20%	Lighter and more fragmented sleep, daytime naps

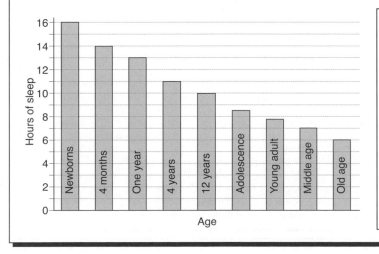

Why do the changes occur?

Different theories have different explanations for the changes in total and REM sleep with age (see theories of sleep). For example, young children may sleep more than adults because of:

- Greater need to conserve energy for body and brain growth.
- Greater physical fatigue due to weaker muscles.
- Less need for physical activity, e.g. food-searching.
- Greater needs to keep out of trouble, avoid predators.
- Greater needs to process / consolidate new learning.

9.6 Theories of the function of sleep

SLEEP DEPRIVATION – IS SLEEP NEEDED?

ANIMAL STUDIES:
- Jouvet (1967) deprived cats of sleep by putting them on a floating island in a pool of water so that when they fell asleep they fell in and woke up. The cats developed abnormal behaviours and eventually died.
- Rechtschaffen *et al.* deprived rats of sleep. They had all died after 33 days.

HUMAN STUDIES:
- Psychological effects – increased desire to sleep, difficulty sustaining attention (however, problem solving is less impaired), delusions, and depersonalisation.
- Physiological effects – minor changes, such as problems with eye focusing, but no significant major adverse effects. Sleep after deprivation is not cumulative (not much longer than usual), although more time is spent in REM sleep (a REM rebound effect). However, sleep deprivation studies are not indefinite.

THEORIES OF SLEEP FUNCTION

RESTORATION THEORY
Oswald (1966) suggests that the function of sleep, especially REM sleep, is simply to restore bodily energy reserves, repair the condition of muscles and cells and to allow growth to occur. Sleep could also allow brain neurotransmitters to replenish and aid psychological recovery.

Evaluation
For:
- Longer sleep (particularly stage 4) occurs after large amounts of physical exercise, and in growing children (REM occupies 50% of sleep in babies, 20% in adults).
- Growth hormones are released during stage 4 sleep, deprivation of which causes physical problems such as fibrositis.
- Sleep is greater after periods of stress and improves mood.

Against:
- Sleep duration is not reduced with lack of exercise.
- Deprivation of REM sleep does not produce significantly adverse effects.
- REM sleep involves an increase in energy expenditure and blood flow which *inhibits* protein synthesis.

MEMORY CONSOLIDATION THEORY
Empson and Clarke (1970) propose that sleep, especially REM sleep, facilitates the reinforcement of information in memory.

Evaluation
For:
- Subjects exposed to information before sleep remember less in the morning if deprived of REM sleep rather than non REM sleep.
- Perhaps more REM sleep occurs in younger humans because they have more to learn.

Against:
- There is little evidence against the theory, but memory consolidation can occur without sleep.

EVOLUTIONARY THEORY
All mammals sleep (the porpoise even shuts down one side of its brain at a time to do so), although the length of time varies according to the species. Given its universal nature and the fact that this unconscious and defenceless state seems a dangerous behaviour to show, sleep probably has an important evolutionary survival function, possibly to
- conserve energy when food gathering has been completed or is more difficult (e.g. at night), and/or
- avoid damage from nocturnal predators or accidents by remaining motionless.

Meddis (1975) suggests the duration of sleep a species shows depends upon its food requirements and predator avoidance needs.

Evaluation
For:
- Lions (which have few predators and meet their food needs in short bursts) and squirrels (who have safe burrows) sleep longer.
- Cattle (which have many natural predators) and shrews (which have high metabolic rates) sleep very little.

Against:
- Some evolutionary arguments suggest that animals who are highly preyed upon need to sleep little to keep constant vigilance for predators, however others suggest the opposite – that they need to sleep longer to keep them away from harm by remaining motionless.

9.7 Explanations of insomnia

WHAT IS INSOMNIA?

- Insomnia is a disruption in a person's natural sleep pattern (difficulty falling or staying asleep) and the perception of inadequate sleep quality or quantity.
- *Acute* insomnia (short duration) is common (up to a third of adults suffer in any one year).
- *Chronic* insomnia (three nights a week for a month or longer) is less common (about 10% of adults seek medical advice) and can last for years if untreated.
- Insomnia increases with age and is more common in women.
- Insomnia can be divided into primary and secondary forms.
- Insomnia has important negative effects, including:
  Affective effects - feelings of tiredness/fatigue, irritability, anxiety and depression.
  Cognitive effects - reduced alertness and ability to concentrate, learn or remember.
  Behavioural effects - lack of energy, daytime sleepiness can cause accidents.

Evaluation: The diagnosis and frequency assessment of insomnia is often made on the basis of self-reports of insufficient sleep rather than laboratory observation, but people vary significantly in their sleep needs and may underestimate their actual sleep.

- **Primary insomnia** refers to sleep disturbance that occurs without any specific underlying medical or psychiatric condition to cause it and is the most common form of insomnia.
- **Secondary insomnia** refers to sleep disturbance where a specific underlying condition can be identified as the cause, is rarer, and requires evaluation by a doctor.

PRIMARY INSOMNIA EXPLANATIONS

Learnt maladaptive sleep patterns

Primary insomnia may be produced and maintained through behavioural classical conditioning by associating:

- Alertness, active thinking, stress, anxiety, sleeplessness, etc. with
- the bed/bedroom you sleep in.

Insomnia may occur because people repeatedly work, read, watch television, think about or discuss problems, and even eat in bed, thus associating the bed with activity or stress rather than sleep.
Once insomnia occurs, it may be maintained as the bed/bedroom also becomes associated with repeated sleeplessness and anxiety about sleeplessness.

Evaluation
Stimulus control treatment of insomnia works by trying to re-associate the bed/bedroom with sleep by:
1 Only allowing the use of the bed/bedroom for sleep.
2 Only going to bed when tired.
3 Leaving the bedroom if sleep is not achieved in 20–30 minutes (then back to step two).

Poor sleep hygiene

Poor sleep habits, especially at times of stress and anxiety, can also account for primary insomnia, e.g.:

- Going to bed, napping during the day and waking up at irregular times.
- Having an uncomfortable bed and not eliminating noise and light sufficiently from the bedroom.
- Drinking stimulants (e.g. caffeine) or alcohol, eating heavy meals and exercising within 4 hours of going to sleep.

Evaluation
Improving sleep hygiene can reduce the chances of insomnia by establishing and maintaining a more stable circadian body rhythm as well as limiting internal and external sources of sleep disruption.

SECONDARY INSOMNIA EXPLANATIONS

Sleep apnea
Apnea is a sleep disorder of frequent awakening when breathing repeatedly stops (five times an hour or more) for at least 10 seconds, lowering blood oxygen levels and triggering brain activation to wake/gulp air. It is usually due to airway blockage by the muscles responsible for snoring, but is more serious - causing excessive daytime sleepiness and cardiovascular problems.

Medical and psychiatric conditions
Insomnia is commonly reported by those with chronic medical (e.g. respiratory or pain-inducing) conditions and by those with mental disorders (e.g. depression).

Restless Legs Syndrome
This is a sleep disorder caused by unpleasant night time sensations in the legs or feet and repetitive leg twitches (Periodic Leg Movements) that wake people.

Drug side effects

Many drugs can cause secondary insomnia, e.g.:

- Everyday drugs (e.g. caffeine, nicotine, alcohol),
- Illegal recreational drugs (e.g. stimulants, ecstasy),
- Psychiatric drugs (e.g. antidepressants, beta blockers),
- Medicinal drugs (e.g. decongestants, sleeping pills!).

Evaluation
- Certain secondary insomnia causes (e.g. apnea, leg movement) occur more in the elderly due to biological age changes. However, the elderly also have lighter sleep (less stage 4 deep sleep) and apnea is a possible cause of SIDS (sudden infant death syndrome).
- Apnea can be treated by Continuous Positive Airway Pressure (CPAP) – wearing a nose mask pressure splint to allow normal breathing in sleep. However, drug treatment for medical/psychiatric conditions can itself cause insomnia and most sleep medication is not effective because it produces addiction, tolerance and withdrawal effects – including 'rebound insomnia'.

9.8 Explanations of sleep disorders

NARCOLEPSY

Narcolepsy is a serious, but relatively uncommon, sleep disorder causing sudden sleep, lack of muscle control and dream experiences at inappropriate times during the day. The main symptoms are:

- Excessive daytime sleepiness – feeling tired with an overwhelming need to sleep during the day, despite a good night's sleep and situations demanding full alertness.
- Sudden and uncontrollable attacks of sleep (that can even occur during conversations or while driving) that can last from 30 seconds to 30 minutes or more.

Auxiliary symptoms can include:

- Hypnagogic hallucinations – visual dreamlike hallucinations experienced at sleep onset or on waking.
- Temporary paralysis – partial or total paralysis while awake causing an inability to move or speak.
- Cataplexy – sudden partial or total decreased muscle tone, usually triggered by an emotional event, that can cause collapse to the ground in a conscious state, risking injury.

Narcolepsy is thought to affect 1 in 10,000 people and starts in adolescence. The symptoms can be dangerous and frightening for the sufferers (and other people), and may harm their personal and professional relationships.

Explanation

Narcolepsy seems to have a biological cause relating to malfunction in the brain areas responsible for controlling sleep and wakefulness, in particular REM sleep onset. Patients with narcolepsy frequently go directly into REM periods when they sleep, without the usual initial NREM period of deep sleep, meaning they may be less rested. Worse still, the auxiliary symptoms occur when REM sleep (with its paralysis and dreaming) intrudes into wakefulness.

Evaluation

The exact cause of the REM sleep advance is not yet known, although deficiencies in the brain proteins orexin and hypocretin (which play a role in sleep patterns) and variations in chromosome 6 may be involved.

REM SLEEP BEHAVIOUR DISORDER

REM sleep behaviour disorder occurs when:

- Sleep is disrupted by complex, active or violent behaviour which can cause damage to the dreamer or those sharing the bed.
- Sleeping behaviour is associated with or reflects vivid dream thoughts and images which are recalled on waking.

It occurs most often in the middle-aged or elderly.

Explanations

The disorder represents pathology of REM sleep whereby the normal muscle paralysis of this type of sleep does not occur or is not maintained, often due to neurological diseases that are more common in older adults.

The disease may affect structures of the brainstem, e.g. the pons, responsible for suppressing muscle movement during REM sleep.

Evaluation

Laboratory observation and EEG recording may be necessary to distinguish the disorder from night terrors, panic attacks or seizures, although the recollection of dream content and the higher frequency in adults helps diagnosis.

SLEEPWALKING

Sleepwalking (somnambulism) refers to recurring episodes of complex behavioural movements, each lasting from around 15 seconds to 30 minutes, usually involving:

- Sitting up, getting out of bed and moving around while in a state of sleep. Eyes are open but unfocused allowing navigation around or outside the home and fairly complex interactions (even driving) with the environment.
- No (or partial and vague) recall of the event.

Sleepwalking may be preceded by night terrors, in which case there can be less responsiveness to external stimuli and fleeing/defence movements may be more energetic/ violent. Sleepwalking is more common in children than in adults. It is most likely to occur during the first third of the night during the first NREM period.

Explanations

Oliviero *et al.* (2008) suggest a lack of the neurotransmitter GABA (which inhibits the motor system during sleep) may be involved, since the GABA system develops slowly in childhood. Twin concordance studies show a genetic influence and sleepwalking is aggravated by stress and certain medications. In the elderly sleepwalking is more often due to waking disorientation caused by dementia.

Evaluation

EEG monitoring confirms that sleep is maintained throughout sleepwalking, which occurs during the deep, delta slow-wave, stages 3 and 4 of NREM sleep.

SLEEP TERRORS

Sleep terrors (pavor nocturnes) are sleep disturbances when:

- Moaning and/or thrashing may occur, followed by screams, a terrified appearance and agitation lasting several minutes – all often without full wakefulness.
- Signs of sympathetic nervous system over-activity occur, including accelerated heart and breathing rate, pupil dilation, sweating, and increased blood pressure.
- There is complete amnesia or only partial recall (e.g. vague memories of threat or danger) of the event.

Like sleepwalking, sleep terrors occur early in the night and are most common in children (up to 5% may suffer, though this decreases during adolescence).

Explanations

Sleep terrors in childhood can be triggered by emotional stress, over-tiredness or disruption to normal sleep rhythms affecting an underdeveloped sleep system. In adults, post traumatic stress disorder may be implicated.

Evaluation

EEG monitoring confirms that sleep terrors usually occur during stages 3 and 4 of NREM sleep.

Sleep terrors can be distinguished from nightmares by the occurrence of amnesia for the event.

Sleep terrors may overlap with sleepwalking, implying a possible link in the brain processes involved, but further research is needed.

10.1 Types of memory

ENCODING TYPES OF MEMORY

The human sensory systems, such as our eyes and ears, receive many different forms of stimulation, ranging from sound waves to photons of light. Obviously the information reaching our senses is transformed in nature when it is represented in our brains, and encoding refers to the process of representing knowledge in different forms.

Imagery memory

- Some memory representations appear to closely resemble the raw, unabstracted data containing original material from our senses, such as the extremely brief iconic (visual) and echoic (auditory) after images that rapidly fade from our eyes and ears. Yet even after these have gone, we retain the ability to recall fairly vivid visual images of what we have seen and to hear again tunes we have experienced.
- Baddeley and Hitch (1974) have investigated this sort of short term imagery ability by suggesting that we have a 'visuospatial scratchpad' for summoning up and examining our visual imagery.
- Photographic (eidetic) memory is an extremely rare ultra enhanced form of imagery memory, shown in a weak form by perhaps 5% of young children (Haber, 1979).

Procedural memory

- Also known as implicit memory, this is the memory for **knowing how** to do things such as talk, walk, juggle, etc. Although we retain these skills and abilities, we are often completely **unable to consciously introspect upon or describe** how we do them. Procedural memory is similar to Bruner's enactive mode.
- Procedural knowledge is very resistant to forgetting (we never forget how to ride a bicycle) and is also resistant to brain damage that eradicates other forms of memory – anterograde amnesiac patients, who forget simple events or verbal instructions after a few moments, are often able to learn new procedural skills such as playing table-tennis.

Declarative memory

- Sometimes termed explicit memory, this type concerns all the information that we can **describe or report**, and as such has been the focus of the *majority* of research on memory. Declarative memory includes:
  - **a semantic memory** – this concerns memory for meaning, the storage of abstract, general facts regardless of when those facts were acquired e.g. *knowing what* a word means.
  - **b episodic** – this is 'knowing when' memory based upon personal experience and linked to a particular time and place in our lives. Episodic memory can be quite precise – Lindsay and Norman (1977) asked students "what were you doing on a Monday afternoon in the 3rd week of September, 2 years ago?", and found many actually knew. Very vivid episodic memories have been termed 'flashbulb' memories (Brown and Kulik, 1977) which involve recalling exactly what you were doing and where you were when a particularly important, exciting or emotional event happened.

DURATION TYPES OF MEMORY

Ever since William James (1890) distinguished between *primary* memory which feels like our present conscious experience, and *secondary* memory which seems like we are 'fishing out' information from the past, cognitive psychologists have been very interested in the possibility of different types of memory store based on the duration of time memories last for. Cognitive psychologists have proposed **three types** of time based store, each with differences in duration, capacity, coding and function.

Sensory memory

(Sometimes called the short term sensory store or sensory register.)

- The sense organs have a limited ability to store information about the world in a fairly unprocessed way for less than a second, rather like an afterimage. The visual system possesses **iconic** memory for visual stimuli such as shape, size, colour and location (but not meaning), whereas the hearing system has **echoic** memory for auditory stimuli.
- Coltheart *et al.* (1974) have argued that the momentary freezing of visual input allows us to select which aspects of the input should go on for further memory processing. The existence of sensory memory has been experimentally demonstrated by Sperling (1960) using a tachistoscope.

Short-term memory

- Information selected by attention from sensory memory, may pass into short-term memory (STM).
- STM allows us to retain information long enough to **use** it, e.g. looking up a telephone number and remembering it long enough to dial it. Peterson and Peterson (1959) have demonstrated that STM lasts approximately **between 15 and 30 seconds,** unless people rehearse the material, while Miller (1956) has found that STM has a **limited capacity** of around **7 'chunks'** of information.
- STM also appears to mostly **encode** memory **acoustically** (in terms of sound) as Conrad (1964) has demonstrated, but can also retain visuospatial images.

Long-term memory

- Long-term memory provides the lasting retention of information and skills, from **minutes** to a **lifetime.**
- Long-term memory appears to have an almost **limitless capacity** to retain information, but of course its capacity could never be measured – it would take too long!
- Long-term information seems to be encoded mainly in terms of **meaning** (semantic memory), as Baddeley has shown, but also retains procedural skills and imagery.

10.2 Research on sensory memory, short-term and long-term memory

SENSORY MEMORY

- Since sensory memory lasts less than a second, most of the material in it will have been forgotten before it can be reported! *Sperling* studied the sensory memory for vision (the iconic store) by using a **tachistoscope** – a device that can flash pictoral stimuli onto a blank screen for very brief instances. Using this device, Sperling was able to ask subjects to remember as many letters as they could from a **grid of 12 symbols** that he was going to display for just **one twentieth of a second**, and found that while they could only recall around **four** of the symbols before the grid faded from their sensory memory, they typically reported seeing a lot more than they had time to report.
- **Capacity** – Sperling presented the 12 symbol grid for 1/20th of a second, followed immediately by a **high, medium** or **low tone,** which indicated which of the three rows of four symbols the subject had to attend to from their iconic memory of the grid. In this partial report condition, recall was on average just over 3 out of the 4 symbols from any row they attended to, suggesting that the iconic store can retain **approximately 76%** of all the data received.

Step 1 Show grid	Step 2 Ring tone	Step 3 Recall letters
7 1 V F		? ? ? ?
X L 5 3	Medium tone	X L 5 3
B 4 W 7		? ? ? ?

- **Duration** – If there was a delay between the presentation of the grid and the sounding of the tone, Sperling found that more and more information was lost (only 50% was available after a 0.3 second delay and only 33% was available after a 1 second delay).

SHORT-TERM MEMORY

- **Duration** – Peterson and Peterson (1959) investigated the duration of short-term memory with their **trigram experiment**. They achieved this by
  1 asking subjects to remember a single nonsense syllable of three consonants (a *trigram* of letters such as FJT or KPD).
  2 giving them an *interpolated task* to stop them rehearsing the trigram (such as counting backwards in threes from one hundred).
  3 testing their *recall after* 3, 6, 9, 12, 15 or 18 seconds (recall had to be perfect and in the correct order to count). While average recall was very good (about 80%) after 3 seconds, this average dropped dramatically to around 10% after 18 seconds.

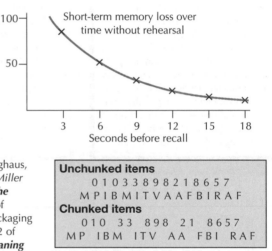
Short-term memory loss over time without rehearsal (% recall vs Seconds before recall: 3, 6, 9, 12, 15, 18)

- **Capacity** – Many early researchers in the area of memory, including Ebbinghaus, noted that short term memory appears to have a limited storage capacity. *Miller* (1956) investigated this limited capacity experimentally, refering to it as '**The magical number seven, plus or minus two'**. Miller found that the amount of information retained could be increased by **chunking** the information – packaging it into larger items or units, although the STM can still only retain 7 + or – 2 of these chunks. Chunking is greatly improved if the chunks already have **meaning** from LTM.

Unchunked items
0 1 0 3 3 8 9 8 2 1 8 6 5 7
M P I B M I T V A A F B I R A F
Chunked items
0 1 0   3 3   8 9 8   2 1   8 6 5 7
M P   I B M   I T V   A A   F B I   R A F

- **Encoding** – It has been argued that the main way information is encoded or retained in STM is through sound – an **acoustic code**. Regardless of whether we see or hear material, we tend to find ourselves repeating the information verbally to ourselves to keep it in mind (STM), and hopefully pass it on to long term storage. Conrad (1964) demonstrated acoustic STM encoding, finding that rhyming letters were significantly harder to recall properly than non rhyming letters, mostly due to acoustic confusion errors, e.g. recalling 'B' instead of 'P'. Baddeley found similar effects for rhyming vs. non-rhyming words.
Den Heyer and Barrett (1971) showed that STM stores visual information too.

1) **B T C P G E D**
2) **F T Z Q W R N**
3) **MAT, CAT, SAT, BAT, HAT, RAT, FAT**
4) **PIE, SIX, TRY, BIG, GUN, HEN, MAN**

Acoustic confusion errors are made when recalling lists 1 & 3, even though the letters are visually presented. This shows the material is retained acoustically in STM.

LONG-TERM MEMORY

- **Duration** – Ebbinghaus tested his memory using nonsense syllables after delays ranging from 20 minutes to 31 days later and found that a large proportion of information in LTM was lost comparatively quickly (within the first hour) and thereafter stabilised to a much slower rate of loss.
Linton used a diary to record at least 2 'every day' events from her life each day over 6 years, and randomly tested her later recall of them. She found a much more even and gradual loss of data over time (approx. 6 % per year).
- **Capacity** – Enormous but impossible to measure.
- **Encoding** – Baddeley (1966) showed that LTM stores information in terms of meaning (semantic memory), by giving subjects four lists to remember.
If recall was given immediately, list A was recalled worse than list B, but there was little difference between the recall of lists C and D, indicating acoustic STM encoding.
After 20 minutes, however, it was list C that was recalled worse than D since words with similar meanings were confused, indicating semantic LTM encoding.

Baddeley's (1966) lists:

List A – Similar sounding words
e.g. man, map, can, cap.

List B – Non similar sounding words
e.g. try, pig, hut, pen.

List C – Similar meaning words
e.g. great, big, huge, wide.

List D – Non similar meaning words
e.g. run, easy, bright.

10.3 Multi-store model of memory

- Much research was devoted to identifying the properties of sensory, short-term, and long-term memory, and cognitive psychologists such as Atkinson and Shiffrin (1968) began to regard them as *stores* – hypothetical holding structures.
- Atkinson and Shiffrin proposed the two-process model of memory, which showed how information flowed through the two stores of short-term and long-term memory, but like many of the models, they assumed the existence of a sensory memory that precedes the short-term memory, and so it is sometimes termed the multi-store model.

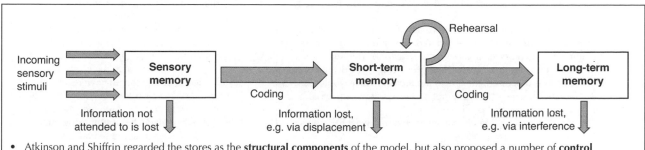

- Atkinson and Shiffrin regarded the stores as the **structural components** of the model, but also proposed a number of **control processes,** such as attention, coding and rehearsal, which operate in conjunction with the stores.

In addition to the research on the differing durations, capacities, etc. of the memory stores there are two main lines of evidence that support the model's assumptions about the way information flows through the system and the distinct existence of short-term and long-term memory stores – free recall experiments and studies of brain damaged patients.

FREE RECALL EXPERIMENTS

- In free recall experiments, subjects are given a number of words (for example 20) in succession to remember and are then asked to recall them in any order ('free recall'). The results reliably fall into a pattern known as the **serial position curve**. This curve consists of

  a **primacy effect** – Subjects tend to recall the first words of the list well, which indicates that the first words entered short-term memory and had time to be rehearsed and passed on to long-term memory before the STM capacity was reached. The primacy effect, therefore, involves recall from long-term memory.

  b an **asymptote** – The middle portion items of the list are remembered far less well than those at the beginning and the end. This is probably because the increasing number of items fills the limited capacity of the STM and these later items are unable to be properly rehearsed and transferred to LTM before they are displaced.

  c a **recency effect** – Subjects usually recall those items from the end of the list first, and tend to get more of these correct on average than all the earlier items. This effect persists even if the list is lengthened (Murdock, 1962), and is thought to be due to recall from the short-term memory store – since the items at the end of the list were the last to enter STM and were not displaced by further items.

- Further evidence for the primacy/recency effects comes from two other findings:

  a Slower rates of presentation can improve the primacy effect perhaps due to more rehearsal time, but have little or no influence on the recency effect.

  b The recency effect disappears if the last words are not recalled straight away. Glanzer and Cunitz (1966) gave subjects an interference task immediately after the last word of the list and found a primacy but no recency effect.

STUDIES OF BRAIN DAMAGED PATIENTS

Cases of **anterograde amnesia** such as H.M. (Milner *et al.*, 1978) or Clive Wearing (reported in Blakemore, 1988) provide strong evidence for the distinction between STM and LTM. Anterograde amnesia is often caused by brain damage to the hippocampus and those suffering from it seem incapable of transferring new factual information between STM and LTM. With this inability, they are essentially trapped in a world of experience that only lasts as long as their short-term memory does. Patients afflicted by anterograde amnesia often retain most of their long term memory for events up until the moment of brain damage and maintain their procedural memories. While they seem incapable of gaining new long-term declarative memory for semantic or episodic information most are able to learn new procedural skills (like playing table-tennis).

If these people are given free recall experiments, they show good recency effects but extremely poor primacy effects (Baddeley and Warrington, 1970).

CRITICISMS OF THE MULTI-STORE MODEL

It is too simplistic, in that:

a It under-emphasises interaction between the stores, for example the way information from LTM influences what is regarded as important and relevant to show attention to in sensory memory and helps the meaningful chunking of information in STM.

b STM and LTM are more complex and less unitary than the model assumes. This criticism is dealt with by the Working Memory model of STM by Baddeley and Hitch (1974) and by research into the semantic, episodic, imagery and procedural encoding of LTM.

c Mere rehearsal is too simple a process to account for the transfer of information from STM to LTM – the model ignores factors such as the effort and strategy subjects may use when learning (**elaborative** rehearsal leads to better recall than just maintenance rehearsal) and the model does not account for the type of information taken into memory (some items, e.g. distinctive ones, seem to flow into LTM far more readily than others). These criticisms are dealt with by the Levels of Processing approach of Craik and Lockhart (1972).

10.4 Levels of processing and working memory

LEVELS OF PROCESSING APPROACH TO MEMORY – CRAIK AND LOCKHART (1972)

THE APPROACH

- Craik and Lockhart's important article countered the predominant view of fixed memory **stores**, arguing that it is what the person **does** with information when it is received, i.e. how much attention is paid to it or how deeply it is considered, that determines how long the memory lasts.
- They suggested that information is more readily transferred to LTM if it is *considered*, *understood* and related to past memories to gain *meaning* than if it is merely *repeated* (maintenance rehearsal). This degree of consideration was termed the '**depth of processing**' – the deeper information was processed, the longer the *memory trace* would last.
- Craik and Lockhart gave three examples of **levels** at which verbal information could be processed:
  1 **Structural** level – e.g. merely paying attention to what the words *look* like (very shallow processing).
  2 **Phonetic** level – processing the *sound* of the words.
  3 **Semantic** level – considering the **meaning** of words (deep processing).

EVIDENCE

- Craik and Tulving (1975) tested the effect of depth of processing on memory by giving subjects words with questions that required different levels of processing, e.g.
  'table'
  Structural – 'Is the word in capital letters?'
  Phonetic – 'Does it rhyme with "able"?'
  Semantic – 'Does it fit in the sentence "the man sat at the _____"?'
- Subjects thought that they were just being tested on reaction speed to answer yes or no to each question, but when they were given an unexpected test of recognition words processed at the semantic level were recognised more often than those processed phonetically and structurally.

MODIFICATIONS

Many researchers became interested in exactly what produced **deep** processing:

- **Elaboration** – Craik and Tulving (1975) found complex semantic processing (e.g. 'The great bird swooped down and carried off the struggling __') produced better cued recall than simple semantic processing (e.g. 'She cooked the ___').
- **Distinctiveness** – Eysenck and Eysenck (1980) found even words processed phonetically were better recalled if they were distinctive or unusual.
- **Effort** – Tyler *et al.* (1979) found better recall for words presented as difficult anagrams (e.g. 'OCDTRO') than simple anagrams (e.g. 'DOCTRO').
- **Personal relevance** – Rogers *et al.* (1977) found better recall for personal relevance questions (e.g. 'Describes you?') than general semantic ones (e.g. 'Means?').

EVALUATION

- **Strengths** – good contribution to understanding the processes that take place at the time of learning.
- **Weaknesses** – There are many problems with defining 'deep' processing and why it is effective.
- Semantic processing does not always lead to better retrieval (Morris *et al.*, 1977).
- It describes rather than explains.

THE WORKING MEMORY MODEL – BADDELEY AND HITCH (1974)

THE MODEL (AS OF 1999)

The working memory model challenged the unitary and passive view of the multi-store model's short-term memory store.

Working memory is an **active** store to hold and manipulate information that is currently being consciously thought about. It consists of 3 separate **components:**

- **The central executive** – a modality-free controlling attentional mechanism with a limited capacity, which monitors and co-ordinates the operation of the other two components or slave systems.
- **The phonological loop** – which itself consists of two subsystems,
  a The *articulatory control system* or 'inner voice' which is a verbal rehearsal system with a time-based capacity. It holds information by articulating sub-vocally material we want to maintain or are preparing to speak.
  b The *phonological store* or 'inner ear' which holds speech in a phonological memory trace that lasts 1.5 to 2 seconds if it does not refresh itself via the articulatory control system. It can also receive information directly from the sensory register (echoic) or from long-term memory.
- **The visuospatial sketchpad** – a visual cache that holds visual and spatial information from the sensory register (iconic) or LTM and an inner scribe.

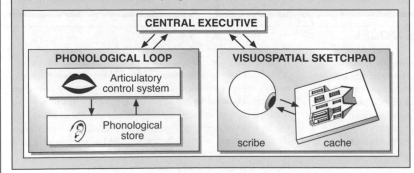

EVIDENCE

- The existence of separate systems in working memory has been shown experimentally by using concurrent tasks (performing two tasks at the same time) – if one task interferes with the other, then they are probably using the same component.
- Thus, if articulatory suppression (continually repeating a word) uses up the phonological loop, another task involving reading and checking a difficult text would be interfered with, but not a spatial task.

EVALUATION

- Working memory provides a more thorough explanation of storage and processing than the multi-store model's STM.
- It can be applied to reading, mental arithmetic and verbal reasoning.
- It explains many STM deficits shown by brain-damaged patients.
- However, the nature and role of the central executive is still unclear.

10.5 Reconstructive memory

WHAT IS THE RECONSTRUCTIVE APPROACH TO MEMORY?

- In contrast to much cognitive research on memory, which focuses on quantitative tests of how many randomly selected digits, words or nonsense syllables can be remembered under strictly controlled conditions, the reconstructive memory approach has tended to concentrate more on *qualitative changes* in what is remembered, often of more *everyday material* such as stories, pictures or witnessed events under more *natural conditions*.
- The pioneer of reconstructive memory research was **Bartlett** (1932) who argued that people do not passively record memories as exact copies of new information they receive, but *actively* try and *make sense* of it *in terms of what they already know* – a process he called *'effort after meaning'*. Bartlett therefore proposed that information may be remembered in a distorted way since memories are essentially 'imaginative reconstructions' of the original information in the light of each individual's past experiences and expectations; rather than remembering what actually happened we may remember what we think should or could have occurred. Bartlett termed the mental structures, that held past experiences and expectations and could influence memory so much, **schemas**.

SCHEMA THEORY

More recent research by cognitive psychologists in the 1970's aimed to specify in more detail the properties of schemas and how they affect memory. Rumelhart and Norman (1983), for example, described how schemas:

1 *represent* both simple and complex *knowledge of all kinds* (e.g. semantic, procedural, etc.)
2 *link together* to form larger systems of related schemas (e.g. a restaurant schema links to other 'eating location' schemas) or smaller systems of sub-schemas (e.g. a restaurant schema consists of sub-schemas of ordering, eating and paying schemas)
3 have slots with *fixed values* (defining, unchangeable characteristics), *optional values* (characteristics that may vary according to the specific memory the schema is storing) and *default values* (the most typical or probable characteristic a schema is likely to encounter)
4 acquire their content through generalised personal *experience* or the taught beliefs and stereotypes of a group or society.
5 operate as *active recognition devices* – all schemas constantly try to make sense of new information by making the best fit with it.

An example of a picnic schema is given by Cohen (1993) below. Notice that if the food eaten at a particular picnic was forgotten, then it may be assumed that sandwiches were eaten by default. Cohen also points out five ways in which schemas may influence memory – by providing or aiding selection and storage, abstraction, integration and interpretation, normalisation and retrieval. These properties mean that there are both advantages and disadvantages of schemas for memory:

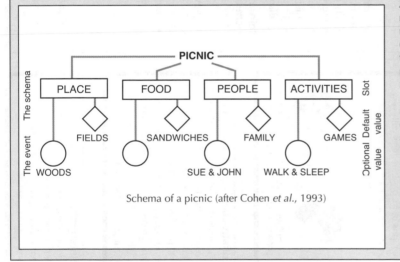

Schema of a picnic (after Cohen *et al.*, 1993)

Advantages – schemas enable us to store the central meaning or gist of new information without necessarily remembering the precise details (abstraction, selection and storage), unless perhaps the details were particularly unusual. This saves memory resources. Schemas also help us understand new information more readily (integration and interpretation, normalisation) and fill in or guess missing aspects of it through the default values (retrieval). This makes the world more coherent and predictable.

Disadvantages – information that does not quite fit our schemas, especially the minor details, may be ignored and forgotten (selection and storage) or distorted (normalisation) so as to make better sense to us, while the guesses/filling-in of memory by the default values (integration and interpretation, retrieval) may be completely inaccurate. This may cause inaccurate, stereotyped and prejudiced remembering.

EVIDENCE FOR SCHEMAS RECONSTRUCTING MEMORY

- Bartlett (1932) found strong evidence for reconstructive memory by asking people to reproduce stories and pictures either serially (by remembering another person's reproduction) or by testing the same person on a number of occasions. When testing English subjects with an unfamiliar North American folk story, 'The War of the Ghosts', Bartlett found their recall became shorter (indicating the gist of the story had been removed) and also distorted by their culture (they omitted unfamiliar details and 'rationalised' the story to make it more coherent and familiar, e.g. recalling the ghosts in 'boats' not 'canoes').
- Brewer and Treyens (1981) tested memory for objects in an office that 30 subjects had waited in individually for 35 seconds. Their 'office schema' seemed to strongly affect their recall. *Expected* objects (e.g. a desk) that were in the room were recalled well but *unexpected* objects (e.g. a pair of pliers) were usually not. Some subjects *falsely* recalled *expected* objects that were not actually in the room (e.g. books and pens).
- Bransford and Johnson (1972, 1973) showed how schemas help to encode and store difficult to understand or ambiguous information.

EVALUATION OF RECONSTRUCTIVE MEMORY

- Bartlett's original research was more ecologically valid than most, but was criticised for its informal nature and lack of experimental controls. However, many recent and well-controlled experiments have consistently shown the reconstructive effect of schemas on memory.
- Bartlett and other reconstructive memory researchers have been accused of over-emphasising the inaccuracy of memory and using unfamiliar material to support the reconstructive effect of schemas on memory. Even quite complex real life material can often be accurately recalled.
- Often unusual information that cannot be easily incorporated into existing schemas (like a skull in the office of the Brewer and Treyens study) is well remembered. This distinctiveness effect has long been noticed and can be accounted for by the schema-plus-tag model of Graesser and Nakamure (1982).
- The concept of a schema and its action is still a little vague.

10.6 Retrieval and forgetting

TYPES OF RETRIEVAL

There are many ways that information may be either retrieved from long-term storage or demonstrate its existence in storage in a less direct manner. Some types are more powerful and accurate than others:

Recall – This involves the active searching of our memory with very few external memory cues, e.g. recalling a list of previously memorised digits or the timed essay situation (we have the question but have to search for the answer).

Memorise   Recall

Recognition – This involves a sense of familiarity with external material whether we can name/identify it or not, for example recognising a face or the correct answer in a multiple choice. In recognition, the material to be retrieved is matched to its external likeness. Recognition is an extremely powerful form of retrieval compared to recall – Standing (1973) showed that subjects in a memory test could correctly identify 10,000 previously presented photographs in recognition tests with very low error rates and little sign of an upper boundary for its capacity.

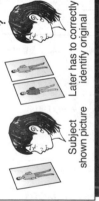

Subject   Later has to correctly
shown picture   identify original

Re-learning – This involves not necessarily being able to recall or even recognise previously presented material, but being better able to re-learn it on later occasions. Ebbinghaus investigated this type of retrieval and found that there were re-learning savings (it took less time to re-learn material perfectly the more times the list was re-learnt). An everyday example could be re-learning a language that you have not studied for years – you may be unable to recall or even recognise some of the words you had previously learnt, but it would take you less time to re-learn them compared to other, unexperienced words.

Reconstruction – This involves retrieval that has **distorted** the original information due to our interpretation of it – based upon our past experiences, beliefs, schemas and stereotypes. Bartlett's subjects not only remembered less of the 'War of the Ghosts' story he presented them, but distorted the story when retelling it by making it more coherent and westernised.

Redintegration – This is where patchy details of an experience will pop into consciousness regardless of what is currently thought about and gradually become more coherent.

Confabulation – This involves the usually unintentional **manufacture** or invention of material to fill in missing details during retrieval. The material added often serves the purpose of making the story more coherent and is likely to occur under conditions of high motivation or emotion.

PROBLEMS WITH RETRIEVAL (FORGETTING)

When considering theories of forgetting it is useful to distinguish between the concepts of availability and accessibility.

Availability of memory refers to whether the material is actually there to be retrieved – it is not possible to retrieve what has not reached/lasted in long-term storage.

Accessibility of memory refers to the problems involved in retrieving available information – the tip of the tongue phenomena illustrates this type of difficulty.

There is however a **'grey area'** of ambiguity between these two concepts since we can never be 100% sure that what we have forgotten is unavailable – we may not have found the correct memory cue to 'jog our memory', and what cannot be directly recalled or recognised may still exist as a memory trace to aid re-learning.

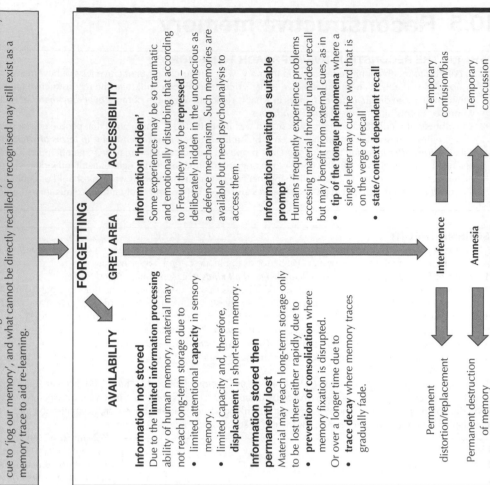

FORGETTING

AVAILABILITY

Information not stored
Due to the **limited information processing** ability of human memory, material may not reach long-term storage due to
- limited attentional **capacity** in sensory memory.
- limited capacity and, therefore, **displacement** in short-term memory.

Information stored then permanently lost
Material may reach long-term storage only to be lost there either rapidly due to
- **prevention of consolidation** where memory fixation is disrupted.
Or over a longer time due to
- **trace decay** where memory traces gradually fade.

GREY AREA

ACCESSIBILITY

Information 'hidden'
Some experiences may be so traumatic and emotionally disturbing that according to Freud they may be **repressed** – deliberately hidden in the unconscious as a defence mechanism. Such memories are available but need psychoanalysis to access them.

Information awaiting a suitable prompt
Humans frequently experience problems accessing material through unaided recall but may benefit from external cues, as in
- **tip of the tongue phenomena** where a single letter may cue the word that is on the verge of recall
- **state/context dependent recall**

Interference

Permanent distortion/replacement

Temporary confusion/bias

Amnesia

Permanent destruction of memory

Temporary concussion

10.7 Forgetting in short-term memory

Short-term memory contains information that is present in our minds and is currently being thought about at any one time, but which soon slips into the past – hopefully to long-term memory so that we can access it again.

Peterson and Peterson (1959) found 90% of STM information was forgotten after just 18 seconds without rehearsal, while memory span studies reveal that forgetting starts once more than 7+/- 2 items enter STM.

We have all been caught out by STM forgetting, e.g. when we forget some of the names of a large group of people we have only just been introduced to, or forget what we were about to say or do next. Cognitive psychologists have provided theoretical explanations of STM's limited duration and capacity.

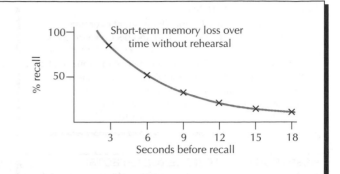

TRACE DECAY THEORY

- Trace decay theory seems to focus on explaining STM forgetting in terms of its limited duration.
- Donald Hebb (1949) suggested that information in STM created an active trace or engram in the form of a brief excitation of nerve cells that, unless refreshed by rehearsal, would spontaneously fade away or decay over time.
- Peterson and Peterson originally argued that the forgetting they found over their 3 to 18 second time delays occurred through trace decay.

Evaluation

- Pure trace decay is very difficult to test. Ideally no new information should be presented in the time between when the trace is acquired and when it is recalled to prevent confounding variables like displacement, yet Peterson and Peterson asked subjects to count backwards to stop them rehearsing.
- Reitman (1974) asked subjects to detect tones between presenting and recalling information, thinking this would hopefully prevent rehearsal without providing any new displacing material. Only about a quarter of information was forgotten after a 15 second delay which was more likely to be due to spontaneous trace decay than the Petersons' result.
- Baddeley and Scott (1971) concluded that 'something like trace decay occurs in the Peterson task, but is complete within five seconds, and is certainly not sufficiently large to explain the substantial forgetting that occurs in the standard paradigm' (quoted from Baddeley, 1997).

DISPLACEMENT THEORY

- Displacement theory seems to focus on explaining STM forgetting in terms of its limited capacity.
- Miller (1956) argued that the capacity of STM is approximately 7+/- 2 items of information. Despite the fact that these items can be chunked to increase their capacity, displacement theory suggests that there are only a fixed number of 'slots' for such information and that once they are full (capacity is reached) new information will push out or displace old material (which may be lost unless it was processed sufficiently to pass into LTM).
- In Peterson and Peterson's experiment, therefore, the increase of forgetting over time may have been a result of the counting backwards task increasingly displacing the original trigrams.

Evaluation

- Waugh and Norman (1965) used the **serial probe technique** where 16 digits are rapidly presented to subjects who are then given one of those digits (the probe) and have to report the digit which followed it. It was found that the nearer the end of the 16 digit sequence the probe was presented, the better was the recall of the following digit. This seems to support displacement theory since digits nearer the end of the sequence have fewer following digits to displace them.

> Order of Sequence presented **3 7 2 9 0 4 5 6 3 1 9 0 7 8 2 6**
>
> If probe = 8 then recall of digit (2) is good (little displacement)
> If probe = 4 then recall of digit (5) is poor (greater displacement)

- The poorer recall (asymptote) shown in the middle of the serial position curve that results from free recall studies could similarly be attributed to displacement.

EVALUATION OF STM THEORIES OF FORGETTING

- In some of the research it is unclear what the relative influences of displacement and trace decay are on STM forgetting. Researchers such as Shallice (1967) have found that presenting digits at faster speeds in serial probe tests increases the ability to recall the digits presented earlier in the sequence. Thus trace decay may be responsible for some of the STM forgetting, since the faster presentation means the digits nearer the beginning of the sequence have less time to decay before being tested.
- It is also unclear how distinct the concepts of displacement and trace decay really are. For example displacement in STM works on the assumption that it has a limited capacity, which is measured in terms of memory span (usually 7+/-2 items or chunks). However Baddeley et al (1975) have shown that fewer words can be retained in STM if they take *longer* to pronounce. It seems STM capacity for words depends on the *duration* of pronunciation (how long it takes to say them) rather than the *number* of meaningfully chunked items – in this case words.
- Finally it is also unclear what is actually happening in trace decay and displacement to cause the forgetting. Is the trace really fading or, because it is so fragile, is it being degraded by other incoming information? Similarly with displacement, is the new material nudging aside, overwriting or distracting attention from the old material (or just making it harder to discriminate)? While **interference theory** has some of the same kinds of questions to answer, it has been more successful in explaining STM forgetting by showing how the **similarity** of competing information from the interpolated task used (as well as from previous trials) can affect the recall of the Petersons' trigrams (see interference theory).

10.8 Forgetting in long-term memory

INTERFERENCE THEORY
- One explanation of LTM forgetting is that over time more and more material will be stored and become confused together.
- Interference is most likely to occur between similar material.
- **Proactive interference** is where material learnt first interferes with material learnt later.
- **Retroactive interference** is where material learnt at a later time interferes with material learnt earlier.

OLD MATERIAL	PROACTIVE INTERFERENCE →	NEW MATERIAL
	← RETROACTIVE INTERFERENCE	

RESEARCH ON INTERFERENCE EFFECTS
- *Proactive interference* – Underwood (1957) found that the more nonsense syllable lists his students had previously learned, the greater their forgetting of new nonsense syllables was after a 24 hour delay. This was because the new nonsense syllables became increasingly confused with those from the old lists. Wickens *et al.* (1963) found subjects could be released from proactive interference effects by changing the nature (and thus reducing the similarity) of the new items to be learned, e.g. from nonsense syllables to numbers.
- *Retroactive interference* – McGeoch and Macdonald (1931) presented subjects who had learnt a list of words with various types of interference list to learn for ten minutes afterwards. Recall of the original words was then tested and those students given an interference list of *similar meaning* words recalled on average far less (12.5%) than those given unrelated words (21.7%) or nonsense syllables (25.8%). Best recall (45%) was gained for subjects who were given no interference test at all.

EVALUATION
1. **Artificiality** – Some of the research has been conducted using nonsense syllables often learned under artificially compressed laboratory conditions (rather than the more everyday distributed learning over time) and so interference theory has declined in popularity as an explanation of forgetting. However, many interference studies have been conducted with greater ecological validity, e.g. Baddeley and Hitch (1977) found rugby players' forgetting of the names of teams they had played depended more on interference from the number of rugby matches played since than on the passage of time.
2. **Applications** – Release from proactive interference has been applied by Gunter *et al.* (1981) to increase recall of news items by ensuring dissimilar items followed each other. Retroactive interference has been applied, e.g. by Loftus, to understand the effect of post-event information such as leading questions on the recall of eyewitness testimony.
3. **Reason for interference** – Some believe interference occurs when information is unlearned (Underwood, 1957) or overwritten (Loftus, 1979) by other information. Tulving however, argues that interference of retrieval cues rather than stored material is responsible. Tulving and Pstoka (1971) found that the retroactive interference effect on a word list disappeared if cues (e.g. category headings of the words) were given for it.

CUE DEPENDENT RETRIEVAL FAILURE
Information may be *available* to recall but *temporarily inaccessible*, for example:
- Tulving (1968) found that different items from a list might be recalled if people are tested on it on three separate occasions, probably because of the different cues present in each test.
- The tip of the tongue phenomenon. Brown and McNeill (1966) induced this 'state in which one cannot quite recall a familiar word' by reading definitions of infrequently encountered words and found the first letter and number of syllables could be identified before complete recall.

Memory **cues** or **prompts** may therefore be necessary to access information.

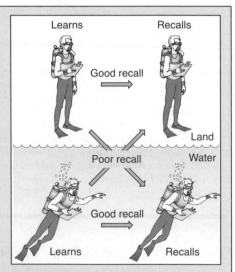

WHAT CUES AID RETRIEVAL?
Much research has investigated the type of cues that, depending upon their presence or absence, will determine retrieval failure.
- Tulving and Pearlstone (1966) studied intrinsic cues (those meaningfully related to the material to be remembered) by asking subjects to memorise lists of words from different categories. Subjects given the category headings as retrieval cues recalled more of the words than those who were not. Tulving proposed the *encoding specificity principle* to account for this – items committed to memory are encoded with the precise semantic context present at the time of learning.

Evaluation – Thomson and Tulving (1970) confirmed this, but later research found cues not around at the time of learning can help too.
- **Context-dependent forgetting** is caused by the absence of *external* environmental cues that were present at the time of learning. Godden and Baddeley (1975) asked divers to learn word lists either on land or under water and found they recalled about 40% less in the opposite environmental context than in the same one. However, no effect was seen if a recognition test was used.
  Smith (1979) found more forgetting occurred a day later if subjects who had learnt 80 words in a distinctive basement room were then asked to recall them in a very differently furnished 5th floor room (12 words) compared to the original room (18 words). Interestingly, almost as many words were recalled (17.2) by a third group who sat in the 5th floor room but were asked to remember as much as they could about the basement room before recall.

Evaluation – Differences in environmental contexts have to be quite large before they significantly affect memory. However, imaginative context recreation can be applied to improve recall in eye-witness testimony.
- **State-dependent forgetting** is caused by the absence of *internal* bodily cues that were experienced at the time of learning.
  Bower (1981) found that his subjects recalled more memories learnt when sad if he tested them when hypnotised to be in a sad mood than a happy one. State-dependent effects have been found for alcohol (Goodwin et al, 1969) and other state-altering substances.

Evaluation – However, true state-dependent memory involving mood has not always been found for emotionally neutral information.

10.9 The role of emotion in forgetting

What effect do emotions have on forgetting?
Cognitive psychologists have sometimes neglected emotions in their models of memory, perhaps because of their focus on the information processing comparison with computers – who do not have them (yet!). However two concepts, repression and flashbulb memory, have created interest in the effect of emotion on memory – the first suggesting it could increase forgetting, the second that it could prevent it. Cognitive psychologists have tried to use their theories (e.g. of rehearsal, interference and cue dependency) to explain such emotional effects.

REPRESSION

- Repression is a concept from **psychodynamic** psychology which focuses heavily on emotion. Freud proposed that forgetting is **motivated** by the desire to **avoid displeasure**, so embarrassing, unpleasant or anxiety-producing experiences are repressed – pushed down into the **unconscious**.
- Repression is a protective **defence mechanism** that involves the ego actively blocking the conscious recall of memories – which become **inaccessible**. Direct recall attempts will either fail, lead to distorted recall or digression from the topic. Psychoanalytic techniques, such as dream interpretation, free association etc., are necessary to access repressed memories.
- Freud argued that repression was the most important of defence mechanisms and that it not only accounted for his patients' anxiety disorders (the result of repressing more traumatic experiences) but was a common cause of everyday forgetting.

Evaluation

- Theoretically, forgetting more unpleasant than pleasant memories could just mean that people rehearse upsetting material less because they do not want to think, or talk to others, about it. It is also difficult to tell to what extent the repressor chooses not to search their memory or is unable to.
- Experimental evidence is difficult to gather due to the ethical problems of probing for traumatic memories or creating them by exposing subjects to unpleasant, anxiety-provoking experiences.
- Those studies that have been conducted show mixed results and, where negative emotions have been found to increase forgetting, there has been debate over the cause – emotion can affect memory without the need for an ego.
- Mild anxiety has been produced in the laboratory by giving false 'failure feedback', which does impair memory. However rather than causing repression, Holmes (1990) argues that it causes people to think about the failure which distracts attention away from the memory test (**interference theory**), since giving 'success feedback' also impairs recall.
- Higher anxiety was produced by Loftus and Burns (1982) who showed two groups a film of a bank robbery, but exposed one of the groups to a far more violent version where a young boy was shot in the face. The group that saw this version later showed far poorer recall of detail than the control group. Freud might have suggested repression, but Loftus (1987) could explain the forgetting with the **weapons focus** effect, where fearful or stressful aspects of a scene (e.g. the gun) channel attention towards the source of distress and away from other details. Alternatively people may need to be in the same state (i.e. anxious) to recall properly – this is a **cue-dependent** explanation.

FLASHBULB MEMORY

- Brown and Kulik (1977) suggested some events can be remembered in almost photographic detail – as if they are imprinted upon the mind. They called this type of recall 'flashbulb memory' and found it was most likely to occur when the event was not only surprising to the person but also had consequences for their own life.
- Thus they found around 90% of people reported flashbulb memories associated with personal shocking events, but whether they had such memories for public shocking events like assassinations depended upon how personally relevant the event was for them – 75% of black participants in their research had a flashbulb memory for the assassination of black-rights activist Martin Luther King, compared to 33% of white participants.
- Brown and Kulik (1977) argued that flashbulb memory was a **special** and **distinct** form of memory since:
1 The emotionally important event triggers a neural mechanism which causes it to be especially well imprinted into memory.
2 The memories were more detailed and accurate than most.
3 The structural form of the memory was very similar – people nearly always tended to recall where they were, what they were doing, who gave them the information, what they and others felt about it and what the immediate aftermath was, when they first knew of the event.

Evaluation

- Neisser (1982) however, disagrees that flashbulb memories are distinct from other episodic memories, since:
1 The long-lasting nature of the memory is probably due to it being frequently **rehearsed** (thought about and discussed afterwards) rather than being due to any special neural activity at the time. Existing memory theory, e.g. levels of processing, would explain meaningful and distinctive events lasting longer.
2 The accuracy of such memories has often been shown to be no different from most other events, e.g. McCloskey et al.'s (1988) study of memory after the Challenger space shuttle explosion and Wright's (1993) of the Hillsborough football tragedy.
3 The similar form of 'flashbulb memories' may just reflect the normal way people relate information about events to others.
Despite such criticisms some research still supports the notion of flashbulb memory. Conway et al. (1994) argue that studies that use events that are really relevant to peoples' lives (e.g. their own on Margaret Thatcher's resignation) find more accurate flashbulb memories over time. Cahill and McGaugh (1998) think that because it is adaptive to remember emotionally important events animals have evolved arousing hormones that help respond in the short term and aid storage of the event in the long term.

SO ARE THE EFFECTS OF EMOTION POSITIVE OR NEGATIVE ON MEMORY?

- Research findings are mixed, e.g. Levinger and Clark (1961) found free associations to emotional words (e.g. 'quarrel' and 'angry') harder to immediately recall. However, other researchers found that after a longer delay the effect reversed and the emotional words were recalled better. Generally positive long-term effects on memory are found for slightly above average levels of arousal (perhaps supporting flashbulb memory), but negative effects for very high levels of arousal. Typical laboratory studies only produce lower arousal levels and have not provided much support for everyday repression, whereas profound amnesia might result from very traumatic or long-term negative emotional arousal which cannot be laboratory-generated.

10.10 Strategies for memory improvement

RECOMMENDATION	RESEARCH BASED ON	EVALUATION
REPETITON • **Practice** makes perfect. The more times information is memorised, the more accurate the recall and the less time it takes to **re-learn** the material. Revise more than once!	• Ebbinghaus (1895) found re-learning savings – the greater the number of repetitions the less time it took to re-learn the lists. Since the majority of material was lost within the first day, perhaps the best time to test memory is after that time delay. Linton found that everyday memories last longer if they are occasionally remembered.	• Ebbinghaus only tested himself and used nonsense syllables. • Advertisers and psychologists have found that simple verbal repetition is not very effective. • Bekerian and Baddeley found that frequently repeated radio information did not produce strong memory.
ELABORATION • Information to be remembered should be made as **meaningful** as possible. New material will be remembered better if it is **integrated** with **existing** knowledge and if it is richly **associated** with other information.	• Craik and Tuiving found deep semantic level processing increased recall. • Morris *et al.* (1981) found that football fans recalled a list of football results far better than non football fans. The fans' interest and knowledge made the scores more meaningful and deeply processed. • Ley (1978) found patients remembered medical information better if they had existing background medical knowledge.	• Many mnemonic techniques work by creating associations with existing memories (the method of loci links items on a list to well known locations) or enriching associations (Bower, 1972), found linking material with vivid visual imagery is especially effective). These methods involve extra learning.
MEMORY CUES • Often memorising cues or **memory jogs** will **help access** larger amounts of information. **Recreating** the **conditions** under which material was learnt can act as a trigger for memory.	• Tulving and Pearlstone (1966) found that cues such as category headings could improve recall of lists of words under those headings. • Godden and Baddeley (1975) showed how state or context could act as a powerful memory jog when testing diver's recall of material under water and on land.	• Mnemonic techniques such as acronyms (like ROY.G.BIV to stand for the colours in the spectrum) or the peg word system and method of loci work by providing memory cues. • Freudian free association may also jog repressed memories.
ORGANISATION • Information is better remembered if it is **presented** in a **structured** way. The structure may aid recall by **linking** information in a **meaningful** way, **grouping** or **ordering** material more **manageably** or by taking advantage of the mind's existing ways of **representing** knowledge (for example in semantic categories).	• Bousfield found in free recall studies that information is automatically organised in LTM in semantic clusters. Bower *et al.* found higher recall for words organised in meaningful hierarchies. • Miller showed how the capacity of STM could be improved by organ-ising/chunking information into larger meaningful units, while many studies have supported the primacy/recency effect where word order affects memory.	• Ley et al (1973) found presenting medical information in a structured way improved patients' recall by 25%. • in a later study Ley (1978) found that many patients remembered the first information received better (the primacy effect). This finding and others were included in an advice booklet for doctors, which improved patients' recall of medical information by 15%.
IMPROVING CONSOLIDATION • Memory can be improved by limiting disruption to it (e.g. through preventing interference or trauma) or by strengthening it (e.g. through the use of memory enhancing drugs).	• Jenkins and Dallenbach (1924) found memory was less disturbed if material was learnt before going to sleep, while McGeoch and MacDonald (1931) found interference effects were greatest if two sets of information were learnt close together in time and were similar. • Cameron *et al.* (1963) has claimed that heavy doses of RNA can improve the memory of elderly people with memory difficulties, while a precursor of RNA, orotic acid, is commonly included in 'smart drugs'.	• Cameron's results were tainted by a lack of proper control data (perhaps memory improvement was due to a Hawthorne effect from the attention the elderly received) and replication failure. • While memory retention can be affected by drugs in laboratory animals, there is little evidence for smart drug effectiveness. • Caffeine may improve memory indirectly by increasing attention, or via a state dependent effect.

11.1 Visual perceptual organisation

GESTALT THEORY OF PERCEPTUAL ORGANISATION
Gestalt psychologists, such as Wertheimer and Koffka, believed that the brain possesses innate organisational properties with which it structures, orders and makes coherent sense of sensations from the environment.

EMERGENT PROPERTIES
The organisation of environmental stimuli into groups produces '**emergent properties**' in them – that is to say, groups of stimuli have '**gestalt**' or 'whole' properties that produce perceptions that are more than the sum of the sensory stimuli that make them up (the whole is greater than the sum of its parts).

Evidence
- Wertheimer's phi phenomenon – a series of separate lights turned off and on, one by one, in sequence will give the perception of continuous movement.
- Navon (1977) found, using figures like those opposite, that subjects were able to identify the large (whole) letter without being influenced by the smaller letters (parts) that made it up, but took longer to identify the smaller letters if the larger one did not correspond. This is evidence for the gestalt notion that the whole image is perceived before the parts that make it up.

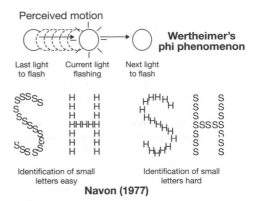

Wertheimer's phi phenomenon

Last light to flash · Current light flashing · Next light to flash

Identification of small letters easy · Identification of small letters hard

Navon (1977)

THE LAW OF PRAGNANZ
Gestalten (organised wholes) are derived from combinations of sensations via the '**Law of Pragnanz**' - the organisation of sensory stimuli will always follow the most simple or stable shape. The organisation will always be as 'good' as possible, so for example:
- The patterns or figures perceived will always be the ones requiring the least descriptive information.
- The unseen or missing parts of figures will be predicted from the seen parts in the most economical way.

Evidence
Pomerantz (1981) found that subjects would join dots in the same way to produce 'good', simple figures. For example, when shown the dots arranged in configuration 'a', subjects tended to join them as pattern 'b' rather than 'c' or 'd'.

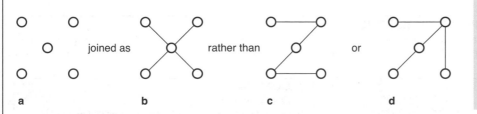

a   joined as   b   rather than   c   or   d

Perception following 'good form'

This shape is perceived as a rectangle and a triangle rather than a complex 8-sided figure.

Pragnanz, and thus perceptual grouping and feature detection, is achieved through organising principles such as proximity, similarity, continuity, closure, figure-ground, and common fate.

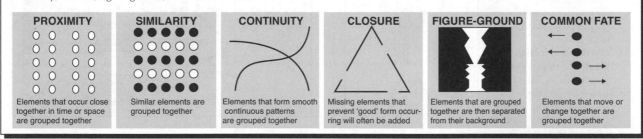

PROXIMITY	SIMILARITY	CONTINUITY	CLOSURE	FIGURE-GROUND	COMMON FATE
Elements that occur close together in time or space are grouped together	Similar elements are grouped together	Elements that form smooth continuous patterns are grouped together	Missing elements that prevent 'good' form occurring will often be added	Elements that are grouped together are then separated from their background	Elements that move or change together are grouped together

EVALUATION
- Gestalt principles tended only to be applied to two-dimensional drawings rather than three-dimensional objects.
- However, Johansson (1975) found that subjects watching films of actors made completely invisible (by wearing black on a black background) except for dots of lights attached to their joints, could identify the actors' movements, posture and even gender. Cutting and Kozlowski (1977) even found subjects could identify their friends filmed under these conditions (requiring quite a degree of joining the dots!).
- The objects gestalt psychologists investigated were usually viewed in isolation, not as part of real scenes.
- Some gestalt concepts are rather vague – what is a 'good' figure and why?
- Gestalt psychology describes how features are grouped rather than explains.

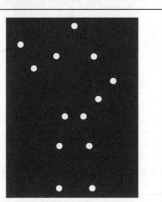

Johansson (1975)

11.2 Bottom-up theories of perception

WHAT DOES PERCEPTION INVOLVE?

Perception is the process of interpreting and organising the environmental information received by the senses. For visual perception, this involves taking the constantly fluctuating patterns of light, which arrive from all over the environment, up-side-down, on to our two-dimensional retinas and achieving:

1 **Feature or object detection** – detecting the shape of objects in the environment, e.g. distinguishing features from each other and their background.
2 **Depth perception** – establishing location in three-dimensional space, e.g. interpreting a two-dimensional retinal image as a three-dimensional object at a specific distance in three-dimensional space.
3 **Pattern or object recognition** – recognising an object in terms of its shape, size, brightness and colour, despite its:
   - Viewpoint – an object seen from different angles will cast images of different shapes upon the retina, yet will be recognised as the same object (a phenomenon known as **shape constancy**).
   - Distance – the same object at longer distances will cast smaller images on the retina but will be identified as the same size (a phenomenon known as **size constancy**).
   - Luminescence – an object will be perceived as the same brightness despite changes in the overall level of luminosity (a phenomenon known as **brightness constancy**).

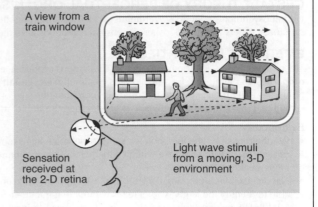

A view from a train window

Sensation received at the 2-D retina

Light wave stimuli from a moving, 3-D environment

BOTTOM-UP THEORIES

- These theories emphasise the richness of the information entering the eye and the way that perception can occur from using all the information available.
- Gibson believes perception occurs directly from sensation, feature detection theories examine the processes involved in assembling perception from sensations.

Hmm... arms, legs, body, a head...

Experience Knowledge Stereotypes

Aah... that is a person over there.

GIBSON'S THEORY OF DIRECT PERCEPTION

Gibson proposed that the optical array contains all the information needed to directly perceive a three dimensional world with little or no information processing needed. Light reaching the eye contains invariant information about the depth, location and even function of objects. 'Sensation is perception'.

1 DEPTH

Monocular depth cues
(capable of perception by one eye)

- **Texture gradients** – closer objects can be seen in greater detail than distant ones.
- **Overlap and motion parallax** – closer objects obscure more distant ones.
- **Linear perspective** – lines known to be parallel converge in the distance.

Binocular depth cues

- **Retinal disparity** – each eye sees a slightly different view, which gives us a three dimensional impression.
- **Ocular convergence** – our eyes converge the closer an object is to us.

2 LOCATION

Optic flow patterns
The point to which we are moving remains stationary while the rest of the view rushes away from it, giving information on speed and direction of movement.

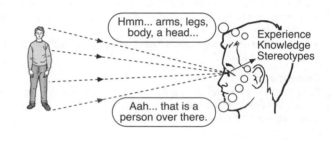

3 FUNCTION

Affordances
Gibson even argued that the perceptual system has evolved to inform us directly of the function of a perceived object, i.e. chairs are for sitting on.

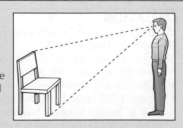

For: Gibson put perception back into the real world, stressing the importance of movement for perception and the richness of information available at the retina.

Against: Affordances are debatable and the theory neglects much of the processing that must take place in perception. Direct perception may apply more to innate reflexes where environmental stimuli directly affect behaviour, but much of human behaviour is governed by higher-order intervening processes between stimulus and response.

11.3 Top-down theories of perception

TOP-DOWN THEORIES

- Sometimes referred to as constructivist theories, these theories stress the factors in the construction of reality that go beyond the information received from the senses.
- Gregory's theory and perceptual set theory regard perception as a very active process, whereby the individual's past knowledge, expectations and stereotypes seek out sensory data to 'complete the picture'.

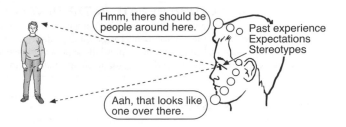

GREGORY'S PERCEPTUAL INFERENCE THEORY

Gregory suggests that we go beyond the available sensory information in perception, 'a perceived object is a hypothesis, suggested and tested by sensory data'. Gregory points out that sensory information alone cannot account for perception – often all the information required is not present or we need to select information to prevent sensory overload – and he uses illusions and perceptual constancy to support his suggestion.

1 ILLUSIONS

Distortions
e.g. The Ponzo illusion. The retinal images of the horizontal lines are equal, yet the top one is usually perceived as longer due to the diagonal lines acting as depth cues from our memory.

Ambiguous Figures
e.g. The Necker cube. Perception of the cube's angle differs according to our focus of attention.

Fictions
e.g. The Kanizsa triangle. The subjective contours of the triangle go beyond the available information.

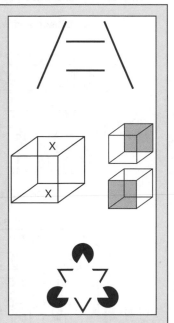

2 PERCEPTUAL CONSTANCY

e.g. Size constancy. The same sized object seen from different distances will cast different sized images upon the retina, yet will be perceived as the same size due to the brain scaling the image.

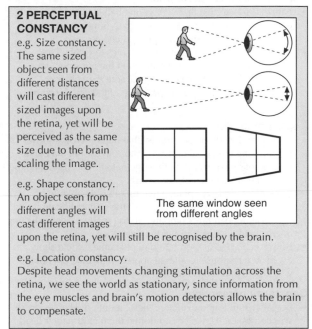

The same window seen from different angles

e.g. Shape constancy. An object seen from different angles will cast different images upon the retina, yet will still be recognised by the brain.

e.g. Location constancy. Despite head movements changing stimulation across the retina, we see the world as stationary, since information from the eye muscles and brain's motion detectors allows the brain to compensate.

For: Illusions and constancy show how the brain uses memory, expectation and unconscious processing to interpret environmental stimuli.
Against: Illusions are artificial stimuli and do not contain the rich amount of detail and information naturally received by the retina.

PERCEPTUAL SET THEORY

Perceptual set theory stresses the idea of perception as an active process involving selection, inference and interpretation. Perceptual set is a bias or readiness to perceive certain aspects of available sensory data and to ignore others. Set can be influenced by many factors such as:

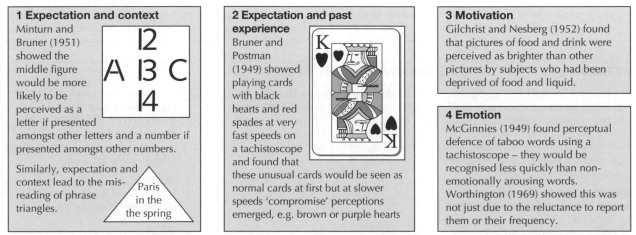

1 Expectation and context

Minturn and Bruner (1951) showed the middle figure would be more likely to be perceived as a letter if presented amongst other letters and a number if presented amongst other numbers.

Similarly, expectation and context lead to the mis-reading of phrase triangles.

2 Expectation and past experience

Bruner and Postman (1949) showed playing cards with black hearts and red spades at very fast speeds on a tachistoscope and found that these unusual cards would be seen as normal cards at first but at slower speeds 'compromise' perceptions emerged, e.g. brown or purple hearts

3 Motivation

Gilchrist and Nesberg (1952) found that pictures of food and drink were perceived as brighter than other pictures by subjects who had been deprived of food and liquid.

4 Emotion

McGinnies (1949) found perceptual defence of taboo words using a tachistoscope – they would be recognised less quickly than non-emotionally arousing words. Worthington (1969) showed this was not just due to the reluctance to report them or their frequency.

For: Set theory links with many other areas in psychology, such as schemata and stereotypes, and has been supported by many studies.
Against: The experimental findings concerning perceptual defence and the validity of tachistoscope presentation have been much debated.

11.4 Development of perception 1

THE NATURE-NUTURE DEBATE IN THE DEVELOPMENT OF PERCEPTION

The research in this area aims to determine what particular aspects of perception are present at birth and what aspects are developed through experience with the environment. The physiology of the eye and brain can only tell us so much about this debate, so many different approaches have been taken to investigate it. All the approaches have their own strengths and weaknesses, however, and there is evidence for both nativist and empiricist views – suggesting an interaction of innate and environmental factors in the development of perception.

HUMAN INFANT STUDIES

Neonates (new born babies) are born with most of the features, such as rods and cones, of the adult eye and quickly demonstrate many perceptual abilities as their eyes and brain systems mature.

EVIDENCE SUPPORTING THE ROLE OF NATURE IN PERCEPTUAL DEVELOPMENT

Pattern and shape perception
- Fantz (1961) argued that very young babies are able to distinguish between patterns, and by 2–3 months prefer looking at complex stimuli if given a choice.
- Bower (1966) conditioned 2 month olds to respond to a triangle with a bar across it and found the response was generalised to a complete triangle (more than other possibilities), indicating the presence of the gestalt law of continuity and closure.

Depth perception
- Gibson and Walk (1960) argued that depth perception was innate using the visual cliff apparatus. Six month old babies would not crawl over the cliff edge onto the deep side, neither would newly born chicks or lambs.
- Campos *et al.* (1970) placed two month old babies (who cannot crawl) onto the deep side of the visual cliff and found a decrease in heart rate compared to the shallow side, reflecting interest and a recognition of the difference.
- Bower *et al.* (1970) found 20 day old babies would show an avoidance response to a large approaching box, but not if it was filmed and projected on a screen.

Constancy perception
- Bower (1966) found evidence that 2 month old babies possess size constancy. Having conditioned them to turn their head whenever they saw a 30 cm cube at a distance of 1 metre (using an adult playing 'peek-a-boo' as a reinforcer), Bower found they would respond more to the same 30 cm cube at a distance of 3 metres than they would to a 90 cm cube at 3 metres (which would cast the same size retinal image as the original 30 cm cube).
- Bower (1966) also showed shape constancy develops in the first few months by conditioning babies to respond to a shape and then rotating it.

Evaluation:
- Obviously it is impossible to rule out any environmental experience since birth.
- If neonates lack a perceptual ability, it may be due to a lack of biological maturation rather than lack of experience.
- The certainty of perception in babies is less reliable because of their lack of verbal report. Therefore, non-verbal methods of perceptual response have to be used, such as preferential looking, conditioned body movement or sucking, heart and brain activity changes.

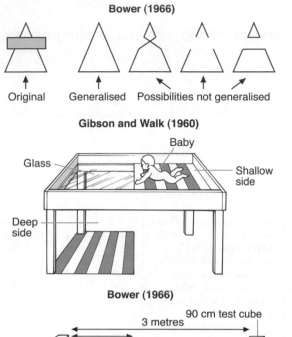

Bower (1966)

Original   Generalised   Possibilities not generalised

Gibson and Walk (1960)

Glass   Baby   Shallow side

Deep side

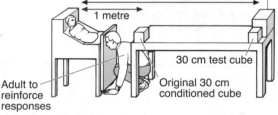

Bower (1966)

90 cm test cube

3 metres

1 metre

30 cm test cube

Adult to reinforce responses

Original 30 cm conditioned cube

PERCEPTUAL ADAPTATION & RE-ADJUSTMENT STUDIES

These studies assume that if perception can be adjusted to cope with artificial perceptual distortions, then perceptual abilities are more flexible and open to environmental influences – lending support to the nurture side of the nature-nurture debate in this area.

Evidence supporting the role of nature in perceptual development
- Studies on animals, e.g. Sperry's (1943) rotation of salamander eyes through 180 degrees, found they could not adjust their perception.

Evidence supporting the role of nurture in perceptual development
Using devices which invert or distort visual stimuli many researchers have found that human perception can re-adjust itself, e.g.
- Stratton (1896) wore an inverting telescope and had adjusted completely after 8 days, with only a location constancy after image afterwards.
- Ewart (1930) found inverting binoculars only produced motor

adaptation (vision-body co-ordination) not true perceptual adaptation.
- Snyder and Pronko (1952) used inverting and reversing goggles and found that the adaptation gained after 30 days lasted for years.

Evaluation:
- What is learnt is not necessarily a new way of perceiving but a new set of body movements.
- Showing that adults can learn to perceive does not mean that babies learn to perceive.

11.5 Development of perception 2

ANIMAL EXPERIMENTS

Animal studies into the development of perception usually involve the deprivation or distortion of the animal's normal visual experience from birth and noting the consequences for later perceptual abilities. Much of the evidence appears to emphasise the need for environmental stimulation for normal perception to develop. However, whether this involves learning to perceive, is less certain.

Evidence supporting the role of nurture in perceptual development

These studies imply that there are no innate abilities in perception and show that **active environmental stimulation** of **normal patterned light** is necessary for normal perceptual development in animals, e.g.

- Riesen deprived animals such as chimpanzees and kittens of either:
  a All light – for the first 16 months of life and found no visual perception because retinal cells failed to develop properly. When then allowed light, normal object recognition was shown at 21 months, although if light was denied until 33 months, the subsequent development of perceptual abilities was poorer.
  b Just patterned light – the animals wore translucent goggles, which only allowed unpatterned light to be seen, and found that only general aspects of brightness, colour and size could be responded to. No object or pattern recognition was immediately evident.
- Blakemore and Cooper (1970) exposed kittens to an environment consisting of either only vertical or only horizontal lines and found that they would only respond to a pointer presented in the same orientation. Furthermore, the cells of each cat's primary visual cortex would only fire in response to lines presented in the orientation they had been raised in and not to lines of the opposite orientation.
- Held and Hein (1963) claimed active interaction with the environment is needed for the development of perception. Their 'kitten carousel' enabled two kittens to experience exactly the same kind and amount of environmental stimulation, but one did so actively, the other passively (it could not move itself). When tested, only the active kittens were able to visually guide their paws or respond to approaching objects.

Blakemore and Cooper (1970)

Evaluation:

- There are major ethical problems with these studies. In one study Riesen tested the blindness of a light deprived chimpanzee by seeing if it would avoid a visually presented object that was associated with a painful electric shock.
- These studies aim to prevent or distort environmental experience or learning to **stop perceptual abilities being acquired** from the environment and thus may imply that there are no innate abilities in perception. However,
  a deprivation may physically **damage** or **prevent** the **maturation of innate abilities** rather than prevent learning – chicks kept in the dark from birth to 10 weeks cannot recognise and peck at grain, whereas normal chicks can do this immediately on hatching without learning (Govier and Govier, cited in Radford and Govier, 1991).
  b distortion of normal visual experience may merely **distort** the **development of innate abilities** – in Blakemore and Cooper's study, the stimulated visual cortex cells may have grown to dominate cells of other orientations that would otherwise have naturally responded.
- Animals cannot report their subjective experience and their perception can only be inferred from behaviour – Held and Hein's passive kitten probably lacked the ability to co-ordinate motor actions with perception rather than perception itself.
- Animal perception and development may be qualitatively different to human perceptual development.

HUMAN CATARACT PATIENTS

- Patients who have undergone cataract operations are provided with sight for the first time as adults and may shed light upon whether perceptual abilities are innate, i.e. shown immediately after the cataracts are removed, or are dependent upon experience and learning.
- Hebb (1949) studied the reports of 65 cases of cataract removal by von Senden and concluded that some aspects of vision were innate (figural unity) while others were learned (figural identity).
- Gregory and Wallace (1963) studied a 52 year old patient, S.B., who had undergone a corneal graft to restore his sight after being blind since he was 6 months old. Some aspects of vision were very quickly shown, others were not – implying a mixture of nature and nurture.

Evidence supporting the role of nature in perceptual development

- Hebb found that figural unity – the ability to fixate upon, scan, follow and detect shapes from their background (figure-ground perception), was shown by those patients whose sight had been restored, indicating these abilities were innate.
- Gregory and Wallace found that S.B. could quickly detect objects, walk around the hospital guided by sight alone and identify objects by sight that he had experienced through touch (showing good cross-modal matching). These abilities may have been aided by his experience of vision in his first 6 months of life.

Evidence supporting the role of nurture in perceptual development

- Hebb found that the cataract patients had great problems with figural identity – recognising objects. The patients could detect and scan a shape such as a triangle but would not be able to identify it by sight unless they counted the angles. They also lacked perceptual constancy.
- Gregory and Wallace found that S.B. had problems with identifying objects by sight that he had not experienced through touch before, detecting mood by visual facial expressions and depth perception (thinking a 40 foot drop from a window was manageable).

Evaluation:

- The adult patients' sensory systems would not be the same as those of babies due to adaptation to the loss of vision. Visual systems present at birth may have deteriorated through disuse or other sensory systems have over-developed to compensate, so interfering with vision.
- Methodologically these studies can be regarded as natural experiments, and so there is a lack of control over variables such as the degree of visual experience before the cataract developed, the age when the cataract was removed, and the emotional trauma of cataract removal.

11.6 Culture and perception

WHY STUDY CROSS-CULTURAL DIFFERENCES IN PERCEPTION?

A major assumption of cross-cultural research is that differences between cultures are more likely to be caused by the differing physical and social environments experienced by the members of those cultures, whereas similarities across cultures are more likely to reflect biological, inherited abilities common to the whole species. Cross-cultural differences in perception might therefore be caused by differing experiences influencing perceptual set.

Many studies have shown individual experience can affect perceptual set and thus perception. Bugeleski and Alampay for example (1961) discovered that subjects presented with pictures of animals and then the ambiguous 'rat-man' figure were more likely to see the rat than a control group who were more likely to see the man. The culture a person is raised in may therefore affect not only object recognition but also the more basic perceptual processes such as size constancy and depth perception.

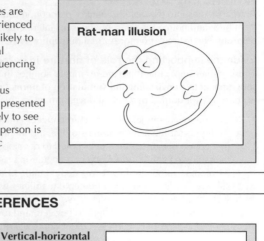

Rat-man illusion

CROSS-CULTURAL DIFFERENCES

ILLUSION STUDIES

- Rivers (1901) in a very early study discovered that Murray Islanders, both adults and children, were more susceptible to the vertical – horizontal illusion but less susceptible to the Muller-Lyer illusion than English subjects.
- Allport and Pettigrew (1957) found that a rotating trapezoid was more likely to be seen as a swaying rectangle by western cultures and urban Zulus who are used to seeing rectangular windows but more likely to be seen for what it was by non-urban Zulus.
- Segall *et al.* (1963) conducted a very large scale study, testing around 1,900 subjects over a six year period, and argued that Africans and Filipinos were less susceptible than European subjects to the Muller-Lyer illusion because they did not live in such a 'carpentered world' where right angles are so frequently encountered that they are readily learnt as depth cues.
  However the 'carpentered world hypothesis' cannot account for findings that some groups of subjects living in rectangular constructed environments also fail to show susceptibility to the Muller-Lyer illusion (Mundy-Castle and Nelson, 1962) or that no difference has been found in its perception between urbanised and non-urbanised aborigines (Gregor and McPherson, 1965).

SIZE CONSTANCY

- Turnbull (1961) suggested that size constancy may be lacking in pygmies living in dense rain forests without the open space required to develop the ability. When taken to an open plain to see a herd of buffalo in the distance one pygmy reported being unable to identify such 'strange insects' and was amazed at what happened as they drove closer to the herd and the insects appeared to grow into buffalo. This was not a rigorously controlled experiment however.

OBJECT RECOGNITION IN PICTURES

- Western missionaries and anthropologists have often reported that the non-western cultures they made contact with had difficulty in recognising western pictures of objects. However, differences in the materials and artistic styles used in the pictures may have influenced their recognition ability.

DEPTH PERCEPTION IN PICTURES

- Hudson (1960) discovered that people from African cultures have difficulty perceiving two-dimensional pictures as 3 dimensional objects. However, the unnatural materials and lack of natural depth cues such as texture gradient may have influenced the African subjects' perception.

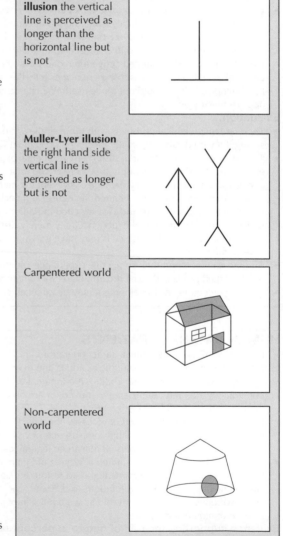

Vertical-horizontal illusion the vertical line is perceived as longer than the horizontal line but is not

Muller-Lyer illusion the right hand side vertical line is perceived as longer but is not

Carpentered world

Non-carpentered world

EVALUATION

Cross-cultural differences in perception are often regarded as evidence for the idea that perception is flexible and so influenced by learning. However, the evidence:
- is not always conclusive and does not always show very large differences,
- ignores the vast similarity in perceptual ability across cultures,
- may only reflect the artificial methodologies and un-ecological materials used
- may even be due to biological factors since, for example, there is evidence that physiological differences in the eye can account for differences in susceptibility to the Muller-Lyer illusion in different subjects.

11.7 'Pictorial perception and culture' Deregowski (1972)

AIM

To present studies to show that different cultures perceive pictures in different ways. Cross-cultural studies of picture perception:
1 provide an insight into how perception works (indicating the role played by learning in perception) and
2 investigate the possibility of a universal cross-cultural means of communication (a 'lingua franca').

EVIDENCE

Pictorial object recognition studies

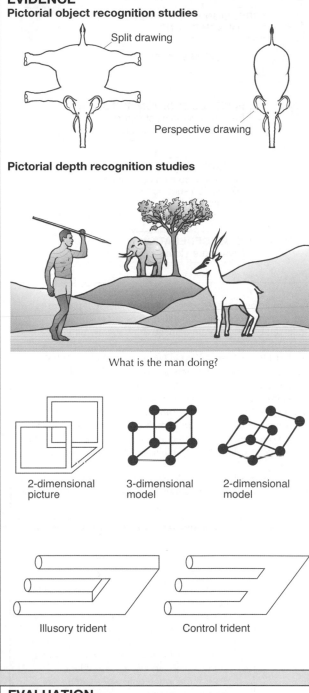

Split drawing

Perspective drawing

Pictorial depth recognition studies

What is the man doing?

2-dimensional picture

3-dimensional model

2-dimensional model

Illusory trident

Control trident

- Anecdotal reports from missionaries and anthropologists living among remote cultures have shown these cultures to have difficulties recognising objects from pictures, especially from accurate perspective drawings which do not represent all aspects of an object. Some studies have shown that African subjects from remote villages can pick out the correct toy from pictures of familiar animals (e.g. lions) though not unfamiliar ones (e.g. kangaroos).
- Hudson showed that African children and adults prefer split drawings to correct perspective drawings.

Hudson tested South African Bantu workers to see whether they could interpret a combination of three pictorial depth cues as a three dimensional representation:
- Familiar size – where the larger of two objects is drawn further away,
- Overlap – where nearer parts of a picture obscure farther away parts, and
- Perspective – where lines known to be parallel converge at the horizon.

The subjects were asked questions about the relationship between objects in the picture to see whether they had two- or three-dimensional vision. For example in the picture opposite, a three-dimensional viewer would say that the man is about to throw his spear at the antelope, a two-dimensional perceiver would say that the man is about to throw his spear at the elephant.

Hudson found two-dimensional perception in African tribal subjects across all ages, educational and social levels, and this finding was confirmed by pictorial depth measuring apparatus developed by Gregory.

Hudson showed Zambian subjects a drawing of two squares (arranged so that western subjects perceive them as a three-dimensional cube) and asked them to build a model of it out of modelling clay and sticks. Most of the Zambians built two-dimensional models, whereas the few who showed three-dimensional perception built a three-dimensional cube.

A group of Zambian school children, having been divided into two- and three-dimensional perceivers, were shown a picture illusion which three-dimensional western perceivers become confused by (since they attempt to see it as a three-dimensional picture of a trident). Three-dimensional perceivers spent longer looking at the illusory trident than a normal control trident, compared to the two-dimensional perceivers who showed no significant difference in viewing the two, when asked to copy the tridents.

EVALUATION

Methodological:

Design – A wide range of methods used in the subject's own environment. However, most involve natural experiments, with a consequent lack of experimenter control over the independent variable (culture) and extraneous variables during testing.

Apparatus – Pictures lacked important depth cues, such as texture gradient, and were presented on paper rather than on ecologically natural materials.

Theoretical: Three explanatory theories are given, but little evidence is used to support or decide between them. There is an ethnocentric assumption that western methods of pictorially representing objects especially involving depth cues are more correct than others and should be universally recognised.

Links: Nature-nurture debate in perception. Cross-cultural psychology.

11.8 Face recognition

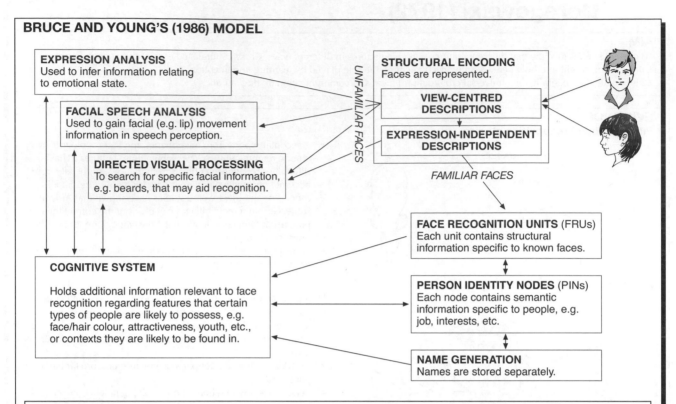

BRUCE AND YOUNG'S (1986) MODEL

EXPRESSION ANALYSIS
Used to infer information relating to emotional state.

FACIAL SPEECH ANALYSIS
Used to gain facial (e.g. lip) movement information in speech perception.

DIRECTED VISUAL PROCESSING
To search for specific facial information, e.g. beards, that may aid recognition.

UNFAMILIAR FACES

STRUCTURAL ENCODING
Faces are represented.

VIEW-CENTRED DESCRIPTIONS

EXPRESSION-INDEPENDENT DESCRIPTIONS

FAMILIAR FACES

COGNITIVE SYSTEM
Holds additional information relevant to face recognition regarding features that certain types of people are likely to possess, e.g. face/hair colour, attractiveness, youth, etc., or contexts they are likely to be found in.

FACE RECOGNITION UNITS (FRUs)
Each unit contains structural information specific to known faces.

PERSON IDENTITY NODES (PINs)
Each node contains semantic information specific to people, e.g. job, interests, etc.

NAME GENERATION
Names are stored separately.

Research studies
- Cognitive neurological studies – have confirmed that familiar and unfamiliar faces are recognised through different processes. Studies of brain damaged individuals reveal that some have problems in recognition tests of familiar faces but not unfamiliar ones, whereas others show the opposite tendency. Brain scans of individuals without brain damage show slightly different areas are used when recognising familiar and unfamiliar faces.
- Experimental studies – regarding familiar face recognition, Young et al. (1986a, 1986b – cited in Eysenck and Keane, 1995) confirmed that face recognition is achieved first, personal identity second and name generation last as the model predicted. They presented pictures of well known faces and found that decisions relating to the familiarity of a face were made faster than decisions relating to the occupation associated with the face, which in turn were made faster than decisions regarding the name.
- Diary/self-report studies – Young et al (1985) found that incidents of everyday face recognition problems recorded by their participants in diaries seemed to confirm the model's predictions. Sensing familiarity (activation of FRUs) before being able to remember anything else about the person (activation of PINs) occurred more often than remembering personal details (activation of PINs) but not the name (activation of name generation). Recalling the name without being able to recall anything else about the person was never reported.
- However, studies of brain damaged individuals who can match faces with names but not recall any personal information or those who show covert recognition (access to information about a person without necessarily consciously recognising them) cannot be explained by this model.

EXPLANATIONS OF PROSOPAGNOSIA

Prosopagnosia (or face blindness) refers to difficulties in identifying faces, even those of family members.
- *Acquired prosopagnosia* results from *brain damage* causing a *loss* of face recognition ability.
- *Developmental prosopagnosia* results from factors which cause face recognition not to develop at all, e.g. *genetic* causes, *early* brain damage or *severe eyesight problems*.

Brain regions for object and face recognition have been identified, but there is still debate over whether prosopagnosia is due to problems with:
- *face-specific mechanisms*
- curved, holistic or configured *pattern recognition in general*
- *expertise* at dealing with *classes* of objects.

Evaluation
There are many individual differences between people with prosopagnosia – some also have other recognition problems, e.g. with non-face objects, emotions, speech or navigation.

Case studies of prosopagnosia
Case studies are useful for studying rare examples of behaviour in in-depth detail. For example:
- Duchaine et al. (2006) studied Edward, a 53-year-old physicist with developmental prosopagnosia (he had difficulties recognising faces, including his father's, during childhood and was unaware of any causal head trauma). His sister reported difficulties with facial identity and emotion as a teenager, but not as an adult. Edward managed in most social situations by using context, body shape, gait, voice and object recognition of hair or unusual features to aid person recognition.
- With exhaustive testing, Duchaine et al. managed to eliminate all other explanations for Edward's problem except deficits in face-specific mechanisms.

12.1 The cognitive developmental approach to psychology

ORIGINS AND HISTORY

- Researchers can be said to adopt a cognitive developmental approach when they not only focus their research on the *inner mental processes of thinking and reasoning* (as do cognitive psychologists in general) but are also interested in how these *change over time* and *can account for behaviour* shown at different ages.
- The study of the development of knowledge and understanding (epistemology) has long interested philosophers and a variety of psychologists have also attempted to explain cognitive development, but have differed in their views on *why* cognitive abilities change over time – whether it is more due to nature (e.g. biology, genetics) or nurture (e.g. environment, social instruction). There has also been some debate as to *how* the changes occur over time – whether qualitatively (in discrete stages) as most suggest or quantitatively (gradually in degree rather than type).
- Piaget is probably the best known cognitive developmental researcher who suggested thinking progressed through qualitative changes (in stages) due to the increasing biological maturity of mental structures with age and environmental interaction. He applied his stage theory to explain a wide variety of children's comments, judgements and actions, for example how their morality developed over time.
- Other researchers have disagreed with Piaget, for example over the cause of cognitive development (e.g. Vygotsky and Bruner believe society plays a more important role) or over the cognitive structures that are changing (e.g. information-processing theorists).
- Most cognitive developmental research has focused on the changes of mental abilities in childhood, however the approach has been applied throughout the life span, for example to the changes of old age.

Jean Piaget
'What makes their [cognitive] theories 'developmental' is the belief that the ways in which we process experience – be it physical, mathematical, or moral experience – normally change in an orderly, increasingly adaptive, species-specific fashion.' Flanagan (1984)

ASSUMPTIONS

Cognitive developmental psychologists assume that:

1 It is necessary to refer to *inner mental concepts* such as thoughts, beliefs and cognitive structures in order to understand behaviour.
2 These mental concepts *change in important ways* over time, particularly in childhood, and these changes have a major influence on people's behaviour, judgement and attitudes at different ages.

METHODS OF INVESTIGATION

Cognitive developmental psychologists have used methods such as:

- Observation – e.g. Piaget's naturalistic observations of children's everyday statements and play.
- Longitudinal study – e.g. Piaget's study of changes in his own children over the course of their childhood or Kohlberg's study of moral reasoning in the same adults over many years.
- Experimentation – e.g. cross-sectional experiments comparing the ability of two different age groups to pass conservation tests.

CONTRIBUTION TO PSYCHOLOGY

Cognitive developmental psychologists have sought to explain:

- *Cognitive changes* – e.g. in the intellectual abilities of children and older adults.
- *Social cognition* – e.g. moral behaviour and reasoning about moral situations at different ages.
- *Social behaviour* – e.g. play and helping behaviour.
- *Socialisation* – e.g. gender and self-development.

CONTRIBUTION TO SOCIETY

The cognitive developmental approach has had a fairly specialised range of applications, for example to:

- *Education* – e.g. the application of cognitive developmental theory to improve classroom practice and aid student progression.
- *Child care* – e.g. to facilitate care in play and peer relations.
- *Criminology* – e.g. children's ability to understand and be held responsible for their crimes, or the link between moral development and criminal behaviour in adolescence and adulthood.

STRENGTHS

The cognitive developmental approach has:

- Overcome the rather static view of mental processes that has dominated traditional cognitive psychology, and has tried to account for the origin of such processes.
- Shown that a straightforward link between age and behaviour cannot be fully made or understood without considering the changing nature of underlying mental structures.
- Had useful practical applications and implications for society.
- Usually conducted scientific and objective research to support its theories.

WEAKNESSES

Unfortunately the cognitive developmental approach has:

- Had a fairly specialised and thus limited contribution to psychology and society.
- Tended at times to underestimate the discrepancies between cognition and behaviour, e.g. between what people say and do about moral situations, and between the ability a child possesses and shows (e.g. due to demand characteristics).
- Not always justified whether cognitive changes are best viewed as occurring in qualitatively different stages rather than in a more gradual quantitative manner.
- Neglected individual differences in cognitive development.

12.2 Piaget's theory of cognitive development

BACKGROUND
- Jean Piaget, although a zoologist by training, was involved in the early development of intelligence tests. He became dissatisfied with the idea that intelligence was a fixed trait, and came to regard it as a process which developed over time due to biological maturation and interactive experience with the world, which adapted the child to its environment.
- Piaget was interested in the kind of mistakes that children make at different ages, thinking that these would reflect the cognitive progress they had made, and so spent many years studying children (especially his own) via the clinical interview method, informal experiments, and naturalistic observation.

Jean Piaget

Intellectual development occurs through <u>active interaction</u> with the world
Increased understanding only happens as the child actively interacts with and *discovers* the world, children do not passively receive their knowledge, they are *curious* and *self-motivated*.

Intellectual development occurs as a <u>process</u>
Piaget thought that children think in *qualitatively* different ways from the adult, we are not born with all our knowledge and understanding 'ready-made', but have to develop our intelligence in **stages**.

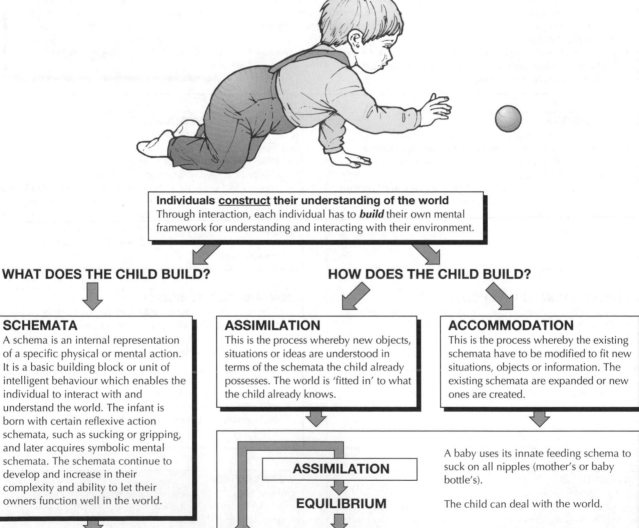

Individuals <u>construct</u> their understanding of the world
Through interaction, each individual has to **build** their own mental framework for understanding and interacting with their environment.

WHAT DOES THE CHILD BUILD?

HOW DOES THE CHILD BUILD?

SCHEMATA
A schema is an internal representation of a specific physical or mental action. It is a basic building block or unit of intelligent behaviour which enables the individual to interact with and understand the world. The infant is born with certain reflexive action schemata, such as sucking or gripping, and later acquires symbolic mental schemata. The schemata continue to develop and increase in their complexity and ability to let their owners function well in the world.

OPERATIONS
In middle childhood, **operations** are acquired – these are higher order mental structures which enable the child to understand more complex rules about how the environment works. Operations are logical manipulations dealing with the relationships between schemata.

ASSIMILATION
This is the process whereby new objects, situations or ideas are understood in terms of the schemata the child already possesses. The world is 'fitted in' to what the child already knows.

ACCOMMODATION
This is the process whereby the existing schemata have to be modified to fit new situations, objects or information. The existing schemata are expanded or new ones are created.

ASSIMILATION
↓
EQUILIBRIUM
↓
NEW SITUATION
↓
DISEQUILIBRIUM
↓
ACCOMMODATION

A baby uses its innate feeding schema to suck on all nipples (mother's or baby bottle's).

The child can deal with the world.

The baby encounters a drinking beaker for the first time.

The baby's sucking schema is not appropriate – a big mess is made!

The baby has to modify its feeding schema so it can use all beakers (ie return to assimilation).

(Adapted from Gross, 1996)

12.3 Piaget's stages of cognitive development 1

Piaget proposed four stages of cognitive development which reflect the increasing sophistication of children's thought. Every child moves through the stages in a sequence dictated by biological maturation and interaction with the environment.

1 THE SENSORIMOTOR STAGE

(0 to 2 Years)

The infant at first only knows the world via its immediate senses and the actions it performs. The infant's lack of internal mental schemata is illustrated by:

- profound **egocentrism** – the infant cannot at first distinguish between itself and its environment.
- lack of **object permanence** – when the infant cannot see or act on objects, they cease to exist for the child.

Throughout this stage internal representations are gradually acquired until the **general symbolic function** allows both object permanence and language to occur.

Evidence for

Piaget investigated his children's lack of object permanence during this stage by hiding an object from them under a cover. At 0 to 5 months, an object visibly hidden will not be searched for, even if the child was reaching for it.
At 8 months the child will search for a completely hidden object.

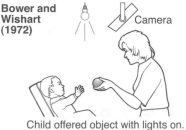

Bower and Wishart (1972)

Child offered object with lights on. Child begins to reach for object.

Evidence against

Bower and Wishart (1972) offered an object to babies aged between 1 to 4 months, and then turned off the lights as they were about to reach for it. When observed by infra-red camera, the babies were seen to continue reaching for the object despite not seeing it.
Bower (1977) tested month-old babies who were shown a toy and then had a screen placed in front of it. The toy was secretly removed from behind the screen, and when the screen itself was taken away, Bower claimed that the babies showed surprise that the toy was not there.

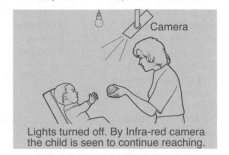

Lights turned off. By Infra-red camera the child is seen to continue reaching.

2 THE PRE-OPERATIONAL STAGE

(2 to 7 Years)

The child's internal mental world continues to develop, but:

- is still **dominated by** the external world and the **appearance** of things.
- shows **centration** – the child only focuses on one aspect of an object or situation at a time.
- **lacks** the mental sophistication necessary to carry out logical **operations** on the world.

The pre-operational child, therefore, shows:

- **class-inclusion problems** – difficulty in understanding the relationship between whole classes and sub-classes. The child focuses on the most visibly obvious classes and disregards less obvious ones.
- **egocentrism** – the difficulty of understanding that others do not see, think and feel things like you do.
- **lack of conservation** – the inability to realise that some things remain constant or unchanged despite changes in visible appearance. By only focusing on the most visible changes, the child fails to conserve a whole host of properties, such as number, liquid and substance.

Evidence for

Class-inclusion tests – if a child is shown a set of beads, most of which are brown but with a few white ones, and is asked 'are there more brown beads or more beads', the child will say more brown beads.

Piaget and Inhelder (1956) – demonstrated the egocentrism of pre-operational children with their 'Three-Mountain Experiment'. Four year olds, when shown a mountain scene and tested to see if they could correctly describe it from different view-points, failed and tended to choose their own view. Six year olds were more aware of other viewpoints but still tended to choose the wrong one.

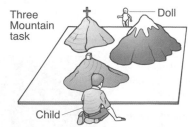

Three Mountain task
Doll
Child

Conservation experiments – Piaget tested for many different types of conservation. The child would fail in each case, since it lacked the necessary operations.

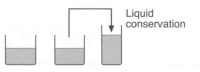

Liquid conservation

Evidence against

McGarrigle et al modified Piaget's class inclusion tasks to make them more understandable and appropriate. They first asked pre-operational children (with an average age of 6) a Piagetian type question – 'Are there more black cows or more cows?' They then turned all of the cows on their sides (as if asleep) and asked 'Are there more black cows or more sleeping cows?' The percentage of correct answers increased from 25% to 48%.

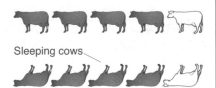

Sleeping cows

Hughes demonstrated that 3.5 – 5 year olds could de-centrate and overcome their egocentrism, if the task made more 'human sense' to them. When these children had to hide a boy doll from two policemen dolls (a task that required them to take into account the perspectives of others but had a good and understandable reason for doing so) they could do this successfully 90% of the time.

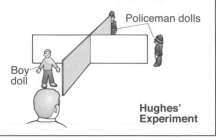

Policeman dolls
Boy doll
Hughes' Experiment

12.4 Piaget's stages of cognitive development 2

3 CONCRETE OPERATIONAL STAGE

(7 to 11 years)

At the concrete operational stage, the child's cognitive complexity allows it to:

- carry out mental **operations** on the world – that is logical manipulations on the relationships between objects and situations. Two such operations are **compensation**, and **reversibility**.
- **de-centrate** – that is more than one aspect of an object or situation can now be taken into account at the same time.

An important limitation on the child's thought at this stage, however, is that the mental operations cannot be carried out purely in the child's head – the physical (concrete) presence of the objects being manipulated is needed. Thus, although the conservation tests can be successfully completed, the child needs to see the transformation taking place.

Evidence for
Liquid conservation

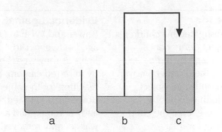

a   b   c

When liquid is poured from **b** to **c**, a concrete operational child can compensate for increasing height with decreasing width and can mentally reverse the pouring, therefore conserving liquid (realising that the amount of liquid remains the same).

Number conservation

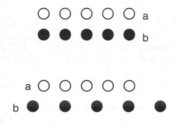

When row **b** is spread out, the concrete operational child can realise that the number remains unchanged, despite the alteration in appearance.

Piaget conducted many tests of conservation on concrete operational children and found that their mental operations allowed them to think about problems in new ways.

Evidence against

McGarrigle and Donaldson (1974) demonstrated that pre-operational children of between 4 to 6 years could successfully conserve if they were not misled by demand characteristics into giving the wrong answer. McGarrigle and Donaldson therefore added an 'accidental transformation' condition where a 'naughty teddy' arrives and disarranges one of the rows. Under this condition more children (63%) could conserve number since the transformation was not meant to have been deliberately intended.

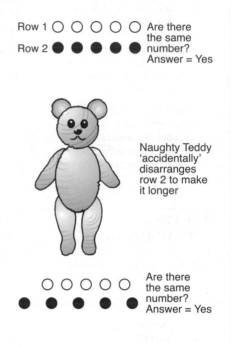

Row 1 ○ ○ ○ ○ ○   Are there the same number?
Row 2 ● ● ● ● ●   Answer = Yes

Naughty Teddy 'accidentally' disarranges row 2 to make it longer

○ ○ ○ ○ ○   Are there the same number?
● ● ● ● ●   Answer = Yes

4 FORMAL OPERATIONAL STAGE

(11 onwards)

At the formal operational stage, the child's mental structures are so developed and internalised that:

- ideas can be manipulated in the head and reasoning/deductions can be carried out on verbal statements, without the aid of concrete examples.
- the individual can think about hypothetical problems and abstract concepts that they have never encountered before.
- the individual will approach problems in a systematic and organised way.

Evidence for
Transitive inference tasks - the child can follow the abstract form of arguments, e.g.

if A > B > C, then A > C.

They can solve problems, such as 'Edith is fairer than Susan. Edith is darker than Lily. Who is the darkest?', *without* needing to use dolls or pictures to help them.

Deductive reasoning tasks - problems, such as the pendulum task, where the child is given string and a set of weights and is asked to find out what determines the swing, are carried out logically and systematically.

Evidence against

Gladwin (1970) is one of many investigators who have questioned the appropriateness of Piagetian experimental tasks for testing non-western cognitive development. Often detailed investigation has found that formal operational thought has been acquired, but in a culturally specific manner. For example, the Pulawat navigators of Polynesia show complex formal operational thought when guiding their canoes at sea, yet will tend to fail standard western tests of cognitive development.

12.5 Evaluating Piaget's theory of cognitive development

THEORETICAL CRITICISMS

AGES
- Much research has seemingly demonstrated that children possess many of the cognitive abilities that Piaget outlined at ages much *earlier* than he expected.
- Often improving upon, or altering, the method of testing/assessing the child reveals their cognitive abilities better (see Bower, Hughes, McGarrigle, etc. below).
- In addition, Piaget seemed to have over-estimated people's formal operational ability - some research has even suggested that only one third of the population actually reach this stage.

CONCEPTS
- While Piaget's theory provides us with a detailed description of development, some have said that it does not really provide us with an explanation of it.
- Some of the concepts are vague, and the stages often show so much overlap (decalage) that development is perhaps better regarded as a *continuous process*.
- By focusing on the child's mistakes, Piaget may have over-looked important abilities that children do possess, or may have wrongly deduced the reason for their failure.

NEGLECTS
- Piaget neglected many important *cognitive* factors that could have accounted for the *individual differences* in development that children show, such as *memory* span, motivation, impulsiveness, practice, etc.
- Overall, in many researchers' view (e.g. Bruner, Light, etc.), he severely underestimated *social influences* on development. By concentrating on individual maturation and *self* construction of mental life, Piaget neglected:
  a the role of society in facilitating and providing increased understanding,
  b the child's understanding of social situations (especially in Piaget's experimental situations), and
  c children's ability in and use of language at different ages.

METHODOLOGICAL CRITICISMS

INAPPROPRIATE TESTS
- A frequent criticism is that Piaget's experiments were *over-complicated* and *difficult to relate to*.
- By simplifying the tasks and ensuring that they made what Donaldson has termed 'human sense', researchers such as Bower and Wishart (1972) (with their object permanence experiment), and Hughes (1975) (with his 'Policeman Doll' experiment) have demonstrated cognitive abilities in children who would not be expected to show them.

DEMAND CHARACTERISTICS
- Even in fairly uncomplicated tasks, Piaget's experiments *ignored* the child's *social understanding* of the test, and may have led the child to give a socially desirable or expected answer instead of what the child really thought and understood.
- McGarrigle and Donaldson (1974) with their 'Naughty Teddy' Experiment, and Rose and Blank (1974) with their one question variation, both demonstrated significantly greater conservation rates in pre-operational children.

OVERALL METHODS
- Piaget's use of the clinical interview method, informal experimentation, and small sample sizes, *lacked scientific rigour*.
- Although these methods had their advantages, the generalised conclusions drawn from them may have been somewhat biased.

STRENGTHS

THEORETICAL IMPORTANCE
- Piaget's theory has received a lot of longitudinal, cross-sectional and cross-cultural *support* over many years, and while the theory has been subject to modification and criticism, many fundamental aspects of his theory are still accepted as valid contributions today.
- Many psychologists have taken Piaget's ideas far more rigidly than they were intended. Piaget modified his theory to take into account certain criticisms and hoped that one day it could be integrated with other theories that dealt with aspects of children's internal life that he had ignored (for example Freud's theory of emotional and personality development).

PRODUCTIVITY
- Piaget's ideas *generated* a huge amount of critical *research* which has vastly increased our understanding of cognitive development.
- Bruner and more socially orientated theorists have used Piaget's views as a 'spring board' to develop their own and to answer many of the issues raised by Piaget's research.

APPLICATIONS
- Piaget's views have had an important impact on *educational* practice – changing the way children are taught today and hopefully making education more effective and enjoyable.
- Piaget has also contributed to psychological theories of children's play and moral development.

12.6 'Asking only one question in the conservation experiment' Samuel and Bryant (1984)

AIM

To support, using a more detailed procedure and a wider age range of subjects, Rose and Blank's experimental criticism of Piaget's conservation studies. Piaget and Szeminska (1952) found pre-operational children (below the age of seven) could not conserve (realise that some properties, such as number, volume, and mass, remain the same despite changes in their physical appearance) by conducting experiments, whereby:

1 They showed 2 rows of counters and asked a pre-transformation question 'are there the same number in each row?' The answer was usually '**yes**'.

2 They then lengthened one of the rows and asked the (same) post-transformation question 'are there the same number in each row?' The answer given was then usually '**no**'.

Piaget took the 'no' answer to mean that the children thought there were now a greater number of counters in the lengthened row and that these children could not conserve. However, Rose and Blank (1974) disagreed with this conclusion. They argued that Piaget had made a methodological error by imposing **demand characteristics** – when an adult deliberately changes something and asks the same question twice, children think that a different answer is **expected**, even though they may well be able to conserve. Rose and Blank (1974) conducted a study where they only asked one question (the post transformation one) to reduce these misleading expectations, and found that more children were able to conserve when they only had to make one judgement than when they had to make two in the standard Piagetian presentation.

Samuel and Bryant (1984) wanted to replicate this study on a larger scale using:
- four age groups (5, 6, 7 and 8 year olds),
- three types of conservation test (number, mass, and liquid volume), and
- three ways of presenting the tests (standard Piagetian way, one judgement/question way, and fixed array with no visible transformation).

METHOD

Subjects: Independent measures design was used. 252 boys and girls were divided into 4 age groups (of 5, 6, 7 and 8 year olds).
Procedure: In each age group every child was tested 4 times each for conservation of number, mass, and liquid volume in one of three ways:

- The standard Piagetian way: (asking the pre- and post-transformation questions)

- The one judgement way: (asking only the post-transformation question)

- The fixed array way: (asking only the post-transformation question, *without seeing* the transformation)

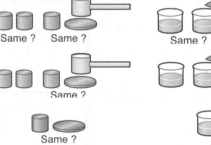

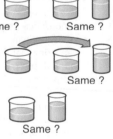

In all three methods of presentation, the 12 conservation tests each child experienced were systematically varied to prevent order effects. Two different versions of each type of conservation test were given to ensure the child could show a proper understanding of the concepts involved.

RESULTS

Mixed design analysis of variance and Newman-Kreuls tests showed that:
- Children were significantly more able to conserve in the one judgement task.
  This supports Rose and Blank's (1974) experiment and criticism of Piaget's methods.
- Older children did significantly better than younger children in conservation.
  This supports Piaget's theory of cognitive development in general.
- The conservation of number task was significantly easier than the other tasks.
  Indicating support for Piaget's notion of decalage.

MEAN ERRORS OUT OF 12 CONSERVATION TESTS

Age	Standard	One judgement	Fixed Array
5	8.5	7.3	8.6
6	5.7	4.3	6.4
7	3.2	2.6	4.9
8	1.7	1.3	3.3

EVALUATION

Methodological: *Good methods –* The study used a control group, different tests of conservation, and different aged subjects.
Good data analysis – The data was extensively analysed to reveal its significance.

Theoretical: *Implications –* The study supports some of Piaget's notions and some of those of his critics.

Links: Child cognitive development Sament. Research methods – demand characteristics.

12.7 Bruner's theory of cognitive development

BRUNER'S ASSUMPTIONS

Jerome Bruner was a cognitive scientist who agreed with Piaget that active interaction with the world could increase a child's underlying cognitive capacity to understand the world in more complex ways. Bruner differed from Piaget, however, in that he:

- Was more concerned with **how** knowledge was **represented** and organised as the child developed, and therefore proposed different **modes** of representation.
- Emphasised the importance of **social** factors in cognitive development, in particular the role of language, social interaction and experience, which could pull the child towards better understanding. Cognitive growth depends upon the mastery of 'skills transmitted with varying efficiency and success by the culture' and occurs 'from the outside in as well as from the inside out' Bruner (1971).

MODES OF REPRESENTATION

Bruner's theory is concerned with **ways** of **representing** or thinking about knowledge at different ages, not stages as such. Bruner proposed **three modes** of representation that develop in order and allow the child to think about the world in more sophisticated ways, but all exist in the adult (we do not lose these ways of thinking like in Piaget's stages). The modes are:

- The enactive mode (0–1 years) – this mode of representation is dominant in babies, who first represent or interact with the world through their actions. Knowledge is therefore stored in '**muscle memory**'.
- The iconic mode (1–6 years) – this mode represents knowledge through visual or auditory **likenesses** or **images**. Children dominated by their iconic mode have **difficulty** thinking beyond the images, to categorise the knowledge or understand relationships between objects.
- The symbolic mode (7 years onwards) – this mode enables children to encode the world in terms of information storing symbols such as the words of our language or the numbers of mathematics. This allows information to be **categorised** and summarised so that it can be more readily **manipulated** and considered. The symbolic mode allows children to think beyond the physical images of the iconic mode.

THE ROLE OF LANGUAGE AND EDUCATION

Like Vygotsky, Bruner stressed education and social interaction as major influences upon cognitive development, and in particular proposed that society provides our language which gives us symbolic thought. Unlike Piaget, who thought that language was merely a useful tool which reflects and describes the underlying symbolic cognitive structures such as operations,

Bruner believed that language is symbolic/logical/operational thought – the two are inseparable. According to Bruner therefore, **language training** can speed up cognitive development, a suggestion that Piaget's theory rejects (since he believed that cognitive structures could only be developed through the child's individual maturation and interaction with the world).

LANGUAGE ACCELERATING DEVELOPMENT

- Francoise Frank (reported by Bruner, 1964) showed how the ability of pre-operational children to give the correct answer in liquid conservation tasks could be improved if they were encouraged to use and rely upon their linguistic descriptions (i.e. their symbolic mode) of the task.
- Frank reduced the visual (iconic mode) effect of the conservation changes by screening most of the beakers during the experiment. Once the children were less dominated by their iconic mode, they could concentrate on their verbal (symbolic mode) descriptions of what was happening, and were more able to conserve.
- Once the 5 and 6 year olds had used their language to solve the conservation task, they showed an increased ability to pass other non-screened conservation tasks. 5 year olds showed an increase from 20 to 70%.
6–7 year olds increased from 50 to 90%.

Step 1 Show standard beakers with equal water and a wider beaker of the same height.

Step 2 Screen the beakers so the water level is hidden, but mark the level of the water on screen.

Step 3 Pour water from the standard beaker into the screened wider beaker.

Step 4 Ask the child, without it seeing the water 'which has more to drink or do they have the same?'
Result - in comparison with an unscreened pre-test there is an increase in correct answers:
4 year olds – increase from 0% to 50%
5 year olds – increase from 20% to 90%
6 year olds – increase from 50% to 100%
Children justify their response linguistically by saying for example 'You only poured it'.

Step 5 The screen is removed and:
4 year olds – all revert to the pre-test answer of less water in the wider beaker, overwhelmed by the appearance of the water (iconic mode).
5-6 year olds – virtually all stick to the right answer, relying on their previous verbal justification (symbolic mode) 'You only poured it from there to there'.

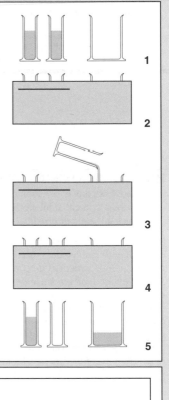

Sonstroem et al. (1966) encouraged children who failed conservation of substance tests to use all of their modes of representation to increase their ability to conserve. The children who rolled the plasticine into a ball themselves (enactive mode) while watching their own actions (iconic mode) and verbally describing what was happening, e.g. 'it's getting longer but thinner' (symbolic mode) showed the greatest improvement in conservation.

a   b

a   b

When the ball 'b' is rolled into a sausage, pre-operational children think there is more plasticine.

12.8 Vygotsky's theory of cognitive development

VYGOTSKY'S APPROACH
- Vygotsky was a Russian psychologist whose ideas on cognitive development were very similar to Bruner's. Vygotsky focused on the importance of *social interaction* and *language* as major influences on children's development of understanding.

SOCIAL INTERACTION
- Vygotsky sees the whole process of cognitive development as being social in nature – *'we become ourselves through others'*.
- At first the child responds to the world only through its actions, but society provides the *meaning* of those actions through social interaction.
- Vygotsky illustrates this with the example of pointing – the child may reach towards an object and fail to grasp it, but the parent will *interpret* this as a pointing gesture.
- 'The original meaning to this unsuccessful grasping movement is thus imparted by others. And only afterwards, on the basis of the fact that the child associates the unsuccessful grasping movement with the entire objective situation, does the child himself begin to treat the movement as a pointing gesture. Here the function of the movement itself changes: from a movement directed towards an object, it becomes a movement directed towards another person, a means of communication, the grasping is transformed into pointing.' Vygotsky (1978).

INTERNALISATION AND LANGUAGE
- Cognitive development, therefore, proceeds, according to Vygotsky, as the child gradually *internalises* the meanings provided by these social interactions. The child's thinking and reasoning abilities are at first primitive, crude and do not involve the use of language, and so the greatest advance comes when we internalise *language*.
- Speech starts off as communication behaviour that produces changes in others, but when language becomes internalised, it converges with thought – *'thought becomes verbal and speech rational'* Vygotsky (1962). Language allows us to 'turn around and reflect on our thoughts' – directing and *controlling* our thinking, as well as communicating our thoughts to others.
- Eventually, language splits between these two functions as we develop an abbreviated inner voice for thinking with, and a more articulate vocabulary for communicating with others. Internal language vastly increases our powers of problem solving.
- The use of language can be said to progress in three stages:
1 Pre-intellectual social speech (0–3 years), where thinking does not occur in language and speech is used to provoke social change.
2 Egocentric speech (3–7 years), where language helps the child control behaviour but is spoken out loud.
3 Inner speech (7 years +), where the child uses speech silently to control their own behaviour and publicly for social communication.

ZONE OF PROXIMAL DEVELOPMENT
- Because cognitive development is achieved by the *joint* construction of knowledge between the child and society, it follows that any one child's potential intellectual ability is greater if working in *conjunction* with a more expert person / other than alone. Vygotsky defines the *zone of proximal development* (ZPD) as:

'the distance between the actual developmental level as determined by individual problem solving and the level of potential development as determined through problem solving under adult guidance or in collaboration with more capable peers. The zone of proximal development defines those functions that have not yet matured but are in the process of maturation, functions that will mature tomorrow but are currently in an embryonic state. These functions could be termed the "buds" or "flowers" of development rather than the "fruits" of development'.

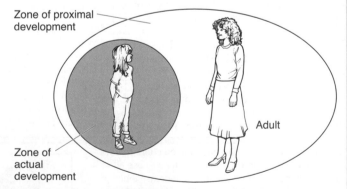

Zone of proximal development

Zone of actual development

Adult

EVALUATION OF VYGOTSKY'S THEORY
Vygotsky's ideas have:
- become increasingly popular as it became clear that Piaget had under emphasised the role of social factors in cognitive development.
- been developed by others such as Bruner who have conducted more research to provide evidence for them than Vygotsky himself did.
- been successfully applied to education.

12.9 The information-processing approach to cognitive development

ASSUMPTIONS

- The information-processing approach to cognitive development is a recent approach that aims to apply experimental cognitive psychological research from a number of areas, such as attention, perception and memory, to explain children's development of understanding.
- In the usual cognitive psychological style, children's minds can be regarded as computers that gradually develop in their ability to process information – to receive it, store it and use it appropriately. Just as the efficiency of a computer depends upon the speed of its processor, the amount of RAM it has to manipulate information at any one time and the sophistication of its software programs, so young children will, at first possess similar limited information-processing abilities.

PROCESSING SPEED

- Young children are actually physically slower at transmitting information along neurones – as the brain matures, nerve fibres become myelinised and can transmit their electrical messages faster, thereby increasing their processing speed.

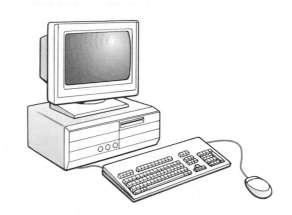

Siegler's (1978) balance beam tests show how children's ability to solve problems is directly related to the number of aspects of a problem they can recognise and combine at the same time. (Processing skill is needed to identify the aspects of the problem, processing capacity is needed to combine them at the same time).

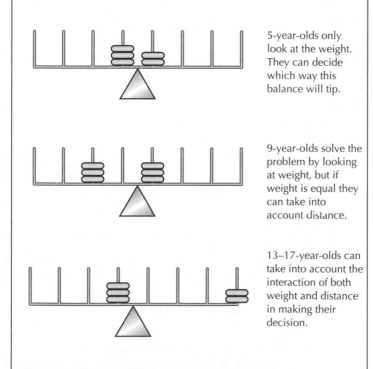

5-year-olds only look at the weight. They can decide which way this balance will tip.

9-year-olds solve the problem by looking at weight, but if weight is equal they can take into account distance.

13–17-year-olds can take into account the interaction of both weight and distance in making their decision.

PROCESSING CAPACITY

- Case (1992) proposes that young children have a limited 'mental space' or working/short-term memory with which to hold and think about information – thus making it difficult to take into account more than one aspect of a problem at a time (Piaget called this centration, and argued that it led to conservation errors). As the child grows older, 'mental space' increases as:
  a neural processing speeds up and
  b strategies for processing information become more automatic with practice and, therefore, need less conscious attention – thus freeing up 'mental space' for other work (rather like experienced drivers being more able to concentrate on other tasks while driving when their driving skills become automatic through practice).

Evidence

- Tests on short-term memory capacity support the idea that processing capacity increases with age – people's ability to recall digits after hearing them just once improves with age (adults can recall around seven, plus or minus two).

PROCESSING SKILLS

- As the child grows and gains experience in the world, its skills for processing information (organising, categorising and problem-solving) develop, becoming faster, more complex and flexible. More efficient strategies can be used, such as chunking and organising information, to improve short- or long-term memory, and heuristics or 'rules of thumb' enable problems to be solved more quickly.
- Fischer (1980) has developed a theory that shows how skills develop and, like many other researchers in the area, argues that different children will develop particular skills or talents in different 'domains' of ability depending upon their environmental experience. Domain skills may not be entirely dependent on environmental stimulation, however, since Baron-Cohen (1990, 1995) proposes that autism, now widely held to be a congenital disorder, is due to a lack of 'theory of mind' – the domain of mental representation and social understanding.

Evidence

- Chi (1978) found that children skilled at chess could remember patterns of chess configurations better than adults who were inexperienced at chess, indicating that domain skill rather than general capability was most important. In computer terms a more efficient program on a less powerful machine was more efficient.

12.10 Nativist explanations and early infant abilities

WHAT ARE NATIVIST EXPLANATIONS?

- Nativist explanations argue that innate, biologically-programmed factors exert a strong influence on human development and so focus on the 'nature' side of the 'nature–nurture' debate.
- Nativist explanations propose that certain cognitive abilities and knowledge are 'built into' the human brain so are 'present' at birth and require only brain maturation and exposure to the environment to naturally and automatically show evidence of their presence.
- According to nativist assumptions, these innate abilities help infants to understand and impose order upon environmental experience rather than resulting from it – thus the nativist explanations contradict theories that suggest early infant abilities are learnt, e.g. Skinner (1957), or constructed in a step-by-step manner from interactions with the environment, e.g. Piaget (1952).

EXAMPLES OF NATIVIST EXPLANATIONS

PERCEPTION

Research, (e.g. Bower, 1960, 1966; Fantz, 1961), on human infant **pattern, shape, depth** and **constancy perception** seems to support a nativist view of these perceptual abilities (see 'The development of perception 1'). However, these studies cannot rule out all learning experience since birth and rely on non-verbal measures.

INTELLIGENCE

Quantitative research on **IQ** indicates a strong role for **genetic influences** (see 'Development of IQ test performance' pages 148–149), although environmental factors are also vital. However, **qualitative** research on intelligence has been influenced by Piaget's ideas on the construction of mental schemas through environmental interaction *constrained* by maturation.

LANGUAGE

Chomsky (1959) argued that human infants are born with a '**language acquisition device**' that provides them with an innate knowledge of language and grammar to help decode and produce the language they are exposed to. However, this view was opposed by Skinner's (1957) learning theory of language acquisition.

INFANT KNOWLEDGE OF THE PHYSICAL WORLD

Piaget (1954) proposed that infant knowledge of the physical world is extremely limited (to physical sensorimotor interactions) at birth. Such knowledge is gradually acquired through individual interactions with the environment and limited by biological brain maturation.

For example, Piaget suggested infants of less than eight months of age **lack object permanence** (the ability to realise that objects still exist when they cannot be physically sensed, e.g. seen or touched) and **only develop a proper mental representation** of objects and knowledge of permanence **after the age of 18 month.**

Piaget based this idea on observations that infants of:

- less than 8 months fail to search for an object they find interesting if it is completely concealed from their view
- 8 to 12 months search for a hidden object, but in places where they previously found it rather than were they last saw it placed (known as the 'A, not B, error')
- 12 to 18 months search for a hidden object where it was last seen, but cannot infer invisible displacements (that something happened to the object out of their view).

However, studies such as Baillargeon's (1987) seem to suggest that babies have **an innate knowledge of object permanence,** thus supporting a nativist view. An infant's failure to search for an object in Piaget's object permanence situations may be due to poorly developed memory (at 1–4 months if an object is hidden too long, the infant forgets about it) or motor skills (maturational development in the frontal lobes helps 12-month-old infants inhibit the previous motor search patterns for objects at locations they know are incorrect).

BAILLARGEON'S (1987) STUDY

Baillargeon tested infant knowledge of object permanence without using active searching as a measure. She did this by showing $3\frac{1}{2}$ to $4\frac{1}{2}$-month-old infants a screen that pivoted towards and away from them through 180 degrees until they habituated to it (i.e. lost interest). Baillargeon then showed:

- **A possible event** – the pivoting screen rose, obscured and was then stopped by a yellow box placed behind it.
- **An impossible event** – the screen rose, obscured and then continued to rotate through the yellow box (an illusion).

The infants showed surprise and renewed interest (staring longer at the screen) when they saw the impossible event, implying that they expected the box to still be behind (and thus block the progress of) the screen, *even though the box could not be seen* at that point – so showing object permanence.

Evaluation

- It is not possible to rule out the occurrence of some perceptual learning about objects before $3\frac{1}{2}$.
- Basic object permanence may be an innate aspect of our perceptual systems, but sophisticated conceptual knowledge about objects probably does develop during infancy as Piaget suggests.
- The study shows that it is easy to misinterpret the cognitive implications of non-verbal infant behaviour (Piaget took a lack of searching to indicate a lack of knowledge). Similarly, Baillargeon's study assumes increased infant 'looking behaviour' indicates surprise at the impossible event rather than just interest at seeing the box again.

12.11 Cognitive developmental theories of moral development 1

COGNITIVE DEVELOPMENTAL THEORIES

PIAGET'S THEORY

- Piaget proposed that the level of **moral reasoning** a child showed would change in a qualitative way over time. Piaget suggested two main types of moral thinking:

  1 **Heteronomous morality** – Shown mostly by 5–9 year old children who regard morality as **obeying other people's rules** and laws. The thinking of this stage is typical of **pre-operational** thought and shows **moral realism** – rules and laws are understood as almost real and **fixed** things that are to be strictly obeyed or automatic punishment will follow (**immanent justice**). Immoral acts are judged by their **observable consequences** rather than intentions – a large amount of *accidental* damage is seen as worse than a small amount of *deliberate* damage.

  2 **Autonomous morality** - Shown mostly by those above 10 years, who regard morality as **following their own set of rules**/laws. The thinking of this stage is typical of **concrete** and later **formal operational** thought and shows **moral relativism** – rules and laws are understood as social creations agreed by mutual consent and the **intentions** of actions can be taken into account.

- Piaget believed the moral thinking of 7–9 year olds and sometimes even adults can be a mixture of heteronomous and autonomous morality, but the main shift from the former to the latter occurs when the child no longer shows egocentrism and is less dependent on the authority of adults. This implies that both cognitive development and social experience are required.

KOHLBERG'S THEORY

- Kohlberg attempted to produce a more detailed theory of moral development by presenting individuals of all ages with moral dilemmas in the form of short stories to solve.
- The dilemmas involved ten universal moral issues, such as the ethics of punishment, liberty and truth; and the reasoning used to justify the answer indicated the level of moral development.
- Kohlberg proposed six universal stages, reflecting three major levels of morality, which everyone progresses through in order.

Level	Stage	Moral reasoning shown
Pre-conventional	1 Punishment & obedience orientation.	Rules are kept to avoid punishment.
	2 Instrumental – relativist orientation.	'Right' behaviour is that which ultimately brings rewards to oneself.
Conventional	3 Good boy – nice girl orientation.	'Good' behaviour is what pleases others – conformity to goodness.
	4 Law & order orientation.	Doing one's duty, obeying laws is important.
Post-conventional	5 Social contract orientation.	'Right' is what is demo-cratically agreed upon.
	6 Universal principles orientation.	Moral action is taken based on self chosen principles.

Heinz's wife is dying of cancer. Only one man has the drug to help her but is charging 10 times what it cost to make it. Heinz can only get half the money but the druggist refuses all pleas. Heinz steals the drug in desperation. Should Heinz have stolen the drug? Why?

EVALUATION OF COGNITIVE DEVELOPMENTAL THEORIES OF MORAL DEVELOPMENT

Piaget supported his theory of moral development by questioning children about their understanding of rules (in **games** like marbles) and by presenting them with **moral stories**, whereas Kohlberg presented people with **moral dilemmas**.

Piagets stories have been criticised for over-emphasising consequences. Kohlberg's dilemmas are criticised as:
- **too difficult** for children to relate to,
- **too hypothetical**,
- **too culturally biased**, and
- **too biased towards male** ideas of morality, such as justice, rather than female moral notions like caring, sympathy and responsibility (**Gilligan** 1982).

Piaget and Kohlberg **ignored** the **relationship** between a person's moral **thought** and **behaviour** – knowing what should be done does not always lead to doing it.
- **Bandura and McDonald** (1963) found children would imitate a model's immoral behaviour regardless of their level of moral development

Some of Kohlberg's ideas and studies have been successfully supported:
- **Longitudinally** – Colby *et al.* (1983) studied 58 American males over 20 years and found they went through 4 of Kohlberg's stages.
- **Cross-culturally** – Snarey (1985) found evidence for Kohlberg's first 4 stages in many cultures. Cultures differ, however, in their moral priorities.
- **Cross-sectionally** – Fodor (1972) found that delinquents operated at lower levels of moral development than non-delinquents.

Some studies have found that stage six morality is rarely reached and that some people may actually **skip stages** or **revert** to earlier stages, which goes against Kohlberg's ideas. Eisenberg (1986) has found parallels with Kohlberg's stages in pro-social helping in dilemmas.

12.12 Cognitive developmental theories of moral development 2

EISENBERG'S THEORY OF PROSOCIAL MORAL REASONING

Eisenberg et al (1983) investigated the moral reasoning behind **prosocial** behaviour, typically concerning situations where another person required help that would inconvenience the potential helper in some way. **Dilemmas** were presented to children of different ages, such as the 'Mary dilemma' below, that involved deciding whether to help another person, but where the alternative was to just satisfy one's own needs rather than breaking any laws or moral rules (as was more the case with Kohlberg's dilemmas).

Eisenberg suggested that such prosocial moral reasoning would change over time as general cognitive development allowed individuals to take on the **perspective** of other people, **empathise** with others and gain some **insight** into their own motives for helping.

Eisenberg et al found that moral reasoning was **not** always **consistent**, but generally progressed through **five levels**.

EISENBERG'S FIVE LEVELS OF PROSOCIAL MORAL REASONING

Level	Helping behaviour based on...	Age range
1 Hedonistic (self-centred)	Concern for oneself – if help provides benefits for oneself.	Pre-school to early primary school.
2 Needs- (of others) orientated	The needs of others – but without much evidence of guilt or sympathy.	Pre-school to mostly primary school.
3 Approval- orientated	Doing what is perceived as good and approved of by others.	Primary school to secondary school.
4 Empathetic or transitional	Inner motives of sympathy and guilt – based on perspective role-taking. Some vague consideration of abstract principles and values.	Older primary school to secondary school.
5 Strongly internalised	Strongly internalised values, norms and principles – to maintain self-respect.	Very few at secondary school.

Source: based on Eisenberg, Lennon and Roth (1983)

Evaluation
- Despite some similarities to Kohlberg's research, Eisenberg's theory has drawn attention to a different aspect of, and has emphasised the role of **emotion** in, moral reasoning.
- Some of Eisenberg's findings have **contradicted** those of Kohlberg, e.g. the occasional *reverting* to lower levels of moral reasoning.
- Although Eisenberg et al found moral reasoning was not always consistent, they did find some evidence that the level of prosocial reasoning was linked to appropriate prosocial behaviour. Younger children who gave 'needs of others' responses to dilemmas were more likely to later show more spontaneous sharing with others than those who replied with 'hedonistic' reasoning, while more mature moral reasoners were more likely to help someone they disliked if they really needed it compared to less mature reasoners.

Mary will miss all the ice cream, cake and games at her friend's birthday party if she helps a girl who has fallen down and hurt her leg. What should Mary do? Why?

Help, or she will not be able to respect herself

Not help - she will miss all the cake!

Adult interviewer

Level 5 child

Level 1 child

GENDER AND MORAL REASONING

Gilligan (1982) argued that Kohlberg's theory was **biased** towards men because:
- It was developed based upon interviews with males.
- Men show a 'morality of justice' – that everyone should be treated the same, whereas women reason based upon a 'morality of care'– that no one should be hurt. Gilligan (1982) suggested that female morality progresses towards an ideal of nonviolence via 3 stages:
  Stage 1 – Care for one's own survival.
  Stage 2 – Care for others.
  Stage 3 – Care for integrity (for self and others).

Women may therefore be rated as morally inferior (e.g. at Kohlberg's stage 3) using male moral standards, which are more likely to portray men as reaching stage 4.

Evaluation
- Although Gilligan found some evidence that women favour a morality of care over one of justice, most research shows men and women use both types of reasoning.
- Walker (1984) found that women are not rated differently using Kohlberg's dilemmas.

DISTRIBUTIVE JUSTICE REASONING

Damon's (1973, 1975) research on distributive justice (the choices people make when allocating resources to themselves and other people) used clinical interviews and sharing dilemmas on 4- to 10-year-olds. He found children's reasoning about fair sharing progressed in stages:

Level	Criteria for distributing resources
0A	Self-interest governs distribution
0B	Self-interest justified by physical features (e.g. age, size)
1A	Strict equality influences sharing
1B	Merit (e.g. effort, performance) affects sharing
2A	Equity – sharing based on competing claims to merit
2B	Equity based on merit, needs, reciprocity, group goals

Evaluation
- Longitudinal studies support the stage progression with age (Damon 1980, Enright *et al.*, 1984).
- The 3 levels correlated well with Piaget's pre-operational, concrete operational and formal operational stages.
- Distributive fairness reasoning can be affected by social class and culture (e.g. Carson and Banuazizi, 2008).

12.13 Moral development – the psychodynamic approach

FREUD'S THEORY OF MORAL DEVELOPMENT

DEVELOPMENT

- Freud proposed that **moral feelings** come from the **superego** – that part of the psychic apparatus that develops as a result of the **Oedipus complex**.
- The Oedipus complex occurs in the phallic stage of psychosexual development and involves the child's feelings of attraction towards their opposite sex parent. However, because the **boy fears** that his father will **castrate** him and the **girl fears** that she will **lose** her mother's **love**, both end up identifying with their same sex parent. **Identification** involves internalising all the same sex parent's moral behaviour, and the superego is therefore an 'inner parent' rewarding good actions and punishing bad ones.

THE SUPEREGO

- There are two main aspects of the superego, the **conscience** and the **ego-ideal**.
- The conscience represents the **punishing** parent and imposes feelings of **guilt** for immoral thoughts or deeds, whereas the ego-ideal represents the **rewarding** parent and is responsible for feelings of **pride** and satisfaction for 'good' thoughts or deeds.

SUPEREGO

CONSCIENCE → Imposes guilt → Represents the punishing parent

EGO-IDEAL → Imposes pride → Represents the rewarding parent

PREDICTIONS

- Moral behaviour will be fairlyy **consistent** across different situations, since the child internalises a **fixed impression** of its parent's morality during the Oedipus complex which becomes a permanent part of the personality.
- **Strength** of morality depends upon
  a the strength of the parent's morality, and
  b the **motive for identification** – Freud claimed that **males** have **stronger consciences** than females, because they identify out of a stronger motive (fear of castration rather than loss of love).
- **Greater wrong-doing** leads to **less guilt**. Since guilt is aggression directed against the self, **releasing aggression** via immoral acts leaves less to punish yourself with.

THE OEDIPUS COMPLEX

IDENTIFICATION

Parent

Child

Inner parent

EVALIUATION OF FREUD'S THEORY OF MORAL DEVELOPMENT

- There is **little evidence** to support Freud's theory in general and the Oedipus complex in particular, especially the motives for identifying with the same sex parent. The superego, and thus Freud's view of morality, is therefore of **doubtful validity**.

- Cognitive developmental theorists have pointed out that morality does **not** stop developing after the phal l ic stage, but develops and matures from childhood to adulthood. Zahn-Waxier (1979) found moral feelings are shown by 18 month old children.

- There is no evidence to support Freud's view that women are morally inferior to men. **Hoffman**, in a review of the literature, found that if anything, **females** were slightly **more** able to **resist** temptation than males.

- Freud's **hydraulic theory** of an **inverse** relationship between moral behaviour and guilt has fallen into disrepute. **MacKinnon's** (1938) study,.however, does provide some evidence for Freud's ideas. Almost 100 subjects were given a difficult task to do, but were subtly given the chance to cheat. Around 50% did, and these **cheaters** usually felt **less guilty** than the non-cheaters. Furthermore, the cheaters showed strong feelings of restlessness and aggression during testing (perhaps letting out their pent-up aggression), and were more likely (than non-cheaters) to have received physical rather than psychological punishment as children.

- An internal personality based conscience implies moral consistency across a variety of moral situations (although Freud's notion of irrational behaviour does allow some inconsistency). Thus people who have internalised a strong superego, might be expected to be consistently honest across a variety of situations. **Hartshorne and May's** (1932) study, however, found that **cheating** was **fairly situation specific**, although a later re-analysis of the data did reveal a small significant amount of consistency in honesty.

12.14 The development of social cognition of self

WHAT IS SOCIAL COGNITION?

- Social cognition refers to how individuals think about and understand themselves and other people.
- Researchers who study the development of social cognition are interested in the changes and progression over time of the thinking people show about their own and other people's thoughts, beliefs, motives, intentions, emotions, desires, and behaviour.

WHAT IS THE SELF?

Self concept
(a general term for what we think about ourselves)

Self image
(our perception of what we are)

Self esteem
(our evaluation of our worth)

Ideal self
(our image of what we would like to be)

Body image
(our notion of physical self)

Catagorical self
(our self-labelling with classifying identity terms)

Psychological self self
(our conception of ourselves as thinking beings)

THE DEVELOPMENT OF A CHILD'S SENSE OF SELF

AGE
0
1
2
3
4
5
6
7

Body – environment differentiation
The first aspect of the self to develop is the body image recognition that we are physically separate from our environment. Piaget suggested infants overcome their profound egocentrism (inability to distinguish themselves from their environment) as they move from primary circular reactions (learning to control and repeat bodily actions, e.g. thumb sucking) to secondary circular reactions (learning to control and repeat actions on external objects, e.g. squeaky toys) in the first 8 months.

Self-recognition
Once a body image has been distinguished from the environment, it has to be identified as 'me' rather than someone or something else.
According to Piaget, this internal mental concept of a distinct, individual self can only emerge once object permanence and the general symbolic function fully develop at 18–24 months.
Lewis and Brooks-Gunn (1979) found that by 20 months 75% of infants would touch their own nose if a mirror reflection showed it was coloured with rouge, and many correctly identified photos as 'me', so demonstrating self-recognition.

Categorical self
Once a body image has been formed and identified as the self, it forms the basis of other descriptive labels. Infants first classify themselves based upon physical social categories, such as sex (by $2\frac{1}{2}$ to 3), age, and later ethnicity, although an accurate understanding of these concepts is not fully achieved until around 5 to 7 years of age. Category identities become increasingly abstract and social in nature as new social roles are understood and acquired, e.g. 'cousin', 'student'. Keller et al. (1978) found 3– to 5-year-old children asked to describe themselves mostly mentioned physical appearance, performance, or possessions. Self-esteem develops as children decentre and see their categorical selves from others' perspectives.

Personal agency
Infants as young as 2 months can learn to kick their legs to produce interesting stimuli (Lewis et al., 1990). However, the concept that one can produce intentional, purposefully-planned actions increases in sophistication from the age of 8 months as, according to Piaget, the child enters the co-ordination of secondary schemas sub-stage and starts producing actions upon the environment *deliberately* rather than accidentally. Intentional behaviour develops further with tertiary circular reactions from 12–18 months as infants try different actions to achieve the same intention.

Development of Theory of Mind
Theory of Mind refers to the understanding of private mental states, processes and knowledge in oneself and other people.

- At 2–3 years of age children refer to mental states, e.g. desires and emotions, in themselves and other people, but assume other people's behaviour reflects their desires not beliefs.
- At age 3 children start to understand that thinking and knowledge occurs in the head and cannot be observed by other people or touched, but do not fully realise that others act on beliefs that may be inaccurate or different from theirs.
- Around age 4 children develop a Belief-Desire Theory of Mind that enables them to understand the nature of mental knowledge and so realise people can act on false and different beliefs.

Four-year-olds pass false-belief tests such as the Sally-Anne Test (see Baron-Cohen et al., 1985) that three-year-olds fail, and also show deceptive behaviour that reflects an understanding of private knowledge and the false beliefs of others.

Psychological self-concept
While 3- to 5-year-olds have a basic concept of psychological trait descriptions (Eder, 1990), full understanding of psychological self attributes and values requires formal operational thinking at 11.

12.15 The development of social cognition of others

PIAGET'S COGNITIVE DEVELOPMENTAL THEORY

Piaget's theory of cognitive development has been used to explain age-related changes in children's understanding of other people.

Evaluation
- Research shows that very young infants react differently towards interesting objects and people, implying the possession of innate concepts about people.
- Piaget's theory focuses more on understanding objects or concepts than people.

PIAGET'S STAGES AND SOCIAL COGNITION

Age	Stage	Changes in social cognition
0–2	Sensorimotor	Infants gradually develop the ability to distinguish people from other things, and themselves from other people, when they acquire internal schemas and object permanence.
2–7	Pre-operational	Children understand the separate physical and mental existence of other people, but focus mostly on their observable external appearance, actions, and possessions.
7–11	Concrete operational	De-centration, conservation, and classification development allows understanding of other people's perspectives, motives, and stable psychological traits/attitudes.
11+	Formal operational	Abstract thinking allows comparisons with other people on psychological dimensions.

SELMAN'S ROLE-TAKING THEORY

Selman (1976) focused more directly on social cognition than general cognitive development, but his role-taking theory and progression of his stages is underpinned by Piaget's sequence of cognitive development. Like many other researchers, Selman used children's reasoning about dilemmas to illustrate that social role-taking is an important influence on social cognition.

Evaluation
- Selman (1980) reported significant reliability and validity in the testing of his stage theory and dilemmas.
- Selman's theory triggered extensive research and has been applied to the development children's friendship, social competence, popularity, and pro-social behaviour.

SELMAN'S STAGES OF SOCIAL PERSPECTIVE TAKING

Age	Stage	Description
3–6	0 – Egocentric perspective	Aware that others have thoughts and feelings, but only follows own perspective and assumes others will view a situation in the same way.
6–8	1 – Social-informational role taking	Knows that others have different perspectives, but attributes this to their access to different information. Tends to focus on one perspective.
8–10	2 – Self-reflective role taking	Understands other's different view (despite access to the same information) and reaction to their own view, but cannot consider both at the same time.
10–12	3 – Mutual role taking	Can simultaneously consider own and other's perspectives, or even the view of a third party, and understands others can do the same.
12–15+	4 – Societal role taking	Starts to understand others' perspectives in their wider social context.

BIOLOGICAL EXPLANATIONS OF SOCIAL COGNITION

Biological explanations of social cognition focus on the brain areas involved in processing information about other people and their mental life. Research indicates that aspects of person perception may involve specialised brain areas distinct from those that deal with object recognition (see Prosopagnosia), while mirror neurons could play an important role in understanding others' intentions/emotions.

Mirror neurons are **brain cells that fire when an animal performs an action and when it sees the same action performed by others** (especially of the same species), thus mirroring another's behaviour.

Evaluation
- Gallese et al. (1996) discovered, using direct neuronal recording of the inferior frontal cortex in macaque monkeys, that certain hand-movement neurons would fire when the monkey grasped an object or when it saw another monkey or person perform a similar action.
- Similar studies on monkeys have found mirror neurons for other actions and in the parietal cortex, while fMRI imaging studies of human brains have revealed activity that indicates mirror neuron systems in similar brain areas and for a variety of behaviours.
- However, human social cognition requires many other brain areas.

THE ROLE OF THE MIRROR NEURON SYSTEM IN SOCIAL COGNITION

Social imitation – Mirror neurons provide 'embodied simulation' and so aid social development, e.g. in language acquisition – mirror neurons have been found for mouth movements during human speech, but not dog barking (Buccino et al., 2004).

Understanding intentions – Mirror neurons can fire in an anticipatory way for a sequence of actions, thus enabling the prediction of behaviour and intentions (Fogassi et al., 2005). Mirror neurons may thus form the basis of a Theory of Mind.

Empathy – Mirror neurons have been found that fire when humans experience an emotion or see it in the facial expression of another (Wicker et al., 2003).

Evaluation
- Deficiencies in cortical mirror neurons, and thus the above functions, may explain autism.
- Mirror neurons cannot explain all social cognition.

13.1 Theories of intelligence 1

THE PSYCHOMETRIC APPROACH TO INTELLIGENCE

WHAT IS THE PSYCHOMETRIC APPROACH?
- Psychometric theories involve the measurement of psychological characteristics, such as extraversion and intelligence.
- Characteristics are regarded as traits which all humans possess, but differ upon in a way that can be quantitatively measured with standardised tests/questionnaires to enable the comparison of individual scores.
- Psychometric tests are used for selection purposes and thus have important social implications.

PSYCHOMETRIC THEORIES OF INTELLIGENCE
- The psychometric approach has dominated psychological research on intelligence and was built on the early work of Binet and Simon who were asked by the French government to create a test to distinguish 'dull' from 'normal' children. They measured general mental ability in the classroom by developing a large selection of cognitive tasks on different kinds of reasoning and comprehension, which were later classified by age to provide each tested child with a mental age score. Terman (1916) derived '*intelligence quotient*' (IQ) scores by dividing the mental age by the actual age of the test taker (× 100), but this procedure is no longer used – even though the term 'IQ' is still applied to describe intelligence test scores.
- Today IQ tests exist for adults as well as children, contain a variety of verbal and non-verbal items, and are standardised to have a mean score of 100 and a standard deviation of 15 (so that around 95% of the population have scores within two standard deviations of the mean, i.e. between 70 and 130).

Factor analysis
Researchers from the psychometric approach have investigated the concept of intelligence by *statistically analysing the scores* of different types of test item (e.g. verbal, spatial) using a method known as factor analysis.
Factor analysis identifies groups or *clusters of test items that correlate highly together*, but less so with other types of item, thus indicating they measure the same, distinct aspect of intelligence, e.g. 'verbal' rather than 'spatial' intelligence.
However, this type of analysis has led to disagreement among different psychometric researchers over exactly how many types of intelligence there are.

Spearman's 'g'
Spearman's (1927) factor analysed children's scores on a variety of test items, concluding they were all moderately correlated so must be derived from *a single general mental ability* he termed '*g*'. Any inconsistent performance on a particular type of test item he termed '**s**' for a specific 'special ability'.

Thurstone's primary mental abilities
Thurstone's (1938) factor analysis revealed ***seven*** distinct clusters or factors of IQ test performance which he called primary mental abilities - verbal meaning, word fluency, numerical reasoning, inductive reasoning, spatial ability, memory and perceptual speed - all of which accounted for Spearman's 'g'.

PSYCHOMETRIC THEORIES OF INTELLIGENCE

Guilford's structure of intellect model
Guilford (1967) suggested that intelligence could be divided into *180 distinct mental abilities* based upon classifying cognitive tasks on a combination of 3 dimensions:
- Content – 5 types of task subject
- Operations – 6 types of task thinking
- Products – 6 types of required answer.

Cattell's fluid and crystallised factors
Cattell (1963) found 'g', primary mental abilities, and other test items can be factored into two dimensions:
Fluid intelligence – the ability to solve new, abstract, unlearnt, culture-free problems, e.g. inductive reasoning or perceptual speed.
Crystallised intelligence – the ability to solve problems based on acquired knowledge, e.g. verbal meaning.

EVALUATION OF THE PSYCHOMETRIC APPROACH TO INTELLIGENCE
- Individual psychometric measurements of IQ ('g') remain stable over time and predict academic achievement well.
- Distinguishing primary mental abilities has been useful for the identification and selection of specifically required skills.
- Distinguishing fluid and crystallised intelligence has been useful in understanding developmental changes in IQ scores over time, e.g. crystallised intelligence increases in old age, but fluid intelligence decreases.

- Different factor-analytic theories reflect different ways of dividing up abilities associated with intelligence; some prefer an integrated hierarchical model with 'g' at the top, subdividing down into more specialist types.
- However, there is still disagreement over what 'g' actually represents – is it generalised abstract reasoning, neural processing speed, or just a statistical regularity?
- Many criticise the psychometric approach for cultural bias, artificiality, and ignoring important mental abilities or intelligence in practical, everyday situations.

13.2 Theories of intelligence 2

THE INFORMATION PROCESSING APPROACH TO INTELLIGENCE

The information processing approach aims to investigate the **underlying cognitive processes involved in intelligence** rather than just measure it (as the psychometric approach does). Sternberg's Triarchic Theory incorporates an attempt to understand the information processing underlying different types of intelligence.

STERNBERG'S TRIARCHIC THEORY

Sternberg (1985) investigated three aspects of intelligence:

Analytical intelligence – this is what IQ tests measure, but Sternberg's *componential subtheory* is more concerned with the cognitive information processes that underlie academic problem-solving abilities. The theory proposes that different components contribute to the development of analytical intelligence: metacomponents are higher-order processes that analyse and select strategies for performance components (basic cognitive processes like mental calculation) to implement, whereas knowledge components are processes or strategies for acquiring and memorising new information.

Creative intelligence – the *experiential subtheory* suggests that the ability to respond to novel situations and consciously apply existing knowledge to new problems is a good indicator of intelligent reasoning. However, the ability to rapidly automatise information processing strategies with practice (i.e. 'picking up' skills quickly) also reflects intelligence. Automatisation speeds up task performance and frees attention to apply other mental processes to a problem.

Practical intelligence – the *contextual subtheory* argues that intelligence also involves successfully adapting to, shaping or selecting environments to achieve desired goals. This implies that social intelligence or 'street smarts' should also be measured in IQ tests and that the types of behaviour regarded as intelligent may vary with context and culture.

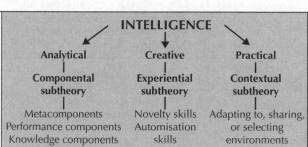

Evaluation

- Understanding the cognitive processes underlying intelligence helps us understand IQ test performance and provides ideas on how intelligence can be improved.
- The theory highlights the point that traditional IQ tests neglect aspects of creative and practical intelligence that would help predict future performance in the wider world, not just in academic, educational settings. Sternberg and others have developed tests of 'tacit knowledge' that predict job performance fairly well.
- The triarchic theory shows how IQ tests may be biased, e.g. against creative people (e.g. by only having a single correct answer arrived at by a single method) or different cultures (e.g. who may not be familiar with, and thus not yet have automatised, formal academic test skills).

GARDNER'S THEORY OF MULTIPLE INTELLIGENCES

Gardner (1983) also criticises psychometric theories of 'g' and argues that psychometric tests only investigate certain types of mental ability (mostly linguistic, spatial and logical intelligence). Gardner proposes **seven types of intelligence** (although he allows there may be others) which may predict success in different vocations and real-life tasks:

1 *Linguistic* – e.g. verbal meaning and fluency, which could predict careers in writing, journalism, etc.

2 *Logical-mathematical* – e.g. inductive, numerical and systematic reasoning, which may predict success in certain scientific careers.

3 *Spatial* – e.g. perceiving or manipulating visual-spatial relationships, which help in engineering, artistic, architectural or navigational jobs.

4 *Body-kinaesthetic* – e.g. using the body skilfully to achieve goals, which helps athletes, dancers and surgeons.

5 *Musical* – e.g. sensitivity to tone, rhythm and melody, of use to musicians, composers, conductors, sound engineers or cardiologists.

6 *Interpersonal* – e.g. skill in understanding and interacting with other people, which may help therapists, politicians, and salespeople.

7 *Intrapersonal* – e.g. the ability of self-insight and understanding – of use to everyone, particularly in assessing one's own strengths and weaknesses to choose the most suitable vocation.

Evaluation

- Psychometric studies of the seven intelligences (especially the first three) indict they correlate reasonable well together, suggesting a possible common underlying factor ('g'?).
- There is some dispute over the use of the term 'intelligence', which some regard as applying more to the first three types than to the other 'skills' or 'specialist talents'.

EVIDENCE OF DISTINCT INTELLIGENCES

Unlike the psychometric approach, Gardner provides a variety of evidence for distinguishing different mental abilities (rather than just a factor-analytic division of IQ test results), including:

- *Brain damage isolation evidence* – different intelligences seem to have their own neurological basis since brain damage that affects one, e.g. loss of speech, leaves the others intact.
- *Cases of exceptional talents* – some individuals show extraordinary levels of one intelligence, e.g. musical child prodigies, despite having normal levels of other intelligences (or even subnormal levels, e.g. 'idiot savants' with outstanding artistic or mathematical intelligence).
- *Distinct developmental progression* – different intelligences develop in different ways, e.g. linguistic ability develops quickly without direct instruction for the majority of children, whereas logical-mathematical ability takes longer and requires some form of tuition for most people.

Gardner's theory also has implications for findings relating to group differences, e.g. sex differences in verbal and spatial intelligence (women on average score higher on the former, men on the latter) or cultural ones, e.g. the focus on logical-mathematical rather than interpersonal intelligence in North American education and IQ tests.

13.3 Classical conditioning

Classical conditioning is concerned with **learning by association**, and refers to the **conditioning of reflexes** – how animals learn to **associate new stimuli with innate bodily reflexes**. The principles of classical conditioning were first outlined by **Pavlov**, and were then adopted by behaviourists, such as Watson, who attempted to use them to explain how virtually all of human behaviour is acquired. Pavlov was a physiologist who, while studying the salivation reflex, found that the dogs he was using in his experiments would sometimes start salivating before the food had reached their mouths, often at the sight of the food bucket. Clearly the dogs had learnt to **associate new external stimuli** (such as sights and sounds), with the **original stimulus** (food) that caused the salivation reflex. In a series of thorough and well controlled experiments, Pavlov found many new stimuli could be associated with reflexes and went on to introduce special terms for, and investigated many aspects of, the conditioning process.

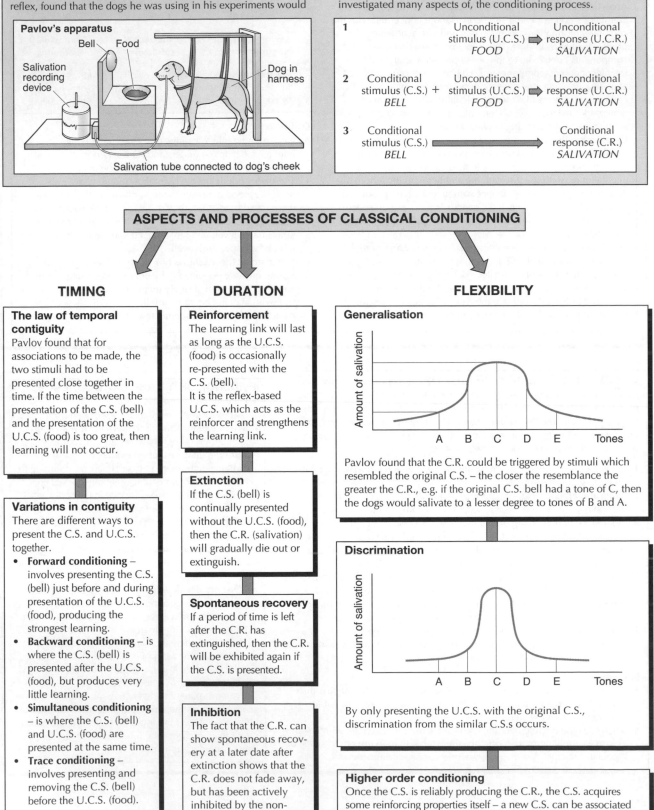

Pavlov's apparatus

Bell   Food

Salivation recording device

Dog in harness

Salivation tube connected to dog's cheek

1   Unconditional stimulus (U.C.S.) ➡ Unconditional response (U.C.R.)
    FOOD   *SALIVATION*

2   Conditional stimulus (C.S.) + Unconditional stimulus (U.C.S.) ➡ Unconditional response (U.C.R.)
    BELL   *FOOD*   *SALIVATION*

3   Conditional stimulus (C.S.) ⟶ Conditional response (C.R.)
    BELL   *SALIVATION*

ASPECTS AND PROCESSES OF CLASSICAL CONDITIONING

TIMING

The law of temporal contiguity
Pavlov found that for associations to be made, the two stimuli had to be presented close together in time. If the time between the presentation of the C.S. (bell) and the presentation of the U.C.S. (food) is too great, then learning will not occur.

Variations in contiguity
There are different ways to present the C.S. and U.C.S. together.
- **Forward conditioning** – involves presenting the C.S. (bell) just before and during presentation of the U.C.S. (food), producing the strongest learning.
- **Backward conditioning** – is where the C.S. (bell) is presented after the U.C.S. (food), but produces very little learning.
- **Simultaneous conditioning** – is where the C.S. (bell) and U.C.S. (food) are presented at the same time.
- **Trace conditioning** – involves presenting and removing the C.S. (bell) before the U.C.S. (food).

DURATION

Reinforcement
The learning link will last as long as the U.C.S. (food) is occasionally re-presented with the C.S. (bell).
It is the reflex-based U.C.S. which acts as the reinforcer and strengthens the learning link.

Extinction
If the C.S. (bell) is continually presented without the U.C.S. (food), then the C.R. (salivation) will gradually die out or extinguish.

Spontaneous recovery
If a period of time is left after the C.R. has extinguished, then the C.R. will be exhibited again if the C.S. is presented.

Inhibition
The fact that the C.R. can show spontaneous recovery at a later date after extinction shows that the C.R. does not fade away, but has been actively inhibited by the non-presentation of the U.C.S.

FLEXIBILITY

Generalisation

Amount of salivation

A   B   C   D   E   Tones

Pavlov found that the C.R. could be triggered by stimuli which resembled the original C.S. – the closer the resemblance the greater the C.R., e.g. if the original C.S. bell had a tone of C, then the dogs would salivate to a lesser degree to tones of B and A.

Discrimination

Amount of salivation

A   B   C   D   E   Tones

By only presenting the U.C.S. with the original C.S., discrimination from the similar C.S.s occurs.

Higher order conditioning
Once the C.S. is reliably producing the C.R., the C.S. acquires some reinforcing properties itself – a new C.S. can be associated with the original C.S., until the new C.S. will also produce the C.R.

13.4 Operant conditioning

THE BASIC THEORY

Operant conditioning involves learning through the consequences of behavioural responses. The principles of operant conditioning were first investigated by **Thorndike**, and were then thoroughly developed by the famous behaviourist Skinner, who applied them to explain how many aspects of human behaviour are acquired. Thorndike studied the way cats would learn to escape from his puzzle box by **trial and error**. Cats did not immediately acquire the desirable escape behaviour, but gradually increased in their ability to show it over time. Nevertheless, Thorndike found that any response that led to desirable consequences was more likely to occur again, whereas any response that led to undesirable consequences was less likely to be repeated – a principle which became known as the **Law of Effect**.

However, as with classical conditioning, the law of contiguity applies – associations between responses and consequences have to be made close together in time for learning to occur.

Thorndike's puzzle box

Cats had to emit the response of pulling the string inside the box to release the catch on the door to provide escape (a pleasant consequence). Time to escape decreased with each trial (the number of times the cat was put back in the box).

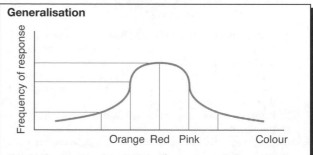

Skinner box

Rats had to press a lever to receive a food pellet, which would increase the likelihood of the lever pressing response reoccurring.

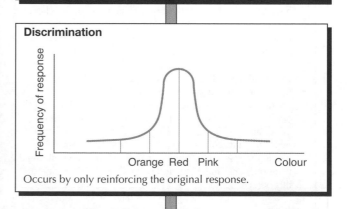

ASPECTS OF REINFORCEMENT

CONSEQUENCES

Positive reinforcement
This increases the likelihood of a response by providing pleasant consequences for it, e.g. food.

Negative reinforcement
This increases the likelihood of a response that removes or provides escape from unpleasant consequences, e.g. stopping an electric shock.

Punishment
This decreases the likelihood of a response being repeated if it is followed by inescapable negative/unpleasant consequences, e.g. an electric shock.

Secondary reinforcement
Secondary reinforcers are those that are associated with naturally occurring primary reinforcers (e.g. food, water, warmth, etc.), for example money, tokens, or parents.

FREQUENCY

Schedules of reinforcement
Continuous schedules – involve reinforcing every response made.
Partial schedules – involve reinforcing responses in varying frequencies to affect response and extinction rates, for example:
- *Fixed ratio schedule* – reinforcing a fixed number of responses (e.g. a food pellet for every ten lever presses in a Skinner box).
- *Variable ratio schedule* – reinforcing an average number of responses (e.g. a food pellet on average every ten lever presses, sometimes after 8 sometimes after 12 presses).
- *Fixed interval schedule* – reinforcing after a fixed amount of time (e.g. a food pellet for a lever press each minute in a Skinner box).
- *Variable interval schedule* – reinforcing after an average amount of time (e.g. a food pellet on average each minute, sometimes after 50 seconds sometimes after 70).

Extinction
If the response is not reinforced, it will gradually die out or extinguish.

FLEXIBILITY

Generalisation

Skinner found animals would make responses that resembled the originally reinforced response - a pigeon reinforced for pecking a red key, would also peck (although less frequently) at an orange or pink key.

Discrimination

Occurs by only reinforcing the original response.

Behaviour shaping
By reinforcing responses that increasingly resemble a desired end behaviour in a step by step manner, very complex behaviour can be built up from simple units.
The first responses are reinforced until perfected and then reinforcement is withheld until the behaviour is refined to the next desired behaviour.

13.5 Evaluation of classical and operant conditioning

EVALUATION OF METHODOLOGY

STRENGTHS – The theories of classical and operant conditioning were the product of behaviourist psychology with its emphasis on observable behaviour and laboratory experimentation. With such objective and standardised methodology the principles of classical and operant conditioning could be reliably replicated while reducing the effect of possible confounding variables. Animals such as dogs, cats, pigeons and rats were frequently used as experimental subjects since the behaviourists believed the laws of learning were universal and they have the advantage of being practically and ethically easier to test (they can be tested under more controlled conditions, do not try to work out the nature of the test and are given less ethical rights etc.).

WEAKNESSES – Unfortunately the methods employed also had disadvantages. The experimental subjects often demonstrated learning of only a small range of unnatural responses, e.g. animals pressing levers or pushing buttons, under artificially controlled conditions, e.g. Albert B was not allowed to suck his thumb (he failed to show the same fear response when he did so). This may have led the behaviourists to ignore behaviour their subjects might have found difficult to learn and neglect other influences upon the learning process. This criticism was especially relevant to the study of non-human animal learning which may be qualitatively different to human learning in important ways. There were also serious ethical problems with some of the procedures used in classical and operant conditioning studies.

EVALUATION OF CLASSICAL AND OPERANT CONDITIONING THEORIES

STRENGTHS – The behaviourists used the theories of classical and operant conditioning to explain a wide variety of psychological phenomena, from the processes of learning to the products of it such as phobia and language acquisition. In addition many practical applications of the theory were developed, from animal training to human education and the treatment of disordered behaviour. In many cases such applications have been shown to be efficient in producing behavioural change.

WEAKNESSES – Unfortunately classical and operant conditioning did not take into account the role of inherited and cognitive factors in learning, and are thus incomplete explanations of the learning process in humans and other animals. By focusing on just a few species such as rats or pigeons and generalising the results to all animals, the behaviourists not only ignored the differing cognitive influences on learning that different species show (e.g. the ability of humans to learn by observation and imitation), but importantly neglected the innate abilities in learning that every species will have evolved to better adapt themselves to their environmental niche.

INNATE BIASES IN LEARNING ABILITY

Ethologists would argue that animals have 'built-in' biases in natural learning ability that they have evolved to better adapt them to their environment. The laws of learning are therefore not the same for all species, for example:

- **Selectivity of associations and phobias** – Garcia and Koelling (1966) found that rats given a novel tasting solution and made to feel sick up to 3 *hours* afterwards would still learn to associate the two events and avoid that solution on future occasions, even after *only one* such trial in some cases. It therefore seems likely that rats have evolved a highly sensitive learning capability between taste and sickness, especially since this sensitivity makes 'evolutionary sense' – it aids survival. Seligman (1970) proposed the concept of **biological preparedness** and argued that humans have also evolved selective associations for survival reasons, in the form of **phobias** for example. The most frequently occurring phobias, e.g. of heights, snakes, spiders, etc., all share the evolutionary characteristic of being dangerous to us, and these sort of stimuli have been experimentally shown to be more easily classically conditioned with fear than non-dangerous stimuli such as flowers and grass, which are far more rarely found as phobias. Also of interest is the finding that modern day dangerous objects such as guns and cars are also rare phobias since evolution has not had time to *prepare* us for these stimuli.

- **Imprinting and language acquisition** – Lorenz (1935) showed an increased learning sensitivity to particular stimuli could occur at *certain times* in an animal's life when it is most important to acquire this learning. In his studies of imprinting he found that goslings would form strong attachments to moving, conspicuous objects in their environment during the first hours after hatching, and will follow and stay close to this object.

  In a similar way some researchers have argued that human *language acquisition* takes place during a sensitive time period early in life. A species-specific, evolved human potential for language (a Language Acquisition Device according to Chomsky) would account for the ease with which young children learn to speak and understand complex grammar as well as the failure to teach human language to apes to the same standard.

COGNITIVE FACTORS IN LEARNING

Classical and operant conditioning also ignore the cognitive factors between the stimulus and response that influence learning. In operant conditioning for example, a number of researchers have demonstrated that learning does not always happen by trial and error, reinforcement is not always necessary for learning to occur and learning can produce changes in mental representations rather than just behaviour.

- **Insight learning** – Kohler found primates often seem to solve problems in a flash of insight (involving a cognitive rearrangement of the elements of the problem) rather than by laborious trial and error.
- **Latent learning** – Tolman found rats will learn mazes without reinforcement and that they acquire mental maps of the mazes rather than a series of left and right turning behaviours.
- **Social Learning theory** – suggests:
  1 Humans can learn *automatically* through *observation* rather than requiring reinforcement through personal experience.
  2 Observed behaviour may be *imitated* if desirable consequences are expected (whole 'chunks' of behaviour can be copied without the need for gradual trial-and-error practice).

13.6 Social learning in non-human animals

EXPLANATIONS OF SOCIAL LEARNING

WHAT IS IT?
Social learning refers to behaviour that is acquired as a result of experience with others rather than that acquired alone (individual learning). Individual learning in animals has been shown to occur through classical and operant conditioning, but there is debate as to whether additional methods of learning are involved in social learning.

WHY DOES IT OCCUR?
There are many possible benefits of social learning, not least that useful survival behaviour relating to foraging and predator avoidance can be acquired faster and more safely by learning from others than by having to discover them individually by trial and error. The evolutionary importance of social learning is illustrated by the finding that in some species parents spend time and effort helping their offspring acquire important survival techniques.

HOW DOES IT OCCUR?
Heyes (1993) points out that other animals can provide useful information concerning both the environment and behaviour used in interacting with it, however, social learning of this information by observation may occur through different methods:

- **Stimulus enhancement** – involves learning about the **environment** through observing others. It is the tendency to **pay attention to**, and thus interact with, certain **places or objects** in the environment after observing others successfully interacting with them. The **behaviour** of the other animal is **not copied** directly, but it increases the chance that the observer will **learn by individual trial and error** to perform similar behaviour to gain the same **rewards**. Information about the stimulus not response is learned.
- **True imitation** – involves learning about the actual **form of behaviour** by observing others. In true imitation the observation of another's pattern of behaviour is causal to changing the observer's pattern of behaviour and allows **novel** (not previously shown) and **complex actions** to be **automatically learned** without the need for reinforcement. Performing the behaviour may or may not depend on reinforcement. True imitation, learning about responses rather than stimuli, is rarely shown in animals.

STUDIES OF SOCIAL LEARNING

BIRDS
Foraging – Fisher and Hinde (1949) suggested that the ability of blue tits and other birds to open the tops of milk bottles to gain the cream was due to imitation, given the rapid spread of the behaviour from town to town. However, since pecking and tearing objects are pre-existing foraging behaviours of these birds rather than novel actions, stimulus enhancement is a more likely explanation – the attention of birds was drawn to bottle tops opened by others, thus increasing the chance of pecking being directed at that particular stimulus. The birds already knew how to peck; they only learned what and where to peck. Similarly, birds may learn where to nest, migrate or not be afraid by following others to certain locations. The presence of other birds may also have a social facilitation effect – encouraging behaviour by increasing motivation or reducing fear (Sherry and Galef, 1990).

Bird song – is more likely to represent a limited form of true imitation in some species, e.g. chaffinches who imitate local dialects or parrots and mynahs who can mimic human speech.

MONKEYS
Foraging – Itani (1958) reported how, in one colony of Japanese macaques, a juvenile named 'Imo' discovered how to wash sweet potatoes and separate food from sand with water, and the behaviour spread to her playmates and their mothers. Rather than imitation, the behaviour (which took a long time to spread) was likely to be due to stimulus enhancement and individual learning (as Imo drew attention to potatoes and water) or inadvertent reinforcement by the researchers who provided the food. However, macaque mothers do guide stimulus enhancement by pulling away their infants from strange food or objects and modelling certain styles of potato washing (Kawai, 1963, 1965a).

PRIMATES
Foraging – Boesch (1991) reported that chimpanzee mothers actively 'teach' their young how to open nuts with stone tools. This involves elaborate stimulus enhancement through the provision of materials, demonstration and corrective intervention. Imitation cannot be ruled out, but is thought to be less likely if the 'simpler' and well-established processes of stimulus attention and trial-and-error learning can adequately explain the learning.

Problem solving – Many studies have shown that 'enculturated' primates seem to show complex forms of delayed imitation. However, Call and Tomasello (1995) found orang-utans do not readily use imitation to solve problems. This is in contrast to observations by Russon and Galdikas (1995) of orang-utans being rehabilitated in Indonesia who have been seen using complex sequences of imitated behaviours to attempt to re-light a fire (by using kerosene scooped out of a drum with a cup and fanning the embers with a cooking lid) or even to steal laundry (by emptying a canoe of water and using it to sneak past a guard) and wash it (using soap and scrubbing brush).

13.7 Intelligence in non-human animals

WHAT IS ANIMAL INTELLIGENCE?

The assessment of intelligence in non-human animals is hampered by the difficulty of defining what intelligence is. Intelligence is an abstract concept and attempts to define and test it may be biased by the values and conceptions of the definers and testers – this has already happened with human testing and becomes even more problematic when attempting to judge other animals by human criteria. In general terms, intelligence has been defined as the ability to learn from experience and to adapt to changes in the environment as a result – acquiring and using knowledge efficiently. The extent to which organisms can learn and adapt depends upon:

* The range of abilities they have – e.g. perceptual, learning, reasoning, memory, spatial, numerical, linguistic, meta-cognitive, etc.
* The complexity of those abilities – e.g. higher level types of learning and reasoning (more intelligent species may be able to use imitation and insight rather than trial-and-error learning, or use self-monitoring and social attribution to select the best strategies).
* The efficiency and speed of applying those abilities – e.g. based on physical ability and/or experience/practice (highly trained or enculturated animals show more complex and rapid adaptive behaviour).

Two particular examples of abilities that have been associated with intelligence in animals are self-recognition and theory of mind.

EVIDENCE FOR INTELLIGENCE IN ANIMALS

SELF-RECOGNITION

Self-recognition may be the physical sign of self-awareness in animals, which may be important in enabling animals to monitor their own thoughts, feelings and behaviour. Self-awareness may help animals to predict the outcome of behaviour, select appropriate strategies and understand other animals' motivations and behaviour (see theory of mind).

* Self-recognition has only been found (using the mirror self-recognition test) in humans and primates (chimpanzees, gorillas and orang-utans).
* Gallop (1970) found that chimps could learn to recognise themselves in mirrors since they:
  1 Gradually stopped reacting (e.g. threatening or calling) as if another animal was present.
  2 Learned to use the mirrors to explore parts of their body they could not normally see.
  3 Touched areas on their heads that had been coloured red more often when in front of a mirror than not.
* Criticisms have been made of Gallop's mirror recognition method since, for example, the red marks had to be applied under anaesthetic which may have affected body touching behaviour and the same results are not reliably found.
* However, Savage-Rumbaugh and Lewin (1994) report that chimpanzees will react to their own image on live-video monitors (e.g. making faces, bobbing up and down, or using it with a torch to look down their own throats) and can use such information to guide arm movements they cannot directly see (e.g. to retrieve food through a small arm hole), but will respond differently to previously taped images of themselves. Also the interest and use of mirrors differs across individual chimpanzees and within the same individual over time, which may account for the unreliability of the mirror test results.
* There is also doubt over whether self-recognition is a valid indicator of conscious self-awareness (rather than of just a body image).

THEORY OF MIND

Theory of mind refers to the ability to realise that others also have intentions, knowledge, beliefs and emotional states, but that these may differ from one's own. A theory of mind allows the possessor to attribute knowledge to others and, practically, to use differences in knowledge to deceive others.

Experimental studies

* Povinelli *et al.* (1990) found chimpanzees could attribute knowledge to humans by selecting the correct hiding place for food (which they could then eat) when two researchers each pointed to a different possible location, but only one had been seen to have knowledge of the true location (the other was outside when the chimp had seen the researcher hide the food but behind a screen).
* Woodruff and Premack (1979) found chimps, who knew the location of hidden food that they could not reach, tended to indicate the correct location to an unaware researcher if that researcher had been cooperative (given the food to the chimp). However, if the researcher had been competitive (keeping the food if directed to the correct location) but the chimp had received the food if it had indicated the wrong location, then the chimps tended towards deception. This involved an attribution of intent to the humans by the chimps.
* However, in both of these laboratory experiments, the chimps may just have been responding to some other cue, such as learning to associate different researchers with different rewards through operant conditioning.

Naturalistic observations

* Byrne and Whiten (1987) gathered reports of examples of tactical deception (where the animal intends to deceive by using 'an 'honest act' from his normal repertoire in a different context, such that even familiar individuals are misled') from over a hundred researchers studying animal behaviour in the wild. By applying strict criteria they found relatively few examples, all of which were shown by apes, mostly chimpanzees (Savage-Rumbaugh and Lewin, 1994). These usually involved deceptions over food by, for example, pretending not to have seen food that others had failed to notice in order to avoid sharing or losing it.

13.8 Teaching human language to primates

WHAT IS LANGUAGE?

Hockett (1960) and Aitchison proposed various *design criteria to define language* as opposed to animal signalling, including:

Structure – the form of language should show:
- *Arbitrariness* – the symbols used do not have to resemble the objects they stand for.
- *Duality and organisation* – the language should be divisible into subcomponents which can be combined.
- *Structure dependence* – the possession of grammatical rules for combining units of language.

Delivery – language should transmit messages:
- *Spontaneously* – the sender can initiate language at will and does not have to wait for triggers or cues.
- *By turn taking* – users can alternate conversational turns.

Function – language should allow:
- *Interchangeability* – the sending and receiving messages.
- *Semanticity* – the use of symbols to stand for or refer to objects, situations, events, concepts, etc.
- *Displacement* – communication about non-present things.
- *Productivity* – creating infinite new messages/meanings.
- *Prevarication* – the creation of conversation about things that have not happened, e.g. fiction or lies.
- *Learnability and transmission* – the acquisition of language and transferral to the next generation.
- *Reflexiveness* – using language to talk about language.

EXAMPLES OF LANGUAGE STUDIES WITH PRIMATES

Study	Result	Evaluation
WASHOE – Gardner and Gardner (1969) taught American Sign Language to Washoe, a female common chimpanzee.	**Semanticity** – she comprehended and used over 130 distinct signs by the age of 4. **Productivity** – generalised signs to similar situations, e.g. called a swan 'water bird'. **Transmission** – taught signs to her children and other chimpanzees.	Four-year-old human children would have acquired around 3000 words. Terrace accused the experimenters of unconsciously cueing the production of signs indicating imitation rather than understanding of meaning.
LANA – Rumbaugh (1977) taught the common chimpanzee Lana an artificial language of symbols (Yerkish) on a computer keyboard.	**Productivity** – e.g. Lana created 'green banana' for a cucumber. **Grammatical structure** – understood the word order difference between 'Tim groom Lana' and 'Lana groom Tim'.	Lana could monitor and correct the signs she typed into the computer by watching a screen that displayed them, perhaps indicating reading ability.
KOKO – Patterson (1978) taught a gorilla, Koko, American Sign Language using operant conditioning and modelling.	**Productivity** – e.g. created self description 'red, mad gorilla' and insult 'dirty toilet'. **Reflexiveness** – e.g. 'good sign Michael'. **Displacement** – e.g. apologised for biting 3 days before. **Prevarication** – lied and joked.	Terrace said apes do not spontaneously initiate conversation, but merely respond to cues or stimuli they have been reinforced for. However, Koko often initiates requests and signs to herself and her dolls when alone.
NIM CHIMPSY – Terrace (1979) taught the male common chimpanzee, Nim, American Sign Language using operant conditioning and modelling.	Grammatical structure – there is some evidence that Nim showed two word order 'pivot grammar' similar to young human children (i.e. put the verb first in a two word utterance in 83% of cases).	Terrace argued that Nim only produced language behaviour without understanding of meaning, rarely produced more than two word utterances and did not develop turn-taking interaction.
KANZI – Savage-Rumbaugh (1986) studied the male Bonobo chimpanzee Kanzi, who spontaneously learnt language by observation using a computer lexigram – a 'speaking' keyboard of visual language symbols.	Displacement – requests/discusses events over the telephone. Ignores present oranges if asked to fetch one from elsewhere. Grammatical understanding and use – uses two word grammatical ordering of verb before action.	One of the most successful attempts. Used very careful double-blind testing conditions and all studies were videotaped. Kanzi is regularly tested under ecologically valid conditions (travelling through woodland each day).

CONCLUSIONS

- **Productivity vs. comprehension** – there is much debate over the relative importance of these. Savage–Rumbaugh has suggested that true ape *comprehension* of human language could be regarded as a cognitive equivalent of having acquired it.
- **The importance of grammar** – apes have shown comprehension of fairly complex grammatical sentences and produced two-word pivot grammar, but have not progressed much further. However, word order is not always consistent in human language.
- **Comparative abilities** – The speed and extent of language and grammar acquisition in other animals, however, is far slower than in humans. A human child at the age of four is more linguistically competent than any other older animal.
- **Comparative physiology** – Some researchers think primates lack brain structures to support language; however a study by Gannon *et al.* found chimpanzee brains with signs of language areas similar to humans on the left side of the cortex.
- **Objectivity of research** – Some argue the attachments animal language researchers develop to their subject matter and their tendency to show anthropomorphism to animal behaviour, distorts the objectivity of the studies leading to over-exaggerated findings. The researchers counter that attachment, close interaction and support is necessary to teach language to apes.
- **Alternative explanations** – Many animal language researchers disagree with Terrace's view that ape language-like behaviour just reflects sophisticated operant conditioning responses to gain reward, not understanding of the meaning of those responses.

13.9 'Spontaneous symbol acquisition and communicative use by pygmy chimpanzees'

Savage-Rumbaugh *et al.* (1986)

INTRODUCTION

Previous research on the language acquisition capacity of three out of the four species of great apes had revealed they could learn by **personal association** to use **symbols** (e.g. with American Sign Language or by indicating visual images on a keyboard) to produce desirable events.

Common chimpanzees given intensive and maintained sub-skill training had also learned to use these symbols **referentially** (i.e. with meanings independent of the immediate personal context or situation), e.g. to indicate future intended behaviour or to orientate the attention of others.

The transition from associative to referential/representational symbol use is regarded as a vital step in the development of human language acquisition, and is seen in human infants when they spontaneously begin to initiate activities with words and respond to them appropriately 'in the absence of context-dependent gestures or routines'. However, the authors argue that **ape** research had **not** yet objectively demonstrated:

* spontaneous **referential** symbol **production** without intensive training
* spontaneous referential symbol comprehension of **spoken English**
* referential language in **pygmy** chimpanzees (the 4th great ape species).

AIMS

The study was initiated after observations that an infant pygmy chimpanzee, Kanzi, seemed to have started using symbols spontaneously.

The aim of the study was to investigate language acquisition capability in the pygmy chimpanzee. In particular, the authors aimed to:

* Provide detailed data to provide a **complete record of all language behaviour.**
* **Objectively** investigate Kanzi's language development with controlled naturalistic and formal **tests** of **referential** language use and **spoken English comprehension**.
* To **compare** Kanzi's language use and development with his younger half-sister, two common chimpanzees studied at the same research centre, previous chimpanzee studies, and human infants.

METHOD

Design
Case study
Longitudinal design

Variables studied:
Symbol use, measured as:
* Correct
* Incorrect (to avoid accusations of data selection)
* Imitation (of symbols emitted just before by others)
* Structured (initiated by question, request or gesture)
* Spontaneous (with no prior prompting).

Participants
* Kanzi – a pygmy chimpanzee born in captivity, sent to the language research centre at six months of age with his wild-caught mother Matata, who was given training in language symbols in his presence. When separated from his mother at 2.5 years of age, he spontaneously began to use the language symbols despite having received no training himself.
* Mulika – Kanzi's younger half-sister (same species) who started using symbols at 11 months of age.
* Austin and Sherman – two common chimpanzees given formal language training on the same symbol system from the ages of $1\frac{1}{2}$ and $2\frac{1}{2}$ respectively.

Procedure
From age 2.5, for a 17-month period, researchers recorded Kanzi's use of a lexigram keyboard (a board covered with geometric visual symbols that represent words, brighten when touched, and activate a speech synthesiser to produce the appropriate spoken word). Unlike Sherman and Austin, no formal language training was given to Kanzi and Mulika, who were just exposed to humans using the keyboard as well as spoken English and gestures to describe everyday objects, activities and interactions with the apes and each other. All ape symbol use was recorded with notes on context (with high inter-rater reliability based on video analysis) both inside the language centre and outside in a 55-acre forest.

Tests of language:
Spontaneous symbol use, verified by **behaviour concordance** measures (checks that behaviour reflected symbol meaning) on 9 out of 10 occasions, was the criteria for vocabulary acquisition.

Informal structured utterance tests (responding correctly to everyday questions/requests) assessed symbol comprehension.

Formal laboratory matching tests of vocabulary – e.g. matching photographs to lexigrams, spoken English to lexigrams and synthesised speech to lexigrams, on 3 out of 3 occasions (with controls to exclude experimenter cues and chance selection).

Formal naturalistic tests of spontaneous referential symbol use – e.g. spontaneous selection of 1 of 6–10 food images followed by correctly guiding a person (blind to the test) to one of 17 locations in the 55-acre forest where that food could be found.

RESULTS
* Kanzi performed almost perfectly on all tests.
* Kanzi spontaneously used symbols referentially (in the absence of context-dependent gestures or routines), without specific training or consistent use of food rewards, and without confusing similar items, to initiate activities and indicate future intentions/events.
* Kanzi understood spoken English in the absence of cues, without having received formal training.
* Kanzi used 3-word novel combinations, 36% of which referred to actions involving agents other than himself.
* Although younger, Mulika's data corroborate Kanzi's.
* Sherman and Austin did not show referential symbol use without training or understand spoken English.

DISCUSSION
* The study represents the first properly documented account of referential symbol acquisition and spoken English comprehension without specific training in a non-human species, suggesting linguistic abilities similar to our own.
* Kanzi's linguistic development, from associational routines to referential symbols extracted from commonalities in different examples, seems to mirror human processes.
* Pygmy chimpanzees naturally differ (e.g. in cognitive ability, gestures, and vocalisations) from other apes in ways that might better predispose them to language acquisition.
* Limited sample/generalisability, but pygmy chimps are rare and language research requires expensive, in-depth, labour-intensive and time-consuming longitudinal case studies.

13.10 Evolutionary factors in the development of human intelligence

ECOLOGICAL FACTORS

Human intelligence and brain size could be associated with ecological factors, such as environmental complexity. This could involve the challenges encountered in foraging and the unpredictability of the environment, for example:

- The distribution food may require sophisticated search skills or cognitive maps of the environment.
- The capture of food may require co-ordinated planning and attack strategies, or the fabrication of tools and invention of food processing strategies.
- The unpredictability of food sources may require adapting or inventing new strategies.

Thus the development of hunting skills to provide more protein rich meat may have caused the increase in hominid brain size.

Evaluation

- Although environmental complexity and unpredictability may provide more cognitive challenge, many primates, mammals and even birds show co-ordinated hunting and foraging over large ranges with much smaller brains.
- Although specific brain structures may increase in size to match environmental demands, overall brain size does not correlate well with environmental complexity.
- Hunting for meat may have evolved to feed already large energy-demanding brains rather than vice-versa.
- Intelligence involves more than foraging and spatial ability.

SOCIAL FACTORS

Human 'Machiavellian' intelligence and thus brain size may have evolved to adapt humans to the social requirements of living in large social groups. Social group complexity and cognitive challenge may result from:

- The need to achieve the most individual gain while still co-operating to maintain the foraging and defensive benefits of living in a group. Intelligence may be required to keep track of co-operative alliances and enemies, manipulate others without detection, ensure that favours are repaid, etc.
- The need to predict the behaviour of others, which may require the development of a 'theory of mind'.
- Larger groups, which will inevitably involve more numerous and complex relationships.

Thus the development of social intelligence to cope with larger social groups may have caused increasing hominid brain size.

Evaluation

- A positive correlation has been found in many species between group size and ratio of brain neo-cortex.
- High social intelligence is not just shown by humans but by many mammals with smaller brains, e.g. vervet monkeys.
- Social intelligence is only one type of intelligence – vervets can be very unintelligent in non-social matters.
- Orang-utans have large brains and are thought to be intelligent but do not live in large social groups.

BRAIN SIZE AND INTELLIGENCE

Why is brain size associated with intelligence?

- The brain is regarded as the source of mental abilities such as intelligence.
- The human brain has trebled in size over the last 2.5 million years (compared to the australopithecines that marked the beginning of human evolution from that of the apes). This increase correlates with the development of behavioural signs of hominid intelligence, e.g. the fabrication of sophisticated stone tools, cave painting, etc.
- The human brain is 3 times larger than expected for a primate of our body size. Apes in turn have higher encephalisation quotients than most other mammals. We regard ourselves as more intelligent than apes, and apes as more intelligent than many other mammals.
- The human brain is evolutionarily very costly to develop. It uses a fifth of our basic metabolic rate but is only 2% of our mass. Increased brain size has increased the risk of childbirth death and has resulted in premature and helpless infants who require more care.
- Human intellectual abilities increase with brain development through childhood.

CULTURAL FACTORS

Human intelligence and brain size may actually result from both social and ecological pressures, as **copying skills** gained from **social interaction** in groups allowed new skills, discoveries and inventions that had **ecological survival value** to be rapidly transmitted between, and accumulate within, individuals. The copying skills, as well as all the survival skills and knowledge acquired, would require larger and more powerful brains.

Blackmore (1999) suggests this kind of selective cultural pressure occurs as a result of meme-gene co-evolution made possible by imitation. Blackmore proposes that true imitation, which is rarely found in animals, evolved as a result of social skills (such as theory of mind or reciprocal altruism) that themselves evolved as a result of the 'Machiavellian' social intelligence gained from social group living. Furthermore, she suggests that the ability humans have to show true imitation of others enabled them to rapidly copy any useful skills, ideas or behaviours (memes), such as stone tool making, that others had discovered by trial and error. The evolutionary survival value of such memes meant that there would be selective pressure to imitate others, especially the most proficient imitators, and mate with them. However, since cultural skills, ideas and behaviours readily combine and change very rapidly 'the genes have been forced into creating brains capable of spreading them – big brains' (Blackmore, 1999).

Evaluation

- Blackmore presents many persuasive arguments to support her theory and has suggested certain empirical tests of her ideas, e.g. that species who imitate the best should have larger brains for their size, and that brain scans should reveal that imitative tasks use more energy and produce more activity in the evolutionary newer areas of the brain.
- Because of its recency the theory has not been thoroughly evaluated and tested at present.

13.11 The development of IQ test performance – nature approach

EVIDENCE FOR GENETIC CAUSES   EVALUATION

Selective breeding studies

- Thompson (1952) selected rats that were 'maze-bright' or 'maze dull' by timing how long they took to negotiate a maze. By selectively breeding the two types of rats (only letting them breed with rats from their own group) Thompson found that the maze learning differences between the offspring of the maze-bright and maze-dull rats increased with the number of generations, until, by the sixth generation, the bright rats made approximately 80% fewer mistakes than the dull rats.
- Henderson (1970) found that the ability of rats to negotiate obstacles to find food would not always improve if their environmental conditions were enriched (as nurture orientated theorists would predict). However, the fact that some of the rats did show some improvement, indicates at least some interaction between genetic abilities and environmental experience.

- Cooper and Zubek (1958) found that there was no significant difference in the performance of selectively bred maze-bright and maze dull rats if they were both raised in either very deprived or enriching environmental conditions (which there should have been if maze learning was under genetic control). Studies of rats raised in enriched environments indicate that physiological changes in the synaptic connections of their brains occur as a result.
- In Thompson's (1952) experiment, it is important to note that only maze-learning was genetically transmitted, not the learning of other tasks.
- Studies on the selective breeding of rats are useful, since we can not selectively breed humans, but there are problems in generalising the results to humans.

Genetic relatedness and IQ

- Family resemblance studies on the heritability of IQ have been conducted on the assumption that the closer the genetic relationship between two people, the closer their IQs will be.
  However, it is equally likely that more closely related people will probably live together in very similar environments, and so the best evidence for genetic influences in this area is gained from studying the similarity of IQ between genetically identical subjects (monozygotic/identical twins) who have been raised in different environments, due to adoption for example (a high positive correlation between them would strongly support a large role for genetic factors in the development of IQ).
- Bouchard and McGue (1981) conducted a review of 111 world-wide studies on family IQ, ignoring studies which they claimed had methodological deficiencies, and came up with the following average correlations of IQ.

	Average correlation
Identical twins reared together	.86
Identical twins reared apart	.72
Non-identical twins reared together	.60
Siblings reared together	.47
Siblings reared apart	.24
Cousins	.15

Bouchard and McGue (1981)

The strongest evidence for genetic influences on IQ from these results is the finding that identical twins raised apart have more similar IQs than non-identical twins raised together.
- Bouchard et al. (1990) have continued this line of investigation in their Minnesota Twin Study, but have focused more on studying the IQ similarity of identical twins reared apart. From their intensive studies of the twins so far, they estimate that 70% of the variance in IQ scores are due to genetic inheritance, a larger estimate than that made by Bouchard & McGue (1981) in their earlier review.

Methodologically, studies on genetic relatedness and IQ have been subject to many criticisms, e.g. by Kamin (1977):

1. It is very difficult to control for environmental influences to arrive at an accurate estimate of the genetic contribution to intelligence. Even studying adoption cases is problematic, since:
   - Different environments can not be guaranteed – in some cases an effort has even been made to place the adopted children in similar family environments.
   - The infants may not have been separated exactly from birth and share the same womb experience anyway.
   - The self-selecting sampling techniques employed in studies such as Bouchard et al's (1990) Minnesota Twin Study have been accused of leading to an exaggeration of the similarities between separated identical twins.
   - The different types of IQ test used in the different studies makes it hard to compare the results since they are standardised in different ways.

2. The experimenter bias sometimes exhibited in this controversial area has led to:
   - The questioning of the validity of some findings, e.g. Cyril Burt's data on separated identical twins, which was used to support the claim that 80% of the variance in intelligence is genetically determined, but was thoroughly rejected by Kamin (1977).
   - An overly genetic interpretation of the data in some studies and a neglect of environmental influences, e.g. the noticeable differences in Bouchard & McGue's (1981) correlations between:
   a. Identical twins reared together and identical twins reared apart (a difference of .14).
   b. Siblings reared together and siblings reared apart (a difference of .23).
   In both cases, the genetic relatedness is the same and the differences are more attributable to environmental experiences.

13.12 The development of IQ test performance – nurture approach

EVIDENCE FOR ENVIRONMENTAL CAUSES	EVALUATION

Effects of early privation on IQ

If measured intelligence can be significantly reduced by environmental privation, then support is provided for the nurture approach.

- Sameroff and Seifer (1983) identified ten environmental factors, such as the mental health and educational level of the mother, the presence of the father, etc., each of which could lead to a loss of approximately 5 IQ points.
- Vernon (1965) in a cross cultural study revealed that children from disadvantaged backgrounds with little education and a poor home life scored lower on IQ tests, even on the spatial and non-verbal items.
- Many studies, e.g. Koluchova (1972) have shown that measured intelligence can be drastically reduced by extreme early environmental privation, but can also be dramatically improved, even to normal levels, by later normal or enriched conditions.

The dramatic recovery of IQ after extreme privation does seem to indicate the strong motivating effects of genetic influences. Correlational studies often neglect the possibility that genetic influenced behaviour can elicit different reactions – children with lower IQ may be rejected or abused by their parents or just cause their parents to give up attempts to educate them.

Environmental enrichment and IQ

If measured intelligence can be significantly increased through environmental enrichment, then support is provided for the nurture approach.

- Caldwell and Bradley (1978) devised the Home Observation for Measurement of the Environment (HOME) checklist, which is capable of measuring the quality of the home environment for children and its implications for intellectual development. Using the HOME checklist it has been found that factors like the emotional responsiveness and stimulation of the child by the parents are of key importance.
- Operation Headstart was an attempt by the government of the USA in 1965 to provide extra learning experiences for pre-school children from disadvantaged backgrounds. It produced some short lasting gains in IQ, but a longer term 'sleeper effect' in improved academic grades and attitudes to academic work (Collins, 1983).
- Scarr and Weinberg (1976, 1983) found that black children adopted from poor backgrounds and raised in white families of higher income and educational level showed an average IQ of 106 (110 if adopted within 12 months of birth) compared to a control group from a similar background who had an average IQ of 90.
- Skeels (1966) reports the case of 13 infant orphans who, with an average IQ of 64 were transferred to a special institution and given enriching interaction with older girls. By the age of seven they had gained an average of 36 points compared to a control group of orphans who remained in the orphanage and whose IQ dropped by an average 21 points from an original average of 86.
- Lynn and Hampson (1986) have reported rises in the national average IQ of Britain (by 1.7), Japan (by 7.7) and the USA (by 3.0) over a 50 year period (1932–1982), which can not be accounted for in terms of genetic factors.
- Howe (1990) has argued that the degree of hard work and practice shown by children with exceptional abilities is often underestimated – even genius needs to be fuelled.

The nature approach would predict that if IQ is under largely genetic control then IQ scores should remain reasonably consistent over time. Jensen (1969) argued that projects like Headstart were a waste of time and resources since poor and minority children were genetically less able to take advantage of them. The strategies employed in projects like Headstart have been accused of:

- not producing the long term effects they were designed for.
- being inappropriate for the children they were applied to.
- being overly focused on improving and measuring IQ.

However, Headstart did provide some long term gains and other intervention projects have been more successful.

Attempts at 'hothousing', or intensively educating children, can have negative effects on other areas of functioning and be stressful to the children.

EVALUATION OF NATURE-NURTURE DEBATE IN IQ DEVELOPMENT

All researchers in the area agree that both genetic and environmental influences interact in very complex ways – the genotype of an individual can only be expressed through a phenotype that is the product of genes building physical structures from environmental resources. The environmental influences on intelligence begin in the womb, indeed Denenberg et al have even shown that rats with inherited brain abnormalities which are transplanted into the wombs of healthy rats do better on learning tests than rats with the same abnormality raised in 'unhealthy' wombs. This indicates that the 'uterine environment can have long-term broad and beneficial behavioural effects' (Denenberg quoted in *New Scientist*, March 1998) and is important for the development of cognitive abilities.

The precise genes involved in intelligence have proven difficult to locate, perhaps due to the lack of funding provided for this socially sensitive area of research in the Human Genome Project. However, Plomin (1997) has claimed to have discovered a gene called IGF2R which can account for 2% of the variation in IQ test results.

Plomin's finding reflects another major problem – that not only are IQ tests often lacking in reliability as measures of intelligence, but intelligence may not be a unitary phenomenon – some aspects may be under more genetic control than others. IQ tests do take into account some different 'kinds of intelligence' and the Minnesota Twin Study has found that, whereas verbal ability correlations between separated identical twins are high, the correlations for memory are lower and spatial ability are variable.

13.13 The influence of culture on IQ test performance

THE CULTURE AND IQ DEBATE
- 'Culture', in the context of IQ test performance, usually refers to the set of social beliefs, values, experiences, etc. associated with different social groups (often ethnic or national groups, although gender differences have also been investigated).
- The influence of culture on intelligence test performance has long been an extremely controversial and important topic in Psychology because of the significant theoretical, practical, social, and political issues involved. For Psychology, this topic represents not only another example of the nature-nurture debate, but also the opportunity to prove itself an impartial science capable of conducting valid and reliable research to properly inform society and political policy.
- Unfortunately, in the early days of Psychology this was not always the case; heavily culturally-biased IQ tests were sometimes administered in discriminatory ways with the results interpreted non-objectively to serve discriminatory political ends with profound social implications (e.g. Gould, 1982).
- More recently, Hermstein and Murray's (1994) book *'The Bell Curve'* proved controversial with its discussion and interpretation of the finding that the mean African American IQ score in the USA has generally been found to be lower, especially for 'g', than the mean Caucasian IQ score (in the 1970s there was a difference of 15 points – one standard deviation).
- The influence of culture on IQ test performance is still not fully understood, but psychologists suggest that it is important to avoid confusion between the concept of intelligence (whatever it is!) and IQ tests, and between the notions of culture and race.

What causes cultural differences in IQ test performance?

Are differences real or due to bias?

Are real differences due to nature or nurture?

CULTURE AND IQ TEST CONSTRUCTION BIAS

Dominant cultural conceptions of intelligence, or prejudice, in a society may affect the construction and administration of IQ tests and thus influence the performance of different cultural groups.

Evaluation

Test administration – equal opportunity and anti-discrimination policies have ensured that IQ tests have increased in standardisation and fairness of testing conditions, especially for children of different ethnic origins growing up within the same cultural educational system. In pre-testing standardisation of modern IQ tests in the USA, any items not answered equally by groups of White, Hispanic, and African American children may be dropped.

Operationalisation of intelligence – given that the purpose of IQ tests is to measure certain socially-desired mental abilities that predict certain forms of socially-desired success in a culture, then IQ tests are inevitably biased against other cultures or subcultures, e.g. verbal IQ test items or instructions in English bias tests against cultures with other first languages. Often, other cultures favour concepts of intelligence that are not tested, like Gardner's interpersonal intelligence. Okagaki and Sternberg (1993) found immigrant parents from a variety of countries thought social and practical abilities were equally or more important for intelligence than cognitive skills (only native-born Anglo-American parents thought the opposite). People from cultures unfamiliar with test items may perform more slowly due to different attitudes towards time or lack of automatisation.

CULTURAL INFLUENCES ON IQ TEST PERFORMANCE

Cultural influences that cause 'real' differences in IQ test performance relate to ***environmental effects***, such as social discrimination in opportunities and expectations based on skin colour or ethnicity, culturally-related SES (socio-economic status), and the learning of different cultural values and attitudes.

Evaluation

Social discrimination – lower African American test scores may reflect the negative environmental influences on the development of IQ associated with their lower mean SES, e.g. poorer nutrition and educational opportunities. SES does negatively correlate with IQ, but matching Blacks and Whites for SES lowers rather than eliminates the differences in their scores. Also, the direction of causation between IQ and social status is difficult to determine.

Expectations – prejudiced expectations on the part of teachers (and disillusioned parents) regarding the likelihood of African American children succeeding in academic (rather than, say, sports) tests may create a self-fulfilling prophecy by affecting effort optimism (Ogbu, 1978).

Motivation – disadvantaged minorities in many cultures perform worse on IQ tests, perhaps reflecting different views of intelligent behaviour and a rejection of, disinterest in, and alienation from the dominant culture's academic system and testing (Boykin, 1994).

Cultural/environmental influences on IQ test performance are strongly supported by the world-wide increase in IQ results (the 'Flynn Effect'), which is actually rising at a faster rate in African Americans (perhaps indicating greater social integration and opportunities).

'RACE' AND IQ TEST PERFORMANCE

'Race' refers to ***supposedly biological/genetic differences*** between ethnic groups of humans that some think cause differences in IQ test performance, e.g. the view that 'black' people in the USA are naturally less intelligent on average than 'white' people.

Evaluation

Concept of 'race' – race as a genetic concept in humans is of little value, being based primarily on skin colour and often confused with culture.

Given the great variety and overlap of skin colours and ethnic origins (e.g. 'white' North Americans originally came from dozens of countries and have interbred for generations) and the fact that there is greater variation between individuals of the same 'race' than between members of different 'races', many have questioned the validity and political purpose of biological studies of race.

The effect of genes – research on individual differences on IQ test performance seems to indicate an important influence of heredity, but also show that genes can only be expressed through a complex combination of environmental factors (see 'The development of IQ test performance' pages 138–139). Apart from the problems of defining 'race' above, revealing any biological group differences would require studies that matched test participants on all other factors, such as age, sex, diet, and home, educational, social, peer group, toxicological and physical environments – an extremely difficult if not impossible and futile task.

14.1 Freud's psychoanalytic theory of personality

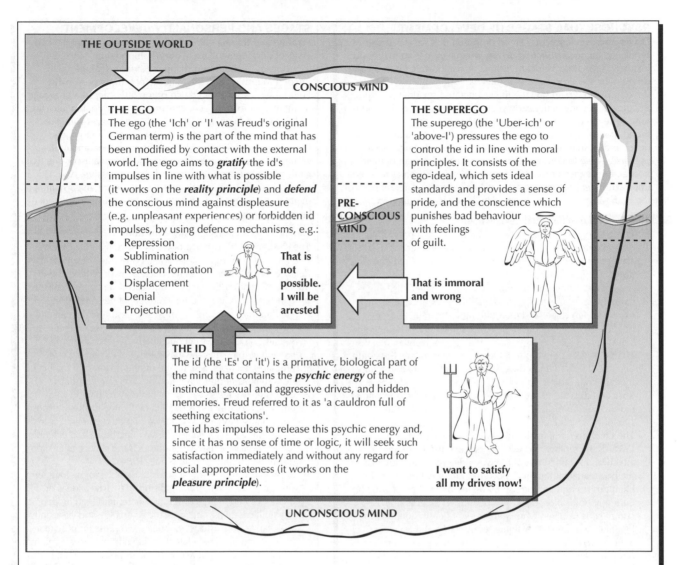

THE OUTSIDE WORLD

CONSCIOUS MIND

THE EGO
The ego (the 'Ich' or 'I' was Freud's original German term) is the part of the mind that has been modified by contact with the external world. The ego aims to **gratify** the id's impulses in line with what is possible (it works on the **reality principle**) and **defend** the conscious mind against displeasure (e.g. unpleasant experiences) or forbidden id impulses, by using defence mechanisms, e.g.:
• Repression
• Sublimation
• Reaction formation
• Displacement
• Denial
• Projection

That is not possible. I will be arrested

PRE-CONSCIOUS MIND

THE SUPEREGO
The superego (the 'Uber-ich' or 'above-I') pressures the ego to control the id in line with moral principles. It consists of the ego-ideal, which sets ideal standards and provides a sense of pride, and the conscience which punishes bad behaviour with feelings of guilt.

That is immoral and wrong

THE ID
The id (the 'Es' or 'it') is a primative, biological part of the mind that contains the **psychic energy** of the instinctual sexual and aggressive drives, and hidden memories. Freud referred to it as 'a cauldron full of seething excitations'.
The id has impulses to release this psychic energy and, since it has no sense of time or logic, it will seek such satisfaction immediately and without any regard for social appropriateness (it works on the **pleasure principle**).

I want to satisfy all my drives now!

UNCONSCIOUS MIND

FREUD'S TOPOGRAPHICAL MODEL
This divided the mind into three levels or layers of consciousness (these can be illustrated with the iceberg analogy above):
1 **The Conscious** – This contains all we are directly aware of, but only represents 'the tip of the iceberg' since although we may think we know why we do things, we often do not. According to Freud, unconscious causes are of great importance.
2 **The Pre-conscious** – This contains material that can become conscious.
3 **The Unconscious** – The part of the mind that is not accessible and contains our inner drives and repressed experiences. It is also where the unconscious struggles that affect our behaviour take place. The unconscious mind resembles a hydraulic closed energy system (like a steam engine) in that psychic energy from the drives builds up and, if not released, causes inner pressure or anxiety.

FREUD'S STRUCTURAL MODEL
Freud also suggested a model that involved dynamic struggle between three aspects of the mind – the **id**, **ego** and **superego** (illustrated above). The ego has the task of satisfying the demands of the id, superego and society, as well as attempting to keep unpleasant experiences out of consciousness. These **conflicting influences** have many important **consequences** for human behaviour, including **dreams**, **the development of personality traits** and **disordered behaviour**.

FREUD'S DREAM THEORY
• Freud suggested that dreams represent **unfulfilled wishes** from the id, which try to break into consciousness and seek satisfaction while we are 'off guard'. Dreams are the way these id wishes are *disguised* by the dream censor using defensive measures such as **symbolism** (using a dream image or event to stand for an id wish), condensation (the merging of many unconscious meanings into one dream image) and **displacement** (where emotions are separated from their true source and attached to trivial sources in the dream). Dreams still demonstrate many aspects of id 'thinking', being so disjointed, illogical, and generally showing little appreciation for time and reality, but can still act as the '**guardians of sleep**' to protect us from our own unconscious while asleep.
• Dreams are thus a very important source of unconscious information since, by undoing the 'dreamwork' of the **manifest content** of the dream (what is consciously remembered) the **latent content** (the hidden id impulses or meaning) can be discovered. This is achieved by free associating to each element of the manifest content to trace it back to the latent content, decoding the symbolism of the manifest content (some symbols are personal but many have universal meanings, e.g. phallic symbols such as guns and knives) and identifying the event (within the previous 24 hours according to Freud) that acted as the trigger for the dream.

14.2 Freud's stage theory and personality development

PSYCHOSEXUAL STAGES OF DEVELOPMENT

Drives and development – Freud proposed that we are driven or motivated by our *instinctual drives*, which come from two basic instincts. Thanatos, the death instinct, is responsible for aggressive drives, whereas Eros, the life instinct, is responsible for the sex drive or libido. Freud saw the life instinct and sex drive as exerting the most influence in the early years of life and thus childhood is a time of key importance in personality development.

Freud proposed a stage theory of infantile psychosexual development that suggested that children are polymorphously perverse – able to derive sexual pleasure from any part of their bodies, but as they grow older the sexual drive becomes focused upon (and seeks expression and satisfaction from) different parts of the body. The stages are governed by biological maturation.

The stages of psychosexual development

- **Oral stage** – where pleasure is gained first from passively and dependently sucking and swallowing (the oral receptive sub-stage) and later, as the teeth emerge, from biting and chewing (the oral aggressive sub-stage).
- **Anal stage** – gratification shifts to the anus where pleasure is gained first from expelling and playing with faeces (the expulsive sub-stage) and then, during toilet training, from holding on to and controlling bowel movements (the retentive sub-stage).
- **Phallic stage** – from around 3 to 5 or 6 years of age the libido becomes focused upon the genitals, and pleasure involving them becomes directed towards the opposite sex parent. Both boys and girls at this age unconsciously desire the opposite sex parent, but differ slightly in the way they deal with this situation, which Freud termed the Oedipus Complex.
  The Oedipus complex for boys involves sexual attraction towards the mother and wishing his rival for the mother's affection, his father, out of the way (ideally dead). However, the boy fears that the more powerful father will discover his illicit desires and will punish by depriving the boy of what he currently holds most dear – his phallus. This 'castration complex' is resolved when, out of fear of castration, the boy identifies with the father figure, introjecting all his values, attitudes and behaviour, so that in becoming like his father the boy can indirectly have the mother through his fantasies and later grow up to have mother-like figures in the same way as his father.
  The Oedipus complex for girls (sometimes referred to as the Electra Complex) involves the girl's desire for the father. The girl believes that she has already been castrated, and out of penis envy she turns to her father to provide her with a symbolic penis substitute – a baby. However, out of fear of losing her mother's love plus the symbolic gains of imitating a person the father is attached to, the girl identifies with her mother and by becoming like her she too can indirectly satisfy her sexual desires.
- **Latency stage** – after the turmoil of the phallic stage the child enters a stage where the child's desires diminish somewhat.
- **Genital stage** – occurs with the onset of puberty and involves the reawakening of the libido and its attachment to external love objects outside the family.

Id, ego and superego development – Freud suggested that by the end of the phallic stage, the three main aspects of the mind would have developed – the id, ego and superego. Babies begin life dominated by the unsocialised id, seeking immediate gratification (crying for food, sleeping and defecating) with no regard for time and place (as parents will testify!). The ego gradually develops through contact with the external world with all its restraints on behaviour, thus toilet training during the anal stage is a particularly important time for its development. The ego is free from moral constraint until the superego develops, mainly as a result of the internalisation of parental values in the Oedipus complex.

STAGES AND PERSONALITY DEVELOPMENT

Fixation and trauma – Freud therefore believed that the early years of development are of utmost importance, since the experiences of childhood shape the structure of the unconscious mind and the majority of human personality. Freud suggested that too much or too little pleasure at a stage might lead to *fixation* at it, causing the individual in later life to still want to indulge in its pleasures (stage *regression*). For example fixation at the oral receptive stage due to over-indulgence (the slightest whimper brought food and oral gratification) may lead to an optimistic personality or one that gains pleasure from being dependent and passive. Any traumatic events, especially of a sexual nature, in early life might also become hidden in the unconscious and influence later behaviour.

Defence mechanisms and stage fixations

The ego cannot allow many of the id's sexual and aggressive impulses to reach respectable, adult, conscious life and so uses defence mechanisms to control, alter, deny or redirect the impulses whenever they may occur. Ego defence mechanisms used to cope with fixations may thus affect personality, e.g.:

- **Sublimation** – usually the most successful defence, it allows the expression of id impulses through behaviour that is a socially acceptable symbolic alternative. For example fixation at the oral stage may later lead to seeking oral pleasure, not from sucking the mother's breast in public, but from sucking at one's thumb, pen or cigarette. Anal expulsive desires to handle faeces may lead to an enjoyment of pottery. A phallically fixated desire to expose one's penis may lead to a later sublimated career choice of a fireman, who can happily drive large hoses and extending ladders with much attention through the streets, after sliding down the fire station pole (Kline, 1984).
- **Repression** – not a very successful defence in the long term since it just involves forcing disturbing wishes, ideas or memories into the unconscious where, although hidden, they will create psychic pressure or anxiety and constantly seek expression. Thus someone may repress homosexual feelings and become a latent (hidden) homosexual who may consciously report attraction to the opposite sex, but has to use other defence mechanisms, such as denial or reaction formation, to control their unconscious urges.
- **Reaction formation** – if unconscious impulses become too powerful then the ego can only maintain control by forcing the individual to consciously feel and act in *exactly the opposite* way to that unconsciously desired. Thus latent homosexuals may feel and show an excessive hatred of overt homosexuals, while those with an 'anal character' (an exaggerated concern for orderliness, cleanliness, control and routine) may be reacting against their anal expulsive desire to mess. If while reading this you are getting a little *too* angry in your objection to some of Freud's ideas, then your ego is probably helping you react against your anxiety provoking unconscious recognition of their truth!

There are many other defence mechanisms, like *displacement* where feelings are expressed by redirecting them onto something or somebody powerless and convenient rather than the original cause (we do not slam a door because we hate it!). They make humans and their society the way they are. Without the restraints defence mechanisms impose, civilisation would not be possible.

Balance – Freud also argued that the overall balance between the id, ego and superego would affect personality. A strong superego, for example, might result in a very moral person while a very weak one may result in an emotional psychopath. An over influential id might lead to irresponsible and impulsive behaviour or even violence and crime.

14.3 Jung's analytical psychology

JUNG & ANALYTICAL PSYCHOLOGY ASSUMPTIONS

Carl Gustav Jung (1875–1961) was a Swiss psychiatrist who worked in a Zurich mental hospital before moving on to his own private practice. He was, at first, a favourite disciple of Freud's, and applied psychoanalytic concepts to his study of schizophrenics, but increasingly developed his own theories that differed from Freud's Psychoanalysis and the two men parted company on bad terms in 1913. Jung pursued his 'Analytical Psychology', and developed a range of theories on personality and mental disorder.

In contrast to Freud, Jung put greater emphasis on:

* Processes occurring *within* the individual rather than on the relationships between individuals and society. Jung regarded the goal or end point of development as *individuation* – the self-actualisation of the individual's potential and the achievement of psychic balance, the integration of opposites and self-realisation.
Thoughts, emotions and behaviour result from a *self-regulating* psyche / mind that constantly tries to *seek balance* and integration between the conscious and unconscious, and between different aspects of personality. Imbalance will cause *compensations*. Compensations result in personality characteristics, dreams and symptoms of mental disorder.
* Spiritual and religious rather than physical aspects of human nature – people seek more than honour, power, wealth, fame, and the love of women as Freud put it. Jung believed everyone needs a myth or set of beliefs to live by to give their life some meaning and purpose. These myths do not necessarily have to be objectively 'true' to have this positive function. If people become alienated from their beliefs, as indeed Jung himself felt alienated from Orthodox Christianity, anxiety and a sense of incompleteness results.

METHODS

Jung employed similar methods to Freud, but often used and interpreted them in different ways.

* **Analysis and interpretation of symbolism** – Jung spent more time on the cross-cultural study of symbolism in mythology. He frequently found important similarities in the myths and symbols of cultures that did not seem to have any contact with each other, especially mystical 'mandala' symbols, such as circular shapes, crosses or other divisions of four, that represent psychic balance and harmony. He interpreted this as evidence for a collective unconscious.
* **Word association tests** – like free association, a person has to reply with the first word that comes to mind that is associated with other words. Jung carried this out in a more scientific way, not just recording the associated word but also measuring the exact time it took for an association to be made to each word in his list as well as the physiological response to it (recorded by skin conductance using a polygraph or 'lie-detector' apparatus). Collections of words that produced variations from normal responses would indicate a common emotional link or 'complex'.
* **Dream interpretation** – Jung disagreed with Freud that dreams are always disguised wish fulfilment resulting from past circumstances. Jung suggested that dreams reflect current preoccupations and may be compensations for conscious attitudes and behaviour that are causing imbalance. Dreams are a symbolic language, difficult to always understand in linguistic terms, but not deliberately disguised. Dreams come from everyday emotional problems in the personal unconscious (and may suggest ways of solving such problems in the future) or from images/symbols from the deeper collective unconscious.

THEORY OF THE UNCONSCIOUS

INDIVIDUAL CONSCIOUSNESS

INDIVIDUAL PERSONAL UNCONSCIOUS

SHARED COLLECTIVE UNCONSCIOUS

Consciousness – similar to Freud's view, it is all we are aware of.

Personal unconscious – the unconscious of each individual, it contains temporarily forgotten as well as truly repressed material and 'complexes' (clusters of linked emotions, memories and attitudes in the personal unconscious that can form mini sub-personalities in themselves) resulting from personal experience.

Collective unconscious – a level of consciousness shared with other members of our species that contains common archetypes. Archetypes are inherited predispositions to feel, act and experience the world in certain ways, thus people may behave in similar ways as their ancestors and people in other cultures they have never met. Important archetypes include The Persona (our social mask), The Shadow (our animal urges, similar to the id but more positive in its influence) and The Anima/Animus (our female or male sides).

THEORY OF PERSONALITY

Jung's analytical psychology suggests the psyche has many aspects and that personality can be influenced unconsciously by complexes and archetypes. In addition, however, Jung suggested that personality is also shaped by how we consciously react towards and experience the world.

Extraversion and introversion – These are two attitudes or ways of directing our libido (Jung saw this as more of a general life force rather than just sexual energy) towards the world. *Introverts* direct their libido inwards towards their mental world and so prefer to keeps themselves to themselves, avoid excessive social contact, and may be somewhat self-absorbed. *Extraverts* direct their libido outwards to the external world and so have an outgoing, confident and friendly nature that adapts easily to situations and seeks social stimulation.

The four functions – These are ways of experiencing the world:
Sensation (registering the existence of things)
Thinking (identifying and understanding things)
Feeling (judging the pleasantness or worth of things)
Intuition (anticipating or predicting things).

Jung suggested one function might predominate, and that sensation and intuition were opposed to each other, as were thinking and feeling. Thus those guided by emotion might not think logically through decisions, while those always anticipating the future might be blind to things happening under their very noses.

Thinking

Sensing ← → Intuiting

Feeling

14.4 Evaluation of Freud's and Jung's theories

Freud's methods
- Freud used an unrepresentative sample and lacked objective data upon which to base his theory. He mostly studied himself, his disordered patients and only one child in detail. Freud thought this unimportant, believing in only a quantitative difference between people – we are all neurotic to some extent, including himself. Freud's case notes consisted of his memories of his clients' memories (often of early childhood), however since he regarded many childhood recollections as fantasies anyway he guessed at what had taken place in his patient's past.
- Freud may have shown researcher bias in his interpretations – since he originally wanted a general theory of sexual causation that would "open all secrets with a single key" he may have tended to interpret all symbols as sexual, only pay attention to or remember information that supported his theories and ignore information or other explanations that did not fit them. E.g. Little Hans' horse phobia may have resulted from his fright on seeing a horse collapse rather than an unconscious fear of castration from the father (Hans had actually been threatened with castration, but by his mother).

Psychoanalytic Theory
- Freud over-emphasised sexual causes – Breuer even said Freud was prone to "excessive generalisation".
- Freud's theory was biased by a cultural, sexist male viewpoint, e.g. on female inferiority and penis envy.
- The unconscious is difficult to test objectively.
- The theory is very good at explaining but not predicting behaviour. Symbolism is so vague and subjective, and defence mechanisms are so flexible, that they can be used to support any theory of the unconscious, indeed they seem to make Freudian theory unrefutable (incapable of being shown wrong) and thus unscientific e.g. any research finding the exact opposite of what Freudian theory would predict could be explained through the defence of reaction formation. Kline (1972) argued that psychoanalytic theory can be broken down into testable hypotheses if they are made **two-tailed** to predict either outcome and refutable by finding no significant effect.

Freud's contribution
- Freud developed his theory throughout his life and proposed explanations for a huge variety of phenomena, from humour and forgetting to crowd behaviour, customs and warfare. Many psychologists and psychoanalysts, although often disagreeing with some of his ideas, have been inspired by his theories to develop their own. Psychoanalytic terms and concepts have become ingrained into western psychology and society, and Psychoanalysis is still practised today.
- Philosophers and writers had long considered the importance the unconscious, dream interpretation, defence mechanisms, etc. whereas Freud's more original ideas concerning them have been criticised, leading psychologists, e.g. Eysenck (1985), to agree with Ebbinghaus that "what is new in these theories is not true, and what is true is not new".
- More negatively, Freud's Oedipus complex may have led to genuine cases of child abuse being dismissed as childhood sexual fantasies.

EVALUATION OF FREUD'S PSYCHODYNAMIC THEORIES

Subsequent research
- Reviews of research attempting to scientifically validate Freudian concepts are largely negative in their conclusions, because it is difficult to show that the unconscious mechanisms Freud proposed are responsible.
- Freud emphasised the importance of the Oedipus complex, calling it the `kernel of neurosis` yet while Social Learning Theory research has found imitation of same sex parents does occur, there has been no conclusive evidence that unconscious motives like castration fear are responsible.
- Freud regarded repression as 'the cornerstone on which the whole of psychoanalysis rests', yet although research has linked trauma to amnesia, the degree to which repressed events are truly unconscious has been questioned and other causes have been suggested as more likely.
- While *Kline and Storey* (1977) found evidence for oral and anal personality traits by using personality questionnaires, it has not been demonstrated that these traits have been caused by Freudian fixation at a stage.

- Freud suggested that a woman's desire for a baby was a symbolic substitute for their desire to gain the penis they envy in men and feel they have been deprived of. Harris and Campbell (1999) investigated whether unconscious motivations might be involved in pregnancy. They thought pregnancy might involve other symbolic gains. Harris gave semi-structured interviews to 128 North London women designed to measure the quality of their lives and sexual partnerships and their degree of **secondary gain** from becoming pregnant (e.g. an improvement in their circumstances or relationships). Women with unplanned pregnancies were found to be significantly more likely to have been in a situation of secondary gain, especially relating to their partnerships, than women with planned pregnancies or no pregnancy. This was particularly the case for those women with unplanned pregnancies who were shocked when they found out they were pregnant. Unfortunately the study cannot conclusively demonstrate that the motivations were truly unconscious – the women were not asked to rate the secondary gain themselves and there are problems relying on retrospective data (based on their memory of events before they were pregnant) gained from interview and self report methods (the secondary gain scale only had an inter-rater reliability of .69)

- **Developmental theory** – Jung focuses very much on the development of the *individual* and their inner life, and tends to ignore human relationships, the past and childhood experiences.
- **The collective unconscious and archetypes** – While evolutionary theory also argues for inherited species-specific characteristics and tendencies, the cross-cultural similarities in myth and symbolism Jung found could just have resulted from similar *experiences* shared by different cultures rather than a shared unconscious.

EVALUATION OF JUNG'S ANALYTICAL PSYCHOLOGY

- **Therapy** – Jung's therapy became increasingly focused on middle-aged clients with high levels of insight, time and money, and with relatively minor problems or just those seeking more meaning in their lives. Lacking objective therapeutic outcomes, it is unclear when full individuation is reached.
- **Contribution to psychology and society** – Jung's ideas have not been as popular as Freud's, perhaps because they were a little more mystical and obscure, and less clearly explained. However, some of Jung's ideas influenced humanist psychology and Eysenck used introversion and extraversion as the basis for his personality dimensions.

14.5 Erikson's psychosocial theory of development

ERIKSON'S PSYCHOSOCIAL STAGE THEORY

Erikson, a psychodynamic theorist influenced by Freud's psychoanalytic ideas and psychosexual stages, suggested that all humans pass through *eight* genetically-determined *psychosocial crises* in their lives, each of which could have a *positive or negative outcome* for healthy personality development depending on how the ego resolves the crisis society presents it.

AGE (approx.)	STAGE OF PSYCHOSOCIAL DEVELOPMENT	EVALUATION
0 to 1	**Basis trust versus mistrust** – the 1st stage involves learning to trust caregivers to provide for basic needs. Insufficient or inconsistent care may result in future mistrust of other people.	These stages correspond to Freud's oral, anal, phallic, and latency stages of psychosexual development. A strength of Erikson's theory is his focus on the more observable, social aspects of child development and his continuation of research from Freud's genital stage onwards.
1 to 3	**Autonomy versus shame/doubt** – in the 2nd stage, efforts for independence may be encouraged/successful, leading to autonomy, or frustrated, leading to later shame and self doubt.	Erikson applied his theory to children's *play*, agreeing with Freud on many points (e.g. by suggesting that girls construct inner spaces while boys build towers and protrusions when they play, reflecting genital differences), but focusing more on
3 to 6	**Initiative versus guilt** – the 3rd stage involves the outcomes of conflict between the child's goals/desires and those of their parents or siblings, resulting in a sense of initiative or guilt.	how play helps the ego deal with *current, external*, social problems or crises rather than inner id impulses and past issues. Erikson saw the importance of play as extending throughout the life span.
6 to 12	**Industry versus inferiority** – the 4th stage concerns feelings resulting from the child's mastery of social and academic skills relative to their peer group in educational contexts.	
12 to 20	**Identity versus role confusion** – the 5th stage occurs during a socially created *moratorium* (delay in becoming an adult) when adolescents can try out different roles, attitudes, beliefs, and even occupations to achieve a stable identity. Failure to do so, or choosing an identity too early (premature foreclosure of the moratorium), can result in identity/role confusion. This could lead to adopting an *extreme negative* identity (e.g. delinquent) rather than have no *identity* at all, problems with intimacy in close relationships, problems with *time perspective* in making plans for the future, or problems with the level of *industry* (e.g. being unable to concentrate or concentrating too much on one task).	Marcia (1980) divided Erikson's 5th crisis into *4 identity statuses* (diffusion/confusion, foreclosure, moratorium, and achievement) and used interviews to empirically test them. Marcia found evidence for increasing identity achievement with age, but the process may take longer than Erikson thought and may vary with gender and parental style of upbringing, and across historical time periods and cultures. There could also be many aspects of identity, not all of which may be achieved at the same time (or ever).
20 to 40	**Intimacy versus isolation** – according to Erikson the 6th stage challenge of early adulthood is to achieve intimacy in relationships. Friendships become important and successful resolution of the crisis enables one to love and show commitment and compromise in relationships. A stable identity from the previous stage of development is required so as not to lose oneself in the relationship, otherwise fear of commitment and an inability to form loving relationships results in isolation.	According to Sugarman (1986) there is much disagreement among researchers over the age boundaries for Erikson's adult stages, for example some see the intimacy versus isolation stage ending at 40 (Havighurst, 1973), others at 34 (Turner and Helms, 1979), and still others at 25 (Bee and Mitchell, 1984).
40 to 65	**Generativity versus stagnation** – in the 7th stage, generativity refers to concern over 'establishing and guiding the next generation' Erikson (1980). The individual may express generativity through parenthood or other creative or altruistic contributions to society. Caring only for oneself leads to self-centredness and stagnation.	Other theorists have proposed different stages: Levinson *et al.* (1978) described a *life structure* theory of adult development, suggesting that people experience a series of alternating **stable** (structure-building) and *transitional* (structure-changing) *phases*, based on interviews with 40 men between the age of 35 and 45. Gould (1978), based on psychiatric work and a questionnaire given to over 500, 16- to 50-year-old
65 +	**Ego integrity versus despair** – reviews of one's life in the 8th stage produce satisfaction and meaningfulness or frustration and regret, depending on the resolutions of previous stages.	people, suggested the evolution of adult consciousness occurs as we *lose false childhood assumptions* and accept control over our own lives.

Evaluation of the existence of crises and transitions

Other researchers have pointed out that there may be considerable variation in the timing and nature of the transitions across individuals, genders, cultures, and historical time periods (a better approach may be to focus on certain critical life events, regardless of when they occur). Although there are broad similarities in biological, psychological, and social changes over time, not everyone shares the same social and cultural experiences/lifestyles, or indeed reacts to life changes in the same way.

14.6 Social learning theory and personality development

SOCIAL LEARNING THEORY AND PERSONALITY DEVELOPMENT

- Social Learning Theory (later re-named Social Cognitive Theory by Bandura) was developed to create a learning theory that went beyond the behaviourist learning theories (e.g. of operant conditioning) to incorporate the important *cognitive processes* that humans seem to possess between the environmental stimuli they receive and the behavioural responses they make.
- Personality refers to relatively permanent characteristics possessed by individuals that may distinguish them from others and influence their behaviour in different situations. **Bandura and Walters** (1963) in their book '*Social Learning and Personality Development*' suggested that such characteristics would be acquired over time from *environmental experience* through *observational learning*. The 'development' of personality according to this theory would result from a continuous accumulation of experiences with age from every different environment encountered, which would rule out any fixed stages of development and would seem to imply an inconsistent 'personality', lacking permanent characteristics, that changed with every new experience.
- However, unlike behaviourist learning theorists who saw people as being passively programmed by their environment, Bandura saw humans as *actively influencing their environment* through their *cognitive abilities*, *acquired beliefs* and the *effects of their behaviour*, which may lead to some characteristics persisting longer than might otherwise be expected in a changing environment.

THE ENVIRONMENT
Includes the physical and social environment. **Models** provide information about *behaviour* (actions, statements, skills etc.) and its *consequences* (whether it leads to positive or negative outcomes). Important sources of models are:

| The media | The family | The peer group |

THE PERSON
Bandura perceives the person as actively influencing the world as well as being influenced by it. Every person possesses:

- **Observation learning ability** – being able to automatically learn behaviour from just being exposed to models, without the need for reinforcement.
- **Cognitive processes** – such as *attention* and *memory* abilities that may change with age and allow the person to:
  1. focus on relevant models and behaviour, e.g. based on past memories of who and what is most useful and appropriate to imitate in a given environment.
  2. store a memory representation of how to reproduce what was said or done.
  3. remember information concerning the past consequences of the behaviour, e.g. whether they saw it rewarded in others, whether they were rewarded for it themselves or if they felt good about it last time (self-reinforcement).
- **Cognitive beliefs** – such as *self-efficacy* (the person's belief in their ability to effectively achieve their goals) or the morality of behaviour (conscience).
- **Physical characteristics** – which also affect interactions with the environment and the ability to imitate certain behaviour.

BEHAVIOUR
Behaviour is imitated if:
- proper attention is paid to the model that produced it.
- the behaviour is effectively stored.
- desirable consequences are expected for the behaviour (or at least unfavourable ones are not expected).
- the person believes they are able to successfully imitate the model (self-efficacy).
- the person is physically capable of imitating the model.

A person's behaviour influences other people and the environment, which in turn will influence the person's future behaviour. This interaction of influences is known as **reciprocal determinism**.

EVALUATION OF SOCIAL LEARNING THEORY OF PERSONALITY
- The theory incorporates many important social, cognitive and learning influences upon the development of personality.
- It is questionable just how much Social Learning Theory can tell us about the *development* of personality and how enduring and consistent learnt personality characteristics really are.
- The theory neglects the role of innate, biological factors upon the development of personality, e.g. the genetic inheritance of traits.

14.7 Attachment in infancy 1

WHAT IS MEANT BY ATTACHMENT?
- An attachment is a strong, long lasting and close emotional bond between two people, which causes distress on separation from the attached individual.
- Psychologists have been particularly interested in the development of first attachments in infancy since they appear to have important consequences for later healthy development, especially concerning later relationships.

HOW DOES ATTACHMENT DEVELOP?
Attachment in infancy occurs gradually over a sequence of phases:

• Pre-attachment phase	0 – 3 months	Infant preference for humans over other objects is shown by preferential looking and social smiling (before 6 weeks the infant is said to be asocial).
• Indiscriminate attachment phase	3 – 7 months	Infant can distinguish between people and allows strangers to handle it.
• Discriminate attachment phase	7 – 9 months	Infant develops specific attachments to certain people and shows distress on separation from them. Avoidance or fear of strangers may be shown.
• Multiple attachment phase	9 months onward	Infant becomes increasingly independent and forms other bonds despite the stronger prior attachments.

THEORIES OF ATTACHMENT

LEARNING THEORY
Learning theory suggests attachment behaviour forms due to:
Classical conditioning – parents become associated with pleasant stimuli such as food via repeated association.
Operant conditioning – parental proximity and care-taking behaviour are negatively reinforced by the reduction of unpleasant infant crying behaviour. Parents may also find baby smiling resulting from care innately positively reinforcing.

Evaluation
- Harlow and Harlow (1969) showed rhesus monkeys had an innate preference to form attachments to surrogate mothers that provided contact comfort rather than food.

	Unconditional Stimulus		Unconditional Response
	FOOD	=	PLEASURE/SATISFACTION

Conditional Stimulus	Unconditional Stimulus		Unconditional Response
PARENT +	FOOD	=	PLEASURE/SATISFACTION

Conditional Stimulus			Conditional Response
PARENT		=	PLEASURE / SATISFACTION

Classical conditioning of parent – child attachment

PSYCHOANALYTIC THEORY
Freud believed infants become attached to people who satisfy their need for food at the oral stage. Oral gratification causes drive reduction, which is experienced as pleasant.

Evaluation
- Freud was probably right that attachment is important for later development.
- Freud's drive theory and idea that attachment is due to food has not been supported (see above).

COGNITIVE THEORY
Schaffer (1971) suggests infants usually form attachments once they can reliably distinguish one caregiver from another and with the caregivers that stimulate and interact with them the mostly intensely.

Evaluation
- This contradicts Bowlby's monotropy, but not necessarily the rest of his theory.
- Supports research showing that quality of care affects attachment formation.

BOWLBY'S ATTACHMENT THEORY
Bowlby (1951) was influenced by evolutionary theory, ethological studies on imprinting in animals, and psychoanalytic ideas. He suggested human infants:
- Were genetically programmed to form attachments.
- Formed an important primary attachment to a single carer (usually the mother): the theory of monotropy.
- Had to form attachments within a critical time period (approx. 2[typesetter: insert half fraction] years). If attachments are not formed by the end of the critical time period then a number of negative effects result (see deprivation and privation).
- Formed a long-lasting working model for later relationships based on their first attachment bond – the continuity hypothesis.

Bowlby argued that attachment between infant and caregiver has evolved because it is an adaptive behaviour that aids survival. In particular, attachment provides food, security, a safe base from which to explore the world, exposure to important survival skills shown by the parent, and an internal working model of relationships with others. For the parent it ensures a greater likelihood of their offspring surviving (and thus passing on their own genes for attachment formation). Various innate social releasers have also evolved to elicit care-giving, such as crying and smiling.

Evaluation
- Bowlby's theory was very influential, but research indicates that multiple attachments can be formed within a sensitive time period (Rutter, 1981) – see deprivation and privation research.
- Some studies have indicated that attachment style may influence later relationships and behaviour – see adult relationship research.

14.8 Attachment in infancy 2

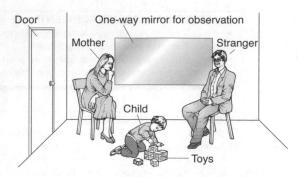

Door — One-way mirror for observation
Mother — Stranger
Child
Toys

HOW DO WE KNOW AN ATTACHMENT HAS FORMED?

Attachment can be tested via the 'Strange Situation' method developed by Ainsworth et al (1971), where the mother and child are taken to an unfamiliar room and subjected to a range of timed, increasingly stressful (for an attached child) set of scenarios, such as:

1 A stranger is introduced to the child in the presence of the mother.
2 The mother leaves the infant with the stranger.
3 After the mother returns and re-settles the infant, it is left alone.
4 A stranger enters and interacts with the lone infant.
5 Mother returns again and picks up infant.

WHAT DIFFERENT KINDS OF ATTACHMENT ARE THERE?

Ainsworth *et al.* (1978) discovered three main types of infant attachment using the Strange Situation, which occurred in various proportions:

Type A – Anxious-avoidant or **detached** (approx. 20% of sample)
The infant ignores the mother, is not affected by her parting or return and although distressed when alone is easily comforted by strangers.

Type B – Securely attached (approx. 70% of sample)
The infant plays contentedly while the mother is there, is distressed by her parting, is relieved on her return and although not adverse to stranger contact treats them differently from the mother.

Type C – Anxious-resistant or **ambivalent** (approx. 10% of sample)
The infant is discontented while with mother, playing less, is distressed by her parting, is not easily comforted on her return and may resist contact by mother and stranger.

Replicating studies have revealed slightly different proportions.

WHAT CAUSES DIFFERENCES IN ATTACHMENT?

Parental sensitivity – Ainsworth *et al.* (1978) suggested that secure attachment is dependent upon emotionally close and responsive mothering, whereas insecure attachments result from insensitive mothers. Although other factors are involved the effects of maternal sensitivity have been supported.

Infant temperament – Researchers such as Kagan (1982) suggest innate differences in infant temperament and anxiety may cause certain kinds of parental reaction and attachment.

Family circumstances – Attachment type may vary over time and setting with social and cultural environmental conditions, e.g. if a family undergoes stress (Vaughn *et al.*, 1979).

Reliability of classification – Strange Situation methodology has been criticised and other attachment types proposed, e.g. D, insecure-disorganised/disorientated.

CROSS-CULTURAL DIFFERENCES IN ATTACHMENT

Using the Strange Situation method (Ainsworth *et al.*, 1978) cross-cultural studies of differences in attachment types have been conducted. Van Ijzendoorn and Kroonenberg (1988) compared the results of 32 cross-cultural studies and found that there was often more consistency across cultures than within them in terms of variation in attachment. However, while the majority of children in each culture seem to be securely attached, there do seem to be variations in the proportion of avoidant and resistant attachments in certain countries. German infants appear to have a slightly higher proportion of avoidant attachments which Grossman et al (1985) have suggested might result from a cultural tendency for German parents to maintain a large interpersonal distance and wean offspring early from close contact. Some studies of Israeli children raised on kibbutzim have revealed a higher proportion of resistant attachments, e.g. Sagi *et al.* (1985), which may result from the fact that the children have contact with parents but are mainly raised communally in a large group. However, the Strange Situation may be based on American cultural assumptions and therefore be a flawed technique for making cross-cultural comparisons.

Country	Number of studies	Percentage of each type of attachment		
		Secure	Avoidant	Resistant
WEST GERMANY	3	57	35	8
GREAT BRITAIN	1	75	22	3
NETHERLANDS	4	67	26	7
SWEDEN	1	74	22	4
ISRAEL	2	64	7	29
JAPAN	2	68	5	27
CHINA	1	50	25	25
UNITED STATES	18	65	21	14
Overall average		65	21	14

Percentages to nearest whole number reported by Van Ijzendoorn and Kroonenberg (1988).

14.9 Deprivation of attachment in infancy

BOWLBY'S MATERNAL DEPRIVATION HYPOTHESIS

Bowlby (1951) proposed that if infants were deprived of their mother (whom he regarded as their major attachment figure), during the critical period of attachment of the first few years of life, then a range of serious and permanent consequences for later development would follow. These included mental subnormality, delinquency, depression, affectionless psychopathy and even dwarfism.

Evidence for:

- Goldfarb (1943) studied children raised in institutions for most of the first three years of their lives, and found they later showed reduced IQ compared to a fostered control group.
- Bowlby (1946) studied 44 juvenile thieves and argued that their affectionless psychopathy was the result of maternal deprivation.
- Spitz and Wolf (1946) investigated infants in South American orphanages and found evidence for severe anaclitic depression in them.
- Harlow and Harlow (1962) researched the effects of social deprivation on rhesus monkeys. Deprived of an attachment figure, they interacted abnormally with other monkeys when they were eventually allowed to mix with them and were unable to form attachments to their own offspring after being artificially inseminated.

Evidence against:

- All the above studies had their methodological flaws, from failing to take into account the amount of environmental stimulation available in institutions, to generalising from animal studies.
- Rutter (1981), in 'Maternal Deprivation Reassessed', a thorough review of research in the area, concluded that Bowlby:
  1 was not correct in his ideas about monotropy (attachment to one figure only) or strict critical periods for attachment.
  2 failed to distinguish between the effects of deprivation (losing an attachment figure) and privation (never having formed an attachment).

POSSIBLE EFFECTS OF DEPRIVATION

SHORT-TERM EFFECTS

- Symptoms of the 'Syndrome of Distress:
  1 Protest – the infant expresses their feelings of anger, fear, frustration, etc.
  2 Despair – the infant then shows apathy and signs of depression, avoiding others.
  3 Detachment – interaction with others resumes, but is superficial and shows no preferences between other people. Re-attachment is resisted.

- Temporary delay in intellectual development.

LONG-TERM EFFECTS

- Symptoms of 'Separation Anxiety':
  1 Increased aggression.
  2 Increased clinging behaviour, possibly developing to the point of refusal to go to school.
  3 Increased detachment.
  4 Psychosomatic disorders (e.g. skin and stomach reactions).

- Increased risk of depression as an adult (usually in reaction to death of an attachment figure).

Evidence

Robertson and Bowlby (1952) based their conclusions regarding the short-term effects of deprivation on observations of the behaviour of children aged between 1 and 4. These children were being hospitalised or placed in residential nurseries. However, the emotional and behavioural effects of the attachment separation may be difficult to distinguish from effects relating to their new environment and situation.

Cockett and Tripp (1994) found more long-term attachment deprivation effects in children from re-ordered families (where parents had divorced and the child now lived away from a parental attachment figure) than those children who lived in intact but discordant (arguing parent) families. However, factors relating, for example, to the disruption of moving house rather than attachment deprivation could also be responsible.

EVALUATION

According to Rutter (1981), there are many sources of individual differences in vulnerability to the short and long-term effects of deprivation, including:

- Characteristics of the child, e.g.:
  1 Age – children are especially vulnerable between 7 months and 3 years (Maccoby, 1981).
  2 Gender – boys, on average, respond worse to separation than girls.
  3 Temperament – differences in temperament, like aggressiveness, may become exaggerated.

- Previous mother-child relationship – The infant's reaction to separation may depend upon the type of attachment, e.g. secure, anxious-resistant or anxious-avoidant (Ainsworth et al., 1978).

- Previous separation experience – Infants experienced in short-term stays with (for example) relatives are more resistant to the effects of deprivation (Stacey et al., 1970).

- Attachments to others – Since Schaffer and Emerson (1964) revealed that multiple attachments are possible (in opposition to Bowlby's (1951) ideas), infants who are not deprived of all attachment figures manage the effects better.

- Quality of care – Research has revealed that both the short- and long-term effects of deprivation can be dramatically reduced by high quality care in crèches and institutions respectively.

- Type of separation – Some research has indicated that long-term separation due to death or illness, if accompanied by harmonious social support, has less of a long-term effect than separation due to divorce.

14.10 Privation of attachment in infancy

- According to Rutter (1981), the most serious long-term consequences for healthy infant development appear to be due to privation – a lack of some kind – rather than to any type of deprivation/loss. However, in his review of the research, Rutter found that the many proposed adverse effects of privation were **not** always **directly** due to a lack of an emotional attachment bond, but often to a deficiency of other important things that an attachment figure may provide (e.g. food, stimulation or even family unity), but an orphanage or dysfunctional family may not. An extreme example of this is the case of Genie (Curtiss, 1977).

MAJOR CONSEQUENCES OF PRIVATION AND THEIR PRECISE LIKELY CAUSES
Rutter (1981)

Intellectual retardation
Due to a deficiency of stimulation and necessary life experiences.

Developmental dwarfism
Due mainly to nutritional deficiencies in early childhood.

Affectionless psychopathy
Due to failure to develop attachments in infancy.

Anti-social behaviour/delinquency
Due to distorted intra-familial relationships, hostility, discord or lack of affection.

Enuresis
Bed-wetting is mainly associated with stress during the first six years.

MEDIATING FACTORS
Factors likely to affect the severity of privation effects include:
- **Type of childcare available** – orphanages, for example, which provide a high standard of care may reduce the effects of lack of stimulation or stress, but may still have a high turnover of staff that prevents attachments forming with the orphans.
- **The duration of the privation** – the longer the time delay before making an attachment, the greater the chance of failure to form an attachment and thus developing affectionless

psychopathy. Although research unequivocally says that experiences at all ages have an impact it seems likely that the first few years do have a special importance for bond formation and social development.
- **Temperament and resilience of the child** – perhaps most importantly, there has been the repeated finding that many children are not excessively damaged by early privation, and that the effects of it can be reversed.

EVIDENCE FOR THE REVERSIBILITY OF PRIVATION EFFECTS

CASE STUDIES OF EXTREME PRIVATION
Freud and Dann (1951) studied six 3-year-old orphans from a concentration camp who had not been able to form attachment to their parents. These children did not develop affectionless psychopathy, probably because they formed close attachments with each other (rather like the two twins raised in extreme privation studied by Koluchova, 1972), and despite developing a number of emotional problems, their intellectual recovery was unimpaired.
Such extreme case studies clearly involve many sources of privation, not just of attachment figures, but also indicate the strong resilience that children's development can show.

ISOLATED RHESUS MONKEYS
Novak and Harlow (1975) found that rhesus monkeys kept in social isolation from birth could develop reasonably normally if they were given 'therapy' by later being allowed to occasionally play with monkeys of their own age.
However, despite indicating the possibility of recovery from total social isolation, generalising the results from rhesus deprivation studies to human deprivation ignores the large differences between the two species.

ADOPTION STUDIES
Hodges and Tizard (1989) found that institutionalised children (who had not formed a stable attachment), adopted between the ages of two and seven, could form close attachments to their adoptive parents.
However, the children returned to their own families had more problems forming attachments and all the institutionalised children had problems with relationships outside their family.
Kadushin (1976) studied over 90 cases of late adoption, where the children were over five years old, and found highly successful outcomes, indicating that early privation does not necessarily prevent later attachment.

14.11 'Social and family relationships of ex-institutional adolescents' Hodges and Tizard (1989)

AIM

To investigate (longitudinally and with a matched comparison group of control children) whether experiencing early institutionalisation with ever-changing care-givers until at least two years of age will lead to long term problems in adolescence for adopted and restored children. Early studies by Bowlby (1951) and Goldfarb (1943a) found that there were many short and long term effects of the early institutionalisation of children, which were attributed to maternal deprivation or privation and were regarded as largely irreversible. However, later studies by Tizard and others on a group of adopted, fostered and restored children with early institutional experience showed that there were markedly less dramatic effects on intellectual and emotional development (probably due to improved conditions) but still difficulties in interpersonal relationships. The children were studied at age 4 and again at age 8, by which time the majority had formed close attachments to their parents, but showed, according to their teachers, more problems of attention seeking behaviour, disobedience, poor peer relationships and over-friendliness. The present study was conducted as a follow up study to see:

- If these children would continue to 'normalise' and lose further effects of early institutionalisation at age 16 or worsen with the stresses of adolescence.
- If adopted children would continue to do better than restored children by age 16, as earlier studies had indicated.

METHOD

Subjects:

All 51 children studied at age 8 were located, of which 42 were available to study at age 16. From these, 39 were interviewed: 23 adopted (17 boys, 6 girls), 11 restored (6 boys, 5 girls) and 5 in institutional care (3 boys, 2 girls). A comparison group of children who had not experienced institutionalisation was gathered for the **family** relationship study, matched, for example, in terms of age, gender, parental occupation and position in the family. Another comparison group of children who had not experienced institutionalisation was formed for the **school** relationship study from the classmate nearest in age of the same sex.

Procedure:

- The adolescents were interviewed on tape and completed the 'Questionnaire of Social Difficulty' (Lindsay and Lindsay, 1982).
- Mothers or careworkers were interviewed on tape and completed the 'A' scale questionnaire (Rutter *et al.*, 1970).
- Teachers were asked to complete the 'B' scale questionnaire (Rutter *et al.*, 1970) on the adolescent's behaviour.

RESULTS

- Institutionalised children differed in their degree of attachment to their parents in that:
  a adopted children were **just as attached** to their parents as the comparison group
  b restored children were **less attached** to their parents than the comparison group and adopted children.
- Institutionalised children had **more problems** with siblings than the comparison group, especially the restored children.
- Adopted children were **more affectionate** with parents than restored children (who were **less** affectionate than the comparison group).
- No difference was found in confiding in, and support from, parents between institutionalised children and comparisons, although the former were less likely to turn to peers.
- Institutionalised children showed significantly worse peer relationships, were less likely to have a particular special friend, and were noted by teachers to be more quarrelsome and less liked by, and show more bullying of, other children.

EVALUATION

Methodological:

Longitudinal methods – Many advantages and disadvantages, e.g. loss of subjects using this method.

Design – Lack of control over this natural experiment, since children were obviously not randomly assigned to adoptive, restored and control groups, there always remains some doubt over the effect of the children's personality characteristics on the results.

Procedure – Problems of self-report questionnaires and interviews as far as socially desirable answers or deception is involved on the subject's part, and experimenter expectation on the interviewer's part.

Data analysis – A thorough statistical analysis was conducted on the results.

Ethical problems – Of asking children and their guardians questions that might disrupt their interpersonal relationships, e.g. asking mothers if they loved all their children equally.

Theoretical: Implies that while Bowlby was wrong about many of the more dramatic effects of early institutionalisation, some long lasting effects on interpersonal relations do persist into adolescence. Further follow up study needs to be conducted to see if adolescent behaviours and feelings persist into adulthood, however. There are some important practical implications for adoption practices from this study.

Links: Child attachment, longitudinal studies.

14.12 Different forms of day care and social development

FORM OF CARE	DAY CARE				PARENTAL CARE
	Nursery/Crèche	Childminding in other homes	Home care by: Nanny	Relative	
Separation from home environment	HIGH	HIGH	LOW	LOW	LOW
Separation from siblings/family	HIGH	HIGH/MEDIUM	MEDIUM	MEDIUM/LOW	LOW
Adult carer initial familiarity	LOW	LOW/MEDIUM	LOW	MEDIUM/HIGH	HIGH
Adult carer presence stability	LOW–HIGH	HIGH	HIGH	HIGH	HIGH
Adult carer attention per child	LOW	MEDIUM/HIGH	HIGH	HIGH	HIGH
Number of other children	HIGH	MEDIUM/LOW	LOW	LOW	LOW

IMPACT ON ATTACHMENT

Some suggest day care could result in the child being unable to form an attachment (causing *privation effects*) or disruption to the bond if attachment had already been made (causing deprivation effects).
- Belsky and Rovine (1988) found infants were more likely to develop insecure attachments if they received day care for over 20 hours per week before they were a year old (i.e. when attachments were forming). However, perhaps parents who use day care differ in their home interactions with infants.

IMPACT ON AGGRESSION

A number of studies, both *longitudinal* and *cross-sectional*, have indicated day care children show higher levels of aggression and behavioural problems, e.g. Haskins (1985) found day care was associated with increased school aggression. However:
- Children with *pre-existing* aggressive temperaments may be more likely to be placed in day care.
- Measurements of 'aggression' may just reflect greater independence or the need to assert/defend oneself among a greater number of peers in day care.
- Much of the research has been conducted in the US where day care provision is less subsidised and monitored for quality by the government (e.g. compared to Sweden) and different norms of aggression exist. *Lower* levels of aggression in day care than home care children have been found in Canada.

IMPACT ON PEER RELATIONS

It has been suggested that increased interaction with peers in day care could help develop sociability and social skills, so leading to more positive social relations. However research has revealed **mixed results**:
- Andersson's (1989) longitudinal study found public day care in Sweden was positively associated with social competence, positive peer relations and play. Andersson (1992, cited in Durkin 1995) later reported evidence that children who had entered day care before the age of 12 months also scored higher on measures of adjustment and social competence at ages 8 and 13. Clarke-Stewart *et al.* (1994) found peer relationships were more advanced in children who had experienced day care.
- However, some research in America has linked greater child care with worse peer relationships and Bates *et al.* (1994) found day care was associated with negative social adjustment in Kindergarten.
- Kagan *et al.* (1980) set up their own nursery with consistent, high quality day care and compared 33 infants from a variety of backgrounds who attended it from 3.5 months of age with a matched home care control group. They found no significantly consistent differences in the groups' sociability.

EVALUATION

Since much of the research is based on **natural experiments** (children are not randomly assigned by the experimenter) and **correlations**, there is a **lack of control** over many important variables.
Durkin (1995) concludes that there are **multivariate explanations** for the different research findings (e.g. the child's pre-existing attachments, temperament, peer group experience, and home environment), but that a **crucial issue is quality of day care** – 'the ratio of staff to children, the professional skills and warmth of the staff, staff turnover, staff-parent communication, and educational materials provided. Research demonstrates consistently that high quality is associated with more favourable outcomes.'
There is a **lack of research** on the **specific effects of the different types of day care**, e.g. between home care by relatives and childminding in other homes, however quality of care again seems the key issue.

14.13 Implications of attachment/day care research for child care

ATTACHMENT/DAY CARE RESEARCH	IMPLICATIONS FOR CHILD CARE PRACTICES
Identity of attachment figure(s) Psychological research has criticised Bowlby's notion of monotropy of attachment and indicates that infants can form multiple attachments and to individuals other than the mother.	**Multiple care-givers** Under the correct conditions, children can form attachments to multiple care-givers, both inside and outside the home, and do not need to be looked after exclusively by the mother. Indeed this is the norm in many cultures (thus mothers should not feel guilty about working and leaving their children with others).
Causes of attachment Research has shown that attachments do not only form to those who give physical care and satisfy food needs, but also those who provide high quality emotional interactions and stimulation (which also promotes cognitive development).	**Quality of care** Quality of interaction and stimulation is therefore an important factor to consider in: a establishing attachments before sending a child to day care. b choosing a suitable day care provider. c maintaining attachment bonds on returning from work.
Attachment privation/deprivation Research indicates that a lack of, or disrupted access to, constant attachment figures within a sensitive time period in infancy may result in negative privation or deprivation effects (Rutter, 1981).	**Age, time spent and constancy in day care** Attachments are more likely to be formed and maintained if: a infants are not put into day care too young or before they have formed stable attachments. b infants do not spend too many hours per week in day care. c day care providers are constant so can be attached to.
Day care research A consistent theme in the effects of day care (whether by other people or relatives, or in nurseries, other homes, or the child's own home) is quality of care. Quality of care is defined by carer: • warmth • stability (in terms of a low turnover of carers) • ability/resources to adequately stimulate the child. In addition, supervised, positive, and stimulating interactions with other children and adults may help develop mature and pro-social behaviour, interpersonal skills and peer relationships.	**Choosing the best type of day care** • *Day care and childminders* – in the UK they are regulated and financed by the government. Based on attachment and day care research, nurseries are inspected to ensure good practice, e.g. that they provide well-trained staff, aim to ensure low turnover of staff, keep group sizes and adult-to-child ratios within specified limits, and ideally provide each child with a key worker (a responsible adult to provide security, warmth, and support throughout the day). • *Relative carers* – usually offer high levels of warmth and stability, but may also need to be provided with suitable support and resources (or in even training in some cases) to help properly stimulate the child's development.
Methodological problems in attachment and day care research Evaluation of attachment and day care research reveals a great number of variables at work in the studies (not all of which are always controlled for), leading to a variety of possible positive and negative effects on children's development.	**Caution with recommendations** Parents should consider a range of factors when evaluating the pros and cons of day care, including: • Individual difference in their child's temperament, experience of others, and attachment behaviour • The quality of, and number of hours spent in, day care • Their own behaviour and interactions with the child at home.

14.14 Development of friendships

AGE	BEHAVIOURAL TRENDS IN PEER RELATIONSHIPS *e.g. who is interacted with and how*		COGNITIVE TRENDS IN PEER RELATIONSHIPS *e.g. the underlying basis of peer relationships or understanding of friendship*
1	0–6 months – peer interest shown by looking only. 6–12 months – infants smile, vocalise and gesture towards peers, but these actions are often not noticed or returned due to a lack of social skills. Parallel play is shown.		
	12–18 months – infants begin to look more at peers than parents and show reactions to each other's gestures. Peers are regarded as responsive toys. 18–24 months – infants show co-ordinated and reciprocal interactions with peers, e.g. imitating each other. Attachment may occur to **preferred playmates** and interactions with these 'friends' are qualitatively different to those with other peers.		18–24 months – infants are able to show self-recognition and can discriminate themselves from others.
2 **3** **4**	2–4 years – **increased social skills and complexity of behavioural interactions** with peers. Increase in association and co-operative play. More sophisticated pretend play, affection and approval is shown with peers who are friends rather than acquaintances. Play occurs in small groups – usually of 2–3 friends.	2-year-old girls already prefer to play with other girls (La Freniere *et al.*, 1984) and by age 3 boys seek boy playmates more than girl playmates.	2–3 years – children increasingly use the general symbolic function and show motor co-ordination improvements (they stop 'toddling').
		3–6 years - children are found to be 'generally willing to give up their own valuable play time to perform a dull task if their efforts would benefit a friend; yet this same kind of self-sacrifice was almost never made for a mere acquaintance. Young children also express more sympathy in response to the distress of a friend than to that of an acquaintance, and they are more inclined to try to relieve the friend's distress as well' (Kanfer *et al.*, 1981, Costin and Jones, 1992 – reported in Shaffer, 1996). Children do this *before* they say such behaviour is important for friendship.	3–4 years – ability to show metarepresentation (understanding others have beliefs) allows more sophisticated social pretend play and **planning** of play to occur.
4 **5**	4–5 years – **ethnic preference** in playmates and friends begins to emerge and may create ethnic groupings in the playground, although this is not inevitable.		4–5 years – basic ethnic identity emerges.
	5–6 years – play group size and **number of friends begins to increase**, especially with boys.		Selman (1980) suggested cognitive development in social perspective or role-taking skills increasingly allows children to understand the meaning of friendship. (The following ages are approximations.)
6 **7** **8** **9**	6–10 years – true, stable and regular **friendship groups** emerge that have a shared identity and set of norms that regulate behaviour, as well as an organisational structure and/or hierarchy. Groups begin to segregate more strictly according to sex. Friendships are predominately of a same-sex nature. By age 6½, children spend 10 times as much time with playmates of the same rather than opposite sex (Maccoby, 1988), perhaps due to incompatible play and interaction styles. Receptivity to peer group pressure to commit anti-social behaviour steadily increases (reaching a peak by the age of 15). *Best* friendships remain stable.	6–14-year-old Scottish and Canadian children were asked by Bigelow and LaGaipa (1980) (cited by Smith in Bryant and Colman, 1995) to write an essay about their expectations of best friends. Based on a content analysis of these essays, they arrived at a 3-stage model of friendship expectations that suggested 'a shift towards more psychologically complex and mutually reciprocal ideas of friendship during middle school years, with intimacy and commitment becoming especially important in later adolescence'. Up to 8 years – 'Reward-cost' stage – based on common activities, living nearby and having similar expectations. 9–10 years – 'Normative' stage – emphasised shared values, rules and sanctions. 11–12 years – 'Empathetic' stage – showing a more mature conception of friendship based on understanding and self-disclosure as well as shared interests. Cairns and Cairns (1994) found honesty and loyalty was more important to adolescent friendship in girls than boys.	3–6 years – children are egocentric and are dominated by the appearance of situations. A friend is therefore anyone who the child has met and successfully played with. 6–8 years – children still base their friendships upon common activities and although they now realise that others may have different views and choose to be friends, relationships are still very much one-way. If a peer does not follow the child's views and desires, they are not a friend. 8–10 years – children can now better understand how their views and interests differ or coincide with those of their friends. Psychological similarity rather than common activities, and mutual or reciprocal fairness in the friendship become important. 10 onwards – children increasingly develop expectations of how a good friend should behave – not necessarily always agreeing, but showing intimacy, loyalty and mutual understanding.
10 **11**	10–11 years – the number of peers regarded as friends begins to drop as children approach adolescence, particularly with girls who tend to play in pairs more often and emphasise intimacy and exclusiveness in their friendships to a greater degree.		

14.15 Causes and consequences of popularity and rejection

MEASURING POPULARITY AND REJECTION

Popularity in childhood is measured by two main sociometric methods:

observation – e.g. of play to record the amount and kind (positive or negative) of interactions children have with their peer group.

self-report – e.g. using questionnaires or interviews to ask children to rate their classmates/peers on a scale for popularity/degree of friendship, or simply nominate their three best friends (or peers they like least).

From these methods researchers can then construct and allocate individuals to sociometric status categories.

SOCIOMETRIC STATUS CATEGORIES

Popular Liked by many, disliked by few	**Controversial** Liked by many but also disliked by many
Average Moderately liked	
Neglected Neither liked or disliked	**Rejected** Disliked by many, liked by few

(vertical axis: Liked most rating) (horizontal axis: Liked least rating)

Evaluation

- According to Smith (in Bryant and Colman, 1995) there may be ethical problems with asking children to rate their peers positively or negatively, for example such questions might bring about increased negative behaviour to disliked peers, 'but so far ill effects have not been found (Hayvren and Hymel, 1984)'.
- Observational studies of behavioural interactions may not reflect the children's opinions of popularity, while asking them relies upon their self-reports (which may be inaccurate or biased by social desirability). Shaffer (1996), however, reports that 'Even 3- to 5-year-olds can respond appropriately to sociometric surveys (Denham *et al.*, 1990); and the choices (or ratings) that children provide correspond reasonably well to teacher ratings of peer popularity, thus suggesting that sociometric surveys provide valid assessments of children's social standing in their peer groups (Hymel, 1983)'.

CAUSES OF POPULARITY AND REJECTION

- Popular children – are consistently found to be outgoing, co-operative and supportive. They are able to assess and show behaviour that is socially acceptable for the peer group. They contribute positively to peer group activities without becoming disruptive and resolve disputes peacefully.
- Rejected children – show characteristics that annoy peers, for example by being aggressive and disruptive in joint activities or by showing behaviour that differs from the social norm.
- Neglected children – do not show characteristics of rejected children and may possess some of the qualities of popular children, but tend not to initiate interactions or draw attention to themselves.
- Controversial children – are often aggressive but use their aggression in socially skilled ways to gain peer group status.

Correlates of popularity and rejection

- Physical attractiveness – facially attractive children and those with athletic builds are more likely to be popular than unattractive children among their peers from an early age (Langlois, 1986). This could result from the positive reactions attractive children receive from adults and peers due to 'the beautiful is good' stereotype (Dion, 1972), which becomes a self-fulfilling prophecy. Negative reactions to unattractive children could lead to feelings of rejection and anger, which could create anti-social behaviour, which in turn would lead to further unpopularity.
- Rate of maturity – among boys, those who mature early are often rated as more popular than those who mature late, perhaps due to greater physical competence and success in peer competition.
- Similarity – children who appear different from the majority, e.g. in terms of ethnicity or even possession of a non-common name, may become less popular. According to Social Identity Theory, those who appear different are more likely to be categorised as 'out-group' members and therefore discriminated against.
- Studies conducted on children of all ages have revealed that personality, behavioural style, and social/cognitive skills are also very important influences on popularity. These characteristics may result from different attachment bonds, parental styles, birth order (later-born children may have more experience interacting with older siblings), innate temperaments, and/or cognitive ability.

CONSEQUENCES OF POPULARITY AND REJECTION

Shaffer (1996) reports studies indicating a variety of consequences of social rejection:

- Fewer friendships and greater feelings of loneliness.
- Greater deviant, anti-social, or serious adjustment problems in later life.
- Aggressive rejected children in particular are more likely to display conduct disorder in school, become chronically hostile, and commit criminal acts of violence in later life.
- Non-aggressive rejected children who show socially awkward or unusual behaviour and hypersensitivity to teasing run a greater risk of being bullied, developing low self-esteem, and suffering from emotional disorders such as clinical depression.
- Popular children, however, are more likely than rejected children to gain more friends, integrate smoothly and achieve higher peer group status when tested in new groups of unfamiliar peers.

EVALUATION

- Many concepts used in the research of this area are difficult to define and vary with culture, e.g. social competence or physical attractiveness.
- There are often problems isolating which are the causes and which are the consequences of popularity in the correlational research, e.g. how much does popularity in turn affect perceptions of physical attractiveness and the development of social skills. In addition, other factors such as family upbringing could account for aggression, rejection, and later problems with social functioning.
- Rejected children may require social skills training in order to avoid the many negative consequences of their status, e.g. modelling, coaching, and social problem-solving or role-taking interventions.

14.16 Gender development – terms and issues

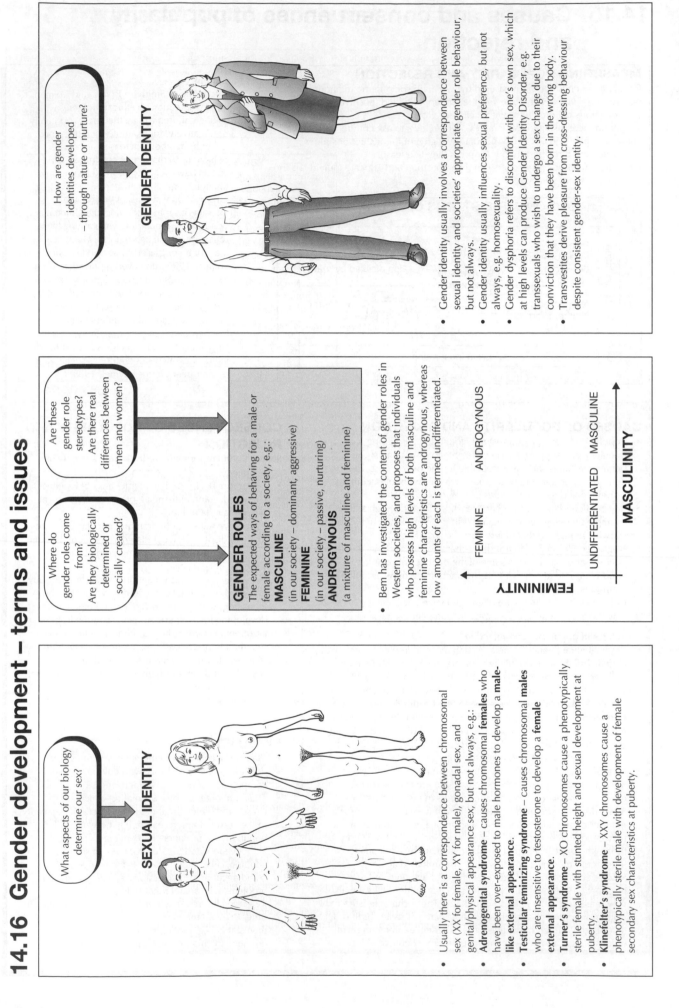

GENDER IDENTITY

How are gender identities developed – through nature or nurture?

- Gender identity usually involves a correspondence between sexual identity and societies' appropriate gender role behaviour, but not always.
- Gender identity usually influences sexual preference, but not always, e.g. homosexuality.
- Gender dysphoria refers to discomfort with one's own sex, which at high levels can produce Gender Identity Disorder, e.g. transsexuals who wish to undergo a sex change due to their conviction that they have been born in the wrong body.
- Transvestites derive pleasure from cross-dressing behaviour despite consistent gender-sex identity.

GENDER ROLES

Are these gender role stereotypes? Are there real differences between men and women?

Where do gender roles come from? Are they biologically determined or socially created?

GENDER ROLES
The expected ways of behaving for a male or female according to a society, e.g.:
MASCULINE
(in our society – dominant, aggressive)
FEMININE
(in our society – passive, nurturing)
ANDROGYNOUS
(a mixture of masculine and feminine)

- Bem has investigated the content of gender roles in Western societies, and proposes that individuals who possess high levels of both masculine and feminine characteristics are androgynous, whereas low amounts of each is termed undifferentiated.

FEMININE   ANDROGYNOUS

FEMININITY

UNDIFFERENTIATED   MASCULINE

MASCULINITY

SEXUAL IDENTITY

What aspects of our biology determine our sex?

- Usually there is a correspondence between chromosomal sex (XX for female, XY for male), gonadal sex, and genital/physical appearance sex, but not always, e.g.:
- **Adrenogenital syndrome** – causes chromosomal **females** who have been over-exposed to male hormones to develop a **male-like external appearance.**
- **Testicular feminizing syndrome** – causes chromosomal **males** who are insensitive to testosterone to develop a **female external appearance.**
- **Turner's syndrome** – XO chromosomes cause a phenotypically sterile female with stunted height and sexual development at puberty.
- **Klinefelter's syndrome** – XXY chromosomes cause a phenotypically sterile male with development of female secondary sex characteristics at puberty.

14.17 Gender development – biologically based theories

THE BIOLOGICAL APPROACH

- The biological approach proposes that the development of gender is dictated by **physiological processes** within the individual and occurs as **biological maturation** takes place.
- From an **evolutionary** point of view, the human male appears to have been equipped with greater physical strength, aggression and visuospatial ability (perhaps adapting them better for hunting/competition), whereas women seem to have evolved greater social sensitivity and verbal ability (perhaps adapting them better for more passive/nurturing behaviour). See also evolution and sexual selection/parental investment.
- These supposedly natural behavioural tendencies are regulated by **hormone** levels – just as hormones trigger the physical changes of puberty, so they also affect the thoughts and behaviour of males and females. The hormone **testosterone** seems especially active in triggering the increased amounts of aggression and 'rough and tumble' play that males show even at young ages.

EVIDENCE FOR THE BIOLOGICAL APPROACH

- **Money** (1972) studied 25 girls with **adrenogenital syndrome** due to an overdose of male hormones while in the womb, and found that 20 of them showed '**tomboyish**' behaviour – showing greater interest in outdoor activity and less in dolls, childcare and self adornment.
- **Imperato-McGinley et al.** (1974) studied members of the **Batista family** who, due to a mutant gene, were born with the external features of (and grew up as) young girls, but **physically changed into men** at puberty. The large increase in testosterone at puberty activated a process that should have occurred during embryonic development and their vaginas healed over, their testicles descended, they grew full sized penises and became men – showing **masculine behaviour** (including marrying women).
- **Animal studies** have shown that female monkeys **given testosterone** show male monkey behaviour, such as increased aggressiveness, dominance and even sexual behaviour.

CRITICISMS OF THE BIOLOGICAL APPROACH

- Girls with adrenogenital syndrome may show more masculine behaviour because they look like males, and therefore may be **treated like males**, rather than because of the testosterone.
- The Batistas may have been able to adopt masculine behaviour more readily, despite being raised as girls, because of their **supportive environment**, rather than biological changes.
- The evidence of the link between testosterone levels and aggression is often correlational. Studies have shown that testosterone levels can increase **after** successful dominant behaviour.
- It is not legitimate to generalise from animal gender studies to human gender behaviour.

THE BIOSOCIAL APPROACH

- The biosocial approach moves **away from the direct** influence of **physiological** factors on gender behaviour and identity, and focuses on the **interaction** of biological and social factors:
  - **a** **Biological predispositions** for male babies to be more irritable and harder to pacify than female babies may lead to different **social reactions** from the caregivers around them. Male babies may, therefore, be treated as more independent and aggressive than female babies, and may become so.
  - **b** The **anatomy** (physical appearance) of males and females may serve as a **cue** for the **social labels** and expectations that society possesses for masculine and feminine behaviours.
  - **c** **Social** factors have a **greater influence** upon gender identity and behaviour than biological ones, but there may be a **critical** or **sensitive time period** to acquire gender identity.

EVIDENCE FOR THE BIOSOCIAL APPROACH

- **Money and Ehrhardt** (1972) studied girls with adrenogenital syndrome who were raised and treated as boys because of their male looking genitalia. If the mistaken classification was discovered and **corrected before the age of three**, then adjustment to the new gender usually proceeded without many problems. However, this was not the case after three years.
- **Money and Ehrhardt** (1972) also studied chromosomal males with testicular feminizing syndrome, which caused them to be raised as females due to their female external appearance. In the majority of all cases these individuals identified fully with their (female) role of upbringing regardless of their underlying biology.
- Cases of **sexual reassignment** for penis amputation and hermaphrodites have also supported the notion that social and psychological factors outweigh the influence of biological factors in the development of gender identities.

CRITICISMS OF THE BIOSOCIAL APPROACH

- There have been some cases which have **contradicted** the **critical age** of reassignment idea, such as the Batistas.
- Most of the studies supporting the biosocial approach involve individuals with **unusual biological conditions**, and so may **not** be **representative** of gender role development in the majority of the population.

14.18 Gender development – psychological theories

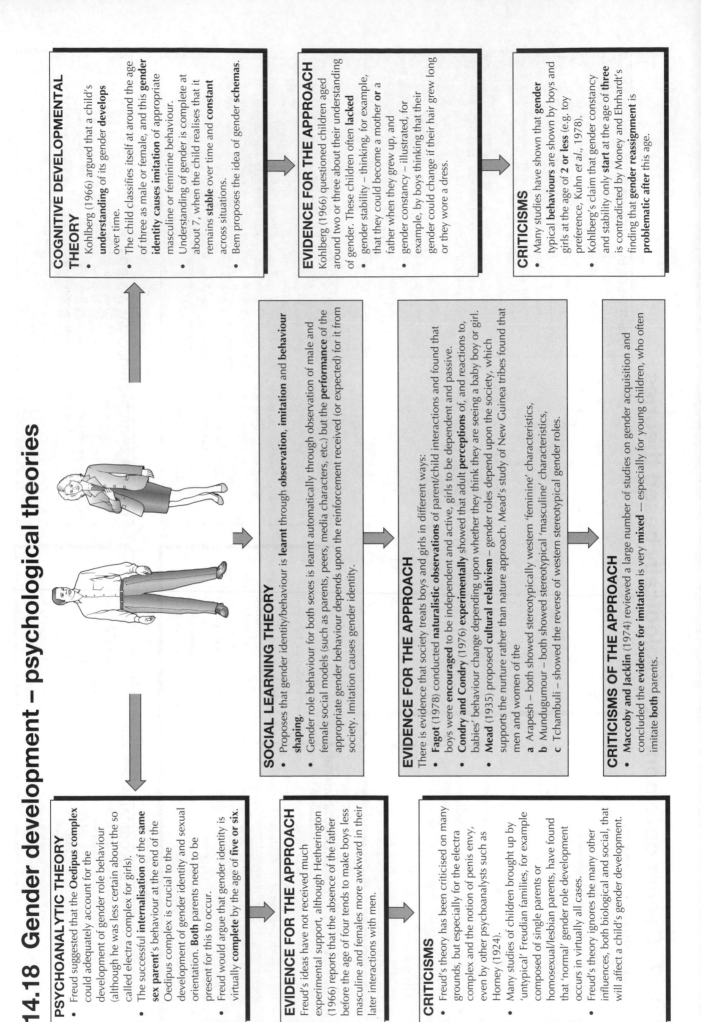

PSYCHOANALYTIC THEORY

- Freud suggested that the **Oedipus complex** could adequately account for the development of gender role behaviour (although he was less certain about the so called electra complex for girls).
- The successful **internalisation** of the **same sex parent**'s behaviour at the end of the Oedipus complex is crucial to the development of gender identity and sexual orientation. **Both** parents need to be present for this to occur.
- Freud would argue that gender identity is virtually **complete** by the age of **five or six.**

EVIDENCE FOR THE APPROACH

Freud's ideas have not received much experimental support, although Hetherington (1966) reports that the absence of the father before the age of four tends to make boys less masculine and females more awkward in their later interactions with men.

CRITICISMS

- Freud's theory has been criticised on many grounds, but especially for the electra complex and the notion of penis envy, even by other psychoanalysts such as Horney (1924).
- Many studies of children brought up by 'untypical' Freudian families, for example composed of single parents or homosexual/lesbian parents, have found that 'normal' gender role development occurs in virtually all cases.
- Freud's theory ignores the many other influences, both biological and social, that will affect a child's gender development.

COGNITIVE DEVELOPMENTAL THEORY

- Kohlberg (1966) argued that a child's **understanding** of its gender **develops** over time.
- The child classifies itself at around the age of three as male or female, and this **gender identity causes imitation** of appropriate masculine or feminine behaviour.
- Understanding of gender is complete at about 7, when the child realises that it remains **stable** over time and **constant** across situations.
- Bem proposes the idea of gender **schemas.**

EVIDENCE FOR THE APPROACH

Kohlberg (1966) questioned children aged around two or three about their understanding of gender. These children often **lacked**

- gender stability – thinking, for example, that they could become a mother **or** a father when they grew up, and
- gender constancy – illustrated, for example, by boys thinking that their gender could change if their hair grew long or they wore a dress.

CRITICISMS

- Many studies have shown that **gender** typical **behaviours** are shown by boys and girls at the age of **2 or less** (e.g. toy preference, Kuhn *et al.*, 1978).
- Kohlberg's claim that gender constancy and stability only **start** at the age of **three** is contradicted by Money and Ehrhardt's finding that **gender reassignment** is **problematic after** this age.

SOCIAL LEARNING THEORY

- Proposes that gender identity/behaviour is **learnt** through **observation**, **imitation** and **behaviour shaping.**
- Gender role behaviour for both sexes is learnt automatically through observation of male and female social models (such as parents, peers, media characters, etc.) but the **performance** of the appropriate gender behaviour depends upon the reinforcement received (or expected) for it from society. Imitation causes gender identity.

EVIDENCE FOR THE APPROACH

There is evidence that society treats boys and girls in different ways:

- **Fagot** (1978) conducted **naturalistic observations** of parent/child interactions and found that boys were **encouraged** to be independent and active, girls to be dependent and passive.
- **Condry and Condry** (1976) **experimentally** showed that adult **perceptions** of, and reactions to, babies' behaviour change depending upon whether they think they are seeing a baby boy or girl.
- **Mead** (1935) proposed **cultural relativism** – gender roles depend upon the society, which supports the nurture rather than nature approach. Mead's study of New Guinea tribes found that men and women of the
  a Arapesh – both showed stereotypically western 'feminine' characteristics,
  b Mundugumour – both showed stereotypical 'masculine' characteristics,
  c Tchambuli – showed the reverse of western stereotypical gender roles.

CRITICISMS OF THE APPROACH

- **Maccoby and Jacklin** (1974) reviewed a large number of studies on gender acquisition and concluded the **evidence for imitation** is very **mixed** — especially for young children, who often imitate **both** parents.

14.19 Explanations for psychological androgyny and gender dysphoria

PSYCHOLOGICAL ANDROGYNY
- In psychological androgyny, an individual's **basic gender identity corresponds to** his or her **sexual identity**, but shows **equally high** levels of **masculine** and f**eminine gender role characteristics**.
- Androgyny has been measured by the Bem Sex Role Inventory (Bem, 1981), constructed from 20 words thought to describe masculine traits and 20 for feminine traits (randomised with 20 unrelated traits), which individuals rate themselves upon for how well each fits their character.
- High scores on both masculine and feminine traits imply psychological androgyny, which has been found to be associated with higher: adaptability/flexibility of behaviour, self-esteem, achievement motivation, parental effectiveness, and marriage/life satisfaction.

GENDER DYSPHORIA
- Gender dysphoria refers to discomfort with one's own sexual identity – a major symptom of Gender Identity Disorder, where a person's **basic gender identity does not correspond to** his or her **sexual identity**. In such cases individuals believe they have been born into the wrong body and show high levels of (transsexual) **gender role behaviour opposite to their sexual identity**.
- Gender Identity Disorder can be diagnosed using DSM IV-TR criteria to distinguish it from gender dysphoria associated with physical sex conditions such as hermaphroditism (being born with both male and female genitalia) and from unrelated transvestism (gaining pleasure from cross-dressing).
- The gender dysphoria associated with Gender Identity Disorder can start as young as four years of age and cause a strong, persistent and upsetting dissatisfaction with one's physical sexual appearance or gender role that often leads to cross-sex behaviour, social dysfunction, and a desire for a physical sex change.

EXPLANATIONS

SOCIAL LEARNING THEORY (SLT)
SLT suggests children's observational learning, imitation, and reinforcement for masculine and feminine behaviour is dependent on the social environment. Thus parents, peers, schools, and the media are all capable of defining and shaping the relative balance of imitation of 'masculine' and 'feminine' behaviour.

Evaluation
Shaffer (1996) quotes studies that show:
- Androgynous parents tend to raise androgynous children (Orlofsky, 1979).
- Daughters of working mothers are more likely to perceive fewer differences between the sexes and be androgynous themselves than daughters of mothers who stay at home (Hoffman, 1989).
- Younger (more than older) children can be easily taught androgynous attitudes (Katz and Walsh, 1991).

GENDER SCHEMA THEORY
Implies androgynous children may develop a less restrictive, dichotomous, or stereotyped gender schema, which influences their tendency to classify and identify with both masculine and feminine behaviour and characteristics. Perhaps such androgynous schemas result from parental styles that do not emphasise the labelling of 'boy' vs. 'girl' objects and activities.

Evaluation
- Bradbard et al.'s (1986, cited in Shaffer, 1996) study supports the effect of gender labelling objects on gender schemas. Four to nine-year-olds were shown gender neutral objects, but were told some were 'for boys' while others were 'for girls'. Boys and girls then proceeded to explore their own 'gender appropriate' items significantly more and were more likely to recall them a week later.

EXPLANATIONS

GENETICS
Research shows, perhaps unsurprisingly, that gender dysphoria is associated with genetic disorders causing ambiguous genital and/or secondary sexual characteristics, e.g. Klinefelter's, Turner's, Adrenogenital or Testicular Feminizing syndromes.

Evaluation
- Gender dysphoria in these conditions is readily explained by the Biosocial approach (e.g. Money and Ehrhardt, 1972).
- However, those with Gender Identity Disorder do not usually have any external sexual anatomical ambiguity that could trigger confusion and dissatisfaction.

HORMONES AND BRAIN DEVELOPMENT
Many researchers suggest a biological basis for Gender Identity Disorder due to its early, persistent and upsetting development in the face of normalising social influences. For example, insufficient or mistimed androgen hormone surges, both before and after birth, may incompletely masculinise the male brain – thus leading to later gender dysphoria and identity problems.

Evaluation
- Post-mortem studies on male-to-female transsexuals, non-transsexual men, and non-transsexual women, have found a significant difference in the volume of sections of the hypothalamus responsible for sexual behaviour (Zhou et al., 1995, cited by Vitale, 1997).
- However, the cause of hormonal disruption and its role in *female* gender dysphoria is unclear.

SOCIAL LEARNING THEORY (SLT)
SLT suggests children automatically learn both male and female gender role behaviour by observation, but that imitation depends on reinforcement. Perhaps cross-gender behaviour is internally rewarding or reinforced by the attention it gains.

Evaluation
- The theory explains behaviour rather than identity problems and that the many negative reactions (punishment) to cross-sex behaviour in most societies should decrease its frequency.

14.20 Social and cultural influences on gender role

INFLUENCE OF PARENTS

Social Learning Theory holds parental influence works by:

1. modelling (through their own behaviour and by gender labelling objects and actions, e.g. clothing, allocation of toys and 'gender-appropriate' joint activities)
2. direct reinforcement of children's gender role imitation.

Evaluation

- *Modelling* – Lytton and Romney's (1991) meta-analysis of many studies found evidence of parental initiation of sex-typed activities, e.g. mothers cooking with daughters rather than sons. Other studies indicate that although children have a tendency to imitate same-sex models (Barkley *et al.*, 1977), the gender-labelling of the model's activity was more important (Masters *et al.*, 1979).
- *Reinforcement* – Maccoby and Jacklin's (1974) review, and others, have found little evidence for direct parental reward or punishment of gender role behaviour in children, although Langlois and Downs (1980) found greater discouragement of cross-sex play in fathers.

INFLUENCE OF THE MEDIA

Social Learning Theory's concepts of observational learning and vicarious reinforcement imply gender role behaviour can be automatically acquired from media sources, e.g. films, TV programmes/adverts, or teenage magazines, and imitated if desirable consequences for those behaviours are observed. The social psychological concepts of informational and referent social influence also provide motivation to conform to and imitate media portrayals of gender role behaviour.

Evaluation

- Many studies find women are more likely to be presented in domestic, child-care, or sexual contexts and shown in submissive or minor roles in prime-time TV and adverts.
- Distinct sex-typing is found in toy adverts and catalogues.
- Some studies have found positive correlations between heavy TV viewing and: sex-typed activity preferences, highly stereotyped gender perceptions, and sexist views in both children and adults; although Durkin (1985) warns the effects are not strong and cannot indicate causation.

INFLUENCE OF SCHOOLS

Despite educational efforts to the contrary, school environments may reinforce gender role behaviour via:

- *Teacher expectations* – which could create self-fulfilling prophecies.
- *Subject choice* and career advice – choosing traditionally stereotypical 'masculine' or 'feminine' subjects, e.g. physics or home economics may consolidate gender roles and lead to traditionally stereotypical careers.
- *Greater exposure to gender role peer group* play and sporting *activities*.

Evaluation

- Gender role development before school attendance and possible innate sex differences in verbal and spatial ability may be a cause rather than effect of later choices.

GENDER ➡ **ROLE**

INFLUENCE OF PEERS

Peer groups can exert influence on gender role behaviour through the Social Learning processes described above and are a particularly powerful source of normative, informational and referent social influences. Conforming to gender roles avoids ambiguity of social behaviour, peer group ridicule and identity confusion.

Evaluation

- Fagot (1985a, cited in Shaffer, 1996) reports peer pressure for sex-appropriate play is even shown at 2 years of age – boys criticise and disrupt each other for playing with girls or their toys, while girls are also critical of other girls who choose to play with boys.

CROSS-CULTURAL STUDIES OF GENDER ROLE

Cross-cultural studies are often presented as evidence for the impact of cultural and environmental factors on gender role development. Mead's (1935) study of different sex-role behaviour in three New Guinea tribes seems to count against innately, fixed gender roles:

- The Arapesh men and women both showed stereotypically Western 'feminine' characteristics, as boys and girls were raised to be sensitive to others, co-operative and non-aggressive.
- The Mundugumour raised both sexes to show aggressive and emotional traits typical of 'masculine' Western gender roles.
- The Tchambuli tribe showed a reversal of Western stereotypical gender roles – women were dominant and independent, men were passive, socially sensitive, and participated in child birth.

Durkin (1995) cites a study (Goodale, 1980) of another Papua New Guinea tribe, the Kaulong, who raise their girls to strike and chase boys with sticks in preparation for later gender roles as women who dominate mate selection (sometimes even capturing men). He also cites evidence of cross-cultural differences in maternal style associated with gender role aggression (Kornadt, 1990).

Evaluation

- Gender role norms and influences can change *within* cultures over time as well as between cultures; e.g. Glascock's (2001, cited in Giles 2003) content analysis of prime-time television in the late 1990s revealed increases in the representation of women as main characters, the variety of jobs or roles they were shown in, and the frequency of less traditional 'feminine' behaviours, compared to the 1970s.
- Despite some striking cross-cultural examples of gender role differences, there are some stable cross-cultural characteristics across the majority of cultures, e.g. the tendency for males to participate in warfare more than women (even in the Arapesh).
- Cultural gender role differences may result from a combination of innate evolutionary adaptive tendencies, biosocial suitability/predispositions of anatomy, and environmental upbringing strategies.

15.1 Defining abnormality

STATISTICAL INFREQUENCY

Abnormality can be defined as deviation from the average, where statistically common behaviour is defined as 'normal' while **statistically rare behaviour** is 'abnormal'. Thus autism is sufficiently statistically rare (it occurs in 2–4 children per 10,000) to be 'abnormal', as is multiple personality disorder. This does not necessarily mean the behaviour concerned is qualitatively different from 'normal' – many human characteristics are shown by everyone in the population to a certain degree, and if they can be measured every individual can be placed upon a dimensional scale or continuum that will reveal how common their score is in comparison to everybody else's. These comparisons can be standardised by the use of **normal distribution curves**. Many characteristics could be placed upon normal distribution curves as dimensions, such as intelligence. Most people fall somewhere in the middle of these continuums, but if an individual shows an extreme deviation from this average then they may be regarded as abnormal.

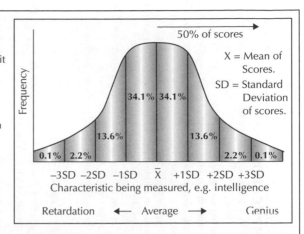

X = Mean of Scores.

SD = Standard Deviation of scores.

50% of scores

34.1% 34.1%

13.6% 13.6%

0.1% 2.2% 2.2% 0.1%

–3SD –2SD –1SD X̄ +1SD +2SD +3SD
Characteristic being measured, e.g. intelligence

Retardation ← Average → Genius

Evaluation

1 There are problems deciding how statistically rare (2 or 3 standard deviations?) behaviour has to be to be considered abnormal.
2 Some currently accepted mental disorders are probably not statistically rare enough to be defined as abnormal, e.g. phobias.
3 Statistical deviation from the average does not tell us about the desirability of the deviation – both mental retardation and genius are statistically rare but only the former is regarded as abnormal.
4 By this definition different subcultures may show behaviour that is statistically rare in the majority culture and be defined as abnormal.

DEVIATION FROM SOCIAL NORMS

Norms are expected ways of behaving in a society according to the majority and those members of a society who do not think and behave like everyone else break these norms and so are often defined as abnormal. The definition is based on the facts that:

1 Abnormal behaviour is seen as vivid and unpredictable, causes observer discomfort and violates moral or ideal standards (Rosenhan and Seligman, 1989) because it differs from most other people's behaviour and standards.
2 Abnormal thinking is delusional, irrational or incomprehensible because it differs from commonly accepted or usual beliefs and ways of thinking.

The deviation from social norm definition of abnormal behaviour is thus a **socially based definition** and is explained by social constructionism and social identity theories. Researchers such as Szasz (1960) have argued that 'abnormality', especially relating to certain mental disorders, is a socially constructed concept that allows people who show different, unusual or disturbing (to the rest of society) behaviour to be labelled and thus treated differently from others – often confined, controlled and persecuted. Social identity theory would argue that people who do not share similar behaviour and beliefs are not included in the 'in-group' (in this case the majority in a society) and are therefore categorised as 'other' (abnormal) and discriminated against.

Evaluation

Since deviation from social norms is a socially based definition, it implies that different societies with different norms will define different behaviours as abnormal and may even disagree over whether the same behaviour is abnormal. This means that an objective definition of abnormal behaviour that is fixed and stable across cultures and time is difficult if not impossible to achieve, and this may lead to unfair and discriminatory treatment of minorities by majorities. Indeed concepts of abnormal behaviour have been shown to differ cross-culturally (a belief in voodoo in one culture may be thought to be paranoia in another) and in the same culture over time (unmarried mothers in Britain and political dissidents in the Soviet Union have been confined to institutions for their 'abnormal' behaviour).

FAILURE TO FUNCTION ADEQUATELY

Maladaptive behaviour, which causes a failure to function adequately in the social and physical environment, seems a more objective way of defining abnormality. Everyone experiences difficulties coping with the world sometimes but if an individual's abnormal behaviour, mood or thinking adversely affects their well being (e.g. ability to maintain employment, a bearable quality of life, normal social relations etc.) then the definition will draw attention to the fact that help is needed. On a more extreme level, if an individual's abnormal behaviour becomes a danger to their own safety (e.g. neglecting self care, self mutilation, suicidal etc.) or the safety of others (e.g. dangerous behaviour) then they may be defined as abnormal and institutionalised ('sectioned' under the Mental Health Act, 1983, for example).

Evaluation

Failure to function adequately may not be recognised (e.g. by those who are in a psychotic state) or cared about (e.g. those with anti-social personality disorder), so the definition may have to be applied by others in society. However difficulties in functioning adequately may be the result of social rejection and 'adequate' functioning is, to some extent, a social judgement which may be based more on threats perceived by the majority in society than actual threats or a genuine concern to help.

DEVIATION FROM IDEAL MENTAL HEALTH

The idea that a single characteristic can be used as the basis of a general definition of abnormality has been rejected by some in favour of a set of criterion characteristics of abnormality or normality. Jahoda (1958) has described several characteristics that mentally healthy people should possess, such as the ability to introspect, integration and balance of personality, self-actualisation, autonomy, ability to cope with stress and see the world as it really is, and environmental mastery.

Evaluation

Unfortunately this criterion approach has also had its problems as a definition, since just how many of these characteristics do you have to lack or possess, and to what degree, to be regarded as normal or abnormal? Jahoda's characteristics of mental health have been regarded as too idealistic, in fact it is 'normal' to fall short of such perfect standards, and humanistic psychologists such as Maslow would argue that very few people actually reach self-actualisation. Not everyone agrees with the ideal characteristics or that all are necessary for mental health, for example other cultures may disagree with the ideals of autonomy and independence, and view other characteristics as more important.

15.2 The biological/medical model of abnormality

MEDICAL MODEL ASSUMPTIONS

Also known as the somatic, biological, or physiological approach.

NOTION OF NORMALITY

- Properly functioning physiology and nervous system and no genetic pre-dispositions to inherit mental disorder.

NOTION OF ABNORMALITY

- Like physical illness, **mental illness** has an **underlying physical/bodily cause.**

- **Genetic, organic, or chemical disorders** cause mental illness, which gives rise to behavioural and psychological **symptoms.**

- These symptoms can be classified to **diagnose** the **psychopathology,** which can then be treated through **therapy** in psychiatric **hospitals** to **cure** the **patient.**

- Note the use of medical terminology which this approach has borrowed.

ETHICAL IMPLICATIONS

There are both positive and negative ethical implications of the medical model definition of abnormality:

1 Positively for the abnormal individual, the idea that they are mentally 'ill' means that the individual is **not** to be held **responsible** for their predicament – they are more likely to be seen as a **victim** of a disorder that is **beyond their control** and, therefore, they are **in need of care** and **treatment.** The medical model is, therefore, intended to be a more caring and humane approach to abnormality – especially given the blame, stigmatisation, and lack of care for abnormality that had been the norm before the approach.

2 Negatively, the medical model's assumptions have produced many unfavourable ethical consequences.

a The assumption that abnormal people are mentally ill and, therefore, **not responsible** for their actions can lead to:
- the **loss of rights**, such as the right to **consent** to treatment or institutionalisation, and even the right to vote if sectioned under the Mental Health Act.
- the **loss of an internal locus of control**, loss of self-care, and an abdication of responsibility to others.
- the assumption that **directive therapy** is needed for the benefit of the mentally ill individual. The concept of directive therapy may be less debatable with acute schizophrenia, where insight may be totally lacking, but becomes more controversial when we consider the rights of depressed patients to withdraw from electro-convulsive therapy which may prevent their suicide.

b The assumption that there is always a **biological underlying cause** for mental disorder may be incorrect and, therefore, lead to the **wrong** diagnosis and/or treatment being given.
- There is not always a clearly identifiable underlying biological cause for disorders.
- Many disorders have a large psychological contribution to their cause, such as the learning theory explanations of phobia acquisition.
- Heather (1976) suggests that the basis of defining abnormality is often governed by social and moral considerations rather than biological – thus the inclusion of psychosexual disorders such as paedophilia.

c The assumption that mentally ill people are **distinctly different** from mentally well people can lead to **labelling** and **prejudice** against those defined as abnormal under the medical model.

PRACTICAL IMPLICATIONS

The use of the medical model to define abnormality as mental illness can lead to:

1 **The use of sectioning** under the Mental Health Act (1983) – the compulsory detention and even treatment of those regarded as mentally ill, if they represent a danger to their own or others' safety. This is based on the medical model assumption that mental illness leads to a loss of self-control and responsibility; but note that a social worker is required to section somebody, in addition to a GP and a psychiatrist (implying that social as well as physical factors need to be taken into account).

Section 2 of the Act can be used to detain people for up to 28 days for observation and assessment of mental illness.

Section 3 of the Act involves the enforced application of treatment and loss of rights.

Power is firmly in the hands of society, since

a Section 5 of the act can prevent the right of even the nearest relative to withdraw the sectioned individual from care.

b Section 136 gives the police the right to arrest in a public place anybody deemed to show mental illness to maintain security.

c Section 139 removes all responsibility for mistaken diagnosis from those involved in sectioning, providing the diagnosis was made in good faith and the legal procedures were carried out correctly.

2 **Institutionalisation** – which can have both positive and negative implications:
- **Positively,** institutionalisation allows the removal to a controlled environment of individuals who may represent a danger to themselves or others. The controlled environment allows the close monitoring, support, and treatment of those suffering from mental illness.
- **Negatively,** institutionalisation may worsen the condition of the patient, providing them with an abnormal environment and causing the internalisation of the passive and dependent role of 'mental inmate'. Rosenhan's study 'On Being Sane in Insane Places' revealed the often negative treatment received in mental institutions.

3 **Biological treatments** – which include the administering of drug treatment, electro-convulsive therapy, or even psychosurgery, all of which have their dangers and side effects as well as the possibility of beneficial effects.

15.3 Psychological models of abnormality

THE PSYCHOANALYTIC APPROACH

Notion of normality

Balance between id, ego, and superego. Sufficient ego control to allow the acceptable gratification of id impulses. No inconvenient fixations or repression of traumatic events.

Notion of abnormality

Emotional disturbance or neurosis is caused by thwarted id impulses, unresolved unconscious conflicts (e.g. Oedipus complex), or repressed traumatic events deriving from childhood. Psychological and physical symptoms are expressions of unconscious psychological causes. Conflict and neurosis is always present to some extent – the difference between the 'normal' and 'abnormal' is only quantitative.

ETHICAL IMPLICATIONS

- **Directive therapy** – due to the unconscious cause of psychological problems and the resistance patients put up to unconscious truths, the patient must trust the therapist's interpretation and instructions. However, psychoanalysis does occur under voluntary conditions.
- **Anxiety provoking** – psychoanalysis can reveal disturbing repressed experiences.
- **Humane** – psychoanalysts do not blame or judge the patient, who is not responsible for their problems.

PRACTICAL IMPLICATIONS

- **Expensive** – Freud argued you do not value what you do not pay for.
- **Long term** – several sessions a week for many months are usually required, although Mallan's Brief Focal Therapy is faster.
- **No institutionalisation** required.
- **Low success rates** – with many disorders, e.g. psychoses.

THE BEHAVIOURAL APPROACH

(Also known as the behaviourist or learning theory approach)

Notion of normality

A learning history that has provided an adequately large selection of adaptive responses.

Notion of abnormality

Maladaptive responses have been learnt or adaptive ones have not been learnt. Observable, behavioural disorder is all abnormality consists of. Abnormal behaviour is not a symptom of any underlying cause.

ETHICAL IMPLICATIONS

- **Directive therapy** – due to the environmental determinism of behavioural problems, patients need to be re-programmed with adaptive behaviour.
- **Stressful** – behaviour therapy can be painful and disturbing, e.g. flooding and aversion therapy.
- **Humane** – specific maladaptive behaviours are targeted, the whole person is not labelled.

PRACTICAL IMPLICATIONS

- **Relatively cheap** – due to the fairly quick nature of treatments.
- **High success rates** – with certain disorders.
- **Institutionalisation** – may be required to ensure environmental control with certain treatments, e.g. selective reinforcement for anorexia.

THE COGNITIVE APPROACH

Notion of normality

Properly functioning and rational cognitive thought processes that can be used to accurately perceive the world and control behaviour.

Notion of abnormality

Unrealistic, distorted, or irrational understanding and thoughts about the self, others, or the environment. Difficulty in controlling thought processes or using them to control actions.

ETHICAL IMPLICATIONS

- **Semi-directive therapy** – due to the client's problems controlling their thoughts, external aid has to be provided by the therapist, although this will vary in its directiveness depending on how forceful the persuasive techniques used by the therapist are.
- **Stressful** – rational emotive therapy can be disturbing although most cognitive therapy is humane.

PRACTICAL IMPLICATIONS

- **Relatively cheap** – depending on length of therapy.
- **Fairly high success rates** – with certain disorders and when combined with behavioural therapies.
- **No institutionalisation** is usually necessary.

THE HUMANISTIC APPROACH

(Also known as the phenomenological or existential approach)

Notion of normality

Positive self regard, ability to self actualise, healthy interpersonal relationships, and responsibility and control over life.

Notion of abnormality

It is wrong to talk of abnormality, since everyone is unique and experiences 'problems with living' occasionally. These problems stem from interpersonal relationships (which prevent individuals being true to themselves) and thwarting environmental circumstances (which prevent self actualisation). The client should not be labelled or directed.

ETHICAL IMPLICATIONS

- **Non-directive therapy** – clients have free will and, therefore, the responsibility and capability to change their thoughts and behaviour (with insightful help).
- **Humane** – the happiness of the client is of most importance. The client is given unconditional positive regard.
- **Non-labelling** – humanist therapists believe labelling is counter-productive and irrelevant, since each person is a unique individual.

PRACTICAL IMPLICATIONS

- **Fairly expensive** – based on length of therapy required.
- **No institutionalisation** – is necessary, since treatment is completely voluntary.
- **Low success rates** – with many disorders, e.g. psychoses. Better success with 'problems with living' in interpersonal areas.

15.4 Diagnostic classification systems

THE PURPOSE OF CLASSIFICATION

The classification of mental disorder involves the **identification of groups** or patterns of behavioural or mental **symptoms** that reliably occur together to form a **type** of disorder. This process of classification allows:

- psychiatrists, doctors and psychologists to **identify** and talk more easily about **groups** of similar sufferers

- a **prognosis** (prediction about the future course of the disorder) to be made

- researchers to **investigate** these groups of people to determine what the **causes** (aetiology) of the disorder are

- a suitable **treatment** to be developed and administered to all those showing similar symptoms

Thus, classification fulfils important communicative and investigative functions, ultimately serving to benefit the individual who has been identified.

CLASSIFICATION SYSTEMS

Emil Kraepelin developed the first comprehensive classification system for mental disorders, believing that they could be diagnosed from observable symptoms, just like physical illness.

Two major western classifications systems exist today - the American Psychiatric Association's 'Diagnostic and Statistical Manual of Mental Disorder' (DSM IV), and the World Health Organisation's 'International Classification of Diseases' (ICD 10).

These systems have undergone many revisions, e.g. from the first, very unreliable DSM in 1952, to the DSM II in 1968, DSM III in 1980, the revision of this (DSM III-R) in 1987, the DSM IV in 1994, and currently the DSM IV-TR (text revision) in 2000.

Compared to the DSM, the ICD lists the same disorders but some are given different names and are classified under different headings. The ICD has no separate axes and is more likely to indicate causes rather than purely symptoms

TECHNIQUES OF ASSESSMENT

Behavioural observation, e.g. behaviour coding systems and rating scales.
- **Advantages** – provides direct and detailed information.
- **Weaknesses** – problems with inter-observer reliability and subject reactivity. Some symptoms cannot be observed.

Clinical interview, e.g. open-ended questions or the more standardised and reliable structured interview (such as 'The Schedule for Affective Disorders and Schizophrenia').
- **Advantages** – a detailed, flexible, and sensitive method.
- **Weaknesses** – lacks objectivity. Self report responses are interpreted by the therapist, and subjects may be unable or unwilling (due to embarrassment) to give accurate data.

Psychological tests, e.g. IQ tests or personality inventories (such as The Minnesota Multiphasic Personality Inventory).
- **Advantages** – objectively rated, quick, and standardised.
- **Weaknesses** – personality tests rely on self report and literacy.

Physiological tests, e.g. static brain scans (magnetic resonance imaging) or dynamic scans (positron emission tomography).
- **Advantages** – gives precise data on brain structure or activity
- **Weaknesses** – expensive and cannot be used to diagnose disorders alone.

THE DSM IV CLASSIFICATION SYSTEM

The 'Diagnostic and Statistical Manual of Mental Disorder' defines a mental disorder as a clinically significant syndrome associated with distress, a loss of functioning, an increased risk of death/pain, or an important loss of freedom.

The manual emphasises that the problem should stem from within the individual, but does not specify whether it is biological, behavioural, or psychological in nature.

The manual describes over 200 specific diagnostic categories for mental disorder and lists the **specific diagnostic criteria** that have to be met for a diagnosis to be given.

Assessment is usually made on five axes to provide a more complete picture of the individual.

AXIS 1 CLINICAL SYNDROMES

Axis 1 refers to the major diagnostic classification arrived at by the clinician, e.g. 'catatonic schizophrenia', 'major depressive disorder', 'generalised anxiety disorder', etc.

AXIS 2 DEVELOPMENTAL AND PERSONALITY DISORDERS

Additional diagnostic classifications that may contribute to an understanding of the Axis 1 syndrome.

AXIS 3 MEDICAL CONDITIONS

Physical problems relevant to the mental disorder.

AXIS 4 PSYCHOSOCIAL STRESSORS

All potentially stressful events (e.g. loss of job) or enduring circumstances (e.g. poverty) that might be relevant to the disorder are rated for severity on a scale ranging from 1 (none) to 6 (catastrophic) for the past year.

AXIS 5 GLOBAL ASSESSMENT OF FUNCTIONING

Rates the highest level of social, occupational, and psychological functioning on a scale of 1 (persistent danger) to 90 (good in all areas) currently and during the past year.

15.5 The practical and ethical implications of diagnostic classification 1

PRACTICAL IMPLICATIONS – CAN CLASSIFICATION BE EFFECTIVELY MADE?

RELIABILITY

For classification systems to be reliable, different diagnosticians using the same system should arrive at the same diagnosis for the same individual. The reliability of the early systems, e.g. the DSM II was very poor:

Beck et al. (1962)
Found that agreement on diagnosis for 153 patients (where each patient was assessed by two psychiatrists from a group of four), was only 54%. This was often due to vague criteria for diagnosis and inconsistencies in the techniques used to gather data.

Cooper et al. (1972)
Found New York psychiatrists were twice as likely to diagnose schizophrenia than London psychiatrists, who were twice as likely to diagnose mania or depression, when shown the same video-taped clinical interviews

Rosenhan (1973)
Found that 8 'normal' people could get themselves admitted to mental hospitals as schizophrenics merely by claiming to hear voices saying single words like 'hollow' and 'thud'. Rosenhan also found that the staff of a teaching hospital, when told to expect pseudo-patients, suspected 41 out of 193 genuine patients of being fakers.

Classification systems have improved in reliability due to a multi-axial approach, more standardised assessment techniques (e.g. the Schedule of Affective Disorders and Schizophrenia), and more specific diagnostic criteria, but are still far from perfect.

Di Nardo et al (1993)
Studied the reliability of the DSM III-R for anxiety disorders. Two clinicians separately diagnosed each of 267 people seeking treatment for anxiety and stress disorders, and used the Kappa statistic to test how similar diagnosis was (the nearer 1 the value is, the closer the agreement). They found high reliability for obsessive-compulsive disorder but lower reliability for generalised anxiety disorder, due to problems with interpreting how 'excessive' a person's worries had to be (see table on the right). The DSM IV corrected this fault.

Diagnostic category	Kappa
Obsessive-compulsive disorder	.80
Generalised anxiety disorder	.57
Panic disorder with agoraphobia	.72
Social phobia	.79
Major depression	.65

VALIDITY

For a classification system to be valid it should meaningfully classify a real pattern of symptoms, which result from a real underlying cause, which can, therefore, lead to a suitable treatment and prognosis (predictive validity). Very few underlying causes are known, however, and there are a wide range of treatments for the same disorder. Some classifications such as 'undifferentiated schizophrenia' (for those whose symptoms do not fit into any of the other sub-types of schizophrenia), are rather meaningless as diagnostic categories. Valid diagnosis for mental disorder is more difficult than physical disorder, due to the lack of objective physical signs of disorder like temperature, blood pressure, etc.

BIAS

Since diagnostic classification is not 100% objective and reliable, bias may result from the expectations or prejudices of the diagnostician. Diagnosticians are likely to expect that people seeking psychiatric help are disturbed and are more likely to make what social psychologists call the fundamental attribution error – over-emphasising personality rather than situational/environmental causes of behaviour.

Temerline (1970)
Found that clinically trained psychiatrists and clinical psychologists could be influenced in their diagnosis by hearing the opinion of a respected authority. After watching a video-taped interview of (a completely psychologically 'healthy') individual, some subjects heard the respected authority state that, although the person seemed neurotic, he was actually quite psychotic. These diagnosticians were highly influenced by the statement in their own diagnosis of the individual.

ETHICAL IMPLICATIONS – SHOULD DIAGNOSIS BE MADE CONSIDERING THE DIFFICULTIES OF CLASSIFICATION?

Szasz questions both the validity and purpose of classification, arguing that in many cases diagnosis is made on a political and social basis, rather than a psychological or biological one, and suggests that the majority in power in a society attach stigmatising labels to those who show different or frightening behaviour and so justify their control and treatment.

Szasz in his book *The Manufacture of Madness* goes so far as to say that mental illness is actually created by society, and adds that where the biological causes of mental disorders are known, they should be defined as 'diseases of the mind', but if there is not a supportable underlying cause of disorder, then the term 'problem with living' should be used. Scheff (1966) proposes a similar criticism of the basis of classification, suggesting that labelling people as abnormal helps society overcome its anxiety and establish clear norms of reality and appropriate behaviour. The major ethical implication here is that the classification systems serve the purposes of the majority in society only, and that it is wrong to assume they are helpful.

Some would argue that society has merely tried to 'medicalise' disruptive behaviour – to find a cause 'within' the person for bad behaviour, rather than looking to the environment for causes. Thus, classifications such as anti-social personality disorder, or kleptomania, are really only medical terms for evil or bad people. Originally the medical model of mental illness was just a useful metaphor, but the underlying assumption has developed that there are underlying biological causes for mental disorder.

A counter argument to Szasz's proposal that we are merely labelling eccentric people, is the fact that medical and behavioural treatments have helped people to overcome their disorders, and that many people (such as those suffering from anxiety and depression) volunteer for treatment.

Classification aims to help those with mental disorders, and, therefore, fulfils a potentially very useful function – medical diagnosis had, and still has, problems with classification, yet we would not think of rejecting it today. The classification systems have led to the development of many effective therapies and treatments that have helped to either cure, alleviate, or control a wide variety of disorders. Perhaps diagnosis should be made more idiographic, and focus on particular problems rather than grouping people together in a category that may not be helpful, especially where biological causes are not known. However many categories have demonstrated themselves to be useful.

Diagnostic classification has improved as the classification systems have developed. Rosenhan's pseudo-patients would probably not succeed in gaining admission to mental hospitals today (or would have to lie a lot more!).

15.6 The practical and ethical implications of diagnostic classification 2

PRACTICAL IMPLICATIONS – WHAT ARE THE CONSEQUENCES OF CLASSIFICATION?

TREATMENT

Since there are problems with the validity of diagnostic classification, unsuitable treatment may be administered, sometimes on an involuntary basis. There are many practical and ethical problems involved in choosing and applying different treatments and therapies.

INSTITUTIONALISATION

Institutionalisation can lead to loss of responsibility. Rosenhan's study found that institutionalisation can lead to depersonalisation, dependency, and a loss of self care skills, thereby worsening the disorder. Goffman (in *Asylums*) speaks of the 'career' of the mental inmate, where the identity of the patient is gradually lost to the institution.
Patients may actually be taught abnormal behaviour from those around them in the institution, and conditions do not help normal functioning since they are not treated as normal people would be.

CARE IN THE COMMUNITY

Rosenhan talked of the 'stickiness' of diagnostic labels – when an individual returns to society, their record of mental illness goes with them (the pseudo-patients left with a diagnosis of 'schizophrenia in remission'). This can lead to stigmatisation, stereotyping, and discrimination against those who have been mentally disordered, making reintegration back into the community difficult.

LABELLING

Scheff (1966) points out that diagnostic classification "labels' the individual, and this can have many adverse effects, such as:

- **Self-fulfilling prophecy** – Patients may begin to act as they think they are expected to act – Goffman argues that they may internalise the role of 'mentally ill patient' and this could worsen their disorder rather than improve it. Doherty (1975) points out that those who reject the mental illness label tend to improve more quickly than those who accept it, although this is not always the case, since accepting the label of 'alcoholic' can help alcoholics recover.

- **Distortion of behaviour** – Diagnosis of mental disorder tends to label the whole person – once the label of diagnosis is attached, then all the individual's actions become interpreted in the light of the label. Sometimes even normal behaviour is ignored or interpreted as a sign of the individual's mental disorder – in Rosenhan's study, the pseudo-patients' behaviours were regarded as symptoms of their psychopathology.

- **Oversimplification** – Labelling can lead to reification – making the classification a real, physical disorder, rather than just a descriptive term to help diagnosticians talk about patients or a hypothesis about what is troubling the person. Labelling may have a major effect not just on an individual's identity, but also on their self-esteem.

LEGAL IMPLICATIONS

Sectioning under the Mental Health Act (although rare) can lead to loss of rights and enforced treatment. Legally, the insane can be found not guilty due to a lack of responsibility for their actions.

ETHICAL IMPLICATIONS – SHOULD DIAGNOSIS BE MADE CONSIDERING THE CONSEQUENCES OF CLASSIFICATION?

An ethical decision has to be made regarding the justification of classification, given the profound implications of being classified as mentally disordered.

- Do the benefits of classification (care, treatment, safety) outweigh the costs (possible misdiagnosis, mistreatment, loss of rights/self responsibility, and prejudice due to labelling)?

Gove (1970, 1990) has found that the stigmatising effects of labelling are only short-lived, while Major and Crocker (1993) have found that the effect of labelling on a person's self-esteem is difficult to predict.
Prejudice from society clearly does occur, however, and is even shown by mental health professionals. Langer and Abelson (1974) showed a videotape of a younger man telling an older man about his job experience. If the viewers were told that the man was a job applicant, he was judged to be attractive and conventional looking, whereas if they were told that he was a 'patient', he was described as tight, defensive, dependent, and frightened of his own aggressive impulses.

- Is society right to administer treatment when misclassification is quite likely and the underlying causes are not known?

Some researchers have argued that, overall, there are too many criticisms of the basic assumptions of classification to justify its use and consequences.
The assumption that mental disorder can be classified into types is ethically questionable. Classification ignores the fundamental uniqueness of human minds and goes against the right of every person to be treated as an individual.
An idiographic, rather than a nomothetic, approach to mental disorder may be more appropriate, considering the huge individual variations in patients' symptom expression and individual circumstances. If nomothetic comparisons have to be made, then perhaps it is best to regard mental health and disorder as on a continuum, so that there is only a quantitative rather than qualitative difference between them. Classification only works if there are enough differences **and** similarities between patients.

- Should individuals lose their rights of consent and self-responsibility?

Humanists would argue that the classification systems are overinfluenced by the medical model's assumptions about lack of control and freewill. In some cases these assumptions have been used as a method of political control.

- Why does society have double standards about responsibility and mental disorder?

Legally, the insane can be found not guilty due to a lack of responsibility for their actions. However, 'insanity' is a decision made by the legal system and, due to society's need to blame people to make them account for their crimes, this verdict may not be given. Many criminals have been clearly mentally disordered, but have been found guilty of their crimes and sent to prison.

15.7 'On being sane in insane places' Rosenhan (1973)

AIM

To illustrate experimentally the problems involved in determining normality and abnormality, in particular:
- the poor reliability of the diagnostic classification system for mental disorder at the time (as well as general doubts over its validity)
- the negative consequences of being diagnosed as abnormal and the effects of institutionalisation

METHOD

Subjects: Eight sane people (3 women and 5 men from a small variety of occupational backgrounds), using only fake names and occupations, sought admission to a range of twelve hospitals (varying in age, resources, staff-patient ratios, degree of research conducted, etc.).

Procedure: Each pseudo-patient arranged an appointment at the hospital and complained that he or she had been hearing voices. The voices were unclear, unfamiliar, of the same sex and said single words like 'empty', 'hollow', and 'thud'. Apart from the aforementioned falsifying of name and occupation and this single symptom, the pseudo-patients did not change any aspect of their behaviour, personal history or circumstances. On admission to the hospital ward, every pseudo-patient immediately stopped simulating any symptoms and responded normally to all instructions (except they did not swallow medication) and said they were fine and experiencing no more symptoms. Their tasks were then to
- seek release by convincing the staff that they were sane (all but one pseudo-patient were very motivated to do this)
- observe and record the experience of the institutionalised mentally disordered patient (done covertly at first, although this was unnecessary)

RESULTS

Admission: Pseudo-patients were admitted to every hospital, in all cases except one with a diagnosis of schizophrenia, and their sanity was never detected by staff – only by other patients (35 out of 118 of whom voiced their suspicions in the first three hospitalisations). To check the poor reliability of diagnosis, and to see if the insane could be distinguished from the sane, a later study was conducted where a teaching hospital (who had been informed of Rosenhan's study) was told to expect pseudo-patients over a three month period. During that time 193 patients were rated for how likely they were to be pseudo-patients – 41 patients were suspected of being fakes, 19 of which were suspected by both a psychiatrist and one other staff member, even though no pseudo-patients were sent during that time.

Release: Length of stay ranged from 7 to 52 days, with an average of 19 days. All except one were released with a diagnosis of 'schizophrenia in remission', supporting the view that they had never been detected as sane.

Observation results:
- **Lack of monitoring** – very little contact with doctors was experienced, and a strong sense of segregation between staff and patients was noted.
- **Distortion of behaviour** – all (normal) behaviour became interpreted in the light of the 'label' of 'schizophrenia', for example:
  a A normal case history – became distorted to emphasise the ambivalence and emotional instability thought to be shown by schizophrenics.
  b Note taking – pseudo-patients were never asked why they were taking notes, but it was recorded by nurses as 'patient engages in writing behaviour', implying that it was a symptom of their disorder.
  c Pacing the corridors out of boredom – was seen as nervousness, again implying that it was a symptom of their disorder.
  d Waiting outside the cafeteria before lunch time – was interpreted as showing the 'oral-acquisitive nature of the syndrome' by a psychiatrist.

- **Lack of normal interaction** – for example, pseudo-patients courteously asked a staff member 'Pardon me, Mr (or Dr or Mrs) X, could you tell me when I will be presented at the staff meeting?' or 'When am I likely to be discharged?'. They found mostly a brief, not always relevant, answer was given, on the move, without even a normal turn of the head or eye-contact (psychiatrists moved on with their head averted 71% of the time and only stopped and talked normally on 4% of occasions).
- **Powerlessness and depersonalisation** – was produced in the institution through the lack of rights, constructive activity, choice, and privacy, plus frequent verbal and even physical abuse from the attendants.

EVALUATION

Methodological:
Lack of control groups – Only the experimental condition was conducted.
Data analysis – Was mostly qualitative rather than quantitative.
Ethical problems – The study involved deception, but it might be argued that the hospitals had the power not to be deceived and were in fact being tested in their jobs. In addition, the study's ends (its valuable contribution) outweighed its slightly unethical means, and kept data confidentiality.

Theoretical: Despite the fact that 'schizophrenia in remission' is an unusual diagnosis according to Spitzer (1976), the study is widely held to have fulfilled its aim of showing the deficiencies of the classification system for mental disorder at the time (the DSM II) and the negative consequences of being labelled and institutionalised for mental disorder. Studies like these led to pressure to revise and improve the accuracy of the classification systems.

Links: Problems with the diagnosis and classification of mental disorders. Stereotyping.

15.8 Multiple personality disorder

WHAT IS MULTIPLE PERSONALITY DISORDER?

Multiple Personality Disorder (MPD) or Dissociative Personality Disorder (DPD) refers to a mental disorder involving:

- **Dissociation of the self** – the self becomes divided into two or more distinct personalities, each with their separate thoughts, characteristics and memories.
- **Alternation of control by the personalities** – bodily control and access to consciousness switches between the personalities, although some may be more dominant than others and thus spend more time in control.
- **Amnesia and unconscious barriers between personalities** – there may be a mutual or one-way lack of conscious awareness and memory access between personalities. Some may experience 'blackouts' or lost time when others take control, some can be directly aware of other personalities' existence, thoughts and memories.

A case of MPD

A famous example is Sybil (Schreiber, 1973) who had 16 alternative personalities of varying genders (those named 'Mike' and 'Sid' were male) and ages ('Ruthie' was only 2 years old), possibly as a result of being beaten and tortured by her (probably) schizophrenic mother. Each personality had a name and was reported by her psychiatrist to have different vocabulary, handwriting, speech patterns, body images, attitudes to sex, jealousies (including those relating to each other's knowledge and memories), interests, religious attitudes, taste in books, painting ability and vocational ambitions. Sybil (the primary personality) was initially unaware of the existence of these other personalities until her psychiatrist diagnosed her condition. In common with other cases of MPD it was suggested that each personality emerged for a particular reason and fulfilled a particular psychological function (e.g. expressive or defensive) by representing certain people, emotional events or abilities. Hypnosis was used to try and integrate the personalities, apparently with some success.

IS MULTIPLE PERSONALITY DISORDER A SPONTANEOUS OR IATROGENIC PHENOMENON?

HAVE THERAPISTS JUST CLASSIFIED A MENTAL DISORDER OR CREATED ONE?

MPD AS A SPONTANEOUS PHENOMENON

MPD could represent a spontaneous, pre-existing mental disorder that therapists discovered and classified, and then were able to diagnose and treat. Many theories have been proposed to try and explain the origin of MPD, including psychodynamic, cognitive and behavioural learning ones. For example it has been suggested that MPD can spontaneously result from:

- Defensive amnesia or repression of traumatic childhood events.
- Self-hypnotic role playing escapism as a coping mechanism.
- Powerful state-dependent memory effects.
- Selective reinforcement for different behaviours in different social contexts.

Evaluation

- Evidence for MPD comes from numerous hours of interviews, observation and personality tests from many case studies.
- Evidence is occasionally provided from physiological methods, e.g. electroencephalograms, galvanic skin responses, and brain scans.
- The disorder is often developed in childhood and is associated with traumatic or disturbed family relationships (the causes far precede therapy).
- MPD is more common in women than men, which may reflect the higher level of childhood abuse suffered by girls than boys.
- Increased rates of MPD may reflect increased public awareness of the disorder, which could have enabled or encouraged therapists and sufferers to more readily recognise the symptoms and seek or provide treatment for it.
- Just because cases of MPD have been simulated and may have been faked to avoid responsibility for crimes, does not mean there are no genuine cases.

MPD AS AN IATROGENIC PHENOMENON

Alternatively, MPD may not be a spontaneous disorder but one created by therapists themselves through:

- **Treatment techniques that suggest the disorder** – the mistaken theoretical *expectation* that MPD can explain memory lapses or erratic behaviour may lead therapists to suggest its presence in the patient. Leading and suggestive interviews, selective attention and social reinforcement, and hypnotic suggestion and prompting may actually have created, maintained and legitimised MPD.
- **The construction of a mistaken diagnostic label** – this may have unconsciously led other people who heard about the disorder to think they have the problem, explain their memory lapses or troubled and poorly understood behaviour in terms of it, and thus seek treatment for it. Others may use the disorder to escape responsibility for their actions and consciously fake it.

Evaluation

- Self-report and non-experimental methods may have made it easier for therapists to have been duped or misled about the existence of MPD in the first place or to transmit their expectations to the patient.
- Physiological differences could just reflect the different demands of role-playing different personalities and, of course, the therapist could still have created the personalities.
- False memories of early abuse could be invented by fakers of MPD (although some cases have been independently verified) or created by therapeutic suggestion and hypnosis (false memory syndrome).
- If MPD is due to spontaneous repression of abuse, escapism, state-dependent memory and selective reinforcement, it might be expected to occur more frequently than it does.
- Cases of MPD have dramatically increased with media coverage and public awareness of it in recent times, and mostly in the USA rather than other countries (suggesting a culturally created disorder). The vast majority of MPD cases are reported by just a minority of therapists (are they specialised at diagnosing or creating MPD?).
- Simulators can convincingly fake MPD (any differences could just be due to lack of practice) and if fakers recall memories they should not be able to, they can easily switch identities or create a new one.

15.9 'A case of multiple personality' Thigpen and Cleckley (1954)

AIM

To describe the case study of a 25-year-old married woman referred to two psychiatrists for severe headaches and blackouts, but soon discovered to have a multiple personality. The article presents evidence for the existence of this previously rare condition in the subject, in a cautious but convinced manner.

SUMMARY OF THE CASE

The first few interviews with the woman, Eve White, only found her to have 'several important emotional difficulties' and a 'set of marital conflicts and personal frustrations'. The first indication of multiple personality was when the psychiatrists received a letter from Eve that she did not remember sending and which contained a note at the end written in a different and childish handwriting. On her next visit, after a period of unusual agitation, she reported that she occasionally had the impression that she heard a voice in her head – and then suddenly and spontaneously showed a dramatic change in her behaviour, revealing the character (and answering to the name) of Eve Black. Over a period of 14 months and around 100 hours of interview time, the two psychiatrists investigated the two Eves, first using hypnosis, but later without the need for it. Eve White was found not to have access to the awareness and memories of Eve Black (experiencing blackouts when Eve Black took over control) although the reverse was true for Eve Black (who often used the ability to disrupt Eve White's life by taking over and getting her into trouble or by giving her headaches).

Later during the course of therapy, a third personality emerged called Jane – again suddenly and with a different set of characteristics. Jane had access to the consciousness of both Eves, but incomplete access to their memories before her emergence, and could only emerge through Eve White.

The authors admit the possibility of fakery, although they think it highly unlikely, and argue for more research to answer some fundamental questions concerning the multiple personality phenomena.

EVIDENCE FOR THE EXISTENCE OF MULTIPLE PERSONALITY

Personality distinctions gained through interview:

- Character – Eve White – self-controlled, serious, matter of fact, and meticulously truthful.
  Eve Black – childish, carefree, shallow, mischievous, and a fluent liar.
- Attitudes – Eve White – distressed about failing marriage, warm love for daughter.
  Eve Black – thought Eve White's distress and love was silly, seemed 'immune to major affective events in human relationships'.
- Behaviour – Eve White – responsible and reserved.
  Eve Black – irresponsible, pleasure and excitement seeking, sought the company of strangers to avoid discovery.
- Mannerisms – 'A thousand minute alterations in manner, gesture, expression, posture, of nuances in reflex... of glance' between the two Eves.

Personality distinctions gained through independent psychological testing:

- Psychometric tests – IQ of Eve White was 110, IQ of Eve Black was 104, differences between the two were found in memory function.
- Projective testing – Rorschach revealed
  a Eve Black to show regression and hysterical tendencies, but to be far healthier than Eve White.
  b Eve White to show repression, anxiety, obsessive-compulsive traits, and an inability to deal with her hostility.
  The psychologist was of the opinion that the tests revealed one personality at two stages of life – that Eve Black represented a regression to a carefree state, as a way of dealing with her dislike of marriage and maternal pressures.

Personality distinctions gained through physiological EEG testing:

Eve White and Jane were found to show similar Electroencephalograph readings, with Eve Black definitely distinguishable from the other two.

Evidence for multiple personality as a distinct and valid disorder:

- Clearly distinguishable from other disorders, such as schizophrenia, but with some similarities to disorders like dissociative fugue.
- Eve's behaviour showed such remarkable consistency within characters that two psychiatrists were persuaded she was not deliberately faking.
- Shows similarities of symptoms with other multiple personality cases such as patterns of amnesia between personalities and similar causal circumstances that provoke a denial of parts of the self.

EVALUATION

Methodological:

Case study method – Lack of objectivity when involved with the patient, especially when trying to help through therapy, rather than attempting rigorous experiments to test the possibility of fakery.

Unreliability of testing – Those tests that were conducted were of doubtful validity, because they could have been affected by deliberate attempts to fake (except perhaps the EEG test, although what the differences found represented is open to interpretation) and projective tests are also of doubtful reliability due to the subjective nature of their interpretation.

Theoretical: Doubts about the validity of this study are caused by Chris Sizeman (the real name of Eve) later revealing that she had other personalities before (and after) 1954, yet these were not detected or mentioned at the time. Doubts about the validity of multiple personality disorder in general are caused by the fact that they are often investigated through hypnosis and are becoming increasingly common in America but not other countries. There are ethical and legal implications involved in accepting multiple personality as a valid disorder, e.g. culpability.

Links: Abnormality (particularly problems in diagnosing), personality, freewill, case studies, hypnosis.

16.1 Schizophrenia – symptoms and diagnosis

BACKGROUND
Some studies indicate that there is approximately a 1% life time risk of developing schizophrenia. Kraepelin (1902) described the symptoms of 'dementia praecox' (senility of youth) as being delusions, attention deficits, and bizarre motor activity, due to a form of mental deterioration that began in youth. Bleuler (1911) observed that deterioration did not continue and often began after adolescence, and so introduced the term 'schizophrenia' (split mind) to describe how psychological functions had lost their unity.

DIAGNOSIS
The DSM IV diagnostic criteria are:
1 **Two** or more of the following symptoms present for a significant amount of time in a one month period:
   - **Hallucinations** (if there are extensive auditory hallucinations of voices, then no other symptoms have to be present)
   - **Delusions** (if these are very bizarre, then no other symptoms have to be present)
   - **Disorganised speech**, e.g. incoherent
   - **Catatonic or disorganised behaviour**, e.g. repetitive movements or gestures
   - **Negative symptoms**, e.g. emotional blunting

2 Disturbance must last for 6 months (including 1 month of the above symptoms).

3 The symptoms must have produced a marked deterioration in functioning at work, in social relations, and in self care (axis 5 of the DSM IV).

SYMPTOMS

EMOTIONAL
Emotions can be either:
- flat, unresponsive and insensitive, or
- inappropriate to the situation and changeable

BEHAVIOURAL
Somatic disturbance, e.g.:
- psychomotor agitation – fixed, repetitive gestures
- catatonic stupor – keeping the same position for long periods of time

PERCEPTUAL
- Auditory hallucinations, usually voices commenting upon behaviour and thoughts in the third person, are heard.
- Visual hallucinations, such as size, space, and colour distortions occur.

COGNITIVE
Disruption occurs to:
- **thought processes** – schizophrenics show **cognitive distractibility** (they are unable to maintain a consistent train of thought); **attentional deficits** (focusing on irrelevant stimuli); and **thought passivity** (where they think that others block, insert or withdraw the thoughts in their head).
- **thought content** – includes delusions, e.g. of persecution, control, or grandeur.

SUBTYPES OF SCHIZOPHRENIA
The DSM IV lists five sub-categories of schizophrenia, because of the huge variety of symptoms shown.

DISORGANISED SCHIZOPHRENIA
Symptoms mostly involve:
- **incoherent** thoughts and speech
- **bizarre** delusions and hallucinations
- **inappropriate** emotions and behaviour

UNDIFFERENTIATED SCHIZOPHRENIA
The classification for those whose symptoms are not classifiable under any of the other subtypes. This is the least useful of the diagnostic classifications.

CATATONIC SCHIZOPHRENIA
Involves alternating between:
- catatonic **stupor** and **negativism**, and
- catatonic **excitement** – prolonged, frenzied, even violent behaviour

PARANOID SCHIZOPHRENIA
Involves organised and complex delusions (often of persecution), mostly auditory hallucinations, and relatively few other symptoms.

RESIDUAL SCHIZOPHRENIA
Involves the gradual development of many minor problems, e.g. unusual behaviour, social withdrawal, emotional blunting, and apathy.

ALTERNATIVE TYPOLOGIES
- **Type 1 schizophrenia** – is characterised by positive symptoms, e.g. hallucinations and delusions
- **Type 2 schizophrenia** – is characterised by negative symptoms, e.g. emotional blunting and avolition

16.2 Explanatory theories of schizophrenia

BIOLOGICAL THEORIES

GENETIC CAUSES

Family studies – Children of two schizophrenic biological parents are around 46% likely to develop the disorder. These studies do not rule out environmental learning though.

Twin studies – Studies from many countries have produced different estimates, but Gottesman (1991) suggests that monozygotic identical twins (who have the same genes) have significantly higher concordance rates (48%) for schizophrenia than dizygotic non-identical twins (17%). Concordance rates refer to whether **both** twins develop the disorder.
However, identical twins also share more similar environments.

Adoption studies – When adopted subjects' environments are matched, the rates of schizophrenia are higher for adoptive children with schizophrenic biological parents compared to adoptive children with non-schizophrenic biological parents (Kety *et al.*, 1975). Ideally, identical twins with schizophrenia, raised apart in different adoptive environments, would be the best evidence for genetic causes, but obviously these cases are extremely rare.

Genetic factors do not account 100% for schizophrenia, however. People probably inherit a genetic predisposition for schizophrenia, which **may** be triggered by environmental factors.

BIOCHEMICAL CAUSES

A very popular theory of schizophrenia was the dopamine hypothesis – that over-activity of the neurotransmitter dopamine in the synapses of the brain caused type 1 positive symptoms of schizophrenia. Evidence for the hypothesis included the findings that:

- large doses of amphetamines (which increase dopamine activity) can create amphetamine psychosis, which closely resembles acute paranoid schizophrenia. Small doses can trigger symptoms in schizophrenics.
- anti-schizophrenic drugs like chlorpromazine work by blocking the post synaptic receptor sites of dopamine, thereby reducing its activity. If schizophrenics are given too much of these drugs, they develop symptoms similar to Parkinson's disease (caused by too little dopamine).
- post-mortems and Positron Emission Tomography scans have found higher amounts of dopamine and dopamine synaptic receptor sites.

However, the dopamine hypothesis is an over simplistic explanation, since new anti-schizophrenic drugs (e.g. clozapine) work by affecting other neurotransmitters, especially serotonin.

BRAIN STRUCTURAL CAUSES

Enlarged ventricles – research has found that these fluid filled cavities in the brain are larger in schizophrenics due to brain cell loss. Cell loss in the temporal lobes of the brain (responsible for cognitive and emotional functions) has been associated with negative symptoms. However, the evidence is correlational – enlarged ventricles may be a symptom not a cause, and non-schizophrenics can also show them.

Brain area activity – schizophrenics' brain scans do not show the usual prefrontal activation of the cortex when given problem solving tasks. Brain scanning can not yet predict the presence of schizophrenia.

PSYCHOLOGICAL/ ENVIRONMENTAL THEORIES

PSYCHOLOGICAL CAUSES

A variety of theories have sought to explain schizophrenia at the psychological level, including:

Psychoanalytic theory – Freud suggested that regression to a state of 'narcissism' in the early oral stage could be responsible, where there is no developed ego to test reality. Psychotic thought resembles the id's primary process thinking, and is untreatable through psychoanalysis because the narcissistic person has given up any attachment to the outside world (preventing transference, for example).

Existential theory – Psychiatrists, such as Laing, have proposed that people withdraw from reality as a normal response to the pressures of a mad world. Schizophrenia is a social and interpersonal experience which can be regarded as a potentially beneficial journey of self discovery.

Labelling theory – Scheff (1966) has argued that schizophrenia may be largely a social role that, once assigned by diagnosis, is conformed to and becomes a self-fulfilling prophecy. The internalisation of the schizophrenic role is strengthened by the reactions of other people and hospitalisation. Szasz has taken these ideas further to argue that schizophrenia is a myth created by society to control those who are different.

Cognitive theory – Frith (1979) proposes that disruption to an attentional filter mechanism could result in the thought disturbance of schizophrenia, as the sufferer is overloaded with sensory information. Studies on continuous performance and eye-tracking tasks indicate that schizophrenics do show more attentional problems than non-schizophrenics. Perhaps reduced short-term memory capacity could account for some schizophrenics' cognitive distractibility.

SOCIAL/ENVIRONMENTAL CAUSES

Social or environmental factors could act to trigger schizophrenia in those with a genetic predisposition.

Family stresses – Faulty interpersonal relationships in the families of schizophrenics have been found by Fromm Reichmann (who proposed the idea of the 'schizophrenogenic mother'); Bateson (who discovered ambivalent 'double bind' communication between schizophrenic children and their parents); and Lidz and Fleck (who described 'schism' and 'skew' in the families of schizophrenics).
However, the evidence is correlational – perhaps schizophrenics cause stress and disturbance in their families.

Environmental stresses – Some studies have found schizophrenia is 8 times more common in the lower socio-economic groups. However, this could be a cause (providing greater stress) or a result (of downward social drift) of schizophrenia.

Viruses – Many viruses, e.g. influenza have been proposed to trigger genetic causes of schizophrenia.

16.3 Mood disorders – symptoms and diagnosis

BACKGROUND

Mood disorders are one of the most frequently occurring psychopathologies, the risk of developing one is around 9%. The DSM IV distinguishes between two main categories of mood disorder: unipolar depression and bipolar (manic) depression. Major unipolar depression occurs at least 5 times more frequently than bipolar depression (it has been called 'the common cold of mental illness'), and mania can occur on its own (although this is very rare). It is important to remember that we all have our emotional 'ups and downs' but these mood disorders differ in degree from 'normal', natural reactions, both in their severity, frequency and duration, and may lead to suicide attempts.

UNIPOLAR DEPRESSION

Diagnosis – Unipolar depression can present four types of symptoms.
The DSM IV states that either depressed mood or loss of pleasure, plus at least another 4 symptoms (out of those listed opposite) must be shown during the same two-week period for the diagnosis to be made.

Prevalence – There is at least a 5% lifetime risk of developing unipolar depression. It appears cross-culturally, but is diagnosed twice as often for women.

EMOTIONAL SYMPTOMS
Intense feelings of sadness or guilt, along with a lack of enjoyment or pleasure in previous activities or company.

MOTIVATIONAL SYMPTOMS
Passivity and great difficulty in initiating action and making decisions.

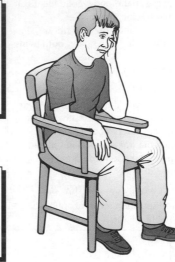

COGNITIVE SYMPTOMS
Frequent negative thoughts, faulty attribution of blame (blame themselves), low self-esteem, and irrational hopelessness.

SOMATIC SYMPTOMS
Loss of energy or restlessness. Disturbance of appetite, weight, and sleep.

BIPOLAR DEPRESSION

Diagnosis – Bipolar depression involves the symptoms of depression, followed by mania or hypomania (shorter, less severe mania). Mania involves 4 types of symptoms.
The DSM IV states a manic episode must involve 'a distinct period of abnormally and persistently elevated, expansive or irritable mood, lasting at least a week', plus at least 3 additional symptoms (out of those opposite).

Prevalence – There is around a 1% lifetime risk of developing bipolar depression.

EMOTIONAL SYMPTOMS
Abnormally euphoric elevated or irritable mood, and increased pleasure in activities.

MOTIVATIONAL SYMPTOMS
Increase in goal-directed activity and increase in pleasurable activities that have a high risk of painful consequences.

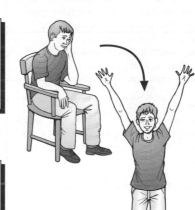

COGNITIVE SYMPTOMS
Inflated self-esteem or grandiosity, racing ideas and thoughts, distractibility of attention.

SOMATIC SYMPTOMS
Decreased need for sleep, psychomotor agitation, more talkative and rapid, pressured speech.

OTHER MOOD DISORDERS

The DSM IV and ICD 10 list many other varieties of mood disorder, including:

- **Dysthymia** – A classification given to those who suffer chronic mild depression over a period of not less than two years, where a depressed mood and other symptoms of mild depression are suffered **a** for most of the day, **b** on more days than not, and **c** without a break of more than two months in the two year period.
- **Cyclothymia** – The bipolar equivalent of dysthymia. It is a classification given to those who suffer from mild depression, interspersed with periods of hypomania, for more than two years.
- **Mania** – A classification given to those who suffer from full blown symptoms of mania without corresponding periods of depression. The symptoms must last for at least one week and must be sufficiently severe to interfere with social and/or occupational functioning.
- **Seasonal affective disorder** – A classification given to those who suffer a mood disorder that systematically varies with seasonal changes, often involving depression in winter months and sometimes also bipolar mania in the summer.

16.4 Explanatory theories of mood disorders

BIOLOGICAL THEORIES

Genetics
There is moderate evidence for a genetic predisposition to suffer from unipolar depression, but much stronger evidence for the role of genes in bipolar depression. Monozygotic twin **concordance** studies and family studies have led Katz and McGuffin (1993) to suggest that genetic factors account for 52% of the variance in unipolar depression, but up to 80% of the variance in vulnerability in bipolar depression.

Neurochemicals
One of the most popular theories is that a **lack** of the neurotransmitters **norepinephrine** (noradrenaline) and **serotonin** are responsible for depression. These biochemicals are involved in the areas of the brain involved in emotional behaviour, and evidence for their involvement in depression comes from studies into the action of anti-depressant drugs (which increase their activity) and the drug reserpine, which causes depression (because it decreases norepinephrine and serotonin levels).
The very successful effect of lithium carbonate in treating bipolar depression indicates a strong role for biological causes in this disorder.
Some studies have indicated that hormones, such as cortisol, have a role to play in unipolar depression.

Evaluation
The role of the above neuro-transmitters and hormones in depression is extremely complex, and anti-depressant drugs have effects on many other neurochemicals, apart from norepinephrine and serotonin, so we cannot guarantee that these are the only substances involved.

PSYCHOLOGICAL THEORIES

Learning theory
Looks at the role of **reinforcement** and **punishment**. Depressives may suffer from a lack of positive reinforcement that may lead to 'sad' behaviour which, when noticed, may itself be reinforced by the attention it draws. However, since depressed people tend to be avoided in the long run, this only leads to further lack of reinforcement and a vicious circle.
Seligman found that dogs repeatedly subjected to unavoidable punishment would no longer initiate any action to avoid electric shocks when it was made possible to do so. Seligman argued that the dogs had **learned helplessness** and showed behaviour similar to that showed by human depressives.

Cognitive theory
Based on his experiments on **learned helplessness**, Seligman proposed a cognitive theory suggesting that people become depressed when they **believe** that nothing they do will improve their situation.
Learned helplessness makes the depressive see
- causes as internal (blaming themselves not the situation)
- situations as stable (showing extreme pessimism about the future)
- failure as global (not specific to one situation)
In other words the depressed person thinks 'its me, its going to last forever, and everything I do will go wrong'.

Aaron Beck came up with some similar ideas by proposing his **cognitive triad** of negative thoughts (about the self, present experience, and the future) and looked at the depressive's **errors in logic** (distortions of thought processes, such as false magnification or minimisation of events, over-generalisation, personalisation, etc.).
Cognitive psychologists emphasise faulty attributions.

Psychoanalytic theory
Focuses on **unconscious** causes of depression. According to Freud, depressives turn their aggressive drive and anger that they feel towards other people or situations inwards and are, therefore, punishing themselves.

Evaluation
Learning theory does not take into account the idea that different people sharing a similar set of environmental experiences will not always become equally depressed. Seligman's finding on animals can not be legitimately generalised to humans. The psychoanalytic theory of depression lacks scientific support.

ENVIRONMENTAL THEORIES

Life events
Depression occurs not only after major stressful life events (particularly the early loss of attachment figures), but is also reliably linked with continual levels of stress and 'hassles'.

Socio-economic background
Depression is proportionally more common in women, but especially in 'working class', house-bound women with three or more children. Clearly, stress and lack of environmental reinforcement is greater in these circumstances.

Seasonal variation
Seasonal affective disorder may be caused by the variations in daylight hours that occur as the seasons change. Less daylight in the winter months may account for the higher reports of depression at this time.

Evaluation
These factors should perhaps be regarded as **triggers** of depression for people who are already predisposed to suffer from it, since not all people will react in the same way to these environmental stresses – some cope, others do not.

INTERACTION EXPLANATIONS
Researchers, such as Checkley (1992), have pointed out that stress causes the release of adrenal steroid hormones, such as cortisol, and these hormones are thought to play a role in regulating the effect of genetic influences.

Other researchers such as Weiss and Simson (1985) have found that rats exhibiting the behavioural symptoms of learned helplessness induced by unavoidable shock, often showed large decreases in the production of the neurotransmitter norepinephrine.

16.6 Anxiety disorders – symptoms and diagnosis

PHOBIAS

Diagnosis

The symptoms are unambiguous and diagnosis is easy:
- Persistent fear of a specific situation out of proportion to the reality of the danger.
- Compelling desire to avoid and escape the situation.
- Recognition that the fear is unreasonably excessive.
- Symptoms not due to another disorder, e.g. schizophrenia.

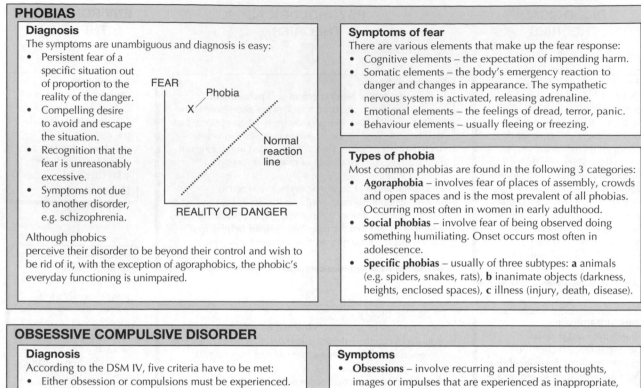

Although phobics perceive their disorder to be beyond their control and wish to be rid of it, with the exception of agoraphobics, the phobic's everyday functioning is unimpaired.

Symptoms of fear

There are various elements that make up the fear response:
- Cognitive elements – the expectation of impending harm.
- Somatic elements – the body's emergency reaction to danger and changes in appearance. The sympathetic nervous system is activated, releasing adrenaline.
- Emotional elements – the feelings of dread, terror, panic.
- Behaviour elements – usually fleeing or freezing.

Types of phobia

Most common phobias are found in the following 3 categories:
- **Agoraphobia** – involves fear of places of assembly, crowds and open spaces and is the most prevalent of all phobias. Occurring most often in women in early adulthood.
- **Social phobias** – involve fear of being observed doing something humiliating. Onset occurs most often in adolescence.
- **Specific phobias** – usually of three subtypes: **a** animals (e.g. spiders, snakes, rats), **b** inanimate objects (darkness, heights, enclosed spaces), **c** illness (injury, death, disease).

OBSESSIVE COMPULSIVE DISORDER

Diagnosis

According to the DSM IV, five criteria have to be met:
- Either obsession or compulsions must be experienced.
- The sufferer has to recognise that the obsessions or compulsions are excessive or unreasonable.
- The obsessions or compulsions are time consuming (taking over one hour a day), interfere with occupational or social functioning, and cause marked distress.
- The obsessions or compulsions are not confused with the preoccupations of other disorders, e.g. food with eating disorders, or drugs with substance abuse disorders.
- The obsessions or compulsions are not directly caused by medication or other known physical conditions.

Symptoms

- **Obsessions** – involve recurring and persistent thoughts, images or impulses that are experienced as inappropriate, intrusive and anxiety provoking, and are not just excessive worries about real life problems. The sufferer realises that these thoughts, etc. are the product of their own mind, and attempts to ignore or suppress them, often by thinking another thought or performing some action.
- **Compulsions** – involve repetitive and rule following behaviours (e.g. hand washing, checking) or mental acts (e.g. counting, praying) that the sufferer feels driven to perform (often in response to an obsession) to reduce distress or to avoid an imagined catastrophe. These acts are excessive and not realistically linked with what the sufferer is trying to avoid.

PANIC ATTACK

Diagnosis

According to the DSM IV a panic attack involves
- a discrete period of intense fear or discomfort, reaching a peak within 10 minutes.
- at least four (out of a list of 13) other symptoms occur very rapidly.

Symptoms

Somatic symptoms – such as sweating, trembling, palpitations, breathlessness, chest pain, nausea, dizziness, numbness, tingling or hot flushes.

Emotional symptoms – such as feelings of choking, smothering, derealization, depersonalisation, and fear of losing control, going mad or dying

GENERALISED ANXIETY DISORDER

Diagnosis

According to the DSM IV generalised anxiety disorder involves
- excessive, and difficult to control, worry and anxiety.
- significant distress and disruption to functioning.
- worry occurring more days than not for at least 6 months.
- worry not involving another disorder (e.g. depression).

Symptoms

Three additional symptoms must also be shown, e.g.
- restlessness and irritability,
- muscle tension, rapid physical fatigue, and sleep disturbance,
- concentration problems.

POST-TRAUMATIC STRESS DISORDER

Diagnosis

According to the DSM IV, post-traumatic stress disorder (PTSD) involves exposure to a traumatic event that was responded to with fear, helplessness or horror, plus the presence of the following symptoms for more than 1 month:
- The traumatic event is persistently re-experienced, e.g. as recurrent and intrusive recollections, flashbacks or dreams.
- Persistent avoidance of stimuli associated with the trauma and numbing of general responsiveness.
- Persistent symptoms of increased arousal, e.g. sleep difficulty, anger outbursts, exaggerated startle response, concentration difficulty.

16.6 Explanatory theories of anxiety disorders

BIOLOGICAL THEORIES

Genetics
The usual methods have been employed to assess the genetic causes of anxiety disorders:

- **Twin studies** – anxiety disorder concordance rates for monozygotic twins are fairly high, especially in comparison with dizygotic twin rates (Carey & Gottesman, 1981).
- **Relative studies** – some studies have shown that people with first degree relatives (e.g. mother, brother) who have experienced panic attacks are 10 times more likely than controls to also have them. Relatives of obsessive compulsives, however, are not more likely to develop obsessive compulsive disorder itself, but are more likely to suffer from some kind of anxiety disorder.

It appears that agoraphobia and panic disorder have the most **specific** genetic transmission, whereas other disorders seem to transmit a general tendency to inherit some kind of anxiety.

The genes for anxiety disorders have proven difficult to isolate however, and their method of action is unknown.

Evolutionary reasons for phobias
Seligman has talked of the 'biological preparedness' of phobias – that we are instinctively biased to acquire certain phobias because they have good evolutionary survival functions. Evidence for this comes from analysing the survival functions of the most common phobias (which usually involve dangerous stimuli, e.g. heights, snakes, the dark, etc.) and conditioning experiments, for example on monkeys which can be conditioned to fear snakes but not leaves or flowers. This also accounts for why modern dangerous objects, such as guns and cars, are rarely involved in human phobias – they have no evolutionary history.
Marks & Nesse argue that anxiety has evolved as 'a normal defence mechanism... People who are afraid of heights, for example, may "freeze" when confronted by a sudden drop, thereby reducing the chances of a fall'.
This does not explain why some people develop a particular phobic response compared to others.

Immediate biological causes
An excess of sodium lactate has been proposed as an explanation of panic attacks – infusions of this substance will provoke panic attacks in susceptible subjects significantly more than in controls. The same substance could be involved in phobias. Lactate may work by increasing blood carbon dioxide levels, thereby increasing respiration rates and provoking panic, or it may reduce serotonin, thereby reducing this neurotransmitter's calming effects. Evidence comes from the fact that anti-anxiety drugs block lactate effects.
PTSD may disrupt the locus coeruleus – the brain's alarm and arousal centre in the brain stem. This may be responsible for the PTSD symptoms of hyperalertness, difficulties in concentration and sleep, and exaggerated startle response.
Biological theories on their own can not provide a complete explanation – bodily effects still need to be cognitively interpreted, and an explanation of why certain people develop certain anxiety disorders needs to be provided.

PSYCHOLOGICAL THEORIES

Psychoanalytic theory
Freud proposed that phobias are caused by the displacement of unconscious anxiety onto harmless external objects. The anxiety stems from unconscious conflict, which has to be resolved before the phobia can be dealt with – even if one phobia goes, another will take its place until the underlying disorder is treated. The classic evidence that Freud provided was the case study of 'Little Hans' (1909), where Hans's unconscious fear of castration was displaced onto a fear of being bitten by white horses (which symbolised the father). Freud would have attributed PTSD to repressed traumatic events.
There are many criticisms of this approach and therapy.

Learning theory
Learning theorists propose that phobias come about as an originally neutral stimulus becomes associated with an unpleasant or traumatic experience and so becomes a fear-eliciting conditional stimulus. The classic example is the case of 'Little Albert' demonstrated by Watson & Rayner (1920).

Neutral Stimulus	+	Unconditional Stimulus	→	Unconditional Response
RAT	+	SUDDEN LOUD NOISE	→	FEAR
Conditional Stimulus			→	Conditional Response
RAT			→	FEAR

The persistence of phobias (i.e. why they do not extinguish easily) is explained by Mowrer's (1960) 'Two-factor' theory. It suggests that phobias are acquired through classical conditioning (as above) but are maintained through negative reinforcement – as the avoidance of unpleasant phobic situations is reinforced.
The degree of PTSD suffering is related to the severity of the trauma experienced, perhaps indicating a strong form of classical conditioning is involved.
Behaviourist views of phobia learning have to compromise with:
- biological preparedness (not all fears are equally easy to learn)
- vicarious learning of fear responses via social learning theory.

Cognitive theory
Clark (1986) proposes that faulty cognitive processes (thinking) are to blame for panic attacks. The sufferers tend to focus their attention internally, so are more aware of bodily sensations, and are more likely to misinterpret those sensations as catastrophic. This thinking can lead to a vicious circle as an increased heart rate is misinterpreted as a sign of impending harm – this leads to anxiety – which in turn leads to increased heart rate!
People suffering from generalised anxiety disorder show the attentional problem of over-vigilance – they are extremely sensitive to even minor danger cues.
Expectancies are important in determining whether traumatic events will cause PTSD. If people in the emergency services are not prepared for traumatic events, they are likely to suffer PTSD.
Obsessive compulsives appear to use their obsessive thoughts and compulsive actions as a way of **suppressing** or controlling some underlying anxiety or worry. These thoughts and actions may be negatively reinforced by providing momentary escape from the underlying anxiety.

16.7 'Analysis of a phobia in a five-year-old boy' Freud (1909)

AIM
To present the case study of Little Hans, a young boy who was seen as suffering from anxiety that led to a number of phobias. Freud uses this case study as strong support for his psychoanalytic ideas concerning:
- **Unconscious determinism** – Freud argues that people are not consciously aware of the causes of their behaviour. Little Hans was not consciously aware of the motivations for his behaviour, fantasies, and phobias.
- **Psychosexual development** – Psychoanalytic theory proposes that the sex drive seeks gratification through different erogenous zones at different ages, e.g. oral stage (0–1 years), anal (1–3 years), phallic stage (3–5 or 6 years). Little Hans was currently experiencing the phallic stage, according to Freud, gaining pleasure through masturbation and showing an interest in his own and other people's genitals.
- **The Oedipus complex** – Central to Freud's theory of personality, this occurs during the phallic stage as young boys direct their genital pleasure towards the mother and wish the father dead. However, young boys fear that their illicit desires will be found out by the father who will punish in the worse way possible – castration. Out of castration anxiety, the boy identifies with the father. Little Hans was regarded as a 'little Oedipus' wanting his father out of the way so he could be alone with his mother.
- **The cause of phobias** – Freud believed that phobias were the product of unconscious anxiety displaced onto harmless external objects. Little Hans's unconscious fear of castration by the father was symbolically displaced as a fear of being bitten by white horses.
- **Psychoanalytic therapy** – Aims to treat disturbed thoughts, feelings and behaviour by firstly identifying the unconscious causes of the disturbance, and secondly bringing them 'out into the open' to consciously discuss and resolve them. Thus Little Hans' behaviour was analysed, and its unconscious causes inferred and confronted.

SUMMARY OF THE CASE
Little Hans started showing a particularly lively interest in his 'widdler' and the presence or absence of this organ in others, and his tendency to masturbate brought threats from the mother to cut it off. When he was three and a half, he gained a baby sister, whom he resented, and consequently developed a fear of the bath. Later Hans developed a stronger fear of being bitten by white horses which seemed to be linked to two incidents – overhearing a father say to a child 'don't put your finger to the white horse or it will bite you' and seeing a horse that was pulling a carriage fall down and kick about with its legs. His fear went on to generalise to carts and buses. Little Hans, both before and after the beginning of the phobias, expressed anxiety that his mother would go away and was prone to frequent fantasies including imagining: **a** being the mother of his own children, whom he made to widdle, **b** that his mother had shown him her widdler, **c** that he had taken a smaller crumpled giraffe away from a taller one, **d** that a plumber had placed a borer into his stomach while in the bath on one occasion and had replaced his behind and widdler with larger versions on another occasion, and **e** that he was the father of his own children with his mother as their mother and his father as their grandfather. Having received 'help' from his father and Freud, his disorder and analysis came to an end after this last fantasy.

METHODS OF ANALYSIS
Little Hans was analysed and treated through his father (a firm believer of Freud's ideas) based on the latter's reports of Hans's behaviour and statements. Treatment was achieved by:
- inferring the unconscious causes of Hans' behaviour through rich interpretation and decoding of psychoanalytic symbols
- confronting Hans with the unconscious causes by revealing to him his hidden motivations and consciously discussing them

RESULTS OF ANALYSIS

Event	Freudian Interpretation	Conclusion
Anxiety of mother's desertion	Sexual arousal of being taken into mother's bed for comfort	Oedipus complex love for the mother
Fear of bath	Death wish against sister due to jealousy over mother's attention	
Asking why mother did not powder his penis	Seduction attempt	
Taking smaller giraffe from the bigger one	Taking mother away from father	
Fear of heavily loaded carts and buses	Fear of another birth due to jealousy over mother's attention	
Fear of being bitten by white horses	Father (with spectacles and moustache) symbolic of white bus horse (with black blinkers and muzzle), bitten finger symbolic of castration	Fear of castration by father
Fantasy of plumber providing larger widdler	Wanting to be like (identifying with) his father	Resolution of Oedipus complex
Fantasy of being father with his mother	Fulfilment of growing up to have mother while making his father a grandfather instead of killing him	

EVALUATION
Methodological:

Case study method – Advantageous for therapeutic use but also many disadvantages, e.g. generalising results.

Lack of objectivity – Analysis was conducted second hand via the father and all data interpreted in the light of psychoanalytic theory. Freud was aware of objectivity problems and putting words in Little Hans' mouth, but argued 'a psychoanalysis is not an impartial scientific investigation but a therapeutic measure. Its essence is not to prove anything, but to alter something'.

Theoretical: There are many other explanations of Little Hans' behaviour that are more credible, e.g. those of Fromm (castration anxiety from the mother), Bowlby (attachment theory) and learning theory (classical conditioning of phobias).

Links: Freud's theory of socialisation, personality development and abnormality (its causes and treatment).
Links to case study of Thigpen and Cleckley in methodology.

16.8 Classical conditioning and phobias

PHOBIAS AS CONDITIONED EMOTIONAL RESPONSES

Behaviourist learning theorists such as Watson suggested that phobias were conditioned emotional responses. Certain stimuli, such as sudden loud noises, naturally cause fear reactions, and stimuli that become associated with them will acquire the same emotional response. In classical conditioning terms, if a rat does not originally produce fear, it can be made to do so by being associated with a loud noise, as follows.

First – test emotional response to rat	**RAT** (neutral stimulus)	⟶	**NO EMOTIONAL RESPONSE**
Second – test natural fear reaction to loud noise		**SUDDEN LOUD NOISE** (unconditional stimulus) ⟹	**FEAR** (unconditional response)
Third – associate rat and loud noise (more associations produce stronger learning)	**RAT** **+**	**SUDDEN LOUD NOISE** ⟹	**FEAR**
Fourth – test emotional response to rat *without* the loud noise	**RAT** (conditional stimulus)	⟶	**FEAR** (conditional response)

THE CASE OF LITTLE ALBERT – WATSON & RAYNER (1920)

Watson and Rayner aimed to provide experimental support for the conditioning of emotional responses such as phobias using a 'stolid and unemotional' young infant, Albert B, to test four questions:

1 **Can a fear of an animal e.g. a white rat be conditioned by visually presenting it and simultaneously striking a steel bar to create fear?**
   - At approx. 9 months Albert, who had been reared almost from birth in a hospital environment, was suddenly presented with stimuli such as a white rat, a rabbit, a dog, a monkey, masks (with and without hair), cotton wool and burning newspapers. Albert showed no fear reaction at any time – a typical response since he practically never cried and had never been seen to show either fear or rage before.
   - Two stimuli were used to try and produce a fear response in Albert – the sudden removal of support (dropping and jerking the blanket he was lying on) and sharply striking a suspended steel bar with a hammer behind his head. The first stimuli was tried exhaustively but was not effective in producing a fear response, while the second stimuli caused Albert to start violently, catch his breath and raise his arms on the first blow, do the same but pucker and tremble his lips on the second blow, and burst into tears on the third blow.
   - At 11 months and 3 days of age the bar was struck behind Albert's head as he began touching the white rat that had been suddenly presented to him. He jumped violently and fell forward, burying his face in the mattress. When he touched the rat with his other hand, the steel bar was struck a second time – having the same effect and causing him to whimper.
   - At 11 months and 10 days of age, Albert was presented with the rat and appeared apprehensive about touching it. After five further joint presentations of the rat and the noise, the rat was again presented alone. The instant he saw it he began to cry, fell over, and then crawled away so fast that he was caught with difficulty before reaching the edge of the table.

2 **Is there transfer (stimulus generalisation) of the conditioned emotional response to other objects?**
   - At 11 months and 15 days of age, Albert was presented with a variety of stimuli. He reacted with most fear to the rat and rabbit, slightly less fear to the dog and a seal fur coat and showed avoidance towards cotton wool, Watson's hair and a Santa Claus mask. He played happily with his blocks (smiling and gurgling) and with the hair of other people however.
   - At 11 months and 20 days the reactions to the rat and rabbit were not as violent so the bar was struck again with the rat, rabbit and dog to strengthen the response before Albert was moved to a different room. The fear did transfer to this new location, but with less intensity.

3 **What is the effect of time upon conditioned emotional responses?**
   Since Albert was due to leave the hospital, only a one-month delay could be left before further testing. At 1 year and 21 days of age Albert showed avoidance of the Santa Claus mask, fur coat, rat, rabbit and dog. He cried on contact with the coat, rabbit and dog, but not the rat (he just covered his eyes with both his hands).

4 **Can conditioned emotional responses be removed?**
   Albert was removed from the hospital on the day the above tests were made and so the authors stated 'the opportunity to build up an experimental technique by means of which we could remove the conditioned emotional responses was denied us'. They suggested they might have tried continually presenting the fearful stimuli to encourage fatigue of the fear response, associating the fearful stimuli with pleasant stimuli, e.g. stimulation of the erogenous zones or food, and encouraging imitation of non-fearful responses.

EVALUATION

Methodological The study has serious ethical problems. Watson and Rayner reported that they hesitated about proceeding with the experiment but comforted themselves that Albert would encounter such traumatic associations when he left the sheltered environment of the nursery anyway. This is not a very good ethical defence, especially since they believed such associations might persist indefinitely and did not leave sufficient time to remove them afterwards, despite knowing Albert was due to leave.

Theoretical The authors claim the study supports the conditioning of emotional responses and point out that their ideas contradict Freudian theories on the primacy of the emotion of love/sex and the origin of phobias. Nevertheless Albert did show a good deal of resistance to the conditioning process and did not show a fear reaction if he was allowed to suck his thumb.

16.9 Autism – symptoms and diagnosis

BACKGROUND

- Autism is one example of an Autism Spectrum Disorder – others include Asperger Syndrome and Childhood Disintegrative disorder. For example, those with Asperger Syndrome show many of the same symptoms as autism, but have average to high IQ scores and no delay in language development.
- Autism is a developmental disorder – it starts in early childhood and is unremitting with no 'cure'.
- Autism is a syndrome in that it consists of a range of conditions (see 'Diagnostic symptoms' below).

Prevalence

- The number of those diagnosed with autism has increased dramatically in the past two decades, with present estimates of around 1 or 2 cases per 1,000 people for autism, but 1 in 200 for ASD in general. This may reflect changes in diagnostic practice, educational assessment in schools, increased awareness of autism in society and/or developments in psychological research and testing methods.
- Boys are more likely to be affected than girls, with ASD averaging a 4.3 : 1 male-to-female ratio, although research suggests that girls may be more severely affected when they do have autism.

DIAGNOSIS

The DSM IV TR (2000) defines autism as showing at least six symptoms including a minimum of:

- Two social interaction symptoms
- One social communication symptom
- One restricted and repetitive behaviour symptom.

Onset must also occur before the age of three with delays/dysfunction to at least one of the following:

- Social language
- Social interaction
- Symbolic/imaginative play.

NON-DIAGNOSTIC ASSOCIATED SYMPTOMS

Other symptoms that can be shown with autism are:

- Excellent memory or attention to detail.
- Islets of ability and exceptional skill.
- Sensory processing problems - over-sensitivity or under-sensitivity in the senses, e.g. to sound, pain, body awareness.
- Physical problems - e.g. seizures affect 15 to 30% of those with autism, poor coordination or fine movement control, sleep problems.
- Behavioural problems, e.g. aggression, tantrums, unusual eating behaviour, self-harming behaviour.
- Learning disabilities (but not necessarily low IQ).

DIAGNOSTIC SYMPTOMS

Qualitative impairments in social interaction

- Non-verbal body language impairments, e.g. lack of joint attention/eye contact, absence of normal facial expressions.
- Failure to develop normal peer relationships and friends.
- Lack of spontaneous seeking of others and shared activities.
- Lack of social or emotional reciprocity.

Qualitative impairments in communication

- Developmental delays in speech.
- Impairment in initiating or maintaining social conversation.
- Stereotyped, repetitive or unusual use of language.
- Lack of spontaneous imaginative or imitative play.

Restricted, repetitive and stereotyped patterns of behaviour, interests and activities

- Intense preoccupation with at least one stereotyped and restricted behaviour pattern or interest.
- Compulsive (apparently) non-functional rituals or routines.
- Stereotyped, repetitive motor actions, e.g. hand flapping.
- Persistent preoccupation with parts of objects.

GROUPING SYMPTOMS

Some researchers, e.g. Frith (2003), have found it useful, in terms of theoretical or biological explanations, to distinguish between different groupings of symptoms. For example, using mindblindness theories to explain the *triad of social impairments*:

- *social interaction difficulties* – being unaware of what is socially appropriate, appearing distant or insensitive, finding socialising (e.g. chatting, small-talk) difficult, finding it very difficult to express feelings and relate to others to develop friendships.
- *social communication problems* (verbal and non-verbal) – with understanding gestures, body language, facial expressions and tone of voice, making it difficult to empathise with people's feelings and understand jokes, sarcasm, and non-literal expressions.
- *social imagination impairments* – such as not enjoying or taking part in imaginative role-play games, difficulties in understanding and predicting other people's behaviour, guessing the thoughts of others and imagining social intentions.

INVESTIGATING SYMPTOMS

Different methods have been used to investigate aspects of autism, such as mindblindness, for example:

- The Sally-Anne experiment – (see Baron-Cohen *et al.*, 1985) using two dolls to test autistic children's inability to attribute false belief, i.e. that one doll falsely believes a marble is in the place she left it (when another doll moved it in her absence). The test is a little artificial, since dolls do not 'believe'.
- The 'Smarties tube' test – studies false beliefs by showing that autistic children who see that a tube of Smarties contains a pencil rather than the expected sweets say another person will expect a pencil, too.
- Comic strip stories – shows autistic children have problems putting pictures in order to tell a story if that story concerns mental states rather than mechanical events or simple behavioural scripts.

16.10 'Does the autistic child have a 'theory of mind'?' Baron-Cohen, Leslie and Frith (1985)

INTRODUCTION

- Baron-Cohen *et al.* describe childhood autism as a severe developmental disorder affecting around 4 in 10,000 children and see the key symptom as being a ***profound problem in understanding and coping with the social environment*** – finding it unpredictable and confusing. This causes impaired verbal and non-verbal communication and a failure to develop normal social relationships – autistic children seem to treat people and objects in the same way and tend to be withdrawn or disruptive in their interactions with others.
- Autistic social problems could be partly caused by other symptoms that such children show – many for example are mentally retarded. However autistic children with normal IQs also lack social competence, while non-autistic retarded children such as those with Down's Syndrome are relatively socially competent. Baron-Cohen *et al.* therefore suggest that autistic children ***lack a specific cognitive mechanism*** that is distinct from general IQ, namely a '**theory of mind**'.
- A theory of mind enables one to realise that '***other people know, want, feel, or believe things***' and as such is vital for social skills. It is a form of '***second–order' representation***' or metarepresentation (a representation of another person's representation of the world, or a belief about another's belief), which also gives the ability to pretend in play – something autistic children are very poor at.

AIM

If a theory of mind that enables one to attribute mental states to others:
1 is specifically lacking in autistic children and is not related to general intelligence
2 allows people to work out what others *believe* about certain situations and thus predict what they will do next
then it can be hypothesised that autistic children whose IQs are in the average range will perform significantly worse on a task that requires such belief based prediction than non-autistic but severely retarded children with Down's Syndrome.

METHOD

Design A natural or quasi experiment was used, employing an independent measures design.
The independent variable was the type of child, naturally manipulated in 3 conditions; autistic, Down's Syndrome, clinically 'normal'.
The dependent variable was the ability to correctly answer the belief question of the Sally-Anne test.
Subjects 20 autistic children aged around 6–16 years old (average approx. 12) of higher average intelligence than the other groups
14 Down's Syndrome children aged around 6–17 (average approx. 11).
27 clinically 'normal' pre-school children aged around 3–5 (average approx. $4\frac{1}{2}$).
Procedure The experimenter sits at a table opposite the child with two dolls, Sally and Anne. Sally puts a marble into her basket, then leaves the scene. Anne transfers the marble and hides it in her box. Sally returns and the experimenter asks the critical ***Belief Question*** – "Where will Sally look for her marble?". If the children point to the previous location of Sally's basket they pass the belief question since they can represent the doll's false belief. If they point to the current location of Anne's box then they fail the question since they cannot take into account Sally's false belief. The scenario was repeated, but this time the marble was transferred to the experimenter's pocket.
Controls –To ensure the validity of the belief question, 3 control questions were asked – the Naming Question asking which doll was which (to ensure knowledge of the dolls' identities), the Reality Question "Where is the marble really?" and the Memory Question "Where was the marble in the beginning?" (to ensure knowledge of the marble's location at each point in the scenario).

RESULTS

% failure on Questions	Autistic group	Down's Syndrome group	'Normal' pre-schoolers
Naming, Reality, Memory	0%	0%	0%
Belief Question	80% on both trials	14% on both trials	15% on both trials

Belief Question differences were significant at P<0.001. All 16 autistic children who failed pointed to the current marble location.

DISCUSSION

The controls rule out explanations of position preference, negativism, random pointing, misunderstanding/forgetting the task or general intellectual ability. The experimenters therefore conclude that the autistic children specifically lacked a theory of mind to enable them to attribute belief to the doll and thus distinguish their own belief from the doll's. The four autistic children who did not fail the Belief Question may have possessed a theory of mind and were predicted by Baron-Cohen *et al.* to show differences from the other autistic children in their type of social impairment and pretend play deficiency (testing of this was not reported). The *conceptual* perspective-taking tested here is distinguished from the *perceptual* perspective-taking tested by Piaget and Inhelder's 'three-mountain' test.

EVALUATION

Methodological The scenario and use of dolls is rather artificial (dolls do not believe!). Realistic tests using people have confirmed the results.
Theoretical The study initiated a large amount of research into theory of mind and links with certain aspects of Piaget's egocentrism.
Links Child cognitive development. Natural or quasi experimentation.

16.11 Explanatory theories of autism

BIOLOGICAL EXPLANATIONS

NEUROLOGICAL EXPLANATIONS

Brothers (1990) identified three brain regions (the 'social brain') that seem particularly involved in empathy or social intelligence:

- the amygdala
- the orbito-frontal cortex (OFC)
- the superior temporal sulcus and gyrus (STG).

Evaluation

Brothers presented many sources of evidence to support her ideas, from animal lesion studies to single cell recording studies.

People with brain damage to the frontal lobes can show abnormal persevering and repetitive behaviour.

Baron-Cohen et al. (2000) presented four lines of evidence for an amygdala deficit in autism.

1 Post-mortem study of adults with autism found microscopic increased cell density in the amygdala.
2 Patients with amygdala lesions show impairments in social judgement similar to autism.
3 Structural magnetic resonance imaging shows autism is associated with reduced amygdala volume.
4 Functional magnetic resonance imaging of adults with high functioning autism or Asperger Syndrome shows significantly less amygdala activation during a 'Reading the Mind in the Eyes' task compared to normal adult controls.

GENETIC EXPLANATIONS

Concordance studies of monozygotic (MZ) twins indicate a high degree of genetic influence and molecular genetics studies have indicated locations on chromosomes with possible associations with autistic symptoms, e.g. on chromosome 7. It is likely that autism will be explained by more than just a single gene mutation or chromosome abnormality.

Evaluation

Bailey et al. (1995) found 60% concordance for autism in monozygotic twins (27 pairs), but 0% for dizygotic same-sex twins (20 pairs).

The International Molecular Genetic Study of Autism Consortium (IMGSAC, 1998, 2001) has conducted large-scale studies, but specific genes for autism have not yet been identified with 100% certainty.

PSYCHOLOGICAL EXPLANATIONS

REFRIGERATOR PARENT THEORY

Bettelheim blamed autism on cold, disinterested parents.

Evidence

None. Distant parenting may result from autistic coldness.

WEAK CENTRAL COHERENCE THEORY

Central coherence is the tendency of the human brain to process incoming information globally, i.e. for gist, general high-level meaning, whole gestalt patterns, etc.

Frith (1989) and Happé (1996) suggested autism may result from weak central coherence – a *cognitive style biased toward specific, detailed* and *local* processing, leading to:

- A *neglect of context*, which can handicap language learning and an *understanding of social situations*.
- A *narrow attention to detail*, which could lead to specific *talents or islets of ability*.

Evidence

- Autistic failure to use context in reading (Happé, 1995).
- Autistic superiority on the Embedded Figures Task.

EXECUTIVE DYSFUNCTION THEORY

Ozonoff et al. (1994) suggest autism involves dysfunction in the executive parts of the mind (e.g. the central executive of the working memory model or frontal lobes of the brain) which allocate attention to tasks, allow flexible planning, and select correct responses or suppress incorrect ones.

Executive dysfunction causes an *inflexible inability to shift attention* from or suppress certain behaviour, thus explaining the *repetitive* and *stereotyped* behaviour as well as the desire for *routine* and *sameness* shown in autism.

Evaluation

Autistic people who also have learning disabilities are more likely to show executive deficits, but this is not specific to autism (e.g. it occurs in Tourette Syndrome and OCD).

This explanation ignores the content of the repetitive behaviour, which may represent a strong interest or preference rather than a lack of ability to shift attention.

THEORY OF MIND DEFICIT THEORY

Baron-Cohen et al. (1985) proposed that autistic children *lack* a specific cognitive mechanism – a theory of mind – that enables people to *attribute mental states* (knowledge, beliefs, desires, and feelings) to others. A theory of mind is a second-order mental metarepresentation of another person's representation (e.g. knowing that someone else knows something) that is *vital for social skills, communication,* and *imagination* (the triad of autistic social impairments).

Evaluation

Baron-Cohen et al. (1985) used the Sally-Anne false belief test to provide evidence for their theory, but some researchers have found autistic children can pass these tests.

Theory of mind alone does not account for other autism symptoms, but Baron-Cohen has developed the idea further (see 'Empathising-Systemising theory' below).

EMPATHISING-SYSTEMISING (E-S) THEORY

Baron-Cohen has since refined his ideas about theory of mind, proposing that it is one aspect of autistic mindblindness and deficits in the normal process of *empathising*, which also involves appropriate emotional reactions (e.g. sympathy) to other people. He also suggests that autistic individuals have a *'Systemising* drive to analyse and build systems, in order to understand and predict the behaviour of non-agentive (inanimate) events' that is either intact or superior. Thus:

- Empathising deficits account for the *triad of social, communication* and *imagination deficits*.
- Systemising strengths account for the triad of *islets of ability, obsession with systems,* and *repetitive behaviour*.

Evaluation

Autistic empathising deficits have been confirmed by more than 30 experimental tests (Baron-Cohen, 1995), including age-appropriate adult tests (Baron-Cohen et al., 1997).

Theory of Mind, Executive Dysfunction and Central Coherence theories each explain different sets of autistic symptoms, but E-S Theory attempts to account for them all.

16.12 'Another advanced test of theory of mind'

Baron-Cohen *et al*. (1997)

INTRODUCTION

The authors suggest that there is 'considerable evidence that the majority of children with autism have impairments in the development of a theory of mind' (ToM) – a core deficit which may underlie the social, communicative, and imaginative dysfunctions of autistic people.

However, some studies (e.g. Bowler, 1992) have found adults with Asperger Syndrome or high-functioning autism can pass second-order ToM tests (reasoning about what one person thinks about another's thoughts) which seems to contradict ToM predictions and research.

The authors reply to this criticism by suggesting that first and second order tests of ToM are not sufficiently complex (normal four- and six-year-olds respectively can pass them and only basic nominal data is usually provided) and thus not suitable for adults – either with or without autism or Asperger Syndrome (AS).

A new test is therefore needed that is suitable for detecting Theory of Mind in adults; this will not only be useful for high-functioning autism/AS, but will also allow more sensitive tests of ToM predictions about mindreading abilities, e.g. that normal females are better than males.

AIMS

Baron-Cohen *et al*. wished to investigate a new, adult test of theory of mind competence – the 'Reading the Mind in the Eyes' Test – with high-functioning adults with autism or AS.

In particular, they predicted that:
- The Eyes Test would show validity as a measure of theory of mind deficits in adults.
- Adults with autism or AS would be unable to interpret state of mind in the Eyes Test and so would perform worse on it than normal adults or those with a different serious developmental disorder.
- If the Eyes Test is valid, it should indicate that normal females would perform better (as suggested by their greater empathising ability) than males.

METHOD

Design
Natural experiment. Matched participants design.

Independent variable:
Type of person likely to have Theory of Mind deficits, tested in three conditions:
- Adults with high-functioning autism or AS
- Normal adults
- Adults with Tourette Syndrome.

Dependent variable:
Score out of 25 on the Eyes Test – which involves looking at 25, black and white, standardised photographs of the eye region of male and female faces, and making a forced choice between which two mental state words (opposites) best describes what the person with the eyes might be thinking or feeling.

Some mental state terms were simple, e.g. sad-happy, friendly-unfriendly, others were more complicated e.g. concerned-unconcerned, sympathetic-unsympathetic. The words for each photo were selected by 4 judges and unanimously confirmed by 8 independent raters.

N.B. Differences in Eyes Test scores (D.V.) between normal males and females (I.V.) were also tested.

Participants
- 16 adults with high-functioning autism (4) or AS (12), of normal IQ, male to female ratio 13:3.
- 50 normal adults, age-matched, with no apparent psychological or IQ problems, male to female ratio 25:25.
- 10 adults with Tourette Syndrome, age-matched, of normal IQ, male to female ratio 8:2.

Controls to ensure validity of Eyes Test of adult ToM
Tourette Syndrome shows no ToM deficits, but is a comparable childhood developmental disorder to autism/AS (it also causes social disruption, affects more males than females, and has proposed genetic and frontal lobe causes).

All autistic/AS and Tourette participants had passed two 1st order and one 2nd order false belief tasks – so any Eyes Test deficits were due to mindreading problems beyond the six-year-old level.

'The Strange Stories Task' (an existing, more advanced test of ToM for 8– to 9-year-olds) was given to compare results to the Eyes Test.

A gender recognition test of the eyes and a basic emotion recognition test of whole faces were also given to control for the possibility of specific difficulties with face or emotion perception.

Procedure
The Eyes Test, Strange Stories Task, and the gender and emotion recognition tests were presented in a random order to individual subjects in a quiet room. Each photo was shown for 3 seconds.

RESULTS
- The Tourette Syndrome adult mean score on the Eyes Test (20.4) was not significantly different from normal adults (20.3), but both were significantly higher (at $p < 0.001$ level or better) than the autism/AS adult mean score (16.3).
- Normal females were significantly better than males.
- There were no significant differences between groups on the gender or emotion recognition tests.
- The autism/AS group made significantly more errors on the Strange Stories Task than the control groups.
- There was no significant correlation between IQ and Eyes Test results in the autistic/AS group.

DISCUSSION
The 'Reading the Mind in the Eyes' Test is a ***valid*** and 'pure' advanced ***Theory of Mind*** test for ***adults***, in that it:
- Distinguishes between those with autism/AS and controls, and between males and females (predictive validity).
- Does not involve problems with face or emotion perception and some adults failed despite passing childhood tests of ToM (internal validity).
- Does not involve executive function or central coherence problems – the alternative theories of autistic/AS symptoms (construct validity), but compares well with the existing, advanced Strange Stories test of ToM (concurrent validity).

However, despite having reasonable ecological validity, the test does not reflect everyday, non-static social situations.

17.1 Somatic/biomedical treatments 1

AIM OF THERAPIES

To cure the underlying physical causes of mental illness or to alleviate the symptoms of these causes.

Physically based treatments for mental disorder have a long and horrific history – ranging from bleeding, vomiting, and high speed rotation, to cold baths, and insulin coma therapy.

Biological treatments have been applied to a range of disorders and have the highest success rates with serious psychoses. However, they involve powerful techniques that can cause many side effects.

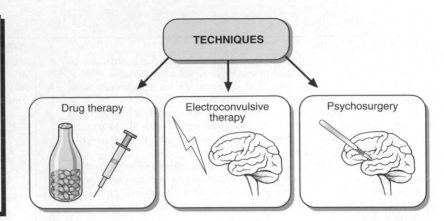

TECHNIQUES

Drug therapy

Electroconvulsive therapy

Psychosurgery

PSYCHOSURGERY

TECHNIQUE

Neolithic skulls with trepanned holes in were perhaps the first attempts at physically rectifying mental problems. When Moniz introduced psychosurgery in the form of prefrontal lobotomy in 1935, some might argue that the scientific justification and techniques were not much more advanced. Prefrontal lobotomy involved severing the connection between the frontal lobes of the brain and the deeper underlying structures (often by hammering a rod through the eye socket and rotating it around) in the hope of producing calm and rational behaviour. Today only very precise bundles of nerve fibres are destroyed, but it should still be noted that the effects are irreversible.

APPLICATION

Psychosurgery was originally performed on tens of thousands for a wide variety of mood, anxiety and personality disorders, but was especially employed for schizophrenia because of its dramatic symptoms and resistance to treatment (before drug therapy). Today it is usually used mainly as a last resort for severe depression or obsessive compulsive disorder, but virtually never for schizophrenia.

EFFECTIVENESS

Psychosurgery was initially hailed as a 'wonder cure' for psychoses, probably due to the need for a cheap, effective, and 'scientific' treatment to give the mental health profession respectability (Valenstein, 1986). However, long term follow up studies of prefrontal lobotomy patients found it to be ineffective at combating the precise symptoms of disorders. A National Commission review of psychosurgery in the USA in 1976, concluded that psychosurgery could be effective for certain disorders, such as severe depression.

APPROPRIATENESS

The indiscriminate use of psychosurgery between 1935 and 1955 led to it virtually becoming a method of social control. The development of drug therapy replaced it. Many undesirable psychological side effects were produced in most patients with prefrontal lobotomies, such as profound changes in personality, motivation, and cognitive abilities (Barahal, 1958). Patients also suffered seizures and a 1– 4% likelihood of death.

ELECTROCONVULSIVE THERAPY

TECHNIQUE

ECT involves applying an electric shock of approximately 100 volts to one side of the brain (unilateral ECT) or both sides (bilateral ECT) to induce a seizure. When the patient recovers, they remember nothing of the treatment, but report a relief of symptoms.

The treatment is usually repeated at least six times over a period of around 3 or 4 weeks. Unilateral shocks are usually administered to the non-dominant hemisphere and muscle relaxants and anaesthetic are given to reduce physical damage.

APPLICATION

ECT was originally applied to schizophrenics under the mistaken assumption that they did not suffer epilepsy (which involves disruptive electrical activity in the brain). Today ECT is rarely applied to schizophrenics but is used to treat severe cases of depression, usually if drug treatment has failed and the risk of suicide is high.

EFFECTIVENESS

ECT is considered a very effective treatment for depression, producing symptom relief in 60–80% of cases. However, its mode of action is unknown. Possible explanations are that the shock
* destroys neurones in brain areas responsible for emotion
* affects the balance of neurotransmitters involved in emotion
* acts as a form of punishment for depressive behaviour or negative reinforcement for recovery behaviour (feeling better to avoid shocks)
* produces memory loss that allows thoughts to be restructured.

APPROPRIATENESS

ECT replaced insulin coma therapy, being a more controllable and less risky procedure. However, ECT has been over-used and abused in the opinion of many and does cause side effects such as memory loss and around a 3 in 10,000 mortality risk.

Ethical problems arise with using a treatment whose mode of action is unknown and also with consent (should ECT be forcibly applied to depressed patients with a high risk of suicide?). ECT can save lives.

17.2 Somatic/biomedical treatments 2

DRUG THERAPY

Many drugs are used to treat a wide variety of disorders. Neuroleptic drugs are thought to have their effect by controlling the activity of brain neurotransmitters at the synapse.

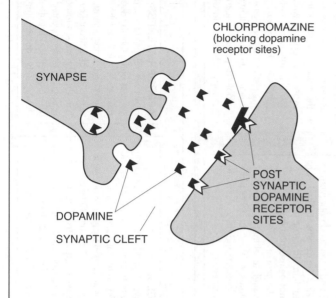

CHLORPROMAZINE (blocking dopamine receptor sites)

SYNAPSE

POST SYNAPTIC DOPAMINE RECEPTOR SITES

DOPAMINE

SYNAPTIC CLEFT

APPLICATIONS

Anti-psychotic drugs

Drugs such as the phenothiazine chlorpromazine are used to reduce the activity of the neurotransmitter dopamine by blocking its post synaptic receptor sites, while a more recent anti-psychotic drug, clozapine, blocks serotonin receptors.

Anti-depressant drugs

Each group of anti-depressant drugs work in a different way:
* Tricyclic anti-depressants, such as imipramine, work by blocking the re-uptake of neurotransmitters like norepinephrine, making more of it available.
* Monoamine oxidase (MAO) inhibitors, increase the amount of norepinephrine available by inhibiting the enzyme (monoamine oxidase) which breaks it down.
* Selective serotonin reuptake inhibitors (SSRIs), such as Prozac, specifically increase the amount of serotonin available in the synaptic cleft.
* Lithium carbonate effectively reduces both the effects of mania and depression in manic depressives.

Anti-anxiety drugs

Often termed minor tranquillisers, drugs like valium have been administered to reduce anxiety disorders and panic attacks.

EFFECTIVENESS OF DRUG TREATMENT

* Anti-psychotic drugs have massively reduced the need for institutionalisation, enabling many schizophrenics to be cared for in the community. However, around 25% of schizophrenics do not improve on traditional neuroleptics and a further 30–40% do not show full remission of symptoms. More recent anti-psychotic drugs, such as Clozapine have been found to improve both positive and negative symptoms in around 50% of those who resisted previous drugs, perhaps because they affect the neurotransmitter serotonin.
* The tricyclic anti-depressants have a delayed effect, providing relief in up to 75% of all cases after 2 to 3 weeks. Although not all patients respond to them, they are generally more effective than MAO inhibitors. SSRIs, like Prozac, have been shown to be of equal effectiveness to prior anti-depressants, are easier to administer, and have less unpleasant side-effects. Lithium carbonate has proven very successful at countering bipolar depression – up to 80% show full or partial recovery, and its use can decrease the risk of relapse.
* Typically, anti-anxiety drugs, such as valium, have been shown to be beneficial for those suffering from generalised anxiety disorder, but not those suffering from panic attacks or obsessive compulsive disorder. Anti-depressant drugs are usually used in these latter cases, and some studies have shown them to be effective for obsessive compulsive disorder in up to 50% of cases.
* The effectiveness of drugs is best tested by using longitudinal studies with placebo (fake pill) control groups and double blind assessment techniques (where neither the patient nor the doctor assessing improvement knows who is receiving the real drug).

APPROPRIATENESS OF DRUG TREATMENT

Side effects:

* Phenothiazines can produce many unpleasant minor side-effects for schizophrenics, such as dryness of the mouth and throat, drowsiness, and weight gain or loss; and two major side-effects – symptoms similar to Parkinson's disease (body stiffness or body spasms), and tardive dyskinesia (involuntary movements of the tongue and mouth).
* Clozapine does not appear to produce the above side-effects in schizophrenics, but does produce a lethal blood condition in about 1% of patients. Weekly white blood cell monitoring is required.
* MAO inhibitors can be lethal if combined with certain foods such as cheese, and tricyclics can produce weight gain, drowsiness, and constipation. SSRIs appear relatively free of side-effects. Lithium carbonate requires close medical supervision.
* Anti-anxiety drugs can produce physiological and psychological dependence or addiction in approximately 40% of cases after 6 months.

Not a complete cure:

* Anti-schizophrenic drugs have been called pharmacological strait-jackets – they only alleviate or contain symptoms rather than providing a complete 'cure'. While they have enabled care in the community, hospital re-admission rates are very high – the relapse rate is around 70% in the first year after discharge if the patient discontinues medication (which is likely given the side effects). Anti-anxiety and depression drugs do not 'cure' either.
* No drug has provided a specific, 100% cure for any mental disorder, and the neurochemical reasons for their effectiveness are still a subject of much debate.
* The biological approach may neglect many important psychological or social factors that contribute to the development of the disorder or its treatment. Social skills training for schizophrenics and their families, for example, will help them readjust to living in society, while cognitive and behavioural therapy may be necessary to overcome anxiety disorders and depression completely.

17.3 Behavioural treatments – behaviour therapy (treatments using classical conditioning techniques)

SYSTEMATIC DESENSITISATION

TECHNIQUE

Aims to **extinguish** the fear response of a phobia, and **substitute** a relaxation response to the conditional stimulus **gradually**, step by step. This is done by

- forming a hierarchy of fear, a list of fearful situations, real or imagined, involving the CS that are ranked by the subject from least fearful to most fearful.
- giving training in deep muscle relaxation techniques.
- getting the subject to relax at each stage of the hierarchy, starting with the least fearful situation, and only progressing to the next stage when the subject feels sufficiently relaxed to do so.

APPLICATION

This therapy was developed mainly by Wolpe (1958). Mary Cover Jones applied systematic desensitisation to infants with phobias, such as the case of 'Little Peter'. Little Peter was a three-year-old child who had a strong phobia of rats and rabbits, and initially 'fell flat on his back in a paroxysm of fear when a white rat was dropped into his playpen', (Walker, 1984). Peter's treatment began by being presented with a rabbit in a cage at the same time as he ate his lunch, and ended 40 sessions later with him stroking the rabbit on his lap with one hand and eating his lunch with the other!

EFFECTIVENESS

This method of treatment has a very high success rate with specific phobias, e.g. of **particular** animals rather than agoraphobia (a **general** fear of being in open spaces), and is thought to work because it seems impossible for two opposite emotions (like fear and relaxation) to exist together at the same time.

APPROPRIATENESS

This conclusion is questioned by studies that claim to have found that neither relaxation nor hierarchies are actually **necessary**, and that the essential factor is just **exposure** to the feared object or situation.
Systematic desensitisation is considered more ethical and less directive because the patient has more control over the treatment - progression only occurs when they feel suitably relaxed.

IMPLOSION/FLOODING

TECHNIQUE

Both methods of forced reality testing aim to produce the **extinction** of a phobic's fear by the **continual** and **dramatic** presentation of the phobic object or situation.
In implosion therapy, the phobic individual is, therefore, asked to continually **imagine** the worst possible situation involving their phobia, whereas in flooding therapy the worst possible situation is actually **physically** and continuously presented.

APPLICATION

Wolpe (1960) forced a girl with a fear of cars into the back of a car and drove her around for 4 hours until her hysterical fear completely disappeared, while Marks et al (1981) used flooding on agoraphobics. Prolonged exposure and compulsive response prevention is used for obsessive compulsives.

EFFECTIVENESS

Marks *et al.* (1981) found continued improvement for up to nine years after the treatment. The key to the therapy is that the dramatic presentation is continuous and **cannot be escaped from or avoided.** Therefore, the patient's anxiety is maintained at such a high level that eventually some process of stimulus 'exhaustion' takes place (you can not scream forever!) and the conditioned fear response extinguishes.

APPROPRIATENESS

These methods are considered to be:
- the most successful at treating phobias, especially flooding, which Marks *et al.*, 1971, found to be consistently more successful than systematic desensitisation, suggesting that *in vivo exposure* is crucial.
- quick and cheap but involve ethical problems of suffering and withdrawal from therapy (which could worsen the phobia).

AVERSION THERAPY

TECHNIQUE

Aims to **remove undesirable responses** to certain stimuli **by associating** them with other **aversive** stimuli; in the hope that the undesirable responses will be avoided in the future. In essence, this therapy actually tries to condition some kind of 'phobia' of the undesirable behaviour, although it is important to note that fear is not always the conditioned response.

APPLICATION

Aversion therapy has been used to treat alcoholism.

Alcohol + Emetic drug → Nausea
Emetic drug → Nausea
Alcohol → Nausea

More controversially, aversion therapy has been used to prevent a number of sexual behaviours, ranging from homosexuality to fetishism. Shocks have been paired with self damaging behaviours to stop them.

EFFECTIVENESS

Some studies have claimed limited success using aversion therapy to treat alcoholism – Meyer and Chesser (1970) found that about half their alcoholic patients abstained for at least one year following their treatment, although O'Leary and Wilson (1987) have reported mixed results. Marks et al (1970) claimed aversion therapy was effective on sexual behaviours for up to 2 years, although Marshall et al (1991) found no effectiveness.

APPROPRIATENESS

However, relapse rates are very high – the success of the therapy depends upon whether the patient can avoid the stimuli they have been conditioned against, to maintain the aversion. If the alcoholic continues to go to bars then the nausea response to alcohol may extinguish under repeated exposure.
There are ethical problems involved in deliberately conditioning aversions.

17.4 Behavioural treatments – behaviour modification (treatments using operant conditioning techniques)

BEHAVIOUR SHAPING

TECHNIQUE

This technique works by positively **reinforcing successive approximations to the desired behaviour** step by step.

Very complex behaviours can, therefore, be acquired from the more simple ones that make them up.

APPLICATION

Lovaas et al. (1967) used behaviour shaping to improve the social interaction and speech of autistic children by

- associating food with verbal approval whenever the child made eye-contact with, or paid attention to, the therapist
- reinforcing any speech sound the child made with food and approval
- gradually withholding reinforcement until the child made the correct sounds, syllables, words then sentences.

EFFECTIVENESS

Lovaas et al. (1976) reported long lasting gains in social and verbal behaviour that were maintained if the children were returned to a supportive home environment and parents who had also been trained in shaping techniques.

APPROPRIATENESS

Many serious psychoses, like schizophrenia, **cannot** fundamentally be 'cured' by learning treatments – when these treatments have been applied to them, they often show superficial short term effects unless continually reinforced.

SELECTIVE POSITIVE REINFORCEMENT

TECHNIQUE

This works by **reinforcing desirable behaviour** with a stimulus the individual finds rewarding, but **withholding** it if the desirable behaviour is not emitted.

The first task of the therapist is to find what is rewarding to the patient, so the therapist will look for a behaviour that the patient shows more frequently than others, presumably because they find it pleasant.

APPLICATION

Stunkard (1976) has successfully used selective positive reinforcement with anorexics to encourage them to eat normally. Once their rewarding behaviours have been identified, i.e. watching television or talking with other patients, then the therapist will **deprive** the patient of them until they first eat a required amount of food. If this is done, then the eating behaviour is positively reinforced with a certain amount of the rewarding behaviour (e.g. each mouthful of a whole meal might be rewarded with five minutes of television) making the eating behaviour more likely to occur again; if not, the reward is withheld.

EFFECTIVENESS

Selective positive reinforcement has been used very successfully for a long time on a number of different behaviours ranging from behaviour problems in educational situations to the eradication of self-mutilating behaviour.

APPROPRIATENESS

Reinforcement needs to be kept consistent and behaviour needs to be monitored closely for selective reinforcement to work efficiently.

Reinforcement for desirable behaviour appears to work better than aversion therapy for undesirable behaviour.

TOKEN ECONOMY PROGRAMMES

TECHNIQUE

Tokens act as **secondary reinforcers,** and many studies have shown that both animals and humans will emit behaviours for tokens that are exchangeable for primary reinforcers at a later time.

APPLICATION

Allyon and Azrin (1968) have used the principle of secondary reinforcement to reward the socially desirable behaviour of long term inmates in psychiatric institutions by giving **tokens** that can later be exchanged for certain primary reinforcers. Each time an appropriate behaviour is demonstrated by the inmate, such as making their bed or brushing their teeth, then a token will be issued - and the more desirable the behaviour, the greater the number of tokens (e.g. 6 tokens for washing up for ten minutes). These tokens can then be used to **buy** desired rewards (e.g. 3 tokens for a favourite TV show).

EFFECTIVENESS

Token economies have produced improvements in self care and pro-social behaviour, even in chronic, institutionalised schizophrenics. Paul and Lentz (1977) found token economies more effective than other hospital management methods.

APPROPRIATENESS

Token economies can make the individuals involved dependent on the tokens. Some patients may become quite mercenary, **only** producing desirable behaviour if they are going to get a token for it, and there may be serious problems in transferring improved behaviour and skills to the outside world. In addition, the beneficial effects of token economy schemes may be, in part, a result of the improved attitude of the staff towards the patients – if the staff are more optimistic about improvements in patients' behaviour, then they may start treating them more positively, and this may become more reinforcing than the tokens.

17.5 Therapeutic programmes for autism

AVERSION THERAPY

WHAT IS IT?

Aversion therapy is a behaviour therapy technique based on the classical conditioning principles of association. The aim of aversion therapy is to remove undesirable behaviour by repeatedly associating it with aversive stimuli in the hope that the undesirable target behaviour will be avoided in the future without the need for the aversive stimuli.

APPLICATION TO SELF-INJURING BEHAVIOUR

Some autistic children exhibit a variety of repetitive self-harming behaviour, from head banging and self-mutilation to eating inappropriate substances. The self-harm behaviour may not be intentional in the sense that it is an outcome of a repetitive, stereotyped action, or routine, and may not be immediately injurious or painful. Since human instruction and social disapproval may not be effective with certain autistic individuals, more extreme behavioural techniques may be required.

Aversion therapy could be employed by repeatedly associating the self-injuring behaviour with the immediate presentation of a short, subjectively aversive, but physically harmless, electric shock. Eventually, the target behaviour is avoided due to its association with noxious results, without the necessity of applying the shock. For example:

	Unconditional Stimulus	Unconditional Response
	Electric shock =	Pain/Anxiety/Fear

Conditional Stimulus	Unconditional Stimulus	Unconditional Response
Head banging +	Electric shock =	Pain/Anxiety/Fear

Conditional Stimulus		Conditional Response
Head banging	=	Pain/Anxiety/Fear

EVALUATION

Favell et al.'s (1982) special task force of 14 expert clinicians and researchers reviewed the research literature on self-injurious behaviour and concluded that 'Aversive electrical stimulation (informally termed shock) is the most widely researched and ... the most generally effective method of initially suppressing self-injury' (cited in Kendall and Hammen, 1995).

However:

- Although aversion therapy may be effective, it should only be used as a last resort in extreme cases that have not responded to other techniques, such as the use of restraints, behavioural modification and shaping through positive reinforcement, the withdrawal of positive stimuli, time-outs, etc.
- The costs of inflicting shock pain should be weighed against the potential damage of the self-harming behaviour (is it the lesser of two evils?).
- There are ethical objections to the use of negative stimuli on autistic patients, especially children.

BEHAVIOUR MODIFICATION

WHAT IS IT?

Behaviour modification refers to a range of techniques based on the operant conditioning principles of positive and negative reinforcement.

The aim is to increase the frequency of desirable behaviours by rewarding them with positive stimuli or by withdrawing negative stimuli, and to decrease undesirable behaviours by punishing them with negative stimuli or the removal of positive stimuli.

APPLICATION TO LANGUAGE TRAINING

Behaviour modification for language training can be effectively achieved through a combination of:

- *Behaviour shaping* – positively reinforcing successive approximations to the desired behaviour of language production in a step by step manner.
- *Selective positive reinforcement* – reinforcing desirable behaviour, e.g. a correctly pronounced word, with a rewarding stimulus, but withholding it if the behaviour is not shown. Rewarding stimuli can be found by looking for a behaviour a patient shows more frequently than others, presumably because they find it rewarding, e.g. eating, drawing.

For example, in language training, rewarding the first of the following steps, then withholding reward until the next step is achieved can shape language:

- **Making verbal sounds**
- **Making verbal sounds at the therapist's verbal prompt**
- **Making sounds closer to the therapist's verbal prompt**
- **Making sounds very similar to the therapist's prompt**
- **Using words exactly like the therapist's**
- **Using words only in the correct context.**

Lovaas gave intensive (40 hours a week, for over 2 years) individual behaviour modification training to nineteen very young autistic children. The aim was to first improve the imitation and following of verbal commands, then to shape fully appropriate language and academic skills, emotional expression, and play (with the goal of integration into normal education).

EVALUATION

Lovaas (1987) reported that 47% of autistic children given intensive behaviour modification were able to be placed in and complete first grade education (compared to 5% with only 10 hours training per week, and 0% with no training). However, there was no random assignment to groups in Lovaas's study, and:

- Progress is slow and time-consuming, and normal language is not always achieved.
- Treatment is more effective on high-functioning children and if started at a very young age.
- Long-lasting gains are often only maintained and generalised to situations outside the clinical setting if parents continue forms of behaviour modification at home. Parental training in such techniques has been shown to increase social responsiveness to parents and language production, and reduce aggression and tantrums. However, IQ, play with peers and stereotyped behaviour was unchanged (Howlin and Rutter, 1987, cited in Kendall and Hammen, 1995).

17.6 Psychodynamic concepts and mental health

FREUD AND THE CAUSES OF MENTAL HEALTH PROBLEMS

A number of Freudian psychoanalytic concepts have been applied to explain the origin of mental disorders:

- **Repression of traumatic events** – traumatic experiences, especially in childhood, may be repressed and become a later source of unconscious anxiety. Freud concluded that neurotics suffer from reminiscences (memories).
  Evidence – research on traumatic events leading to dissociative states like fugue (where people forget their previous life and start a new one) or multiple personality disorder (where a person may have different personalities that are unaware of each other's existence due to amnesic barriers) supports the possibility of repression and its effects.
- **Sublimation into somatic symptoms** – underlying anxiety may be symbolically expressed in physical symptoms as in hysteria. Hysteria, as it was understood in Freud's time was a medical term applied to patients who seemed to be suffering symptoms of disorder to the nervous system (e.g. pain or temporary paralysis or blindness), for which no *physical* neurological cause could be found.
  Evidence – Freud presents numerous case study examples of his patients' hysterical disorders as evidence, e.g. Anna O.
- **Regression** – the disorganised and delusional thinking of schizophrenia may result from a regression to a self absorbed state of 'narcissism' in the early oral stage where the irrational id dominates and there is no well developed ego to make contact with reality. Depression may also result from regression to an early state of dependency due to a loss in later life triggering the emotional effects of a more serious childhood loss.
  Evidence – many studies have supported the idea that early parental loss and childhood trauma are correlated with later mental disorder, but are not able to tell whether repression and regression are the causes.
- **Displacement** – unconscious anxiety may be displaced onto external symbolic objects and situations, resulting in phobias.
  Evidence – Freud regarded the case of Little Hans as good supporting evidence for this.

FREUD AND THE TREATMENT OF MENTAL HEALTH PROBLEMS

Traditional psychoanalytic therapy involves first identifying the unconscious source of disorder (such as the blockage of id impulses or the repression of traumatic experiences) and then trying to relieve the blockage by making the unconscious causes conscious. This is not easy since the patient is not only unaware of what is causing their problems, but will show resistance to the therapist's attempts to interpret them as the ego tries to maintain its defences.

1 **Identifying the problem** – Freud used three methods for un-rooting the unconscious causes of disorder:
- **Free association** – thought associations expressed from the client to the analyst without inhibition could contain clues regarding the source of unconscious anxiety. Pauses in, or drying up of, associations meant unconscious resistance was being met.
- **Dream analysis** – which Freud regarded as the 'royal road' to the unconscious. By unravelling the disguised symbolism of the manifest content of the dream (what was remembered), the latent content (what the dream actually meant) could be revealed.
- **Behaviour interpretation** – Freud believed that both normal (e.g. slips of the tongue) and abnormal behaviour were due to unconscious causes which could be carefully deduced from what people said and did – "He that has eyes to see and ears to hear may convince himself that no mortal can keep a secret. If the lips are silent, he chatters with his finger-tips; betrayal oozes out of him at every pore" (Freud 1901).

2 **Producing improvement** – this is achieved by:
- **Catharsis** – Freud originally thought that discharging the emotion (psychic energy) associated with repressed impulses or traumatic memories brought about improvement, but what seemed more important was that the unconscious conflict was brought out into the open for discussion. This is where transference is important.
- **Transference** – the process whereby unconscious feelings of love and hate are projected onto the analyst. These feelings provide a basis for identifying, accepting and discussing the analyst's interpretation of the problem.
- **Insight** – Freud regarded this as the crucial therapeutic element since it increases ego control over revealed unconscious causes.

JUNG AND THE CAUSES OF MENTAL HEALTH PROBLEMS

Jung generally agreed with Freud's interpretations of hysterical neuroses, but thought his theory of schizophrenia too incomplete. A number of Jung's analytical psychological concepts have also been applied to explain the origin of mental disorders:

- **Individuation and growth** – If a person is not able to proceed in their growth then neurosis will develop. Unlike Freud, Jung believed neurosis was caused by *present rather than past problems*, which only trigger memories of similar troubles from childhood as a result. Neuroses were even sometimes a result of the spirit of the times.
- **Balance** – Mental and behavioural disorder, like dreams and personality traits, are the result of *imbalance* in the psyche. Jung believed excessive introversion might lead to complete withdrawal from reality and schizophrenia, while excessive extraversion may lead to hysteria.
- **Compensation** – Since symptoms are the result of compensation, they can often be regarded as serving a *positive function*, indicating deficiencies and ways in which a more healthy and balanced set of behaviour or attitudes could be achieved in the future. Jung believed that even schizophrenic delusions were attempts of the mind to create new explanations of, or ways of seeing, the world.
- **Archetypes and complexes** – Since the self is not one personality but many, Jung saw the fragmentation of schizophrenic and dissociative disorders such as multiple personality as differing only in extreme (quantitatively not qualitatively) from 'normality' (a term Jung disliked). Problems may result from the imposition of complexes and archetypes, e.g. infatuation with a member of the opposite sex usually involves the projection of the archetypical anima or animus upon them, leading to an exaggerated view of their perfection.

JUNG AND THE TREATMENT OF MENTAL HEALTH PROBLEMS

Jung's therapy was more of a face-to-face (Freud sat out of his client's view, Jung sat opposite them), co-operative and joint process between therapist and client, both seeking answers to the problems. Analysis was less frequent, partly to ensure patients did not lose touch with their everyday lives, and aimed to restore balance and meaning to the client's life. Balance could be restored by bridging the gap between the conscious and unconscious through creative and imaginative activities (such as painting and play) or imaginary dialogues with archetypal figures, and by engaging in activities *opposite* to a dominant attitude (introversion/extraversion) or function (thinking, feeling, intuiting, etc.).

17.7 Traditional psychoanalysis

The debate over the effectiveness and appropriateness of psychodynamic therapies was first sparked off by criticisms of Freudian Psychoanalysis. Many attacks were made on Freud's underlying psychoanalytic theory and methodology, and this naturally led people to question whether a therapy based on such disputed foundations could be worthwhile. Since Freud developed his therapeutic techniques, many other psychodynamic therapists have developed their own variations of the therapy that often differ in important respects from traditional psychoanalysis, and all should not be tarred with the same brush. It is instructive, however, to look at some of the issues surrounding the debate over just how effective and appropriate Freud's therapy is, since the debate is more complicated than it appears.

WHAT ARE THE AIMS OF PSYCHOANALYSIS?

Aims – The notion of a cure, according to Freud, involves not merely eradicating symptoms but identifying the deeper, underlying unconscious mental causes of disorder and dealing with them as best as possible. However, since Freud regarded all humans as neurotic to some extent his notion of a cure was very modest, to 'turn neurotic misery into common unhappiness' by providing the client with more self-control – 'where id was, there shall ego be' (Freud, 1933). Freud discovered the unconscious causes of disorder by interpreting the symbolism of his clients' behaviour, dream reports and free associations. The process (cathartic and transference) of revealing the hidden causes of their behaviour and above all the insights Freud provided regarding them provided the relief of anxiety and ego control required to improve their condition.

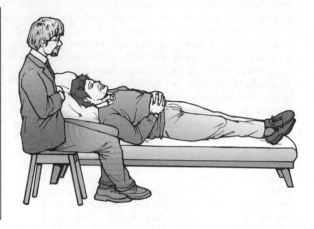

EFFECTIVENESS

Freud's own patients – It has been suggested (e.g. by Webster, 1995) that Breuer and Freud may have misdiagnosed their patients and that many who were supposedly cured through psychoanalysis, including Anna O, continued to show their symptoms after treatment by it. Some patients would have probably been classified as suffering from organic, physical disorders today, such as forms of epilepsy (Anna O), Tourette's Syndrome (Emmy von N, Freud's first hysterical patient treated by psychoanalysis) or even tumours (M-l, who died from a tumour of the stomach, had her stomach pains diagnosed as hysterical by Freud).

Criteria of success and the causes of psychoanalytic effectiveness
This is difficult to assess since psychoanalysis aims to change the unconscious processes that cause disturbed behaviour. However
1   unconscious progress may not always produce immediate observable changes (this affects the criteria and measurement of success)
2   unconscious changes can not be measured and may not be responsible for changes in behaviour.
Lacking an objective goal for therapeutic success, Freud's therapy essentially involved retrieving information about the patient until a cause could be found, but the only way the problem memories could be identified was when talking about them coincided with improvement in the patients symptoms. Freud stated "I accustomed myself to regarding as incomplete any story that brought about no therapeutic improvement". Since psychoanalysis took so long, the symptoms may have spontaneously recovered (disappeared on their own) and the 'story' being recalled at the time could just have been coincidental.

Effectiveness studies
Eysenck (1952) found that psychoanalytic therapy had lower success rates (44%) than alternative psychotherapies (64%) or spontaneous remission (72%). This finding has been hotly disputed, because of its very high spontaneous remission rate (some research suggests 30%) and criteria for success. When the criteria are changed, psychoanalytic success rates improve. A meta-analysis of general therapeutic success rates by Smith and Glass (1977) shows that psychoanalysis is more effective than no therapy at all for most people, but has slightly lower success rates than other therapies. Sloane et al (1975) found psychoanalysis was most effective for clients with less severe problems.

APPROPRIATENESS

Who can benefit? – Rather than asking 'should people undergo psychoanalysis?' a better question might be 'who should undergo psychoanalysis?' Freud applied psychoanalysis to a range of disorders such as hysteria, phobias and obsessive compulsive disorder (e.g. the 'Rat Man'), yet it seems more appropriate for minor neuroses and anxiety disorders, with more intelligent and articulate clients. Freud himself argued psychotic disorders could not be treated because they lacked insight and the ability to form transference attachments to the therapist (although psychoanalysis with schizophrenics has been attempted in combination with drug therapy). In addition free-association may be inappropriate for obsessive-compulsive patients and transference may encourage further dependency in depressed patients.

What are the costs and benefits? – Psychoanalysis offers a therapy distinct from most other therapies and, using certain criteria, can produce progress and self-reports of improvement (although the latter, as with all therapies, may just reflect the patients' and therapists' justification of the time and effort they have committed). In terms of costs, the need for long-term analysis makes psychoanalysis very expensive and time consuming, although shorter versions have been developed, e.g. Malan's Brief Focal Therapy. Ethically speaking psychoanalytic therapy can be distressing for the patient (some say it can be counter-productive for schizophrenics because of its emotional stress) although it is not the only therapy with negative side effects. In terms of therapist-patient power and control the therapy involves complete trust in the interpretations of the analyst. Because of the concept of unconscious resistance, the therapist may directly or indirectly discourage the patient's right to withdraw from therapy since refusing or leaving therapy could indicate ego defence to progress in uncovering hidden truths.

17.8 Psychotherapy – cognitive therapies

> **AIMS OF THERAPIES**
> To cure or alleviate the underlying mental causes of disorder by restructuring the maladaptive thought processes that are causing it. Cognitive therapies aim to alter the way people think about themselves and their environment, to prevent illogical or irrational thoughts and to enable thought to control behaviour and emotion. Cognitive therapists concentrate on current thinking.

TECHNIQUES

There are a variety of cognitive behavioural therapies that differ in technique and directiveness. All, however, aim to alter thought processes (the cognitive part) and monitor the effectiveness of this on everyday behaviour or in role play situations (the behaviour part).

Beck's cognitive restructuring therapy

Beck's therapy (Beck *et al.*, 1979) involves the identification and restructuring of faulty thinking as a collaborative process between the client and therapist. The therapist challenges the client's assumptions by gently pointing out errors in logic and contradictory evidence in their life and letting the client decide for themselves whether their thinking is accurate.

Ellis's rational emotive behaviour therapy

Ellis's therapy (Ellis, 1962) involves identifying generalised irrational and false beliefs (such as 'I must be successful at everything I do' or 'I must be liked by everyone') and forcibly persuading the client to change them, often through reality testing, to more rational beliefs.

Meichenbaum's self-instructional training

Meichenbaum (1975) assumes many problems are caused by negative, irrational and self-defeating inner dialogues – individuals may talk themselves into maladaptive behaviours with internal thoughts such as 'I can't do this' or 'something is going to go wrong'. The therapy identifies these maladaptive inner dialogues and gets the client to substitute them for better inner statements such as 'I can do this' by verbally repeating them until they become internalised, natural, and self guiding.

Kelly's personal construct therapy

Kelly's (1955) therapy is based upon his theory of personality. The client's personal constructs (ways of seeing the world) are identified through the use of the Repertory Grid technique and then altered or 'loosened' so they become more accurate or functional.

APPLICATION

Cognitive therapies have been applied to treat a variety of mental disorders including:

- **Depression** – Beck's therapy aims to correct the cognitive triad of negative thoughts about the self, the environment, and the future.
- **Anxiety disorders** – Beck's therapy and attribution training have been used to counter panic attacks and phobias.
- **Impulsive children** – Meichenbaum's self instructional training has been used to internalise dialogues of self-control.
- **Stress** – Meichenbaum has also applied his ideas to stress management in industry.
- **Schizophrenia** – Cognitive therapists, such as Beck, have even tried to help schizophrenics cope with, if not remove, their delusions and hallucinations.

EFFECTIVENESS

With depression, cognitive therapies have been shown to be just as effective as drug therapy – some studies have even reported higher success rates. Perhaps more importantly, lower relapse rates are gained if cognitive therapy is used in conjunction with medication.

Anxiety disorders also respond well to cognitive behavioural therapy although some research indicates that they are not superior to pure behavioural techniques, such as systematic desensitisation in some cases.

APPROPRIATENESS

Ellis's therapy is more forceful and directive than the others, but generally cognitive therapies aim to empower the patient with self-control strategies. Although cognitive behavioural therapies emphasise thought processes, they do tackle all aspects of a problem and are thus more complete in their approach. As Ellis's (1993) 'ABC' principle illustrates, many therapists assume that an activating event (A), such as being rejected for a job, directly causes an emotional consequence (C), low self-esteem. However, in reality it is often the intervening belief (B), such as 'I am suitable for all jobs', that is responsible for the emotional effect.

17.9 Difficulties assessing treatment

DIFFICULTIES ASSESSING EFFECTIVENESS

WHAT DO WE MEAN BY AN EFFECTIVE TREATMENT?

To consider how effective a treatment is, one must first define what its aim is. Some treatments aim to 'cure' the individual (e.g. flooding for phobias) while others seek only to alleviate or control the disorder (e.g. drugs for schizophrenia).

One major problem, however, is that different therapeutic approaches have different ideas about what constitutes a 'cure' – for behavioural therapists the removal of maladaptive responses may be sufficient, but for psychoanalysts an underlying unconscious solution must be found, regardless of current behaviour. Indeed, given Freud's quantitative views on abnormality, we may all be neurotic to some extent and so a cure may only involve 'reducing neurotic misery to common unhappiness'.

Relapse rates must also be considered when assessing effectiveness – how long should a cure last?

HOW DO WE KNOW WHEN WE HAVE CURED?

There are several difficulties involved in assessing when a treatment has been effective:

- Generalisability – an individual may appear cured in the controlled conditions of the clinician's place of work, but sometimes relapse will occur when the individual returns to the real world. For example, people exposed to token economy systems often do not generalise their improved behaviour, and alcoholics treated with aversion therapy often relapse when returned to public life.
- Monitoring effectiveness – who decides when a treatment has been effective – the therapist or the client? Both the therapist and the patient want to see success and may therefore make type one errors in assessment. The patient may show the 'hello-goodbye' effect, exaggerating their disorder at the beginning to ensure they are taken seriously, and exaggerating their recovery at the end of therapy out of gratitude. Psychometric tests used to monitor improvement may be unreliable.

HOW DO WE KNOW WHAT MADE THE INTERVENTION EFFECTIVE?

There are many factors, other than those the therapy intends, that could affect recovery, such as:

- spontaneous remission – many disorders disappear themselves, without any treatment and, in some cases, without reappearing again. Estimates of spontaneous recovery vary according to the disorder but overall it is generally thought to occur in around a third of all cases.
- mere attention – it has been suggested that just the increased attention and support from another can lead to improvement (the Hawthorne effect). In addition the expectation of recovery can cause self-fulfilling prophecy.

For the above reasons control groups are needed to test therapy effectiveness, e.g. using placebos in drug testing.

ETHICAL ISSUES OF INTERVENTION

TREATMENT VS. NO TREATMENT

The first ethical decision that has to be made, concerns whether treatment should be administered, given that:

- there is a chance that spontaneous remission will deal with around a third of all cases anyway.
- there are potentially many costs involved in intervention, such as money, time, and side-effects.
- some therapies, such as psychoanalysis, have been accused of being less successful than spontaneous remission.

POWER AND CONSENT

One of the most difficult ethical problems involves the issue of power in the therapist-patient relationship.

- Treatment may be enforced if the patient is sectioned under the Mental Health Act (1983).
- The choice of goals in some therapies is determined by the therapist or the norms of society, not the patient. This is especially relevant in psychoanalytic therapy where the patient has to accept the therapist's interpretation.
- The therapist may deem it necessary to discourage the patient from exercising their right to withdraw – for example when close to the unconscious 'truth' in psychoanalytic therapy, during flooding, or when forcibly restructuring thoughts and perceptions in rational emotive therapy.

SUFFERING VS. SUCCESS

Many therapies involve making decisions between success and suffering. Drugs and electroconvulsive therapies can cause many unpleasant side-effects or even death. However, their use could be potentially very beneficial – preventing greater suffering from the disorder or suicide (especially in cases of depression).

TESTING ON HUMANS

Many therapies have to be tested on humans rather than animals for validity. However,

- should patients be given new treatments whose mode of action is unknown? Even in the case of ECT, which has been used for many years, its reason for effectiveness is unknown.
- should patients be allocated to control groups with no treatment? Should not every patient have the right to the best treatment available?

CONFIDENTIALITY

Should the patient's disorder be made publicly known, given the stigmatising effects of labelling in our society?

17.10 Community care and counselling

CARE IN THE COMMUNITY
WHAT IS IT?

Care in the community involves providing treatment and support for those suffering from mental disorder under **more socially integrated**, naturalistic and less controlling conditions, rather than in long-term institutions, wherever possible.

While those with very serious disorders or those who represent a danger to themselves and others (see 'sectioning' under the Mental Health Act, 1983) may require round the clock care, support and control, others may benefit from varying degrees of these factors. Care in the community can therefore take the form of:

- **Short-term inpatient care** in local hospitals or **residential treatment programs** – these involve high degrees of support, control and/or therapy, but for shorter periods than in long-stay institutions.
- **Half-way houses**, **'family group' homes**, **night-care** or **sheltered housing** – these involve higher degrees of support and less official therapeutic measures, but are still tied to less socially integrated residential arrangements. Individuals can indulge in productive and everyday activities during the day, e.g. employment, but still live with others with mental health difficulties and access to support is usually on hand from health care staff.
- **Home care** (ideally with respite care arrangements), **day-care**, **outpatient therapy** at local hospitals or **drop-in centres** – these involve socially integrated independent residence or home residence with relatives, with some access to therapy.

THE ORIGIN AND DEVELOPMENT OF COMMUNITY CARE

Community care in Britain and the USA developed as a response to:
- the many problems of long-term institutionalisation for the mentally ill (see Rosenhan's 'On Being Sane in Insane Places' study)
- a humanistic questioning of the motives behind institutionalisation (e.g. who does it benefit – society or the mentally disordered?)
- financial pressures to find a more efficient use of tax-payers' money (institutions are supposedly more expensive to run, but of course this depends on the quality of community care provided).

In the USA the Joint Commission on Mental Illness and Health began an examination of state hospitals in 1955 and advised in 1961 that no more large institutions be built for the mentally disordered since their function seemed largely custodial rather than therapeutic. In 1963 President Kennedy advanced the Community Mental Health Centres Act that began to implement the Commission's recommendations.

In Britain the trend towards community care and deinstitutionalisation began later, with the first serious changes beginning in 1980 when long-stay institutions for the mentally disordered were phased out. In 1990, The Community Care Act put into legislation the idea that local authorities should be responsible for community care provision and should encourage private and voluntary agencies to provide domestic, day-care and respite care (for relatives looking after those with mental health problems) services.

EVALUATION OF COMMUNITY CARE
Advantages

- The therapeutic rationale for community care is that more normal living conditions and social integration will encourage greater independence, self-care skills, social skills, self-esteem, and 'normal' and productive interactions, activities, relationships and behaviour, compared to care in institutions.
- The various methods of community care can more flexibly meet individual needs and abilities since mental health problems differ in severity between individuals and over time. Work, friend and family relationships can be more readily maintained.

Disadvantages

- Problems are encountered in assessing, monitoring and financing individuals' mental health needs.
- The difficulties of diagnosing and treating mental disorders as well as insufficient government funding and local authority provision means some individuals may not receive all the support, control or therapy they need without the necessary contact with health professionals.
- Practically, stigmatisation and prejudice against the mentally disordered may make social integration difficult. This is not helped by media publicity of the comparatively rare cases where released mentally disturbed individuals have attacked or murdered others.
- Home care may become unbearably stressful for both relatives and the mentally disordered.
- The above problems may lead to patients dropping out of care/not taking medication and becoming homeless.

THE GROWTH OF COUNSELLING
WHAT IS IT?

According to Nelson-Jones (1982), counselling can be viewed as:

- **A helping relationship** – provided by a counsellor who creates 'core conditions' for therapy through certain skills and attitudes.
- **A set of activities or methods** – based on therapeutic principles derived from psychological theories.
- **An area of special therapeutic focus** – catering for the needs of the less seriously disturbed.

'Counselling psychology is an applied area of psychology which has the objective of helping people to live more effective and fulfilled lives. Its clientele tend to be not very seriously disturbed people in non-medical settings. Its concerns are those of the whole person in all areas of human psychological functioning, such as feeling and thinking, personal, marital and sexual relations, and work and recreational activity' (Nelson-Jones 1982).

THE ORIGIN AND DEVELOPMENT OF COUNSELLING

Counselling developed from *psychological approaches* (humanistic, psychodynamic and behavioural learning) that were strongly concerned with how the individual is influenced by, and adjusted to, their *social environment* (e.g. family, friends, partner and work relations). Counselling became more distinguished from clinical psychology and psychiatry in the USA and Britain with the establishment in 1947 of the American Psychological Association's 'Division of Counselling and Guidance' and the creation of the British Association of Counselling in 1977. It has become ever more prevalent and has been applied to marital, family, accident, bereavement and educational problems.

EVALUATION OF COUNSELLING
Advantages

Compared with clinical psychology, counselling psychology:

- Focuses more on *social contexts* and relationships rather than problems within individuals. Thus counselling may involve relatives and partners not just the individual with problems.
- Emphasises well-being and fulfilment rather than sickness and maladjustment – looking for what is right and how to use it, rather than what is wrong and how to treat it (Super, 1977).
- Is more proactive – it can be applied to prevent or limit the development of problems, e.g. trauma counselling, rather than just responding to already developed problems.

Limitations

- Not always suitable on its own for more severe mental disturbance.

18.1 The concept and measurement of stress

THE CONCEPT OF STRESS

The concept of stress has been viewed in different ways. Stress has been regarded as:

1 An *internal bodily response* – an essentially automatic biological *reaction* to external stimuli. This neglects the type of stimuli that causes the reaction.
2 An *external stimuli* that exerts a destructive force upon the organism. This neglects the fact that the same external stimuli will not always produce the same reaction.
3 An *interaction or transaction* between stimulus and response that depends upon *cognitive appraisal* of the situation – the stress reaction will only result if individuals *perceive* a mismatch between the demands of the situation and their ability to cope with it (regardless of actual demands and coping ability). This is currently the most common view and thus a widely used definition of stress is: 'A pattern of negative physiological states and psychological responses occurring in situations where people perceive threats to their well being which they may be unable to meet' Lazarus and Folkman (1984).

Stress can result from:
- changeable or continuous causes (e.g. life-events or steady occupational demands)
- predictable or unpredictable causes (e.g. depending on the experience of control)
- biological sources (e.g. disruption of bodily rhythms, illness, fatigue), social sources (e.g. interpersonal and work related), environmental sources (e.g. noise and pollution) or psychological causes (e.g. locus of control and personality type).

STRESSOR STIMULI
- Demanding situations (e.g. change, overwork)
- Negative external or internal stimuli (e.g. noise, illness)

COGNITIVE APPRAISAL
- Perception of situations/stimuli as stressful
- Perception of inability to cope with stressors (e.g. lack of control)

STRESS RESPONSE
- Physiological stress response (biological effects)
- Psychological stress response (emotional/behavioural effects)

THE MEASUREMENT OF STRESS

METHODS

Physiological measures
- *Monitoring machinery* – measures stress via its associated autonomic nervous system changes in heart rate and blood pressure, e.g. heart monitors, skin conductance polygraphs.
- *Biochemical testing* – e.g. blood and urine sample testing to measure changes in stress-related hormones, catecholamines (such as epinephrine) and corticosteroids (such as cortisol).

EVALUATION

- *Advantages* – these methods provide direct, reliable, objective and quantitative data on stress responses.
- *Disadvantages* – the methods are expensive, require specialist equipment/expertise, and ignore subjective perceptions ('positive' stress produces less cortisol). The measures can be affected by factors like caffeine or test anxiety (especially taking blood samples).

Self-report measures
- *Stressful life event scales* – measure stress retrospectively or prospectively via the amount of reported life change, e.g. Holmes & Rahe's Social Readjustment Rating Scale (SRRS).
- *Self-perception of stress* – measures subjective feelings of stress associated with negative or positive life events, e.g. Sarason et al.'s (1978) Life Experiences Survey (LES).

- *Advantages* – the SRRS provides a relatively quick measure of a variety of stressor stimuli and the LES takes into account the subjective cognitive appraisal.
- *Disadvantages* – while the LES overcomes some of the criticisms of the SRRS (see Change and stress), subjective measures may be unreliable, change over time, and confuse the causes and effects of stress.

Combined approaches
- *Interview schedules* – measure stress based on self-reports of events and feelings, but analysed and scored by a trained interviewer, e.g. Brown and Harris's (1978) Life Events and Difficulties Schedule (LEDS).
- *Behavioural indicators* – measure the frequency of events commonly associated with stress, e.g. in records of work absenteeism, illness and intake of stress-related medication.

- *Advantages* – introducing an external assessor in self-report interviews and behavioural indicators of stress aims to provide a more objective and complete measure of stress stimuli, perceptions and responses.
- *Disadvantages* – interview data can be more difficult to quantify and behavioural indicators are more indirect measures of stress (e.g. medication may be taken to avoid anticipated rather than actual stress).

18.2 Stress as a bodily response

THE BODY'S RESPONSE TO STRESS

The pituitary-adrenal system and sympathomedullary pathway

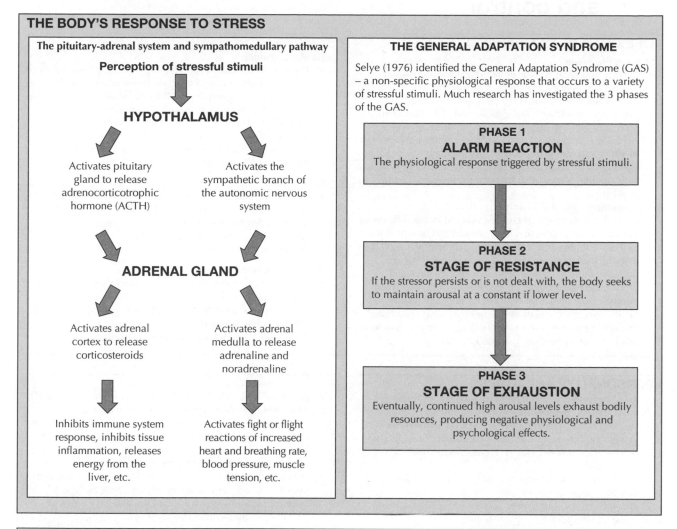

Perception of stressful stimuli

⬇

HYPOTHALAMUS

↙   ↘

Activates pituitary gland to release adrenocorticotrophic hormone (ACTH)

Activates the sympathetic branch of the autonomic nervous system

⬇   ⬇

ADRENAL GLAND

↘   ↘

Activates adrenal cortex to release corticosteroids

Activates adrenal medulla to release adrenaline and noradrenaline

⬇   ⬇

Inhibits immune system response, inhibits tissue inflammation, releases energy from the liver, etc.

Activates fight or flight reactions of increased heart and breathing rate, blood pressure, muscle tension, etc.

THE GENERAL ADAPTATION SYNDROME

Selye (1976) identified the General Adaptation Syndrome (GAS) – a non-specific physiological response that occurs to a variety of stressful stimuli. Much research has investigated the 3 phases of the GAS.

PHASE 1
ALARM REACTION
The physiological response triggered by stressful stimuli.

⬇

PHASE 2
STAGE OF RESISTANCE
If the stressor persists or is not dealt with, the body seeks to maintain arousal at a constant if lower level.

⬇

PHASE 3
STAGE OF EXHAUSTION
Eventually, continued high arousal levels exhaust bodily resources, producing negative physiological and psychological effects.

STRESS-RELATED ILLNESS AND THE IMMUNE SYSTEM

1 Physiological effects:

Stress has been associated with many illnesses, ranging from headaches (Gannon et al., 1987) and asthma (Miller and Strunk, 1979), to colds (Stone *et al.*, 1987), stomach ulcers (Brady, 1958), and cancer (Jacobs and Charles, 1980). This could be due to:

* **Reduced resistance to infection** – Studies on both animals and humans have shown that stress, especially in the long-term, can adversely affect the immune system as corticosteroids suppress its activity and thus increase vulnerability to infection. Cohen *et al.* (1993) found participants infected with a cold virus were more likely to develop colds if they had experienced higher levels of stress, negative emotions, and stressful life events in the last year. This finding is supported by Segerstrom and Miller's (2004) meta-analysis of nearly 300 studies on stress and the immune system which indicated long-term stress has been consistently shown to suppress human immune systems (cited in Green *et al.*, 2008).
* **Heart and circulatory disorders** – Stress-triggered increases in heart rate and blood pressure, as well as levels of glucose/fatty acids released into the blood stream, may result in the deterioration and blocking of blood vessels and thus increased cardiovascular disorder.
* **Stress-induced negative affect and behaviour** – Stress may also indirectly cause illness since it leads to unhealthy emotions (see opposite) and behaviour, e.g. lack of exercise, drinking, and smoking.

2 Psychological effects:

* **Anger and frustration** – Can cause a vicious circle of stress production as they contribute to a more stressful environment. Hostility may be a key stress-provoking factor in Type A behaviour.
* **Depression and helplessness** – Seligman (1975) found continual and unavoidable stress caused learned helplessness and depression, which would be inappropriately generalised to different situations.
* **Anxiety** – Different types of stressful situation can produce different types of anxiety disorder, e.g. persistent, irresolvable stress could lead to generalised anxiety disorder, whereas 'one-off' traumatic events could cause post-traumatic stress disorder.

18.3 Sources of stress – change, personality and control

LIFE CHANGE AS A CAUSE OF STRESS

Stressful life events

- Holmes and Rahe (1967) suggested that stress is caused by *change* and may lead to greater susceptibility to physical and mental health disorders. They compiled the 'Social Readjustment Rating Scale' (SRRS), a list of 43 life events, both 'positive' and 'negative', involving stressful change requiring re-adjustment, and rated them for their severity out of 100 (e.g. death of a spouse = 100, marriage = 50, change in school = 20, etc.). Scores of over 300 life change units in a year would represent a high risk for stress-related health problems.
- *Evaluation* – The SRRS has been criticised for its over-generalised approach. There are many individual differences in what events people find most stressful and how they react to them, e.g. for some a divorce may represent the end rather than the beginning of stress and divorces differ in their duration, difficulty, and extent of change. Positive and predictable changes may be less stressful than negative and unpredictable ones. The evidence for the scale relating to health is mostly correlational, illness may have contributed towards the development of stressful life events such as losing employment, rather than vice versa.

Hassles and uplifts

- The researchers Lazarus and Kanner have proposed that more *everyday problems or pleasant* occurrences are more likely to affect stress levels and health. They designed the 'Hassles and Uplifts Scale' to measure these incidents and their effects.
- *Evaluation* – The 'Hassles and Uplifts Scale' has proved a better predictor of health. Continuous diary monitoring of everyday stresses has enabled a causal link to be made with later illness (Stone *et al.*, 1987).

Catastrophic stress

- *Single traumatic events*, e.g. natural disasters, warfare, or violent assault can provoke long-lasting stress and health problems. Mental disorder classification systems term this Post-traumatic Stress Disorder (PTSD).
- *Evaluation* – see PTSD research in anxiety disorders.

Biological changes

- SRRS items relating to changing work and sleep patterns could cause stress through biological changes such as the desynchronisation of body rhythms with new zeitgebers (e.g. activity and light levels).
- *Evaluation* – see Shift work and jet lag research.

PERSONALITY AND STRESS

- Friedman and Rosenman (1974) argued that some people have '*Type A' personalities* that create and maintain higher levels of stress in their life styles. 'Type As are often more aggressive, competitive, driven, perfectionist, unwilling to delegate and impatient (than 'Type B' personalities who are the opposite).
- Kobasa (1979) suggests people with '*Hardy personalities*' are less vulnerable to the effects of stress because they have a greater sense of control over, and a more positive attitude towards, stressful events and a stronger sense of purpose.
- Rotter agrees that cognitive style, like a sense of control over stressful events (i.e. an internal rather than external *locus of control*) moderates the effects of stress.

- Rosenman *et al.* (1975) found in a 9-year study involving over 3,000 men that Type A personalities were more prone to suffer heart disease than Type B personalities. However, there is debate over whether the personality traits are a cause or result of stress, and which traits are the most important since some studies have not replicated Rosenman *et al.*'s results.
- Men and those from capitalist/individualistic cultures may be more socialised into aggressive and competitive Type A behaviour towards stressful situations, and have different coping styles and levels of social support.
- Type C personalities (who suppress emotion, e.g. anger) may be more prone to cancer, but the research is mixed.

CONTROL AND STRESS

- The perceived inability to control life event changes, everyday hassles, work schedules/deadlines, and unexpected traumatic events, etc. is a major cause of stress and consequent ill health.
- Weiss (1972) found rats that could *control* electric shocks were less likely to develop gastric ulceration than those who could not, despite receiving an identical number of shocks.
- Workers with little control at the bottom of organisational hierarchies are often found to suffer the most ill health from stress (e.g. Marmot *et al.* 1997) – see 'Stress at work', page 195.
- Rotter (1966) suggested that an 'external locus of control' leads people to think they have a lack of control over their lives and can result in less active coping strategies and greater stress-related illness. Even the illusion or possibility of control in humans can reduce the effects of stress. Feelings of control are thus important in increasing the perception that one has an ability to cope that is sufficient to match the demands of the situation (see 'The concept of stress', page 192). However, very high levels of control can also be stressful, especially when one is responsible for decisions and many choices are available – which may account for the executive stress of

some managers.

- Glass *et al.*'s (1969) study of predictability and control asked participants to work for 30 minutes on simple numerical and verbal tasks while being exposed to *no noise*, *soft* noise, or *loud* (108-decibel) noise. The study also manipulated whether the noise was:

1 *predictable* or unpredictable (random).

2 *controllable* by pressing a button (that they were asked not to do if possible) or uncontrollable.

The noise had little immediate effect on task performance and the physiological arousal provoked by the noise (measured via electrodes) decreased somewhat as the participants managed to adapt.

However, when the participants were then taken to a quiet room and given four puzzles (two of which were insoluble) and a proof reading task, those exposed to the *loud*, *unpredictable*, and *uncontrollable* noise had the *greatest stress after-effect* on *performance* – showing the least persistence on the puzzles (indicating increased frustration) and the most errors in proof reading (Hogg and Vaughan, 1995).

18.4 Sources of stress – stress at work

WHY STUDY STRESS AT WORK?
According to Frese (1998) 'Work is interesting because it can contribute not only to well-being (consider the fact that depressed unemployed people become well again, when they find a job) but also to ill health … . Stress at work is a major factor contributing to ill health, to human suffering and to productivity loss. Rosch and Pelletier (1989) have estimated the costs of stress at work to be US$150 billion in the USA because of increased absenteeism, diminished productivity, compensation claims, health insurance and medical expenses.'

WHAT CAUSES STRESS AT WORK?
Many *physical*, *organisational*, and *social* factors in the workplace can become sources of stress, usually exerting a relatively *long-term*, *stable*, and *chronic* influence. Work overload or underload, lack of control, role ambiguity or conflict, job insecurity or poor interpersonal relations at work may all contribute to distress, ill health and eventual burnout (physical, emotional and mental/attitudinal exhaustion, depersonalisation, and perceived inadequacy/low personal accomplishment).

WORK OVERLOAD/UNDERLOAD
Work overload or underload refers to the *demands* of a job in terms of its *workload*, *complexity* and *responsibilities*.
Work overload can be:
- *Quantitative* (too much to do in too little time), or
- *Qualitative* (the work itself is too demanding on cognitive and emotional abilities, e.g. requiring high levels of concentration, complexity or responsibility).

Stress often depends upon individuals perceiving a mismatch between the demands of the situation and their ability to cope with it, but not always. Work underload can also be:
- *Quantitative* (too little work to do in too much time), or
- *Qualitative* (the work itself is too undemanding on cognitive and emotional abilities, e.g. requiring too little concentration, complexity or responsibility).

The above factors may lead to a number of distressing physical, emotional and cognitive effects, e.g. exhaustion, frustration, fear, resentment, feelings of inadequacy, boredom, uselessness and low self-esteem.

Research evidence
Haynes and Feinleib (1980) compared working women, who had been employed outside the home for more than half their adult years, with housewives and men. They found that working women with children (high family and work demand) were more likely to develop coronary heart disease (CHD) – a tendency that increased with the number of children – whereas the incidence of CHD actually decreased with more children for housewives (cited in Gatchel *et al.*, 1989).

CONTROL
Control or job autonomy refers to the level of control workers have over the speed, nature and conditions of work. Control increases as the power to make work decisions and alter work conditions increases.
Control can cause stress if:
- There is far too little job control – the inability to control work schedules, deadlines, the pace of work or the organisation of work tasks is a major cause of stress. Workers with little control at the bottom of organisational hierarchies may therefore suffer the most ill health from stress.
- There is far too much job control – (see **Complexity and responsibility work overload**). Very high levels of control can also be stressful if decision responsibility and importance is extremely high and many choices are available, which may explain executive stress in the highest-ranking managers.

Feelings of control are important in increasing the perception that one has an ability to cope that is sufficient to match the demands of the situation.

Research evidence
Marmot *et al.* (1997) found civil service clerical and office support employees on the lowest grades were four times more likely to die of a heart attack than those on the most senior grades. They were also more likely to suffer from cancers, strokes and gastrointestinal disorders (cited in Eysenck and Flanagan, 2000). Marmot *et al.* identified lower levels of control triggering greater stress as the most important influencing factor.

SPECIFICALLY STRESSFUL OCCUPATIONS
The job strain model
Karasek *et al.* (1982) argues that a **combination** of **low levels of control** and **excessive workload** create **job strain**, which is particularly associated with *high levels* of job-related stress. An analysis of specifically stressful occupations reveals that job strain does result from a combination of work overload and low control.
- Medical personnel such as doctors and nurses have heavy workloads, high levels of responsibility and exposure to suffering, and are required to maintain high levels of concentration over many hours. Control is often lacking, particularly with regard to patient admissions (work rate) and variety of cases (work complexity) in accident and emergency departments, or relating to the ability to improve health in terminal patients.
- 'Production line workers' in factories or the catering industry (e.g. cooks and waiting personnel) may also be subjected to high workloads that that they are unable to control, such as machinery pace or influx of customer demands.

Research evidence
- Wolfgang (1988, cited in Cox, 2000), using self-report questionnaires, found the highest levels of stress to be among nurses.
- Karasek *et al.* (1979, cited in Huczynski and Buchanan, 1991) surveyed American and Swedish workers from a variety of occupations using questionnaires and found that stress was strongly associated with high workload and low job discretion (control) over how the work was done. Those in high-stress jobs with these characteristics included assembly workers, nurses' aids and orderlies, and telephone operators. The main symptoms were exhaustion, sleep problems, depression and anxiety, with a strong link between work stress and the consumption of tranquillisers and sleeping pills.
- Karasek *et al.* (1981) found the job strain model predicted cardiovascular disease and mortality in Swedish workers.
- Theorell *et al.* (1985, cited in Gatchel *et al.*, 1989) reported 'greater systolic blood pressure elevations among those in high demand-low control occupations (e.g. waiters, drivers and cooks) than among those in more controllable or less demanding settings'.

18.5 Managing and reducing stress 1

HOW CAN STRESS BE REDUCED?

1 DEAL WITH THE CAUSES
Those strategies that focus on removing or coping with stressful *stimuli* or *situations* before they produce a stress reaction are known as '**problem-focused strategies**'.

STRESS

2 DEAL WITH THE EFFECTS
Those strategies that focus on *removing* or *coping* with stress *reactions* once they have occurred are known as '**emotion-focused strategies**'.

Problem-focused strategies seem the preferable choice, but unfortunately:
* There are a huge variety of sources for stress, it may therefore be impossible to deal with them all.
* The individual may be unaware of the source of stress or may only realise after the stress reaction has occurred.
* Not all sources of stress can be avoided, some may be an inevitable part of living and working life, others may be mental worries that physical action cannot deal with.

People use a variety of coping strategies in everyday life; however, specific physiological and psychological techniques have also been developed to help individuals who feel unable to deal with sufficiently stress on their own. Most of these techniques are emotion-focused strategies, but some aim to incorporate elements of problem-focused strategy as well.

PSYCHODYNAMIC METHODS

Defence mechanisms – Freud would argue that many naturally-occurring methods of stress reduction are in fact the products of ego defence mechanisms (see Psychoanalytic theory), e.g.:
* *Sublimation* – stress-related emotional energy can be given cathartic release/expression in different forms, e.g. through laughter or physical exercise.
* *Displacement* – negative stressful emotions may be displaced as aggression towards scapegoats, e.g. in aggressive sports or shouting at blameless people, kicking doors, etc.
* *Repression* – causes of stress or its emotional effects may be pushed into the unconscious, although Freud argued this creates anxiety that could later reappear in other forms, e.g. psychosomatic symptoms or even dissociative disorders if long-term stress was experienced.
* *Denial* – a refusal to acknowledge/deal with causes of stress, e.g. patients denying illness or refusing to believe a diagnosis.
* *Regression* – resorting to childish strategies and behaviour typical of early stages of child development, e.g. crying, seeking attachment figures, and temper tantrums.
* *Rationalisation* – explaining away problems with justifying reasons or excuses, e.g. I'm not stressed, just tired.
* *Intellectualisation* – dealing with a stressor in an intellectual, emotionally-detached manner, e.g. regarding one's own illness as an abstract medical problem.

Evaluation
* Freudian defence mechanisms have not always been supported by empirical evidence. If psychodynamic defence mechanisms operate at an unconscious level as Freud suggests, then they are difficult to assess using self-report measures and to study objectively.
* Problems with emotional suppression, especially anger, have been associated with 'Type C' personalities and cancer-proneness, although the extent of the similarity with Freudian repression is debatable.
* Some defence mechanisms may only provide short-term solutions or relief while creating long-term problems (e.g. repression).
* Different defence mechanisms may be successful under different conditions, e.g. intellectualisation could be helpful under controllable, problem-focused conditions to help reduce stress causes.
* However, denial may be maladaptive under controllable problem-focused conditions (e.g. refusing to acknowledge signs of breast cancer that could be treated), but adaptive under uncontrollable emotion-focused conditions (e.g. once cancer is diagnosed and treated is being received).

BEHAVIOURAL METHODS

Biofeedback
* Feedback signals on body processes can help control the adverse autonomic physiological effects of stress, such as increased heart rate and blood pressure. Relaxation techniques are taught and individuals attempt to employ them while wired to machines that provide visual or auditory feedback on their success or failure at controlling functions such as heart rate, blood pressure, muscle tension, or respiration rate.
* Learning theorists suggest the feedback signals of control success/failure act as forms of operant conditioning reinforcement/punishment, allowing participants to gain some measure of voluntary control over these processes that will generalise to real-world settings without feedback signals.

Systematic desensitisation
* This has been used for certain stress-related conditions (see Behaviour therapy and phobias).

Evaluation
* Although there is debate over how it works (some suggest relaxation without feedback is just as effective and requires less equipment), biofeedback has been shown to lower heart rate and blood pressure.
* Biofeedback has no negative side effects, but does require equipment, motivation, and practice.
* However, biofeedback only treats the effects not the causes of stress.

18.6 Managing and reducing stress 2

COGNITIVE-BEHAVIOURAL THERAPY

Cognitive behavioural therapy (CBT) is based on the cognitive appraisal definition of stress and aims to change a person's perceptions and thoughts relating to, and strategies for dealing with, stressful situations.

Stress inoculation training (Meichenbaum, 1977) involves cognitive behavioural techniques designed to increase stress resistance through:

1   *Conceptualisation* – identifying the individual's sources of stress and their cognitive appraisals/misperceptions of, and current methods of dealing with, stressful situations.
2   *Skills training & rehearsal* – a range of problem-focused and emotion-focused skills and strategies are taught for dealing with the individual's:
   •   specific causes of stress, e.g. positive rather than self-defeating self-instructional statements, time-management or social skills, etc.
   •   stress effects/symptoms, e.g. relaxation techniques.
   These are practised under therapist supervision before the next stage.
3   *Real world application and follow-up* – acquired skills and strategies are applied in a sequence of increasingly stressful and varied realistic situations, with periodic follow-up sessions.

Hardiness training (Kobasa, 1986) aims to increase 'hardiness' by:
•   *Focusing* – learning to recognise the physical signs of stress.
•   *Reconstructing stressful situations* – analysing past stressful situations to consider different ways of viewing or dealing with stressors.
•   *Compensating through self-improvement* – performing manageable tasks to reinforce a sense of control in the face of unavoidable stressors.

Evaluation
•   Cognitive behavioural therapies are effective, although it is unsure whether the behavioural aspects (successfully dealing with a stressful situation) are more important than the cognitive ones (stress reducing statements or a sense of control).
•   Clarke *et al.* (1999) found CBT effective for treating stress reactions in panic disorders.
•   The techniques aim to deal with the source as well as the effects of stress and so are potentially more effective in the long term.
•   Cognitive therapies do not have the negative side effects of physiological methods, but are more time-consuming.

PHYSIOLOGICAL METHODS

Anti-stress drugs
•   Beta-blockers – act on the autonomic nervous system to reduce cardiovascular heart rate/blood pressure physiological stress arousal.
•   Anxiolytic drugs – benzodiazepines such as Valium increase the activity of the inhibitory neurotransmitter GABA in the brain.
•   Anti-depressant drugs – less often used, but can be appropriate for severe anxiety.

Other drugs
•   Alcohol is an often sought remedy for stress; its sedative effects slow down neural and bodily functions and its effect on loosening inhibitions can lead to cathartic behaviour.

Evaluation
•   Anxiolytic drugs can cause psychological and physical dependence, tolerance and withdrawal symptoms (*addiction*).
•   Many drugs have unpleasant *side effects*.
•   Drugs are only *short-term remedies* that temporarily reduce stress effects but may make dealing with its causes more difficult or even create further sources of stress (especially alcohol).

SOCIAL METHODS

Social support – individuals who perceive they have social support (e.g. reassurance, advice, and practical aid) suffer less physiological stress effects than those without such support, e.g. those with no intimate friends (Brown and Harris, 1978) or partners (Tache *et al.*, 1979).
Social support has been associated with increased resistance to and recovery from a very wide range of stressors and stress-related illnesses.
Other people may have either a direct or stress-buffering effect to help avoid or cope with stressors by providing (according to Wills, 1985, cited in Gatchel *et al.*, 1989) different kinds of social support:
•   *Esteem support* – by praising, comforting, or protecting our ego.
•   *Informational support* – by providing useful knowledge to help deal with stressors.
•   *Companionship support* – to increase positive stimulation and activities. Some research suggests social events like celebrations and friendly get-togethers can sometimes have a more positive effect on health than negative events have a negative effect, and that a decrease in positive events can have a worse effect than an increase in negative events (Baron and Byrne, 1997).
•   *Instrumental support* – by increasing physical aid, e.g. money.

Evaluation
•   It is *difficult to measure* social support since the quality as well as the number of friendship bonds is involved and self reports of friendship may be biased by socially desirability.
•   There are important *individual differences* in *willingness* (e.g. due to personality) and *ability* (e.g. due to modern living conditions, architecture in high-rise blocks, etc.) *to seek support*.
•   Social support may be more effective for social stressors (e.g. unemployment and bereavement) than environmental ones.
•   Social support is significantly *correlated* with lower mortality rates, but causation is difficult to determine.

19.1 Substance abuse

<table>
<tr>
<td colspan="2">

SHORT-TERM
Physiological and psychological effects of drugs

These refer to the *immediate* effects of the drug at different doses on:

- The brain – the inhibition or activation of neurotransmitters and brain areas.
- Subjective experience – how thoughts, feelings and perceptions are changed.
- Behaviour – how the person is likely to act.

</td>
<td colspan="1">

LONG-TERM
Physiological and psychological effects of drugs

Prolonged and excessive use of drugs (substance abuse) can lead to addiction (substance dependency). According to the DSM IV substance dependency is defined in terms of psychological dependency, either with or without physical dependency:

PHYSICAL DEPENDENCY – when the body adapts to a drug to the extent that it shows:

- **Tolerance** – increasing amounts of the substance are needed to achieve the same desired effect.
- **Withdrawal** – the body is affected when the substance is *not* taken. Abstinence causes severe and unpleasant physical and psychological symptoms (usually the reverse of the drug's effects) and a craving and compulsion to use the drug to relieve or avoid the withdrawal effects.

PSYCHOLOGICAL DEPENDENCY – occurs when the user feels and behaves as if the substance is necessary for their well being. Use of the drug is continued despite knowledge of its negative health or social consequences, despite efforts to reduce consumption, and even despite remission of physical dependency (it thus provokes relapse).

- **Relapse** – when substance use begins again after a period of abstinence or remission.

</td>
</tr>
<tr>
<td>

SHORT-TERM EFFECTS

ALCOHOL

- Physiological effects – possibly increases the inhibitory effects of the neurotransmitter GABA, first in the brain's inhibitory areas (thus suppressing their inhibitory effects on behaviour) then throughout the brain-depressing arousal centres, slowing cognitive functions and affecting movement and balance in the cerebellum.
- Psychological effects – lowers:
➤ Social inhibitions (facilitating behaviour such as sociability, enjoyment or aggression).
➤ Reaction time, co-ordination, memory and alertness (the overall depressant effect can increase sleepiness or anxious and depressive thinking).

</td>
<td>

DEPENDENCY AND TOLERANCE

- Physiological effects – long-term abuse produces many negative physical conditions, e.g. cirrhosis, memory loss, increased vulnerability to infection, physical dependence, increased tolerance (up to about 200%), and severe withdrawal symptoms. Physical dependency is fairly slow to develop, but repeated consumption of over 8 ounces of strong whisky a day is sometimes sufficient to produce addiction in humans (Davidson, 1985).
- Psychological effects – alcohol causes psychological dependence that can cause major disruption to normal social, occupational and recreational activities, depression, and increased risk of accidental death (of others too). It is estimated that more than 10% of all drinkers in the US abuse alcohol, more than half of whom may be physically dependent (Sarafino, 1994).

</td>
<td>

WITHDRAWAL AND RELAPSE

- After-effects of excessive use of alcohol are familiar to many (i.e. hangovers). However, abstinence for those highly physically dependent on alcohol can produce delirium tremens ('the DTs') – a withdrawal syndrome associated with intense anxiety, irritability, nausea, headaches, body tremors and frightening hallucinations. In severe cases death may result from withdrawal.
- The alcoholic will attempt to maintain the habit to avoid withdrawal symptoms, and the long-term psychological dependency produces strong cravings and impulses to drink (especially in social situations) when abstinence is attempted or remission experienced, leading to frequent relapse.

</td>
</tr>
<tr>
<td>

HEROIN

- Physiological effects – Heroin powerfully binds with the brain's natural pain-killing enkephalin and endorphin receptor sites due to its similar structure, then breaks down into morphine, which has similar but less powerful effects.
- Psychological effects – produces short-term but intense feelings of euphoria and pleasure, followed by longer-lasting pain-dulling and numbing effects.

</td>
<td>

- Physiological effects – single use may not result in addiction, but prolonged use quickly leads to physical dependence (due to the brain adapting and producing less of its own natural endorphins), intense withdrawal symptoms and the rapid development of extreme tolerance. Experienced users can tolerate up to 5000% of the dose tolerable by a naïve, first-time user (Kendall and Hammen, 1995). Sharing among users leads to an increased risk of death by overdose (due to differences in tolerance) and infection with HIV or hepatitis.
- Psychological effects – causes psychological dependence that can cause life disruption, increased and persistent anti-social behaviour to gain the drug in order to avoid the onset of withdrawal, and depression and anxiety.

</td>
<td>

- Abstinence for those physically dependent on heroin produces withdrawal symptoms within 6 to 8 hours of the last dose, typically peaking within 2 days and remitting within a week. Symptoms depend upon the tolerance reached (since the brain has been producing insufficient levels of natural pain killers) and include severe physical discomfort, diarrhoea, chills and goosebumps on the skin ('cold turkey') twitching of the extremities (e.g. kicking of legs), irritability, hallucinations and intense craving for the drug (Kendall and Hammen, 1995).
- When remission is experienced, relapse is fairly common.

</td>
</tr>
<tr>
<td>

Evaluation
The short-term effects of drugs may vary across individuals according to their body weight, personality, moods, expectations, and natural or acquired tolerance.

</td>
<td>

Evaluation
The potential for long-term use and abuse of drugs, and thus the severity of their physiological and psychological effects, depends upon many conditions and may vary across individuals (see **Social and psychological Factors affecting addiction**, next page).

</td>
<td>

Evaluation
The risk of relapse after withdrawal or physical dependency on alcohol or heroin:
- Decreases with age.
- Is triggered by high-risk situations, e.g. negative emotional states, social pressure, modelling of use or conflict.

</td>
</tr>
</table>

19.2 Models of addictive behaviour applied to smoking and gambling

BIOLOGICAL MODEL

INITIATION

Genetic vulnerability – some people may be more responsive to drugs or prone to develop addictive personalities or physiological dependency for genetic reasons. Silverstein *et al.* (1982) found biological factors may influence a person's first positive or negative experiences with cigarettes (e.g. nausea, choking), affecting their likelihood of becoming a smoker. If genetics play a role in gambling, it probably involves the inheritance of personality characteristics, e.g. extraversion, sensation-seeking.

MAINTENANCE

Physical/Psychological dependency – studies show a variety of drugs (including nicotine, e.g. Jarvik, 1979) have biologically addictive effects.

- T*he nicotine-titration model* (Schachter *et al.*, 1977) suggests smokers smoke to maintain a certain level of nicotine in their system.
- *The psychological tool model* (Ashton and Stepney, 1982) suggests biological effects also interact with psychological processes, e.g. the effects of nicotine on stress/attention levels or the adrenaline rush/social relaxation of different types of gambling act as rewards to maintain addictive behaviour – see the learning model below (Gatchel *et al.*, 1989).

RELAPSE

Withdrawal effects of drugs not only act to maintain addictions through negative reinforcement of avoidance of unpleasant stimuli, but also increase the likelihood of relapse in some cases, e.g.:

- Nicotine withdrawal is associated with increased irritability and weight gain (Grunberg, 1986).
- Gamblers miss the physiological/psychological rewards of stress reduction or excitement associated with gambling activities/situations.

However, many of the withdrawal effects are more psychological than physical with smoking or gambling than harder drugs like heroin.

COGNITIVE MODEL

INITIATION

Expectancies – Smith's (1980) *Perceived Effects Theory* argues that expectancies regarding the effects of psychoactive substances play a major role in the initiation, maintenance, and excessive use of drugs. Eiser *et al.* (1987) suggested veteran smokers transmit *positive expectations* about the effects of cigarettes to novices who might otherwise be put off by the first negative sensations. Casinos exploit the sight of others winning to encourage positive expectations about the success of gambling.

MAINTENANCE

Attributions – Eiser *et al.*'s (1987, cited in Durkin, 1995) study of 10,000 British adolescents indicated teenage smokers also acquired *expectations of addiction* from veteran smokers and had a greater external locus of control about their health compared to non-smokers.

Cognitive distortions and attribution have also been applied to the persistence of gambling behaviour in the face of repeated losses, e.g.:

- *Flexible attributions* – where gamblers attribute success to their skill, but failure to external influences, bad luck, etc.
- *Fixation on absolute frequency* – focusing on the total number rather than frequency of wins (and so ignoring losses).

RELAPSE

Attitudes/intentions/beliefs – many cognitive theories or models aim to explain failure to abstain from addictive behaviour, e.g.:

- *Locus of control* – those with an external locus of control may fail to take responsibility for changing their own behaviour.
- *Self-efficacy* – those with low self-efficacy may feel incapable of changing the addictive behaviour.
- *The Theory of Reasoned Action* – one's own or others' unhelpful beliefs and attitudes about the benefits of changing addictive behaviour may negatively affect the intention to do so.

LEARNING MODEL

INITIATION

Social learning theory – suggests children automatically learn addictive behaviours like alcohol drinking, smoking or gambling through the *observation* of influential *role models* (e.g. parents, peers, and media celebrities) and, because they often selectively see positive rather than negative *consequences* (e.g. fun, winning, and popularity rather than hangovers, illness, and debt), *vicarious reinforcement* may lead to the imitation of these behaviours.

MAINTENANCE

Operant conditioning – argues short-term pleasure from drugs (e.g. nicotine) or gambling, provides more *immediate positive reinforcement* (reward) than the *longer-term negative effects* (punishment), e.g. of illness, debt, and thus maintains addictive behaviour. Avoiding unpleasant withdrawal symptoms is a potent source of *negative reinforcement* for continued drug taking, while *variable ratio reinforcement* payout *schedules* may maintain gambling. *Tension Reduction Theory* (Conger, 1956) argues that drugs may help avoid stress or fear arousal (negative reinforcement), e.g. of social situations, by reducing inhibitions. Gambling may allow escape from unpleasant realities (Griffiths, 1991).

RELAPSE

Classical conditioning – suggests environmental cues present during the performance of addictive behaviour may become associated with the pleasure provided by the addiction (e.g. a bar may be associated with the pleasure from alcohol, smoking, and gambling on fruit machines). These cues may thereafter act as prompts, creating a craving for the addictive behaviour (see Classical conditioning) and are key factors in psychological dependence and relapse (e.g. walking back into a familiar bar or seeing a friend with a cigarette after giving up alcohol or nicotine).

19.3 'The role of cognitive bias and skill in fruit machine gambling'

Griffiths (1994)

INTRODUCTION

Previous research suggests that gamblers show many irrational cognitive biases that influence and maintain their gambling behaviour, e.g.:

- *The illusion of control* – an expectation of above probability success and perception of skill in chance betting conditions that involve an element of choice, familiarity, involvement, and/or competition.
- *Flexible attributions* – attributing chance successes as due to skill, but failures as due to external factors or 'near wins', often explained away with hindsight bias (e.g. saying 'I knew that would happen.').
- *Illusory correlates* – superstitious gambling behaviours resulting from the chance association of an unrelated behaviour with a past success.

Previous study by Griffiths indicated that regular fruit machine players *believe their gambling to be skilful* and even those who accept they will lose all their money in the long run (who play *with* rather than *for* money) aim to use 'skill' to stay on the machines as long as possible. Cognitive biases and the design of fruit machines (e.g. specialist play buttons that stimulate the illusion of control) may encourage this since pathological fruit machine gamblers show higher levels of skill belief.

AIMS

Griffiths aimed to investigate:

a whether fruit machine gambling *skill* is *real* or just *perceived* by comparing the *success* of regular versus non-regular gamblers

b the *cognitions* of regular and non-regular gamblers while gambling using the *thinking aloud method*

c subjective perceptions of skill through post-experimental semi-structured interviews.

In particular, he hypothesised that:

- There would be no significant differences between regular and non-regular gamblers on (7) objective measures of skill.
- More regular than non-regular gamblers would produce irrational verbalisations.
- More regular than non-regular gamblers would report skill use in the interview.

METHOD

Design
Natural experiment
Independent measures design

Independent variable:
Frequency of fruit machine gambling, tested in two conditions:

- Regular gamblers (gambled at least once a week)
- Non-regular gamblers (once a month or less).

Dependent variables:
Behavioural measures of gambling (7)

- Total number of plays
- Total time in minutes spent playing
- Play rate (total number of plays per minute)
- End stake (total number of ten pence pieces won)
- Wins (total number of wins)
- Win rate for time (total minutes between each win)
- Win rate for plays (total plays between each win).

Content analysis of thinking aloud verbalisations
A coding scheme of 31 categories of statements (including rational and irrational verbalisations) was intuitively constructed by the experimenter after collecting the 30 transcripts.

Post-experimental semi-structured interview of skill perception
Included questions: 'Is there any skill involved in playing fruit machines?' 'How skilful do you think you are compared with the average person?' and 'What skill (if any) is involved in playing fruit machines?' (First two questions answered on 5-point scales.)

Participants

- 30 regular gamblers; 29 male, 1 female (due to male dominance in fruit machine gambling); mean age 21.6 years.
- 30 non-regular gamblers; 15 male, 15 female; mean age 25.3.

Participants mostly recruited via poster advert at a local university.

Procedure
The study was conducted at a local amusement arcade using the same specified fruit machine (unless participants objected).

Each participant received £3 (the equivalent of 30 free gambles) and was asked to try to stay on the machine for a minimum of 60 gambles (to break even and win back the £3).

Any participant who succeeded in reaching 60 gambles had the choice of keeping the winnings or continuing to gamble.

All gamblers were randomly assigned to either a 'non-thinking aloud' group or a 'thinking aloud' group who had to continuously report everything that went through their minds as they gambled, even if seemed irrelevant or was in fragmented sentences.

Thinking aloud verbalisations were recorded via lapel microphone and transcribed within 24 hours so the experimenter could remember the correct context of the verbalisations.

RESULTS

- *Behavioural data on gambling success* – the null hypothesis was mostly supported at the required $p < 0.01$ level. Regular gamblers played faster and showed some skill to stay longer on the machines (at the $p < 0.05$ level), but did not differ in total winnings and were more likely to gamble until they lost all.
- *Content analysis of verbalisations* – regular gamblers made significantly more irrational verbalisations and personalised the machine at the required $p < 0.01$ level, and had a greater tendency to swear at the machine and explain away losses (at the $p < 0.05$ level).
- *Skill questions* – regular gamblers were more likely to attribute skill to gambling and change fruit machine.

DISCUSSION

- The experimenter concludes that, although some basic skill may be involved, regular gamblers 'believe their activity to be far more skilful than it actually is'. However, the author also acknowledges that 'it has yet to be ascertained fully which features of fruit machine gambling are truly skilful.'
- The regular gamblers' greater irrational verbalisations, skill attributions, and desire to change machines, all supported the use of cognitive biases such as the illusion of control. This has implications for cognitive rehabilitation therapy.
- The study was ethical (e.g. permission from volunteers) and controlled (e.g. mostly identical conditions, tape recording) and fairly ecologically valid, but the inter-rater reliability was low due to lack of context and gambling knowledge.

19.4 Vulnerability to addiction

HEREDITARY FACTORS

It is uncertain if individual dispositions for addiction are learned or inherited. A twin is twice as likely to become an alcoholic if an identical rather than non-identical twin is one, and adopted children are around four times more likely to become problem drinkers than other adoptees if their biological parents were alcoholics, regardless of the drinking habits of their adoptive parents (Sarafino, 1994).

Evaluation

- However, most addiction research indicates a complex interaction of biological and psychological causes; e.g. Heather and Robertson's (1997) review of alcohol addiction found that although there seems to be some genetic predisposition towards drinking patterns (especially chronic or teetotal rather than moderate/heavy use), methodological problems mean the relative influence of environmental and inherited metabolic or personality effects are difficult to assess (Marks et al., 2000).

PERSONALITY

People with certain behavioural traits may be more disposed to addiction, e.g. drug abusers have been found to be more rebellious, impulsive, and sensation-seeking than non-users (Stein et al., 1987).

Evaluation

Personality characteristics could be a cause rather than effect of drug use, however longitudinal studies have been conducted (e.g. Shedler and Block, 1990) that found those with poor impulse control, social alienation, and emotional distress at ages 7 and 11 were more likely to use marijuana once a week and have tried at least one other drug at age 18.

SELF-ESTEEM

A psychodynamic view suggests that addiction 'fills psychological holes' such as poor self-concept – an idea linked to the self-medication hypothesis. Khantzian (1997) has even suggested that certain drugs are chosen to gain or manage certain feelings.

Evaluation

- Greenberg et al. (1999) report a survey of college students who rated their personal levels of addiction to common substances (e.g. alcohol, cigarettes, caffeine, and chocolate) and activities (e.g. gambling or exercise), but found no relationship between negative self-esteem and high levels of addiction. However, they did not test people with serious dysfunctional addictions.
- Höfler et al. (1999) concluded that low self-esteem is just one of many correlates of cannabis use.
- Corte and Zucker's (2008) longitudinal prospective family study of alcoholism found negative self-schemas were a risk factor that predicted early drinking onset.

SOCIAL CONTEXT

Cultural norms, attitudes, and availability create the environment in which drug use is exposed, initiated, maintained, and abused. Social psychological processes such as conformity and in-group identities operate to transmit cultural norms of behaviour and positive or negative attitudes towards substances, e.g. the norms for drinking at parties or celebrations. However, differences in these factors will occur across different cultures, and within the same culture over time and at any one time (e.g. in sub-cultural groups).

Peer influence – Vaz (1967) pointed out how peer groups, especially adolescent ones, form cohesive sub-cultural units that operate away from adult/official supervision and may have norms regarding drug use that differ from the majority in society. Subtle competition in risk-taking behaviour (usually defined by defying social norms and laws) may result in 'peer pressure' to seek and experiment with drugs, often to excessive extents, to gain in-group prestige and status (Kendall and Hammen, 1995).

Evaluation

Sarafino (1994) reports a variety of supporting evidence for the role of social factors/peer influence in addiction:

- Leventhal et al. (1985) reported that adolescents typically tried their first cigarette in the company of peers and with peer encouragement, indicating modelling and peer pressure effects.
- Chassin et al.'s (1991) longitudinal questionnaire study found that smoking continued or increased in adolescents who: had at least one parent who smoked; had parents who were unconcerned about smoking; had siblings and friends who smoked; and/or had peer pressure or positive attitudes to smoking.

ATTRIBUTIONS

Expectancies and attributions about the positive effects of drugs can increase the desire to use them. However, Davies (1998) in his book The Myth of Addiction takes attribution theory one step further with his Theory of Functional Attributions by suggesting that the concept of addiction itself is an explanatory attribution rather than a true fact. He argues that 'people take drugs because they want to and because it makes sense for them to do so given the choices available, rather than because they are compelled to by the pharmacology of the drugs they take'.

Davies proposes that the attribution of 'I cannot stop' is not a statement of fact, but is based on the self-observation that the user reliably fails to do so, since once physical dependency dies out after withdrawal is complete any craving effects come from memory rather than physiological reward pathways in the brain. Davies adds that evidence for psychological 'addiction' is based on self-report information, which may be mistaken because the user still wants to indulge his habit, lacks the desire to make the decision to quit, and has made faulty attributions about 'addiction'. Furthermore, it becomes functional for addicts and external observers to attribute addiction to factors beyond the addict's control, but this removes a sense of personal power over the 'addiction' leading to a form of learned helplessness and feelings of lack of control that maintain 'addictive' behaviour.

Evaluation

- Wilson and Lawson (1976) found subjects who expected sexual arousal effects from alcohol did indeed show more arousal if they were given a placebo and told it was alcohol than if they received alcohol but were told it was only a placebo.
- Attributions of illusory perceived control and skill in random games of chance have been associated with pathological levels of gambling (Griffiths, 1990abc).

19.5 The role of the media in addictive behaviour

MEDIA SOURCES

Various media, such as:
- *television/film*
- *radio*
- *internet*
- *newspapers/magazines*
- *posters/billboards;*

provide various forms of influence, e.g.:
- *direct advertising*
- *product placement*
- *media portrayals/use/framing*
- *sponsorship products*
- *news discussion.*

MEDIA INFLUENCES

There is competition in media influence between:
- *Organisations which sell addictive products*, e.g. tobacco advertising (which could encourage initiation, maintenance, relapse, and brand switching in smoking) or government sponsored lottery advertising.

and
- *Health promoting organisations*, e.g. anti-smoking media advertising which seeks to encourage non-smokers not to start and smokers to quit, not relapse or not contribute to second-hand smoke effects.

THEORETICAL EFFECTS AND PATHWAYS

Possible advertising effects include:
- Encouraging experimentation with, and imitation of, addictive behaviour via provision of information, use of role models and reinforcement.
- Acting as cues/reminders to trigger existing addictive behaviour.
- Affecting motivation to quit or resume addictive behaviour.
- Increasing familiarity or prevalence of addictive behaviours or attitudes to them, thus affecting perceptions of social acceptability, normative use, and the dangers of addiction.
- Consolidating self-identities or group membership identities relating to the addictive behaviour.

MODIFYING INDIVIDUAL AND CONTEXTUAL VARIABLES

- **Age** – Pollay *et al.*'s (1996) study of youth and adult smoking surveys over a 20-year period found increased advertising of a brand increased teenage smoking three times more than adult smoking. Anti-smoking advertising also seems to be more effective on younger than older teenagers (Wakefield *et al.*, 2003).
- **Amount of addiction experience** – e.g. anti-smoking advertisements are more effective at preventing smoking initiation than making smokers quit.
- **Gender** – men and women may respond differently to adverts for addictive behaviours due to differences in levels of risk-taking.
- **Culture** – role models have to be salient to the targets since they vary in their importance and appeal among different populations.
- **Family and peer group** – the attitudes and behaviour of parents, siblings, and friends influence susceptibility to advertising effects.
- **Tastes** – advertising may just trigger the switching of brands rather than increase overall consumption.

RESEARCH ON MEDIA EFFECTS ON ADDICTIVE BEHAVIOUR

GAMBLING

Griffiths (2005) suggests the glamorous images of casino advertising and the strategies and pervasiveness of lottery publicity (e.g. in the UK) may be a situational factor in initiating gambling behaviour, particularly in low-income/working class families (who watch more television than, and in some studies bet three times as much as, middle class families).

Evaluation

Griffiths' review concludes there is too little empirical research to draw firm conclusions about the impact of advertising on gambling addiction, but cites some suggestive studies:
- Amey's (2001) gambling survey of 1,500 people in New Zealand found an association between gambling participation and recall of gambling advertising (although the direction of causation is unclear).
- Grant and Won Kim's (2001) study of 131 adult pathological gamblers in the US found 46% reported that TV, radio, and billboard adverts were a trigger to gamble (although this self-report data may be biased by attributions that justify their gambling behaviour).

SMOKING

Wakefield *et al.*'s (2003) literature review suggests that the media:
- both shapes and reflects social values about smoking.
- directly provides: new information about smoking to audiences, models who act as a source of observational learning and teenage imitation, and reinforcement for smoking or not smoking.
- promotes interpersonal discussion and influences 'intervening' behaviours that may make teenage smoking less likely.

Evaluation

Wakefield *et al.* (2003) cites many supporting studies, including:
- Cross-sectional studies showing that 'awareness, exposure and liking of cigarette advertising is associated with smoking status and smoking initiation among teenagers, and are independent of other predictors of smoking such as peer, sibling and parental smoking.'
- Longitudinal studies showing:
  - approval of cigarette advertising to be associated with non-smokers taking up smoking, and disapproval with smokers quitting smoking (Alexander *et al.*'s 1983 one-year study of 10– to 12-year-old schoolchildren).
  - self-reported advertising-induced urges to try smoking to be associated with taking up smoking one to two years later (Armstrong *et al.*, 1990).
  - brand-specific exposure to cigarette advertising in magazines to be correlated highly with brand of initiation among new smokers (Pucci and Siegel, 1999).
  - ownership of cigarette promotional items to be linked with later smoking initiation, especially of the promoted brand (Sargent *et al.*, 2000).

20.1 Intervention 1 – individual-based types of intervention

TYPES OF INTERVENTION
Sarafino (1994) outlines a variety of interventions, including:

AVERSION THERAPY
Aversion therapy involves associating unpleasant stimuli with the addictive behaviour via classical conditioning (see Behaviour therapy), e.g.:
- mild electric shocks with smoking
- nausea inducing drugs with alcohol.

More cognitive versions of aversion therapy involve *imagining* negative scenarios with the addictive substance.

Evaluation of effectiveness
- The use of Antabuse to treat alcohol addiction can be successful for some, but depends on the user continuing an unpleasant treatment and some studies have reported no greater effect than placebo treatment. Reviews of aversion therapy for smoking addiction have also produced mixed conclusions (Davison and Neale, 1996).

SELF-MANAGEMENT
Self-management strategies aim to increase an addict's control over the environmental conditions that maintain addictions, e.g.:
- Self-monitoring – noting contexts and cues to addiction.
- Stimulus control – removing the cues of addiction.
- Response substitution – replacing problem behaviours with positive or incompatible ones.
- Contingency contracting – creating firm conditions, rewards, and penalties for behaviour.

Evaluation of effectiveness
- Hester and Miller (1989) found evidence for the success of these techniques in alcohol addiction.
- It may be more effective with external supervision and support.

BIOLOGICAL TREATMENT
Biological treatments involve the use of drugs to counter the physical and/or psychological dependency of addiction, e.g.:
- Nicotine patches or chewing gum prescribed with a gradual tapering dose over three months to decrease cigarette withdrawal symptoms.
- Methadone to reduce heroin cravings in addicts.

Evaluation of effectiveness
- Double-blind studies show nicotine gum/patches can reduce withdrawal symptoms, but may substitute one dependency for another and produce short-term abstinence rates of less than 40%, indicating other methods are required in conjunction (Davison and Neale, 1996). Methadone also requires continued user motivation.

Modifying factors in intervention

LOCUS OF CONTROL (LoC)
- Locus of Control, (Rotter, 1966) refers to the attribution of responsibility for behaviour to internal or external sources.
- Those with an internal LoC who believe they can influence their addiction (e.g. through effort/willpower) are more likely to quit than those with an external LoC (who attribute the likelihood of giving up their addiction to the effects of drugs or the efficiency of their doctor).
- Some cognitive therapies aim to encourage the idea of an internal LoC.

Evaluation
- Davies (1998), in his book The Myth of Addiction, argues addict and society attributions of addiction to factors beyond the addict's control (external LoC) remove the sense of personal power and control necessary to change 'addictive' behaviour.
- Strickland (1978) reports that those with an internal LoC tend to be more successful in reducing cigarette smoking than those with an external LoC, although the relationship is not strong (Sarafino, 1994).

STAGES OF CHANGE MODEL
The Stages of Change part of the Transtheoretical Model (Prochaska *et al.*, 1992) suggests intervention must consider individuals' readiness to deal with their addiction at 5 stages of intentional behaviour change:
1 *Precontemplation* – never thought about, not seriously considering or against change in the next few months.
2 *Contemplation* – aware of the problem, considering change, but not ready to commit to action.
3 *Preparation* – plan to change in next month, but failed attempts to completely change in the past year.
4 *Action* – initiation of successful and active efforts to change behaviour.
5 *Maintenance* – work to maintain achieved change.
The model proposes that:
- Readiness reflects motivational and self-efficacy levels, which can be assessed through interviewing.
- Different people may need different types of intervention at different stages (e.g. self-efficacy training at stage 1, self-management at stage 5).
- Relapse is part of the process and people can cycle round the stages many times before they manage to quit (a 6th stage, 'termination', was later proposed).

Evaluation
DiClemente *et al.* (1991) confirmed the model's stage predictions for smoking cessation, but others have proposed different stages (e.g. Dijkstra *et al.* 1998).

SELF-EFFICACY
- Self-efficacy (Bandura, 1977) refers to a person's belief in their ability to succeed in tasks and cope with problems.
- Addicts who believe they are incapable of giving up their addictions do not even try to do so and failure to succeed can lower self-efficacy leading to repeated relapse.
- Cognitive behaviour therapies for addictions frequently aim to increase self-efficacy and the concept is a key part of the Stages of Change model and Theory of Planned Behaviour.

Evaluation
- DiClemente *et al.* (1985) found smokers at stage 1 of the Stages of Change Model believed they were incapable of kicking the habit so did not attempt to do so.
- Marlatt *et al.* (1995) indicate there is substantial evidence linking the development of self-efficacy with positive treatment outcomes, while Westerberg (1998) concluded that successful attempts and trying to be successful predict the eventual ability to overcome addiction (Pycroft, 2007).

20.2 Intervention 2 – public health interventions

HEALTH EDUCATION

Health education programmes aim to transmit information required to prevent (**social inoculation**) or change unhealthy behaviour such as addictions. The information provides **knowledge** about the positive and negative effects of health-related behaviour, health or social **skills**, and prompts or **reminders** for those who already know. Repeated prompts and reminders also help establish **social consensus** and so gradually change the norms of a society and encourage **conformity** to them. Different methods have been attempted to convey the information in the most effective manner possible to cause attitude and behavioural change:

MEDIA CAMPAIGNS

Media campaigns use the mass media to transmit health messages via television, radio, newspapers, etc. Media celebrities are sometimes used as role models to establish norms and encourage identification (which increases attention to, and imitation of, behaviour according to Social Learning Theory).

Evaluation of effectiveness
- Media campaigns have the advantage of reaching a wide number and variety of people, but have a more diffused impact.
- Flay (1987) says media campaigns help people avoid or stop smoking, but are more successful on those who already want to change.
- Wakefield *et al.* (2003) conclude that antismoking advertising can have a beneficial effect on teenage smoking, especially: combined with school interventions (doubling the effect), for younger teenagers, and to prevent rather stop smoking. They also cite Pechmann and Knight's (2002) experimental study showing that one antismoking advert was able to offset the impact of three cigarette adverts.

FEAR AROUSAL

Fear appeals that use frightening warnings about unhealthy behaviour to increase healthy behaviour may work by increasing:
- attention to the message
- cognitive dissonance (with incompatible attitudes/behaviour)
- negative reinforcement (to avoid unpleasant consequences).

Evaluation of effectiveness
- Advertisements which elicit strong emotional arousal, e.g. by graphically portraying adverse consequences of smoking, often rate highly among teens and adults, and are associated with increased intention not to smoke (Wakefield *et al.*, 2003).
- Janis (1984) suggests that different levels of fear may have different effects on different people in different situations or issues. Very high fear levels can thus sometimes interfere with message processing and cause denial or only short-term effects.
- Self and Rogers (1990) suggest fear arousal only works if people perceive they can do something about the situation (see Self-efficacy).

TARGETING RISK GROUPS

Direct advertising, or instruction, targets particular sections of the population at high risk of certain conditions and provides instruction or training on specific health behaviour.

Evaluation of effectiveness
- Targeting may have a greater effect because it is more individual (being specific to exact health needs and avoiding diffusion of responsibility effects) and provides greater opportunity for monitoring, evaluation, and reinforcement.
- Evans *et al.* (1981) employed social learning principles in an attempt to inoculate students against social influences to smoke and provide coping skills to aid refusal by using films and posters to explain the effects of peer, family, and media pressure and model ways of resisting. There was moderate success over 3 years in terms of reduced smoking and intentions to smoke in experimental compared to control groups (Gatchel *et al.*, 1989), but longer-term follow-ups find inoculation programme effects do not persist beyond 4 years (Flay *et al.*, 1989) so may require later booster sessions (Sarafino, 1994).

LEGISLATION

Legislation is designed to lower use of addictive substances by:
- banning their sale partially (e.g. through age limits, doctor prescriptions) or completely.
- reducing exposure to them by banning their advertising partially (e.g. in certain media only) or completely.
- penalising their use through taxation (e.g. making cigarettes more expensive).
- restricting their use (e.g. pub opening hours/smoking bans).

Evaluation of legislation effectiveness
- *Alcohol* – Griffiths (2005) points out that Chaloupka *et al.*'s (2002) review concluded that advertising bans can reduce alcohol consumption, but other thorough literature reviews such as Nelson's (2001) concluded that the evidence does not support 'a statistically significant or material effect of alcohol advertising bans'. Furthermore, Williams *et al.* (2005) found that increasing the price of alcohol seemed just as effective as banning campus alcohol advertising at reducing heavy student drinking. Saunders (1985) found an association between restrictive or liberalised alcohol legislation and levels of alcohol consumption and alcoholism in Finland.
- *Smoking* – Wakefield *et al.*'s (2003) review concludes that empirical evidence on the impact of tobacco advertising bans on smoking (including Saffer and Chaloupka's 2000 analysis of data from 22 countries from 1970 to 1992) indicates that complete advertising bans influence total cigarette consumption, but partial bans have little or no effect (Chaloupka and Warner, 2000) because the tobacco industry compensates for inability to advertise in one medium by transferring advertising to another.
- *Gambling* – Griffiths (2005) suggests there has been less empirical research on gambling bans, but draws attention to the US National Gambling Impact Study Commission's (1999) recommendation that government agencies should ban aggressive advertising strategies, especially those that target low-income neighbourhoods or youth.

20.3 Health promotion and the theory of reasoned action

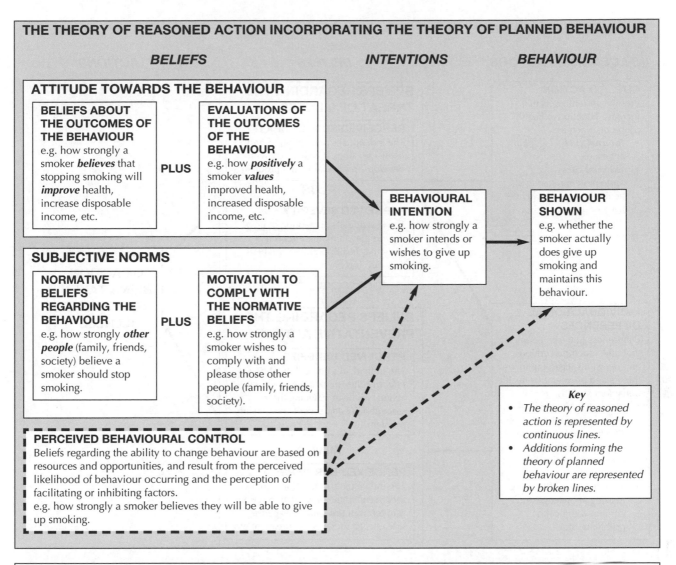

THE THEORY OF REASONED ACTION INCORPORATING THE THEORY OF PLANNED BEHAVIOUR

BELIEFS   *INTENTIONS*   *BEHAVIOUR*

ATTITUDE TOWARDS THE BEHAVIOUR

BELIEFS ABOUT THE OUTCOMES OF THE BEHAVIOUR
e.g. how strongly a smoker *believes* that stopping smoking will *improve* health, increase disposable income, etc.

PLUS

EVALUATIONS OF THE OUTCOMES OF THE BEHAVIOUR
e.g. how *positively* a smoker *values* improved health, increased disposable income, etc.

SUBJECTIVE NORMS

NORMATIVE BELIEFS REGARDING THE BEHAVIOUR
e.g. how strongly *other people* (family, friends, society) believe a smoker should stop smoking.

PLUS

MOTIVATION TO COMPLY WITH THE NORMATIVE BELIEFS
e.g. how strongly a smoker wishes to comply with and please those other people (family, friends, society).

BEHAVIOURAL INTENTION
e.g. how strongly a smoker intends or wishes to give up smoking.

BEHAVIOUR SHOWN
e.g. whether the smoker actually does give up smoking and maintains this behaviour.

PERCEIVED BEHAVIOURAL CONTROL
Beliefs regarding the ability to change behaviour are based on resources and opportunities, and result from the perceived likelihood of behaviour occurring and the perception of facilitating or inhibiting factors.
e.g. how strongly a smoker believes they will be able to give up smoking.

Key
- *The theory of reasoned action is represented by continuous lines.*
- *Additions forming the theory of planned behaviour are represented by broken lines.*

THE THEORY OF REASONED ACTION AND HEALTH
- The theory of reasoned action (Fishbein and Ajzen, 1975), later modified into the theory of planned behaviour (Ajzen, 1985, 1991), is another social cognition model that has been applied to health beliefs and behaviour.
- The theory suggests that health behaviours are based upon intentions, which are formed by a mixture of personal attitudes towards, and social pressure to adopt, a particular health behaviour. Based upon Bandura's (1977) work on self-efficacy, perceptions of the ability to actually implement behavioural changes are also important in explaining and predicting the likelihood that preventative health measures will be taken.
- Marks *et al.* (2000) report two particularly relevant studies.
  - Rise (1992) used a questionnaire based upon the theory of reasoned action to test the behavioural intentions of over a thousand 17–19-year-old Norwegians to use a condom during their next intercourse. Both attitudes and subjective norms were significantly positively correlated with behaviour intentions (0.29 and 0.55 respectively). However, a variable not included in the theory of reasoned action, past behaviour (previous/habitual condom use), was even more significantly positively correlated (at 0.75). This indicates that the theory is incomplete in explaining health behaviour.
  - Conner and Sparks (1995) supported this conclusion, reporting that while the variables of the theory of reasoned action accounted for between 43% and 46% of the variance in the intention to perform health related behaviour, and those of the theory of planned behaviour accounted for up to 50% of the variance, there is still a good deal of behavioural intention unaccounted for by these models. In addition, it must be remembered that intentions to behave in a certain way only correlate between 0.45 and 0.62 with actual behaviour.

EVALUATION OF SOCIAL COGNITION MODELS OF HEALTH BEHAVIOUR
The health belief model, theory of reasoned action and theory of planned behaviour are all regarded as social cognition models that aim to predict health-related behaviour from an analysis of people's beliefs and attitudes. They have been shown to explain and predict health behaviour to varying degrees of precision, however they have also been criticised on a number of grounds:
- They assume that behaviour is rationally thought out and regulated and so ignore the emotional, irrational and habitual influences upon health behaviour.
- They cannot sufficiently measure and incorporate all of the variables that influence health behaviours. These variables may differ depending upon the health behaviour concerned.
- They underestimate the role of external physical and social factors that are unpredictable and act to counteract or facilitate behavioural intentions, e.g. the variations in the availability of cigarettes and condoms.
- The measurement and testing of attitudes and intentions is based upon self-report techniques, which can lack reliability and validity.

20.4 Health promotion and the health belief model

THE HEALTH BELIEF MODEL OF MEDICAL HEALTH USE

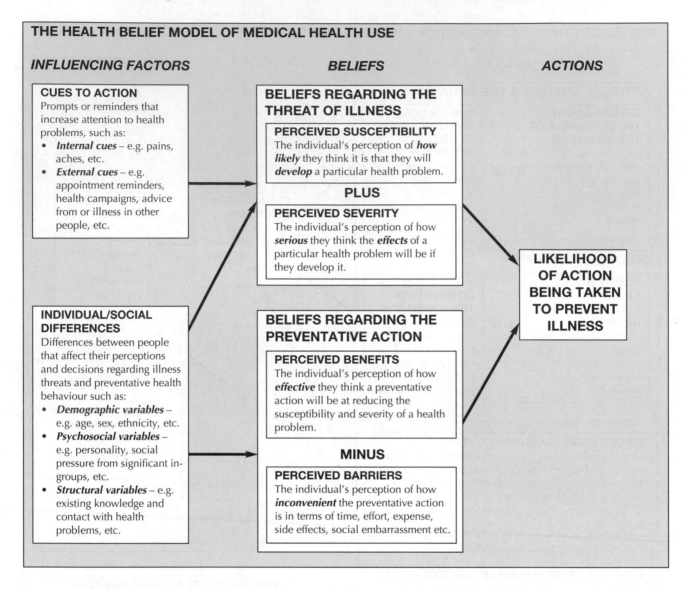

INFLUENCING FACTORS

CUES TO ACTION
Prompts or reminders that increase attention to health problems, such as:
- **Internal cues** – e.g. pains, aches, etc.
- **External cues** – e.g. appointment reminders, health campaigns, advice from or illness in other people, etc.

INDIVIDUAL/SOCIAL DIFFERENCES
Differences between people that affect their perceptions and decisions regarding illness threats and preventative health behaviour such as:
- **Demographic variables** – e.g. age, sex, ethnicity, etc.
- **Psychosocial variables** – e.g. personality, social pressure from significant in-groups, etc.
- **Structural variables** – e.g. existing knowledge and contact with health problems, etc.

BELIEFS

BELIEFS REGARDING THE THREAT OF ILLNESS

PERCEIVED SUSCEPTIBILITY
The individual's perception of **how likely** they think it is that they will **develop** a particular health problem.

PLUS

PERCEIVED SEVERITY
The individual's perception of how **serious** they think the **effects** of a particular health problem will be if they develop it.

BELIEFS REGARDING THE PREVENTATIVE ACTION

PERCEIVED BENEFITS
The individual's perception of how **effective** they think a preventative action will be at reducing the susceptibility and severity of a health problem.

MINUS

PERCEIVED BARRIERS
The individual's perception of how **inconvenient** the preventative action is in terms of time, effort, expense, side effects, social embarrassment etc.

ACTIONS

LIKELIHOOD OF ACTION BEING TAKEN TO PREVENT ILLNESS

THE HEALTH BELIEF MODEL
- The health belief model (Rosenstock, 1966, Becker and Rosenstock, 1984) helps explain and predict people's preventative health behaviour and compliance to medical advice. The model has undergone some elaboration over the years, for example by adding a general health motivation component – how important health in general is to the individual (not included above) – that has led some to argue that the model is increasingly hard to test.
- For example, the likelihood of people using a condom to prevent sexually transmitted diseases such as AIDS could depend upon factors such as:
  - How likely they think they are to acquire HIV and AIDS from unprotected sex with a particular individual.
  - How severe they believe the symptoms or risk of death from AIDS are.
  - How effective they think condoms are at preventing transmission of HIV.
  - How inconvenient they believe condoms are to use, e.g. in terms of reduced pleasure or remembering to carry them.
  - Whether they have been recently exposed to cues to action, e.g. AIDS awareness publicity campaigns or contact with those suffering from AIDS.
  - The nature of the person, e.g. their existing knowledge regarding AIDS or exposure to peer group social pressure or norms to use them.
- The health belief model has been applied to many preventative health behaviours and although each key variable does seem to be significantly correlated with the behaviour studied, they typically only account for around 10% of the variance in behaviour when combined (Marks *et al.*, 2000).

USING THE HEALTH BELIEF MODEL IN HEALTH PROMOTION
By specifying the factors involved in why people do or do not follow health advice and behaviour, health promoters can work out how to better implement their interventions. For example, health education on a particular topic may benefit from targeting certain:
- Perceptions (e.g. by providing clear, accurate and up-to-date information on the prevalence and effects of certain health problems and the prevention methods available).
- Populations (e.g. some populations may be less willing to adopt health behaviour or respond to different techniques).
- Medical procedures (e.g. providing postcard reminders for screening tests).
- Barriers to use (e.g. by challenging social embarrassment or providing social skills to negotiate the use of condoms between sexual partners).

20.5 Adherence to medical regimes

MEASURES OF NON-ADHERENCE

PHYSIOLOGICAL

Physiological measures conducted by medical professionals include:

- Biochemical blood or urine tests of prescribed medicine consumption.
- Physical outcome tests of health improvement, e.g. Lustmann et al. (2000) measured blood sugar levels for adherence to diabetes treatment.

Evaluation

- Testing for drug levels in the body provides limited snapshots that do not always reveal adherence to regularity or dosage instructions.
- Physiological sampling is time-consuming and expensive.
- Improvement in health may be the outcome of spontaneous recovery, e.g. Hays et al.'s (1994) four-year study of over 2,000 patients found adherence was not a good predictor of improved health (Russell, 2005).

SELF-REPORT

Asking patients if and how they adhere to treatment with interviews or questionnaires.

Evaluation

- The most common, easy, and economical method.
- Patients may lie, exaggerate, or be mistaken in their self-reports to please the doctor, avoid criticism or because they forget.
- Gordis et al. (1969) found reports of 83% adherence to antibiotic use, but 92% of urine samples showed no sign of the drug (Marks et al., 2000).
- Choo et al. (2001) found 21% of patients reported missing doses once or more a week, but electronic medication monitors showed the real figure was 42% (Legge et al., 2005).

BEHAVIOURAL

Observational methods include:

- Pharmacy prescription fulfilment.
- Pill counting – of untaken medicine or by electronic dispenser records.
- Doctor or family assessment

Evaluation

- More objective than self-reports.
- Patients may acquire medicine from the pharmacy, but not take it.
- Pill counting does not reveal if the correct dose was taken regularly.
- Deceptive patients may throw away medicine they are supposed to take, even if using electronic recording dispensers. Roth et al. (1970) found a disparity between adherence based on pill counts and blood drug levels in patients with peptic ulcers (Marks et al., 2000).
- Families are often more accurate in assessing adherence than doctors.

REASONS FOR NON-ADHERENCE

Researchers such as Meichenbaum and Turk (1987) have identified many reasons for non-adherence, including:

Patient factors

- *Personal characteristics* e.g. external locus of control, low self-efficacy, depression, personality traits.
- *Social characteristics* e.g. difficulty of life situation, poverty, and lack of social support.
- *Health beliefs* e.g. low perceived: illness threat, trust in doctor and convenience/effectiveness of treatment.

Evaluation

See Health Belief Model and Theory of Reasoned Action. McAuley (1993) found higher self-efficacy was linked to greater adherence to exercise programmes (Russell, 2005). Patient traits interact with doctor and treatment factors.

Doctor and treatment factors

- *Doctor communication style* – can result in the patient failing to: attend to, understand, believe, perceive as relevant and/or remember treatment information.
- *Doctor-patient relationship* – e.g. doctor-centred vs. patient-centred styles, status, perceived expertise.
- *Rational non-adherence* – patients deliberately choose not to adhere for reasons perceived as rational, e.g. due to the side effects, cost, or ineffectiveness of treatment.
- *Treatment requirements* – adherence can decrease with the length, complexity, and demands of treatments.

Evaluation

Ley's (1981) Model of Compliance research suggested adherence reflects patient satisfaction, which results from understanding and memory of medical information. Bulpitt (1988) found male patients did not adhere to hypertension medication due to side effects of impotence. Cramer et al. (1989) found daily dose complexity reduced adherence (88% for 1 dose, 77% for 3 doses, 39% for 4).

IMPROVING ADHERENCE

Many of the recommendations for improving adherence stem directly from research on reasons for non-adherence:

Consider individual differences

- *Treating depression* – Lustmann et al. (2000) treated the depression of diabetics and found their adherence to their diabetes treatment increased.
- I*ncrease social support* – involving family members may help since adherence increases with perceptions of social support (DiMatteo and DiNicola, 1982).
- *Evaluate health beliefs and perceptions* – including highlighting the seriousness of the illness and health dangers of non-adherence. This is difficult and time-consuming for a doctor to do in practice, but may save the costs of relapse and further appointments.

Communication improvement

- *Improve presentation of medical information* – e.g. stressing important information (improves recall by 15%), simplifying vital facts (raises recall by 13%), and presenting the most important information first (the primacy effect increases recall by 36%) based on studies by Ley (1972) and Bradshaw et al. (1975) (in Russell, 2005). Leaflets may compensate for the approximately 50% of facts forgotten after consultations.
- *Match doctor style to patient expectation* – see evaluating health belief and perceptions above.
- *Use motivational and cue techniques* – such as reinforcement, reminders, and alarms, e.g. Watt's (2003) study of the 'Funhaler' (an asthma inhaler for children incorporating a toy designed to increase the effectiveness of inhalation technique and motivation to follow treatment) found it improved adherence of use by 38% and of proper dosage by 60%.

21.1 Neural mechanisms involved in eating and satiation

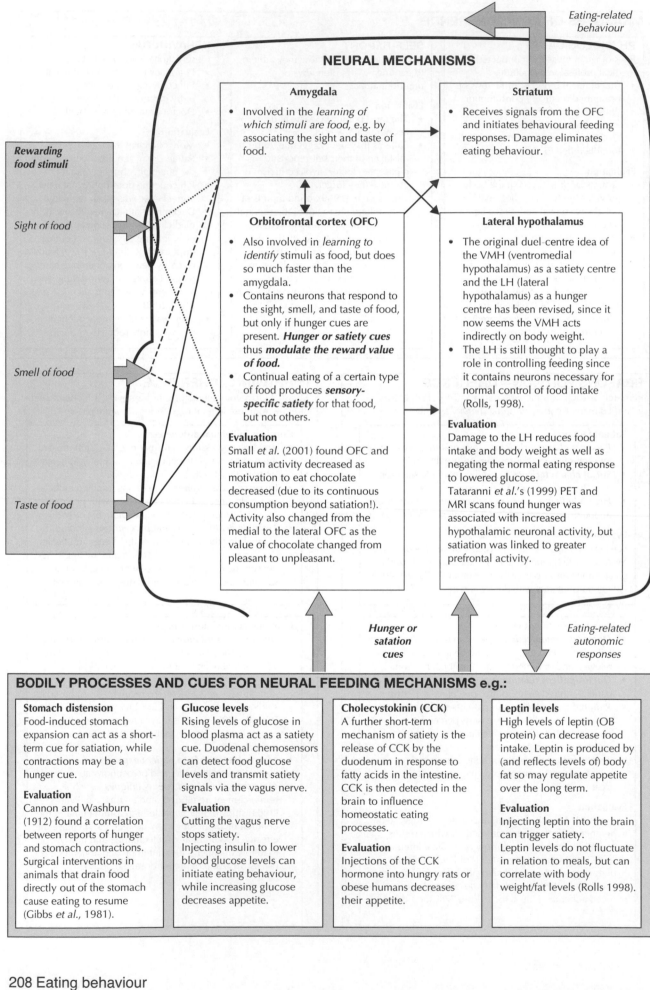

NEURAL MECHANISMS

Eating-related behaviour

Amygdala
- Involved in the *learning of which stimuli are food*, e.g. by associating the sight and taste of food.

Striatum
- Receives signals from the OFC and initiates behavioural feeding responses. Damage eliminates eating behaviour.

Rewarding food stimuli

Sight of food

Smell of food

Taste of food

Orbitofrontal cortex (OFC)
- Also involved in *learning to identify* stimuli as food, but does so much faster than the amygdala.
- Contains neurons that respond to the sight, smell, and taste of food, but only if hunger cues are present. **Hunger or satiety cues** thus **modulate the reward value of food.**
- Continual eating of a certain type of food produces **sensory-specific satiety** for that food, but not others.

Evaluation
Small *et al.* (2001) found OFC and striatum activity decreased as motivation to eat chocolate decreased (due to its continuous consumption beyond satiation!). Activity also changed from the medial to the lateral OFC as the value of chocolate changed from pleasant to unpleasant.

Lateral hypothalamus
- The original duel-centre idea of the VMH (ventromedial hypothalamus) as a satiety centre and the LH (lateral hypothalamus) as a hunger centre has been revised, since it now seems the VMH acts indirectly on body weight.
- The LH is still thought to play a role in controlling feeding since it contains neurons necessary for normal control of food intake (Rolls, 1998).

Evaluation
Damage to the LH reduces food intake and body weight as well as negating the normal eating response to lowered glucose.
Tataranni *et al.*'s (1999) PET and MRI scans found hunger was associated with increased hypothalamic neuronal activity, but satiation was linked to greater prefrontal activity.

Hunger or satation cues

Eating-related autonomic responses

BODILY PROCESSES AND CUES FOR NEURAL FEEDING MECHANISMS e.g.:

Stomach distension
Food-induced stomach expansion can act as a short-term cue for satiation, while contractions may be a hunger cue.

Evaluation
Cannon and Washburn (1912) found a correlation between reports of hunger and stomach contractions. Surgical interventions in animals that drain food directly out of the stomach cause eating to resume (Gibbs *et al.*, 1981).

Glucose levels
Rising levels of glucose in blood plasma act as a satiety cue. Duodenal chemosensors can detect food glucose levels and transmit satiety signals via the vagus nerve.

Evaluation
Cutting the vagus nerve stops satiety.
Injecting insulin to lower blood glucose levels can initiate eating behaviour, while increasing glucose decreases appetite.

Cholecystokinin (CCK)
A further short-term mechanism of satiety is the release of CCK by the duodenum in response to fatty acids in the intestine. CCK is then detected in the brain to influence homeostatic eating processes.

Evaluation
Injections of the CCK hormone into hungry rats or obese humans decreases their appetite.

Leptin levels
High levels of leptin (OB protein) can decrease food intake. Leptin is produced by (and reflects levels of) body fat so may regulate appetite over the long term.

Evaluation
Injecting leptin into the brain can trigger satiety.
Leptin levels do not fluctuate in relation to meals, but can correlate with body weight/fat levels (Rolls 1998).

21.2 Evolutionary explanations of food preference

EVOLUTION OF TASTE AVERSION

Humans and other animals are thought to have evolved an innate ability to more readily learn associations between taste and sickness/nausea than other associations that make less 'evolutionary sense' (e.g. between light/sound and sickness). Such rapid learning aids survival and increases fitness by helping to avoid poisonous, illness-causing foods – many of which taste bitter and repel us.

Evaluation

- Garcia et al. (1972) showed taste aversions in rats could be acquired in a single trial and with a delay of up to 24 hours between food consumption and illness, whereas traditional learning theory suggests many repetitions of associations occurring close together in time are needed.
- Taste aversions are acquired most easily with nauseous gastrointestinal illness (Pelchat and Rozin, 1982).
- Profet (1992) argued that the heightened taste aversions and nausea of pregnancy (morning) sickness evolved to protect the developing embryo from levels of toxins that would be harmful to organ development in the first trimester. Pregnancy sickness disappears when organ formation is complete and the foetus's main need is for energy for growth.

EVOLUTION OF TASTE PREFERENCES

Human taste preferences also serve evolutionary functions:

- **Sweetness** – to attract us to fruit and other foodstuffs that contain ready sources of energy-rich sugars.
- **Protein** – humans possess the unami taste receptor for amino acids and can develop protein cravings when on carbohydrate only diets.
- **Fat** – omnivorous humans have the adaptive ability to learn to prefer which of their wide variety of food sources contain high amounts of calories (Booth et al. 1982).
- **Sensory specific satiety** – to encourage us to eat a variety of foodstuffs to gain different nutrients and avoid over-consumption of any one food-based toxin.

Evaluation

- Neonates show distinct facial responses to sweet and bitter substances before any feeding experience (Steiner, 1979). Genes for different tastes have been identified and humans cross-culturally prefer sweet to bitter foods.
- Wurtman and Wurtman (1983) suggested food cravings for protein versus carbohydrates are balanced by brain chemistry, e.g. high carbohydrate diets raise serotonin levels and induce a craving for protein, presumably by heightening the reward value of unami taste.

Adaptations to variable food types

Evaluation

For food preferences to be evolved rather than learned they should be:

- Cross-culturally widespread.
- Ancient – due to slow evolutionary processes.
- Not better explained by commonsense discovery.

EVOLUTIONARY ADAPTATIONS

Evolutionary explanations focus on the ultimate functional origin of food preferences, suggesting that what and how much we prefer to eat is influenced by our nomadic hunter-gatherer ancestors' past adaptations to variability in food type/quality and availability/quantity in their environment.

Evaluation

Many food preferences are culturally determined or could be accidental by-products of other adaptations, e.g. some bitter-tasting drugs are liked as they contain molecules that trigger pleasant bodily processes.

Adaptations to variable food quantities

EVOLUTION AND OBESITY

Overeating today could result from evolutionary adaptations to survive past variability in environmental food levels, e.g.:

- The ability to efficiently store extra calories as body fat to survive in times of famine – is no longer so adaptive in Western societies with an abundance of food.
- The reward value of human taste preferences – the higher availability of calorie-rich, sugary foods, and flavourings, increases the reward value of food beyond that of our evolutionary past. Greater food variety and menu courses also reduce the limiting effect of sensory-specific satiety.

Evaluation

- Evidence for the reward value of chocolate comes from research indicating that naloxone (an opiate blocker also used to counter the effect of heroin) can reduce chocolate addiction. Many chocolate products also contain very high levels of fats and sugars.
- Monosodium glutamate (MSG) flavouring is added to foods to stimulate the perception of the unami receptors on the tongue, increasing the reward value of food.
- Fast food companies have been accused of contributing to the US obesity and diabetes epidemic due to the high sugar and fat levels in their products. The evolutionary environments of Pleistocene foragers were likely to contain few high-glycemic index foods (Logue, 2004).

EVOLUTION AND ANOREXIA

Guisinger's (2003) Adapted to Flee Famine Hypothesis of anorexia suggests genetically susceptible individuals who lose too much weight may trigger adaptive mechanisms that helped our evolutionary ancestors (thought to be nomadic foragers) leave environments that were depleted of food. Under these conditions, genes that favoured hyperactivity, compulsion to move, food restriction and starvation denial may have aided survival. These behavioural adaptations to falling fat levels persist today since they are still built into the brains of those who possess the genetic tendency.

Evaluation

- Guisinger suggested that the hypothesis accounts for the form of anorexia's symptoms, but not the initial motive or decision to diet in today's society – probably more due to culturally-produced desires to be thin. The hypothesis also has implications for anorexia therapies.
- However, the hypothesis is perhaps less convincing in explaining why anorexia affects young *adolescent women* the most, causing loss of fertility, continued restriction of food when it is easily available, and serious risk of death if untreated – all of which lower fitness and the ability to pass on genes. Guisinger suggests greater social support to overcome anorexia existed in the past and kin selection could help account for this self-destructive disorder.

21.3 Factors influencing attitudes to food and eating behaviour

CULTURAL INFLUENCES

Cultural differences in *diet, eating patterns,* and *body image expectations* can influence children's acquisition of attitudes towards food and eating behaviour through:

* *Mere exposure* – individuals' acquire preferences as a result of experience. Sociocultural factors have a major influence on the tastes children acquire for foods (Birch, 1989; Rozin, 1989; Schutz and Diaz-Knauf, 1989). Children receive certain foods, but not others, depending on cultural and economic conditions – and simply being exposed to a food may increase a person's liking of it' (Sarafino, 1994).
* *Classical conditioning association* – some fast food restaurants have been accused of trying to addict children to their products at an early age by associating them not only with positive stimuli such as sugar, but also with fun toys, games, and play areas.
* *Social learning theory* – observation, vicarious reinforcement and imitation also affect food attitudes and behaviour. 'Children also observe in person and through television commercials how other people respond to food and tend to become more attracted to it if they see others eat it and like it' (Sarafino, 1994).
* *Social comparison and identification theories* – due to cultural exposure to body size values and important media models (see Explanatory theories of eating disorders).

Evaluation
* Junk food adverts in the U.K. have been banned from television when programmes aimed at young children are being shown (since 2007).
* Giles (2003) reports studies showing magazine reading was the best predictor of body dissatisfaction among undergraduate women (Harrison and Cantor, 1997), whereas magazine reading, music video watching, and soap opera viewing were the best predictors for adolescent girls (Tiggemann and Pickering (1996).

MOOD INFLUENCES
* The immediate pleasurable and positive mood-enhancing effects of eating derive from the taste neurons, e.g. of the orbitofrontal cortex, which are involved in the reward value of food stimuli, based on the body's level of hunger (reward value and pleasure are high when extremely hungry, but decrease with satiation).
* 'Comfort eating', especially of sugar- and fat-rich carbohydrate foods, such as milk chocolate, may overcome the negative moods of irritability, anxiety, and depression by raising serotonin levels in the brain.

Evaluation
* Drugs that increase serotonin neurotransmitter levels in the brain can suppress food cravings and reduce depression.
* Wurtman and Wurtman (1983) suggested the carbohydrate food cravings associated with PMS and Seasonal Affective Disorder are caused or aggravated by insufficient serotonin in the brain (Logue, 2004).

HEALTH CONCERNS

Attitudes and behavioural responses to a wide variety of food-related health concerns, from warnings of the dangers of red meat or high sugar levels to public health promotions designed to increase fruit and vegetable intake, are modelled by:

* *The Health Belief Model* – for example, working out the likelihood of someone avoiding a food product such as sugar by:
  ➤ evaluating the perceived *susceptibility* and *severity* of the threat from eating a food (e.g. how likely they think it is that they will develop diabetes and the seriousness of the disorder)
  ➤ while also taking into account the perceived *benefits* minus the *barriers* to action of doing so (e.g. how effective sugar reduction will be at avoiding diabetes versus the inconvenience of giving up sweet foods).
* *The Theory of Reasoned Action* – e.g., calculating individuals' intentions to eat something in terms of their own attitudes towards the food as well as the attitudes of other people towards one's consumption of that food.
* *The Theory of Planned Behaviour* – e.g., assessing individuals' perceived behavioural control over their eating behaviour (e.g. how much do they believe they can be successful at dieting given their lifestyle, motivation, self-efficacy, etc.).

Evaluation
* See Health and the Theory of Reasoned Action/Health and the Health Belief Model.

21.4 Explanations of dieting success or failure

METHOD OF DIETING FACTORS

RESTRICTION OF FOOD QUANTITY

Abrupt and dramatic restriction of calorie intake can lead to rapid weight loss, but with a greater likelihood of regaining weight and negative side effects than a gradual, long-term reduction to sensible portions.

RESTRICTION OF FOOD TYPE

Some diets specifically eliminate or focus on a food type, e.g. low fat diets, carbohydrate or protein only diets. Different methods have different strengths and weaknesses, especially for different people, e.g. Nordmann *et al.*'s (2006) meta-analysis found low-carbohydrate, non-energy-restricted diets appeared to be at least as effective as low-fat, energy-restricted diets in inducing weight loss for up to 1 year, but also produced changes in different types of cholesterol.

WEIGHT-LOSS GROUPS

Work by providing:
- social support and motivation
- dieting methods/information
- external monitoring.

Workplace dieting schemes are sometimes more effective than voluntary groups because of the greater regularity of monitoring, social pressure, and difficulties in dropping-out.

SELF-MONITORING

Behavioural self-monitoring and contingency management methods work by controlling environmental eating cues and reinforcement. Hollis *et al.* (2008) found dieters who kept a food diary of what they ate lost twice as much weight as those who did not.

Evaluation

- Problems assessing success – success rates are often affected by sample attrition (drop-out) or self-report bias.
- Individual differences – different methods may be effective with different people, e.g. weight-loss groups for those with an external locus of control, but self-monitoring for dieters with an internal LoC.
- Exercise – combined with diet increases effectiveness (muscle burns more calories than fat).
- Medical intervention – in some cases, e.g. life-threatening diabetes, appetite suppressants or surgery (gastric bypass/stomach reduction) may be required.
- Combining methods – Wing and Phelan (2005) found weight loss maintenance was associated with high levels of physical activity, eating a low-calorie, low-fat diet, eating breakfast regularly, self-monitoring of weight, and consistent eating patterns across weekdays/weekends.

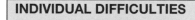

DIETING SUCCESS OR FAILURE

Wing and Phelan (2005) reported that only 20% of those who lose 10% of their body weight are able to maintain that loss for a full year. There are many possible reasons why.

THEORETICAL MODELS

The Health Belief Model and Theory of Reasoned Action can be applied to dieting success or failure.

GENERAL DIFFICULTIES

PHYSIOLOGICAL DIFFICULTIES

Once weight is acquired it becomes difficult to lose because:
- Fat cells increase in size and number with weight gain, but only decrease in size, not number, thereafter (Brownell, 1982).
- Fat tissue is less metabolically active than lean tissue, thus lowering metabolic activity and making weight loss more difficult (Sarafino, 1994).

EVOLUTIONARY FACTORS

The greater availability and tastiness of food today, combined with an efficient evolutionary tendency to store extra energy as fat makes weight loss difficult in general (see Evolution and obesity).

However, some studies show little difference in food intake between the obese and non-obese, indicating individual factors are involved.

INDIVIDUAL DIFFICULTIES

GENETIC FACTORS

Monozygotic twins raised together or apart show greater overweight concordance than non-identical twins, and adoption studies show a child's overweight correlates better with biological than adoptive parents (Stunkard *et al.* 1986, in Sarafino, 1994). Some diets could fail due to inherited disorders of satiety indicators, e.g. lower leptin production/sensitivity.

PHYSIOLOGICAL FACTORS

Endocrine problems can cause weight gain, making dieting difficult, but these are relatively rare (Robinson and Lawler, 1977).

Individual set-point theory suggests each body strives to maintain a set body weight by homeostasis so that lower food intake initiates hunger signals for compensatory eating until the set-point is re-attained. Set-points may be influenced by genetics or early eating patterns.

PSYCHOLOGICAL FACTORS

Restraint theory suggests restrained eaters, who constantly worry about and resist eating what they want to, are more likely to break their strict diets with binge eating because any minor violation triggers disinhibition – the perception that they have lost control so might as well overindulge (Sarafino *et al.*, 1994). Successful diets require long-term balance.

LIFESTYLE FACTORS

Dieting success is also affected by environmental conditions, such as:
- Activity patterns at work/home, e.g. commuting methods, desk jobs, amount of TV watched.
- Stress, anxiety, and depression.
- Eating patterns, e.g. snacking between meals, heavy meals at night, alcohol consumption.

21.5 Eating disorders – symptoms and diagnosis

BACKGROUND

Eating disorders like anorexia and bulimia are fairly recent arrivals to the classification manuals – appearing for the first time in the DSM III in 1980. There is debate over whether these disorders have always existed, but what is certain is that they have increased in prevalence in recent years. This could be due to increasing media publicity drawing attention to the disorder and thus making referral and diagnosis more common, or due to the media actually influencing the increase in the frequency of the disorder (see theories). These disorders are ten times more common in women than men and often occur together in the same individual.

ANOREXIA NERVOSA

DIAGNOSIS: 'Anorexia' comes from the Greek term for 'loss of appetite' and involves problems maintaining a normal body weight.
The DSM IV states that the four symptoms below must be shown for the classification to be made.
The DSM IV also suggests two sub-types:
The 'restricting type' maintains low body weight by refusing to eat and/or indulging in frequent exercise.
The 'binge-eating/purging type' maintains low body weight by refusing to eat in combination with bingeing and purging (like bulimia below but usually less frequently)
PREVALENCE – 0.5 – 1% of females in adolescence to early adulthood.

BEHAVIOURAL SYMPTOMS
1 A refusal to maintain a body weight normal for age and height (weight itself is less than 85% of that expected).

COGNITIVE SYMPTOMS
2 Distorted self-perception of body shape (over-estimation of body size) and over-emphasis of its importance for self-esteem. Denial of seriousness of weight loss.

EMOTIONAL SYMPTOMS
3 An intense fear of gaining weight even though obviously under-weight.

SOMATIC SYMPTOMS
4 Loss of body weight and absence of menstruation for 3 consecutive months.

BULIMIA NERVOSA

DIAGNOSIS: 'Bulimia' is derived from the Greek for 'ox appetite' and involves binge eating followed by compensatory behaviour to rid the body of what has just been consumed.
The DSM IV states that the symptoms opposite must be shown for the classification to be made, and includes a 'non-purging' subtype who binges but uses excessive physical exercise instead of purging to compensate.
PREVALENCE – Around 1–3% of females in adolescence to early adulthood.

BEHAVIOURAL SYMPTOMS
1 Recurring binge eating – excessive quantities consumed within a discrete period of time (e.g. 2 hours) without a sense of control over what or how much is consumed.
2 Recurring inappropriate compensatory behaviour to prevent weight gain – such as self-induced vomiting, misuse of laxatives or fasting.
3 Binge eating and compensatory behaviours occur on average at least twice a week for three months.

COGNITIVE SYMPTOMS
4 Self-image is overly influenced by body size and shape.

HOW SIMILAR ARE THE TWO DISORDERS?

- The main differences are that bulimia sufferers usually maintain their weight within the normal range (although bulimia causes much other damage to their bodies) and, despite some anorexia sufferers being obsessed with food and reporting hunger, bulimia involves an urge to overeat that often causes bingeing long before purging and other methods are used as compensations.
- However, some researchers think anorexia and bulimia should be thought of as two variants of the same disorder, since they have many features in common, are often both found in the same person (anorexia can progress to bulimia with age), and have similar theories provided to explain them.

21.6 Explanatory theories of eating disorders

BIOLOGICAL THEORIES

PSYCHOLOGICAL THEORIES

Genetics

Family studies have shown that there is a higher risk of developing anorexia or bulimia if a first-degree relative suffers from it, while monozygotic (MZ) twin concordance studies have suggested there may be a stronger genetic link with anorexia than bulimia.

Holland et al (1984) found the likelihood of one identical (*MZ*) twin also getting *anorexia* if the other developed it was *55%*, compared to *7%* for non-identical, dizygotic (*DZ*) twins.

Kendler et al (1991) reported concordance rates of *23%* for *MZ* twins and *8.7%* for *DZ* twins with bulimia however.

Physiology

Early research found damage to the hypothalamus could severely affect eating behaviour, perhaps implying homeostatic imbalance and satiety indicators could be involved in eating disorders.

Kaye *et al.* (2005) report that PET brain imaging studies indicate altered brain activity (e.g. in the frontal, parietal, and temporal areas of the cortex) in those with anorexia nervosa and bulimia nervosa, both during illness and after recovery. They suggest dysregulation of serotonin pathways in the cortex and limbic system may affect mood (e.g. anxiety), impulse control, and feeding motivation mechanisms in such individuals. Eating disorders have been linked to depression which has also been connected with serotonin dysfunction.

Evaluation

Some twin studies have not always controlled for the effect of similar shared environments (e.g. by using adoption studies) or have found more environmental than genetic influences in eating disorders. Since concordance rates are nowhere near 100% for MZ twins, environmental triggers do seem to be involved. It is also uncertain what is actually inherited to cause the eating disorder, some researchers suggest personality traits such as perfectionism, others a predisposition to inherit mental disorder in general.

The biological cause and effect of eating disorders is difficult to determine since the physical disorders found in anorexia and bulimia may be an effect of starvation and purging rather than a cause. Post mortem studies have not revealed damage in the hypothalamus of those with eating disorders, however anti-depressants that increase serotonin levels are also effective in treating bulimia.

Psychoanalytic theory

Psychoanalytic theory has produced various explanations for eating disorders. The anorexic's refusal to eat has been interpreted as an unconscious denial of the adult role and wish to remain a child (in figure at least) provoked by the development of sexual characteristics in puberty. The timing of onset in anorexia and the loss of menstruation support this idea.

Another psychoanalytic interpretation is that anorexics are unconsciously rejecting their bodies as a reaction to sexual abuse in childhood.

Cognitive theory

Cognitive psychologists have suggested that irrational attitudes and beliefs, and distorted perception are involved in eating disorders. These beliefs may concern unrealistic ideals or perception of body shape, or irrational attitudes towards eating habits and dieting (e.g. the disinhibition hypothesis – once a diet has been broken, one might as well break it completely by bingeing).

Cognitive researchers have also proposed that sufferers of anorexia and bulimia may be seeking to assert control over their lives to an excessively idealistic extent - Dura and Bornstein (1989) found this drive for perfection in hospitalised anorexics extended to academic achievements which were at a much higher level than their IQ scores would predict.

Learning theory

Learning theory explains eating disorders in terms of reinforcement consequences for eating behaviour.

Social praise or respect from a society that places a high value on slim female appearance may reward weight loss or control. Alternatively, the attention and concern shown towards someone with an eating disorder may be reinforcing. Social learning theory would suggest that thin or dieting role models would be imitated, while some learning theorists have proposed that a weight gain phobia is involved in eating disorders.

Evaluation:

Psychological level theories gain more strength when integrated with the following, social, cultural and family research findings.

The idea that cultural exposure to socially desirable conceptions of body shape is responsible for eating disorders has received much support. For example, anorexia and bulimia occur most in:

- Cultures where thinness is socially desirable, e.g. North America, Western Europe and Japan. Indeed evidence suggests that immigrants to these countries show higher levels of eating disorder than their native countries.
- Western women – physical attractiveness is the best predictor of self-esteem in western girls.
- Groups where thinness is particularly valued, e.g. ballet dancers, models and gymnasts.

Many researchers have found that the families of children with eating disorders show the following characteristics:

- Less emotional and nurturing – this may lead to eating disorders developing as an attention-gaining tactic.
- Overly protective – restricting independence may force the child to assert its own control and autonomy through the eating disorder.
- Middle class, overachieving parents – whose high expectations of success may lead to overly idealistic notions of success in matters of weight control.

However, although anorexics may develop their symptoms at puberty and may have been sexually abused in some cases, the effects of these events are often more convincingly explained in non-psychoanalytic terms. While cultural and family experiences do seem correlated with eating disorders, it is difficult to always work out the cause and effect and not all people will react in the same way to these experiences – some under-eat, others over-eat.

22.1 Defining and measuring crime

WHAT IS CRIMINAL AND FORENSIC PSYCHOLOGY?

Howitt (2006) suggests *Criminal Psychology* is generally taken to refer to the study of criminal behaviour and its origins, while *Forensic Psychology* concerns the application of psychological knowledge or methods to the legal system (e.g. in the preparation of evidence concerning victims, witnesses, and investigators, as well as criminals, the analysis of legal decision-making processes, or even work in prisons/rehabilitation). However, he also argues that the disciplines today are perhaps better regarded as 'inseparable rather than two separate things combined'.

PROBLEMS DEFINING CRIME

According to the legalistic approach, a crime occurs when a person breaks the legally established laws of a country. A criminal is therefore a person who has been arrested, found guilty of an offence and has a criminal record. This legal definition has the advantages of providing a simple and agreed upon framework for research, but poses problems for the criminal psychologist.

Crime as normative problems

A legal definition of crime as the act of breaking the law is over-inclusive – the majority of people in a society (unwittingly or otherwise) break some kind of law in their lives, and some may do so without coming to the attention of the authorities. This aspect of the legal definition is thus of little use in identifying 'criminals' for research and may include criminal behaviours of little interest to criminal psychologists.

Criminal record under-inclusiveness problems

There are many stages in the legal system before a criminal record is gained, during which 'crimes' or 'criminals' of interest to psychologists may escape the definition, e.g.:
- criminals who escape detection (i.e. successful ones)
- crimes not reported to the police (e.g. traumatic crime or minor crimes that may be early indicators of greater ones)
- crimes with insufficient evidence to proceed
- criminals falsely found not-guilty or false convictions.

Crime as a social construct problems

Laws represent the morals and values of those with power in a society, so are neither created nor enforced in a neutral way. Laws vary across societies and within the same society over time, e.g. age limits for criminal responsibility and laws relating to drug-taking, homosexuality, stalking, and terrorism. The social construction of crime therefore has implications for the identification of 'criminals' and the causes of 'crimes'.

Crime as a useful psychological construct problems

The concepts of 'crime' and 'criminals' may be too broad to be accounted for by any one theory, whereas alternative general concepts of 'anti-social behaviour' or 'deviance' run into similar problems of subjectivity of definition. Criminal psychologists may thus find it more constructive to focus on the specific causes of specific types of 'criminal' behaviour rather than assuming all criminals share common traits.

PROBLEMS MEASURING CRIME

Psychological studies have assessed stealing in the context of moral development, but more ecologically valid measures include:

OFFICIAL STATISTICS

Many countries compile detailed crime statistics, e.g.:
- The UK Home Office's yearly 'Criminal Statistics' report compiled from regional police forces around Britain.
- The US FBI's annual 'Crime in the United States' report compiled from the Uniform Crime Report of offences reported to, or uncovered by, the police in different states.

Official statistics are used to present crime rates, e.g. as the incidence of crime per 100,000 of the population. This allows the comparison of the types and locations of crimes, so enabling police resources to be directed where needed.

Evaluation
- Official crime statistics under-report crime, e.g. due to crimes not being declared to or discovered by the police, or subsequently not recorded or proceeded with by them.
- Official measures at different stages in the legal system provide different definitions of crime and its incidence, e.g. depending on whether they are taken from police reports, court statistics, or prison records.
- Official crime statistics fluctuate with policing policies, crackdowns, solve rates, offence re-classifications, political pressure, etc. rather than actual crime rates.

SELF REPORTS

Self-report measures of crime can be gained from:
- Victim surveys, e.g. the UK 'British Crime Survey' or the 'International Crime Victimisation Survey' (2001).
- Offender surveys, e.g. of uncaught offenders in the general population or convicted criminals in prisons.

Evaluation
- Victim surveys indicate a greater incidence of crime than official figures and identify different frequencies in certain types of crime (e.g. violent assaults not recorded in police figures). Victim surveys can also indicate victim reactions to, and perceptions of, crime that are not revealed by official statistics.
- Surveys of uncaught offenders, e.g. adolescent delinquents, can reveal important information about the development of crime, while surveys of convicted offenders can provide data on the prevalence and motives of their criminal behaviour.
- All surveys suffer from the problems of self-report measures, e.g. refusal to participate, deception, distortions of exaggeration (boasting) or minimisation (due to shame), and memory corruption or forgetting.

22.2 Psychological theories of offending – learning and upbringing

SOCIAL ENVIRONMENT AND UPBRINGING FACTORS

DISRUPTED FAMILIES

Research has not only shown that crime runs in families, but has also identified possible mechanisms for the transmission of criminal behaviour through parental upbringing, e.g. direct role modelling, parental discipline style, marital instability, and quality of care effects on attachment bonds (see below).

- The 'Cambridge Study' of delinquent development, a prospective longitudinal study of 411 males, found 40% of criminal children had a criminal father whereas only 13% of non-criminal children did (e.g. Farrington 1991).
- Farrington et al. (1996) found 53% of men with a criminal conviction also had convicted family member (compared to 24% in men without one).

Evaluation

Howitt (2006) argues it is difficult to disentangle cause and effect, and parental upbringing effects from other social influences and genetic inheritance, citing for example:

- Farrington et al.'s (1996) finding that 83% of men with a criminal conviction also had a convicted wife, although wives share neither genes nor parents with their husband.
- Johnson et al.'s (2004) 25-year longitudinal study found parents with criminal and violent behaviour caused anti-social behaviour in their offspring through their problematic parenting styles. Controlling other variables and statistical analysis allowed the researchers to infer a causal effect of the parents' inconsistent rule enforcement, marital arguments, and anger interactions with the child.

PSYCHOLOGICAL THEORIES OF CRIMINAL BEHAVIOUR ACQUISITION

LEARNING THEORIES

Social Learning Theory – proposes that criminal behaviour is automatically acquired through observational learning, but imitation depends on its expected reinforcement consequences.

Operant conditioning – suggests criminal behaviour is maintained by social approval or the immediate positive reinforcement of crime, e.g. stolen 'rewards', compared to the more distant punishment received if caught.

Evaluation

- See Social Learning Theory of aggression and media violence evidence.
- Learning theories take into account all social influences, e.g. family, peers, and society, and so interact well with the social environment and upbringing research.

PSYCHODYNAMIC THEORIES

Psychoanalytic theory suggests identification with the same-sex parent, as a result of the Oedipus Complex in the phallic stage, could result in a superego that provides low moral control over potentially criminal impulsive id desires, e.g. due to internalising the values of a criminal parent, acquiring a weak superego conscience, etc. (see Moral development).

Evaluation

- Parenting may exert its effect via different processes, e.g. learning (see opposite) or attachment privation causing psychopathy (see Bowlby's theory of attachment).
- Freud neglected non-family influences (but see Erikson) and proposed weaker female morality (but most crime is male).

COGNITIVE THEORIES

Environmental experience provides, and is interpreted by, attitudes, attributions, etc. (see Cognition and crime).

LEARNING ENVIRONMENT

Sutherland's (1939) Differential Association Theory (DAT) of crime suggests people become criminals:

- through personal contact with others in intimate primary groups, e.g. family or peers rather than via the media.
- by learning specific criminal techniques, pro-criminal attitudes, motivations and justifying rationalisations.
- when intensity and exposure to law-breaking attitudes is greater than exposure to law-abiding attitudes.

Evaluation

- The theory applies to different crimes and socioeconomic environments, not just general, working-class criminals – exposure to middle-class criminal attitudes and behaviour may lead to middle-class crimes, e.g. fraud or tax evasion.
- The DAT is supported by family and peer group criminal socialisation studies, but does not explain why some become criminal and others do not in the same situation.

POVERTY AND DISADVANTAGED NEIGHBOURHOODS

The 'Cambridge Study' of delinquent development found large family size, low income, and poor accommodation were associated with later criminality (Farrington, 1995). SCoPiC (Social Contexts of Pathways into Crime) studies, such as the Peterborough Adolescent Development Study, aim to investigate how individual characteristics interact with social contexts (especially in disadvantaged urban areas) over time to produce offending behaviour.

Evaluation

- The Peterborough Youth Study (precursor to the later SCoPiC study) found youth predispositions (e.g. low self-control, low shaming, weak pro-social values) and social situations (e.g. low parental monitoring, weak family/school bonds) were strong offending predictors in disadvantaged contexts (Wikström, 2003).

22.3 Cognition and crime

CRIMINAL THINKING PATTERNS

Yochelson and Samenow's (1976) *criminal personality theory* proposed:

- Criminality results from *conscious, free will choices* and decisions to participate in a lifestyle of crime from an early age, e.g. delinquents choose to associate with criminal peers and to reject normal employment rather than being passively affected by social and environmental conditions.
- The origin of criminal choices may stem from early family or peer interactions and a persistent enjoyment of the forbidden.
- Criminals show *distinct criminal thinking patterns*. Yochelson and Samenow identified many different traits and *cognitive biases and distortions* in criminals which lead them to make automatic and crime-related *thinking errors*, e.g.:
  - ➤ An irresponsible, self-centred character driven by fear, anger, and a need for power and control.
  - ➤ Manipulativeness, chronic lying, and a lack of empathy and trust towards others.
  - ➤ Excessive optimism about criminal success, fantasising about criminal acts, and distorted perceptions of property ownership and victimisation.

Evaluation

Yochelson and Samenow based their conclusions on a sample of 255 male offenders, however this sample:

- may have been unrepresentative of criminals in general since it consisted of male, captured (unsuccessful) criminals, many of whom were committed for psychiatric evaluation (and therefore may have been just as easily described in terms of existing DSM or ICD personality disorder diagnostic classifications).
- lacked an appropriate control group so it could not be established that the identified traits and thinking patterns were unique to criminals.
- was studied using Freudian clinical interviews so may have lacked reliability or validity due to:
  - ➤ researcher expectations (although Yochelson and Samenow completely revised their assumptions during the course of the study)
  - ➤ self-report deceit (common in psychopaths).
- suffered from enormous sample attrition – the 40% treatment success rate claimed at the end of the study was based on just 30 remaining offenders of the 255.

SOCIAL COGNITION AND CRIME

Gudjonsson (1984) proposed that the way criminals attribute responsibility/blame for their actions affects their feelings of guilt about the crimes they commit. This in turn can influence their likelihood of re-offending, readiness to confess, legal defence, and responsiveness to rehabilitation.

Gudjonnson's *Blame Attribution Inventory* of offenders' perceptions of their crime is a self-report measure of:

- *External attribution* (EA) – tendencies to blame external causes, e.g. provocation or social/environmental factors.
- *Mental Element Attribution* (MEA) – tendencies to blame out-of-character mental states, e.g. low mood or temporary loss of self control (this still reduces self-responsibility).
- *Guilt* – the amount of remorse felt about their crime.

It is possible that attributions, especially EA ones, function to reduce anxiety and guilt feelings about criminal acts.

Evaluation

Gudjonsson (in Cox, 1998) summarised a number of studies showing the interaction of attribution style with:

- *Offence type* – Gudjonsson and Singh (1988) analysed the attributions and guilt of 171 offenders and found that:
  - ➤ Crimes against people (sex and violent offences) produced more guilt than property offences.
  - ➤ Guilt was positively correlated with MEA (cross-cultural replications indicate coefficients of 0.41 to 0.57 at a P<0.01 significance level or better).
  - ➤ Guilt was negatively correlated with EA (coefficients of –0.22 to –0.33 at the P<0.05 level in replications).

This may support the role of attribution in guilt reduction, since EA involves less internal responsibility than MEA.

- *Cognitive distortion* – Gudjonsson (1990a) found a strong positive correlation (0.62 at the P<0.001 level) between EA and self-justifying cognitive distortion in child molesters.
- *Personality* – EA correlates positively with measures of psychoticism on Eysenck's Personality Questionnaire, suggesting emotional coldness and lack of empathy may be the most important causes of EA.
- *Remorse, confession and outcomes* – Gudjonsson suggests guilt facilitates confession, but shame inhibits admission. Furthermore, MEA has implications for 'mens rea' (legal guilty intention) and successful therapeutic rehabilitation.

MORAL DEVELOPMENT AND CRIME

Although not necessarily intended to be applied to criminal behaviour, the cognitive developmental theories of moral development of Piaget, Kohlberg, Eisenberg, and Selman all have implications for it, e.g. lower levels of moral and pro-social reasoning, and the inability to adopt other perspectives may contribute towards anti-social actions (see Cognitive theories of moral development).

Evaluation

- Nelson *et al.*'s (1990) meta-analysis of 15 studies found that delinquents do tend to reason at lower levels of moral development than control groups, while Palmer and Hollin (1998) reported these moral reasoning differences were greatest for issues that were especially relevant to criminal behaviour (Howitt, 2006).
- The Peterborough Youth Study found low moral/pro-social values were a strong predictor of offending, even when social contexts were controlled for, implying that voluntary cognitive decision making is important in the development of youth delinquency and that perspective-taking interventions in youth may help to reduce later criminality (Wikström, 2003).
- Of course, all the evaluative points for theories of moral development have implications for the validity of their application to criminal behaviour (see Moral development).

22.4 Biological theories of offending 1

ATAVISTIC FORM THEORY

Lombroso (1876) applied atavism to criminals, arguing that they could be identified by their primitive evolutionary appearance and behaviour, e.g. low cranial capacity and intelligence, large jaws, and the 'ferocious instincts of primitive humanity' and apes.

Evaluation

- Lombroso pioneered the use of data collection, statistics, and typology in criminology.
- However, his ideas were not supported by later research and he has been criticised for poorly applying the scientific method and for incriminating individuals based on their appearance, e.g. by Gould (1981).
- Gould (1981) re-analysed Lombroso's own data on cranial capacity in criminals and non-criminals, concluding it provided weak evidence for his ideas.

EYSENCK'S CRIMINAL PERSONALITY THEORY

Eysenck argued that *high extraversion* (E), *neuroticism* (N) and *psychoticism* (P) scores on the Eysenck Personality Questionnaire were associated with criminality due to underlying **inherited differences in nervous system functioning**, e.g. extraverts' natural CNS under-arousal making them more impulsive, sensation-seeking, and difficult to socially condition (i.e. learn conditioned emotional responses to punishment – see Classical conditioning).

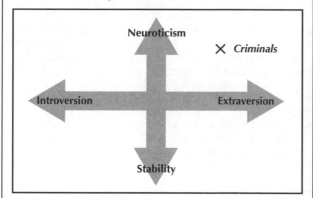

Evaluation

- Research reveals little support for the biological basis of Eysenck's personality theory, i.e. the strong genetic origin and physiological differences in arousal and conditioning.
- However, research reviews indicate that prisoners tend to score higher on P and N, but not E (although delinquents do, based on self-reports).
- Given the weakness of Eysenck's biological explanation, these findings could be attributed to:
  - ➤ the worrying, anxiety-provoking, and depressing (i.e. N) effects of prison
  - ➤ the fact that the P scale probably measures psychopathic rather than psychotic tendencies
  - ➤ delinquents scoring higher on the impulsiveness aspect of E.

SOMATOTYPE THEORY

Sheldon (1949) also suggested criminals could be identified by their appearance depending on their somatotype (body build). Sheldon argued that the muscular build of *mesomorphs* made them more self-assertive or aggressive and thus more likely to engage in criminal activity (than thin, self-conscious ectomorphs or fat, sociable, comfort-loving endomorphs).

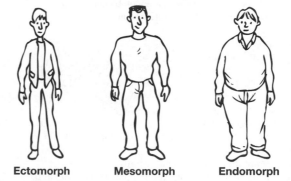

Ectomorph   Mesomorph   Endomorph

Evaluation

- People vary in their degree of somatotype, but rating on a 7-point scale Sheldon found higher levels of mesomorphy in delinquents – a result that other studies have replicated.
- However, the cause of the mesomorph link to crime is debatable, with explanations ranging from social labelling theory to higher testosterone levels.

GENDER AND CRIME

Evolutionary psychologists propose that males have evolved behavioural and physiological adaptations that predispose them to behaviours that are regarded as criminal offences in modern society, e.g.:

- greater risk-taking and sensation-seeking
- higher levels of dominance and violent aggression and competition
- greater average physical size/musculature
- higher testosterone levels.

Daly and Wilson (1988) suggest that evolutionary differences in parental investment and sexual selection pressures have therefore led to greater male:

- Intra-sexual competition, e.g. male-male homicide.
- Inter-sexual aggression, e.g. jealous violence and rape.
- Co-opting of resources, e.g. theft of property/territory.

Evaluation

- See Evolutionary theories of aggression evidence.
- Historically and cross-culturally (even in remote tribes) men commit more crime than women, indicating inherited influences as well as biosocial and environmental ones (such as labelling, expectations, and social learning).
- Evolutionary theory provides fundamental explanations for both behavioural and physiological gender differences.
- Learning theory, psychoanalytic, and feminist psychologists have criticised such evolutionary explanations for:
  - ➤ Ignoring more immediate *family* dynamics and socialising influences.
  - ➤ Playing down wider *modern-day* cultural, social, and environmental influences on male crime.
  - ➤ Justifying unacceptable male criminal behaviour as natural and unavoidable, while ignoring the general female ability to inhibit physically violent and criminal tendencies.

22.5 Biological theories of offending 2

GENES AND CRIME

Ishikawa and Raine (2002) propose that:

- Genes do not directly cause crime, but may provide 'varying degrees of predisposition to criminal behaviour' via heritable physiological processes such as nervous system and neurotransmitter functioning (see below).
- Criminal behaviour is influenced by genetics and environment, and their interaction.
- Genetic research applies to populations, not individuals, so cannot explain why a specific person commits crime and does not claim that 'crime is destiny'.

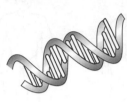

The influence of genetic factors on criminality has been studied through:

1 Family studies of criminal records.
2 Twin studies, e.g. comparing monozygotic (MZ) and dizygotic (DZ) twins for criminal concordance (similarity).
3 Adoption studies – to see if criminality in adopted children is more related to criminality in their biological parents (genetic influences) or their adoptive parents (environment/upbringing).

Evaluation

- Ishikawa and Raine's (2002) meta-analysis of twin studies produced average concordances of 44% for MZ twins and 21.6% for DZ twins. Even after controlling for political or sampling bias, accuracy of zygosity testing and age of study, MZ twins were still 1.5 to 3 times more likely to be concordant for criminality.
- Grove et al.'s (1990) study of 32 sets of MZ twins reared apart (tested for zygosity and adopted soon after birth away from the family) found correlations of 0.41 for childhood conduct disorders and 0.28 for adult antisocial behaviours.
- Mednick et al.'s (1984) study of over 14,000 Danish adoptees found that they were more likely to have a criminal conviction if a biological but not adoptive parent had one (20%), than if an adoptive but not biological parent had one (14.7%). In addition, this finding was independent of socioeconomic status or age at adoption and there was a positive correlation between biological parent and adoptee in the number of convictions.
- Interestingly, although results from adoption studies have consistently revealed a relationship between biological parent and adoptee criminal behaviour, the finding has applied much more to minor offences and property crime than violent crime – even though many studies that do not use criminal records have indicated a genetic influence on aggression.
- However, the concordance rates are still fairly low, indicating strong environmental effects.
- See Evaluation of family, twin and adoption studies.

BRAIN PHYSIOLOGY AND CRIME

Proposed physiological correlates of crime include:

- **Brain disruption** – e.g. poor functioning of the prefrontal region of the brain (e.g. Raine et al., 1998) or amygdala/limbic system (e.g. Blair et al., 1999), thought to be involved in: impulsivity, the inhibition of violent behaviour, fearlessness, and a failure to learn the negative effects of antisocial behaviour, and psychopathy and poor empathetic response.
- **Hormone level** – e.g. testosterone (see Gender differences in crime and hormonal influences on aggression research and evaluation).
- **Neurotransmitter dysfunction** – low serotonin has been consistently correlated with increased irritability, aggression, impulsivity, and conduct disorder, while recent research indicates an intriguing role for the neurotransmitter-metabolising enzyme monoamine oxidase A (MAOA) – see opposite.
- **Low physiological arousal** – e.g. Raine (1997) argues lower resting heart rate is a medium to strong correlate of antisocial behaviour and aggression in childhood and crime in adolescence. Ishikawa and Raine (2002) suggest this may be because it reflects fearlessness and resistance to punishment conditioning (e.g. not responding to the negative aspects of fighting, such as injury and social punishment) or because individuals with low arousal seek out aggressive, criminal, and other antisocial stimulation to increase their arousal to more optimal levels (see Eysenck's theory).
- **Large body build** – e.g. Sheldon's (1949) theory of criminality and mesomorphs (see Somatotype theory and evidence).

Evaluation – Monoamine oxidase and crime

- Brunner et al. (1993) studied a Dutch family in which several males were affected by a syndrome of borderline mental retardation and abnormal behaviour, include impulsive aggression, arson, attempted rape, and exhibitionism. Analysis of urine samples indicated a complete and selective deficiency of the neurotransmitter-metabolising enzyme monoamine oxidase A (MAOA) caused by a point mutation in the MAOA structural gene on the X chromosome in each of the five men affected, which was postulated to have triggered their impulsive aggression. Such an extreme mutation is thought to be rare, thus limiting the applicability of the results.
- Caspi et al. (2002), however, in their longitudinal study of a large sample of male children from 3 to 26 years of age in New Zealand, found genetic differences in the amount of MAOA produced mediated the effect of childhood maltreatment in the development of antisocial behaviour. Capsi et al. found 85% of males with a low-activity MAOA genotype who were severely maltreated developed some form of antisocial behaviour, and concluded 'Maltreated children with a genotype conferring high levels of MAOA expression were less likely to develop antisocial problems. These findings may partly explain why not all victims of maltreatment grow up to victimise others, and they provide epidemiological evidence that genotypes can moderate children's sensitivity to environmental insults.' This was a well-controlled and intriguing study of gene-environment interaction, but needs to be replicated.
- As with all potential genetic or physiological 'causes' of criminal behaviour, research on MAOA may have important legal and ethical implications for criminal liability and responsibility.

22.6 'Brain abnormalities in murderers indicated by positron emission tomography'
Raine *et al.* (1997)

INTRODUCTION
Previous research using a variety of techniques (e.g. brain damage effects and EEG measurements) on both humans and other animals has indicated that dysfunction in certain localised brain areas may predispose individuals to violent behaviour. Such brain structures include the prefrontal cortex, corpus callosum, left angular gyrus, amygdala, hippocampus, and thalamus.

AIM
By using recent brain imaging techniques on a large group of violent offenders who have committed murder and a control group of non-murderers, this study hypothesises that dysfunction in the above brain structures should be found more often in the murderers than

1 dysfunction of the same areas in non-murderers
2 dysfunction in other areas of the murderers' brains that have been implicated in *non*-violent psychiatric disorders (e.g. the caudate, putamen, globus pallidus, midbrain, and cerebellum)

METHOD
Subjects – The 'murderers' were 41 prisoners (39 male, 2 female) with a mean age of 34.3 years (standard deviation of 10.1), charged with murder or manslaughter in California. They were referred for brain imaging scans to obtain evidence or information relating to a defence of not guilty by reason of insanity, incompetence to stand trial or diminished capacity to reduce sentencing having been found guilty. The reasons for scanning referral were very diverse, ranging from schizophrenia (6 cases) to head injury or organic brain damage (23 cases). No murderer had psychoactive medication for 2 weeks before scanning (each was urine screened).

Controls – Each murderer was matched with a 'normal' subject for age, sex and schizophrenia where necessary. Each was screened to exclude physical and mental illness, drug taking and, of course, a history of murder.

Procedure – After practice trials, all participants were injected with a tracer substance (fluorodeoxyglucose) that was taken up by the brain to show the location of brain metabolism (activity) while they conducted a continuous performance task (CPT) requiring them to detect target signals for 32 minutes. A positron emission tomography (PET) scan was then immediately given to show the relative brain activity (glucose metabolised) for 6 main cortical areas (the outside of the brain) and 8 subcortical areas (inside the brain).

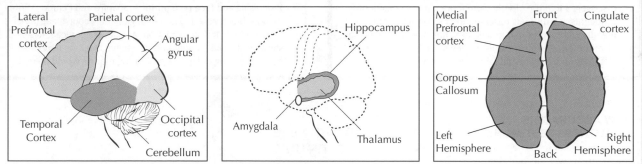

RESULTS

	Brain structure	Murderers' metabolic activity level	Interpretation
Cortex	Prefrontal cortex	Lower activity than controls	Linked to loss of self control and altered emotion.
	Parietal cortex	Lower activity than controls especially in the left angular and bilateral superior gyrus	Lower left angular gyrus activity linked to lower verbal ability, educational failure and thus crime.
	Temporal cortex	No difference compared to controls	No difference was expected.
	Occipital cortex	Higher activity than controls (unexpected)	May compensate on CPT for lower frontal activity.
Subcortex	Corpus callosum	Lower activity than controls	May stop left brain inhibiting the right's violence.
	Amygdala	Lower activity in left than right side of the brain in murderers than controls	These structures form part of the limbic system (thought to control emotional expression).
	Medial (inner) temporal including hippocampus	Lower activity in left than right side of the brain in murderers than controls	Problems with these structures may cause a lack of inhibition for violent behaviour, fearlessness and
	Thalamus	Higher activity on right side in murderers	a failure to learn the negative effects of violence.
	Cingulate, caudate, putamen Globus pallidus, midbrain and cerebellum	No significant differences were found in these structures between murderers and controls.	No differences were expected in these structures (which are involved in other disorders), supporting the specificity of brain areas involved in violence.

No significant differences were found for performance on the CPT, handedness (except left-handed murderers had significantly less abnormal amygdala asymmetry than right handed murderers), head injury or ethnicity.

DISCUSSION
Strengths – a large sample was used with many controls to rule out alternative effects on brain activity.

Limitations – the PET scan method can lack precision, the findings apply only to a subgroup of violent offenders (not to other types of violence or crime) and caution in the interpretation of the findings is needed, which need to be replicated.

The findings do not mean violence is caused by biology alone (other social, psychological and situational factors are involved), do not demonstrate that the murderers are not responsible for their actions, do not mean PET scans can diagnose murderers and do not say whether the brain abnormalities are a cause or effect of behaviour.

EVALUATION
Methodological	No control over the level of violence used in the murder. Brain scans can be difficult to interpret.
Theoretical	Previous findings on brain structures involved in violence are supported and new findings revealed.
Links	Brain scanning. Cortical functions. Freewill. Ethical implications of socially sensitive research.

23.1 Memory research and eye-witness testimony

THE NATURE OF THE WITNESS AFFECTING EYEWITNESS TESTIMONY

RECONSTRUCTIVE MEMORY e.g. Bartlett's work on how schemas, expectations and stereotypes change memory has been applied to explain the effects of:

- **Prejudice** – Allport and Postman (1947) found that prejudice influenced the recall of whether a black or white person was holding a cut throat razor in a picture.
- **Inferences** – Harris (1978) found that over 60% of subjects would infer information not present in testimony based on their expectations, even when trained not to. For example if given the testimony 'I ran up to the burglar alarm in the hall' many would later assert that the burglar alarm had been rung.
- **Expectations** – List (1986) found subjects who had watched videos of shop-lifting incidents a week earlier recalled more of the actions that had a high probability of occurring during shoplifting than a low probability. They even falsely remembered high probability actions they had not witnessed on the video.
- **Stereotypes and face recognition** – Bull (1982) revealed people were willing to identify strangers as criminals just by their appearance. Yarmey (1982, 1993) found people readily stereotype faces as 'good guys' and 'bad guys' and discovered that the elderly were more likely to misidentify innocents as criminals based on their stereotypes of what they thought a criminal looked like. Racial stereotypes may also influence eyewitness testimony since Shepherd et al (1974) found cross-racial face recognition is poor.

THE NATURE OF THE EVENT AFFECTING EYEWITNESS TESTIMONY

CUE-DEPENDENT MEMORY e.g. state- and context-dependent retrieval have been applied to explain the effects of:

- **Stress** – Clark et al. (1987) suggest that recall of violent crime may be more difficult because it occurs in a less aroused state.
- **Face recognition and context** – Shapiro and Penrod (1986) suggest matching witnessed faces to mug shots, photo-fits or line-ups may be difficult because of the different contexts on witnessing and recall; mug-shots and photos-fits being 2-dimensional and without expressive movement may provide insufficient cues, while line-ups involve different locations and clothing. Crime re-enactments may help by recreating context.

MEMORY PROCESSING MODELS e.g. rehearsal and depth of processing have been applied to explain the effects of:

- **Timing** – Clifford and Richards (1977) found better recall of details for a person who had approached police officers for 30 rather than 15 seconds. Potential jurors rated crime duration, and thus time to get a good look at the suspect, the 4th most important influence on eyewitness accuracy out of 25 variables (Lindsay, 1994). Greater exposure may allow more processing.
- **Processing and face recognition** – Shapiro and Penrod (1986) found subjects asked to make judgements about a face rather than just look at it showed more accurate later recall. Research shows that more familiar and distinctive faces are remembered better after long delays, as processing models would predict.

HOW ACCURATE IS EYEWITNESS TESTIMONY?

Cognitive research has been applied to answer this question…

EYEWITNESS TESTIMONY

POST EVENT INFORMATION AFFECTING EYEWITNESS TESTIMONY

INTERFERENCE THEORY and **RECONSTRUCTIVE MEMORY THEORY** have been applied to the following:

- Loftus has shown how information received after a witnessed event (especially in the form of leading questions) can have a retroactive interference effect on the memory of that event. Information can be:

1 **Added to an account** – Loftus and Zanni (1975) showed subjects a film of a car accident, and got more subjects to incorrectly recall seeing a broken headlight by asking 'Did you see *the* broken headlight?' than asking 'Did you see *a* broken headlight?'. Loftus (1975) even got subjects to recall seeing a non-existent barn in a picture by using a similar technique of adding post-event information.

2 **Distorted** – Loftus and Palmer (1974) received higher estimates of speed when asking 'How fast were the cars going when they *smashed* into each other?' than when the verb '*hit*' was used.

3 **Substituted** – Loftus et al. (1978) changed the recognition of a 'stop' sign to a 'yield' sign with misleading questions.

However there are many debatable issues involved in this area:

1 **Artificiality** – Yuille and Cutshall (1986) found the eyewitness testimony of a **real life** and quite traumatic event was very accurate and resistant to leading questions. This was only a single case study however.

2 **Demand characteristics** – McCloskey and Zaragoza (1985) suggest that subjects may just be following the expectations to recall the (misleading) information that was last given to them. However warnings that incorrect post event information has been given does not appear to stop incorrect information being recalled (Lindsay, 1990).

3 **Degree of interference possible** – Loftus (1979) has shown that *obviously* incorrect post event information has little or no effect on accurate recall. Interference is most likely to occur with minor details and if post event information is given after a long time delay.

4 **Nature of interference** – Loftus (1979) is convinced that post event information replaces the original information – which cannot be recalled even if money is offered for accurate information. McCloskey and Zaragoza (1985) disagree – they showed that if subjects are given misleading information and are later offered a choice of the original or a neutral alternative, they tend to choose the original, indicating that the original material is not 'overwritten' or permanently distorted.

- **Interference and face recognition** – Davis and Jenkins (1985) found the accuracy of face recognition is significantly reduced if subjects are shown composite photo-fit pictures of other faces beforehand. Gorenstein and Ellsworth (1980) found witnesses are more likely to identify (correctly or otherwise) a person from a line-up if they had appeared in mug shots the witness had searched beforehand.

23.2 'Reconstruction of automobile destruction' Loftus and Palmer (1974)

BACKGROUND

There is much support for the idea that most people, when they are witnesses to a complex event, such as a traffic accident, are very inaccurate when reporting numerical details like time, distance, and especially speed, even when they know that they will be questioned on them (e.g. Marshall, 1969). As a consequence, there can sometimes be large variations in estimates between witnesses and so it seems likely that such inaccurate testimony could easily be influenced by variables such as the phrasing of questions or 'leading' questions.

AIM

Loftus and Palmer, therefore, aimed to investigate the effect of leading questions on the accuracy of speed estimates in, and perceived consequences of, a car crash.

EXPERIMENT ONE

Subjects: 45 students, tested in groups of different sizes.

Design: Laboratory experiment.

Procedure:

7 films of traffic accidents, ranging in duration from 5 to 30 seconds, were presented in a random order to each group.

After each film, the subjects had to give a general account of what they had just seen and then answer more specific questions about the accident. The critical question, 'About how fast were the cars going when they hit each other?' acted as the independent variable, since it was manipulated in five conditions. Nine subjects heard the sentence with the verb 'hit' in it, and then an equal number of the remaining subjects were asked the same question but with the verb 'smashed', 'collided', 'bumped' or 'contacted' instead of 'hit'. The estimated speed was the dependent variable.

Results

Speed estimates for the verbs of experiment one		Significance of result	Accuracy of subjects' speed estimates		
Verb	Mean speed estimate	Results were significant at the P < .005 level, according to analysis of variance of the data.	In 4 of the 7 films the speed of the cars was known.		
				Actual speed of collision	Mean speed estimate
Smashed	40.8		Film 1	20 mph	37.7 mph
Collided	39.3		Film 2	30 mph	36.2 mph
Bumped	38.1		Film 3	40 mph	39.7 mph
Hit	34.0		Film 4	40 mph	36.1 mph
Contacted	31.8				

Discussion

The results indicate that not only are people poor judges of speed, but they are systematically and significantly affected by the wording of a question. However, this finding could be attributed to either response-bias (the subject remembers accurately but is pressured by the word to increase or decrease the estimate) or a genuine change in the subject's memory of the event (the word makes the subject recall the event as worse than it was). If the latter explanation is true, then the subject might be led into recalling details that did not occur. The second experiment was designed to determine which explanation of different speed estimates was correct.

EXPERIMENT TWO

Subjects: 150 students, tested in groups of different sizes.

Design: Laboratory experiment.

Procedure:

A film lasting just less than a minute was presented to each group which featured four seconds of a multiple traffic accident. After the film, the subjects had to give a general account of what they had just seen and then answer more specific questions about the accident. The critical question concerning the speed of the cars was the independent variable, and it was manipulated by asking 50 subjects 'About how fast were the cars going when they hit each other?', another 50 'About how fast were the cars going when they smashed into each other?' and another 50 acted as a control group who were not asked the question at all. One week later the dependent variable was measured – without seeing the film again they answered ten questions, one of which was a critical one randomly positioned in amongst the ten questions, asking 'Did you see any broken glass? Yes or no?'. Although there was no broken glass it was expected that some might be falsely remembered if the leading question of a week ago had changed the memory of the event to seem worse than it was.

Results

Verb	Mean estimate	Response	Smashed	Hit	Control	Probability of seeing broken glass with speed estimate			
						Verb	1–5 mph	6–10 mph	11–15 mph	16–20 mph
Smashed	10.46 mph	Saw broken glass	16	7	6	Smashed	.09	.27	.41	.62
Hit	8.00 mph	Did not see glass	34	43	44	Hit	.06	.09	.25	.50

Discussion

The authors conclude that the results show that the verb 'smashed' not only increases the estimates of speed, but also the likelihood of seeing broken glass that was not present. This indicates that information from the original memory is merged with information after the fact, producing one distorted memory. This shift in memory representations in line with verbal cues has received support from other research.

EVALUATION

Methodological: A well operationalised and controlled experiment, but lacked the ecological validity of having real life events and involved witnesses.

Theoretical: The research supports the idea that memory is easily distorted and has implications for eyewitness testimony in court.

Links: Interference and forgetting in memory, practical applications of memory, laboratory experimentation.

22.3 Recall under hypnosis – repression and false memory

WHAT IS HYPNOSIS?

The word 'hypnotism' is derived from the Greek for sleep – 'hypnos', however there are distinct differences between the two phenomena. Hypnosis is characterised by:

1 **Relaxation and suspension of planning** – hypnotised subjects sit quietly and do not seem to plan or initiate activity. Control is given over to the hypnotist.
2 **Suggestibility** – hypnotised subjects will respond to suggestions and obey instructions with little sign of inhibition, even if the request is unusual or seemingly impossible to do.
3 **Atypical behaviour** – hypnotised subjects can apparently perform behaviours that they would not normally be willing or able to do, such as controlling severe pain, experiencing hallucinations and, of course, retrieving forgotten memories.

Depth of hypnosis can be measured, e.g. by the Stanford Hypnotic Susceptibility Scale – a list of 12 hypnotic suggestions that are increasingly difficult to follow. About 15% of people are highly hypnotisable, 15% are very resistant to it, and the rest are somewhere in between.

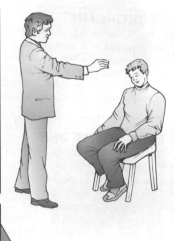

Cognitive psychological research on repression, interference, reconstructive memory and cue dependent memory can be used to help understand the accuracy of memories retrieved through hypnosis in two main situations - during therapy and police investigation. The former tends to focus on the victim's memory, while the latter has been applied to both victim and eyewitness recall.

CLINICAL HYPNOSIS AND MEMORY

Much debate has been generated over the accuracy of memories of childhood abuse, satanic abuse and even alien abduction retrieved using hypnosis during therapy that had not been remembered up until that point. It is often assumed that such *recovered memories* are due to the *repression* of these traumatic events and that *hypnotic regression* was required to retrieve them. Victims frequently find that the recovered memories help them make sense of disturbances in their behaviour, beliefs or emotions.

Evaluation of hypnosis for recovering repressed memory
For – there may be many genuine cases, since:

- child abuse is disturbingly common and amnesia for such traumatic events does occur – Herman and Schatzow (1987) found 28% of female incest victims reported severe childhood memory losses, especially the more violent the abuse.
- hypnotic age regression is an established technique (it is item 7 on the Stanford Hypnotic Susceptibility Scale) and may work through reducing recall inhibitions, overcoming memory blocks through accessing a different level of consciousness or even aiding context recreation of the time (*cue-dependent memory*).

Against – given the sensitivity and implications of such claims, many researchers think hypnotically recovered memories should not be relied upon without objective corroborative evidence, since:

- The concept of psychoanalytic repression and the extent of the unavailability it claims to produce has been criticised.
- Hypnosis may lead to *false memory syndrome*. Therapists may give *leading suggestions* before or during hypnosis which may distort original memories by acting as *retroactive interference* or encourage confabulation of fictitious memories by aiding *imaginative reconstruction*. Support for this is that:
1 Hypnosis increases the ability to imagine and even hallucinate.
2 Very hypnotisable people may be even more imaginative and/or have a 'fantasy-prone personality' (Wilson and Barber, 1983)
3 Hypnosis can produce experiences of future or even past lives.
4 Certain therapists tend to retrieve certain types of recovered memory – some frequently find abuse, others alien abduction (a more recent culture-bound and less credible phenomena).
5 Clients want to find causes for their problems and, being unaware of them, may readily believe they forgot others were to blame.
6 Independent corroboration has refuted many recovered memories.

POLICE HYPNOSIS AND MEMORY

In contrast to the clinical use of hypnosis to recover memories the client did not know they had, forensic or investigative hypnosis is usually employed in criminal investigations to try and access consciously forgotten information that victims or witnesses think they do, or might, possess.

The information gained can be used as forensic evidence or for investigative purposes to create leads that can be corroborated. Far more objection is raised to the former use than the latter.

Evaluation of hypnosis for victim and witness testimony
For - Police officials hope that the relaxed and focused state of hypnosis, as well as the more specific hypnotic techniques such as context recreation (based on *cue-dependent memory* theory) and the 'freeze-framing' of mental scenes to focus on detail, will greatly increase the amount and accuracy of previously inaccessible material recalled (a property termed hypermnesia).

- Geiselman and Machlowitz (1987) reviewed 38 experimental studies on hypnosis; 21 found significantly more correct information recalled, 4 significantly less and 13 no difference. However 8 experiments found an increase in errors while 10 showed no effect on error rate. Hypnosis was most effective in the studies using interactive interviews (not fixed questions), on more realistic material, after longer time delays.

Against – Gudjonsson (1992) suggests the highly suggestible, compliant and imaginative state of hypnosis may lead witnesses to greater *confabulation* and vulnerability to *leading questions*, as well as overconfidence in the accuracy of their recall.

- Putnam (1979) revealed that hypnotised subjects made more errors and were more likely to follow misleading information when answering questions on a videotape of an accident.
- Sanders and Simmons (1983) discovered hypnotised subjects who had witnessed a pick-pocket on video were less accurate in their interview answers (although just as confident) and identity parade identification (which they were more likely to be misled on) compared to non-hypnotised subjects.
- Geiselman et al (1985) found American law enforcers using the Cognitive Interview technique (which involves context recreation and different recall perspectives) produced greater correct recall of a violent crime video (41.2 items) than a standard interview conducted under hypnosis (38 items).

23.4 Identification procedures

Wells and Bradfield (1998) state that 'the identification of innocent persons from line-ups and photo spreads is the primary cause of wrongful conviction, accounting for more convictions of innocent persons than all other causes combined.' They add that this conclusion is supported by forensic DNA techniques that have overturned wrongful imprisonment. It is important, therefore, to understand the limitations of identification techniques, human memory, and facial recognition processes.

CONSTRUCTION OF LIKENESSES USING COMPOSITE SYSTEMS

Originally, construction of likenesses was attempted using artist impressions (drawings or sketches based on verbal descriptions and visual feedback from the witness). These were thought to be time-consuming and expensive, so various composite systems have been developed, including:

- **Identikit systems** – witnesses choose the most representative line drawings of each individual feature, which are assembled to form the composite image.
- **Photofit systems** – the same as the identikit system, but with photographs of individual features.
- **E-FIT or PRO-fit** – computer programmes similar to Photofit systems, but with the ability to select and resize individual features in the context of the whole face.
- **EvoFIT software** – evolves and blends witness selections of whole faces to create increasing suspect resemblance.

Evaluation

- Frowd *et al.* (2004) asked participants to inspect a photo of a celebrity they did not know for 1 minute, then 3 to 4 hours later gave them a cognitive interview followed by one of five different likeness reconstruction methods. Independent judges who knew the celebrities were best able to correctly name the composites of the E-FIT and PROfit systems (20% of the time), followed by artist's sketches (10%), Photofit (5%), and EvoFIT (3.5%).
- Frowd *et al.* (2005) found testing after a more realistic period of two days produced lower average naming and a shift in method efficiency (e.g. sketches 8.1%, EvoFIT 3.6%, and E-FIT/PROfit less than 2%). However, testing composites against a line-up of photographs led to correct identifications of 60% for E-FIT, 46.7% for sketches, 40.6% for PROfit, but only about 30% for EvoFIT.
- Despite poor laboratory results for the identification of even familiar faces, composite images can still help the police by narrowing suspect characteristics. However, perhaps the incorrect images exert distorting retroactive interference effects on the original memory trace.

IDENTIFICATION LINE-UPS

Rather than relying on the cued recall of composite systems, identification line-ups are able to use the more powerful memory process of recognition by presenting either the actual suspect or an established likeness – a photograph. Nevertheless, there are still many problems with the methods used in this approach, ranging from misplaced familiarity and the retroactive interference of post event information to witness assumptions and expectations, e.g.:

- **The 'show-up' method** – where only one photo is presented for identification. Witnesses may assume this is because the police are confident that person is the only suspect.
- **Photo spreads** – a choice of mug shots are presented. Two-dimensional images lack animation and may not resemble the suspect if not recent. As with identification parades, witnesses may expect the suspect to be present and feel pressure to select one of the options presented.
- **Simultaneous identification parades (line-ups)** – a suspect is physically lined up with other people (foils – often 7) who are of a similar appearance for witnesses to identify. If the foils are not sufficiently similar to the witness, the functional size of the line-up is reduced. According to relative judgment theory, witnesses may compare members of the line-up to find the one most like the culprit, even if the culprit is not present, and falsely identify that person.
- **Sequential identification parades** – where witnesses see line-up members one at a time to encourage comparison with their memory rather than with the other members to limit relative judgement. Misidentification can still occur, e.g. if witnesses have previously been shown a mug shot of the (innocent) suspect or if the suspect looks nervous.

Evaluation

- Lindsay and Wells (1985) found sequential presentation reduced misidentification from 43% (simultaneous line-up) to 17% when the true suspect was not in the line-up.
- Ainsworth (1995) found subjects were more likely to pick out a photo of a helpful bystander (48%) than the suspect (38%) a week after seeing images of both in a media report.

FACE RECOGNITION PROCESSES – FEATURE ANALYSIS OR HOLISTIC FORMS?

- **Feature analysis theory** – Research indicates that faces can sometimes be identified from just one distinctive facial feature, and that certain features may be more important than others, e.g. eyes, then mouth, then nose. Sadr *et al.* (2003) have even suggested that eyebrows could be even more important than eyes, finding recognition of 50 celebrity faces was significantly poorer if the images lacked eyebrows than if the eyes were missing. This may be due to the contrast visibility and stability of eyebrows as facial features or their role in conveying emotions and other nonverbal communication.
- **Holistic form theory** – Research on facial recognition supports the idea that, although feature processing is important, faces are also identified through the spatial arrangement of features and head shape. Some studies show the configuration of individual facial features can override their identity value. Young *et al.* (1987) found that combining features of the top half of one face with the bottom half of another face made identification of the two distinct identities very difficult unless the two halves of the face were misaligned, indicating holistic context affects the processing of individual features. If people store holistic images of faces rather than individual features, the best identification should come from holistic retrieval methods (i.e. of whole faces) – something the latest computer reconstruction programmes such as EvoFIT try to incorporate.

23.5 Interviewing witnesses

THE COGNITIVE INTERVIEW TO IMPROVE RECALL

The cognitive interview (Geiselman *et al.* 1984) aims to use psychological principles to improve witness recall by:

- **Reporting everything** – by encouraging free-recall of all details regarding the past incident, no matter how trivial or irrelevant they might seem, the witness's memory is not immediately constrained, distracted or directed by closed or potentially leading interviewer questions. More potential information can be uncovered which may trigger further associated memories.
- **Context reinstatement** – by asking witnesses to first recall the general scene, surrounding events and emotions, the encoding specificity principle suggests state and context-dependent memory effects will provide cues to prompt recall.
- **Reverse order and changed perspective recall** – requesting that witnesses try to remember events in a different order or from another's viewpoint may help to reduce the effect of the witnesses pre-existing schemas, expectations and scripts, as well as providing different mental routes or cues to further memories.

The enhanced cognitive interview of Fisher and Geiselman suggests additional interviewer training on communication skills, such as building rapport, handing control of the interview to the witness, appropriate pausing and body language, and clear presentation of questions (to prevent hurrying, intimidating, confusing or leading the witness) improves the results of the basic cognitive interview, which according to Fisher *et al.* (2002) should proceed as follows:

- **Introduction** – building rapport, explanation of method
- **Open-ended narration** – free-recall, interviewer note taking
- **Probing** – developing memories, use of other recall methods
- **Review** – and accuracy checking of the evidence provided
- **Close** – paperwork, invitation to re-contact if later recall.

Evaluation

- Geiselman *et al.*'s (1984) first test of the cognitive interview (CI) found interviewers with just 20 minutes training could gain up to 35% more correct details about simulated events than untrained interviewers with no increase in errors.
- Köhnken *et al.*'s (1999) meta-analysis of studies in which both children and adults were witnesses found the CI outperformed comparison interviews in 54 of 55 cases with an overall accuracy rate of 85% (compared to 82% for other interviews).
- The CI has also been found to increase witness recall of correct details in:
  - ➤ learning disability adults (Milne *et al.*, 1999)
  - ➤ preschool children (Holliday, 2003)
  - ➤ senior citizens (Wright & Holliday, 2005)
  - ➤ non-college educated Brazilian cleaning employees witnessing a simulated armed abduction (Stein and Memon, 2006).
- Although not always applied in its full form, the CI has been successfully used by police officers:
  - ➤ Fisher *et al.* (1990) found Miami detectives using the CI increased recall by 46% (with 90% accuracy) compared to standard interviews.
  - ➤ Ginet and Py (2001) found no problems training French officers to use the CI, which increased correct witness recall of information by 36 %.
- Davis et al. (2005) found a less time-consuming version of the CI resulted in little information loss.

CHILDREN AS WITNESSES

Pipe *et al.*'s (2004) review of recent research on children's testimony about experienced and witnessed events concluded that 'children are capable of providing accurate information about their experiences, although their ability to convey the information is affected not only by the qualities of their memories, but also by the types of retrieval mechanisms employed and the quality of the communication between them and their interlocutors' e.g. interviewers.

This means interviews with children should take into account:

- Very young children's limited
  - ➤ memory capacity and linguistic ability to describe events
  - ➤ abstract reasoning and understanding of certain events and concepts such as dates, time, counting, distance, etc.
  - ➤ motivation and ability to concentrate for extended periods.
- The value of free-recall as a way of avoiding adult pressure and leading questions.
- The importance of simple questions and statements, e.g.
  - ➤ avoiding long sentences that overload memory capacity
  - ➤ avoiding grammatically complex constructions, such as passive phrases and question tags
  - ➤ taking into account children's limited understanding of key words and legal terms.

Evaluation

- Deffenbacher *et al.*'s (2004) meta-analysis of 12 studies of witness recall by children aged from 3–10 years found face identification accuracy under conditions of high and low stress was virtually identical to adults.
- Woolley (1997) concluded that, by the age of 6, children are probably little different from adults in terms of their ability to distinguish fantasy from reality, while Lamb et al. (1999) found even fantasy-prone children are not more likely to make false reports when giving evidence (Howitt, 2006).
- Krackow and Lynn's (2003) experiment asked children of 48–70 months of age a false leading question in one of two ways. Children who were asked 'Did Amy touch your bottom?' were almost always accurate in their answer, whereas those asked 'Amy touched your bottom, didn't she?' produced nearly 50% false agreement (Howitt, 2006). This supports the idea that leading questions/question tags are to be avoided with younger children.

23.6 Interviewing suspects

INTERROGATION TECHNIQUES

Although legislation in some countries, such as the Police and Criminal Evidence Act in the UK, aims to limit coercion in interrogations (e.g. by tape recording interviews and having legal representatives present), coercive techniques used by the police include:

- **Maximisation** – e.g. exaggerating the amount and strength of incriminating evidence, the seriousness of the crime, and the severity of punishment for it.
- **Minimisation** – e.g. underplaying the severity of the crime, showing sympathy and understanding for the reasoning behind the offence, hinting at lenient treatment after co-operation and confession.
- **Tone and body language variation** – from intimidating robust confrontation and invasion of personal space to softer challenge and empathetic moral appeals.
- **Questioning style** – e.g. using multiple questions to overload the suspect's memory and ability to lie, questioning contradictions in suspects' accounts and using leading questions that assume suspects' guilt.

INBAU *ET AL.*'S (1986) 9 STEPS FOR OBTAINING CONFESSIONS

1 **Confront and accuse** suspect of crime.
2 **Develop themes** to minimise or justify the suspect's actions.
3 **Interrupt denials** of the accusation and themes.
4 **Overcome objections**, e.g. by ignoring claims of innocence.
5 **Prevent withdrawal/passivity**, e.g. with eye contact, proximity.
6 **Handle suspect's mood**, e.g. with sympathy, victim empathy.
7 **Present alternative incriminating accounts** of the crime with one that allows the suspect a more face-saving explanation.
8 **Encourage suspects to describe details** of the crime after they accept an incriminating account to provide oral confession.
9 **Convert oral to written confession** to prevent later retraction.

Evaluation

- Inbau *et al.*'s method is the most widely used by US police, but has been criticised by some psychologists, e.g. Gudjonsson (2003). There is a danger that coercive interrogation techniques could lead to false confession (see below) and conviction given the powerful influence of confession on judge and jury willingness to convict.
- Russano *et al.* (2005) found minimisation interrogation techniques increased the rate of both true and false confessions.

FALSE CONFESSIONS

Researchers such as Gudjonsson (1992) have proposed different types of false confession:

- **Voluntary** – where people falsely confess without police coercion, e.g. due to mental illness, need for attention or gang pressure to 'take the rap'.
- **Coerced compliant** – where suspects knowingly make a false confession due to:
  - ➢ the need to escape the stress of interrogation; Ofshe and Leo (1997) call this 'stress compliant confession'
  - ➢ rational choice if witnesses believe police strategies of *maximisation* (e.g. of the strength of incriminating evidence and the severe consequences of denial), and *minimisation* (e.g. of lenient treatment if they confess).
- **Coerced internalised** – where suspects come to believe their own guilt after continual police suggestions (e.g. due to memory/intelligence problems or high susceptibility to suggestion – see Hypnosis and obedience to authority). Ofshe and Leo call this 'persuaded false confession'.

Evaluation

- Kassin and Kiechel (1996) found false confession could be obtained by using pressurising conditions *and* a false witness under laboratory conditions. Although the study lacked the ecological validity of negative consequences for confession, Horselenberg et al. (2003) replicated the results after adding financial penalties for confession.
- Gudjonsson (1992) and others have found false confessors are often younger, more vulnerable to coercive interrogation techniques on Gudjonsson's Susceptibility Scale, and may have a history of drug dependency.

DETECTING LIES

Various lie detecting methods have been studied, e.g.:

- **Behaviour analysis** – based on the idea of leakage of lying cues, e.g. asymmetrical facial expressions, abrupt emotional onset, etc. Universal indicators of lying can lack reliability; a better approach is to look for deviations from an individual's normal base-line behaviour, but of course this can change with the situation.
- **Polygraphs** – measure changes in physiological responses that indicate emotional reactions to statements. However, emotional reactions vary with the type of lie and the liar, may reflect anxiety about not being believed rather than lying, and may also occur to the control questions.
- **Statement validity analysis** – involves content analysis of statements using a 19 item checklist of true testimony indicators, e.g. unstructured production, spontaneous corrections, quantity of details, admission of memory deficiency, description of interactions/conversations, etc.

Evaluation

- Ekman and O'Sullivan (1991) evaluated the ability to detect lying in 509 people, including law-enforcement personnel (e.g. members of the US Secret Service, CIA and FBI polygraphers, and Californian police), judges, psychiatrists, college students, and working adults. A videotape showed 10 people who were either lying or telling the truth in describing their feelings. Only the Secret Service performed significantly better than chance.
- Vrij and Mann (2001) showed videos of British press conferences of victims' relatives (some of whom had actually committed the crime) to Dutch police officers who only identified the liars at chance levels (Howitt, 2006).
- Patrick and Iacono's (1991) study found polygraphs had a success rate of 98% in identifying the guilty (higher than most studies), but only 55% in identifying the innocent.
- Undeutsch has claimed success for Statement Validity Analysis in legal cases, but it is difficult to assess this. Laboratory and field studies also have methodological problems but generally support SVA effectiveness, although some criteria are more effective than others and its suitability as court-worthy evidence is questioned.

23.7 Offender profiling

THE AIMS OF OFFENDER PROFILING
Offender profiling aims to aid the identification, apprehension and conviction of an unknown criminal by providing:
- Descriptions of the likely social (e.g. employment, marriage), physical (e.g. age, race) and mental (e.g. IQ, education, motivational) characteristics of the offender.
- Predictions about when, where and against whom they are likely to commit their next offences.
- Possible interview strategies to elicit confession of guilt or information relevant to their crimes (e.g. motivation or missing evidence).

DIFFERENCES IN TECHNIQUE
Boon and Davies (1992) drew a basic distinction between the original American and British approaches to offender profiling in terms of the way their profiles seem to be created and applied.

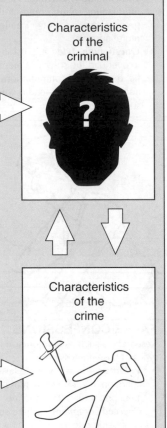

Focuses more on aspects of the criminal

Characteristics of the criminal

Characteristics of the crime

Focuses more on analysis of data provided by the crime

THE US 'TOP-DOWN' APPROACH TO PROFILING
Pioneered by members of the FBI such as Ressler, Burgess and Douglas. The approach seems to rely more on:
- The **creation** of general typologies of criminal behaviour and motivation based on **interviews with captured criminals** and **impressions of past crime scenes**.
- The **intuitive analysis** of data based on **personal experience** in law enforcement.
- Matching a particular **type** of criminal to the features of a **particular crime**.

FBI investigators initially interviewed 36 serial murderers to fill out a 57-page document relating to factors such as what led to the offending, what early warning signs there were, what encouraged or inhibited their offences etc. (Douglas and Olshaker, 1995). From the insights they gained and a thorough analysis of the crime details they distinguished between typologies such as *organised* and *disorganised* offenders. Organised offenders are often of above average intelligence, in a skilled occupation and socially/sexually competent, and their crimes typically appear planned, controlled in execution and involve the removal of evidence. Disorganised offenders, however, are often of below average intelligence, in unskilled work and live alone, and tend to commit crimes spontaneously, with little control and leave evidence at the crime scene.

Gaining data from interviews with volunteering, manipulative offenders has been criticised, although the interviewers suggest their thorough briefing on the facts of the case helped detect deception.

THE BRITISH 'BOTTOM-UP' APPROACH
Pioneered by psychologists, particularly David Canter and Paul Britton, working with the police. This approach seems to focus more on:
- The data-driven, building up of more individualistic profiles through the identification of specific associations between particular **characteristics of the offence** and the **offender**.
- The use of **scientific statistical analysis** and the **application of psychological principles**.
- Finding what kind of criminal behaviours were associated together and therefore might be the work of the same type of criminal.

Canter's initial profiles were based on an individualistic analysis of particular serial crimes, but he began to statistically analyse larger numbers of solved crimes (using techniques like ***smallest space analysis***, which reveals clusters of events that commonly occur together) in order to derive typologies. In each case the ***behaviour*** of the criminal (e.g. their choice of, and interactions with, victims, the location and timing of their offences, content analysis of speech, etc.) was used as a data source rather than interviews with the actual offenders. Canter also used environmental psychological concepts such as mental maps to understand offender behaviour, e.g. finding that most British serial rapists lived within their 'offence circle' of rape locations.

Canter's approach seeks to make the process of profiling scientifically explicit rather than intuitive.

POINTS OF COMPARISON IN TECHNIQUE
The above distinctions between the US and British approaches mostly appear to concern their different emphasis on scientific methodology resulting from their originators' different backgrounds and access to data, and hide many common assumptions, for example:
- Use of typologies – Canter and Heritage (1990) have built up their own typologies, e.g. those based on the statistical analysis of rape acts that seem to involve the victim as a person, object or vehicle for the rapist's needs.
- The offender consistency hypothesis – both approaches assume that criminal behaviour (especially extreme behaviour) will reflect characteristics that are typical of that person and will remain relatively consistent across offences.
- Evolution of criminal careers – both approaches propose that criminals may well adjust their modus operandi as a result of experience, increased forensic awareness, etc., but also suggest that there are fundamental motivations or needs ('signatures' in Douglas's terms, 'central narrative themes' in Canter's) that will remain more static.
- Similar strengths and weaknesses – both approaches have had high-profile, spectacular successes that have drawn attention away from profiling failures. Studies actually reveal similarly low rates of success for each approach; Holmes (1989) reported that only 17% of FBI profiles contributed to arrests, while Copson and Holloway (1997) found British detectives believed UK profiles helped to solve 16% of cases they were used in (Harrower, 1998). Nevertheless, such figures still represent a significant contribution to police work, providing inaccurate profiles do not outweigh it by misdirecting cases and wasting valuable time and money.
- Range of application – both approaches have been applied to a range of crimes, e.g. burglary, arson, blackmail, hostage-taking, etc.

24.1 Persuading a jury

THE EFFECT OF WITNESS CONFIDENCE

Researchers such as Penrod and Cutler (1987) have suggested that although the relationship between witness confidence and accuracy is rather weak, especially under sub-optimal viewing conditions (Deffenbacher, 1980), jurors are strongly influenced by confident witnesses.

Evaluation

- Deffenbacher *et al.*'s (1986) meta-analysis of 35 tests of the eyewitness confidence-accuracy relationship found the average correlation to be 0.25, significant but low.
- Wells, Lindsay, and Ferguson (1979) reported that witness confidence accounted for 50% of the variance in jurors' belief in the witness testimony.
- Cutler, Penrod, and Dexter's (1989) study of testimony found that, of the ten factors they manipulated, only one, witness confidence, had a statistically significant and substantial effect on participants' verdicts and perceptions that the identification was correct. Although witness confidence accounted for a substantially smaller proportion of jurors' verdicts than in the Wells, Linsay, and Ferguson experiment, 54% of jurors convicted if the eyewitness was 100% confident compared to 39% convictions if the witness was 80% confident.

THE EFFECT OF SHIELDS AND VIDEOTAPE WITH CHILDREN'S EVIDENCE

These methods aim to protect children from added trauma.

Evaluation

Ross et al. (1994) conducted experiments to assess the impact of protective shields and videotaped testimony on conviction rates in a simulated child sexual abuse trial. Mock jurors watched a videotaped simulation of a 10-year-old child witness testifying in one of three different ways:

1 The child testified in court while directly confronting the defendant (open court condition).
2 The child testified in court with a protective shield placed between the child and the defendant (shield condition).
3 The child testified outside the courtroom and the child's testimony was presented to the jury and defendant on a video monitor (video condition).

When the mock jurors judged the defendant's guilt:

- Immediately after the child's testimony – jurors in the open court condition were more likely to convict the defendant than those in shield and videotape conditions.
- After watching the entire trial – the modality of child testimony had no impact on conviction rates.

THE EFFECT OF EVIDENCE RULED INADMISSIBLE

Much mock juror research has been conducted into the influence on juries of judge instructions to disregard evidence that is inadmissible (e.g. because it is unreliable, prejudicial, or illegally obtained). However, different studies have found instructions to disregard inadmissible information can produce the desired effect, no significant effect, or even the opposite effect:

Evaluation

- Broeder (1959) found a 'boomerang effect' – mock jurors awarded greater damages when instructed to disregard information (indicating the defendant was insured) than when it was not ruled inadmissible, perhaps because the instruction to disregard increased the importance of the evidence.
- Mallard and Perkins (2005) found mock jurors in a murder trial successfully disregarded evidence from an inadmissible wiretap.
- Steblay's (2006) meta-analysis of 48 studies with 8,474 participants found instructions to ignore inadmissible evidence did not effectively eliminate its impact. Contested evidence ruled admissible had an even greater impact on verdicts, but if judges gave a rationale for ruling inadmissibility, juror compliance increased.
- Kassin and Sommers (1997) found mock jurors disregarded inadmissible testimony thought unreliable, but were influenced by inadmissible evidence obtained illegally – perhaps because they wanted a 'fair' verdict regardless of legal technicalities.

THE EFFECT OF TESTIMONY ORDER

Pennington and Hastie's (1981, 1992) *Story Model for Judicial Decisions* suggests jurors spontaneously construct 'one or more plausible accounts or stories describing "what happened" during events testified to at the trial' and use their preferred story as a basis to interpret and understand the evidence to reach their verdict. The theory predicts that witnesses and evidence presented in a way that provides a coherent, logical, and consistent story will influence verdict outcomes more than evidence and witnesses presented in other ways.

Evaluation

- Devine and Ostrom (1985) found greater discounting of an inconsistent witness occurred when evidence was organized in story order.
- Pennington and Hastie (1988) varied the order of presentation of evidence 'to manipulate the ease with which one story (favouring the prosecution side of the case) or another (favouring the defence) could be constructed. The order manipulation had clear effects on verdicts; easier-to-construct stories dominated the decisions'.
- Pennington and Hastie (1992) found stronger and more confident decisions in favour of evidence organised by story than by legal issue.

THE EFFECT OF EXPERT WITNESSES

Krauss and Sales (2001) point out that:

a In the USA the 'Daubert Ruling' emphasises that any methods used by expert witnesses should show scientific validity and reliability.
b The US legal system assumes jurors are capable of distinguishing the value of expert clinical opinion testimony from expert testimony based on scientific evidence and that if they cannot the adversary process (i.e. opposite lawyers) will do so,

but argue that research studies on expert testimony and juror decision-making suggest these assumptions are dubious.

Evaluation

- Krauss and Sales (2001) investigated whether 208 mock jurors were more influenced by clinical opinion expert testimony or expert testimony based on scientific research and found:
  ➤ expert testimony, regardless of type, influenced the mock jurors
  ➤ adversary procedures could lessen the influence of expert testimony
  ➤ clinical opinion testimony was more effective than scientific-based expert testimony in persuading jurors, even after adversary process
  ➤ mock jurors may not have realised they were influenced by one type of testimony more than the other.

However, the study used college students rather than actual jury members and the trial procedure lacked the ecological validity of a real legal proceeding (e.g. in its length and range of evidence), especially since it aimed to mimic a capital sentencing hearing.

24.2 The effects of defendant characteristics on the jury

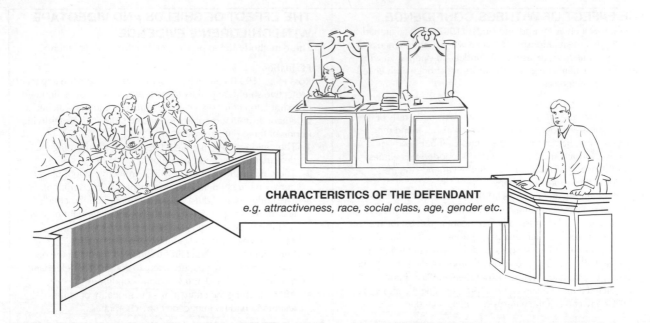

CHARACTERISTICS OF THE DEFENDANT
e.g. attractiveness, race, social class, age, gender etc.

PHYSICAL ATTRACTIVENESS

As Baron and Byrne (1997) note 'One of the more consistent findings is that attractive defendants are at an advantage compared to unattractive ones with respect to being acquitted, receiving a light sentence, and gaining the sympathy of the jurors.' They suggest that evidence indicates this effect is due to the 'beautiful-is-good stereotype' whereby attractive physical features seem to be associated with attractive or positive psychological characteristics. In a similar way stereotypes relating to criminals being physically unattractive may also have an effect on legal decision-making.

- Michelini and Snodgrass (1980) found that physically attractive defendants were more likely to be acquitted.
- Sigall and Ostrove (1975) found experimental participants shown an attractive photograph of a defendant charged with burglary recommended almost half the average sentence of those shown no photo or an unattractive one.
- Stewart (1980) conducted an observational study of American judges' decisions regarding 74 male defendants and found that attractive defendants tended to receive lighter sentences and were less likely to receive prison sentences than unattractive ones (Lippa, 1990). Downs and Lyons (1991) found a similar effect on the setting of bail or fines by 40 judges in 1500 court cases involving misdemeanours (Baron and Byrne, 1997).

Factors that influence the effect of the defendant's physical attractiveness include:

- **The seriousness of the crime** – the attractiveness effect is strongest with serious but nonfatal crimes such as burglary, but ceases to have an effect with extremely serious crimes.
- **The nature of the crime** – Sigall and Ostrove's (1975) experiment also found attractive defendants charged with fraud received higher average recommended sentences than unattractive defendants and those with no photo, perhaps because they used their looks to accomplish their crime.
- **The gender of the defendant** – physical attractiveness seems to have a stronger effect with female defendants, perhaps because women are judged as attractive on a more physical basis then men, especially by men (see the evolution of sex differences in mate choice).
- **The attractiveness of the victim** – Castellow *et al.* (1990) found that in cases of sexual harassment the relative level of attractiveness between the defendant and victim was important. For example, an unattractive male defendant was more likely to be judged guilty of harassing an attractive female, than an attractive male defendant was of harassing an unattractive female (Baron and Byrne, 1997). Kerr's (1978) mock jury experiment found that an attractive victim of theft was more likely to provoke a guilty verdict for the defendant than an unattractive victim.

RACE / ETHNICITY

Race or ethnicity is another characteristic of defendants that could influence judge and jury decision-making due to stereotyping and prejudice. However the effect of defendant ethnicity upon verdicts is less consistent than that of physical attractiveness, and depends upon many factors, e.g.:

- **The race of the jurors** – variable effects have been found here and depend on the degree of prejudice.
  Baldwin and McConville's (1979) study of British real-life trials revealed that a black defendant was more likely to be perversely convicted than perversely acquitted, even by mostly black juries.
  Pfeifer and Ogloff (1991) found that white university students were more likely to rate black defendants as more guilty than white defendants. Skolnick and Shaw (1997) found little difference between black and white student mock jurors in their verdicts concerning black defendants, however compared to white jurors, the black jurors were significantly more likely to find a white defendant guilty, but half as likely to find them not guilty, than black defendants (Brewer, 2000)
- **The nature of the crime** – Gordon *et al.* (1988) found that defendants charged with burglary were given longer sentences if they were black rather than white, but the reverse was true if the crime was embezzlement (Coolican, 1996).
- **The race of the victim** – Pfeifer and Ogloff (1991) found that white students were even more likely to rate black defendants as guilty if the victim was white. However, Henderson and Taylor (1985) report that, regardless of a defendant's race, those who kill a white victim are more likely to be sentenced to death than those who kill a black victim.

Evaluation

In some studies on defendant race and attractiveness, if an emphasis is put on proving the facts beyond a reasonable doubt the effects are reduced or disappear completely.

24.3 Jury decision-making 1

INDIVIDUAL / MINORITY INFLUENCES ON JURY DECISION-MAKING

WHAT JUROR CHARACTERISTICS MAY INFLUENCE JURY DECISION-MAKING?

If certain juror characteristics such as age, sex, race, socio-economic status, occupation, education or personality can be linked to a willingness to convict defendants generally, or for certain crimes, then efforts to scientifically select jury members could affect the outcome of court cases. The characteristics of jurors are of interest to the defence and prosecution since lawyers and attorneys in Britain and the USA have the right of 'peremptory challenges' or 'voir dire' (to object to a limited number of potential jurors) and so may try to select jurors more sympathetic to their case.

SUPPORT FOR SELECTION OF JURORS

Some studies have found that:

- Jurors with previous jury experience are more likely to convict (see foreperson election).
- Younger jurors are less likely to convict.
- Female jurors are more likely to convict rapists and child abusers (although longer deliberation may modify this effect).
- Jurors with authoritarian personalities are more likely to convict (perhaps because of their support of convention, police authority and their tendency to be dogmatic in sticking to one possible view).
- The race of the juror may affect their willingness to convict defendants of different races (see characteristics of the defendant).
- Those who do not oppose the death penalty are more likely to convict such cases (disturbing, since those who do object are excluded from such trials).

EVIDENCE AGAINST SELECTION OF JURORS

Overall, the research seems to find a lack of empirical support for scientific juror selection, e.g.:

- Baldwin and McConville (1979) concluded that British research, and Hastie *et al.* (1983) concluded that American research, indicates that no single social / demographic factor leads to significantly consistent effects on verdicts.
- Zeisel and Diamond (1978) found that jurors rejected by attorneys but still asked to attend the trial (forming a shadow jury) would have influenced the verdict in 3 out of 12 cases.
- Olczak *et al.* (1991) found that lawyers were not accurate at predicting the verdicts of jurors and were no better than students at doing so.
- Acre (1995) suggests that studies on the effects of juror characteristics on verdicts have tended to neglect the type of case (some personality variables only respond to certain kinds of crime or victim) and factors such as the strength of the evidence or persuasiveness of the lawyers.

HOW MIGHT JUROR CHARACTERISTICS INFLUENCE VERDICTS?

JUROR'S CHARACTERISTICS INFLUENCING OWN VERDICT

Pennington and Hastie (1990) suggest that jurors make their decisions by creating hypothetical reconstructive stories that could explain the evidence and then match the story to a verdict.

However, people may differ in:

- The kinds of stories they tend to construct or believe based upon their personality, attitudes and experience.
- The complexity and number of alternative stories they are willing and able to consider.
- How early they form their stories and how selective they are in attending to evidence that supports or refutes them.

MINORITY INFLUENCE UPON OTHERS' VERDICTS

Moscovici (1976) suggests that one or a small minority of like-minded individuals may influence the majority vote by conversion over a longer period of deliberation, if they:

- Are consistent and committed in their opinions and arguments.
- Seem to be acting on principle rather than out of self-gain and incur some cost (e.g. in terms of group acceptance and more time spent arguing).
- Are not overly rigid and unreasonable in their opinions and arguments.

FOREPERSON INFLUENCES UPON OTHERS' VERDICTS

The foreperson of the jury regulates the discussion in the jury room, may be perceived as a leader and thus may be able to influence the verdict. This could be important since studies show that elected forepersons are generally men, those of higher socio-economic status, those who first start discussion and those who have had previous jury experience. However, Baldwin and McConville (1980) found no relationship between the social characteristics of forepersons and jury verdicts, and McCabe and Purves (1974) found forepeople did not seem to overly influence jury deliberation.

24.4 Jury decision-making 2

SOCIAL / MAJORITY INFLUENCES ON JURY DECISION-MAKING

WHAT EFFECTS MAY SOCIAL PRESSURE HAVE ON JURY DECISION-MAKING?

An important assumption behind trial by jury is that group decisions should be of better quality than individual decisions since a greater range of life experiences and group deliberation should enable more alternative interpretations of the evidence to be expressed, more errors in reasoning to be spotted and individual biases to be countered. However, based on studies of real juries (before this was made illegal) Kalven and Zeisel (1966) proposed the 'liberation hypothesis' – that jurors have usually decided on a verdict before they retire to deliberate and jury deliberation consists of merely trying to persuade others to the same opinion. Social group pressure may thus lead to illogical, biased and ill-considered verdicts from juries, for a number of reasons:

GROUP POLARISATION
A group tends to make more extreme decisions (either riskier or more cautious) through a process of social comparison and increasing conformity to the group's initial majority decision, e.g. many studies find juries make more lenient decisions than individuals.
- Kalven and Zeisel (1966) found that out of 215 juries with an initial majority vote, 97.2% then went on to reach the same final verdict.
- Tanford and Penrod (1986) found the side with the majority verdict at the first ballot in mock jury studies were 95% likely to achieve the same final verdict. (Hastie et al, 1983, found around 75%).
- Nemeth (1977) found that juries are more likely to agree with a majority not guilty verdict than a majority guilty verdict.
- Baldwin and McConville (1980) found the chances of acquittal virtually doubled if juries deliberated for more than 3 hours.

CONFORMITY
Group pressure to agree with majority verdicts may result in a lack of consideration for alternative, minority opinions. Social pressure may result from uncertainty over the verdict and the need to refer to others for guidance (informational social influence) or from the need to behave in socially approved of ways (normative social influence). The pressure may increase with:
- ***The severity of the crime/sentence*** – more severe penalties may actually discourage conviction.
- ***The need for a majority rather than unanimous verdict*** – juries only required to make majority decisions, e.g. 10:2, spend less time discussing the case and put more pressure on the minority to agree (Hastie *et al.*, 1983).
- ***The size of the jury*** – in 6-person juries a minority of 1 against 5 could be less able to resist majority pressure than a proportional minority of 2 against 10 (see Asch's ally effect). However, Vollrath and Davis's (1980) review suggests jury size does not significantly affect verdicts.

GROUPTHINK
Illogical decisions may be made under pressure by cohesive and isolated groups dominated by a directive leader. Groups of individuals with similar opinions are more likely to show groupthink through confirmatory bias – not equally considering evidence against their joint beliefs. Smaller, 6-person juries may be even less representative of the population and produce homogenous (similar) jurors.
- Acre *et al.* (1992) found that homogenous groups were more likely to change their initial opinions to agree with each other.

SOCIAL LOAFING
Individuals in the jury may be inclined to deliberate less than they would alone and let others think for them.

DO THESE EFFECTS OCCUR?

The accuracy of jury decision-making
Whether juries make different decisions because of group pressure could be discovered by comparing their verdicts with those of others.
- Kalven and Zeisel's (1966) classic questionnaire survey of 3576 trials revealed that judges agreed with their jury's verdict in 75% of cases and concluded from this that juries were competent decision-makers. However, this is still a high degree of disagreement that on further analysis by Stephenson (1992) revealed a great deal more disagreement over not guilty compared to guilty verdicts.
- A number of questionnaire studies in Britain (e.g. Zander, 1974) have found around 6 – 12% of verdicts were reported as 'perverse acquittals' by judges and solicitors.
- Studies of shadow juries (where a mock jury sits in on the trial and their deliberations can be recorded and analysed), e.g. by McCabe and Puves (1974), reveal that decisions are made similar to those from real juries.

Problems assessing the accuracy of jury decision-making
- Comparing the verdicts of juries with other sources implies that one source is more likely to be accurate and objective than the other. It is significant that the rate of 'perverse acquittals' varies according to who one asks, e.g. the prosecution and police, judges or the defence.
- Questionnaire studies have their problems (the Kalven and Zeisel one has been heavily criticised for its unrepresentativeness – it only sampled 3% of all trials and only 15.8% of judges responded) and experimental jury simulations and shadow juries can never replicate the realism, pressures and responsibilities with 100% accuracy.

24.5 Imprisonment

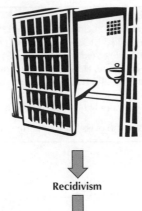

The effectiveness of custodial sentencing
The effectiveness of prison depends upon its perceived role.
• As a retributive punishment, prisons inflict considerable psychological damage on most inmates.
• However, in terms of crime reduction, rates of recidivism can be extremely high (see Alternatives to custodial sentencing).

Retribution   Recidivism   Reform

DEPRESSION AND SUICIDE RISKS

Prison is known to produce a variety of negative emotion effects (see also the SPE opposite), particularly on arrival before adjustment can occur. These include increased levels of:
• anxiety
• depression
• psychotic breaks.

Evaluation
• Dooley (1990) studied the case notes of 295 suicides in prisons in England and Wales between 1972 and 1987 and found:
  ➤ 17% occurred within a week, 29% within a month, of prison entry.
  ➤ The increase in the suicide rate was far in excess of the rate of rise in the prison population.
  ➤ The most common method was by hanging, usually at night.
  ➤ There was a frequent history of psychiatric treatment/self-injury.
  ➤ People charged or convicted of violent or sexual offences were over-represented, as were those serving life sentences.
  ➤ There was an association between suicide and both guilt for the offence and being charged or convicted of a homicide offence.
• Dexter and Towl (1995) found:
  ➤ Two-thirds of suicides occurred within the first 3 months, and 80% within a year, of prison entry.
  ➤ Longer sentences were associated with higher suicide rates.
• Crighton (2000) studied 525 suicides from 1988 to 1998 and found:
  ➤ An exceptionally high risk during the first 24 hours of entering prison or being moved to a new prison.
  ➤ The rate of suicide in prison was still increasing.
  ➤ Over 30% of suicides involved those with a history of drug abuse.
  ➤ 51% had expressed a prior intent to commit suicide.

PRISON SITUATIONS AND ROLES

The adverse environment and intensive exposure to other criminals may:
• reinforce criminal identities
• reinforce anti-establishment attitudes
• increase exposure to criminal knowledge, contacts, and techniques
• trigger violent/anti-social behaviour
• lead to institutional dependence.

Evaluation
• See Haney, Banks, and Zimbardo's (1973) Stanford Prison Experiment.
• Haney and Zimbardo (1998) reflected on the lessons of their Stanford Prison Experiment (SPE) 25 years after conducting it, concluding for example that:
  ➤ US Prison Policy has ignored the findings of the SPE and other psychological research that shows prison environments are potentially damaging situations regardless of the people put in them; custodial sentencing has significantly increased and prison conditions have worsened over the years, resulting in the current crisis in American corrections.
  ➤ The 'long-term legacies of exposure to powerful and destructive situations, contexts, and structures means that prisons themselves can act as criminogenic agents ... thereby serving to increase rather than decrease the amount of crime that occurs within a society. Department of corrections data show that about a fourth of those initially imprisoned for nonviolent crimes are sentenced a second time for committing a violent offence. Whatever else it reflects, this pattern highlights the possibility that prison serves to transmit violent habits and values rather than to reduce them.'
• See research on recidivism rates in 'Alternatives to custodial sentencing'.

PLANS AFTER RELEASE AND RECIDIVISM

Research has shown that:
• Offenders leaving prison have a high risk of unemployment.
• Unemployment of offenders is associated with higher recidivism.
• Offenders report employment is important in avoiding recidivism.
• Effective employment-focused interventions/education programmes can reduce recidivism.

Evaluation
• Lipsey's (1995) meta-analysis of studies from 1950 to 1990 found the most effective factor in reducing recidivism was employment (a 37% effect size).
• Motiuk (1996) reported a study where 69% of Canadian offenders were unemployed at the time of their arrest.
• Gillis, Motiuk, and Belcourt's (1998) study of repeat offending found that unemployed men were more likely to re-offend (41%) than employed men (17%) one year after prison release.
• Steurer et al.'s (2001) study of 3,170 released American inmates found those who had participated in educational programmes had a 29% re-incarceration reduction compared to non-participants after three years, despite initially equal motivation levels to not re-offend.
• Bridges (1998) argues that vocational guidance without practical skills can increase recidivism slightly due to disappointment of job expectations.
• Hurry et al.'s (2006) literature review of 10 of the best quasi-experimental studies available found that 6 out of 7 intervention programmes were successful at producing significantly higher levels of ex-offender employment after six months compared to control groups.
• The costs of successful prison-based interventions are more than offset by the reduced costs of re-imprisonment.

24.6 Alternatives to imprisonment

Why try to find alternatives to custodial sentencing?
The US Federal Bureau of Justice (2002) study of recidivism in 272,111 prisoners found:
- 67.5% were rearrested for a new crime and 51.8% were back in prison within 3 years of release.
- Nearly two-thirds of all the recidivism during the 3-year period occurred within the first year.
- Property offenders had the highest re-arrest rate (73.8%) followed by released drug offenders (66.7%), while the lowest re-arrest rates were for homicide (40.7%), rape (46.0%), and other sexual assault (41.4%).
- Re-arrest increased with the number of previous convictions.
- Prisoners with longer prior records were more likely to be re-arrested than those with shorter records.

Perhaps alternative methods could decrease the overall level of crime and better serve the victims of it.

Change environment   **Help victim**   **Eliminate offender**

PROBATION

Probation concerns the supervision of convicted offenders in the community, e.g. those subject to a court order or released on licence from prison.

The aim is to avoid the negative environment of prison while restricting behaviour, administering 'punishment', or attempting reform.

Stevenson (2007), Director of the Smith Institute, argues, 'The collateral damage of imprisonment is considerable – a third of prisoners lose their home while in prison, two-thirds lose their job, over a fifth face increased financial problems and more than two-fifths lose contact with their family. This is damaging not only to individual offenders but also to society as whole, which pays the price – in a variety of ways – for not reducing reoffending.'

Evaluation

The research is mixed and properly controlled studies are difficult to find, e.g. because participants cannot always be randomly assigned, most offenders in non-incarceration programmes are lower-risk, non-violent, and have less extensive criminal records.

- Gendreau *et al.*'s (1999), meta-analysis of 27 recidivism studies (from the US and UK, with male and female, adult and juvenile, high- and low-risk offenders), that met the criteria for inclusion, found a 7% increase in recidivism for ex-prisoners compared to offenders given community or other sentences.
- Villettaz *et al.*'s (2006) stricter meta-analysis of 27 studies found re-offending after a non-custodial sentence was lower than after a custodial one in 11 cases, not significantly different in 14 cases, and higher in two. However, when only considering the five best controlled studies, non-custodial sanctions were not found to have lower rates of re-offending beyond random effects.

RESTORATIVE JUSTICE

According to the Smith Institute (an independent think tank) Report (2007), 'Restorative justice [RJ] is a process that brings victims of crime into communication, either directly (face to face) or indirectly (through a mediator), with the person who has offended against them. This process is facilitated by a trained practitioner who can ensure the safety and support of all participants … RJ is always a voluntary process for both the victim and the offender – no one is forced to take part.'

Evaluation

The Smith Institute highlights a variety of research findings on RJ, including:

- The British Crime Survey – suggests around half of victims would like to communicate with their offender to achieve emotional closure.
- Ministry of Justice research in 2007 of RJ pilot studies found:
  - 85% of victims were satisfied with their experience of RJ (compared with 33% for conventional justice).
  - 78% of victims participating in RJ said they would recommend it.
  - Victims participating in RJ are far more likely to receive an apology from the offender than at court.
- Sherman and Strang's (2007) review of international randomised control studies found that, compared to conventional justice, overall RJ:
  - reduced victim post-traumatic stress
  - reduced victim desires for revenge
  - improved victim satisfaction
  - reduced recidivism more than prison with adult offenders or as well as prison with youths.

The Smith Institute report concludes: Although RJ 'is no magic wand', it can substantially reduce repeat offending and its related costs for some offenders, humanising justice for the benefit of all. RJ evidence is far more extensive and positive than it has been for many other national policies and is ready to be put to far broader use.

THE DEATH PENALTY

Regardless of moral viewpoint on the ethical justification of the death penalty, most would agree that such an extreme solution to criminal behaviour should be applied fairly and without prejudice. Unfortunately, studies have shown that this is far from the case.

Evaluation

Eberhardt *et al.*'s (2006) 'Looking Deathworthy' study showed that, in cases involving a White victim, the more stereotypically Black a defendant was perceived to be, the more likely that person was to be sentenced to death. The study controlled for many factors:
- ➤ aggravating circumstances
- ➤ mitigating circumstances
- ➤ severity of the murder
- ➤ defendant socioeconomic status
- ➤ victim socioeconomic status
- ➤ the defendant's attractiveness.

The authors report that:
- 24.4% of Black defendants falling in the lower half of the stereotypicality distribution received a death sentence compared to 57.5% of those who fell in the upper half.
- The death-sentencing rate for Black male defendants convicted of murdering *Black* victims was only 27% compared to 41% for White victims.

Eberhardt *et al.* explained the results in terms of prior research, which found:
- Racial stereotypes are more readily applied to Blacks who are thought to look more stereotypically Black than those less so (Blair *et al.*, 2004).
- Black physical traits are particularly associated with criminality and the more stereotypical the traits appear to be, the more criminal the person is perceived (Eberhardt *et al.*, 2004).
- Perceived stereotypicality correlates with judges' sentencing decisions (Blair et al. 2004); defendants with the most stereotypically Black facial features served up to 8 months longer in prison for felonies than those with the least stereotypical features.

24.7 Treatment programmes for offenders

COGNITIVE SKILLS PROGRAMMES AND ANGER MANAGEMENT

Cognitive skills programmes and offenders

- Friendship *et al.* (2002) measured the effectiveness of a prison-based cognitive behavioural treatment programme in England and Wales involving 'the enhancement of thinking skills for the purposes of self-control (thinking before acting), interpersonal problem-solving skills, analysis of social situation, critical reasoning skills, cognitive style of living, and understanding the values that govern behaviour.'
- The 2-year reconviction rates for the 670 volunteer adult male offenders with custodial sentences of 2 years or more who had participated in Cognitive Skills programmes were up to 14 % lower than matched controls, even when the influence of other variables related to reconviction were considered.
- However, later studies (e.g. Cann *et al.*, 2003) have not always replicated this finding.

Anger management and offenders

Beck and Fernandez (1998) report that many anger management therapies are derived from Meichenbaum's stress inoculation training (SIT), i.e. using a coping skills approach structured into three phases:

- ***Cognitive preparation*** – identifying situational triggers of anger and positive or negative self-statements.
- ***Skill acquisition*** – acquisition of relaxation skills and rehearsing cognitive self-statements to reframe the situation and facilitate healthy responses (e.g. 'Relax, don't take things so personally' or 'It isn't important enough to blow up over this').
- ***Rehearsal*** – exposure to anger-provoking situations using imagery or role-plays to practise the cognitive and relaxation techniques until the mental and physical responses can be achieved automatically and on cue.

Beck and Fernandez (1998) add that the 'basic outline of SIT can also be supplemented with alternative techniques such as problem-solving, conflict management, and social skills training.'

Evaluation

- Ireland (2004) found a brief group-based anger management intervention produced significant improvements in 50 young male offenders compared to 37 controls according to two measures taken two weeks before and eight weeks after the intervention:
  - ➤ A self-report anger questionnaire (Anger Management Assessment questionnaire).
  - ➤ A prison officer assessment of angry behaviour (Wing Behaviour Checklist: WBC).
- Beck and Fernandez (1998) meta-analysis of 50 studies involving 1,640 subjects found Cognitive Behavioural Therapy (CBT) for anger management on a variety of populations (including offenders):'*produced a grand mean weighted effect size of .70, indicating that the average CBT recipient was better off than 76% of untreated subjects in terms of anger reduction. This effect was statistically significant, robust, and relatively homogeneous across studies. These findings represent a quantitative integration of 20 years of research into a coherent picture of the efficacy of CBT for anger management.'*

EAR ACUPUNCTURE FOR DRUG REHABILITATION

Aim

Mike Wheatley conducted a study on the use of auricular acupuncture to treat substance misusing male prisoners in six high security prisons in partnership with SMART-UK and University of Cambridge Institute of Criminology. Previous research had indicated the positive effects of acupuncture in different contexts and the programme had already proven popular with prison inmates and staff so, given the highly significant role of drug addition in criminal behaviour, an evaluative study was undertaken.

Method

After screening, comparisons were made between prisoners going through a 4-week period of the ear acupuncture programme (twice weekly treatments) plus standard care, versus those on standard care only, using quantitative scales and qualitative methods.

Results

Quantitative measurements (Smart-UK synopsis 2007):

- The treatment group's health distress symptoms improved by 43% compared to a 25% improvement in the control group receiving standard care).
- Worry levels reduced by 30%.
- Muscle tension reduced by 42%.
- Drug craving reduced by 47%.
- Physical well-being improved by 31%.
- Psychological well-being improved by 53%.
- Stress levels reduced by 20%.
- Energy levels increased by 23%.
- 27% increase in confidence to address drug and alcohol problems and likelihood to recommend acupuncture.

Qualitative measurements (HM Prison Service magazine)

Wheatley reports that other treatment effects included: sleep promotion, improved relaxation, better coping skills, reduced nicotine cravings, amended cognitions, general health improvements, greater engagement in prison and support activities, and greater inclination to communicate with their families and engage in offending behaviour programmes or education classes.

Prisoners also reported fewer suicidal and self-harm tendencies, while prison staff commented on less conflict and aggression between inmates.

Evaluation

- It is difficult to assess the precise role of acupuncture, given that it is just one of the many interventions used for drug rehabilitation – indeed Wheatley is quick to point out that ear acupuncture should not be seen in isolation and is used with 'good clinical services that offer detox medications, quality cognitive behavioural therapy and comprehensive social and after care support services'. (*HM Prison Service magazine*).
- It is popular with management and staff since it is easily taught and administered and is very low-cost.
- It is popular with prisoners since it does not require high levels of motivation and is more non-verbal and non-confrontational compared to other therapies.

25.1 Traits and sport

THE TRAIT APPROACH TO PERSONALITY

Personality traits refer to the **characteristics of individuals** (such as how they typically think, feel and behave) that are supposed to remain reasonably **consistent across situations** and **over time**, but that may **vary between individuals** in degree. Two major personality trait theories established through statistical factor analysis (although using slightly different approaches) have been proposed by **Eysenck and Cattell**:

- Eysenck suggested three basic personality types that vary between people along dimensions and are mostly biologically based. The extremes of the dimensions are introversion / extraversion, neuroticism / stability, and psychoticism, and can be measured using the EPI or EPQ (Eysenck Personality Inventory/Questionnaire).
- Cattell suggested 16 basic source personality traits, again varying between people along dimensions and measured using the 16PF (Sixteen-Personality Factor Questionnaire).

Eysenck's personality types:

- **Extraverts** – are sociable, crave excitement and change, take chances, and are impulsive. They tend to be carefree, optimistic, unreliable and lose their temper fairly quickly. Eysenck suggests they get bored more quickly, are less responsive to pain and are poor at extended periods of concentration if change and excitement is not involved.
- **Introverts** – are reserved, socially retiring, plan their actions and control their emotions. They tend to be serious, reliable and pessimistic, and do not lose their temper easily.
- **Neurotics** – are anxious, worrying, moody and overly emotional and reactive, finding it difficult to calm after upset.
- **Stables** - are emotionally calm, unreactive and unworried.
- **Psychotics** – are unempathetic, solitary and often uncaring, troublesome, aggressive or cruel towards others.

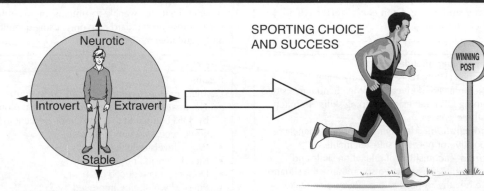

SPORTING CHOICE AND SUCCESS

TRAITS AND SPORT CHOICE AND SUCCESS

Much research has been devoted to trying to link specific personality traits to the choice of sport in general, different sports in particular, and sporting success. The research was undertaken in the hope that individuals could be selected for their potential for different sports or their suitability for training.

Traits and sport choice

- Kroll and Crenshaw (1970) – assessed the personality profiles of individuals highly skilled in American football, wrestling, gymnastics and karate using Cattell's 16PF questionnaire. Similar profiles were gained for the American footballers and wrestlers, but distinct profiles were found for those involved in gymnastics and karate (Woods, 1998).
- Kirkcaldy (1982) – assessed 199 team athletes and 124 individual sport athletes aged 22–24 using the EPI, but found no significant differences between those involved in team or individual sports (unlike previous research that has found team players to be more anxious and extravert). However, on analysing the within-team differences, males in offensive positions scored significantly higher on psychoticism and extraversion than midfield players, while defenders tended to score slightly higher than forwards on stability (Banyard and Hayes, 1994).
- Daino (1985, also cited in Banyard and Hayes, 1994) found 66 teenage tennis players scored higher on extraversion and lower on neuroticism, psychoticism and anxiety than an age matched control group who played no sport.

Traits and sporting success

- Williams and Parkin (1980) found the 16PF profiles of international standard male hockey players were different from those of club standard players (Woods, 1998).
- Garland and Barry (1990, cited in Jarvis, 1999) found that the 16PF traits of tough-mindedness, extraversion, group dependency and emotional stability accounted for 29% of the variance in the skill ratings of American college athletes.

EVALUATION OF THE TRAIT APPROACH TO SPORT PSYCHOLOGY

- Despite hundreds of studies, there have been many contradictory findings and the effects of personality traits on sport choice and success seem to range from none to minor.
- Researchers such as Ogilvie and Tutko (1972) have argued that personality profiles emerge most consistently at elite levels of competition, while Fisher et al (1978) report that personality traits appear in general to explain no more than 10% of the behavioural variability in sporting situations.
- Personality profiles may have better success at predicting more extreme sporting activities (e.g. rock-climbing and sensation-seeking).
- Personality traits appear to be better at predicting sport choice rather than success. This may be due to studying individuals who have stuck at a sport because they were more successful at it compared to unsuccessful players who gave it up, thus obscuring a significant proportion of the success.
- There are many methodological problems in trait research. Correlational data means that sporting choice and success could cause or shape, rather than result from, personality traits. Longitudinal research is needed to measure whether traits lead to sport activity and remain stable through sporting careers.
- There are many other more important factors than personality that influence sporting choice and success, e.g. interests, abilities, motivation, and experience. Interactionism of personality and situation is a more likely explanation.
- Personality traits may not actually remain stable across situations and time, and personality tests have many problems with their reliability and validity, e.g. mood and motivation may affect the results.
- There are better ways of predicting sporting performance and suitability, e.g. actual performance trials.

25.2 Sport and socialisation 1

SOCIAL LEARNING THEORY AND INDIVIDUAL DIFFERENCES IN BEHAVIOUR

Social Learning Theory (Bandura, 1962, Mischel, 1973), proposes that individual differences in behaviour result from different environmental experience. It suggests that in addition to behaviour being learned through personal experience (via the behaviourist processes of classical and operant conditioning), individual differences may be acquired by just observing others' modelled behaviour and its consequences, via the following processes:

- **Observation learning** – being able to automatically learn behaviour from just observing models, without the need for reinforcement. Models provide information about **behaviour** (actions, statements, skills etc.) and its **consequences** (whether it leads to positive or negative outcomes).
- **Cognitive processes** – such as **attention** and **memory** abilities that allow the person to focus on relevant models and behaviour, e.g. based on past memories of who and what is most useful and appropriate to imitate in a given environment. A memory representation of how to reproduce what was said or done is stored with information concerning the past consequences of the behaviour. Models most likely to be imitated are those who are rewarded for their behaviour (e.g. high status and successful models) or regarded as socially appropriate, relevant and similar to the observer (e.g. those of similar gender, age and interests).
- **Imitation** – involves the motor reproduction (copying) of previously witnessed and stored actions with varying degrees of accuracy.
- **Motivation** – the imitation of behaviour depends upon the expected consequences of behaviour, based upon whether it was seen to be rewarded in others (vicarious or indirect reinforcement) or punished, whether individuals were rewarded or punished for it themselves, or if they felt good about it last time (self-reinforcement).

Thus each person will have a unique actual and vicarious reinforcement history depending upon the particular set of environmental and social interactions they have experienced and witnessed, although common life events and a shared culture will mean individuals will also show marked similarities in behaviour.

EVALUATION

- The theory incorporates many important social, cognitive and learning influences upon the development of sport behaviour.
- The theory neglects the role of innate, biological factors upon abilities and personality traits that may affect sport choice and behaviour.

Social learning theory and sport behaviour

Individual difference in sporting behaviour may result, according to Social Learning Theory, from:

- **Exposure** to sport and sporting models – the interest in and opportunity to attend or watch sporting events determines the degree of attention paid to sport behaviour and skills.
- **Observation of models** who are:
  1 highly successful, famous or well paid in sport (especially if attention is drawn to them through media exposure)
  2 similar to the observer in gender and sporting interests (this has implications for gender differences in imitation of certain athlete role models and sports).
- **Cognitive ability** to represent and store sport related skills (this perhaps relates to procedural and visuo-spatial memory encoding and retrieval abilities).
- **Motor skill** and strength to reproduce stored sport-related actions – a mixture of innate capacity, age and practice determines this.
- **The degree of encouragement** for imitated or personally acquired (through trial and error) sporting performance. This depends upon the relative degrees of positive reinforcement (e.g. praise, success), negative reinforcement (e.g. avoidance of criticism, failure) and punishment (e.g. criticism and failure) actually or vicariously received.

Note. Social learning theorists would also accept that positive or negative emotional responses (e.g. due to enjoyment) can be associated with sporting activity through classical conditioning, thus affecting attitudes to sport.

THE EFFECT OF SOCIALISATION ON SPORTING BEHAVIOUR

Socialisation refers to the process of acquiring the behaviour, beliefs, values and attitudes of one's society. As indicated above, Social Learning Theory suggests that environmental experience can shape sporting attitudes and behaviour, and that different patterns of reinforcement history result from different kinds of environmental influence. Three major socialising influences that can affect sport participation, choice, attitudes and behaviour include family, culture and gender.

- **Family influences** – socialisation begins in the home and parental or sibling interest and participation in sport act as important first role models and sources of reinforcement. Children often attempt to emulate and compete with their sibling peers; success may lead to a similar choice of sport, while failure may result in switching to other sports or a lack of further participation. Parental encouragement of children's sporting participation and performance often triggers a life-long interest and is vital for sport participation outside of school.
- **Cultural influences** – it has long been accepted, at least since Roman gladiatorial times, that the general norms and values of a society can affect attitudes toward sport and the kind of sports indulged in. Sipes (1973) in an observational anthropological study found that 9 of 10 warlike societies had combative sports, but only 2 of 10 peaceful societies did. Sipes also found a positive correlation between military activity and the popularity of combative sports in the United States. Individualistic cultures like the USA tend to emphasise individual achievement and competition more than collectivistic cultures, perhaps socialising their children to be competitive but less willing to be good team players. This socialisation actually appears to cause many American children to drop out of sport due to the emphasis on winning, since interviews with young children typically reveal that their initial participation in sport is due to the desire to make or maintain friendships and have fun rather than to win.

Gender socialisation and sporting behaviour

The way boys and girls are socialised in general can have a profound influence on their attitudes towards, and performance in, sport.

- Duquin (1978) reports 'support for the notion that parents, other adults, teachers, textbooks, and the media all affirm the idea that sport, vigorous physical activity, and risk-taking are all appropriate behaviours for males [but not] for females' (Oglesby, 1984).
- Many studies (e.g. Fagot, 1977) indicate that females are reinforced for dependency, passivity, low competitiveness, and less aggression and rough-and-tumble play.
- Gill and Deeter (1988) found that males scored higher than females on competitiveness and win orientation using the Sport Orientation Questionnaire, while females scored a little higher on goal orientation (reaching personal goals) in sport (Woods, 1998).
- Coolican (1996) reports that, compared to boys, girls have been found to prefer non-competitive activities (Weinberg and Jackson, 1979), value sport less (Eccles and Harold, 1991) and be perceived as less physically competent when matched on performance (Brawley et al, 1979).

25.3 Sport and socialisation 2

THE EFFECT OF SPORT ON SOCIAL DEVELOPMENT

- Rather than just reflecting socialisation, sport may actually be an important socialising influence itself.
- Sports people are, in social learning theory terms, widely publicised and admired role models, while sporting activities and games effectively represent the goals, norms and personal qualities found in, or desired by, a society.
- Since socialisation refers to the process of acquiring the behaviour, beliefs, values and attitudes of one's society, we should not necessarily expect this influence to be entirely positive, as is often thought.
- A society's sports and role models may, unwittingly or otherwise, portray, communicate and reinforce the socially undesirable behaviour and attitudes of a society to its children.

SPORT AND AGGRESSION

Psychologists have argued that sport legitimises aggression that would otherwise be prosecuted, e.g. boxing, and socially sanctions, expects and rewards it. The socialising effect of sport to create aggression has been found in many studies:

- Smoll and Smith conducted extensive field studies of Little League teams in North America and found that the coaches they interviewed reported little in the way of character building in the children they coached. However, the researchers concluded that competitive sport could have a beneficial effect on the children depending on the coach's behaviour and the degree to which adult pressure to win affected the children.
- Silva (1981) found that while the constitutive (official or formal) rules of sport were designed to promote pro-social behaviour, the normative (informal or unwritten) rules of some team sports socialised children to be violent, cheat, foul and negatively stereotype injure, intimidate and dehumanise their opponents. Silva argues that anti-social normative behaviour is reinforced by success, praise and social pressure, and cites the study of McMurtry (1974) who found that ice hockey players who refused to conform to normative rules concerning aggression against the opposition were negatively labelled and sometimes ostracised from the team.

Viewers and fans of sport may also be affected by the aggression it contains and sanctions, as well as falling prey to the inter-group identity, competition and conflict it creates (thus the violence of football hooliganism, for example).

- Phillips (1983) found homicide rates increased by over 12% on average following heavyweight boxing championship prize fights, especially highly publicised ones (Lippa, 1990). Goldstein and Arms (1971) found the contact sports of wrestling and ice hockey increased aggression in viewers, whereas competitive but non-contact sports such as gymnastics and swimming did not.

THE POSSIBLE EFFECTS OF SPORT

POSITIVE EFFECTS OF SPORT

Character building
- Self-reliance, assertiveness, courage, sportsmanship.
- Dedication, self-discipline and perseverance.

Cognitive skills
- Decision-making skills, moral cognitive development.
- Mastery, competence and self-efficacy.

Social skills
- Co-operation, friendship and communication skills.

Emotional effects
- Positive self-esteem, pride and a sense of accomplishment.

Pro-social effects
- Delinquency avoidance via provision of a sense of purpose and productive use of time.
- Prejudice reduction though the portrayal of positive images of minorities, inter-group contact, super-ordinate team goals and shared in-group identity.
- Transmission of socially desired values (e.g. individual achievement and competitiveness in individualistic societies, teamwork and respect in collectivist societies).
- Transmission of society's norms of acceptable and unacceptable behaviour and rules of fair play.
- Punishment of anti-social behaviour and rule breaking, e.g. via yellow and red cards or fines.

NEGATIVE EFFECTS OF SPORT

Character deterioration
- Selfishness, self-absorption, arrogance, over-competitiveness, and aggressiveness / combativeness.
- Lack of dedication and perseverance if consistent failure.

Cognitive skills
- Lower moral cognitive development, lack of guilt.
- Lack of competence / self-efficacy if consistent failure.

Social skills
- Lack of teamwork or co-operation and social isolation if individual achievement is emphasised or rewarded.

Emotional effects
- Negative self-esteem, fear of failure as a result of failure.

Anti-social effects
- Prejudice reinforcement though the selective media reporting and exposure of majority group sporting events, e.g. male rather than female football, or stereotypes.
- The creation of frustration and inter-group conflict, competition, stereotyping, dehumanisation and violence.
- Transmission of socially undesirable values (e.g. gamesmanship, aggression, cheating without discovery, and disrespect of rules and authority, i.e. referees).
- Encouragement of anti-social behaviour and rule breaking (e.g. through the ineffective use of punishment or the higher rewards of winning over offending).

25.4 Intrinsic and extrinsic motivation and sport

WHAT IS MOTIVATION?

As Silva and Weinberg (1984) point out, "Like many other psychological constructs, *motivation* has been defined in a variety of ways, but in general it refers to the intensity and direction of behaviour. The direction of behaviour indicates whether an individual approaches or avoids a particular situation, and the intensity of behaviour relates to the degree of effort put forth to accomplish the behaviour. Thus, motivation can affect the selection, intensity, and persistence of an individual's behaviour, which in sport can obviously have a strong impact on the quality of an athlete's performance."

ENJOYMENT
MASTERY
COMPETENCE
INNER STANDARDS
SELF-WORTH

INTRINSIC MOTIVATION

EXTRINSIC MOTIVATION

INTRINSIC MOTIVATION AND SPORT

- Intrinsic motivation comes from, or is perceived to come from, **within** the individual.
- In the context of sport it may refer to the spontaneous enjoyment of sporting activities, the sense of mastery and competence in acquiring skills, the inner need to achieve, and the feelings of self-worth at having achieved *personal* standards or goals.
- When not being controlled by external goals or limits, the above intrinsic influences are self-perpetuating and remarkably persistent forms of motivation.
- A sense of voluntary, self-determining choice and control over one's sporting activities is central to the individual regarding their sporting activity as intrinsically motivated.
- Intrinsic motivation occurs spontaneously in individuals and is evident from very young ages.
- Intrinsic motivation and inner standards, rewards and punishments are incorporated into psychodynamic, humanistic, cognitive and social learning psychological theories.

EXTRINSIC MOTIVATION AND SPORT

- Extrinsic motivation comes from, or is perceived to come from, **outside** the individual.
- In the context of sport it may refer to the positive or negative reinforcement of sporting achievement through physical means, such as the possibility of gaining or losing prizes (e.g. trophies and money), or social means, such as praise or the avoidance of criticism. Extrinsic motivation may also involve competition with others to achieve *external* standards or goals.
- External rewards or goals may set limits on motivation and need to be maintained to keep motivation persistent.
- A sense of lack of voluntary, self-determining choice and control over one's sporting activities is central to regarding sporting activity as extrinsically motivated.
- Extrinsic motivation may be applied at any age depending upon the type of reinforcer used, e.g. very young children are not readily motivated by competition with others.
- Extrinsic motivation and reinforcement is a key assumption of behaviourist learning theory psychology.

INTRINSIC AND EXTRINSIC MOTIVATION AND SPORT PSYCHOLOGY

Psychologists originally assumed that providing extrinsic motivators for an interesting activity would add to the intrinsic motivation. However Deci's (1975) Cognitive Evaluation Theory suggests that extrinsic motivation can undermine intrinsic motivation if it:

- Removes the individual's sense of voluntary control or choice over performing an activity.
- Provides information that decreases the individual's sense of competence or self-worth in the activity.

Competition can also undermine intrinsic interest by reducing enjoyment and 'turning play into work'.
Coaches should therefore:

- Use extrinsic rewards to encourage activities not originally found intrinsically interesting, then gradually phase them out.
- Use extrinsic motivators carefully, e.g. praise rather than punish, and reinforce the athlete's sense of competence rather than control their performance.
- Emphasise intrinsic motivations in competitive sports, e.g. enjoyment, mastery and personal goals, especially after losing.
- Take into account that different athletes (e.g. genders) may find different stimuli reinforcing.

STUDIES OF INTRINSIC AND EXTRINSIC MOTIVATION

Deci (1971) found that participants paid to conduct an intrinsically interesting activity (puzzle-solving) later spent almost half the time on it than participants who had not previously been paid for it.

Lepper and Greene (1975) – their field experiment tested nursery school children who had shown a high intrinsic interest in picture drawing. They found those children told to expect a certificate and gold star for their drawing before actually receiving this external 'reward' later showed lower interest in the activity, implying their intrinsic interest had been undermined. Children unexpectedly given the same reward, or those who were neither told about or received it, showed higher levels of interest than the first group in a free-choice situation.

Smith, Smoll and Curtis (1979) – found American children showed greater enthusiasm and enjoyment of sport if their coaches encouraged and reinforced them rather than stressing winning and competition, thus reinforcing rather than undermining their intrinsic motivation.

Deci et al (1981) – found participants given an intrinsically interesting task and told to compete with others were later found to show less motivation in the task than those not instructed to compete.

Deci et al (1977) – found males who competed for a reward showed more intrinsic interest than those who competed for no reward, but females showed the opposite tendency.

Weinberg (1979) – found higher levels of intrinsic motivation in participants after they had won in an activity than lost in it.

25.5 Achievement motivation and sport

WHAT IS ACHIEVEMENT MOTIVATION?

'Achievement' refers to a measure of ability or attainment that reflects progress or an accomplished goal. 'Motivation' refers to the impulse or desire to behave in certain ways. 'Achievement motivation' therefore concerns the desire to do well, succeed and reach standards in one's own eyes and the eyes of others, and reflects a willingness to persist in behaviour that enables higher standards to be reached despite the possibility of failure.

Researchers such as McClelland et al (1953) and Atkinson (1964) extensively studied achievement motivation, the latter suggesting that it could be precisely formulated and calculated by measuring the **desire to succeed** of an individual and **subtracting** from it a measurement of that person's **fear of failure**.

In most early studies, achievement motivation was measured by *projective testing* – for example, people were asked to create a story on a particular topic and their responses were analysed to reveal how much the themes of their stories reflected desires to succeed or fear of failure.

Atkinson regarded achievement motivation as a **personality trait** – differing between individuals but remaining fairly consistent within each person and thus stable across different situations they might encounter. However, it was recognised that achievement motivation *interacted* with **situational factors**, in particular:

- The difficulty of the tasks faced – measured in terms of the probability of success or failure
- The incentive value of success – measured in terms of the importance to the individual of success or failure in a particular task.

ACHIEVEMENT MOTIVATION AND SPORT

Achievement motivation has many implications for sporting attitudes, training and performance. For example, those showing high levels tend to show:

- **Desire for challenge** – seeking challenging opponents (i.e. those of equal or slightly higher ability) or tasks, and demanding but achievable standards or goals. Those scoring low on achievement motivation will either not seek sporting challenge at all or will choose either very easy or very hard opponents, tasks and goals (especially if high on fear of failure) so success is guaranteed or failure justifiable.
- **Concern for excellent standards and value of feedback** – meaning they may respond better to constructive criticism in coaching, training for skill acquisition and practice for skill refinement.
- **Lower fear of failure and more positive internal attributions regarding failure and success** – leading to greater persistence in sport endeavours.
- **Positive attitudes towards evaluation** – in combination with all the above factors may lead to higher standards of performance.

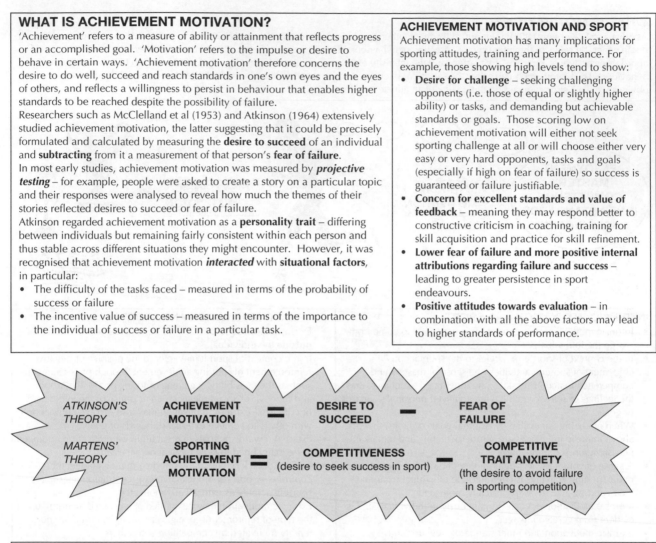

ATKINSON'S THEORY | **ACHIEVEMENT MOTIVATION** = **DESIRE TO SUCCEED** − **FEAR OF FAILURE**

MARTENS' THEORY | **SPORTING ACHIEVEMENT MOTIVATION** = **COMPETITIVENESS** (desire to seek success in sport) − **COMPETITIVE TRAIT ANXIETY** (the desire to avoid failure in sporting competition)

EVALUATING ACHIEVEMENT MOTIVATION IN SPORT

Achievement motivation does not reliably predict performance in sport. Contradictory findings have been produced, probably because research shows that those high in achievement motivation are likely to choose tasks of 0.5 probability (50:50) of success (e.g. equally matched opponents), while those low in achievement motivation are more likely to choose tasks of very high or low probability of success (e.g. very easy or very difficult opponents). Factors like relative ability and attribution may be more important in predicting persistence and performance in sport.

Measures of achievement motivation often lack reliability and validity. Projective tests are of doubtful reliability and validity because of the often subjective nature of their interpretation – different interpreters can arrive at different conclusions (poor inter-rater reliability) and may in fact project their own characteristics on to others' responses (poor validity). There is also the problem of relying on self-report data (which also applies to the use of questionnaires) to measure achievement motivation since people's responses and reported attitudes may not actually reflect how they behave.

Achievement motivation is too general and complex as a concept Cassidy and Lynn (1989, cited in Rolls and Eysenck, 1998) suggest it consists of six components: work ethic (the notion that work is 'good' in itself), pursuit of excellence, status aspiration (will to dominate others), competitiveness, acquisitiveness (desire for money), and mastery (competitiveness against set standards rather than against other people). This means that:

- People high in achievement motivation may possess these components to differing extents
- These intrinsic motives will respond differently to different extrinsic motivating factors or rewards (see intrinsic and extrinsic motivation)
- Achievement motivation may vary across different situations and sports.

- Horner (1972) suggested that *fear of success* is another important factor in achievement motivation, which can explain gender differences. Horner gave female undergraduates projective tests by asking them to create stories about successful female or male figures, and found around two-thirds invented negative consequences for the female figure. Because they did not tend to do this for male story figures, Horner concluded that women have a higher fear of success than men do. However, the research was based on a limited sample (a minority of women) and other studies have found men show equal (Robbins and Robbins, 1973) or higher (Pyke and Kahill, 1983) fear of success (cited in Tavris and Wade, 1990).
- Martens (1977) attempted to make achievement motivation more sport specific by suggesting that sporting motivation and performance can be more precisely predicted by comparing competitiveness (e.g. measured by Gill and Deeter's Sport Orientation Questionnaire) with competitive trait anxiety (which can be measured by Martens's Sport Competition Anxiety Test).

Sports men and women scoring high in competitive trait anxiety are more likely to show cognitive and physical state anxiety in competitive situations that will affect their performance (see **Effects of Anxiety/Arousal**).

25.6 Improving motivation in sport – self-efficacy

WHAT IS SELF-EFFICACY?
Bandura (1977b) regarded self-efficacy as the **cognitive belief** that one **is competent** at a **particular task**. As a concept, it is thus **distinct from** (although it may be linked to):

- Self-esteem because this relates to positive or negative *feelings* about one's ability, rather than the **thought processes** of self-efficacy.
- Achievement motivation because this concerns one's desire or need to be competent and do well, rather than the **actual self-perception of current competence** of self-efficacy.
- General self-confidence because self-efficacy is **situation-specific** (one may have self-efficacy in football but not other sports).

As a measure, self-efficacy refers to the **strength of conviction** that behaviour can be **successfully executed** to produce a certain outcome. It can be regarded as an important **mediating variable** between past and future performance.

WHAT CAUSES SELF-EFFICACY?
Several sources of information can form the basis of the self-efficacy belief, some more valid or important than others, for example:

- **One's own past performance** – the most influential and valid influence on the strength of self-efficacy. The relative levels of past success and failure in the particular sport, skill or task provide *probability information* on the likelihood of future success or failure. Repeated failure, for example, will lead to very low self-efficacy, especially for beginners.
- **Verbal feedback and persuasion** – coaches or other observers may provide positive or negative information on competence or performance in sporting tasks that may modify, favourably or otherwise, the individual's own beliefs. Observers' perceptions and information may be less or more accurate than the performer's, however, and depend upon attributions of cause.
- **The observation of others' performance** – Bandura's Social Learning Theory suggests that other people act as models that provide information regarding the consequences of actions. Through observational learning of models' actions, and their success or failure, the learner may vicariously experience competence, which may affect their own sense of efficacy. Such self-efficacy may be illusory, short-term and easily contradicted by their own ability-based performance, however, as observers find it is not as easy or hard as it looks.

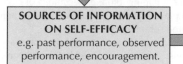

SOURCES OF INFORMATION ON SELF-EFFICACY e.g. past performance, observed performance, encouragement.	→	SELF-EFFICACY Strength of current competence belief	→	SPORTING PERFORMANCE Quality of future performance

WHAT EFFECT DOES SELF-EFFICACY HAVE ON SPORTING PERFORMANCE?
Self-efficacy affects **expectations of success** and performance via:

- **Task motivation** – influencing how much effort and persistence is shown in a task by affecting tolerance of defeat and fear of failure (consistent past success makes self-efficacy and motivation more resistant to a defeat or two). Those high in self-efficacy are also likely to attribute the cause of performance to internal factors that they can work on to improve.
- **Arousal and anxiety** – perceived competence can reduce negative arousal, distracting worrying or negative self-statements. Arousal that is experienced may be interpreted more positively with higher self-efficacy (thinking one is 'psyched up' not 'stressed out'!).
- **Tactical confidence** – self-efficacy might influence the confidence to employ skilful or daring (but productive) tactics, or intimidate / cause self-doubt in the opposition with displays of confidence.

HOW CAN SELF-EFFICACY BE IMPROVED TO INCREASE MOTIVATION IN SPORT?
- **Appropriate goal setting** – since the most important influence on self-efficacy is past experience, coaches should give plenty of opportunity for players to actually practise skills and tasks and to experience success by setting achievable goals, especially for beginners (Bandura and Schunk, 1981). McAuley (1985, cited in Woods, 1998) found guiding gymnasts through a task was more successful than having them watch a model do it, and was more effective at reducing anxiety than verbal persuasion.
- **Positive and constructive feedback** – coaches should provide and reinforce skill, competence and confidence.
- **False feedback** – exaggerating success can increase performance within limits. Wells et al (1993, cited in Jarvis, 1999) found weightlifters duped into thinking they had lifted more weight than they had, later did lift more than weightlifters given accurate feedback.

EVALUATION OF SELF-EFFICACY IN SPORT
- Bandura realised that many other factors are important in influencing sport performance and has applied his ideas to *team* self-efficacy too.
- Self-efficacy does seem associated with increased performance, but it is not always clear exactly how it has its effect, and measures of it are not as good as past performance at predicting future performance.
- The correlational nature of many studies on self-efficacy means it is not always certain how much it is a cause rather than effect of performance.

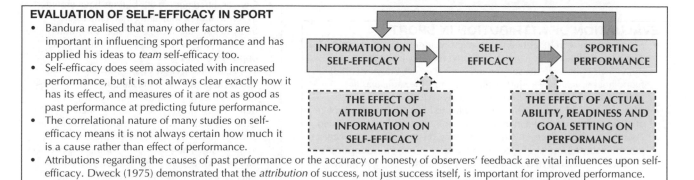

- Attributions regarding the causes of past performance or the accuracy or honesty of observers' feedback are vital influences upon self-efficacy. Dweck (1975) demonstrated that the *attribution* of success, not just success itself, is important for improved performance.

25.7 Improving motivation in sport – attribution

WHAT IS ATTRIBUTION?
- Attribution refers to how individuals **explain the cause of behaviour**.

HOW ARE ATTRIBUTIONS MADE?
Weiner's (1972) model of attribution points out that depending upon a *logical cognitive assessment* of
- whether behaviour is caused by factors relating to the actor or the situation they are in
- whether the cause is stable or unstable over time

an individual will attribute behaviour to one of four kinds of cause (see below). Various theories have been proposed (e.g. Jones and Davis, 1965, Kelley, 1967) to explain how factors like intention, ability, distinctiveness, social desirability, consistency and comparison with others, can be used to rationally derive such attributions.

However, humans often show **biases or errors** in attribution, for example based on their access to, or perception of information, or for motivational reasons (such as to maintain self-esteem).

Biases or errors in attribution include:
- The fundamental attribution error (Ross, 1977) is the general tendency people have *to make internal attributions for others' behaviour* rather than external, situational ones, when there may be equally convincing evidence for both types of cause.
- The actor-observer effect (Jones and Nisbett, 1972) refers to the tendency of people to attribute internal / dispositional causes when observing others' behaviour (as in the fundamental attribution error), but *attribute external / situational causes to their own behaviour* (when they are the actors).
- The self-serving bias effect (Miller and Ross, 1975) refers to the tendency of **actors** to *attribute successful behaviour to internal causes*, but *unsuccessful behaviour to external ones*, thus qualifying the actor-observer effect.

Attributional bias tends to increase with the *seriousness of the consequences* of the behaviour and its *personal (hedonic) relevance*.

WEINER'S MODEL OF ATTRIBUTION

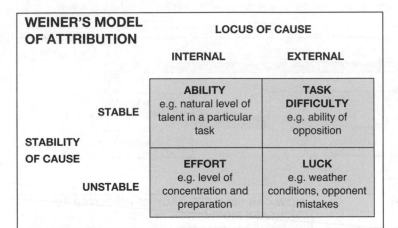

		LOCUS OF CAUSE	
		INTERNAL	**EXTERNAL**
STABILITY OF CAUSE	**STABLE**	**ABILITY** e.g. natural level of talent in a particular task	**TASK DIFFICULTY** e.g. ability of opposition
	UNSTABLE	**EFFORT** e.g. level of concentration and preparation	**LUCK** e.g. weather conditions, opponent mistakes

HOW CAN ATTRIBUTIONS BE IMPROVED TO INCREASE MOTIVATION IN SPORT?
Attributional retraining – coaches should not just provide opportunities for success rather than failure, but should encourage players to attribute those experiences favourably or appropriately (Dweck, 1975). More specifically:
- Beginners should be encouraged to attribute success to internal factors, with an emphasis on stability to draw attention to their natural ability and potential in the sport. This should encourage choice and persistence of sporting activities by increasing self-efficacy.
- Established athletes should be encouraged to attribute success to internal factors, with an emphasis on instability to draw attention to their ability to improve through increasing their own effort (appealing to their intrinsic mastery and achievement motivation).
- Athletes should be encouraged to attribute failure to a mixture of unstable internal factors, to encourage responsibility and further effort, and external factors to maintain self-esteem.

EVALUATION OF ATTRIBUTION IN SPORT
- Some of the research has been contradictory, for example Roberts (1975) found baseball teams as a group attributed more logically than individuals (who used the self-serving bias), whereas Brawley (1980) found hockey teams were just as likely to show the same bias as individuals. Attribution is affected by many factors.
- Although Weiner has added controllability to his model, the kinds of attribution shown may be more complex and integrated than suggested.
- Focus just on the effects of winning or losing on attributions may neglect the athlete's perception of success and failure. A narrow loss against a significantly superior opponent may be regarded as a success, and a team loss may not have the same effect if the individual played well.

WHAT EFFECT DO ATTRIBUTIONS HAVE ON SPORTING PERFORMANCE?
Attributions of sporting success and failure are very important in explaining future expectations of success and performance (and thus for achievement motivation and self-efficacy).
- Consistent failure can lead to negative internal attributions. A sense of learned helplessness may result where failure is attributed to stable internal factors such as lack of ability, rather than unstable internal factors (meaning individuals will think effort will make no difference, so it is not even worth trying). This will lead to a self-fulfilling prophecy effect of the athlete's attitudes on their performance.
- Fortunately, both laboratory and field research generally indicates that athletes tend to make both individual and team attributions in line with the self-serving bias to help maintain their self-esteem – attributing success to internal factors (such as their ability or effort) and failure to external ones (such as strong opposition or bad luck).
- The self-serving bias can lead to false impressions of one's ability or even self-handicapping behaviour, e.g. deliberately choosing difficult opponents or insufficiently preparing to justify or excuse defeat.
- Successful athletes adopt an internal unstable attribution leading them to feel they are responsible for their performance but can also strive to improve it.
- Gender differences in attributions have emerged in some studies, indicating that females are more likely to attribute success to luck, but failure to lack of ability, while males show roughly the opposite tendency.
- The actor-observer effect and self-serving bias can be important in understanding how athletes and coaches perceive the causes of sporting behaviour. Disagreement is more likely over the causes of failure – the athlete will be more likely to blame external factors, while the coach will focus on internal factors of the athlete. Observers and actors are more likely to show agreement on internal attributions when a victory is gained.

25.8 Social facilitation

WHAT IS SOCIAL FACILITATION?

Social facilitation refers to **the effect that the mere presence of other people has on performance**. The effect can be:

- **Positive** – increasing / facilitating performance,
- **Negative** – decreasing / inhibiting performance.

Performance appears to be **facilitated** by the presence of others when **easy** or *well known* tasks are attempted, but **inhibited** with **difficult** or *new tasks*. Social facilitation research has focused on two kinds of situation:

- **Coaction** – when people work individually, side by side on similar tasks
- **Audiences** – when people are watching an individual performing a task.

Triplett (1897) – Performed the earliest experiments on cyclists in cycling trials under three conditions. In the first condition cyclists were told to race *individually* against the clock, in the second condition they were told to race *together* but *not to compete*, and in the third condition they were sent off together and asked to *compete*. The fastest time was recorded for the competing group, but importantly the non-competing group was significantly faster than the individuals.

ZAJONC'S (1965) DRIVE THEORY

Zajonc's drive theory suggests that the *mere presence* of others triggers an innate response of *increased drive* or *arousal*, which *energises the performance of dominant responses*. The theory is based on Clarke Hull's ideas on drives and behavioural responses, which suggests that dominant responses are those most learned and habitual. Zajonc proposed that in *easy* or well-known tasks the *most frequently available (dominant)* responses of an organism *are correct* ones - so these are energised to increase performance. With *complex* or unpractised tasks however, the *most likely or dominant* responses that an organism could make are incorrect ones – and when these are energised performance is bound to decrease! Zajonc proposed that arousal in the presence of others is a biologically *innate* response, thus accounting for his cockroach results, but other researchers have suggested different (and more cognitive) reasons for this arousing effect.

Zajonc reviewed many studies conducted up to 1965 and concluded that his theory could explain the fairly consistent finding that easy/well-practised tasks tend to be facilitated while difficult/novel ones were inhibited by the presence of others. Later research also tended to confirm this finding:

Zajonc et al (1969) – Tested *cockroaches* in easy and difficult mazes and found that they escaped more quickly in the easy maze if two cockroaches ran the maze or an audience of cockroaches watched, but took longer to escape in the more difficult maze under the same conditions.

Michaels et al (1982) – Rated *pool players* as either good or below average, and then stood around and pool table in a small group to watch them play. The *best players* showed an *increase* in shot accuracy by 9%, while the *poor players* showed a *decrease* of 11%, suggesting that tasks which are easy or well known are facilitated, while difficult or unpractised tasks are inhibited by audiences.

Bell and Yee (1989) – Tested 16 skilled and 17 unskilled subjects in karate, both in front of an expert audience and on their own. The task was to kick a target as many times as possible in 15 seconds over four trials. The skilled karate kickers performed equally well under both conditions whereas the *unskilled* performed significantly less kicks in front of the audience.

EVALUATION APPREHENSION THEORY

Cottrell (1968) accepted Zajonc's drive theory of social facilitation but argued that the arousal is triggered by a learned rather than instinctive source – evaluation. Evaluation apprehension theory proposes that social facilitation effects only occur when individuals feel they are under evaluation from, and thus will receive positive or negative outcomes for their performance from, other people, either when working together (coaction) or being directly watched (audience).

Dashiell (1930, 35) – Found social facilitation just by telling subjects that others were performing the same task *elsewhere*. In a later experiment Dashiell carefully arranged the coaction experiment so that the subjects could *not compete*, rather than just telling them not to, and found no coaction facilitation effect.

Paulus and Murdock (1971) – Found that audience effects are stronger in front of *experts* than non-experts.

Cottrell (1968) – *Blindfolded* the audience and found no social facilitation. However, Schmitt et al's (1986) study (see below) contradicts this finding.

DISTRACTION CONFLICT THEORY

Baron (1986) suggests that others have an arousing effect simply because they are a *source of distraction*, regardless of whether they are evaluating us or not. The presence of others puts people into a state of *attentional conflict* over whether to allocate attention to the task or others, and this conflict may raise their drive / arousal level. In addition, *well-known* or simple tasks require *less attention* and so will be less distracted by the presence of others as they are more automatic, whereas difficult tasks require much more attention to be effectively performed and so are more open to distraction from other sources.

Baron, Moore and Saunders (1978) – Found *non-social* stimuli, e.g. noise and lights also produce distraction arousal and social facilitation effects.

Schmitt et al (1986) – Asked subjects to type their name into a computer (easy task) or to type their name backwards (difficult) under one of three conditions – alone, with the experimenter watching, or in the same room with a blindfolded and ear-muffed subject whose back was turned (supposedly waiting for another experiment). The times in seconds revealed that the *mere presence* of another was sufficient to increase the performance of easy tasks and decrease the performance of more difficult ones.:

Results	Alone	Experimenter	Mere presence
Easy task	15 sec	7 sec	10 sec
Difficult task	52 sec	63 sec	73 sec

- The research and theory in this area have tended to *oversimplify* the number of factors at work. In real life, the *reactions of the audience* vary considerably, e.g. the home crowd advantage. *Hostile* audiences may impair the performance of even the simplest tasks and there is often more than one recipient of an audience, individuals may be affected more than teams.
- Each of the above theories relies to some extent on the notion of psychological drive or arousal, however physiological signs of this activation have not been consistently found or linked to performance across subjects. The kind and level of arousal (see optimal arousal theory) also needs to be considered. Other, more purely cognitive, theories of social facilitation have been proposed.

25.9 Teams and performance

TEAM COHESION AND PERFORMANCE
What is team cohesion?
Team cohesion refers to the total field of forces causing members to remain with a group (Festinger et al, 1950), or its resistance to disruptive forces (Gross and Martin, 1952), that keep members together to achieve team goals (Carron, 1982). Rather than being fixed, cohesion undergoes dynamic changes in sports teams and consists of two main forms:

- **Task cohesion** – the level of commitment to work together as a team to achieve common objectives
- **Social cohesion** – the level of friendship and mutual trust and support between team members.

Many factors influence the cohesion of sports teams, some of the most important being:

- *The size and stability of the group* – large groups or constantly fluctuating membership decreases cohesion.
- *The satisfaction of members* – successful teams that enjoy their sport are more cohesive.
- *The similarity of members* – members with similar values and goals are more cohesive.
- *Clarity of roles, goals and communication* – clear understanding of responsibilities and objectives, and conformity to roles, increases cohesion.
- *Leadership* – managers and captains can encourage team unity by adopting strategies designed to improve the above factors.

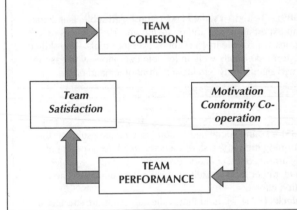

THE EFFECTS OF COHESION ON PERFORMANCE
Possible positive effects
- Increases conformity to team roles, values and goals and thus co-ordination.
- Increases motivation to do well for the team.

Possible negative effects
- Increases conformity to behaviour and attitudes more conducive to social cohesion than task cohesion.
- Socially cohesive sub-groups within a team (cliques) may reduce overall task cohesiveness, e.g. by only passing to friends rather than better-placed individuals.
- Increases team self-deception over weaknesses to avoid conflict.
- Reduces rivalry and competition over standards between team members, and therefore weakens motivation.

These effects probably depend upon the nature of the sport.

- According to Carron (1982), in 'group situations in which the individual's task is either carried out independently (e.g. rifle shooting, bowling) or is under external control for initiation and overall co-ordination (e.g. rowing), group tension, rivalry and intragroup competitiveness can serve to motivate the individual toward better performance'. In each of these sports, lower interpersonal attraction (social cohesion) has been associated with performance success.
- Where teams have to co-operate and co-ordinate themselves more to achieve success, e.g. basketball or hockey, cohesion teamwork and closeness has been associated with increased performance (Arnold and Straub, 1972, Ball and Carron, 1976).

THE EFFECTS OF PERFORMANCE ON COHESION
- Ruder and Gill (1981) found team ratings of cohesiveness in women's volleyball markedly increased after a victory whereas losers' ratings of cohesion decreased slightly (Carron, 1982).

Cohesion and performance can be highly correlated but it is difficult to infer their cause and effect.

- Hacker and Williams (1981), based on their study of women's field hockey teams, suggested that there is a circular relationship between cohesion, performance and satisfaction. This means, for example, that greater cohesion may lead to greater success, which leads to greater satisfaction, which in turn leads to greater cohesion.

THE NEGATIVE EFFECT OF TEAM MEMBERSHIP ON INDIVIDUAL PERFORMANCE
When individuals work in a team with others on a *shared or additive task* **social loafing** can occur. This is where individuals put in less effort than they would alone (a decrease in individual performance), even on the simplest collective tasks (e.g. pulling on a rope or shouting with others). Social loafing could occur for a number of reasons.

Physical factors – such as performance losses due to:
- problems in co-ordination of effort or production-blocking (where group members restrict each others' access to the task and output, causing a certain degree of turn-taking).

Motivational losses – a reduction of actual effort put into the task due to:
- Reduction of evaluation – if a task is not intrinsically motivating and individual performance can not be identified or assessed in a group, then members may think they can get away with putting in less effort.
- Output equity – people expect others will loaf and so put in less effort themselves so as not to become a 'sucker'.
- Lack of common standards – members of a team may not have a clear idea of the standard they are capable of achieving and thus not work to peak performance.

Social loafing can therefore be reduced by improving co-ordination, ensuring individuals know that their performance will be identified, making tasks more intrinsically interesting, giving feedback from other members of high performance and setting high standards.

STUDIES OF SOCIAL LOAFING
- Ringlemann, 1913) had young men pull on a rope (horizontally, as in tug-of-war) individually and together in groups of two, three or eight, and found the force exerted per person decreased as group size increased.

	Average force of pull in kilograms		
	Pull exerted	Pull expected	Force lost
Lone person	63		
Two pulling	118	126	8 (6%)
Three pulling	160	189	29 (15%)
Eight pulling	248	504	256 (51%)

- Ingham et al (1974) replicated Ringlemann's study using pseudo-groups (with confederates who did not actually pull) and found the group force loss was due to both motivation and co-ordination losses.
- Latane et al (1979) found the amount of noise produced per person in shouting and clapping groups was reduced by 29% in groups of two, 49% in groups of four and 60% in groups of six.

25.10 Arousal, anxiety and performance

WHAT ARE AROUSAL AND ANXIETY?

- Arousal refers to the state of **general physiological and psychological activation and alertness** experienced by an individual that varies in degree over time. Increased levels of arousal are associated with greater activity of the sympathetic autonomic nervous system (preparing the body for action) and higher levels of attention and mental processing activity. Arousal levels vary naturally with biological rhythms but also in response to a range of environmental triggers (see **Social Facilitation**, for example).
- Anxiety refers to **arousal that is experienced as a negative emotional state** and is associated with **feelings and thoughts of worry, apprehension and nervousness**. Anxiety has a significant cognitive as well as somatic (physiological) aspect – anxiety is particularly likely to result under 'stressful conditions' when individuals perceive that they may be unable to meet or cope with the demands of a situation, or cognitively interpret and label their arousal as 'distressing' rather than 'exciting'.

Arousal and anxiety both significantly influence behaviour and so have important implications for sporting performance.

HOW DO AROUSAL AND ANXIETY AFFECT PERFORMANCE?

DRIVE THEORY

Drive theory, developed by Hull (1943) and Spence (1956), suggests that increasing levels of drive (arousal) will increasingly energise the performance of habitual (well-learned), dominant responses in a **linear manner**.

$$\text{PERFORMANCE} = \text{DRIVE AROUSAL} \times \text{HABIT STRENGTH}$$

If these responses are correct ones, as is likely in simple or well-practised tasks, then the greater the drive arousal, the better the performance. If the habitual responses are incorrect, as is likely with new or complex tasks, then increased drive will worsen performance by energising them. Thus beginners should practise with low arousal.

Evaluation

- Performance does not always improve with ever-increasing amounts of arousal, too much can inhibit performance (see optimal arousal theory).
- Drive theory ignores the kind of arousal (anxiety may have a negative impact upon performance) and it is difficult to measure how habitual responses are.

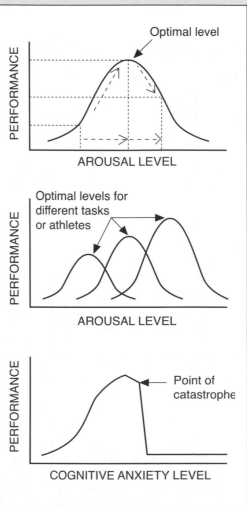

Arousal and the performance of simple or habitual tasks

OPTIMAL AROUSAL THEORY

Optimal arousal theory (the inverted-U hypothesis) suggests that **up to a certain optimal level** arousal will increasingly energise performance, but beyond this point higher levels of arousal will only serve to interfere with and reduce performance. The theory has been developed in several ways:

- Different sporting tasks will require different optimal levels of arousal. Tasks requiring fine motor movements, precision and control (e.g. golf, snooker and shooting) will have lower optimal levels than those requiring speed and strength (e.g. weight lifting, shot-putt and rugby tackling).
- Different athletes will have different zones of optimal functioning (Hanin, 1986) that reflect individual differences in how much arousal is required to reach peak performance and how improved that performance can be (depending on skill and practice levels).
- Performance will not always smoothly change with arousal levels – the inverted-U may only apply to performance under conditions of low cognitive anxiety. If high levels of cognitive anxiety accompany physiological arousal, then a small increase in arousal beyond the optimum may result in a catastrophic drop in performance. Cognitive anxiety may have its negative effect by distracting or inappropriately focusing attention in sporting tasks (Nideffer, 1976b).

Evaluation

Martens and Landers (1970) found boys exposed to moderate levels of stress and with moderate trait anxiety scores (which affects state anxiety levels during performance) performed significantly better than boys with low or high stress and trait anxiety. Klavora (1978) found 95 male basketball players' pre-game state anxiety levels showed an inverted-U pattern with their coach's post-game ratings of their performance – very high or low levels of anxiety were associated with worse performance than moderate levels. Coaches and trainers can use optimal arousal theory to help athletes reach their optimal level either by 'psyching' them up or calming them down depending upon their current state of arousal and anxiety and the nature of the task they are attempting. More specifically, muscle relaxation can be used for somatic over-anxiety/arousal, whereas cognitive self-instructional techniques can be used to stop negative thinking and distracting worry when athletes are high in cognitive anxiety. In practice, however, arousal and anxiety levels will fluctuate during a sporting event and current performance may depend upon how well a sports person has performed up to that point.

Optimal level

Optimal levels for different tasks or athletes

Point of catastrophe

26.1 Behaviourist learning theory applied to education 1

BEHAVIOURAL PRINCIPLES AND THE DELIVERY OF EDUCATION

- The behaviourists focused on **observable, stimulus and response** interactions between the environment and the individual. They believed that **learning by association** from the **environment** was the most important influence upon behaviour, and developed the **theories** of **classical** and **operant conditioning** to explain how experience could change observable behaviour without the need to refer to the cognitive workings of the mind.
- Their contribution to education therefore involves guidelines on how to **alter environmental stimuli**, e.g. classroom conditions, presentation of information, performance consequences and teacher behaviour, to produce repeated behavioural responses that reflect educational requirements. For example, providing a pleasant classroom environment and atmosphere may create *positive conditioned emotional responses* (feelings or attitudes) towards the subject matter or learning in general through association via the process of classical conditioning. Clearly *emphasising* important aspects of information (stimuli) to be attended to, providing positive consequences (*reinforcement*) for correct responses and *pointing out associations* between old and new stimuli, will encourage the correct responses to be made, repeated and generalised to new situations.
- Skinner suggested that the application of behavioural principles could be optimised through *programmed learning*.

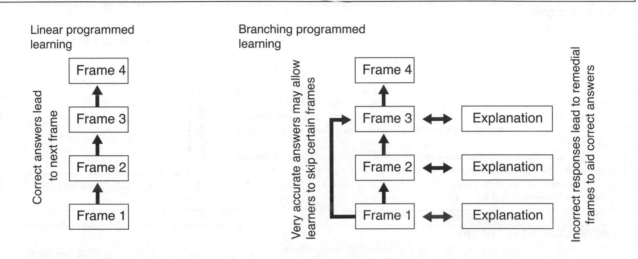

PROGRAMMED LEARNING

How does programmed learning work?

1 Information is broken down into manageable units (known as **frames**) which are presented in a logical order. In **linear** programmes very **small** amounts of information are presented. **Branching** programmes present **larger** frames.
2 Questions are asked in each frame. In **linear** programmes very **simple** questions with helpful prompts are asked (making it difficult to get the answer wrong) and the correct response leads to the next frame. **Branching** programmes present a **range of alternative answers** and learners have to select the correct one, which enables them to proceed more quickly or receive help depending upon the accuracy of their answers.
3 Each learner proceeds through the programme **individually** and is **immediately informed** of whether they have answered correctly. Knowledge of achieving the correct answer is presumed to be reinforcing.

Why is programmed learning needed?

- Many points of information are presented but it is often difficult to distinguish between them.
- The classroom contains many sources of distraction and reinforcement for behaviour that is not conducive to learning desired responses.
- The learner has to progress at the same speed as the rest of the class, which may be too fast or slow – leading to frustration.
- The learner in a class is often passive and has to compete with others for reinforcement – many may know the answer but only one is praised for getting it correct.
- Wrong answers may be punished leading to a fear of responding.

What are the strengths of programmed learning?

- Breaking the information down into manageable units clarifies which responses have to be learnt and does not overload the memory.
- The individualistic nature of programmed learning means it can occur without the distracting presence of others and provides each learner with their own task to focus on.
- Each learner can progress at their own pace through the material. Branching programmes provide extra support.
- The learner is actively involved in the learning process and is individually reinforced for their responses.
- In linear programmes the small amount of information and the ease of the questions presented ensures few mistakes are made and therefore most feedback is positive reinforcement.

What are the weaknesses of programmed learning?

- Not all topics can be broken down into small chunks or taught effectively in this way. The method may be more suitable for learning information rather than skills.
- The presence of others in a class may be a necessary part of education, e.g. for group discussion, task co-operation, social skills and motivation to learn.
- The speed of progress through the programme depends upon the motivation of the learner.
- Not all learners find mere progression through the programme (especially the really easy linear ones) sufficiently interesting or fulfilling.
- The programmes can not be sufficiently flexible to answer all the questions a learner may have, which may stifle curiosity and independence.

26.2 Behaviourist learning theory applied to education 2

BEHAVIOURAL PRINCIPLES AND THE REDUCTION OF PROBLEM BEHAVIOUR IN THE CLASSROOM

The behaviourist would first identify the problem behaviour, e.g. lack of attention, disruptive behaviour, insufficient work rate or quality, etc. and then alter environmental stimuli to change its frequency.

PUNISHMENT

According to behaviourist principles, ***problem behaviour*** can be ***reduced in frequency*** by associating it with ***negative consequences***. These can take the form of:

Applying negative stimuli, e.g.:
* Verbal reprimands – these can be made publicly or privately, harshly or softly, and with or without giving the reasoning behind the reprimand.
* Non-verbal reprimands – such as expressions of facial disapproval, eye contact glaring, negative head-shaking.
* Unpleasant activities – like extra homework or line writing.
* Physical punishment – such as extra push-ups/running laps (in physical education lessons!) or smacking/caning (where legal).

Removing positive stimuli, e.g.:
* Exclusion – such as exclusion from classroom activities (time-outs) or break/home time (detention).
* Penalties – (or response cost punishments) are where a certain amount of already gained credits or privileges are removed per undesirable behaviour.

Evaluation
Strengths
* Punishment brings undesirable behaviour to the attention of both the offender and witnesses, who may then act to avoid future punishment (see negative reinforcement).
* Certain behaviours have to be seen to be unacceptable.
* Non-physical reprimands, made privately and with justification, can be very effective in managing problem behaviour, as can penalty systems, especially if provided by a warm and otherwise accepting authority figure.

Weaknesses
* Physical punishment is ethically objectionable and can be counter-productive (punishing violence with violence only serves to model aggressive behaviour).
* Punishment on its own does not inform those receiving it of what desirable behaviour they should be showing.
* Punishment only inhibits undesirable behaviour and creates further negative feelings and resentment towards authority.
* Exclusion from class may increase the extent to which the excluded individual gets behind and their sense of alienation from normal classroom behaviour.
* Punishment methods have variable effects – reprimands may reinforce undesirable behaviour in those who crave attention, 'psychopaths' may not learn from punishment.

REINFORCEMENT

Reinforcement attempts to reduce the problem behaviour by ***encouraging*** or gradually ***shaping*** the opposite, ***desirable responses***. Reinforcement can take a number of forms:

Positive reinforcement, e.g.:
* Socially rewarding stimuli – such as attention and praise from the teacher (or classmates) for desirable behaviour.
* Educational feedback – like good grades and, in the longer term, examination success.
* Token systems – such as merit points, star charts, etc. These tokens can reflect social praise or be exchanged at a later time for other reinforcers (see below).
* The Premack principle – using behaviour / activities that are liked (frequently shown) to reward desirable, educational behaviour (that may be less frequent / liked!).

Selective positive reinforcement – the same as positive reinforcement above, but in combination with ignoring and withholding reinforcement from problem behaviour to encourage its extinction.

Negative reinforcement – involves maintaining good behaviour by allowing the negative consequences associated with problem behaviour to be avoided, e.g. warnings or threats of punishments for bad behaviour.

Evaluation
Strengths
The behaviourist, Skinner, argued that reinforcement was more effective than punishment in education, since:
* Rewards provide information on desirable behaviour, increase motivation to perform it rather than other behaviour and are associated with pleasant emotions.
* Reinforcement is a very flexible form of behaviour control – selective reinforcement can shape many different types of behaviour and reinforcement schedules mean rewards do not have to be given for every desirable behaviour.

Weaknesses
* Lepper and Greene (1975) found that providing too much extrinsic reinforcement (external rewards) for behaviour can undermine the intrinsic (internal) satisfaction for it, which can reduce self-motivation and produce 'mercenary' attitudes (only behaving when rewarded).
* Reinforcement is most effective if provided immediately, but this is not always possible or practical.
* Rewards can be costly in terms of time (and sometimes expense) to set up and administer.

EVALUATION OF THE USEFULNESS OF THE BEHAVIOURAL APPROACH TO LEARNING

Practically – Many behaviourist principles have been shown to be highly successful in controlling problem behaviour, e.g. O'Leary and Becker (1967), and programmed learning has been found to be at least as successful as normal classroom methods for some topics. However, behaviourists ignore individual differences – different learners find different stimuli punishing and reinforcing and show different levels of intrinsic motivation to learn. Teachers can never control all the competing sources of punishment and reinforcement in the learning environment, e.g. from peers and influences outside the classroom.

Theoretically – behaviourists neglect cognitive influences upon learning – e.g. punishment and reinforcement are most effective if explanations are also given, and the learner's cognitive attributions are important in the decision over whether they are performing behaviour for its own sake or for a reward, whether praise given is genuine, etc.

26.3 Key application – of cognitive developmental theories to education

APPLICATIONS OF PIAGET'S THEORY TO EDUCATION

Piaget did not apply his theory to the classroom himself and most of the following recommendations are what other researchers have proposed based on Piagetian principles. Overall Piaget's theory has applications for *when* and *how* to teach.

WHEN TO TEACH
- Because of Piaget's ideas on stages of development, the notion of '**readiness**' is important – children show qualitatively different kinds of thinking at different ages and should only be taught concepts suitable for their underlying level of cognitive development.

HOW TO TEACH
Because of Piaget's emphasis on the individual child's self construction of its cognitive development, education should be *student centred* and accomplished through **active discovery learning**.

CURRICULUM IMPLICATIONS
- Some researchers have suggested that because of the notion of readiness certain concepts should be taught before others or even in a specific *order* – for example, conservation of number, followed by conservation of weight, followed by conservation of volume.
- New knowledge should be *built on pre-existing schemas*, which should be expanded through accommodation. Concrete operational children should therefore start with concrete examples before progressing onto more abstract tasks.
- However there should be a *balance* between accommodation (learning new concepts) and assimilation (practising and utilising those concepts).

THE ROLE OF THE TEACHER
The role of the teacher in the Piagetian classroom is as a *facilitator*. Teachers should be involved in the indirect imparting of knowledge, not direct tuition and should therefore:
1 Focus on the *process* of learning rather than the end product of it.
2 Assess the *level* of the child's development so suitable tasks can be set.
3 Choose tasks that are *self-motivating* for the child, to engage its interest and further its own development.
4 Set tasks that are challenging enough to put the child into *disequilibrium* so it can accommodate and create new schemas.
5 Introduce abstract or formal operational tasks through *concrete* examples.
6 Encourage *active interaction* not just with task materials but with other children. In small group work children can learn from each other.

LIMITATIONS ON PROGRESS
- Piaget proposed that cognitive development should *not* be speeded up because of its dependence on biological maturation. Teaching children a concept before they are biologically ready prevents them from discovering it for themselves – resulting in incomplete understanding.
- Piaget disagreed with Bruner over the ability of *language training* to advance cognitive reasoning.

THE THEORIES OF BRUNER AND VYGOTSKY APPLIED TO EDUCATION
- Bruner and Vygotsky both disagreed with Piaget's strict notion of readiness and argued that the teacher should *actively intervene* to help the child develop its understanding - instruction *is* an important part of the learning process. The teacher, or more knowledgeable other, provides the 'tools' or 'loan of consciousness' required for the child to develop cognitively by providing structure, direction, guidance and support, not just facts. The following concepts are therefore important in education according to the theories of both Bruner and Vygotsky:

THE SPIRAL CURRICULUM
The '*spiral curriculum*' involves material being structured so that complex ideas can be presented at simplified levels first and then *re-visited* at more complex levels later on. This opposes Piaget's idea of readiness.
Children should be made aware of the structure and direction of the subjects they study, and progression should proceed via an *active problem solving* process.

SCAFFOLDING
'*Scaffolding*' is a kind of hypothetical support structure around the child's attempt to understand new ideas and complete new tasks. The scaffolding allows the child to climb to the higher levels of development in manageable amounts by
1 Reducing degrees of freedom (simplifying the tasks)
2 Direction maintenance (motivating and encouraging the child)
3 Marking critical features (highlighting relevant parts or errors)
4 Demonstration (providing model examples for imitation)

THE ZONE OF PROXIMAL DEVELOPMENT AND EDUCATION
- Tharp and Gallimore (1988) propose the following definition of teaching according to Vygotsky's ideas – "*Teaching consists in assisting performance through the ZPD. Teaching can be said to occur when assistance is offered at points in the ZPD at which performance requires assistance*" and go on to quote Vygotsky (1956) who said that teaching was only good when it "*awakens and rouses to life those functions which are in a stage of maturing, which lie in the zone of proximal development*".
- Teachers should assist performance by working sensitively and *contingently* within the ZPD. Bruner developed this idea of contingency (responding appropriately and flexibly to the child's individual needs only when required) in his own work, and Wood and Middleton (1975) have investigated contingency by watching mothers help their children build a puzzle. The mothers showed contingency by offering different levels of help depending on how much difficulty the child was having.

26.4 Cognitive information-processing theory applied to education

---

COGNITIVE PSYCHOLOGY AND EDUCATION

- The cognitive approach assumes that it is important to study inner mental processes such as attention and memory because such processes actively filter, organise and manipulate the information we receive. It is also assumed that humans, like computers, are information-processors, and that their processing of information can be modelled and scientifically tested.
- What does this mean for education? It means that cognitive psychologists would argue that their scientific models make a sound basis for informing teachers how they can *best adapt teaching to suit the way humans filter, organise, store and manipulate information*, and the *limitations* of their information processing abilities.

AUSUBEL – SUBSUMPTION THEORY

Ausubel's ideas on education are linked to cognitive psychological research on schemas and the organisation of memory.

How does Ausubel think we learn?

- Ausubel suggests that new information is only meaningful if it can be related to previous knowledge / concepts. This means that for learning to occur a new concept must be *subsumed under* (be related to, or a new or slightly different example of) a previously learned concept.
- Because *more specific concepts become subsumed under more general ones*, knowledge is gradually *represented* (stored) in a *hierarchical* way in the mind. This means a cognitive (mental) structure is formed which is arranged so that the most general concepts are at the top and increasingly specific sub-concepts are found beneath.
- Although subsumption involves finding *similarities* between past concepts and new ones, new concepts will only be *remembered* if they are separated or distinguished in some way from previous concepts (Ausubel calls this *dissociative subsumption*). Forgetting occurs, according to Ausubel, when there is *zero dissociability* (or *obliterative subsumption*) because new learning cannot be distinguished from the old.
- Obviously new concepts will vary in how different they are from previous ones and therefore cause different amounts of change in the underlying cognitive structure. 'Derivative subsumption occurs when new material is so similar to what is already known that it could have been derived from it; correlative subsumption involves material that is sufficiently novel that it requires some change in existing cognitive structure' (Lefrancois 1994).

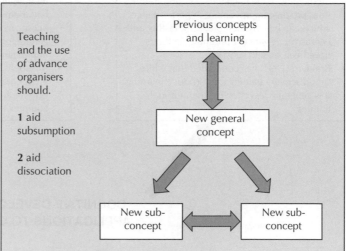

Teaching and the use of advance organisers should.

1 aid subsumption

2 aid dissociation

What should teachers do?

- New material should be *integrated* with previously acquired knowledge through comparison and contrast.
- *General ideas* should be presented first, then more detailed subsumed concepts should be taught and *dissociated* (shown to be different in some way) from each other.

Teachers should therefore present *advance organisers* before teaching new material to create an explicit *link* between what has been learned and what is about to be learned, and to provide an *general* (subsuming) *framework* for understanding new sub-concepts. When the information to be learned is completely new, the advance organisers are termed *expository* organisers, whereas when familiar material is about to be presented, they are termed *comparative* organisers.

GAGNE – CONDITIONS OF LEARNING

Gagne's research has many implications for education since it describes:

What is learned – by identifying the different *outcomes of learning* that can be achieved. Gagne sees the *five main categories* of learning as being: verbal information, intellectual skills, cognitive strategies, motor skills and attitudes.

How learning occurs – by identifying the different *conditions of learning* or *instructional events* that are needed to achieve each kind of learning. Often these instructional events can be sequenced or ordered hierarchically to show how teaching should best progress.

Why learning occurs – by identifying the *cognitive processes* that underlie and explain the success of the instructional events.

Example: Learning outcome = intellectual skill (learning a new concept, e.g. what is a duck?)

Nine instructional events required (in order), *with examples.*		Cognitive process involved
1	Gain attention	*OK, everyone, let's start the lesson…*	Reception
2	Identify objective	*Today we are going to learn about ducks…*	Expectancy
3	Recall prior learning	*What do you remember about our lesson on birds?*	Retrieval
4	Present stimulus	*A duck can be defined and described as…*	Selective perception
5	Guide learning	*Here are several examples of pictures of ducks…*	Semantic encoding
6	Elicit performance	*Now, all of you draw your own picture of a duck…*	Responding
7	Provide feedback	*Correct, correct, no that is wrong I'm afraid…*	Reinforcement
8	Assess performance	*Good, 10/10, looks like a chicken – adjust the beak…*	Retrieval
9	Enhance retention/transfer	*Now, out of all these bird pictures, identify the ducks…*	Generalisation

26.5 Evaluating cognitive applications to education

PIAGET'S APPLICATIONS TO EDUCATION

- Bruner agreed with Piaget that discovery learning was important in teaching.
- Criticisms of Piaget's applications to education have been made both of the notion of readiness and discovery learning.
- Meadows (1988) in her review of the research finds that 'the behaviours typical of different stages ... can certainly be accelerated by training... Contrary to the predictions of the Piagetian account, training does produce improvement in performance which can be considerable, long-lasting and pervasive. A variety of training methods have been seen to succeed...' .
- Brainerd (1983) has concluded that while 'self-discovery training can produce learning, it is generally *less* effective than tutorial training'.

BRUNER AND VYGOTSKY'S APPLICATIONS TO EDUCATION

- Bruner and Vygotsky were correct in assuming that teachers can assist performance by working sensitively and ***contingently*** within the ZPD and training children to understand concepts.
- Wood and Middleton (1975) have supported the idea of contingency by watching mothers help their children build a puzzle. The mothers showed contingency by offering different levels of help depending on how much difficulty the child was having.
- Sonstroem et al (1966) encouraged children who failed conservation of substance tests to use all of their modes of representation to increase their ability to conserve. The children who rolled the plasticine into a ball themselves (enactive mode) while watching their own actions (iconic mode) and verbally describing what was happening, e.g. 'it's getting longer but thinner' (symbolic mode) showed the greatest improvement in conservation.
- Ausubel's ideas support Bruner's on the value of organisational hierarchies and the spiral curriculum method of presenting more general and simple concepts before proceeding to more specific and complex ones.

COGNITIVE DEVELOPMENTAL APPLICATIONS TO EDUCATION

HOW GOOD ARE COGNITIVE APPLICATIONS TO EDUCATION?

INFORMATION PROCESSING THEORY APPLICATIONS TO EDUCATION

AUSUBEL'S APPLICATIONS TO EDUCATION

- Ausubel's ideas are mainly limited to the learning of meaningful verbal / textual information in the classroom.
- Bruner suggests that students should discover and construct their own meaningful hierarchies from the components given them, Ausubel thinks this is a waste of time for older children because teachers can outline complex cognitive structures more efficiently through expository teaching.
- Advance organisers have been shown to facilitate learning.
- Research consistently supports the idea that the more background knowledge a learner has on a particular topic, the greater their ability to learn and understand new information concerning it (Alexander and Judy, 1988).

GAGNE'S APPLICATIONS TO EDUCATION

- Gagne's ideas apply to a range of different kinds of learning and recognise the importance of different learning strategies for different learning outcomes.
- In line with cognitive psychological principles, Gagne's ideas are specific in their suggestions and their effects are scientifically verifiable.
- Gagne may have identified which conditions of learning or instructional events are most suitable for certain learning outcomes, but not which are most suitable for certain students. The theory therefore neglects individual differences in learning style and ability.

26.6 Teaching styles and attitudes

DIDACTIC TEACHING

Refers in general to teacher-centred methods, which tend to be associated with:

Formal style (Bennett, 1976) – e.g. controlling the seating, associations and movement of the students, focusing on student-teacher rather than student-student interactions, and emphasising teacher assessment and motivation of achievement.

Direct style (Flanders, 1970) – e.g. using lecturing, expository and authority based methods of relaying information and opinions. Students are told what to think and do.

How might these affect student performance?

Research suggests that a formal style is associated with greater academic achievement, lower noise levels and suitability for insecure/anxious students than an informal style. The success of a direct style depends upon the subject matter, conditions of leaning (i.e. time-constraints) and student learning style.

STUDENT-CENTRED TEACHING

Refers in general to methods, which tend to be associated with:

Informal style (Bennett, 1976) – e.g. allowing greater student freedom of choice over conditions of learning and emphasising internal motivation and satisfaction over external teacher-based assessment.

Indirect style (Flanders, 1970) – e.g. encouraging student ideas, opinions and behaviour through question asking and the acceptance of student contributions.

Discovery learning (e.g. Piaget and Bruner) – e.g. student self-construction of learning based upon teacher-provided materials.

How might these affect student performance?

Bennett (1979) suggests that an informal style is associated with greater communication between students, but not always higher creativity compared to formal methods. Discursive subject matter may benefit more from an indirect style, while discovery learning may be unsuitable for less-motivated students, learning very complex material under time constraints.

TEACHING STYLES AND THEIR EFFECT ON STUDENT PERFORMANCE

TEACHERS' ATTITUDES/EXPECTATIONS AND THEIR EFFECT ON STUDENT PERFORMANCE

LABELLING AND STEREOTYPING

- Labelling concerns the attachment of a descriptive term onto an individual or group by others. Such descriptive labels for students can be positive, e.g. 'hardworking', 'clever', 'attentive', 'well-behaved', etc, or negative, e.g. 'lazy', 'slow', 'distractible', 'troublemaking', etc.
- Labels may be based upon past experience or an assessment of some kind with the individual or group, or may be attached based upon stereotypes.
- Stereotypes are pre-formed opinions of groups or categories of people that are presumed to share similar typical characteristics. Stereotyping involves allocating people to certain categories based on little more than visible cues (e.g. gender, dress, and skin colour) and assuming they possess the same general descriptive characteristics as the other category members. Stereotyping can exaggerate the differences between groups and cause the prejudgement of student behaviour and performance.

What are the possible effects of labelling and stereotyping?

1 **The creation of lasting and fairly stable impressions** of the labelled individual or group, which take fairly dramatic changes in behaviour to cause a re-assessment. For example, a student's initial bad behaviour, poor performance or group stereotype may create a lasting impression in their teacher of them being a 'troublemaker' or a 'less-able' student.

2 **The creation of distortions in the perception of behaviour** in the light of the attached label. For example, a teacher may become more vigilant for bad behaviour in a labelled 'troublemaker' or have lower expectations for a 'less-able' student. This may lead the teacher to remember the 'troublemaker's' misbehaviour more than good behaviour, and regard the 'less-able' student's poorer performance as normal/more acceptable, thus strengthening the negative opinions.

3 **The creation of self-fulfilling prophecies** in the behaviour of the labelled, through reactions to the behaviour and expectations of the labeller. A labelled 'troublemaker' may stop trying to be good since it does not seem to be noticed and behave as expected out of resentment. The labelled 'less-able' student may develop a negative self-image of their ability, think they are incapable of producing higher quality work, and stop trying to. The teacher may set less demanding work, thus slowing their progress. Marking and assessment may become biased.

Evaluation – Rosenthal and Jacobson's (1968) study is the classic support for the effects of labelling in the classroom – randomly selected students improved in intellectual and academic ability because their teachers were given the mistaken impression that they had been identified as (labelled) intellectual 'spurters'. This study has been criticised (e.g. by Smith and Cowie, 1994) and not always replicated, however Good and Brophy's (1991) review of research suggests teacher expectations do influence student behaviour. Similarly, teacher prejudice based on stereotypes has also been shown to affect students.

It is not always clear whether self-fulfilling prophecy effects result more from teacher reinforcement/neglect/punishment, teacher assessment bias, student reactions to expectation, or changes in student self-image. Positive teacher expectations may actually result in worse performance if more teacher attention is devoted to those perceived as more needy.

26.7 Student variables in learning

INDIVIDUAL LEARNING
- Refers to students learning and completing tasks on their own without regard for others' performance.
- The rewards of learning are independent of those received by others.
- The rewards of learning gained reflect one's own effort and are not limited by other people's performance.
- Self-esteem is based on one's own actions.
- Is less likely to involve social distractions.
- Does not require or provide social skills, may suit the shy.
- Individuals can employ their own learning style and work at their own rate.
- Receives no emotional and intellectual support from peers.

CO-OPERATIVE LEARNING
- Refers to students learning the same material together and completing the same tasks as a group.
- The rewards of learning are the same for each group member and may depend upon the success of the group.
- Rewards may not always reflect one's own effort and be limited by the group's performance, but quality may increase.
- Self-esteem is based on the group's actions. May increase liking of others.
- Is more likely to involve sources of social distraction.
- Requires and provides social skills, may not suit the shy.
- Individuals may have to compromise on their preferred learning style and work at other's rate.
- Receives more emotional and cognitive support from peers.

COMPETITIVE LEARNING
- Refers to students learning on their own, but with regard to other's performance.
- The rewards of learning depend on the success of the individual relative to the success of others.
- Rewards may not always reflect one's own effort and be limited by other's performance.
- Self-esteem is based on one's own actions relative to other's. May decrease liking of others.
- Involves some social distraction.
- Does not require or provide social skills, may not suit the shy.
- Individuals can employ their own learning style and but may feel pressure to work at other's rate.
- Receives little emotional and intellectual support from peers.

 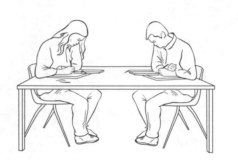 

WHAT LEARNING CONDITIONS MIGHT DIFFERENT STUDENTS PREFER?

STUDENT VARIABLES IN LEARNING

WHAT LEARNING/COGNITIVE STYLES MIGHT DIFFERENT STUDENTS PREFER?

TYPES OF LEARNING/COGNITIVE STYLE

Learning or cognitive styles are preferred ways of acquiring information that are characteristic of different students. They involve differences in students' cognition, emotion, physiology and behaviour that influence how they perform and react when exposed to different methods of teaching. Students are presumed to feel more comfortable and learn/achieve better when the teacher's method of presentation and instruction matches their preferred style. Differences may be found in:

- Cognitive factors – the student's typical way of processing (perceiving, storing, thinking, problem-solving and remembering) information, e.g. whether they prefer to receive information through visual, auditory or tactile (learning by doing) presentation.
- Emotional factors – the way the student feels about their own ability or different teaching and assessment methods, e.g. based upon their confidence, self-image, sociability and levels of (intrinsic or extrinsic) motivation.
- Physiological factors – the differences relating to activity levels, sex, physical handicap, and even body rhythms.

The effectiveness of sex related differences in learning style
Some have suggested that the increasing under-achievement of boys in British schools is due to average differences in their learning style because of their:
- higher physiological arousal levels
- competitive need for immediate feedback
- preference for visual or tactile presentation.

These aspects of learning style do not always suit educational methods, although more negative, culturally produced attitudes towards learning are probably more responsible.

The effectiveness of mastery-orientated and failure-avoiding styles
Greater academic success is usually experienced by those with mastery-orientated rather than failure-avoiding styles.
- Mastery-orientated students are intrinsically motivated to improve their ability to overcome new challenges. Failure motivates them to modify their strategies.
- Failure-avoiding students see their ability as fixed and thus only attempt tasks they feel they can achieve. Their dependence on external assessment and motivation means failure is usually blamed on external factors and may lead to acceptance of failure.

27.1 Media influences on pro– and anti–social behaviour

LABORATORY EXPERIMENTS ON MEDIA VIOLENCE

Bandura's experiments showed that aggression could be learnt and imitated from live, filmed or cartoon models.
Liebert and Baron (1972) found that children who had watched a violent programme were more likely to hurt another child. However laboratory studies may produce artificial results.

CORRELATIONS ON MEDIA VIOLENCE

Eron (1987) found a significant positive correlation between the amount of aggression viewed at age 8 and later aggression at age 30.
Phillips (1986) has found correlations between highly publicised incidents of aggression, such as murder cases or boxing matches, and the number of corresponding incidents in society at large. Correlation is not causation however.

NATURAL EXPERIMENTS ON MEDIA VIOLENCE

Joy et al. (1986) measured children's levels of aggression in a Canadian town one year before and after television was introduced, and found a significant increase compared to the non significant increases in towns that already had television.

FIELD EXPERIMENTS ON MEDIA VIOLENCE

Parke et al. (1977) showed juvenile delinquents in the USA and Belgium either violent or non-violent television for a week in their homes. Aggression was greater for the violent TV group especially in those who had previously shown higher levels. Field studies are hard to control and replicate however.

OBSERVATIONAL LEARNING

Violent behaviour could be learnt by observation and imitated if rewarding.

DISINHIBITION

Watching aggression could reduce inhibitions about behaving aggressively as it is seen as socially legitimate.

AROUSAL

Aggressive emotional arousal or excitement from watching aggression may lead to real violence.

DESENSITISATION

Watching aggression may lead to an increased acceptance or tolerance of it in society.

NEGATIVE EFFECTS (OF MEDIA VIOLENCE)

MEDIATING FACTORS

- The personality of the viewer. The effects of TV violence often depend on what the child brings to the screen.
- The amount of exposure to media violence.

HOW MIGHT THE MEDIA INFLUENCE BEHAVIOUR ?

NO EFFECT

Howitt and Cumberbatch (1974) analysed 300 studies concluding that TV violence has no direct effect on children's behaviour.
Freedman (1984, 1986) argues that although there is a small correlation between levels of viewing and behaving aggressively, the causal connection is very weak.

POSITIVE EFFECTS OF MEDIA VIOLENCE

INOCULATION

Watching antisocial violence could provide the opportunity to discuss its immorality or to see it come to no good (the 'baddie' loses).

CATHARSIS

According to Freud's ideas, watching violence could provide a relief from pent up aggression, as it is released through emotional sympathy.

STUDIES ON THE CATHARTIC EFFECT OF TV VIOLENCE

Feshbach and Singer (1971) claimed that children shown aggressive programs over a 6 week period showed *less* aggressive behaviour than those who saw non-violent TV. However, this study has been accused of methodological flaws, and more recent studies have not replicated or have found the opposite findings.

POSITIVE EFFECTS OF PRO-SOCIAL MEDIA

POSITIVE ROLE MODELS

Just as aggression could be learnt from aggressive media models, so pro-social role models could also provide a basis for observational learning and imitation – especially if their behaviour produces rewards such as public praise, social respect etc. (the 'goodie' always wins in the end).

STUDIES ON THE EFFECTS OF PRO-SOCIAL TV

Sprafkin et al. (1975) found over 90% of children chose to help a puppy instead of personal gain after watching a program that involved helping ('Lassie'), while Baron et al. (1979) found children were more co-operative after watching the 'The Waltons'.
Hearold (1986) analysed approximately 200 studies and concluded that pro-social television has around twice the effect on children's behaviour than anti-social television.

27.2 The effects of video games and computers on young people

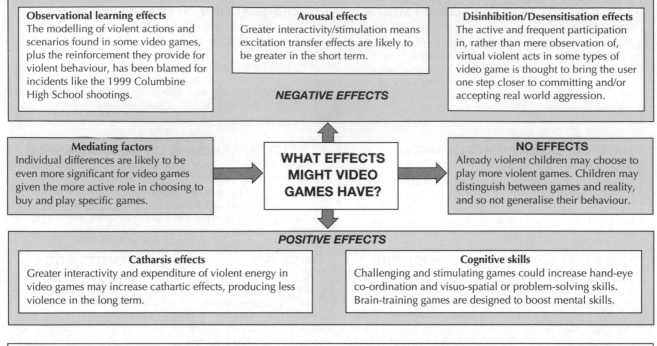

Observational learning effects
The modelling of violent actions and scenarios found in some video games, plus the reinforcement they provide for violent behaviour, has been blamed for incidents like the 1999 Columbine High School shootings.

Arousal effects
Greater interactivity/stimulation means excitation transfer effects are likely to be greater in the short term.

NEGATIVE EFFECTS

Disinhibition/Desensitisation effects
The active and frequent participation in, rather than mere observation of, virtual violent acts in some types of video game is thought to bring the user one step closer to committing and/or accepting real world aggression.

Mediating factors
Individual differences are likely to be even more significant for video games given the more active role in choosing to buy and play specific games.

WHAT EFFECTS MIGHT VIDEO GAMES HAVE?

NO EFFECTS
Already violent children may choose to play more violent games. Children may distinguish between games and reality, and so not generalise their behaviour.

POSITIVE EFFECTS

Catharsis effects
Greater interactivity and expenditure of violent energy in video games may increase cathartic effects, producing less violence in the long term.

Cognitive skills
Challenging and stimulating games could increase hand-eye co-ordination and visuo-spatial or problem-solving skills. Brain-training games are designed to boost mental skills.

Research on the effects of video games
Giles (2003) reports that the research on the effects of video game play:
- Is even more inconclusive than is the literature on media violence in general (Griffiths, 1997).
- Has found evidence that trait aggression in adults may enhance the negative effects of game play (Anderson and Dill, 2000), although this finding was not replicated with adolescents (Warm, 2000).
- Found general increases in short-term hostility for video game play in general, regardless of violent content (Anderson and Dill, 2000).
- Suggests any cognitive skill resulting from repeated video game play is likely to be very localised. Sims and Mayer (2002) found Tetris players showed enhanced performance in mental rotation tasks involving shapes similar to the ones used in the game, but performed no differently from controls on tasks involving other kinds of shapes.

- Pakes and Winstone (2007) cite Bensley and Van Eenwynk's (2001) analysis of 28 research studies which found play with an aggressive video game was often followed by brief aggressive play straight afterward in 4- to 8-year-olds, but was not consistently found for other age groups (due to the design of the studies), leading the authors to conclude that, although video game realism may change in the future, the 'current research evidence is not supportive of a major concern that violent video games lead to real-life violence'.
- Gentile *et al.* (2004) found increased levels of video game playing and anti-social effects in children, even for non-aggressive children, which could be reduced by parental control and limits.

THE EFFECTS OF COMPUTERS

- *Addiction* – Giles, (2003) cites Griffiths (1999) suggestion that heavy Internet users show components of addiction, including salience, mood modification, and tolerance (i.e. the Internet becomes highly important and provides a 'buzz' that the user becomes habituated to and requires greater use to re-experience). However, although some may be 'Internet dependent' with more than 38 hours online a week (Young, 1998), this does not apply to all and does not focus on what this time is spent on.

Subrahmanyam *et al.* (2001) report research on a number of other effects:
- *Displacement of other activities* – research shows computer use lowers television use, but has not properly studied its effect on other activities.
- *Cognitive skills* – computer use may develop computer literacy skills and some studies show correlations with improved visual attention skills (Greenfield *et al.*, 1996) and academic performance (Cole, 1996). However, these findings have not always been replicated and cause and effect relationships are difficult to identify (e.g. greater wealth may explain greater computer use and academic performance).
- *Social relationships* – the effect of computers on relationships is complex. McKenna and Bargh (1998) found socially anxious and lonely people find better relationships through the Internet, while Kraut *et al.*'s (1998) longitudinal study found an association between time online and declines in social and psychological well-being, mainly in the first two years of use.

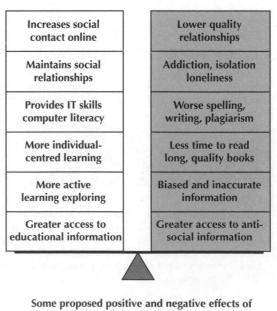

Increases social contact online	Lower quality relationships
Maintains social relationships	Addiction, isolation loneliness
Provides IT skills computer literacy	Worse spelling, writing, plagiarism
More individual-centred learning	Less time to read long, quality books
More active learning exploring	Biased and inaccurate information
Greater access to educational information	Greater access to anti-social information

Some proposed positive and negative effects of computers and the Internet

27.3 Persuasion and attitude change 1

HOVLAND-YALE MODEL

The **Yale Persuasive Communication Model** (Janis and Hovland, 1959) suggests the degree of attitude change produced by persuasive communication depends upon many important variables, including *source factors* relating to the communicator of the information, *message factors* relating to the content and style of the communication itself, *audience factors* relating to the recipients of the message, and *situational factors* relating to the context the communication occurs in.

CONTEXT
More informal environments seem to induce more attitude change than formal contexts.

Communicator	Communication	Audience
Communicator Source factors of communicators: • credibility, (expertise, knowledge) • trustworthiness (motives, beliefs) • likeability (attractiveness, charm, status and race).	**Communication** Message factors of presentation: • spelling out conclusions • one or two-sided arguments • order of presentation • use of emotion.	**Audience** Recipient factors include: • level of education/intelligence/ knowledge • resistance to persuasion/strength of initial attitudes • level of audience participation.

Communicator

Source factors of communicators:
- credibility, (expertise, knowledge)
- trustworthiness (motives, beliefs)
- likeability (attractiveness, charm, status and race).

Evaluation
Studies show equal learning from high and low credibility sources, but more acceptance of information from high credibility sources (although this effect was relatively short-lasting)
Attractive, charming, high-status, and same-sex sources increase persuasion.

Communication

Message factors of presentation:
- spelling out conclusions
- one or two-sided arguments
- order of presentation
- use of emotion.

Evaluation
Studies find one-sided arguments and spelling out conclusions more effective with complex messages and low education audiences, but better-educated ones are more influenced if left to draw their own conclusions. Information presented first (primacy effect) and avoiding extreme use of emotional appeal is more effective.

MESSAGE →

Audience

Recipient factors include:
- level of education/intelligence/ knowledge
- resistance to persuasion/strength of initial attitudes
- level of audience participation.

Evaluation
Studies show greater attitude change with higher audience participation (see cognitive dissonance), but weaker initial attitudes/resistance. Educational level interacts with source and message factors.

ELABORATION-LIKELIHOOD MODEL (ELM)

Petty and Cacioppo's (1981, 1986) ELM suggests the degree of persuasion and attitude change depends upon the probability (likelihood) that people will devote mental effort to (elaborate upon) the information they receive about an issue or product.

Motivation/Ability to elaborate
People's elaboration increases when:
- The issue/product is highly important or relevant to them.
- They are solely responsible or accountable for decisions.
- They are ambivalent or uncertain.
- They have greater intelligence, time, and freedom from distraction

Low motivation/ ability to elaborate = less scrutiny of issue/product information

← **Elaboration-likelihood continuum** →

High motivation/ ability to elaborate = greater scrutiny of issue/product information

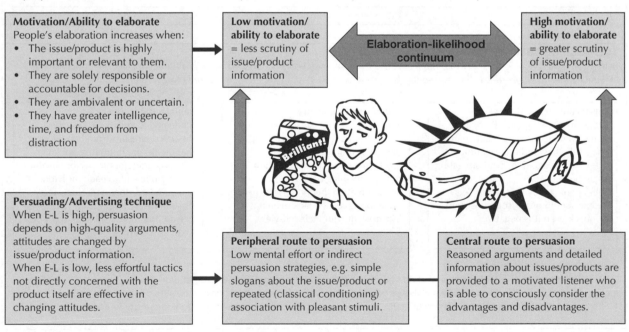

Persuading/Advertising technique
When E-L is high, persuasion depends on high-quality arguments, attitudes are changed by issue/product information.
When E-L is low, less effortful tactics not directly concerned with the product itself are effective in changing attitudes.

Peripheral route to persuasion
Low mental effort or indirect persuasion strategies, e.g. simple slogans about the issue/product or repeated (classical conditioning) association with pleasant stimuli.

Central route to persuasion
Reasoned arguments and detailed information about issues/products are provided to a motivated listener who is able to consciously consider the advantages and disadvantages.

Evaluation
- The peripheral route techniques often produce weaker attitude change, poorly thought-out decisions (e.g. based on superficial characteristics or the number rather than quality of arguments) and other negative effects (e.g. reinforcing stereotypes).
- The ELM has been supported by attitude change studies that vary the quality of arguments and exposure time to messages.

27.4 Persuasion and attitude change 2

THE INFLUENCE OF ATTITUDES ON DECISION MAKING

An individual's positive or negative attitudes (or more specifically, the cognitive and affective components of attitudes) are thought to play an important role in that person's decision making and eventual behaviour. Those who wish to affect decision making and behaviour (e.g. advertisers or governments) have therefore tried to use persuasion techniques to change attitudes and have found it useful to take into account the roles of cognitive consistency/dissonance and self-perception.

THE ROLE OF COGNITIVE CONSISTENCY/DISSONANCE

What are cognitive consistency/dissonance?
Festinger (1957) suggested that cognitive dissonance is a feeling of unpleasant arousal experienced when an individual simultaneously holds two cognitions or attitudes that conflict (are inconsistent) with each other. The arousal acts like a drive state to motivate attempts to restore cognitive consistency and reduce dissonance. Cognitive dissonance can be reduced by:
- *Changing attitudes* or *behaviour* to eliminate the inconsistency (the desired goal of persuaders).
- Dealing with the dissonance in another way, e.g. attributing it to *external influences* (Festinger and Carlsmith, 1959), *minimising* its importance, or distracting oneself with unrelated behaviour such as drinking alcohol (Steele *et al.*, 1981).

How can dissonance affect attitudes?
Persuaders who wish to change attitudes and thus decision making should thus aim to introduce or increase dissonance with an effort to control non-attitude change solutions.
- For example, anti-smoking campaigns have used images of the blackened lungs of dead people to increase the dissonance between the inconsistent (in non-suicidal smokers) cognitions 'I smoke' and 'smoking kills'.
- Additional statements such as 'only *you* are responsible for your own health' or 'you *can* quit' and presenting figures on the number of smoking-related deaths may help prevent individuals dealing with the dissonance by blaming other people and addiction or minimising it (although smokers outside pubs may still go back inside and try to drink the dissonance away!).

Evaluation
A number of studies have shown that more positive attitudes (towards initially counter-attitudinal issues or subjects) can be induced by introducing dissonance, for example by:
- Asking people to tell others that a boring experiment was interesting for just one dollar – participants rated the experiment as more enjoyable ('I did it for $1 so it must have been') than if given a better external reason for their behaviour, i.e. 20 dollars (Festinger and Carlsmith, 1959).
- Having people eat grasshoppers after a request from a dislikeable person (Zimbardo *et al.*, 1963, cited in Petty *et al.*, 2003) – caused more positive ratings of the experience ('Why would I have done that unless it was not too bad?').

Petty *et al.* (2003) point out that, although studies have measured the physiological arousal from dissonance (e.g. Losch and Cacioppo, 1990) and supported its subjective unpleasantness (Elliot and Devine, 1994), dissonance:
1 may not always be due to pure cognitive inconsistency – even pro-attitudinal behaviour can cause dissonance if it has unintended negative consequences (Cooper and Fazio, 1984).
2 is strongly affected by an individual's self-perception (see the role of self perception and dissonance below).

THE ROLE OF SELF-PERCEPTION

Petty *et al.* (2003) review a variety of theories on the role of self-perception in dissonance and attitude change, but conclude the evidence for each is mixed and they are so flexible that they are better at explaining than predicting research results.

Self-inconsistency theory
Aronson (1969) argued dissonance stems from inconsistency between one's self-view and one's actions, e.g. I am a vegetarian, but I am eating a hamburger.
Self-inconsistency theory predicts people should prefer self-consistent feedback even it is negative.

Self-affirmation theory
Steele (1988) suggests dissonance results from any threat to viewing oneself as morally adequate, e.g. I am a good person but I am doing something bad.
Self-affirmation theory predicts people prefer positive feedback even if it is inconsistent with their self-view.

Self-standards theory
Stone and Cooper (2001) suggest dissonance results from behaviour that breaks the normative social values or idiographic personal values that are relevant to each individual.
Self-standards theory predicts less dissonance on issues irrelevant to the person, but more on issues applying to all in society.

Evaluation
Other self-theories have been proposed that do not require dissonance effects to account for attitude change, e.g.:
- Self-perception theory (Bem, 1965) suggests people *infer* their *attitudes from* their *behaviour* so no dissonance occurs.
- Impression management theory (Tedeschi *et al.*, 1971) argues that attitude change results from the desire to *appear* consistent.

27.5 Explanations of the effectiveness of television in persuasion

EXPLANATIONS

HOVLAND-YALE MODEL

Context
More informal environments seem to induce more attitude change than formal contexts.

Communicator
Source factors of communicators:
- Credibility, (expertise, knowledge).
- Trustworthiness (motives, beliefs).
- Likeability (attractiveness, charm, status, race).

Communication
Message factors of presentation:
- Spelling out conclusions, one or two-sided arguments, order of presentation.
- Use of emotion.

Audience
Recipient factors include:
- Level of education/intelligence/knowledge.
- Resistance to persuasion/strength of attitudes.
- Level of audience participation.

ELABORATION-LIKELIHOOD MODEL (ELM)

Motivation/ability to elaborate
Elaboration increases with:
- Personal importance/relevance of the issue.
- Sole decision responsibility/accountability.
- Ambivalence or uncertainty.
- Greater intelligence, time, freedom from distraction.

Peripheral route to persuasion
Low mental effort/indirect persuasion strategies:
- Simple slogans about the issue/product.
- Repeated (classical conditioning) association with pleasant stimuli.

Central route to persuasion
Reasoned arguments and detailed information about issues/products are provided to a motivated listener who is able to consciously consider the advantages and disadvantages.

DISSONANCE/SELF-PERCEPTION

Cognitive consistency/dissonance
Dissonance reduction achieved by changing attitudes or behaviour to eliminate inconsistency.

Self-inconsistency theory
Dissonance stems from inconsistency between self-views and self actions.

Self-affirmation theory
Dissonance results from threats to viewing oneself as morally adequate.

TELEVISION PERSUASION

- Television viewing mostly occurs in the most informal of conditions – relaxing at home.
- News/current affairs programmes watched by more educated viewers invite credible experts with competing points of view.
- Television advertising uses 'white coat' scientists, visual celebrity endorsement of products and celebrity voiceovers.
- Government TV health and safety campaigns use emotion, but at high levels (shock) to create dissonance effects.
- Advertisers exploit the human tendency to shift attention to stimuli that are vivid or novel by focusing on the presentation of the message (peripheral route), not just the message itself (central route). TV adverts are thus made entertaining – humorous, vivid, unique or bizarre.
- Advertisers encourage deeper processing (elaboration) of an advert by deliberately making it bizarre or puzzling.
- TV adverts create pleasant associations of success, sex, happiness, etc. with a product that are not directly related to it. This is usually achieved by linking the product (via classical conditioning) to famous and attractive promoters, humour or appealing fantasy situations. Positive emotions bypass the more analytical parts of the mind and appeal directly to the desires and needs a person finds important.
- Dissonance is created in TV charity fundraising (If you are a moral person, why are you not helping?) which can be reduced through donating, and in TV adverts (You want this, product, can afford it, and others have it, so why don't you have it?) reduced through buying.

Giles (2003) suggests advertisers have shifted away from product-oriented adverts that provide more factual information towards consumer-oriented adverts that focus more on techniques that appeal to the consumer's self-perceptions, e.g.:

- Self-image – psychographic profiling of typical consumers of a product to create adverts that appeal to their assumed personality characteristics.
- Ideal self – targeting adverts to the consumer's supposed aspirations and ideal future selves.

Giles (2003) adds that the relevance of certain products to our self-identity cannot be overestimated; he cites as evidence:

- Snyder and de Bono (1985) found consumers who scored highly on a test of self-monitoring (and were thus more self-conscious and concerned with image) had more favourable attitudes toward soft-sell adverts, whereas low self-monitors with a more pragmatic approach to life preferred more hard sell factual information.
- Cook (1992) asked 248 American adults to grade items on a continuum from 'self' to 'not self' and found male participants ranked cars higher than their own bodily organs and religion in relation to 'self'.

Evaluation
- Changing the affective aspect (liking/disliking) of attitudes does not necessarily predict consumer behaviour.
- Deliberate attempts to influence in advertising may back-fire – they are often recognised and cynically ignored.
- Although TV advertising has a captive audience, 80% of viewers are likely to leave the room during commercial breaks, and most people watching pre-recorded material will fast-forward through them (Comstock and Scharrer, 1999, cited in Giles, 2003).

27.6 The psychology of celebrity and fandom

THE ATTRACTION OF 'CELEBRITY'

Social psychological explanations

- **Familiarity and physical attractiveness** – psychological attraction occurs through repeated exposure and beauty as a positive central trait of impression formation (see Theories of attraction).
- **Heider's balance theory** – liking for celebrities may be a simple matter of maintaining cognitive consistency because we like their music, acting, fashion, views, etc. (see Theories of attraction).
- **Social construction of celebrity roles** – 'celebrity' is constructed by the mass media via advertising for economic gain – the celebrity 'is well-known for their well-knownness' (Boorstin, 1961).
- **Social role identification** – celebrities are attractive and exert referent social power (people wish to be like and identify with them) because celebrities possess traits and abilities found in the ideal-selves of the audience, or symbolise their fans' lifestyle aspirations of achievement and success (McCracken, 1989).

Evolutionary psychology explanations

- **Physical attractiveness and status as fitness indicators** – celebrities usually possess higher levels of both these indicators of reproductive success, confirmed by Buss's (1989) cross-cultural data from 10,000 respondents in 37 countries on the preferred characteristics of potential mates.
- **Talent and sexual selection** – celebrities often come from sports or entertainment industries and so have the chance to show displays of skill that distinguish themselves from their same-sex competitors (e.g. Miller, 2000) in the eyes of potential mates (see Sexual selection in human mate choice).

Evaluation

Social theories do not always explain the ultimate origin of attraction to the physical beauty and other desirable traits of celebrities, whereas evolutionary theories find it more difficult to account for modern celebrity fame based on no particular achievement or quality.

RESEARCH ON INTENSE FANDOM

Celebrity worship

Giles (2003) points out that the word 'fan' comes from the Latin 'fanaticus' meaning 'of the temple' and cites two pieces of research that draw parallels between fandom and religion:

- Jindra's (1994) analysis of Star Trek fans' behaviour argued that it showed enough criteria to be classed as a civil religion, including organisations, dogmas, recruitment systems, and religious rituals.
- Frow's (1998) analysis of fan worship as a 'cult of the dead' proposed that film star images become disembodied and worshipped once they are recorded on film.

Celebrity worship represents an extreme form of *para-social interaction* where people respond to media figures or their media portrayals (e.g. character roles) as if they were real people in their lives – talking about, interacting, and assuming a social relationship with them *despite no actual social contact*.

Such para-social interactions vary in degree, from sympathising with and talking about (or to!) the media figure on television as if they were in a real relationship, to modelling one's behaviour after, seeking contact with, or even stalking them, and experiencing 'para-social bereavement' when they die, e.g. the deaths of Princess Diana and Jill Dando in the UK (Giles, 2003).

Explanations of celebrity worship include:

- *Personality factors* – e.g. fantasy proneness, cognitive-deficits, low self-esteem, low levels of life control.
- *Self-concept over-identification* – fans are often attracted to and identify with celebrities who possess traits and abilities found in their ideal-self. McCutcheon *et al.* (2002) suggest celebrity worship is due to over-identification based on psychological absorption and addiction.
- *Companionship needs* – through repeated exposure and a sense of familiarity and intimacy (due to extensive media details of their private lives), celebrities provide para-social friendships (perhaps as a compensation for loneliness, deficiencies in social life, or dependency on television).
- *Social Identity Theory* – celebrity worship for some may be reinforced by social group benefits of fan group membership, such as the rewarding social interaction of discussion forums or the acquisition of subcultural or countercultural identities (e.g. Jenkins' 1992b study of Star Trek fans).

Stalking

Stalking refers to the obsessive following of individuals (e.g. media figures) usually with unwanted attempts of physical contact and intrusion upon their lives, often leading to harassment, intimidation, or even physical assault.

Pakes and Winstone (2007) point out that although there have been many well-publicised cases of fans stalking celebrities, research indicates that stalking occurs relatively frequently to non-celebrities, often by ex-partners and acquaintances more than strangers, and that there are different types of stalkers and motives for their behaviour.

Explanations of stalking

Sheridan and Boon (2002, cited in Pakes and Winstone, 2007) identified five types based on 124 cases of stalking serious enough to warrant police involvement:

- *Ex-partner harassment/stalking* – often motivated by anger and bitterness and likely to involve impulsive violence.
- *Infatuation harassment* – less malicious, threatening and intrusive stalking motivated by intense yearning for and romantic fantasy about the victim.
- *Dangerous delusional fixation stalking* – often of high-status women or celebrities, motivated by belief of a hidden relationship and a history of mental health problems with a high risk of violence upon rejection.
- *Less dangerous delusional fixation stalking* – again based on a delusional assumed relationship of mutual affection with the victim but one that is 'understandably' thwarted by external factors, e.g. existing marriages, so less likely to lead to violence.
- *Sadistic stalking* – more calculated and likely to escalate to violence, related to psychopathy and desires of control.

Meloy (1989) suggested stalking arises from attachment pathology, a theory that could be supported by Dutton *et al.*'s (1994) finding that individuals with preoccupied and fearful attachments were more likely to show jealousy, following and surveillance behaviour. Kienlan *et al.*'s (1997) study of a small sample of imprisoned American stalkers found the majority had lost their primary caretaker in childhood and had a major loss (usually a personal relationship) in the six months prior to the onset of their stalking behaviour.

28.1 Issues in the study of anomalous experience

What is anomalistic psychology?
- Anomalistic psychology studies **beliefs** in, and **experiences** of, phenomena that **appear** to be **paranormal** in nature, i.e. those that seem to be *inexplicable* in terms of *current scientific knowledge*.
- Anomalistic psychology stems from the field of parapsychology, but assumes there are *psychological explanations for anomalous experiences* and focuses more on investigating beliefs in, rather than the authenticity of, such experiences.

What are the theoretical and methodological issues?
- The academic field that has traditionally studied anomalous experience (parapsychology) has been criticised as being a **pseudoscience**, i.e. that it lacks all or some of the characteristics of a true science.
- Parapsychology has also been accused of having higher levels of **scientific fraud** (than other sciences), which accounts for its significant experimental results.

Why study anomalous experience?
Study is important for a number of reasons:
- Anomalous experiences, and beliefs in them, are *very common*. About 75% of the public believes in psychic phenomena and around 50–65% claim to have had a psychic experience (Henry, 2005).
- Such phenomena are not only intriguing, but have *fundamental implications* for vital issues, e.g. life after death, religious belief, and the *validity of current science*.
- Study in this area nicely illustrates *issues* in the definition of 'science' and *scientific methods, analysis, debate, and progress*.

'SCIENCE' AND THEORETICAL & METHODOLOGICAL ISSUES IN PARAPSYCHOLOGY

UNSCIENTIFIC THEORIES?
Scientific theories are valid, internally-consistent, provide understanding, prediction and control, and generate new precise, testable, and refutable hypotheses. However, parapsychology has been accused of having theories that:
- are vague, un-testable, irrefutable or inadequate
- provide little or no predictive power or control
- fail to generate new hypotheses and research.

UNSCIENTIFIC METHODS?
Scientific methods are objective, standardised, controlled, and replicable. Parapsychology has been criticised for:
- Using (unstandardised, uncontrolled, and unreplicable) *spontaneous* 'paranormal' *case studies* as evidence.
- *Insufficiently controlled* experimental studies allowing participant cheating, sensory leakage of information, and scientific fraud on the part of the researchers.

FILE DRAW EFFECT?
The file draw effect refers to the selective reporting of significant rather than null results, making an effect appear stronger than it is.

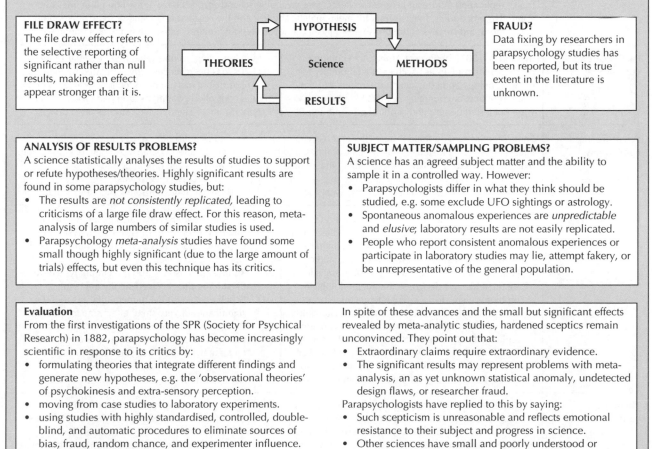

FRAUD?
Data fixing by researchers in parapsychology studies has been reported, but its true extent in the literature is unknown.

ANALYSIS OF RESULTS PROBLEMS?
A science statistically analyses the results of studies to support or refute hypotheses/theories. Highly significant results are found in some parapsychology studies, but:
- The results are *not consistently replicated,* leading to criticisms of a large file draw effect. For this reason, meta-analysis of large numbers of similar studies is used.
- Parapsychology *meta-analysis* studies have found some small though highly significant (due to the large amount of trials) effects, but even this technique has its critics.

SUBJECT MATTER/SAMPLING PROBLEMS?
A science has an agreed subject matter and the ability to sample it in a controlled way. However:
- Parapsychologists differ in what they think should be studied, e.g. some exclude UFO sightings or astrology.
- Spontaneous anomalous experiences are *unpredictable* and *elusive*; laboratory results are not easily replicated.
- People who report consistent anomalous experiences or participate in laboratory studies may lie, attempt fakery, or be unrepresentative of the general population.

Evaluation
From the first investigations of the SPR (Society for Psychical Research) in 1882, parapsychology has become increasingly scientific in response to its critics by:
- formulating theories that integrate different findings and generate new hypotheses, e.g. the 'observational theories' of psychokinesis and extra-sensory perception.
- moving from case studies to laboratory experiments.
- using studies with highly standardised, controlled, double-blind, and automatic procedures to eliminate sources of bias, fraud, random chance, and experimenter influence.
- establishing a number of peer reviewed journals.
- studying 'belief'/'experience' instead of the 'paranormal'.

In spite of these advances and the small but significant effects revealed by meta-analytic studies, hardened sceptics remain unconvinced. They point out that:
- Extraordinary claims require extraordinary evidence.
- The significant results may represent problems with meta-analysis, an as yet unknown statistical anomaly, undetected design flaws, or researcher fraud.

Parapsychologists have replied to this by saying:
- Such scepticism is unreasonable and reflects emotional resistance to their subject and progress in science.
- Other sciences have small and poorly understood or replicated effects, but may have less controlled studies.
- Anomalies are important even if not 'paranormal'.

28.2 Controversies in ESP and psychokinesis studies

	EXTRASENSORY PERCEPTION (ESP)	PSYCHOKINESIS (PK)
Definitions	ESP refers to the *hypothesised* ability to acquire information *without* the use of normal sensory (e.g. visual, auditory, etc.) or reasoning (e.g. inferential, deductive) processes. Different types include: • Telepathy – mind-to-mind information transfer. • Clairvoyance – ESP of inaccessible visual events. • Precognition – ESP of future events.	Psychokinesis refers to the hypothesised ability to influence physical objects or systems through purely mental activity (e.g. wishes, preferences, intentions). Psychokinesis has been studied in the context of: • Macro-PK effects – affecting single large objects, e.g. bending or moving objects, psychic healing. • Micro-PK effects – affecting statistical probability.
Methods of study	A variety of methods have been used to study ESP; *Ganzfeld* studies involve the reduction of normal sensory input through the use of visual, auditory, and kinaesthetic deprivation in isolated participants who have to describe and later identify randomly selected images (usually being viewed by a 'sender') under double-blind conditions controlled for chance guessing and sensory leakage of target information.	Macro-PK has been studied by case study collections of spontaneous occurrences, e.g. watches stopping, falling objects, knocking noises, etc. and case studies of exceptional individuals, e.g. metal benders. Micro-PK studies test the ability of any participant to influence the statistical probability of events over a large number of trials, e.g. dice rolls or displays of the output of random event generators (REGs).
Methods controversy	Early laboratory methods using face-to-face testing of ESP with Zenner cards or PK with dice rolling could eliminate the effects of unknown chance frequency, selective memory, or mental inferences associated with cases of spontaneous ESP and psychokinesis. However, early studies did not always control sensory leakage or participant cheating as effectively as modern, automated, and computer-controlled Ganzfeld ESP or micro-PK REG studies. Nevertheless, even highly controlled studies show replication problems, perhaps due to: • *Experimenter effects*, e.g. sceptical researchers produce more non-significant results (e.g. Wiseman and Schlitz, 1997), even with participants *unaware* of the researcher's belief (e.g. West 1954), perhaps implying a *parapsychological experimenter effect* – the researcher's psychic abilities unconsciously affect the results! • *Participant effects*, e.g. some studies indicate sceptical participants show more non-significant or even psi-missing (significantly *below* chance expectations) results than believers (Lawrence, 1993). To control for bias, other method problems like early stopping (terminating the study after a run of successful trials), replication failure and file draw effects, parapsychologists and sceptics have agreed on guidelines for: controlled procedures, fixed criteria for meta-analytic studies, and the registration of studies in advance. Both calculations and surveys of unpublished studies have now ruled out file draw effects in many meta-analyses.	
Participant fraud controversy	In Randi's (1983a,b) 'Project Alpha', two conjurors presented themselves as psychics at a laboratory for parapsychology and convinced researchers that they could produce 'encouraging results'. However, they were not tested under tightly controlled conditions.	Metal bending, as illustrated by Uri Gellar in the 1970s, has been successfully simulated by many conjurors, but has not been reliably replicated under fully controlled conditions (and participants given the opportunity to cheat in such studies often do so).
Scientific fraud controversy	Some sceptics suggest fraud is a simpler and more rational (being well established) explanation of significant effects in ESP and PK studies than psychic abilities, and point to cases of fraud in parapsychology, e.g. Soal's data fixing in the 1930s and Levy's tampering in the 1970s. However, Irwin and Watt (2007) point out: • Cases of fraud were identified and thoroughly reported by parapsychologists themselves. • Fraud occurs in all sciences and parapsychology has not been shown to have unusually high levels of it.	
Results analysis controversy	Ganzfeld study meta-analysis has varied results: • Hyman's (1985) meta-analysis of 42 studies found highly significant results, but attributed them to serious methodological problems in the studies. • Honorton's (1985) meta-analysis found statistical significance, but disagreed that methodological problems were strong enough to account for it. • Bem and Honorton's (1994) analysis of Ganzfeld studies designed to overcome Hyman's concerns replicated Honorton's (1985) significant results. • Milton and Wiseman's (1999b) analysis found an effect near chance, but included studies that did not replicate the original method (Bem *et al.* 2001).	PK study meta-analysis has also generated debate: • Radin and Ferrari's (1991) meta-analysis of dice-throwing studies revealed a weak but statistically significant PK effect. • Radin and Nelson's (2003) meta-analysis of REG-PK studies also revealed significant results. • Bosch *et al.*'s (2006a,b) meta-analysis found a significant but very small effect size for REG-PK studies and attributed it to a file draw effect. • Jahn *et al.*'s (2000) international, pre-registered meta-analysis showed a slight but not significant tendency for PK effects to be directed in pre-specified directions (one-tailed hypotheses).
Theoretical controversy	• These controversies show even meta-analysis has methodological problems, e.g. the criteria used to code and exclude studies can be subjective and different analyses reveal different interpretations of the data that often reflect the theoretical biases of the researchers. Unfortunately, many other sciences use meta-analysis. • There is no agreed theory of ESP, PK or of which effects are due to clairvoyance, precognition, or telepathy. • Effect sizes are small but would be accepted in any other field of science given the numbers of participants, researchers, trials, controls and highly significant studies (some with billion-to-one against chance results).	

28.3 Cognitive, personality, and biological factors in anomalous experience

COGNITIVE FACTORS

Cognitive psychology research on the attention, perception, and *memory* processes found in *all* humans has been applied to explain anomalous experience, including:

- **Misperception** – studies of the effects of expectation on the perception of ambiguous stimuli and pattern recognition are well documented in psychology and could explain the misperception of movement and form, e.g. in cases of psychokinesis or ghost sightings, especially under conditions of poor lighting and high expectation, e.g. at séances or in places thought to be haunted.
- **Hallucination** – e.g. hypnagogic hallucinations could explain ghost sightings.
- **Faulty memory** – copious psychological research on reconstructive memory, effort after meaning, post-event information, suggestion, and eyewitness testimony shows events can be misremembered and distorted after the fact – leading to exaggeration, increased coherence, or even creation of experienced anomalous events (Loftus and Palmer, 1974; Loftus, 1996; French, 2003).
- **Misattribution** – of coincidental events, e.g. due to confirmatory bias, hindsight bias, neglect of non-events or illusion of control, may account for perceptions of, and belief in, ESP and PK abilities (Marks and Kammann, 1980).
- **Unconscious processes** – information acquired without awareness (e.g. from body language and background conversation on television while engaged in other tasks) or consciously forgotten (e.g. cryptamnesia) may form the basis of impressions of clairvoyance, telepathy, precognition, retrocognition, past life experience, or knowledge shown through psychic mediumship.

Evaluation
- Ghost sightings in daylight by many witnesses seem to eliminate certain cognitive explanations, but of course raise the possibility of others, e.g. informational social influence and suggestion causing conformity under ambiguous conditions.
- These factors are more convincing as explanations of spontaneous anomalous experiences rather than controlled laboratory studies of anomalous events.
- For evidence, see cognitive psychology studies and research on deception and self-deception.
- Cognitive explanations need to combine with personality explanations to discover *who* is more likely to show these effects.

PERSONALITY FACTORS

Research into personality factors investigates the idea that certain people possess a psychological predisposition for anomalistic experiences. Individual differences in the psychometric measurement of certain psychological traits have therefore been correlated with the type and frequency of anomalistic experiences, including:

- **Attitudes and belief** – those who believe in psychic abilities (termed 'sheep') are more likely to have such spontaneous anomalistic experiences than those who reject the possibility (termed 'goats'). This can be explained in terms of the greater probability that sheep will misperceive, selectively attend to, and misremember events in line with their beliefs and expectations. However, the same explanations cannot be applied to the sheep-goat effect found in controlled laboratory tests.
- **Extraversion** – there is evidence that extraversion is correlated with ESP success in laboratory experiments (Palmer and Carpenter, 1998). Critics have argued that extraverts are more likely to cheat in ESP tests, but modern controls and a non-significant correlation with spontaneous ESP experiences contradicts this.
- **Creativity** – although Schlitz and Honorton (1992) had excellent ganzfeld results with creative arts students (e.g. a hit rate of 50% compared to 25% expected by chance) a consistent relationship has not been found between creativity and ESP.

Irwin and Watt (2007) review many other personality factors, including IQ, low neuroticism, low defensiveness, and psychological absorbtion (associated with ESP), and fantasy proneness (linked to anomalous experience and belief in general).

Evaluation
- Schmeidler's 10-year study of over 1,000 subjects found believers in ESP (sheep) tended to score just above chance on such tests while non-believers (goats) on average scored just *below* chance. The effect is small, but significant and often replicated (Palmer, 1977). Perhaps goats use their psychic ability unconsciously to avoid getting the right answer to maintain their belief system.
- Cause and effect is difficult to determine in correlations – does belief facilitate psychic ability, or ability create belief? More research is needed on how personality traits can explain *laboratory* test results.

BIOLOGICAL FACTORS

Brain dysfunction explanations focus on disturbance in brain function that either produce anomalistic experiences (according to sceptical psychologists) or facilitate genuine paranormal abilities (according to believers in paranormal explanations).

Physical signal explanations research the possible external physical conditions or mechanisms that trigger seemingly paranormal phenomena in the brain (sceptical view) or facilitate the transfer of genuine psychic information (paranormal view), e.g. ELF (extremely low frequency) electromagnetic waves that can penetrate walls.

Henry (2005) reports a range of research investigating these explanations:

- Persinger (1985) suggested that certain parapsychology results are better and ESP activity is greater when geomagnetic disturbance is low.
- Zilberman (1995) found French and Russian lottery payouts were higher when geomagnetic activity decreased (with a probability of 400 to 1 against chance).
- Radin (1998) found a relationship in some studies between gambling and the lunar cycle (a possible payout increase of 2% near the full rather than new moon).
- Persinger (1999) replicated a sense of presence and out-of-body experiences in certain participants by magnetic stimulation of the temporal lobe.
- Observational theories based on quantum physics ideas suggest human intentions or conscious observation might modify the probability of events occurring.

Evaluation
If the brain is responsible for genuine ESP, then conditions that increase its receptivity to weak psi signals would produce more significant results, e.g:.

- lower internal arousal levels associated with extraversion, low neuroticism, low defensiveness, and psychological absorbtion.
- relaxation and reduction of external stimulation in Ganzfeld tests.
- longer consideration of interesting targets in remote viewing, dream studies and ESP of video clips.

However psi effects do not seem to be reduced by distance, time or shielding (even with a Faraday cage) and no brain 'receptor' has been identified.

28.4 Psychology of deception, self-deception superstition, and coincidence

DECEPTION

- Deception refers to the intentional faking of paranormal behaviour. Sceptics and professional conjurors have long pointed out the possible existence of deception in those claiming and investigating paranormal abilities.
- Explanations for deception range from sensation-seeking, need for attention and self-satisfaction in duping others, to gaining a living/profit or acquiring/keeping social respect.
- For researchers investigating the paranormal, deception may also result from the desire to prove one's viewpoint, maintain academic employment and funding, or frustration at the difficulty of replicating weak and erratic psi effects.
- A variety of methods of deception have been employed to fake anomalistic phenomena, from cold reading, stooges, eavesdropping, and spying in stage mentalism and fortune-telling to conjuring in ESP or PK studies and simple lying or exaggeration in reports of OBEs or ghost sightings.

Evaluation

Analysis of cold reading techniques (Hyman, 1977) shows how a psychic can fool sitters into revealing personal information about themselves without realising it, e.g. by:

- The initial analysis of the sitter's appearance and speech, e.g. clothing, jewellery, mannerisms, accent, self- introduction, and explanation of the reasons for presence.
- The psychic's use of high probability, flattering, and non-specific/ambiguous statements.
- The analysis of the sitter's facial expressions, verbal responses, and elaborations in response to the statements.
- Hedging, adjusting, reversing, or elaborating on statements in response to the sitter's verbal and non-verbal feedback.
- Blaming lack of success to sitter/spirit uncooperativeness.

Randi's 'Project Alpha' presented conjurors as psychics.

SELF-DECEPTION

- Self-deception in the context of anomalistic psychology refers to sincere but inaccurate beliefs in one's own or other people's paranormal abilities or experiences.
- Many *cognitive biases* in information processing (see Cognitive factors in anomalous experience) work without conscious awareness and so may both *initiate* and *maintain self-deceiving beliefs* about the paranormal.
- For example, misattributing control to oneself after a series of surprising coincidences (see below) may result in the initiation of a self-deceptive though sincere belief in one's possession of psychic talents, which could be maintained by the later misattribution or misremembering of events in line with this new belief (see sheep vs. goat personalities).
- Similarly, a sitter's selective attention to, and memory of, a 'psychic's' cold reading (e.g. inattention to self-revealed information and the number of inaccurate/vague statements, but selective memory of accurate information) could result in a self-deceiving belief in the truth of psychic statements.
- Interestingly, self-deception in parapsychologists may arise through similar processes due to a string of initial positive results (either due to chance or methodological problems), and be maintained by the variable ratio reinforcement (see superstition below) of irregularly replicated results.

Evaluation

- There is much evidence for the existence of cognitive biases in psychology, and some have applied them to paranormal situations (see Wiseman *et al.*'s 2003 study, 'Belief in the Paranormal and Suggestion in the Séance Room') and beliefs (e.g. French, 1992; Irwin, 1993).
- The possibility exists, of course, that it is the sceptics of the paranormal who may be deceiving themselves!

SUPERSTITION

- Superstition refers to beliefs that the presence of certain objects or the performance of certain behaviours/rituals will increase or decrease the likelihood of something happening, e.g. good or bad luck, performance, rainfall, death, etc.
- Since the objects or behaviours are usually unrelated to the desired outcomes in any scientifically demonstrable manner, superstitious behaviour involves beliefs of *paranormal* effects. Nevertheless, superstition can significantly affect behaviour and lead to self-fulfilling prophecies.
- Superstitious behaviour has been found: cross-culturally, throughout recorded history, at all levels of education (e.g. doctors), and at high levels in surveys of modern societies.
- Skinner explained superstitious behaviour initiation and maintainance using *operant conditioning* learning theory. Unrelated behaviour emitted close in time to actions that genuinely produce desirable consequences (reinforcement) is more like to be repeated again – even though it has no causal effect. This *accidentally reinforced 'superstitious' behaviour* is maintained by future sporadic coincidental reinforcement (a *variable ratio reinforcement* schedule that is *resistant to extinction*) or continues to be emitted to avoid undesirable consequences (*negative reinforcement*).

Evaluation

- Skinner provided evidence from animal laboratory studies, although human superstition also involves cognitive factors.
- Evidence of the non-causality of superstitious behaviour comes from a variety of studies, e.g. on the null effects of superstition on lottery payouts (e.g. Smith *et al.*, 1997) and hospital admissions (e.g. Ahn *et al.*, 2002)

COINCIDENCE

- Coincidence in anomalistic psychology refers to the study of *seemingly improbable simultaneous occurrences* of two or more events that may be *attributed to paranormal causes*.
- Spontaneously-occurring anomalies may just reflect surprising coincidences that are interpreted as paranormal due to their unknown frequency of occurrence by chance and the following factors:
  - ➤ People are poor judges of probability (Kahneman *et al.*, 1982) so underestimate the occurrence of chance effects.
  - ➤ Humans have cognitive biases to attend to, perceive and attribute causality and meaning to coinciding events.
  - ➤ The statistical Law of Truly Large Numbers (Diaconis and Mosteller, 1989) states that amazing coincidences occur frequently between events in large populations.
  - ➤ The 'small world effect' predicts common coincidences due to the huge interconnectivity of social relationships.

Evaluation

- Zusne and Jones (1989) 'calculated that the probability of thinking about any of the people we knew of by chance alone within five minutes of learning of their death would be about one in 30,000 per year. Although this would be a rare event for an individual, in a country the size of the USA, about 3,000 adults would have such an experience by chance alone in any given year and so it should not be surprising to hear of such instances' (Milton in Henry 2005).
- However, studies have had mixed results when correlating ability to judge probability with belief in, or experience of, the paranormal. Also, personal coincidences affect belief in the paranormal more than other people's coincidences.

28.5 Research on anomalous experience and beliefs 1

OUT-OF-BODY EXPERIENCES (OBES)

OBEs involve the vivid, subjective impression of a centre of awareness temporarily external to the physical body, often with reports of viewing oneself and the environment from a bird's-eye view. OBEs can also involve the impression of moving around and travelling to other places, control over the event, or even of having an astral body and connecting cord. OBEs can occur spontaneously or be induced in a variety of people, under a variety of conditions (i.e. not just NDEs).

- *Paranormal explanations* are popular cross-culturally and historically (but see NDE paranormal explanation problems).
- *Psychological explanations* involve a breakdown in the normal body image due to a loss of contact with somatic sensations and either *absorption* in a new synaesthetically created experience (Irwin, 1985, 2000) or a viewpoint shift to *memory-imagery* self perspectives (Blackmore 1984).
- *Physiological explanations* concern disruption to the somatosensory areas of the brain (located in the angular gyrus region at the junction of the temporal and parietal cortex) responsible for integrating sensory information into a consistent body image.

Evaluation

- Psychological explanations are supported by studies showing OBE occurrence is associated with high scores on absorption and spatial ability tests, and by physiological theories and studies of body image problems in the brain.
- Blanke *et al.* (2002) triggered an out-of-body experience by stimulating the angular gyrus in the right cortex during surgery for an epileptic patient. Further study showed visual body part illusions in other patients were associated with dysfunction in the temporo-parietal junction of the brain (Blanke *et al.*, 2004) and found transcranial magnetic stimulation of the same area inhibited the imagination of an OBE in healthy patients, but not the imagination of spatial transformation of objects (Blanke *et al.*, 2005).

NEAR-DEATH EXPERIENCES (NDES)

An NDE is associated with seriously life-threatening events, e.g. revival from cardiac arrest, and commonly involves an OBE associated with overwhelming feelings of well-being and of drifting through darkness or a tunnel towards a golden light and communicating with 'presences' or relatives in a world of beauty. A rapid life review in images may also be reported.

- *Paranormal explanations* usually involve literal separation of the 'soul' from the body, but this theory is difficult to test scientifically (plus any ability to access information away from the body could be attributed to ESP) and so any support depends on the elimination of all other explanations.
- *Psychological explanations* include hallucinations triggered by stress and motivated fantasy based on cultural notions of the after-life, e.g. from films, books, religious stories.
- *Physiological explanations* involve hallucinations triggered by the physiological trauma of the event, e.g. temporal lobe seizures, endorphin release, oxygen starvation, excess carbon dioxide, and cortical disinhibition (e.g. of the visual cortex, leading to light and tunnel effects).

Evaluation

- Some studies on the psychological explanations have found no relationship between NDEs and prior religious belief (e.g. Sabom, 1982) or prior knowledge of near-death experiences – even after the publication of the first popular book on the subject (Athappilly *et al.*, 2006). However, there are some cross-cultural variations in NDE reports, e.g. more negative NDEs in Thailand and absence of OBE in India.
- Many of the symptoms produced by proposed physiological explanations do not always exactly match the NDE reports, e.g. they typically produce fear, confused images, or longer-lasting effects than the pleasant, rapid, clear, specific and coherent content of an NDE. Also NDEs occur in people without physical trauma who only *believe* they will die.

PSYCHIC MEDIUMSHIP

- The SPR investigated physical mediumship (moving, apporting or materialising objects) and mental mediumship (obtaining apparently inaccessible information, e.g. from living or dead people) by careful observation of séances and using controls designed to reveal fakery. Many cases of medium fraud were revealed, using techniques of deception and conditions that encouraged self-deception, although certain individuals resisted 'debunking' more than others, e.g. Daniel Douglas Home.
- Explanations of belief in psychic mediumship include:
  - ➤ Motivation to belief, e.g. based on the psychological need to contact dead relatives for reassurance about the after-life and their continued well-being.
  - ➤ Convincing deception – studies using conjuring techniques and cold reading techniques have successfully convinced participants of paranormal effects (see Wiseman *et al.*, 2003).
  - ➤ Self-deception – often in combination with trickery, environmental conditions are created, e.g. dim lighting, expectation, and anxiety, that facilitate self-deception.

Evaluation

Wiseman *et al.* (2003) investigated 'Belief in the Paranormal and Suggestion in the Séance Room' using conjuring tricks employed by fraudulent mediums in the 19th century and pure suggestion in a 'spooky' setting.

Groups of 25 people were taken to a dark, underground former Victorian prison, told a fictitious ghost story and witnessed a fake séance where:

1. certain objects moved and levitated (due to trickery)
2. the medium merely stated that a table was levitating (when in fact it was completely stationary).

Infra-red video recording and questionnaires showed:

- The atmosphere created fear, cold shivers, and even a sense of mysterious presence in some participants.
- 40% of those who had expressed a prior belief in the paranormal thought the ghostly phenomena were real, compared to only 3% of non-believers.
- Over 30% reported seeing the table levitate, although more disbelievers than believers realised it had not.

PSYCHIC HEALING

- Psychic healing refers to the *apparent* ability to *cause positive changes in physical well-being* (in other humans or even animals, plants, and cells) without the use of known medical techniques or effects (e.g. the placebo effect, where a person's belief of being treated causes improvement even when no real treatment is given).
- Forms of psychic healing are found cross-culturally, e.g. the laying on of hands, prayers for the sick, shamanistic healing rituals, etc., and in some cultures are the preferred or only choice for treatment. Explanations range from channelling energy and evoking spirits or deities to psychokinesis.
- Spontaneous cases are difficult to assess because healers keep no or inadequate (if they have no scientific medical training) records, and the placebo effect cannot be ruled out in the many cases where the patients are aware of being treated.
- Since the placebo effect and a person's mental state have been consistently shown to have dramatic effects on physical well-being, the true effects of *psychic* healing can only be tested in controlled double-blind experiments of distance healing (where the healer has no contact with the patient and the patient is unaware of the healer's attempt). Animal and plant studies are also used because they exclude placebo and expectancy effects.

Evaluation

- Benor (2001a,b) reviewed nearly 200 controlled psychic healing studies, including distance ones, on humans, animals and plants and found around two-thirds of them had statistically significant results.
- Serious methodological problems were found with some human studies, but fewer have been identified in animal and plant studies – many of which have shown statistically significant effects, e.g. Wirth *et al.*'s (1992) salamander limb regeneration study and Roney-Dougal and Solfvin's (2003) study on lettuce seed growth.
- Some psychic healing studies have found the patient's subjective improvement, e.g. pain reduction, is greater than their objective physical improvement (this is still an important effect, however).
- Some think that psychokinesis explains psychic healing or even the placebo effect itself because DMILS (direct mental interaction with living systems) meta-analysis studies, e.g. on the ability to affect other people's electrodermal activity or blood pressure, have shown statistically significant results (Braud and Schlitz, 1991, Schmidt *et al.*, 2004).

THE FUNCTIONS OF PARANORMAL BELIEF

PROVISION OF CONTROL AND REDUCTION OF UNCERTAINTY

A function that has received a good deal of support is that certain paranormal beliefs and behaviours help provide a perceived sense of control over threatening or uncertain conditions.

EXPLANATION OF THE UNKNOWN

In pre-scientific times and cultures, 'paranormal' explanatory models of causality form the basis of cultural worldviews and religious beliefs. Psychologists and anthropologists have noted that these paranormal explanatory beliefs fulfil a variety of functions, from the regulation of human social organisation and activities (e.g. hunting and farming) to the need for cognitive consistency or reassurance regarding the loss of loved ones and the 'after-life'.

SOCIAL IDENTITY

Paranormal and related beliefs (e.g. religious) form an important basis for distinguishing different social groups, membership of which provides social support, protection, and a sense of identity (see Social Identity Theory). In modern Western societies, paranormal beliefs may be a key element of groups or cults with anti-conforming identities, e.g. those rebelling against science or traditional religions.

EVOLUTIONARY FUNCTIONS

Dawkins (1989) suggested cultural 'memes' for beliefs replicate from mind to mind, and psychologically attractive ones such as the 'God meme' that provide easy answers to troubling questions and promises of a better world have particular longevity and fecundity in the meme-pool.

Evaluation

Wiseman (2007) reports three interesting *cross-cultural* studies supporting the idea that paranormal belief is due to a perceived *need for control* to reduce uncertainty:

- Malinowski (1922) attributed the magical/superstitious rituals performed by the Trobriand Islanders of *New Guinea* before going out into dangerous open seas, as an attempt to gain perceived control over uncertain conditions since the same rituals were not performed when fishing in the calmer waters of the lagoons.
- Padgett and Jorgenson (1982) found a significant relationship between economic threat (measured in terms of certain wage, production, and unemployment levels) and superstition (based on the number of magazine and newspaper articles on astrology and mysticism) in *German* society between 1918 and 1940. Articles on cooking and gardening served as controls, and the authors attributed the relationship to the effects of increased uncertainty on the tendency to seek a sense of certainty by resorting to irrational ideas of fate.
- Keinan (1994) found more superstitious behaviour developed in areas under higher risk of missile attack in *Israel* during the first Gulf War than lower risk areas.

Irwin (2006) has proposed a psychodynamic model that suggests trauma or the inability to establish a clear sense of control over life events in childhood leads some people to develop paranormal beliefs as a way of establishing 'an illusion of control' over an unpredictable world.

How Science Works

In common with other science specifications (such as Physics, Chemistry, and Biology) Psychology now incorporates 'How science works'. The aim of 'How science works' is to encourage students to understand what science is, how it is best done and communicated, its impact on society, and in turn the influence of society on science. 'How science works' skills, knowledge, and understanding should be integrated with the other specification content.

This book has many examples of 'How science works', with the *Issues and debates*, and *Research Methods* chapters being particularly relevant. The listing below shows the QCA criteria for 'How science works' and some possible examples of these. As for other aspects of the course, for more detail on requirements it is important that you look at a copy of the specification and question styles which can be found on the website of your awarding body (AQA, Edexcel, OCR, etc.).

REQUIREMENTS	EXAMPLES IN PSYCHOLOGY
A Use theories, models and ideas to develop and modify scientific explanations	• The wide variety of alternative theories, models and ideas that psychologists use to explain human behaviour, e.g. cognitive models of mental processes
B. Use knowledge & understanding to pose scientific questions, define scientific problems, present scientific arguments and scientific ideas	• The use of psychological knowledge and theories to generate new hypotheses and research, and to support arguments, views and ideas in psychological topic areas and debates
C. Use appropriate methodology, including ICT, to answer scientific questions and solve scientific problems	• Psychological research methods and techniques, especially choosing appropriate methods (e.g. experiments, self-reports, observations, etc.) and the use of ICT
D. Carry out experimental and investigative activities, including appropriate risk management in a range of contexts.	• Psychological research methods and techniques, especially choosing appropriate and safe procedures, equipment and environmental conditions
E. Analyse and interpret data to produce evidence, recognising correlations and causal relationships.	• Psychological research methods and techniques, especially choosing appropriate descriptive and inferential statistics and their correct interpretation
F. Evaluate methodology, evidence and data, and resolve conflicting evidence	• Psychological research methods and techniques, especially the strengths and weaknesses of different methods, e.g. in terms of reliability and validity
G. Appreciate the tentative nature of scientific knowledge	• The examination of the nature of theories and hypotheses in psychology
H. Communicate information and ideas in appropriate ways using appropriate terminology	• The psychological terminology used for each concept, idea, theory and method in Psychology. Respect conventions for psychological reports
I. Consider applications and implications of science and appreciate their associated benefits and risks	• The applications of psychological knowledge and theories to different areas of interest, e.g. education, crime, therapy, etc., and their evaluation
J. Consider ethical issues in the treatment of humans, other organisms and the environment	• Ethics in human and animal research in Psychology
K. Appreciate the role of the scientific community in validating new knowledge and ensuring integrity	• Accepted methodology and peer review in Psychology
L. Appreciate the ways in which society uses science to inform decision making	• The applications of psychological knowledge and theories to different social areas of interest, e.g. child care

Index

Index